P9-CDN-368

THE PENTATEUCH AND BOOK OF

JOSHUA.

a

AN

HISTORICO-CRITICAL INQUIRY

INTO

THE ORIGIN AND COMPOSITION

OF

THE HEXATEUCH

(PENTATEUCH AND BOOK OF JOSHUA)

BY

A. KUENEN

PROFESSOR OF THEOLOGY AT LEIDEN

TRANSLATED FROM THE DUTCH, WITH THE
ASSISTANCE OF THE AUTHOR

BY

PHILIP H. WICKSTEED, M.A.

London

MACMILLAN AND CO.

1886

𝔒𝔵𝔣𝔬𝔯𝔡

PRINTED BY HORACE HART, PRINTER TO THE UNIVERSITY

TRANSLATOR'S PREFACE.

THE first edition of Professor Kuenen's *Historico-critical Inquiry into the Origin and Collection of the Books of the Old Testament*[1] was exhausted some years ago, and the work here presented to the English reader is the first instalment (the only one that has yet appeared) of the second edition[2]. It is, therefore, properly speaking, the opening chapter of a complete treatise on the Books of the Old Testament.

The special intricacy of the critical questions raised by the Pentateuch and Book of Joshua, the great amount of attention which they have recently excited, and the importance of their bearings upon the history of Israelite religion, have led Professor Kuenen to deal with them at exceptional length; and the same considerations confer upon this portion of his work an independent interest and value which make it unnecessary to offer any apology for laying it before English Students of the Bible—at least provisionally—in the form of a substantive work; but in justice to Professor Kuenen, it should be borne in mind that the subject is treated throughout from the point of view of a general 'Introduction,' not from that of a monograph on the Hexateuch.

So rapid have been the recent growth and change of critical opinion on the Hexateuch that the opening por-

[1] *Historisch-Kritisch Onderzoek naar het ontstaan en de verzameling van de Boeken des Ouden Verbonds.* Three Vols., Leiden, 1861–65.
[2] *Historisch-critisch Onderzoek*, etc. Tweede, geheel omgewerkte Uitgave. Eerste Deel, Eerste Stuk. De Hexateuch, Leiden, 1885.

tions of the 'Inquiry,' though much in advance of the times in which the first edition was issued, had to be completely re-written for the second[1]. The Author would have preferred, on many grounds, to withhold his treatise for the present, and content himself with pursuing his special investigations, and continuing the series of his 'Contributions to the criticism of the Pentateuch and Joshua' in the Dutch *Theologisch Tijdschrift*[2]. For though the main lines of the subject can now be laid down with remarkable firmness and certainty, yet a variety of important, though subordinate, points still remain as to which it will be impossible to pronounce with confidence till yet further researches shall have thrown fresh light upon them.

In Professor Kuenen's view, however, an 'Introduction' should be written not for independent and fully equipped students, but for those who desire to be initiated into the present state of knowledge and the points round which the experts are still engaged in controversy.

Under this aspect it was impossible not to recognise the urgent need, both in Holland and elsewhere, of a concise but complete exposition of the criticism of the Hexateuch which should not only build upon the foundations laid long ago and universally accepted, but should, as it were, construct the whole edifice, from base to pinnacle, before the eyes of the student.

These considerations determined Professor Kuenen to overcome his scruples, and no longer to withhold the first chapter of his new edition.

In his preface (from which many of these details are taken) he lays it down as the primary object of his work,

[1] See Introduction.

[2] Vols. xi., xii., xiv., xv., xviii. These essays are alluded to by Professor Robertson Smith (Preface to Wellhausen's *Prolegomena*, p. ix.) as 'perhaps the finest things that modern criticism can show.'

not so much to advance knowledge as to indicate the point which it has already reached; but inasmuch as it is not always easy to draw the line between the problems which are and those which are not ripe for solution, he has found it impossible to avoid occasional excursions into fields of inquiry which still belong to the domain of the 'mémoire' more properly than to that of the 'hand-book.'

The *Introduction*, on the recent history of the criticism of the Pentateuch, has been compiled, with Professor Kuenen's assistance, from various articles and notices contributed by him from time to time to the *Theologisch Tijdschrift*. The Author had some hesitation in allowing this addition to his work, on the ground that it might seem implicitly to claim for this treatise the character of a monograph on the Hexateuch, complete in itself, whereas it is really, as we have seen, only the long first chapter of an 'Introduction to the Old Testament.' He was, however, induced to withdraw his objection in the face of an urgent representation of the value and interest which such an introductory essay would possess for his English readers.

In executing the translation I have had the advantage of the Author's extremely careful and thorough revision of the proof-sheets; and I cannot refrain from offering him my sincerest thanks for his unfailing patience in rendering me every possible assistance.

The references (both Biblical and others) have been carefully verified throughout. In the very few cases in which I have not been able to consult the books referred to Professor Kuenen has for the most part been good enough to re-verify the references for me. In this way a small number of errors has been removed from the remarkably correct original. I shall be well satisfied if these corrections are found to balance the inevitable additional errors which must accrue, despite every device of checking and verifying, in reprinting so many thousands of figures.

The Biblical references are given to the chapters and verses of the Hebrew ; but where these differ from the numeration of the English versions I have added the latter in square brackets [ ]. This has been done even where the point of the reference is entirely linguistic; and, indeed, in all cases it must be understood that while the chapter and verse of the English are given for convenience, it is the Hebrew Text which is actually referred to, and the point of the reference will not always be obvious from the English versions. The English reader, therefore, must not at once conclude that the reference is erroneous if he does not find anything to the purpose in the passage indicated.

The pagination of the original is given in the margin.

In the spelling of the proper names no uniform system has been followed. The traditional forms have been preserved when they appeared to be completely naturalized. In other cases an approximation to a reasonable orthography has been attempted. More especially the mute final ' h ' has been dropped, and ' y ' has been substituted for ' j.' In the transliteration of Hebrew words a uniform system has been adopted in consultation with Professor Kuenen (note ‎י=y, ‎פ and ‎פ=ph, but ‎ב and ‎ב=b, etc.).

PHILIP H. WICKSTEED.

London, *Feb.* 1886.

CONTENTS.

INTRODUCTION.

Outline of the History of the Criticism of the Pentateuch and Book of Joshua during the last quarter of a Century.

I.

FIVE-AND-TWENTY years ago [1] the defenders of the 'authenticity' of the Pentateuch were never weary of insisting on the mutual disagreement of its assailants. The charge was not altogether baseless, and yet a dominant theory as to the origin of the Mosaic writings was certainly established amongst the representatives of the critical school. The main points upon which unanimity seemed gradually to have been reached were the following : ' The Deuteronomist, a contemporary of Manasseh or Josiah, was the redactor of the Pentateuch and the Book of *Joshua*, and it was he who brought them into the form in which they now lie before us. He interwove or inserted his own laws and narratives into the work of the Yahwist (Jehovist) that dated from the eighth century B. C., and was therefore about a hundred years old in his time. To this Yahwist we owe the first four books of the Pentateuch and the earlier (præ-deuteronomic) recension of *Joshua*. His work was in its turn based upon a still earlier composition — the " Grundschrift " or " Book of Origins "—which came from the pen of a priest or Levite and might be referred to the century of Solomon. Embedded in this " Grundschrift " were still more ancient fragments, some of them Mosaic. The Yahwist expanded and sup-

---

[1] The date at which the first volume of my *Historisch-Kritisch Onderzoek*, etc. was published at Leiden. See Preface.

plemented the Grundschrift with materials drawn in part
from tradition and in part from written sources.'

Wide diversity of opinion still existed on a number of
details, especially as to what laws and narratives should
be regarded as earlier than the 'Grundschrift' and attributed to a so-called 'præ-Elohist'; and again, as to the
sources of the Yahwist. But the great majority of the
critics held by the main lines of the sketch given above.
It seemed to have become almost an axiom that 'the Book
of Origins' (or the earlier Elohist), the Yahwist and the
Deuteronomist succeeded each other in the order I have
indicated. At any rate this was the genealogy of the
Pentateuch drawn up by Ewald and his school, by de Wette,
by Bleek, and by many others.

I myself could not escape from the overpowering influence which such a consensus naturally exercised. But
I may now point out, with pardonable satisfaction, that even
in 1860 I could not accept the dominant theory as it stood
and felt obliged to modify it very considerably.

In the first place (*Onderzoek*, 1st ed., chap. I. § 18) I
followed Hupfeld and others in rejecting the 'Ergänzungshypothese' (cf. p. 159 sqq. of this work). The Yahwist did
not 'fill in' the elohistic 'Grundschrift.' His narratives were
originally independent, and it was not till long after their
composition that they were welded by a redactor into a
single whole with other documents, some earlier and some
later than themselves.

A second departure from the current hypothesis was more
significant. It referred to the 'Grundschrift' or 'Book
of Origins' itself, in which I distinguished successive
elements. I not only followed Hupfeld once more in
recognising a second Elohist, by the side of the author of
the 'Grundschrift' (op. cit. p. 76 sqq.), but I went on to
impugn the unity of the priestly legislation in *Exodus–Num-*

bers with its connected narratives (p. 84 sqq.). For the
hypothesis (of Ewald and others) that these laws and narratives were committed to writing in Solomon's reign, I substituted the contention that they were successive deposits of
the traditions and views of the priestly circles in which they
rose, and had been repeatedly worked over and expanded
before they acquired the form in which we now possess them.

Closely connected with this departure from the critical
tradition was yet another. I still supposed that the priests
had begun to commit their traditions to writing in the reign
of Solomon. But when was the last hand put to the work?
What was the date of that redaction of the priestly passages
which was finally incorporated in the Hexateuch? I
answered: It must have been subsequent to *Deuteronomy.*
The priestly code contains regulations, such as *Lev.* xvi.,
xvii.; *Num.* xvi., xviii., xxxi., which can only be understood
as further developments of the demands made in *Deuteronomy*
(p. 147 sq., 152 sqq., cf. also p. 193 n. on *Josh.* xxi.).

All this necessarily involved a fourth departure from the
received opinion. The Deuteronomist could not have been
the redactor of our present Hexateuch. Such a hypothesis
was excluded alike by chronology and by the way in which
the task was performed. It was evidently from the sacerdotal
corporation of Jerusalem that the Hexateuch received its
present form; and the redactor, accordingly, must have been
a priest of Jerusalem (p. 165 sqq., p.194 sqq.).

I must confine myself to the simple enumeration of these
points, merely adding that some of my deviations from the
then current opinion might be regarded as a return to earlier
hypotheses. The priority of *Deuteronomy* as compared with
the priestly laws had been defended by George[1] and Vatke[2]

[1] J. F. L. George: Die älteren jüdischen Feste mit einer Kritik der Gesetzgebung des Pentateuch, 1835.
[2] W. Vatke: Die biblische Theologie wissenschaftlich dargestellt, I., 1835.

(*Onderzoek*, p. 46 sq.). And when I now re-read the arguments which I then regarded as an adequate refutation of
their views I can but acknowledge the power of tradition
or, if you will, of public opinion, even in the domain of
criticism! Not that the views of these two scholars satisfied
every reasonable requirement, or could even now be accepted
in the form in which they presented them. But they
contained elements of truth to which I was far from doing
justice. The concessions I made were inevitable—but wholly
inadequate. From my present position I regard them on the
one hand as a tribute extorted by the power of truth, but on
the other hand as a humiliating proof of the tyranny which
the opinions we have once accepted often exercise over us.
When we are really called upon boldly to quit our ground
and choose a new site for our edifice we too often attempt to
stave off the necessity by timid and minute modifications in
the plan to which we are already committed.

But it is high time to turn to the proper purpose of this
Introduction and attempt to sketch the course that the
criticism of the Hexateuch has taken since the year 1860.
I pass over Keil's commentary on the Pentateuch (1861
sqq.) and Knobel's Pentateuch and Book of Joshua (1852–
1861), since they exercised no permanent influence on the
criticism of the Hexateuch; but in 1862 appeared the first
part of J. W. Colenso's *Pentateuch and Book of Joshua
critically examined*, which deserves our close attention.

Colenso's work was of course attacked as blasphemous from
the orthodox side; but it was also taxed from the opposite
quarter with falling short of the requirements of modern
scholarship. Those who urged this charge no doubt accorded
more favour to the immediately following Parts II–V. of the
Bishop's work, than they had done to Part I.; but I have
never been able to accept this judgment. In such a sketch

as this, Parts II–V. can occupy but little space. No doubt
they contain much that is interesting. For example, Part III.
includes a very careful analysis of *Deuteronomy*, Part IV. a
number of sound observations on the composition and the
unhistorical character of *Genesis* i.–xi., and Part V. a fresh
investigation of the composition of *Genesis*. But in all this
the writer builds upon foundations already laid, and still
appears as a supporter of what I have called the 'dominant
hypothesis[1].' Where he deviates from his predecessors—
especially in Part II., with reference to the Elohîm- and
Yahwè-psalms—he cannot be said to have improved upon
them. And even if it were otherwise, if all his innova-
tions had been improvements, still he would in the main
have merely worked out and confirmed what was pretty
generally admitted before he wrote. No new light is struck,
no new direction given to research in these volumes.
But it is far otherwise with Part I. Continental criticism
of the Pentateuch had been inconsiderately busying itself
with a constructive work that used these very materials
now so rudely tested by Colenso. For myself I gladly
admit that he directed my attention to difficulties which I
had hitherto failed to observe or adequately to reckon with.
And as to the opinion of his labours current in Germany I
need only say that inasmuch as Ewald, Bunsen, Bleek, and
Knobel were every one of them logically forced—if they
could but have seen it!—to revise their theories in the light
of the English bishop's researches, there was small reason in
the cry that his methods were antiquated and his objections
stale!

It will be remembered that Colenso demonstrated the

---

[1] In Parts VI. and VII. Colenso adopts a new critical position, and partially
allies himself with the opponents of the once 'dominant hypothesis.' The
detailed work contained in Part VI. especially, demands and will receive a
conscientious consideration in the body of this work.

absolutely unhistorical character of sundry narratives in the Pentateuch by applying the test of those universal laws of time and space from which no chain of phenomena can escape. In a certain sense this was nothing new. Colenso was not the first to note that the stories of the Mosaic times were not simple reflections of the facts, but must be regarded as exaggerated and but half historical legends. But his investigations made it clear that this was but half the truth. He showed that the very documents which most expressly put themselves forward as authentic, and make the greatest parade of accuracy, are in reality the most unhistorical of all. In other words it is just the narratives of the 'Grundschrift' or 'Book of Origins' which turn out to be the most helpless before his criticism. This is all the more remarkable inasmuch as Colenso urged his objections without any regard to the separation of the various documents. He was only concerned with the question whether the representations of the Pentateuch, as they stand, correspond or fail to correspond with the actual facts. Again and again he meets with insuperable difficulties, and behold! it is always in the 'Grundschrift' that they occur. With one single exception the twenty chapters of his book are devoted to an absolutely pulverising criticism of the data of the 'Grundschrift.'

The dominant theory of the genesis of the Hexateuch had not prepared us for any such result. In the earliest of the documents we should have expected to find the most faithful reflection of the actual facts. Nor is this all. How are we to reconcile Colenso's results with the form into which the accounts of the 'Grundschrift' are thrown? When we read that the Israelites numbered 600,000 fighting men and then discover that physical impossibilities are involved in any such supposition, it is easy to put down the estimate to the embellishing hand of legend. But when we are presented with two official reports of the census, in *Num.* i. and xxvi. respectively, which accurately define the numerical strength of each tribe, severally, and in conclusion make the totals reach just about the given figure, then surely the case is changed. I must either suppress my difficulties as best I may in the face of the authority with which I am confronted, or—if that is simply impossible—I must frankly declare that the 'authority' is no authority at all, but neither more nor less than *a fiction.* There is no other alternative. Now Colenso's criticism places us again and again in the face of this dilemma. He himself did not perceive the legitimate inferences that flowed from his demonstrations; for in subsequent volumes [1] of his work he accepts the current opinion as to the date and character of the 'Grundschrift.' But the fact only serves to emphasise the impression made by his criticism on an observant reader capable of estimating its true bearings. Such at least was the result in my own case. I had myself pointed out some of the difficulties on which Colenso dwelt (cf. *Onderzoek*, I. 36 under *f.* [on *Ex.* xxxviii. 25 sqq.] and 92, n. 13 [on *Num.* xxxi.]); but massed together as they were by him, and set forth with such imperturbable *sang froid* and relentless thoroughness, they raised a strange presentiment in my mind which gradually ripened into a settled conviction that we had stopped half way in our criticism of the 'Grundschrift,' and must go right through with it before we could reach our goal.

This same year of 1862 witnessed another attack on the 'Grundschrift' from quite another side in a work by the Jewish scholar Dr. J. Popper, entitled *Der biblische Bericht über die Stiftshütte. Ein Beitrag zur Geschichte der Composition und Diaskeue des Pentateuch.* The results of Popper's investigation are in substance as follows: 'The description of the rearing of the tabernacle (*Ex.* xxxv.–xl.),

---

[1] I. e. Parts II–V. Cf. p. xv. *note.*

and of the consecration of the priests to their task (*Lev.* viii.)
is later than the injunctions on these two subjects (*Ex.*
xxv.–xxxi.), and cannot have received its present form until
long after the Babylonian captivity.' This book of Popper's
is in more than one respect a tough piece of reading. The
style is so diffuse as to furnish an unbroken illustration of
the well-known rule on 'l'art d'ennuyer.' And moreover the
question itself is highly involved, for the author bases his
conclusions on a study not only of the Masoretic, but of the
Samaritan text and the Greek translation of *Ex.* xxxv. sqq.
A still greater difficulty, however, was, in the first instance,
raised by the result of the investigation. It departed so
widely from the traditional belief and seemed so far to overstep the limits of all legitimate hypothesis that it took some
time to recover the calm and impartial frame of mind imperatively requisite for the fair consideration of the theses here
maintained. My present judgment on Popper's investigations
may be found in my 'Religion of Israel,' Ch. VIII. and IX.,
and in the body of this work (p. 74 sqq.), but from the first
I was profoundly impressed by his argument, which gave a
shock to the very generally accepted belief in the unity of the
'Grundschrift,' and introduced the idea of a 'continuous *diaskeue*' that was obviously destined to exercise a powerful
influence upon future investigations [1].

With the exception of Geiger and Graf, the recognised
German critics took no notice of this work, brimful of sug-
gestiveness though it was, and thereby they showed but too

---

[1] The quasi-autobiographical character of this introduction justifies, and
indeed almost demands, the mention of another work that might otherwise
have been passed over. I refer to that startling and fascinating book of
Dozy's, 'De Israëlieten te Mekka,' Haarlem, 1864. Though I cannot indicate any considerable obligations to this book on the field of Pentateuchal
criticism, and am still less prepared to defend its dashing and brilliant hypotheses on the field of history, yet the awakening caused by Dozy's rare originality and freedom from traditional restraint produced an effect on my own
studies none the less real and important for being almost entirely indirect.

plainly how the 'dominant hypothesis' had established itself
in their minds too firmly to allow them to see the importance
or the truth of anything that conflicted with it[1].

It was by no means an accident that Graf, almost alone
of German critics, did justice to Popper's work, for he had
very largely shaken off the critical tradition which blinded
the rest. His epoch-making work: *Die geschichtlichen Bücher
des Alten Testaments. Zwei historisch-kritische Untersuchungen*,
bears the date of 1866, but as a matter of fact it appeared
towards the close of 1865.

The second essay (*Das Buch der Chronik als Geschichtsquelle*,
p. 114–247) has a certain connection with the criticism of the
Pentateuch, inasmuch as the Chronicler is often cited as a
witness to the credibility of some of the Pentateuchal narratives and the early existence of many of the laws, and it is
important to determine with certainty the degree of confidence
that may be placed in him. In this respect Graf's careful
investigations yield in general a negative result. He demon-
strates, as others had done before him, but with unprece-
dented thoroughness, the freedom with which the Chronicler
manipulated his materials, and shows that when his authorities
left him in the lurch he had no hesitation in accepting and
setting down as actual fact everything that his historical and
dogmatic convictions assured him must have happened. We
cannot fail to note the special effect of this line of criticism
in depriving the laws and narratives of the 'Grundschrift' of
an important source of confirmation—for the most part,
indeed, of the only support which the whole Old Testament
affords them. Now this same 'Grundschrift' is itself the
chief though not the only subject of the former of Graf's two
essays. Its title (*Die Bestandtheile der geschichtlichen Bücher*

---

[1] Unfortunately it cannot be said that Popper himself, in his subsequent
work 'Der Ursprung des Monotheismus,' Berlin, 1879, realised the legitimate
expectations raised by his essay.

von Genesis i. *bis* 2 *Kings* xxv.) shows that it covers, in some
sort, a much wider field; but whereas it deals with *Judges,
Samuel,* and *Kings* in so summary a manner as to leave many
important questions unanswered, its treatment of the Hexateuch was such as to inaugurate a veritable revolution. And
to this we must now confine ourselves. Graf's first care is
to establish a firm point of departure, or basis of operations;
and this he finds in *Deuteronomy.* In agreement with the
vast majority of critics he identifies Hilkiah's book of Law
(2 *Kings* xxii. sq.) with the deuteronomic code; and he likewise attributes its composition as well as its publication to the
same reign. The details of his criticism will be duly noted in
the body of this work (cf. p. 121 and elsewhere) and need not
detain us here. Taking Deuteronomy as his fixed point
Graf proceeds to inquire which of the laws and narratives of
the Hexateuch are assumed in that work as already existing,
and which of them on the contrary announce themselves as
subsequent to it. His conclusion, put into a nut-shell, is
that the Yahwistic laws (*Ex.* xx.–xxiii.; xiii. 1–16; xxxiv. 10–
27) and the Yahwistic narratives are shown to be præ-deuteronomic by a careful comparison of their form and contents
with the ordinances and statements of the Deuteronomist;
whereas the priestly or ritual laws usually regarded as
belonging to the 'Grundschrift' are post-deuteronomic.
Graf confronts these ordinances one after another with the
precepts of the Deuteronomist and the evidence of the historical books—and always with the same result, *viz.* the
establishment of the priority of *Deuteronomy.* I must refer
to my 'Religion of Israel' (Ch. VIII., and the second note
appended to it) for the details in which I agreed with Graf or
dissented from him at the time. Here we must note that he
still supposed the (curtailed) 'Grundschrift,' the Yahwist, and
the Deuteronomist to follow each other in the accepted order,
and regarded the last of the three as the redactor of a his-

torico-legislative work beginning with the creation of the
world and ending with the death of Joshua. But this work,
he believed, was something very different from our present
Hexateuch; for in this latter the whole mass of the priestly
laws and (*nota bene!*) some priestly narratives were added by
Ezra after the Captivity, forming altogether a colossal interpolation in the work of the Deuteronomist, consisting of
Ex. xxv.–xxxi.; xxxv.–xl., all *Leviticus*, and the greater part
of *Numbers*. If these priestly additions are withdrawn we have
the work of the Deuteronomist left, consisting of *Genesis* and
Joshua in their present form, *Deuteronomy* nearly as we now
have it, and *Exodus* and *Numbers* in their original form.

Such was the genealogy of the Hexateuch as drawn out
by Graf. We note at once that it splits the so-called
'Grundschrift'—Ewald's 'Book of Origins'—into two. The
smaller, or historical portion retains its place as the earliest
element of the Hexateuch, the basis on which the Yahwist
built in the eighth century B. C., and itself therefore still more
ancient. The greater, or legislative section of the supposed
'Grundschrift,' on the other hand, is the latest of all the
great strata of the Hexateuch. Some of it is a little earlier
than Ezra, some of it due to Ezra himself, and some of it—
a genuine discovery of Popper's—even subsequent to 450 B. C.
But how is it possible, one asks at once, that the earliest and
the latest elements of the Hexateuch should hitherto have
been classed together and regarded as portions of one and the
same work? Graf answers (p. 92 sq.) that a certain resemblance of language had misled the critics, but that its true
explanation must be sought not in community of origin, but
in the later priestly author's deliberate imitation of the style
of the 'Grundschrift,' especially such passages of it as *Gen.*
xvii. for example.

The first glance at Graf's essay was enough to satisfy me
that this attempt to split up the 'Grundschrift' was the

Achilles-heel of his whole hypothesis. My attention was continuously directed to this point by a renewed study of the Hexateuch which I had already entered upon in connection with my lectures for 1865–66, before the appearance of Graf's book; and my conviction was soon established that his solution could not be the true one. It was neither one thing nor the other. Anyone who took his stand with Graf on the historical passages which he still recognised as belonging to the ancient præ-Yahwistic 'Grundschrift,' might show that he had no right to make the legislative portions so much later. The historical and legislative sections are dominated by essentially the same conceptions and resemble each other so closely that they cannot possibly be severed by a period of three or four centuries. And conversely, if we are forced to admit with Graf that the ritual legislation is exilian or post-exilian then we must assign the priestly histories to the same period also. Were there any need I would undertake to place this dilemma in so strong a light that it could not be misconceived, but it will be enough simply to refer to *Num.* xx. 22–29; xxvii. 12–23; xxxiv.; xxxv. 1–8; 9–15 (the last three pericopes in whole or in part legislative, and yet assigned by Graf to the 'Grundschrift' proper) and *Josh.* xxi. These passages alone suffice to show how impossible it is to separate the historical sections from the laws, and to make the former some centuries earlier than the latter.

But what then? Must the laws stand with the narratives, or must the narratives fall with the laws? I could not hesitate for a moment in accepting the latter alternative. The reader will see by what has gone before that I was already more than half won over to such a view, and Graf's treatise had itself influenced me powerfully in the same direction. He had supported his thesis that the priestly laws are post-deuteronomic with a host of valid arguments which,

though not severally conclusive in every instance, established
an irresistible case collectively, whereas in recognising the
high antiquity of the historical parts of the 'Grundschrift'
and the use made of them by the Yahwist he had simply
attached himself to the traditions of the critical school without
adducing a single argument to support them. It was obvious
that the question whether these historical passages were
really in their place at the head of the genealogy of the
Hexateuch had never so much as presented itself to him.
Hardly had I begun seriously to ask myself on what
grounds they had been placed there by others and left
there by Graf than I saw more clearly day by day that they
had no real claim whatever to be regarded as præ-Yahwistic.
In a word, not only does the prophetic preaching chronologically precede the priestly legislation, but the prophetic (= Yahwistic) representations of the genesis of the
theocracy precede the priestly historiography. And
may we not ask, in passing, whether the problem when so
formulated does not almost solve itself?

Perhaps I may be permitted at this point to transcribe a
fragment of a letter I received from Graf in answer to the
objections I had urged against this portion of his solution.
His last public utterances were of similar purport, but it is
not without interest to show that in 1866 (his letter is dated
Nov. 12th of that year) a simple expression of the difficulty,
unsupported by any attempt at a proof, had already disposed
him to revise his ideas of the genesis of the Hexateuch.
Writing to the Alsatian (whom moreover the German
governments allowed to remain till his death—not Professor
of Old Testament Exegesis and Criticism at any of the
Universities, but—'Professeur de Français' at the Royal Gym-
nasium of Meissen) I had availed myself of the French
language, in which he likewise answered. 'Je suis loin de
croire que toutes les difficultés soient résolues. Au contraire

vous m'en faites remarquer une bien sérieuse et qui n'a pas manqué en effet de me causer beaucoup de scrupules, la grande ressemblance entre les lois sacerdotales et les parties élohistiques de la Genèse. Je n'ai pu donner moi-même qu'une explication de cette ressemblance quant à la loi sur la circoncision (p. 93) que je suis forcé de reconnaître comme insuffisante et vous avez raison de craindre qu'en s'appuyant sur l'antiquité de ces parties élohistiques on ne puisse soulever de bien graves difficultés contre ma manière d'envisager les origines du Pentateuque. Mais vous me faites pressentir une solution de cette énigme qui m'a frappé d'autant plus vivement qu'elle était tout-à-fait nouvelle pour moi et que cependant j'ai senti à l'instant que c'était là sans doute la solution véritable, c'est que les parties élohistiques de la Genèse seraient postérieures aux parties jéhovistiques. La priorité de l'Élohiste sur le Jéhoviste a été jusqu'à présent tellement hors de doute ou plutôt admise comme une sorte d'axiome, que la preuve du contraire produirait une véritable révolution dans la critique du Pentateuque, principalement de la Genèse ; mais je ne manquerai pas dorénavant de considérer le Pentateuque sous ce point de vue, pour parvenir à me former une conviction raisonnée par rapport à cette priorité.'

My own conclusions, after a special study of the priestly narratives from this point of view, are embodied in my 'Religion of Israel,' and will be further illustrated in the course of this essay. I may therefore pass them over for the present. I may likewise deal very summarily with Riehm's criticism of Graf's book[1]. He protests against the attempt to separate the historical from the legislative portions of the 'Grundschrift,' the essential unity of which he maintains. And he further recalls Hupfeld's attack on the 'Ergänzungshypothese,' and regrets that Graf has paid no attention to it.

---

[1] Studien u. Krit., 1868, p. 350–79.

On both of these points I am completely at one with him. But his arguments in support of the priority of the ritual laws, compared with those of *Deuteronomy*, are so extremely weak that they could hardly have seemed satisfactory to their author himself had he not already been committed to the conclusion they are adduced to support.

In one important point Graf's researches were supplemented by my countryman Dr. W. H. Kosters, whose doctoral essay *De Historie-beschouwing van den Deuteronomist met de berichten in Genesis–Numeri vergeleken*, appeared in Leiden in 1868. Graf had shown that the Deuteronomist was unacquainted with the priestly laws; but which of the narratives of the Pentateuch lay before him? And, specifically, were the priestly or elohistic narratives amongst them? This was the question which Dr. Kosters asked and answered. He compared all the historical data in Deuteronomy with the narratives of *Genesis–Numbers*; and the result—which is always the same—renders it almost certain that the deuteronomic conception of history stands midway between the Yahwistic (prophetic) and the elohistic (priestly). Kosters himself, however, in keeping with the plan of his dissertation, confines himself to the purely negative conclusion that the Deuteronomist shows no familiarity with the priestly narratives. With the character and relative position of these latter he only concerns himself incidentally; but they were soon to be submitted to a luminous examination on their own merits by Nöldeke, whose work comes next in our chronological survey. Is not such a succession of investigations itself a sufficient indication that the results previously regarded as established were no longer felt to be satisfactory, and that a new conception was gradually ripening[1]?

[1] From this point of view I may likewise call attention to M. M. Kalisch's ' *Historical and Critical Commentary, etc.*' *Leviticus*, Part I., 1867, Part II., 1872, London. After having dealt in a prevailingly conservative spirit with

The first and most important of the four essays that make up Nöldeke's *Untersuchungen zur Kritik des A. Testaments* (Kiel, 1869) deals with 'Die s. g. Grundschrift des Pentateuchs.' At the outset Nöldeke explains his belief that the essential elements of the Hexateuch must be assigned to the following sources and writers : (1) The 'Grundschrift;' (2) the Yahwist, who compiled his work out of materials that included an elohistic document, from which he took over entire sections, but which we must carefully distinguish from the 'Grundschrift;' (3) the redactor, who united (1) and (2) into a single whole; (4) the Deuteronomist, who combined his own legislation and the associated historical passages with the work of (3). The bulk of the essay is then devoted to an investigation of the first of these sources. Nöldeke begins by attempting to define its limits. He runs through the whole Hexateuch, watching for the formal and substantial marks of the 'Grundschrift,' which grow ever clearer and fuller as he proceeds. At the close of this investigation (p. 7–108) he reviews the 'Grundschrift' as a whole, and endeavours to sketch the method of its author and determine its historical value. It is in the pages devoted to this task (p. 108–143) that the true and permanent significance of Nöldeke's essay appears to me to lie. He lays down, with the hand of a master, the characteristics of the priestly author, his passion for systematising, for developing a symmetry and an ascending emphasis everywhere, and setting everything before us in a minutely definite shape. His chronology and his figures generally are submitted to a keen inspection, and with striking results. The contrast between the 'Grundschrift' and the Yahwistic narratives

---

Genesis and *Exodus*, Kalisch treated the critical questions suggested by Leviticus with great vigour and independence, and arrived at conclusions essentially in harmony with those of Graf. His independent co-operation was of high value.

comes out with ever growing distinctness. The latter are
legends worked up in the prophetic spirit, the former have
left tradition far behind, and give us instead the offspring
of the fancy, or more often the postulates of the dogmatic
system of their author. To a certain extent all this had been
noted before, but never had it been so displayed in its full extent
and significance. What had previously been no more than a
well-grounded impression was raised by Nöldeke's discoveries
into an established fact. Let me give a single instance. The
two lists in *Numbers* i. and xxvi. might have been pronounced
inventions without the least hesitation, because—well because they could not rest upon tradition. But now came
Nöldeke and showed to demonstration how they were constructed. 'The figure of 600,000 for the whole force of
fighting men was given by the earlier writings. Divided
amongst the twelve tribes this would give an average of
50,000 warriors for each tribe. Now the two lists are so
constructed that, in each case, six of the tribes give more and
six less than the average; but not the same six in the two
lists. Simeon and Naphthali, who muster 59,300 and 53,000
respectively in *Numbers* i., have come down to 22,200 and
45,400 in *Numbers* xxvi., whereas Asher and Manasseh have
risen from 41,500 and 32,200 respectively to 53,400 and
52,700.' Is not a single glance such as this into the work-
shop of the author of the ' Grundschrift' enough to instruct
us as to his method?

I confess that it was a great disappointment to me, and
still remains enigmatical, how Nöldeke, after giving such
a sketch of the character of the ' Grundschrift,' should hold
by the tradition as to its antiquity, or at least decline to
depart anything like far enough from it. There is no need,
he says (p. 141), to make the so-called ' Grundschrift' the very
oldest document of the Pentateuch. It may really be so, but
it may also be contemporary with the work of the Yahwist, or

even somewhat later. But—and this is the limit Nöldeke thinks we must insist on—it is at least præ-deuteronomic, Graf's proofs to the contrary are pronounced inadequate. Taking his stand on the unity of the 'Grundschrift,' which Graf had made the great mistake of sacrificing, and insisting on the antiquity of its narratives, which Graf did not deny, Nöldeke maintains that the laws also must be attributed to some priest of the temple of Solomon. It is true that the laws in question were never carried out, but this is easily explained from the circumstances. The priests must hold the helm of the state before the full realisation of their demands could be so much as thought of. After the Captivity, and under Ezra's influence, the whole Mosaic code was made the rule of faith and conduct; but it was not the post-exilian period that produced that code. It did but bring to light and embody in practice what had long existed in theory or as a demand.

My friend De Goeje, who reviewed Nöldeke's book in *De Gids*, was fully justified in pronouncing this conclusion wholly unsatisfactory. Had Nöldeke disarmed Graf's proofs of the post-deuteronomic origin of the ritual laws? Some of them he had not so much as noticed. Others he admits to be valid in a certain sense, but maintains that they only show the laws to have exercised no practical influence at first. And no doubt we should have to accept this solution if the laws were really proved to have been in existence at an early date. But the proof would have to be a very strong one before it could induce us to believe that a whole system of priestly legislation was codified for no practical purpose, but simply in the hope of better times. Now no such proof is given by Nöldeke at all. His attempts to trace the 'Grundschrift' in Amos and Hosea will be duly noted in the body of this work, but when we compare them with the colossal force of Graf's demonstration Nöldeke appears to

be engaged in an attempt to suspend a 'fifty-six' by a
cobweb; and indeed he admits himself (p. 142) that a sceptic
might, at need, explain all the references to the 'Grundschrift' in the prophets of the Assyrian period, and even
in Jeremiah and his contemporaries, as mere coincidences.
But he goes on to say that 'the Deutcronomist, at any rate,
implies with absolute certainty the existence of the whole
compilation of which the "Grundschrift" is a part.' As
long as Nöldeke simply asserted this I could only let my
denial stand against his assertion. But at a later date he
endeavoured to bring proofs of his position, and these are
duly considered in their proper place (vid. infr., p. 171 sq.).
The weakness of his positive proof, which Nöldeke himself
seems to perceive, is made good in his opinion by an *argumentum ex absurdo* which he brings to reinforce it. The
'Grundschrift' must have been written about the time in
which he places it, because it cannot have been written
later. The post-exilian period, he thinks, was absolutely
incapable of producing such a work. Now this is—or rather
was—the general estimate of the post-exilian period, including the age of Ezra and Nehemiah. I should be glad
to see this conception, against which my 'Religion of Israel'
is one unbroken protest, seriously discussed, and, if unable
to defend its life, honourably buried[1]. That the Jewish
people became dry and unfruitful as soon as it returned
from Babylon must be accepted as soon as it is proved; but
a mere traditional prejudice must not be allowed for a moment
to protect an idea which is in itself equally mournful and
astonishing.

Schrader, in the 8th edition of de Wette's *Einleitung*,

---

[1] This hope, originally expressed in 1870, is now within measurable
distance of its full accomplishment. I may call attention, for instance, to
R. Smend's very interesting sketch 'Über die Genesis des Judenthums'
in the *Zeitschr. f. alttest. Wissenschaft*, II. 94-151.

adopted a position essentially analogous to that of Nöldeke, but he supported it by no fresh arguments of any weight, and his contributions to the discussion will be noticed in detail in the body of this work.

Nöldeke's treatise long remained the most conspicuous and important of all the attempts to refute Graf, and it was likewise the latest that Graf himself ever saw. The few pages which he devoted in Merx's *Archiv* (i. 466–77) to Riehm's and Nöldeke's criticisms were not in the hands of the public till their author had ceased to breathe, and the later contributions to the discussion he had raised never came under his eye. His concessions, in the article just referred to, were important. In the first place, he admits, with Hupfeld, Riehm, and Nöldeke, that the 'Ergänzungs-hypothese' must be abandoned, and that the Yahwist's literary activity must be recognised as independent. In the second place he allows that his attempt to divide the 'Grund-schrift' has failed ; that the legislation and the history must go together and that his own hypothesis of imitation was inadequate to explain their mutal connection. It follows, then, that if the legislation is exilian or post-exilian, then the accompanying narratives must be so too. So far from shrinking from this conclusion Graf embraces it unhesi-tatingly. It is nothing but habit, he declares (p. 468 sq.), that prevents our recognising the 'Grundschrift' as the latest stratum of the Pentateuch. We find it difficult not to think of the creation story in *Gen.* i. as the foundation of that which follows rather than as a later story placed before it. Graf attempts to dispel this prejudice by running through the Hexateuch and indicating the proofs of the later origin of the historical portions of the 'Grundschrift.' At the same time, however, by a kind of inversion of the old 'Ergänzungs-hypothese,' he denies the independence of the 'Grundschrift' and endeavours to show that its narratives not only pre-

suppose those of the Yahwist, but were intended from the
first to supplement them and to constitute a single whole
with them[1]. One need not accept this view of the relations
of the two sets of narratives in order to appreciate the weight
of Graf's arguments for the later origin of the ' Grundschrift'
or the vigour with which he defends his position with regard
to its laws against the attacks of Riehm and Nöldeke. The
idea of the passive existence of these laws for ages before they
had any practical influence is decisively rejected by Graf.
He argues that the transplanting of the foremost representatives of the priesthood, with Jehoiachin, to Babylon, where
they were deprived of the support of a civil and ecclesiastical
organization of their own, was the very thing most calculated
to throw them back upon half traditional, half theoretical
methods of collecting, systematising, developing, and completing
the precepts of their religion, and so stimulating that ' theoretical reconstruction of history and legislation,' which, according to Nöldeke himself (p. 132), is the most prominent
characteristic of the ' Grundschrift.' Ezekiel at the opening
and Ezra at the close (or at least at a decisive turning point)
of this period of Babylonian activity furnish the irrefragable
proof that it is not a mere creature of the imagination.

With this short paper of Graf's the problem may be regarded
as assuming its true form. His great essay had recalled the
criticism of the Pentateuch to the true path, and his frank
recognition of his errors had prevented its being drawn away
again on a side issue. In the discussion that followed he
could take no part, but however much we may lament we
can hardly complain that one who had done so much was
not enabled to do yet more.

We have seen that Graf's hypothesis, in its original form,
had, at first, won no support. Nevertheless, if arguments

---

[1] Vid. infr. p. 299, 301 sq., where the somewhat analogous views put
forward by Maybaum in 1880 are likewise discussed.

are to be weighed, not counted, and if in criticism as elsewhere the heaviest weight is to weigh heaviest, then we
must admit that the ultimate issue could not even then be
doubtful, and that all valid objections to the hypothesis
must be met not by withdrawing it, but by pushing it
through to its legitimate conclusions.

The remainder of this introduction will be devoted to a
brief and summary indication of the principal steps by which
this result has been actually attained.

II.

In 1869 and 1870 my own 'Religion of Israel' appeared
in Holland. It was an attempt to write the religious history
of Israel from the point of view of the newer criticism, and
to show that that criticism not only rested on a firmer objective basis than the theories it sought to overthrow, but would
in its turn serve as the foundation of a constructive treatment of Israel's history in every way more coherent and
rational than had been possible previously.

I had no reason to complain of the reception or the effect
of my work. In Holland and England it was accepted by
many scholars as having laid down the main lines of the
religious development of Israel correctly, and in further
elaborating and defending its fundamental assumptions I was
able to rely on the support of my friends Tiele, Oort,
De Goeje, Kosters, and many others.

I was subsequently able to strengthen whatever impression
I had made by publishing from time to time a more detailed
treatment of special points or aspects of the question in the
eleventh and following volumes of the *Theologisch Tijdschrift*,
in a series of *Contributions to the criticism of the Pentateuch
and Joshua.*

German scholarship, however, long appeared to present an

almost solid phalanx against the newer criticism, and until Germany was won, the battle was, to say the least, ' behind and before.' Merx[1] and de Lagarde[2], indeed, were our allies, and were able to point to utterances which proved that they had reached important points of agreement with us independently of our help. Moreover rumours were abroad of important defections from critical orthodoxy impending but not yet declared. It almost seemed as though our German friends were lying in ambush somewhere watching for their chance. Woe to the enemy when they should spring upon him !

Meanwhile the attack was strengthened by a work which issued (like Graf's) from the school of Reuss. Aug. Kayser published in 1874 *Das vorexilische Buch der Urgeschichte Israels und seine Erweiterungen*, in which he defended the thesis that 'the elohistic document, the so-called Grundschrift, was composed in its entirety (historical and legislative portions alike) after the return from the Captivity.' Inasmuch as Kayser was unacquainted with anything that had been written on the subject since Graf's *Geschichtliche Bücher*, his investigations had hardly less value as an independent confirmation of results already gained by others than they would have possessed had they really been, as he supposed, entirely new in the breadth and scope of their conclusions.

Kayser begins with a fresh analysis of the Pentateuch, which advances the critical position at several points of interest ; but the weight of his essay lies in the very careful examination of the Israelitish literature in order to discover

[1] Cf. Merx in *Prot. Kirchenzeitung* for 1865, no. 17, and in his *Nachwort* to Tuch's *Genesis*, 2nd ed.

[2] Cf. Lagarde in the *Gött. Gel. Anzeigen* for Sept. 28, 1870, p. 1549–1560, containing a reference to his academical lectures in 1864 and the following years.

indications of the form in which the Pentateuchal narratives and laws lay before the other biblical authors. Beginning with Deuteronomy, and running through the whole series of historical books, then returning to trace the prophets down in chronological order, Kayser finds that in all cases the priestly narratives and laws alike are excluded from the field of vision of the præ-exilian and early exilian writers, who build first upon the prophetic and then upon the deuteronomic elements of the Hexateuch, and show not the smallest trace of acquaintance with the Priestly Codex. It will be seen that Kayser's line of investigation was not new; but it was carried out with a comprehensive thoroughness and minuteness that gave it the highest importance, and though Schrader and Nöldeke again stepped forward (and now for the last time) in defence of the critical tradition, they were far from successful in disarming Kayser's demonstration[1].

And here I must desert the order of chronology, for a moment, to note the issue in 1879 of the third part of Édouard Reuss's great work *La Bible,* under the sub-title *L'Histoire sainte et la Loi.* The venerable Strassburg Professor showed himself, in his admirable introduction to this work, to be not so much a distinguished convert to the Grafian hypothesis as its real author. Ever since 1833 he had held and had from time to time uttered opinions, based rather on intuitive insight than on minute and exhaustive investigations, which anticipated the main result of the newer criticism and substituted the succession Prophets, Law, Psalms, for the traditional Law, Psalms, Prophets. In the lecture-rooms of Strassburg, then, we might look, in no small measure, for the ultimate source of Graf's and Kayser's inspiration, and Reuss had the satisfaction of seeing the views he had enunciated in his youth taken up

---

[1] Kayser has made further contributions to the analysis of the Pentateuch in the *Jahrb. f. prot. Theol.,* 1881 (vid. infr. p. 2).

and elaborated by his distinguished pupils and commanding ever increasing assent as he incorporated them, matured and consolidated, into the works of his old age[1].

From this parenthetical notice of the founder of that Strassburg school of criticism which, as we have seen, played such an important part in the history we are tracing, we may now return to our chronological survey, remembering that we have reached the point at which our allies in Holland, England, and Alsatia were awaiting, so to speak, the adhesion of their German friends.

At last, in 1875, Bernhard Duhm, of Göttingen, broke the consensus of the German critics by the publication of *Die Theologie der Propheten als Grundlage für die innere Entwicklungsgeschichte der Israelitischen Religion.*

It is not obvious from the title of this work what bearing it has on the question here at issue; and in truth our problem is attacked by Duhm in quite a new and independent way. It is nevertheless inseparably connected with the subject of his monograph. For to study the theology of the prophets we must know whether Prophecy is an independent phenomenon, or whether it is a link in a chain; and if it is the latter we must distinctly realise its position and its connection with what goes before and comes after it in order rightly to comprehend its character.

Will the traditional succession of Mosaism, Prophecy, Judaism, lead us to a true understanding of the Prophets? Duhm regards this succession as antecedently improbable. In point of fact it makes the legal period precede and follow the prophetic; and moreover Judaism by no means strikes us as a mere falling back upon antiquity. The post-exilian psalms, for example, sung in praise of the Law, are redolent with a freshness of delight which fully justifies

---

[1] See also ' *Die Gesch. der Heil. Schrift. A. T's.,*' by Ed. Reuss., Braunschweig, 1882.

us in believing that the poets must have felt themselves
in a complete and intelligent sympathy with the Law such
as could never have belonged to a 'restoration.' But the
difficulty is far greater in understanding how that very
identical legalism which we know to have been the death
of prophecy in the post-exilian period could have been its
nurse or mother in the earlier times. It is all very well
to say that the prophets maintained the spirit of Mosaism
while neglecting its letter, but in the first place we are
never shown that this assertion has any intelligible sense,
and in the next place no attempt is made to show us that
it is true. Certainly the law itself makes no such distinction
as is here implied, and if the prophets had intended to do
so they could not have helped laying it down and defending
it, while at the same time defining their position towards
the letter.

Prima facie, then, both psychology and history seem
opposed to the succession Mosaism, Prophecy, Judaism; but
we have yet to ask whether a closer investigation of the
documents may not compel us to accept it, or, in other words,
whether it can be shown that the great central mass of
the Tora, narrative and legislative, did really precede the
prophets.

Provisionally accepting the results obtained, on this point,
by Vatke, myself, Kayser, and others, Duhm proceeds to
investigate the historical conditions and the internal development of prophecy, to see whether the whole history, external
and internal, can be consistently traced out on the assumption
of the non-existence of the priestly legislation. The result
is that, in the whole course of his masterly investigation,
he is never once driven back upon the Mosaic Law for
explanations or illustrations of the growth of prophecy.
This is, in itself, an important indication that he has chosen
the right point of view. But there is more. On two occa-

sions his path leads him into immediate contact with the
Tora, *viz.* when he has to deal with Deuteronomy in describing
the historical environment of the prophets of the second
period, and again when his investigation closes, at the time
of Ezra and Nehemiah. Does it appear at these critical
points that he has been following the wrong track? And
does he meet with phenomena here which compel him to
adopt other premises than those from which he started?
On the contrary, he is able, here too, to explain what he
finds before him without violence or difficulty.

Take his section on Deuteronomy (p. 194 sqq.). The
fundamental ideas of the deuteronomic legislation are, he
says, the demand to serve Yahwè alone, and serve him with
the service of the heart; Israel's sanctity, or the consecration
of Israel to Yahwè; the temple at Jerusalem as Yahwè's
only sanctuary; Levi's descendants as the only lawful priests.
Now these fundamental ideas he clearly shows to be derived
specifically from Hosea and Isaiah; so that they presuppose
their activity, but nothing else,—no priestly legislation for
instance. And, we may add, if even Deuteronomy presupposes
such an objective projection of religion as we find in Hosea
and Isaiah, not in Amos or Micah (see the striking passage
in Duhm, p. 199 sq.), how much more must the priestly code
follow rather than precede the same!

This last point is brought out by Duhm himself in his
section on 'the establishment of the Theocracy' (p. 264
sqq.); where, in spite of what seems to me his injustice
towards Ezra's Law, he nevertheless points out its connection
with all that had gone before with irrefragable truth.

Experience had shown that there were scholars who might
remain deaf even to the claims of such historical considerations as these, who would prefer to think that the so-called
'Grundschrift' dropped from the sky some few centuries
before anyone wanted it rather than that it grew up in

its own historical environment when its hour had come. Yet as I read Duhm's book, it seemed as if they must hear at last, so loud and clear was the witness he bore, alike in the passages analysed and throughout his work. 'I have already declared myself absolutely convinced by the arguments of Graf, Kuenen, and others in support of the Grafian hypothesis. The post-exilian origin of the priestly book of religion has been demonstrated more cogently and more abundantly than the exilian origin of the second part of Isaiah' (p. 195). Bold words! yet not too bold. No one who had really grasped the situation could take any other view[1].

Duhm's work was not without its effect, but it was reserved for another scholar finally to break up the German opposition to the ' Grafians,' as we were generally called.

In 1876 and 1877 Dr. Julius Wellhausen, well known by his admirable treatment of various critical and historical subjects connected with the literature and religion of Israel, published his valuable studies on the ' Composition des Hexateuchs' in the *Jahrb. f. deutsche Theologie.* Though mainly devoted to the critical analysis of the Hexateuch, these studies were intimately connected with our question, and their author left no room for doubt as to his position with respect to it[2]. His great contribution to its solution, however, was made in the year 1878, in the first volume of his *History of Israel.* I can fortunately dispense with any detailed account of this work inasmuch as it is now in the

---

[1] Were I criticising Duhm's book, instead of merely pointing out its place in the history of Pentateuchal investigation, I should have to dwell on its involved and perplexing style, its overstrained contrasts and distinctions, and its occasionally unsympathetic tone.

[2] The earlier of these articles were translated and controverted by Colenso, whose objections will be noted from time to time in this work. They are now reprinted as the second volume of the author's *Skizzen und Vorarbeiten,* Berlin, 1885.

hands of English readers[1], but I can hardly describe the delight with which I first read it—a delight such as seldom indeed meets one on the path of learning. At one with the writer *a priori*, not only in principles but in general results, I was able to follow him from beginning to end with almost unbroken assent, and at the same time to learn more than I can say from every part of his work. Now and then my pleasure was—shall I say tempered or increased?—when I noted that Wellhausen had got the start of me as to this or that point that I had expected to indicate for the first time, in my own forthcoming work. But I could not wish that I had been sooner on the field, for in that case I should have missed all the other points which I had not anticipated and by which I could now profit.

Wellhausen's treatment of our theme, for which I must refer to his book itself, was so cogent, so original, and so brilliant, that its publication may be regarded as the ' crowning fight' in the long campaign. Since 1878 the question has been more and more seriously considered in Germany— and in most cases to consider it seriously has meant to decide it in our sense. Some eminent scholars still hold out against the ' Grafian hypothesis[2],' but it is no longer possible to count its supporters or to enumerate *seriatim* the works written in its defence or built upon its assumptions[3]. In

[1] *Prolegomena to the History of Israel, with a reprint of the article Israel from the 'Encyclopædia Britannica,'* by Julius Wellhausen, etc., translated by J. Sutherland Black, M.A. and Allen Menzies, B.D. Preface by Prof. W. Robertson Smith, Edinburgh, A. and C. Black, 1885.

[2] The foremost place amongst them belongs to Dillmann (vid. infr. p. 1), whose view, however, cannot be judged in its entirety till the appearance of his forthcoming commentaries on *Numbers, Deuteronomy,* and *Joshua.* He is supported by Ed. Riehm of Halle, already referred to. A middle position is defended or sought by W. Graf von Baudissin (*Der heutige Stand der alttestamentlichen Wissenschaft,* Gieszen, 1885) and in a certain sense by Delitzsch (vid. infr. p. 2).

[3] I cannot, however, refrain from mentioning the names, if nothing more, of Budde, Giesebrecht, Horst, Smend, Stade, and Robertson Smith,

setting forth in this treatise, for the first time, its complete
and systematic critical justification I am no longer advocating
a heresy, but am expounding the received view of European
critical scholarship. Those who dissent from it may still
appeal to names which command universal respect, but they
can no longer stake their case on the ' consensus criticorum,'
which has at last declared itself against them.

whose writings will be noticed in the body of this work, and F. E. König
(*Der Offenbarungsbegriff des A. T.*, 2 vols., Leipzig, 1882) who combines the
Grafian criticism with a very rigid doctrinal orthodoxy.

ADDENDUM TO PAGE 2.

Since the early sheets of this work left my hand, the translation
of Wellhausen's *Prolegomena* (see p. xxxix) has appeared. References to this, as to other translations, are inserted in square
brackets.

Wellhausen's Articles on the Composition of the Hexateuch are
now published separately as the second part of his *Skizzen und
Vorarbeiten*, Berlin, 1885; but as the pagination of the original
is given in the margin of the reprint, the references in this work
will be available for either form of the essays.—Tr.

THE HEXATEUCH

(PENTATEUCH AND BOOK OF JOSHUA).

LITERATURE. For more than a century past the origin of the Pentateuch, [5] and especially the question whether Moses was its author, has been the subject of diligent inquiry and of violent dispute. The most important of the almost innumerable books and essays that deal with separate portions of the critical inquiry will be mentioned in their proper places in the course of our investigation. The subject, as a whole, is dealt with in the 'Introductions' to the Old Testament (J. G. Eichhorn; L. Bertholdt; W. M. L. de Wette (8th ed. by E. Schrader); F. Bleek (3rd ed. by A. Kamphausen [English translation of 2nd ed. (also by Kamphausen) by G. H. Venables]; 4th ed. by J. Wellhausen); H. A. C. Hävernick (2nd ed. by C. F. Keil [English translation of 1st ed. by W. L. Alexander (general) and A. Thompson (special)]; C. F. Keil [English translation by G. C. M. Douglas], J. J. Stähelin, S. Davidson, and others), and also in the following works, amongst others of less importance :—

a. The Commentaries on the Pentateuch and Joshua. For the older commentaries cf. Kamphausen in Bleek's *Einl.* 3rd ed. p. 156-158 [i. 161-163], and the works there cited. The best known recent Commentaries are: J. S. Vater, *Commentar über den Pentateuch*, 3 Theile (Halle, 1802-1805); M. Baumgarten, *Theol. Commentar zum A. T.*, Erster Theil; *Pentateuch* (Kiel, 1842-1844); A. Knobel, in the *Kurzgefasstes exeg. Handbuch zum A. T.* Lief. xi. (Genesis, 4th ed. neu bearb. von A. Dillmann); xii. (Exodus u. Leviticus, 2nd ed. neu bearb. von A. Dillmann); xiii. (Numeri—Josua); M. Kalisch, *A hist. and crit. commentary on the O. T.* vol. i.-iv. Genesis, Exodus, Leviticus part i. and ii. (London, 1855-1872); C. F. Keil, in the *Bibl. Commentar über das A. T.*, by C. F. Keil and F. Delitzsch, Theil i. *Die Bücher Moses*; Theil ii. 1; *Josua, Richter u. Rut* (Leipzig, 1861 sqq. [English translations by J. Martin; Pentateuch, 3 vols. Josh. etc. 1 vol.] Commentaries on the Book of Genesis have been written by G. A. Schumann (1829); P. von Bohlen (1835) [partial English translation, edited by J. Heywood]; F. Tuch (1838; 2nd ed. by Arnold and Merx, 1871); F. Delitzsch (1852; 4th ed. [6] 1872); E. Böhmer (1862); on Deuteronomy, by F. W. Schultz (1859); on Joshua, by F. J. V. D. Maurer (1831); C. F. Keil (1847) [English translation by J. Martin].

b. The critical researches of J. S. Vater, *Abhandlung über Moses u. die Verfasser des Pentateuchs* (in his Commentar, etc. iii. 391-728); W. M. L. de Wette, *Beiträge zur Kritik des A. T.*, 2 Bände (Halle, 1806-1807); A. Th.

Hartmann, *Hist. Krit. Forschungen über . . . fünf Bücher Mose's* (Rostock, 1831); F. H. Ranke, *Untersuchungen über den Pentateuch*, 2 Bände (Erlangen, 1834-1840), E. W. Hengstenberg, *Die Authentie des Pentateuchs* (in his Beiträge zur Einl. in das A. T., Bd. ii. and iii., 2 Bände (Berlin, 1836-1839) [English translation by J. E. Ryland]; B. Welte, *Nachmosaisches im Pentateuch* (Freiburg, 1841); J. J. Stähelin, *Krit. Untersuchungen über den Pent., die Bücher Jos. Richt. Sam. u. der Könige* (Berlin, 1843); J. W. Colenso, *The Pent. and Book of Joshua critically examined*, part i.-vii. (London, 1862-1879); *Lectures on the Pent. and the Moabite stone* (London, 1873); K. H. Graf, *Die gesch. Bücher des A. T.*, p. 1-113 (Leipzig, 1866); Th. Nöldeke, *Untersuchungen zur Kritik des A. T.*, i.-iii. p. 1-172 (Kiel, 1869); A. Kayser, *Das vorexil. Buch der Urgeschichte Israels u. seine Erweiterungen* (Strassburg, 1874); *Der gegenwärtige Stand der Pentateuchfrage* (Jahrb. für prot. Theol. 1881, p. 326-365, 520-564, 630-665); J. Wellhausen, *Die Composition des Hexateuchs* (Jahrb. f. deutsche Theol. xxi. 392-450, 531-602; xxii. 407-479); *Gesch. Israels*, i. (Berlin, 1878); 2nd ed. entitled *Prolegomena zur Geschichte Israels* (Berlin, 1883); F. Delitzsch, *Pentateuch-kritische Studien*, i.-xii. in the Zeitschr. f. kirchl. Wissenschaft u. kirchl. Leben, Jahrg. i. (Leipz. 1880).

§ 1. *Names, Division, and Contents.*

To the first five books of their Sacred Scripture the Jews gave the name of תּוֹרָה, or teaching. This word is often used in the Old Testament itself, where it generally signifies the teaching given by Yahwè to his people by means of his servants (priests, prophets, etc.)[1], and often, more specifically, Yahwè's revelation to and by Moses, which was [7] written down in a book[2]: whether the books we now possess or not cannot be determined till later on.

[1] On this use of the word see § 10, n. 4.
[2] Cf. *Josh.* viii. 31, 34; xxiii. 6; 1 *Kings* ii. 3; 2 *Kings* xiv. 6; xxii. 8; xxiii. 25; 2 *Chron.* xxiii. 18; xxv. 4; xxx. 16; xxxiv. 14; xxxv. 12; *Ezr.* iii. 2; vii. 6; *Neh.* viii. 1; etc.

The division of the Tora into five books (known by the Jews as חֲמִשָּׁה חוּמְשֵׁי הַתּוֹרָה) is presupposed by the names ἡ πεντάτευχος βίβλος and *Pentateuchus* (liber), current amongst the Hellenists and the Greek and Latin Christians. The division is certainly very old[3]; it seems to have been known to the latest collector of the Psalms[4], and may very well be original, i. e. contemporaneous with the final redaction of the Tora[5]. In the Hebrew text the five books are indicated respectively by their first or almost their first words, whereas in the Greek translation their names refer to their main contents, or some striking portion of them [6]. These Greek names, unchanged or translated into Latin or the vernaculars, subsequently passed into general use.

[3] Flavius Josephus is familiar with it, *c. Apion,* i. 8.

[4] In all probability it was this division that suggested the splitting up of the Psalms into five books.

[5] The division is not forced upon the Tora, but falls in naturally with its contents. *Ex.* i. opens a new section, the history of the people; *Ex.* xl. closes the subdivision of the legislation that refers to the sanctuary; the book of *Leviticus,* though not a well rounded whole, is clearly parted by the colophons in xxvi. 46, xxvii. 34, from *Numbers,* which latter has its own superscription (i. 1) and colophon (xxxvi. 13). Finally, the beginning of *Deuteronomy* obviously coincides with a fresh departure. Cf. Delitzsch, *Die Genesis,* p. 15, and below, § 16, n. 13–15.

[6] Δευτερονόμιον signifies *repetition of the law* (previously delivered at Sinai); τὸ δ. τοῦτο in *Deut.* xvii 18 is a mistranslation of משנה התורה הזאת, i. e. the reproduction or 'the copy of this tora;' how the translator meant τὸ δ. νόμος Μωυσῆ, *Josh.* viii. 32 [Grk. ix. 5] to be taken is not certain, probably '(the book) Deuteronomy, the law of Moses.' Cf. *Th. Tijdschr.* x. 549 sq. (1876).

The book of Joshua takes its name, in which the original and the old translations agree, from the chief personage in the narrative it contains. In the Jewish canon, though immediately following the Tora, it is sharply divided from it, and is assigned to another division of the Sacred Scripture. In this work, on the contrary, the Tora and the [8] book of Joshua are not only treated together, but are included under the common heading of the Hexateuch; for they belong to each other, and their contents form a single whole, and, moreover, they are the final outcome of one and the same literary process. The weight of the latter reason can only be gradually appreciated as we go along, but that of the former will be obvious at once from the following survey of the contents of the books.

This survey aims at being more than a mere table of contents, which the reader might easily draw up for himself. It is intended to prepare for the investigation we have undertaken into the composition of the Hexateuch, and the mutual connection of its parts, by a preliminary indication of the drift, or plan of the whole work; or, in other words, to trace the thread which runs through the whole, and which we shall see at once so holds it together as utterly to exclude any idea of its being a mere chance assemblage of heterogeneous elements.

The election and settlement of Israel, the people of Yahwè, consecrated to him and destined for his service,—such is the main subject of the Hexateuch. The book of Genesis, then, figures as an indispensable introduction, in which the formation of this people is described. But it does not enter upon its proper subject till xi. 27 sqq. (migration of Terah and his family to Canaan) or xii. 1 sqq. (call of Abraham);—what precedes serving to indicate the place of Israel's forefathers in the history of the world, and to connect their origin with the beginning of all things. In i.–iv. the creation of heaven and earth and the fortunes of the first human beings are related. Ch. v. contains a genealogical tree from Adam to Noah. The flood, with the escape of Noah and his sons, is the subject of vi.–ix. After a few records of their descendants in general (x.–xi. 9), a special genealogical tree from Shem to Terah (xi. 10–32) brings us down to Abram, the tribal father of Israel and of the nearest kindred peoples. In this division of *Genesis* the consecration [9] of the sabbath (ii. 1–3), the distinction between clean and unclean beasts (vii. 2 sqq.) and Elohîm's commands to Noah (ix. 1–7), point forward towards the ordinances of the Mosaic time, while the statements as to Terah's offspring (xi. 26–30) await their due expansion in the narratives concerning Abram (xii. 5; xiii. 5 sqq.; xix.; xxii. 20 sqq.; xxiv.; and xv. sqq.).

In xii.–xxv. 11 Abraham is the chief person. A short account of his son Ishmael (xxv. 12–18) is followed by a fuller narrative of the fortunes of Isaac and of his two sons up to the time of Isaac's death (xxv. 19–xxxv. 29); and then in like manner Esau and his race are rapidly dealt with in ch. xxxvi., after which the history of Jacob and his sons, especially of their migration to Egypt and their experiences there, is told at greater length (xxxvii.–l.). The connection of this portion of the narrative with what precedes and follows comes out in the repeated employment of the superscription : '[and] these are the tôlĕdôth of,' etc.[7], in the continuous chronology[8], in the frequent announcements of Israel's settlement in Canaan[9], in the account of the institution of circumcision[10], and so forth.

[7] See *Gen.* ii. 4; v. 1 ('this is the book of the tôlĕdôth of Adam'); vi. 9; x. 1; xi. 10, 27; xxv. 12, 19; xxxvi. 1,9; xxxvii. 2. Graetz, *Gesch. der Juden,* II f. p. 157 sq., truly remarks that אלה תולדות always points *forward*; but it is not true that אלה ה", without the *copula*, always points *backward*, unless we are prepared to alter the text of *Gen.* v. 1; vi. 9; xi. 10; xxxvii. 2; (cf. also *Gen.* xxxvi. 20, 29). If we make *Gen.* ii. 4ᵃ refer to what precedes as well as what follows it, and regard xxxvi. as a single whole, in spite of *v.* 9, we arrive at the conclusion that *Genesis* consists of *ten* tôlĕdôth—which, however, differ so much in length, and are so far from obvious, that we may doubt whether any such division was contemplated by the redactor.

[8] The chronology may be made out from the following passages : *Gen.* v.; vii. 6, 11; xi. 10–26; xii. 4; xvi. 16; xvii. 1; xxi. 5; xxv. 7, 20, 26; xxxv. 28; xxxvii. 2; xli. 46; xlv. 6; xlvii. 9; *Ex.* xii. 40—which last text fixes the year of the exodus, by which again further dates are reckoned in Exodus, Numbers, and Deuteronomy.

[9] The predictions to the patriarchs need not be enumerated here. The following deserve special notice : *Gen.* xv. 13–16 (Egyptian bondage, exodus, settlement in Canaan); xlix. (fortunes and territories of the tribes); l. 25 (Joseph's bones, cf. *Ex.* xiii. 19; *Josh.* xxiv. 32).

[10] See *Gen.* xvii., especially *v.* 10–14, where the ordinance refers to the future [10] as well as the present; cf. xxi. 4; xxxiv. 15 sqq.; also *Ex.* xii. 44, 48, where the rite is presupposed.

The Sinaitic legislation forms the centre of the book of Exodus. The arrival of Israel in the desert of Sinai (xix. 1) is preceded by accounts of the oppression of Jacob's progeny in Egypt (i.), the birth, the early fortunes and the call of Moses (ii.-iv.), his appearance before Pharaoh, the plagues of Egypt, the exodus (v.-xiii. 16)—with which latter the laws of the passover, the feast of unleavened bread, and the consecration of the first-born are connected (xii. 1-25, 43-50; xiii. 1-16),—the passage of the Red Sea (xiii. 17-xv.), the miracles of the manna and the quails (xvi.), the events at Rephidîm (xvii.), and the visit of Jethro, Moses' father-in-law (xviii.). The events at Sinai are related in the following order : the announcement of the revelation of Yahwè's will (xix.); the proclamation of the Decalogue (xx. 1-17); the commandments given to Moses by Yahwè (xx. 18-xxiii.); the covenant between Yahwè and Israel, on the basis of these commandments (xxiv.); further injunctions from Yahwè to Moses concerning the construction of the sanctuary, the ôhel mo'éd, and the consecration of Aaron and his sons to the priesthood (xxv.-xxxi. 17). Between the delivery of these injunctions and their execution (xxxv.-xl.) is inserted the account of Israel's apostasy and its consequences (xxxi. 18-xxxiv.). The arrangement of these events and ordinances rouses our suspicions on more points than one, but in the main it is chronological (xii. 1 sqq. 51; xvi. 1; xix. 1; xl. 2, 17). The approaching settlement of the people in Canaan is constantly spoken of, with references to the promises made to the fathers (iii. 6 sqq.; vi. 2 sqq.; xxiii. 20-33; xxxii. 13; xxxiii. 1, 2; xxxiv. 11-16). The genealogical tree in vi. 14-25 contains a number of names to which the narrative subsequently returns.

The book of Leviticus is almost entirely devoted to legislation; viii.-x. can hardly be regarded as constituting an exception. The book, therefore, contains no chronological statements. From *Ex.* xl. 2, 17, compared with *Num.* i. 1; [11] ix. 1-8; x. 11, it would follow that the laws of *Leviticus* were drawn up after the completion of the ôhel mo'éd

and before the departure of Israel from the Sinaitic desert.
This agrees with the statements as to place in *Lev.* i. 1;
vii. 38; xxv. 1; xxvi. 46; xxvii. 34. We find these statements in the headings and colophons with which some, but
not all, of the laws in *Leviticus* are provided[11]. The laws
themselves deal with offerings (*Lev.* i.–vii.), clean and unclean
animals (xi.), bodily uncleanness, especially leprosy (xii.–xv.),
the celebration of the great day of atonement (xvi.), sacrificing
at the sanctuary, and the blood of the victims (xvii.), the
ethico-religious duties of the Israelite (xviii.–xx.), the qualification and the special duties of the priests (xxi., xxii.), the
festivals (xxiii.), the golden lamp-stand and the shew-
bread (xxiv. 1–9), the punishment of blasphemy and the penal
code in general (*v.* 10–23), the sabbatical year and the year
of jubilee (xxv.), and vows (xxvii.); while viii.–x. refers to the
consecration of the priests to their office and all that goes
with it; and the long discourse in xxvi. sets forth to Israel
the consequences of the observance and of the breach of
Yahwè's precepts. This summary is enough to show that
the arrangement of the ordinances is far from perfect, but
that points of contact with *Exodus* and *Numbers* are not
wanting[12], so that on this ground, as well as on others,
Leviticus should be regarded as an essential portion of the
Tora.

[11] See *Lev.* vii. 38; xi. 46, 47; xiii. 59; xiv. 54–57; xv. 32, 33; xxvi. 46;
xxvii. 34. The superscriptions, including those in vi., vii., will be dealt with
hereafter.

[12] In addition to the mention of the ôhel mo'éd (*Lev.* i.–vi. and viii.–x.
passim; xii. 6; xiv. 11, 23; xv. 14, 29; xvi. *passim*; xviii. 4–6, 9; xix. 21;
xxiv. 3) we may note amongst other things how *Lev.* viii. refers back to *Ex.*
xxix. 1–37; how *Lev.* xvi. is related to *Ex.* xxx. 10 (*Lev.* xxiii. 26 sqq.; xxv. 9);
Num. xxix. 7 sqq.; and *Lev.* xxiii. to *Num.* xxviii., xxix.; how *Lev.* xxv. 32–34 is
connected with the consecration of the Levites in *Num.* iii. sq. and of the
Levitical cities in *Num.* xxxv. 1–8; and *Lev.* xxvii. with *Num.* xxx.

The book of Numbers, partly historical and partly legislative, completes the account of the sojourn of Israel in the

[12] Sinaitic desert, i.–ix. 10. The accounts of the census and
the disposition of the camp (i., ii.), the gifts of the heads of
the tribes at the consecration of the sanctuary (vii.), the
setting apart of the Levites for their functions (viii.), the
celebration of the passover in the second year after the exodus
(ix. 1–14), and the column of cloud and fire (*v.* 15–23), are
interspersed with more or less germane ordinances as to
the Levites and their duties (iii., iv.), the cleansing of the
camp (v. 1–4), the trespass-offering and the offering of jealousy
(*v.* 5–10, 11–31), the Nazirite vow (vi. 1–21), the priestly
blessing (*v.* 22–27), and the sacred trumpets (x. 1–10). A
similar intertwining of matter may be observed in x. 11–xix. :
the narrative is continued in x. 11–28 (march from the desert
of Sinai) ; *v.* 29–36 (details of the journey in the desert) ; xi.,
xii. (Tab'era, Kibrôth-hattaäva, Miriam's leprosy) ; xiii., xiv.
(the dispatch of the spies and its consequences); xvi., xvii.
(revolt of Korah, Dathan, and Abiram); whereas in xv. we
find legal regulations on five miscellaneous subjects; in xviii.
on the income of the priests and Levites ; in xix. on the
purification of the unclean. With xx. the preparation for
Israel's settlement begins : at Kadesh Miriam dies and the
people murmur against Moses and Aaron (xx. 1–13); thence
an embassy is dispatched to Edom (*v.* 14–21); Aaron dies
(*v.* 22–29); the territory of Sihon and of Og is conquered
(xxi.); Balaam blesses Israel (xxii.–xxiv.); idolatry is practised
at Shittîm, and punished (xxv.); the second census takes
place (xxvi.); the rights of heiresses are regulated (xxvii.
1–11); Joshua is appointed and consecrated as Moses' successor (*v.* 12–23); the laws concerning fasts and vows are
supplemented (xxviii.–xxx.); Moses punishes the Midianites
and makes regulations about the booty (xxxi.); he allows the
tribes of Reuben and Gad and half the tribe of Manasseh to
settle in the Transjordanic region (xxxii.); records the
stations of the desert wanderings now ended (xxxiii. 1–49);

orders the extermination of the Canaanites (*v.* 50–56); defines
the limits of Israel's future territory (xxxiv.); issues ordi- [13]
nances concerning the priestly and Levitical cities (xxxv. 1–8)
and the cities of refuge (*v.* 9–34) and supplements the previous
ordinance (xxvii. 1–11) concerning heiresses (xxxvi. 1–12).
The whole is closed by a colophon (xxxvi. 13). It is obvious
that here too the order of succession is often anything but
natural, and challenges further investigation. But neither
chronological arrangement[13] nor connection with the two
preceding books[14] is wanting; while xxvii. 12–14, xxxii.
20 sqq., xxxiv., xxxv. 1–8, 9–34, and other passages, contain
announcements or injunctions, the fulfilment of which we
find in due course in *Deuteronomy* (xxxii. 48–52, xxxiv.) and
in *Joshua* (i. 12–18, xiv. 1–5, &c., xx., xxi.).

[13] See, in addition to the texts already mentioned (i. 1 ; ix. 1–8 ; x. 11),
xiv. 33–35 (announcement of the forty years' wandering); xx. 1 (1st month
[of the 40th year ?]); *v.* 22–29, cf. xxxiii. 38 (fifth month of the 40th year).

[14] The points of contact with *Leviticus* have been indicated in n. 12 ; those
with *Exodus* hardly need to be pointed out : the ôhel mo'éd, the sacred
vessels, and Aaron and his sons as priests, are presupposed *passim*. Further,
compare *Ex.* xxxviii. 25 sq. with *Num.* i.

In the last chapters of *Numbers* the close of the life of
Moses is represented as close at hand (xxvii. 12–14, xxxi. 2),
and we therefore expect the account of his death immediately.
But, as a fact, almost the whole of *Deuteronomy* precedes it,
so that this latter book seems like a huge parenthesis. Its
position after *Numbers* agrees with the date in the superscription i. 1–5 (first day of the eleventh month of the
fortieth year), which is the only chronological datum in the
book. This superscription refers in the first instance to the
address of Moses to the assembled people, contained in i.
6–iv. 40, and chiefly devoted to recalling the events of the
years and months just gone. A short account of the
establishment of the cities of refuge in the Transjordanic
region, iv. 41–43, severs this address from the discourse of

Moses which follows, in v. sqq., and which is referred by a
fresh superscription (iv. 44–49) to the same place and period
as the other. This discourse, at the beginning of which the
[14] Decalogue is repeated (v. 6–18 [6–21]), is hortatory up to
the end of xi., and then, from xii. onward, it is legislative
and runs on unbroken to the end of xxvi.[15] The four following chapters (xxvii.–xxx.) still introduce Moses as the speaker,
but they are not simply a continuation of v.–xxvi., as may be
seen from the fresh headings in xxvii. 1, 9, 11; xxix. 1, and
from the colophon in xxviii. 69. Ch. xxvii. is chiefly concerned with a religious assembly to be held at Mounts Ebal
and Gerizîm (cf. xi. 29–32); and in xxviii.–xxx. the blessing
and the curse of the law are held before Israel. In xxxi. we
read that Moses reduced the law he had proclaimed to writing,
pointed to Joshua as his successor, and composed a song of
solemn warning to his people, which song is given in xxxii.
1–43, and earnestly commended to Israel in *v.* 44–47. A
second announcement of Moses' death *v.* 48–52 (cf. *Num.*
xxvii. 12–14) precedes 'the blessing of Moses, the man of
God,' in xxxiii., and the record of his actual death, ending
with a fitting tribute to his character and services (xxxiv.).

[15] The summary of the contents of the laws is omitted here, but will be
given later on, when a comparison between them and the other legislative
parts of the Tora will be instituted.

The close connection between the book of J o s h u a and
the Tora is unmistakable. In both sections of the former,
i.–xii. (the conquest of Canaan), and xiii.–xxiv. (the partition
of the land, and Joshua's last dispositions) constant and express reference is made to Moses, to his deeds and to his
ordinances[16]. And moreover, material agreement and connection with the Tora become obvious at once in the first part of
the book. After the death of Moses (cf. *Deut.* xxxiv.) Joshua
takes command and prepares the people, especially the Transjordanic tribes (cf. *Num.* xxxii. 20 sqq.; *Deut.* iii. 18–22), for

the passage of the Jordan (i.); he sends out spies (ii.), and on their return accomplishes the passage (iii. iv), which is constantly represented in *Deuteronomy* as close at hand. After this the people are circumcised (v. 1–8) and the passover [15] celebrated (*v.* 9–12). The series of conquests, announced by an angelophany (*v.* 13–15), is opened by the taking of Jericho (vi.), which is immediately followed, after the punishment of Achan's offence, by the fall of Ai (vii. 1–viii. 29). The assembly at Ebal and Gerizîm is held (*v.* 30–35) in accordance with the injunctions of Moses (*Deut.* xxvii. 1–13). The Gibeonites succeed by a stratagem in securing their lives (ix.), but the kings first of southern (x.) and then of northern Canaan (xi.) are defeated by Joshua, their cities taken, and the inhabitants exterminated, in accordance with the Mosaic precepts in *Deuteronomy*. A list of the conquered cities closes this section of the book (xii.).

In the second section the dispositions made by Moses concerning the Transjordanic region are called to mind (xiii.), and the partition of Canaan proper is then described. The introduction (xiv. 1–5) refers back to the indications of *Num.* xxxiv.; and the episode of Caleb's inheritance, which immediately follows (*v.* 6–15), depends upon *Num.* xiii., xiv. and still more directly upon *Deut.* i. 20–46. Territories are assigned respectively to Judah (xv.), Ephraim, and Manasseh (xvi., xvii.), without neglecting the commands of Moses concerning Manasseh (*Num.* xxvii. 1–11; xxxvi. 1–12), and then—at Shiloh, where the ôhel mo'éd (cf. *Exod.* xxv. sqq.) was pitched—to the other tribes also (xviii., xix.). The cities of refuge (xx.) and the priestly and Levitical cities (xxi. 1–40 [1–42]) are next assigned, in execution of the law in *Num.* xxxv. The settlement of Israel thus accomplished (*v.* 41–43 [43–45]), the Transjordanic tribes turn homewards, with rich presents (xxii. 1–8), and by the erection of an altar give the other tribes occasion to manifest their attachment to the one sanctuary (*v.* 9–34). Finally, Joshua takes leave of his people (xxiii.), and at his instance the covenant between Israel and Yahwè is renewed in Shechem (xxiv. 1–28); his two addresses [16] alike presuppose the narratives and exhortations of the Tora throughout. A short account of the deaths of Joshua and Eleazar, and of the interment of Joseph's bones (cf. n. 9) closes the book (*v.* 29–33)[17].

[16] Moses is mentioned in i. 1–3, 5, 7, 13–15, 17; iv. 10, 12; viii. 31–33, 35; ix. 24; xi. 12, 15, 20, 23; xii. 6; xiii. 8, 12, 15, 21, 24, 29, 32 sq.; xiv. 2 sq., 5–7, 9–11; xvii. 4; xviii. 7; xx. 2; xxi. 2, 8; xxii. 2, 4 sq., 7, 9; xxiii. 6 —fifty-six times altogether, against four only in Judges (or five, including xviii. 30) and two in *Samuel.* The other points of contact and agreement with the Tora likewise gain additional significance and weight from the contrast between *Joshua* on the one side and *Judges* and *Samuel* on the other.

[17] In accordance with the purpose of this survey only a few of the chief references to the Tora are included in it; others will come under notice later on, e.g. viii. 29; x. 27 ('about the going down of the sun,' cf. *Deut.* xxi. 22 sq.); xiii. 21 sq. (cf. *Num.* xxxi. 8, 16); xxii. 17 (cf. *Num.* xxv.); xxiv. 9, 10 (cf. *Num.* xxii.–xxiv.; *Deut.* xxiii. 5, 6), etc. etc.

§ 2. *Testimony of the Hexateuch itself as to its author.*

It is but fair to begin an inquiry into the origin of the Hexateuch by weighing any testimony we may find in the work itself as to the author of the whole or of any part of it.

The books of G e n e s i s and L e v i t i c u s contain no statements as to how or by whom they were committed to writing. In E x o d u s we read that Yahwè commanded Moses to record the attack of Amalek in the book (בַּסֵּפֶר), or rather—according to the reading of some of the old translations (בְּסֵפֶר)—in a book (xvii. 14); that Moses wrote down (xxiv. 4) all the words of Yahwè, which had been uttered to him on Sinai (xx. 23–xxiii. 33), and read out this Book of the Covenant to the people (xxiv. 7); that when Yahwè had set forth the commandments, on the basis of which he made a covenant with Israel (xxxiv. 10–26), he commanded Moses to write down these words (*v.* 27). In

Numbers we are told that Moses recorded the camping places of Israel in the desert (xxxiii. 2),—a statement which is immediately followed by the list itself (*v.* 3–49). Finally, the book of Joshua contains the statement (xxiv. 26), that [17] after the solemn renewal of the covenant between Israel and Yahwè, Joshua 'wrote down these words in the book of the tora of God.' Two of these texts, *Ex.* xvii. 14 and *Josh.* xxiv. 26, cannot be accepted as in any way bearing on the authorship of the narratives to which they belong: for what Moses (or Joshua) is there said to have written down by no means coincides with what now lies before us, and must, in the latter case, be very definitely distinguished from it [1]. On the other hand, the remaining passages are most naturally understood as making Moses the author, not of the narratives into which they are incorporated, but of the pericopes to which they refer, i.e. *Ex.* xx. 23–xxiii. 33; xxxiv. 10–26; *Num.* xxxiii. 3–49 [2]. Whether these indications are correct or not we must inquire hereafter. To stretch these statements further and make them apply to the books in which they occur, or even to the Tora as a whole, is at open variance with their obvious meaning [3].

[1] What Moses is to write down, according to *Ex.* xvii. 14, is not the account of the conflict with Amalek which we now possess in *Ex.* xvii. 8–16, but (cf. *Deut.* xxv. 17-19) the treacherous conduct of the Amalekites that will one day be avenged by their utter extinction. Still less can we identify the words written down by Joshua (xxiv. 26) with the passage in *Josh.* xxiv. 1–24; for the latter does not stand 'in the book of the tora of God,' and contains not the obligations entered into by the people, which Joshua was to register, but the description of what took place at Shechem. It is the official document which we do not possess, and not the narrative of its enditement, that is assigned to Joshua. See further n. 3.

[2] Obvious as this interpretation is, it is not the necessary or the only possible one. It is certainly highly probable that 'all the words of Yahwè,' *Ex.* xxiv. 4 (cf. *v.* 3, 'all the words of Yahwè and all the mishphatim'), refers to the precepts in *Ex.* xx. 23–xxiii. 33, so that *e mente auctoris* (cf. *Ex.* xxiv. 7) these precepts are rightly designated the book of the Covenant; but it might be maintained that *Ex.* xxiv. 3-8 refers to some other commandments of Yahwè. Cf. § 5, n. 3.—In *Ex.* xxxiv. 27 Moses receives an order : but does

he execute it? I have expressly refrained from citing *v.* 28, for the subject of
וַיִּכְתֹּב, is not Moses but (cf. *v.* 1–4) Yahwè. The curious relation in which
v. 27 thus stands to *v.* 28—a point to which we shall have to return—makes it
in some sense doubtful whether *v.* 27 really does refer to *v.* 10–26, for which,
however, everything else pleads.—The writer of *Num.* xxxiii. 2 unquestionably
intends it to be understood that his list in *v.* 3–49 is founded on notes by
[18] Moses, but he does not say in so many words that this very list was actually
written by Moses.

³ Hengstenberg, *Authentie*, ii. 149 sqq. [ii. 122 sqq.] ; Haevernick,
Einl. i. 1, p. 19 sqq. [14 sqq.], and the rest who adopt this interpretation, start
from the Masoretic reading בַּסֵּפֶר in *Ex.* xvii. 14 : what can '*the* book' mean,
if not the roll in which Moses regularly recorded all that took place in the desert
and that Yahwè revealed to him? To this day-book the other passages are
also made to refer, and even when it is not mentioned it is supposed to underly
the Tora or even to be identical with it. Against this it may be remarked
(1) that this interpretation of בספר is quite unsupported : the supposed day-
book has never once been mentioned before *Ex.* xvii., and therefore could not
be called '*the* book' ; (2) that even if this were not so, still the identification of
the said day-book with what Moses subsequently wrote (*Ex.* xxiv., xxxiv., etc.)
or with the whole Tora—including *Genesis!*—is arbitrariness itself.—If the
Masorets vocalised *Ex.* xvii. 14 correctly, then '*the* book' must mean the book
destined, or to be provided, for that purpose ; cf. *Num.* v. 23. But the vocali-
sation בְּסֵפֶר (LXX. ; Arab. ; and perhaps other versions, which, however, could
not have expressed the article) here, as in 1 *Sam.* x. 25, has everything in
its favour, including the analogy of *Is.* xxx. 8 ; *Jer.* xxx. 2. Wherever the consonants, i.e. the writers themselves, decide the matter the article is absent.

Far more numerous and of quite a different character are
the testimonies in *Deuteronomy*. In the course of the second
address (iv. 44–xxvi) Moses speaks (xvii. 18 sq.) of 'this
tora' (which he sometimes indicates or paraphrases as the
commandment, the mishphatîm, etc.), which he gives 'this
day⁴.' The expression itself together with these closer definitions raises it above all doubt that the reference is exclusively
to the series of exhortations and commandments which Moses
uttered, shortly before his death, in the land of Moab in the
hearing of all Israel⁵. Concerning 'this tora,' it is related
that Moses wrote it down and gave it to the priests, the
sons of Levi (xxxi. 9, 24–26), commanding them to read it
aloud on the feast of tabernacles every seventh year to the
whole people (*v.* 10–13); which injunction must likewise

be referred to the same deuteronomic tora[6]. But whereas
this code, according to the texts now cited, is in process
of production from v. to xxvi., and only exists in writing
after xxxi. 9, we find 'this tora' mentioned in the first
discourse of Moses (iv. 8, cf. i. 5) as though it were already
in existence; and in passages which follow the second
or legislative discourse, but precede xxxi. 9, the expressions occur 'the words of this tora, written in this book' [19]
(xxviii. 58); 'the book of this tora' (*v.* 61); 'this book of
the tora' (xxix. 20 [21]; xxx. 10); 'this book' (xxix. 19,
26 [20, 27]). Not one of these texts gives the least occasion
for changing the interpretation of the formula 'this tora.'
In testifying that Moses not only pronounced but committed to writing the legislative discourse of v.–xxvi.,
they agree with xxxi. 9. But at the same time they contain a curious *prolepsis*, which is quite incompatible with
the supposition that Moses is the author of the whole book,
and which suggests the idea that we may be in the presence
of one of those literary artifices which so often betray themselves by similar inconsistencies[7].

[4] See v. 1; vi. 6; vii. 11; viii. 1, 11; x. 13; xi. 8, 13, 26–28, 32; xiii. 19
[18]; xv. 5, 15; xix. 9.—In xxvii., too, we have 'all the commandments which
I command you this day' (*v.* 1); 'this tora' (*v.* 3, 8, 26); and in xxxii.
'this tora' (*v.* 46). Further parallels are found in 'this covenant,' xxix.
8, 13 [9, 14]; cf. 'this curse,' *v.* 18 [19]; 'the covenant of Yahwè, that he
makes with you this day,' *v.* 11 [12].

[5] The opinion that the whole tora is intended—defended by F. W.
Schultz in *Das Deut. erkl.* p. 87 sqq., but withdrawn in his work *Die Schöp-
fungsgeschichte nach Naturwissenschaft u. Bibel,* p. viii. sqq.—is inconsistent, not
only with the expressions themselves, but with the colophon, xxviii. 69
[xxix. 1]: 'these are the words of the covenant, that Yahwè commanded
Moses to make with the children of Israel in the land of Moab, besides
the covenant that he had made with them at Horeb.' What the
book itself distinguishes we are not at liberty to identify.

[6] Nothing is more natural than that when 'this tora,' i.e. *Deuteronomy,* had
become a part of a greater whole, the precept in question should have been
referred to that whole, i.e. to the Pentateuch itself. Perhaps Josephus (*Antiquities,* iv. 8. 12), so understands it; at any rate he speaks quite generally of

'the laws' being read aloud. It deserves notice, however, that the Jewish tradition still preserves traces of a true perception of the author's meaning. The passages which the Mishna (*Sotah*, vii. 8) says were read aloud by the king at the feast of the tabernacles in the seventh year all of them belong to *Deuteronomy*. In *Sifri* on *Deut.* xvii. 18 (ed. Bomberg, f. 45 b.; ed. Friedmann, i. f. 105 b.) the question is raised why the passage in question says 'mishnê tora.' The answer is: 'because it was to be transcribed; others say: because on the day of the assembly (ביום הקהל) nothing is read but *Deuteronomy*.' Here 'the day of the assembly' must mean one of the days of the feast of the tabernacles of the seventh year.—The Old Testament itself gives no evidence in this matter. The assembly described in *Neh.* viii.-x. was of quite a special character: it began as early as the first day of the seventh month, and was expressly designed to make the Tora known in its entirety. Moreover there is nothing whatever to show that it took place in 'the year [20] of release,' nor yet to indicate what portions of the Tora were read on the days of the feast (*Neh.* viii. 18).

[7] According to Hengstenberg, *Authentie*, ii. 153 sqq. [ii. 125 sqq.], and others, Moses wrote *Deut.* i.–xxx. and gave the book to the priests (xxxi. 9); but this was a symbolical action; he afterwards received the book back again and added xxxi. 1–23; the sequel, from *v.* 24 to xxxiv. 12, is an appendix taken up into the tora shortly after his death. Exegetically considered this is quite arbitrary: there is not the least indication that the account of Moses writing down the tora, xxxi. 9, is from the hand of Moses himself; nor that a change of authors takes place at xxxi. 24. Moreover it is quite inconceivable that Moses (in xxviii.–xxx) should have referred to the book he was engaged in composing, as already in existence, and even as having been in existence some days before, when he was still speaking to the people. These and other such difficulties, in which the recognition of the absolutely historical character of the statements of *Deuteronomy* involves us, give ample occasion to the doubt which has been expressed in the text, and which will hereafter be expressly justified.

From what has now been said it is obvious that those who ascribe the Tora in its entirety to Moses, and the Book of Joshua to the hero whose name it bears, cannot appeal to the testimony of the Hexateuch itself. The Mosaic origin of certain passages in *Exodus* and *Numbers*, and of a great part of *Deuteronomy*, may be supported by such an appeal, but no more than this. Whether even this can be established thus will be seen later on, but at the very outset, in view of the character of the testimonies themselves, we must pronounce it doubtful.

§ 3. *Investigation and provisional determination of the general character of the Hexateuch. A. The legislation.*

The Jewish and Christian tradition that makes Moses the author of the Tora, and Joshua of the book that bears his name, implies in the first place that the Hexateuch dates from the time in which the books of *Exodus–Deuteronomy*, and the book of *Joshua* place us. Can this supposition be allowed; and if not, by what must it be replaced? The answer to this question must determine the point of view from which we are to regard the Hexateuch, and consequently the method and course of our criticism. With this question in view, therefore, we shall submit the legislation of the [21] Hexateuch to a preliminary investigation in this paragraph, and its narratives to a similar treatment in § 4.

Our survey of the contents of the Hexateuch (§ 1) has already shown us to what source the laws it contains are referred, and in what order they are communicated. Yahwè reveals them to Moses, or sometimes to Moses and Aaron, or after the death of the latter to Moses and Eleazar ; a direction is often added as to the persons to whom Moses is to give them,— whether the children of Israel or Aaron and his sons[1]. From *Deuteronomy* we learn how Moses acquitted himself of his task, for the ordinances which he there delivers to the people have been revealed to him beforehand by Yahwè[2].—As to the arrangement of the laws, it is evident that the Tora, in its present form, was not intended to furnish its readers with a system of legislation; for similar subjects are not treated in immediate succession, and even the regulations that con- cern one single subject are scattered up and down[3]. Indeed we can only speak of any proper arrangement at all within the limits of the several groups or collections of laws, which are sometimes very clearly marked off, such as *Ex.* xx. 23– xxiii. 33; *Ex.* xxv.–xxxi. 17; *Lev.* i.–vii.; *Deut.* xii.–xxvi.

How far there is any real arrangement even here we shall see presently. The Tora, as a whole, gives the laws *in chronological order*, i. e. with reference to the time at which they were revealed to Moses or, in the case of *Deut.* v.–xxvi., at which they were delivered by him to the people [4].

[1] See, for instance, *Ex.* xx. 22; xxi. 1; xxv. 1, 2; xxxi. 12, 13; *Lev.* vi. 1, 2; xi. 1; xiii. 1; *Num.* xxvi. 1, etc. etc.

[2] In *Deut.* v. 28 [31] Moses announces that Yahwè had uttered to him on Horeb ' all the commandments, institutions and mishphatîm which he was to teach to the Israelites, that they might observe them in the land that Yahwè should give them.' This is referred to again in the words of vi. 1, 'these are the commandments, etc., which Yahwè commanded me to teach you, etc.'

[3] Cf. § 1. Thus, for example, the feasts are dealt with in *Ex.* xxiii. 14–17; xxxiv. 18, 22–25; *Lev.* xxiii.; *Num.* xxviii. sq.; *Deut.* xvi. 1–17; and maççôth and the passover in *Ex.* xii. 1–28, 43–50; *Num.* ix. 1–14 as well; vows in *Lev.* xxvii.; *Num.* xxx.; and the Nazirite vow in particular in *Num.* vi. 1–21; [22] the punishment of sabbath-breakers in *Ex.* xxxi. 14; xxxv. 2; *Num.* xv. 32–36. These are but a few out of many instances.

[4] This is obvious enough in the vast majority of cases. Observe that in *Num.* xxvi. 1; xxvii. 2; xxxi. 12, 13 the mention of Eleazar indicates that the ordinances in question were communicated after the death of Aaron; we meet with Eleazar as early as in *Num.* xvii. 2 [xvi. 37]; xix. 3, but only as his father's probable successor (xvii. 18 [3]; xix. 1). Further, note *Lev.* xvi. 1 (cf. x. 1, 2) and, with respect to *Deuteronomy*, not only *Deut.* i. 3, 4 and the corresponding note of locality in iv. 46–49, but the repeated announcements of the approaching passage of the Jordan in v. sqq., such as ix. 1; xi. 31 sq.; xxvii. 2, 4, 12, and of the settlement in Canaan in xii. 29; xv. 4; xvi. 20, etc.—Only a few of the laws are given without any direct indication of the time and place of their delivery, in *Num.* xv. and xix. (before Aaron's death, *v.* 1); and in *Num.* xviii., which latter stands, however, in close connection with the story of Korah's revolt, given in xvi. sq. But in these cases also the intention of the author of the Tora was obviously to indicate by the position assigned to the laws the time of their promulgation.

If we ask whether this distribution of the legislative activity of Moses over the years during which he was guiding Israel accords with probability, we can but answer in the negative. The laws are congested in the first year after the exodus (from *Ex.* xx. to *Num.* x. 10), and the closing months of the fortieth year (from *Num.* xxvii. to the end of *Deuteronomy*). For the thirty-eight years of wandering only some few ordinances are left (*Num.* xv., xviii.,

xix.). This accords but ill with the demands of probability[5]. It is still more obvious that the legislation,
taken as a whole, does not answer in any single respect
to the expectations raised by the supposed time and circumstances of its promulgation. If we grant that Moses, while
still in the desert, may have given laws intended for the
people when settled in Canaan, or, in other words, may have
presupposed the transition of the tribes from the nomad to
the agricultural life, it still remains very strange that he
should have made such an assumption tacitly, and so have
left this great transition wholly unregulated[6]. Nor is it less
surprising that various subjects which at that time belonged
entirely to the future are dealt with at length and down to the
smallest details, though in some cases one would have thought
that the experience subsequently to be gained might well
have been waited for[7]. In strange contrast with this minute- [23]
ness of the legislation stands its incompleteness: regulations
as to the government of the clans, the tribes and the whole
people, though constituting the very first condition of the
introduction and maintenance of any legislation, are nowhere
found, and that too though the tribes, having just escaped
from the bondage of Egypt, can hardly have had a trace of
any such government already in existence. Whenever the
law-giver speaks of the authorities he assumes their existence
and activity, though one would have supposed that, before
Israel's settlement in Canaan, he would have had to institute
them and define their functions[8]. When we put all this together
we cannot avoid the conclusion that the character of the
legislation as a whole is in absolute contradiction with the
setting in which the Hexateuch puts it.

[5] A far stronger expression would be justified when we consider that according to *Num.* xx. 22–29 cf. xxxiii. 38 the mourning for Aaron was not over
till the first day of the sixth month of the fortieth year, so that we have only
five months left (cf. *Deut.* i. 3) for the rest of the march to the Transjordanic

district and its conquest (*Num.* xxi.), the episode of Balaam (xxii.-xxiv.), the worship of Baal-Peor (xxv.), the second census (xxvi.), the chastisement of Midian (xxxi.), and the settlement of the Transjordanic tribes (xxxii.)! The few ordinances contained in *Num.* xxvii.-xxx., xxxiv.-xxxvi. only serve to make the impossibility of such a succession of events all the more conspicuous.

⁶ On the face of the whole legislation, of course, we read that the theatre is the desert; Israel is encamped there; the settlement in Canaan is in the future. With regard to the laws in *Ex.* xxv. sqq.; *Lev.* i. sqq.; *Num.* iv. sqq., xix., etc., this is elaborately shown to be the case by Bleek, *Einl.*, p. 29 sqq. (4th ed.), but it is also applicable in the main to *Ex.* xxi.-xxiii. (see especially xxiii. 20 sqq.), and to *Deuteronomy* (cf. n. 4). In other words it is not only the superscriptions that assign the laws to Moses and locate them in the desert, but the form of the legislation likewise accords with this determination of time and place. Now this may be explained in two ways : either the laws really come from Moses and the desert, or they are merely put into his mouth, and the desert and so forth belong to their literary form of presentment. With this dilemma before us let us examine the phenomena to which the text directs attention, and, to begin with, let us consider the following point :—

The people for whom the laws are destined is a people cultivating the soil and inhabiting cities. I will only select a few of the abundant proofs of this statement. The fourth of the 'ten words' (*Ex.* xx. 10; *Deut.* v. 14) speaks of 'thy man slave and thy woman slave, thy cattle and thy stranger that is within thy gates.' *Ex.* xxi. 1-11 presupposes slavery in quite a developed form : the Hebrew reduced to indigence sells himself or his daughter. *Ex.* xxi. 33, 'if any man opens or digs a pit,' etc.

[24] *Ex.* xxii. 4, 5 [5, 6], the vineyard, the corn, the sheaves, etc. *Ex.* xxii. 28 [29], the surrender of the first-fruits of the harvest, of wine, and of oil. *Ex.* xxii. 30 [31], beasts torn in the field. *Ex.* xxiii. 4, 5 (cf. *Deut.* xxii. 1-4), strayed ox, overloaded ass. *Ex.* xxiii. 10-12, thy land, thy vineyard, thy fig-tree, the stranger. *Ex.* xxiii. 19 (cf. xxxiv. 26), 'the best of the first-fruits of thy land.' *Lev.* xi. 9, 10, fish of the sea and the rivers. *Lev.* xiv. 40, 41, 45, 53, outside the city. *Lev.* xix. *passim*, e.g. *v.* 9, thy harvest; *v.* 10, thy vineyard; *v.* 13 (and a number of others), hirelings or day-labourers. *Lev.* xxv. as a whole, e.g. *v.* 29 sqq., the distinction between houses in cities and in villages, paralleled by that in *Lev.* xxvii. 22 between lands obtained by inheritance and those obtained by purchase. *Num.* xxvii. 1-11 ; xxxvi., regulation of the tenure of land by inheritance. *Deut.* xx. 5, 6, newly-built houses and newly-planted vines. *Deut.* xxi. 3, 'a heifer, that has not been worked with and that has not borne the yoke.' *Deut.* xxii. 6, 7, regulations about bird-nests. *Deut.* xxiii. 16, 17 [15, 16], concerning escaped slaves and their surrender. *Deut.* xxiii. 25, 26 [24, 25]; xxiv. 19-22, etc. etc. Every reader of the Tora will readily admit that its contents are, for the most part, in strange contrast with the words which constantly remind us that Israel is still on the way to Canaan. The authors, so far from contemplating the settlement of the people in a more or less hazy future, constantly assume it as actual, together with all that in the course of time it would bring

into existence. Especially instructive is the distinctive use of תושב, גר, נכרי, and the contrast גר ואזרח.

[7] The feasts, at any rate the festival of first-fruits or of weeks, and the harvest-home or feast of tabernacles, are agricultural; yet the offerings are enumerated in *Num.* xxviii. sq., and even the separate sacrifices for each day of the harvest feast in xxix. 12–38. The regulations as to vows in *Lev.* xxvii., *Num.* xxx., likewise descend to the minutest particulars. And so does the law concerning leprosy and its treatment, *Lev.* xiii., xiv., and the disinfection of (stone) houses, *Lev.* xiv. 33–53.

[8] Cf. Vatke, *Die Religion des A. T.,* p. 204–211, contradicted, but by no means refuted, by Hengstenberg, *Authentie,* ii. 338 sqq. [ii. 276 sqq.] Duly to appreciate the phenomenon under discussion we must bear in mind that regulations about the High Priest, the priests, the Levites, their duties and the limits of their prerogative, their revenues and so on, are not wanting in the Tora (cf. *Lev.* xxi., xxii.; *Num.* iii. sqq.; xviii. etc.) The omission especially concerns the executive and judicial power. Even if what we are told of the heads of the tribes and clans were an accurate reproduction of the real condition of things we should still require an account of the functions and powers of these chiefs and princes; but we find nothing of the sort. The provision for the administration of justice in *Ex.* xviii. 21–26 is unsuited for a settled people, and the narrative itself represents it as a merely temporary arrangement, for it leaves the decision in all important matters to Moses, and no reference whatever is made to it in the rest of the Tora—not even in *Num.* xi., which is worked up into a single whole with it in *Deut.* i. 9–18. In the laws of *Deuteronomy,* 'the elders of the city' appear from time to time as the representatives of the citizens and as judges (*Deut.* xix. 12; xxi. 2–4, 6, 19; xxii. 15–18; xxv. 7–9), without their relation either to the heads of families or to the assistants of Moses in *Ex.* xviii. or *Num.* xi. being defined. And yet these [25] 'elders of the city' are the only persons whom we can think of as charged with the execution of the penal laws, for example, of *Ex.* xxi. 15; xxii. 18; xxi. 32, etc. etc. The priests also appear to exercise a certain judicial authority, but what it is and to what cases it applies is not clear. The injunctions in *Ex.* xxi. 6; xxii. 7, 8 [8, 9] (referring to appearance before Elohîm, and to the sentence there pronounced), are wholly inadequate as they stand. What do they mean? The law-giver *must* have explained this unless he could assume it as known in practice. The same holds good in a still higher degree of *Deut.* xvii. 8–13. Here an appeal is allowed in lawsuits to the Levitical priests officiating at the sanctuary, but associated with them is 'the judge who shall be in those days;' and according to *v.* 12 the sentence is pronounced now by the priests and now by the judge. What decides which it is to be? and who is this 'judge?' The probable answer may be gathered from 2 *Chron.* xix. 8–11, but what sense would such a precept have had if uttered by Moses without the least explanation or supplement?

Vatke, *ibid.,* is fully justified in insisting upon the profound significance of these facts as bearing on the Mosaic origin of the Tora. A people may make a shift without written laws, but the executive and judicial power is indispensable. If this latter is not instituted by the Tora, and is only now and again incidentally referred to, it is obvious at once that the Tora was written for a settled and organised people—such as Israel actually became, but, in the time of Moses, had yet to become.

The representation given in the Hexateuch of the legislative activity of Moses involves the essential unity of the Tora; and this furnishes us with another test of its accuracy. From this point of view let us first examine the form and then the contents of the Tora.

In comparing the several portions of the Tora with respect to their form we must not forget, (1) that they are not represented as being absolutely contemporaneous, for between the Sinaitic group, from *Ex.* xx. to *Num.* x. 10, and the laws which profess to have been promulgated in the fields of Moab, from *Num.* xxvii. to the end of *Deuteronomy*, there is a space of nearly forty years; (2) that, as already seen (§ 2), the actual committal of a great number of the laws to writing (*Ex.* xxv.–xxxi. 17, *Leviticus, Numbers*) is never attributed in so many words to Moses; he is only named as the writer of *Ex.* xx. 23–xxiii. and of the great legislative discourse in *Deut.* v.–xxvi.; all the other laws, though revealed to him and promulgated by him, may—according to the representations of the Hexateuch itself, which we are here following— [26] have been reduced to writing by some other hand or hands; (3) that in *Deuteronomy*, including xii.–xxvi., a different style is adopted to that of the other laws: the oratorical and hortatory element may not be wholly absent in the latter, but in the former it comes prominently into the foreground and permeates, so to speak, the whole style of expression. For all these reasons we have no right to expect absolute similarity of form in all parts of the Tora. But such uniformity is far indeed from being realised. Without going into details, to which we can do more justice in another connection (§ 6 sqq.), we may say at once that each several group of laws has its own linguistic character and is specially marked by certain fixed formulæ which constantly recur, while their absence from the other groups must at any rate seem strange, if we are to assign a common origin to them all, even with the reservations just indicated[9]. The representation of Moses as a law-giver, given in the Hexateuch itself, is therefore contradicted rather than confirmed by the form of the legislation. With respect to the tradition which makes him the actual writer of the whole Tora, we must express ourselves much more strongly: It is absolutely excluded by the difference of form between the several codes[10].

[9] In view of our future investigations I may confine myself here to a few striking examples: 'I, Yahwè, am your God,' or 'I am Yahwè,' occurs in *Lev.* xviii. 2, 4–6, 21, 30; xix. 2, 3, 4, 10, 12, 14, 16, 18, 25, 28, 30–32, 34, 36, 37; xx. 7, 8, 24; xxi. 8, 12, 15, 23; xxii. 2, 3, 8, 9, 16, 30–33; xxiii. 22, 43; xxiv. 22; xxv. 17, 38, 55; xxvi. 1, 2, 13, 44, 45. Except in this group, neither of these expressions is found anywhere but at the head of the Decalogue (*Ex.* xx. 2 ; *Deut.* v. 6) and in *Num.* iii. 41, 45; x. 10 ; xv. 41.—The designation of the months as 1st, 2nd, etc., which we should have expected from *Ex.* xii. 2 to appear in *all* the laws, is absent from *Ex.* xiii.; xx. 23–xxiii.; xxxiv.; *Deut.* xvi., and all the rest of the book except i. 3 ; in these passages the first month is called חדש האביב (*Ex.* xiii. 4 ; xxiii. 15 ; xxxiv. 18; *Deut.* xvi. 1), an appellation which does not appear in the laws that mention the months by number.—For punishment by death the Book of the Covenant uses the Hophal of מות (*Ex.* xxi. 12, 15–17, 29; xxii. 18 [19]); and once the phrase לא תחיה (*Ex.* xxii. 17 [18]). The former expression, which for that matter is perfectly natural and regular, also appears in other laws, such as *Ex.* xxxi. 14 sq.; xxxv. 2 ; *Lev.* xix. 20 ; xx. *passim*, etc.; *Deut.* xiii. 6, 10 [5, 9], etc. But here it alternates with (or is united to) other formulæ, viz. (*a*) in *Ex.–Num.*, 'to be rooted out (נכרת) from,' etc ; *Ex.* xii. 15, 19 ; xxx. 33, 38 ; xxxi. 14, etc. (24 [27] times in all, never in *Deut.*) : (*b*) in *Deut.* the phrase, 'and thou shalt destroy (בערת) the evil (or, the wicked one) out of thy midst;' *Deut.* xvii. 7, 12 ; xix. 19 ; xxi. 21, etc. (12 times in all, never in *Ex.–Num.*) See further, Knobel, *Num. Deut. u. Josh.*, p. 515 sqq., 527 sqq., 587 sqq., from whose copious collection abundant examples may be gleaned.

[10] The position that all the laws of the Tora are from a single hand really does not merit refutation. The very form of these laws, apart from their contents, reduces the supposition to an absurdity. Even where the subjects are identical (e.g. in *Ex.* xxi. 1–6 and *Deut.* xv. 12–18 ; *Lev.* xi. and *Deut.* xiv. 1–21), or the tone similar (*Ex.* xxiii. 20–33 ; *Lev.* xxvi.; *Deut.* xxviii.), the form, the style, and the language are completely different. Only one word

more : according to the chronology of the Hexateuch, *Num.* xxvii.-xxxi., xxxiv.
-xxxvi., and *Deuteronomy*, belong to one and the same year, nay, there would
hardly be a month between the dates at which they were respectively written
by one and the same author. Yet note the difference, for example, between *Num.* xxxv. 9-34 and *Deut.* xix. 1-13,—two laws on the very same
subject !

In inquiring into the unity of the Tora we must now
proceed from the form to the contents of the laws. And
indeed this latter is the more important inquiry. But before
we can enter upon it, we must determine the relation of
Deuteronomy to the legislation of the preceding books. According to the general opinion, which has found expression
in the very title of the book,—though not really supported
by it, since it rests upon a mistake (§ 1, n. 6),—the Sinaitic
legislation is repeated in *Deuteronomy*, and at the same
time brought into harmony with the requirements of the
settlement of Israel in Canaan, now instant. But we
must insist, (1) that in the book itself no previous legislation is assumed except the Decalogue, which is given
in v. 6-18 [6-21]; for though other laws have been revealed to Moses on Sinai, yet inasmuch as they are intended
for the people when living in Canaan, he now delivers
them to Israel for the first time (v. 28 [31]; vi. 1)[11];
the alleged references to an earlier legislation, which are
cited as conflicting with this view, must be explained
otherwise[12]; (2) that the laws of *Exodus–Numbers* are themselves intended for a settled people cultivating the soil (n. 6),
and would therefore need no modification in view of the
impending passage of the Jordan.—There can be no question,
therefore, that if we place ourselves at the point of view of
the Hexateuch itself we are justified in regarding the ordi-
[28] nances of *Exodus–Deuteronomy* as the several parts of a
single body of legislation, and comparing them one with
another as such[13]. The comparison will often reveal important differences, nay, irreconcilable contradictions. This

is especially true of *Deuteronomy* when compared with the laws that stand between *Ex.* xxv. and the end of *Numbers*, so that even if the relation in which *Deuteronomy* has been supposed to stand to the preceding books could be accepted as the true one, it could not in any way bridge over the kind of difference we actually find between them.

The complete demonstration of this fact must be deferred, but a few examples may serve to indicate the mutual relation of the codes. We may note, then, more especially, the laws concerning—

(*a*) The place of worship, *Ex.* xx. 24; *Deut.* xii. and parallel passages; *Lev.* xvii. and parallel passages [14].

(*b*) The religious festivals, *Ex.* xxiii. 14–17 and parallel passages; *Deut.* xvi. 1–17; *Lev.* xxiii. and parallel passages [15].

(*c*) The priests and the Levites, *Ex.* xxviii. sq. and parallel passages; *Num.* iii. and parallel passages; *Deut.* xviii. 1–8 and parallel passages [16].

(*d*) The tithes of crops and cattle, *Num.* xviii. 21–32; *Lev.* xxvii. 32 sq.; *Deut.* xiv. 22–29; xxvi. 12–15 [17].

(*e*) The firstlings of cattle, *Ex.* xxii. 29 [30]; xiii. 12, 13; xxxiv. 19, 20; *Deut.* xv. 19–23; *Num.* xviii. 15–18 [18].

(*f*) The dwelling places of priests and Levites in the land of Canaan, *Deut.* xviii. 6 and parallel passages; *Num.* xxxv. 1–8 and parallel passages; *Josh.* xxi. 1–40 [1–42] [19].

(*g*) The age at which the Levites enter upon their duties, *Num.* iv. 3, 23, 30, 35, 39, 43, 47; viii. 24 [20].

(*h*) The manumission of Israelitish slaves, *Ex.* xxi. 1–6; *Deut.* xv. 12–18; *Lev.* xxv. 39–43 [21].

Without anticipating the sequel of our inquiry, we may lay it down at once that most of the laws which are here brought under comparison answer to wholly different wants and were made in view of widely divergent circumstances, and accord- [29] ingly must, in all probability, be separated from each other by a space, not of years, but of centuries [22].

This conclusion is partially coincident and wholly consistent with the result of our previous investigation (concerning the form of the codes)[23], so that nothing prevents our
making it the provisional epitome of our final judgment on
the legislation of the Hexateuch.

[11] Cf. Graf, *Geschichtliche Bücher*, p. 11 sq.   I do not mean to assert that
the writer of *Deut.* v. 28 ; vi. 1, was not acquainted with any previous code,
such as the Book of the Covenant, *Ex.* xx. 23–xxiii., for instance.   But he
does not assume it as known to his readers, and does not put his own precepts
into any definite relations with these older laws.   If we suppose him to have
intended to repeat them, and at the same time to supplement and extend
them, we cannot appeal to any testimony of his own in support of the supposition.   That ' the covenant ' entered into at Sinai was regarded by our author
as containing no other commands of Yahwè to Israel than ' the ten words,'
is further evinced by his calling the stone tablets upon which these 'words'
were written (v. 19 [22]), ' the tablets of the covenant ' (ix. 9, 11, 15).   It
is also worth noting that in ix., x., where the events at Horeb are recalled,
no mention is made of the Book of the Covenant and its solemn acceptance by
the people (*Ex.* xxiv. 3–8), though this would have placed Israel's sin in a yet
stronger light.

[12] I myself formerly (*Historisch-kritisch Onderzoek*, 1st ed., i. 45) relied
upon *Deut.* xviii. 2, compared with *Num.* xviii. 20 [but the real reference here
is to the election of Levi as the priestly tribe, which *Deuteronomy* itself (x. 8, 9)
places earlier than the time at which Moses is represented as speaking, and
with which election of course the declaration, 'Yahwè is Levi's inheritance,'
would be simultaneous] ; xxiv. 8, compared with *Lev.* xiii., xiv. [but here the
author is not thinking of written laws, but of the oral tora, which the priests
are to utter in accordance with the will of Yahwè ; see below, § 10, n. 14] ;
xxvi. 18, 19, compared with *Ex.* xix. 4–6, *Lev.* xviii.–xx. [but the words of the
author himself, especially ' to-day ' (v. 17, 18), clearly show that he is thinking
exclusively of the union which is there and then being entered upon in the
land of Moab ; it is quite a mistake to see any reference here to *Ex.* xix., etc.].

[13] The different destination of the several codes must of course be kept
in view : the Book of the Covenant (cf. *Ex.* xx. 22 ; xxi, 1) and the legislative discourse in *Deut.* v.–xxvi. are addressed to the people ; other laws, e.g.
Lev. xiii., xiv., to the priests or to the Levites.   But since it remains equally
imperative that the several parts of a single legislation should be in mutual
harmony, this need not affect our conclusions.

[14] In my *Godsdienst*, i. 493–496 [*Rel. Isr.* ii. 81–84], I have shown that
in *Ex.* xx. 24, permission is given to erect altars and offer sacrifices to Yahwè
in different places, and that this permission, which is not contradicted by *Ex.*
xxi. 14 ; xxiii. 14–17, 19ᵃ, agrees with *Ex.* xxi. 6 ; xxii. 8, 9, where the existence of more than one sanctuary of Yahwè is presupposed.—In *Deuteronomy*,
on the other hand, it is repeatedly laid down, with the utmost emphasis, that

only 'in the place which Yahwè shall choose,' that is to say in the one central sanctuary, shall sacrifice be made in his honour (*Deut.* xii. 5, 8, 11, 14, 18, 21, [30] 26; xiv. 23–25; xv. 20; xvi. 2, 6 sq., 11, 15 sq.; xvii. 8, 10; xviii. 6; xxvi. 2). —In *Lev.* xvii., and in a number of other laws, such as *Ex.* xxv. sqq.; *Lev.* i. sqq.; xxiii., etc. etc., the ôhel mo'éd is the only place of sacrifice. So that here again the cultus is centralised in the one sanctuary, the exclusive pretensions of which, however, are not expressly maintained, but rather assumed, and now and then, as it were, incidentally confirmed.

[15] *Ex.* xxiii. (cf. also xxxiv. 18, 22–24; xiii. 3–10) and *Deut.* xvi. agree in the recognition of three yearly feasts at which the Israelites must repair to Yahwè's sanctuaries or sanctuary to see his face (cf. Geiger, *Urschrift*, p. 337 sqq.); though the two codes differ in points of secondary importance. In *Lev.* xxiii., on the other hand, as in *Num.* xxviii. sq., the מועדי יי are seven in number: sabbath, new moon, maççôth in conjunction with phesach, feast of weeks, new moon of the 7th month, day of atonement, feast of tabernacles. Their common mark is the מקרא קדש, i.e. the sacred assembly or gathering of the people at the ôhel mo'éd, with which sacrifices and cessation from work were associated (*Lev.* xxiii. 2, 4, 7, 8, 24, 27, 35–37; *Num.* xxviii. 18, 25, 26; xxix. 1, 7, 12; *Ex.* xii. 16). Now although maççôth, the feast of weeks, and the feast of tabernacles occupy a higher place, even in this second group of laws, than the new moon in general, for example, or the special new moon of the 7th month, nevertheless the absolute silence of the first group of laws concerning these festivals, and also—which is far more significant—concerning the day of atonement (cf. *Lev.* xvi.), remains highly remarkable, and indeed, on the supposition that the solemnities in question were known to the authors, inexplicable. See below, § 11.

[16] According to *Ex.* xxviii. sq. and the laws in *Leviticus* and *Numbers* generally, A aron and his sons are the only lawful priests. It is true that the Levites in a body are set apart for the service of the sanctuary (*Num.* iii. sq., viii., xviii., etc.), but they are excluded from the priesthood (see, for instance, *Num.* xvi. 9, 10; xvii. 5 [xvi. 40]; xviii. 1–3). The line between the sons of Aaron and the other Levites is clearly drawn in these laws; the subordinate position of the latter is unequivocally declared and strictly maintained. It is quite otherwise in *Deuteronomy.* According to x. 8, 9, Yahwè has separated the tribe of Levi 'to bear the ark of the covenant of Yahwè, to stand before Yahwè's face to serve him and to bless in his name'— in a word, to exercise the priesthood. Accordingly, the priests are called throughout this book הכהנים הלוים or בני לוי הכ"ים, the Levitical priests or the priests, sons of Levi (xvii. 9, 18; xviii. 1; xxi. 5; xxiv. 8; xxvii. 9; xxxi. 9; cf. *Josh.* iii. 3; viii. 33), never 'sons of Aaron,' and in *Deut.* xviii. 1, 'the whole tribe of Levi' stands in apposition with 'the Levitical priests,' after which the author thus proceeds: ' the sacrifice (אשי) of Yahwè and his portion (i.e. the portion that falls to Yahwè, נחלתו) shall they eat, and he (i.e. the tribe of Levi) shall have no inheritance amongst his brethren: Yahwè is his inheritance, as he has said to him' (xviii. 1b, 2). The equivalence of priests and Levites could hardly be formulated more distinctly. Does the

[31] author mean, then, that the priestly office was exercised—in the one sanctuary of course—by all the Levites without distinction? Not so, for he tells us that the Levites sojourn as strangers in the different cities of Israel (n. 19). But he considers them all qualified to act as priests. ' If the Levite (i. e. any Levite whatever) comes out of one of your cities in all Israel, where he sojourns as a stranger, and with undivided desire (בכל־אות נפשו) betakes himself to the place which Yahwè shall choose, then he shall serve in the name of Yahwè, his god, like all his brothers, who stand there before the face of Yahwè' (xviii. 6, 7). All this is quite unequivocal; it is a uniform and consistent picture; the passages support and explain each other. One more instance! Inasmuch as *Deuteronomy* knows nothing of priests + inferior servants of the sanctuary, it must of course lay upon the Levitical priests in general all the duties which are divided in *Exodus—Numbers* between the two classes. And so it does. According to *Num.* vi. 23-27, Aaron and his sons pronounce the blessing; in *Deut.* x. 8, 9; xxi. 5, we find the tribe of Levi (or the Levitical priests, or sons of Levi) separated (or, chosen), amongst other things, to bless in the name of Yahwè. The bearing of the ark of the covenant is amongst the duties assigned to the Levites in *Num.* iii. 31 ; iv. 5, 6, 15 ; and in *Deut.* x. 8, also, it is part of the task of the tribe of Levi. It is accordingly ascribed to ' the priests, sons of Levi,' in *Deut.* xxxi. 9, and to ' the Levites' in *Deut.* xxxi. 25. Cf. *Josh.* iii. 3, 6, 8, 13-15, 17 ; iv. 9-11, 16, 18 ; vi. 6 ; viii. 33.

Anyone who is curious to know the harmonising artifices employed to remove this discrepancy between *Exodus–Numbers*, and *Deuteronomy*, may consult Hengstenberg, *Authentie*, ii. 401-404 [ii. 329-332]; Haevernick, *Einl.* i. 2, p. 429 sqq. [311, 312], and more especially S. Ives Curtiss, *The Levitical priests* (Edinb., 1877). It is, of course, *Deuteronomy* in this case that has to be forced into agreement with *Exodus–Numbers*. The harmonists, therefore, attempt to show that the texts of *Deuteronomy* do not necessarily involve the absolute exclusion of the system of *Exodus–Numbers*, but only pass over in silence what is there expressly worked out—viz. the division of the priestly duties amongst the different descendants of Levi ; they do not say, but neither do they deny, that Aaron and his sons have a place of their own apart. No doubt this is what would be the case if the whole Tora were from a single hand; but it is not what actually is the case. *Deut.* xviii. 1-8 and the parallel passages are in no way incomplete or fragmentary: Levi, the priestly tribe, is as clear and finished a conception as that of Aaron and his sons + the Levitical subordinates. The texts of *Deuteronomy* itself are therefore the best and the all-sufficient arguments against these really hopeless efforts of the apologists. Cf. also Kayser, *Jahrbücher f. prot. Theologie*, 1881, p. 336-340, 637-643.

See further, n. 17-19, which show that this discrepancy between *Exodus–Numbers*, and *Deuteronomy*, by no means stands alone ; and also the historical explanation of the phenomenon in § 15.

[17] The practices enjoined in the various passages cited are evidently not identical : the tithes of the harvest according to *Num.* xviii. 21-32, and of the

cattle according to *Lev.* xxvii. 32 sq., are to be given to the Levites, who, in
their turn, must surrender a tenth of them to the priests ; they differ, therefore,
from the tithes of the harvest, which, according to *Deut.* xiv. 22-29 ; xxvi. 12–
15 (cf. xii. 6, 17-19), are to be set aside by the Israelites for sacrificial meals [32]
to which the Levites must be admitted, and are to be wholly given up every third
year to the Levites, widows, orphans, and strangers. In order to make out, in
spite of this, that the passages agree with each other, we must suppose them to
run parallel, or, in other words, must suppose that one and the same law-
giver requires two tithes. That is how the Jews have actually taken it
(cf. so early an authority as *Tobit* i. 6-8), and that is how they must take it,
since they regard the Tora as a single whole. But the very question we have
to decide is whether they are right in this ; and the answer must be in the
negative. The author of *Deuteronomy* knows nothing of any other
tithes, to be given to the Levites, in addition to those he mentions. Had it been otherwise he could not have passed them over in
silence ; he must at least have explained why the Levites—who were already
so richly provided for—were to have a share of his tithes in addition. But
there is more. In *Deut.* xviii. 3, 4, the ordinary revenues of ' the Levitical
priests, the whole tribe of Levi' (cf. n. 16), are summed up, and there, in *v.* 3,
we have their share in the offerings, and, in *v.* 4, the first-fruits that the people
are to give them, but no mention is made of the tithes. If we were to
interpret *Deut.* xviii. 3, 4 as referring to the priests in distinction from
the Levites—which as we have seen in n. 16 would be wrong—we should
still have to say that the tithes of the tithes are not mentioned.
This is inconceivable if the author had known of them.—Conversely, if we
look at *Num.* xviii. 21 sqq. in connection with *Deuteronomy*, as cited above,
our conclusion is the same, for here the Levites receive ' all the tithes of
Israel ' (*v.* 21). How can we suppose, when reading this, that yet other tithes
have been or are to be demanded ? The method which the defenders of the
unity of the Tora ascribe to the law-giver is simply treacherous ; he withdraws
from the Israelites the free disposal of a fifth part of the produce of their
land, and expresses himself throughout as though it were only a tenth which
he claimed for religious purposes. The single law-giver can only be retained
by the sacrifice of his moral character.

On the tithes of cattle cf. § 15, n. 30. Here we need only remark that
Deuteronomy simply mentions the tithes of corn, wine, and oil (xii. 17 ;
xiv. 23 ; as well as xxvi. 12, where תבואה signifies this same produce of the
land), and therefore excludes the tithes of cattle.

[18] The laws on the consecration of the firstlings of animals differ widely one
from another, as the following survey shows :—

(a) *Ex.* xxii. 29 [30] demands the male firstlings of oxen and sheep for
Yahwè ; they are to be sacrificed to him on the eighth day after their birth.

(b) *Ex.* xiii. 12, 13 ; xxxiv. 19, 20 demand the male firstlings of all domestic
animals for Yahwè ; the ass-foal, which cannot be sacrificed, is to be redeemed
by a sheep, or, if not, then killed.

(c) *Deut.* xv. 19-23 (cf. xiv. 22-27 ; xii. 6 sq., 17) says that the male firstlings of oxen and small cattle are sacred to Yahwè, and therefore must not be turned to private use, but must be consumed, year by year, at the sanctuary, in sacrificial feasts in which the Levite is to share.

[33]   (*d*) *Num.* xviii. 15–18 (cf. *Lev.* xxvii. 26, 27) demands for Aaron (*v.* 8), that is for the priests, all (i.e. male and female) firstlings of cattle; the clean beasts, oxen, sheep, and goats must be given to them in kind, and when their blood and fat have been laid on the altar must be eaten by them; the unclean beasts must be bought off from the priests, either at the fixed price of 5 shekels (*Num.* ibid.), or at the valuation of the priest, with the addition of one-fifth: if the possessor is dissatisfied with this the animal is to be sold (*Lev.* ibid.) and the price to be paid to the priest.

The differences between (*a*) and (*b*) may be passed over, and we may confine ourselves to the following points: (1) on comparing *b* with *d* we notice that the former contains a regulation about the ass-foal, which is modified in the latter to the advantage of the priests; the practice which the former allows, viz. breaking the neck of the ass belonging to Yahwè, if its owner cannot redeem it—which would comply with the requirements of consecration, but would not bring in anything to the priest—is not sanctioned by the latter: the priest always receives either the price of the animal's redemption, or the proceeds of its sale; (2) between *c* and *d* there is direct contradiction: that which *Deuteronomy* sets aside for sacrificial feasts is assigned in *Numbers* to the priests. The latest attempt to remove this contradiction is due to Dr. Ives Curtiss, op. cit., p. 39–41, who tries to explain *Num.* xviii. 18 otherwise. 'It is not said in Numbers that all the flesh of the firstlings belongs to the priests, nor in Deuteronomy that the people are to eat all of it.' On the contrary, in saying ' their flesh shall be yours; even as the wave breast and the right shoulder shall it (i.e. their flesh) be yours,' the law-giver means that the priests are to receive the breast and shoulder of the firstlings as of the thank-offerings (*Ex.* xxix. 27, 28; *Lev.* vii. 34). In other words: by his reference to the thank-offering he specifies the sense in which the firstlings of the cattle are assigned to the priests. The priests would think it a fine 'specification' that took back the greater part of what had first been given! If the law-giver had wished to say what Dr. Curtiss reads, he must of course have written ' their flesh shall be yours as that of the thank-offerings,' i.e. not in whole but in part. But he names just those parts of the thank-offering which the priests did receive: the breast and the shoulder. Inasmuch as they obtained these in whole and not in part, it follows that they are to receive the flesh of the firstlings in the same way. We must add that according to Dr. Curtiss's exposition of *Num.* xviii. 15–18 there is no direction as to what shall be done with the rest of the flesh. If the Israelite had taken it away with him out of the sanctuary he would not—always according to Dr. Curtiss's exegesis—have violated the law. But how can this be reconciled with the fundamental conception of all the laws on this subject, viz. that the firstlings belong to Yahwè? 'The grammar certainly allows, and *harmony demands*, that we should understand that the priests received the same proportion of the firstlings of sheep and cattle as of peace-offerings '

(p. 41, n. 3). The words I have italicised furnish the solution of the riddle how any man dare put forward such explanations.

[19] The regulations in *Num.* xxxv. 1–8, which *Josh.* xxi. 1–40 [1–42] represents as having been put into practice when the land was conquered, hardly need any comment: the forty-eight cities, with the pastures belonging to them, are given in fee simple to the priests and Levites; indeed the pastures [34] are inalienable (*Lev.* xxv. 34). If non-Levites may dwell in the cities—as may be gathered *per consequentiam* from *Lev.* xxv. 32, 33—the Levites still remain the owners: the cities are their אֲחֻזָּה (ibid.). This is quite inconsistent with the fact that, according to *Deut.* xviii. 6 (cf. xii. 12, 18; xiv. 27, 29; xvi. 11, 14), the Levites sojourn as strangers in the cities of the Israelites; and are repeatedly (*Deut.* xii. 19; xiv. 27, 29; xvi. 11, 14; xxvi. 11 sqq.) classed with the widows, orphans, and strangers, and commended to the charity of Israel. Let him explain who can how the law-giver, after having made, in the 40th year, such ample provision for the priests and Levites, could assume, a few days later, that his injunctions would not be carried out, and that the Levites would wander about in destitution.

[20] According to *Num.* iv. the Levites serve from their 30th to their 50th year; according to *Num.* viii. from their 25th to their 50th. Hengstenberg, *Authentic*, ii. 391 sqq. [ii. 321 sqq.], fails in his attempt to remove the contradiction: his assertion that *Num.* viii. refers to the service in general, and *Num.* iv. to service as porters, is contradicted by *Num.* iv. 19, 24, 27, 47. Delitzsch, *Die Genesis*, p. 50, admits the divergence and regards *Num.* viii. as a later modification of *Num.* iv. Very probable! But a modification introduced by the same law-giver who had drawn up *Num.* iv.? And did the necessity for it arise while Israel was still in the wilderness and the circumstances remained unchanged? For another view see § 15, n. 28.

[21] The points of difference between the laws in *Ex.* xxi. 1–6 and in *Deut.* xv. 12–18 are not without interest, but both alike are opposed to *Lev.* xxv. 39–43: in the former the Hebrew slave is set free after six years' service; in the latter the brother who has sold himself as a slave is set free in the year of jubilee. How anyone can say (see Hengstenberg, for example, ibid. p. 440 [362]) that the one does not exclude the other is hardly comprehensible. *Ex.* xxi. is taken to mean: he shall serve you six years unless the year of jubilee falls in the interval; and again: the slave, if he choose to do so, shall serve his master all his life long (לְעֹלָם), that is to say, not all his life long, but until the year of jubilee. Next, ' he shall serve you till the year of jubilee' (*Lev.* xxv. 40) is explained to mean: provided always that his six years of service do not terminate sooner! Is there any need to refute such interpretations?

[22] This is the case in particular with the points of difference, to which attention is called in n. 14, 15, and 16–19. Consider, for instance, what the concentration of sacrifices, feasts, etc. in one single sanctuary involves. In fact it will be seen presently that the intervening period is measured by centuries.

[23] The comparison between the contents of the several codes naturally yields

the more positive and definite results. But the differences of form, to which we first turned our attention, lead in general to the same conclusion; and the inappropriateness and want of natural arrangement which characterise the laws when regarded as codes of the desert, disappear or receive their explanation on the hypothesis of a later origin.

[35] § 4. *Investigation and provisional determination of the general character of the Hexateuch. B. The narratives.*

The investigations instituted in § 3 have dealt exclusively with the legislation, but they cannot fail to influence our views as to the narratives of the Hexateuch also. For the laws do not stand alone. Some of them are furnished with historical introductions from which they cannot be detached [1]. Others are so closely united with narratives that the connection must have existed from the first [2]. The result obtained with respect to the laws must therefore be extended to any historical passages which prove to be inseparable from them; and they too must be regarded as coming neither from a single period nor a single hand. But side by side with these passages there are others which are not affected by the inquiry as to the legislation. The narratives in *Genesis* and *Joshua* do not, for the most part, stand in direct connection with the laws. And even in *Exodus* and *Numbers* the connection between legislation and history is often very loose or altogether wanting; in some cases it is quite obvious that the two existed independently at first, and were only subsequently united into a single whole [3]. To form a correct and complete conception of the character of the Hexateuch we must therefore submit its narratives also to an express examination. Indeed, it will be well provisionally to set aside the results arrived at with regard to the laws, and examine the narratives independently.

[1] This is the case with *Ex.* xii. (institution of the passover); *Lev.* xxiv. 10–23 (punishment of blasphemy); *Num.* ix. 1–14 (postponement of the celebration of the passover on account of uncleanness); xv. 32–36 (punishment of

sabbath-breakers) ; xxvii. 1-11 ; xxxvi. (succession of daughters to property) ; xxxi. (cleanness of the camp, partition and consecration of the spoil). All these laws, at any rate in their present form, are inseparable from the narratives which introduce them.

[2] There is a very close connection between *Ex.* xxv.-xxxi. 17 (laws as to the structure of the tabernacle and the consecration of the priests) and *Ex.* xxxv. -xl.; *Lev.* viii., ix. (account of the execution of these directions ; with which, again, *Lev.* x. is closely connected). *Num.* i. and *Ex.* xxxviii. 26 are not, it is true, in harmony with each other, for the reckoning on which the passage in *Exodus* rests must be supposed to precede by some months the census with which its result precisely coincides, but it is utterly impossible that the two pas- [36] sages should have sprung up independently one of the other. *Num.* iii. and iv. are connected with *Lev.* x. by *Num.* iii. 4. *Num.* vii. is closely connected with *Ex.* xxv.-xxxi., etc.; *Num.* x. 11-28 with *Num.* ii. ; *Num.* xviii. with Korah's revolt in *Num.* xvi., xvii. Of course the character of this connection must be more closely determined in each particular case ; it by no means follows that it is always due to one and the same cause—to community of authorship for instance. But however we may explain it, the connection itself is undeniable. All this holds good of *Deut.* i.-iv. 40 ; xxvii.; xxxi. sq., and xxxiv. compared with the great legislative discourse in *Deut.* iv. 44-xxvi. ; and also of *Josh.* xx., xxi. compared with *Num.* xxxv., and, in general, of the partition of the land in *Josh.* xiv.-xix. compared with *Num.* xxxiv. Details will follow later on when we come to the minuter inquiry just promised.

[3] I do not mean to deny that the authors of the narratives in question were acquainted with the laws, or at any rate with some of them ; for the contrary is often evident on a careful comparison. I only mean that as they now stand in the Hexateuch they do not form an integral portion of the legislation which it likewise contains. With respect to *Genesis* and *Josh.* i.-xii. ; xxii.-xxiv. this is obvious at once. But even where laws and narratives stand side by side they often have no connection with each other. Indeed, *Ex.* xxxi. 18-xxxiv. positively breaks the connection between *Ex.* xxv-xxxi. 17 and xxxv.-xl., and *Ex.* xxv.-xxxi. 17, in its turn, is obviously thrust in between xxiv. and xxxi. 18-xxxiv. Observe, for instance, how in *Ex.* xxxiii. 7-11 the existence of the tabernacle, which according to *Ex.* xxxv. sqq. has yet to be built, is already assumed. So again *Num.* xv. is connected neither with xiii. sq. nor with xvi. sq. ; *Num.* xix. neither with xviii. nor xx. ; *Num.* xxviii.-xxx. stands oddly between xxvii. (cf. *v.* 13) and xxxi. (cf. *v.* 2). For the rest these examples, like those in n. 2, are by no means homogeneous, and the indication of the peculiarities of each must be reserved.

Meanwhile the phenomena indicated in. n. 1-3 justify us at once in drawing a conclusion of some importance with reference to the hypothesis put forward by E. Bertheau in his work : *Die sieben Gruppen mosaischer Gezetze in den drei mittleren Büchern des Pentateuchs* (Gött., 1840). I must content myself, however, with referring to the more elaborate criticism in my *Historisch-kritisch Onderzoek* (1st ed., i. 41-44) and remarking ; (1) that each of the 'seven groups' consist of seven series, and each of these again of ten commandments, so that the whole codex which Bertheau believes he can find in *Exodus–Numbers* contains 490 precepts; (2) that the manner in which the seven series and the ten commandments belonging to each of them are indicated and, yet more, the omission of some of the laws from the numbering, as 'supplementary,' is occasionally very artificial, not to say arbitrary; (3) that the mutual contradictions in the laws, already brought out in § 3, and to be further shown in the sequel, make their union into a single systematically arranged code extremely improbable; and, above all, (4) that the intimate connection between some of the laws and some of the narratives (n. 1 and 2) absolutely forbids us to suppose that the former existed at first in a separate form as a book of law, and were not united with the narrative passages or taken up into a continuous history until afterwards. In other words, Bertheau's hypothesis supposes a relation between the legislation and the history which, as a matter of fact, is anything but universal in the Pentateuch, though it certainly does appear sporadically (cf. n. 3).

[37]   In fixing the chronological relations of the narratives of *Exodus–Joshua* to the time of Israel's deliverance from Egypt and settlement in Canaan, we may find a point of departure in *Num.* xxi. and *Josh.* x. Each of these chapters makes a citation, the former (*v.* 14) from the book of the wars of Yahwè, the latter (*v.* 13) from the book of the upright[4]. Both these works are probably collections of songs, and they certainly date from the period of the monarchy[5]. The narratives whose authors appeal to them must, of course, be later still. Indeed the mode of citation, especially in *Num.* xxi., warrants the belief that the authors stood very far from the events which they record: their attitude approaches that of the archæologian who does not simply tell his tale, but defends a specific interpretation of the events and supports it by citations[6].

Perhaps other poetical passages in the Hexateuch are borrowed from the same or similar collections[7], and, if so, their occurrence would strengthen the opinion just expressed. At any rate, the use of the formula 'even to this day' inclines us to place the writers of the Hexateuch long after the times of Moses and Joshua[8]; and here and there a historical or geographical note in the book of *Deuteronomy* forces us to the same conclusion[9]. The traditional view which makes Moses and Joshua themselves come forward as witnesses concerning their own achievements and fortunes is not supported by a single trait in the narratives, and is distinctly contradicted by several [10].

[4] ספר הישר, i.e. the book either of that which is right (sc. in Yahwè's eye), or of him who is right (again, in Yahwè's eye). Without possessing the book itself it is impossible to decide with certainty between these two interpretations. The latter, however, gains some support from the use of ישרון, *Deut.* xxxii. 15; xxxiii. 26, to indicate the people of Israel in its relation to Yahwè.

[5] For the Sepher hayyashár, see 2 *Sam.* i. 18, where we learn that David's dirge on Saul and Jonathan was included in it. Evidence of the date of the Sepher Milchamôth Yahwè is supplied by the title itself: the 'wars of Yahwè' are the wars of Israel against his neighbours in the period of the Judges, under David (1 *Sam.* xviii. 17; xxv. 28), and later on. The collector of the songs referring to these wars presumably lived after their close, when [38] Israel's heroic age was long gone by. Hengstenberg's attempt, *Authentie,* ii. 223–226 [ii. 182–185], to establish the earlier and successive origin of the collection may be left to condemn itself.

[6] In *Num.* xxi. 14, 15 an expression from 'the book of the wars of Yahwè' is cited to prove that the Arnon was the boundary between the Amorites and the Moabites, so that when the Israelites had crossed it ('in the desert,' *v.* 13, east of the Dead Sea) they were in Amorite territory. The writer attaches great weight to this. After having mentioned in *v.* 25 that by defeating Sihon Israel became master of Heshbon and its dependencies, he continues (*v.* 26): 'for Heshbon is the city of Sihon, king of the Amorites, and he had waged war against the first king of Moab and had taken away all his land as far as the Arnon'—a statement which he proceeds to support by a poetical citation, *v.* 27–30 ('wherefore the poets,—here called המשלים,—say'). —What an absurdity to ascribe such a narrative to a contemporary! It gives back the echoes of the disputes between the Transjordanic tribes and the Moabites and Ammonites, in which the question seems often to have been raised who it was that the former had dispossessed (cf. *Judges* xi. 12–28; *Deut.* ii. 9, 19). The writer has a decided opinion of his own on the subject, and he offers proofs in confirmation of it.—Evidence of another kind shows that *Josh.* x. stands in the same category as *Num.* xxi. The quotation runs on to the words עד יקם גוי איביו (*v.* 13ᵃ); what follows ('and the sun stood still in the midst of the heaven,' etc.) is a prosaic paraphrase of what has gone before, and probably a misunderstanding of the poet's meaning.

[7] Especially *Gen.* xlix.; *Ex.* xv. 1–19; 20 sq., 'The song of the well,' *Num.* xxi. 17, 18, though brought into connection, in this passage, with Israel's stay at Beër, may very well have been taken from the mouth of the people, in which case it is not really an 'occasional' poem at all. *Deut.* xxxii.

and xxxiii. will be dealt with later on, when their connection with the rest of the book is investigated.

⁸ *Gen.* xix. 37, 38 ; xxvi. 33 ; xxxii. 33 [32] ; xxxv. 20 ; xlvii. 26 ; *Deut.* ii. 22 ; iii. 14 ; x. 8 ; xi. 4 ; xxxiv. 6 ; *Josh.* iv. 9 ; v. 9 ; vi. 25 ; vii. 26 ; viii. 28 sq. ; ix. 27 ; x. 27 ; xiii. 13 ; xiv. 14 ; xv. 63 ; xvi. 10. As to the passages in *Genesis*, though it is highly probable that they should be brought down far beyond the time of Moses, yet there is nothing in this expression absolutely to preclude the Mosaic date. The same may be said of *Deut.* ii. 22 ; xi. 4. But *Deut.* iii. 14 ; x. 8 ; xxxiv. 6 unquestionably bring us to a later date, and so too, with ever-growing distinctness, do the texts in *Joshua*. Ch. vi. 25 ; xiv. 14 do not refer to Rahab and Caleb, but to their descendants ; xv. 63 points to the time after David, for till then Jerusalem was still completely in the power of the Jebusites (*Judges* xix. 12), but after its capture by David they remained there side by side with the Israelites (2 *Sam.* xxiv. 16, 18 ; 1 *Kings* ix. 20, 21 ; *Ezra* ix. 1, 2 ; *Zach.* ix. 7) ; xvi. 10 we should have to place before Solomon if 1 *Kings* ix. 16 were to be taken literally ; but it is probable that Gezer was at first subject to the Philistines (2 *Sam.* v. 25 ; 1 *Chron.* xiv. 16 ; xx. 4) and did not become tributary to the Israelites till after its conquest by Solomon's father-in-law.—To ix. 27 we shall return presently, but note in the meantime that 2 *Sam.* xxi. 2 shows that the Gibeonites, though persecuted by Saul, were not exterminated by him.

[39]   ⁹ See *Deut.* ii. 10–12, 20–23 ; iii. 9, 11, 13ᵇ, 14. There is not the smallest reason for assigning these notes to any one but the author of *Deut.* i. 1–iv. 40, with which their linguistic character coincides (ירשה, השמיד, ירש, רב, רם, ענקים, etc.). They may, no doubt, be considered as glosses, for it can hardly be intended that Moses communicated these details to the Israelites by word of mouth ; but in that case they are glosses on the speech of Moses made by the hand which committed it to writing. The remark made upon *Num.* xxi. in n. 6 is therefore applicable *a fortiori* to *Deut.* ii., iii. : their author is a scholar, in his own way, and he gives his readers the benefit of his geographical and historical knowledge. Cf. Ewald, *Geschichte*, i. 184 sq. (3rd ed.) [125, 126]. —The questions raised by x. 6–9 are very complex, and must therefore be reserved for future treatment (§ 7, n. 6).

¹⁰ Evidence against the authorship of Moses is supplied not only by *Deut.* xxxiv. (especially *v.* 10), but by *Ex.* vi. 26, 27 ; xi. 3 ; *Num.* xii. 3, 6 sqq. ; *Deut.* xxxiii. 4, in which Moses himself is spoken of in the most objective manner possible. That Joshua wrote the book which bears his name certainly cannot be inferred either from xxiv. 26 (§ 2, n. 1) or from any other passage of the book. Ch. v. 1 has been ascribed to a contemporary, on the strength of the עברנו, but the true reading is עברם (cf. the versions), and the received text is due to the eye having wandered to iv. 23.

This would be the place for an express treatment of the so-called anachron- isms of the Pentateuch, i. e. the texts which illustrate its post-Mosaic origin. As long as the tradition that Moses was the author of the Tora was do- minant, it was natural that great stress should be laid on pointing out these ana- chronisms, or, on the other hand, demonstrating that the passages in question might quite well have come from the hand of Moses. The texts over which the controversy raged are collected by Hengstenberg, *Authentie*, ii. 179–345 [ii. 146–282]; Keil, *Einl.* § 38 [i. 137 sqq.] and elsewhere. But this phase of the critical inquiry now lies behind us. The Mosaic origin of the whole Tora is hardly defended now. Attention is directed to phenomena of wider scope and greater significance, which bear upon the problem as a whole and lead to a positive solution of it. I shall therefore confine myself to the simple enumeration of the most important of these texts, and a reference to my *Historisch-kritisch Onderzoek*, (1st ed.) i. 22–29, where the quality of their apologetic treatment is illustrated by a few examples.

That the Tora was written in Canaan appears from the use of יׄם for the West, and עבר הירדן for the district which we, too, taking our stand in Canaan, call the Transjordanic region; and further, from texts such as *Gen.* xix. 20–22; xxi. 31; xxiii. 2; xxvi. 32 sq.; xxviii. 19; xxxv. 19, where names of places in Canaan are explained—surely not either by or for those who had yet to enter the land!—or again from the detailed—and yet not always really intelligible or correct—information about the regions in which Israel wandered before the conquest, *Deut.* i. 1–5 (cf. Graf, *Geschichtliche Bücher*, p. 6, n.). The historical position of the writers of the Tora betrays itself, for example, in *Gen.* xii. 6; xiii. 7; xl. 15 (the ancient inhabitants are expelled; Canaan has become 'the land of the Hebrews'); *Gen.* xiv. 14; *Deut.* xxxiv. 1 (the name of Laish is already changed to Dan; cf. *Josh.* xix. 47; *Judges* xviii. 29); *Deut.* ii. 12 (Canaan occupied by Israel); iii. 11 (Og's bed a relic of [40] antiquity); iii. 14 (the name *Havvôth-Yaïr* has long been in use); xix. 14ᵃ (the ראשׁנים themselves were living in Canaan); *Num.* xv. 32 (the sojourn in the desert a closed period of history); *Gen.* xxxvi. 31 (Israel governed by kings). Proofs of post-Mosaic origin are particularly numerous in the poetical passages, *Gen.* xlix. (cf. J. P. N. Land, *Disp. de carmine Jacobi*, Lugd. Bat., 1857; K. Kohler, *Der Segen Jacob's*, Berl. 1867); *Ex.* xv. (especially *v.* 13, 17); *Deut.* xxxii. (cf. A. Kamphausen, *Das Lied Mose's*, Leipz., 1862); xxxiii. (cf. K. H. Graf, *Der Segen Mose's*, Leipz., 1857; W. Volck, *Der Segen Mose's*, Erl., 1873); and in the story of Balaam, *Num.* xxii.-xxiv. (cf. B. R. de Geer, *De Bileamo*, Traj. ad Rhen., 1816; Hengstenberg, *Die Gesch. Bileams und seine Weissagungen*, Berl., 1842; H. Oort, *Disp. de pericope Num.* xxii. 2–xxiv., Lugd. Bat., 1860; M. Kalisch, *Bible Studies*, i., London, 1877).

Now the inference drawn from these special phenomena is at once confirmed and rendered more definite by the contents and the general character of the narratives themselves. All the marks which usually appear in subsequent and late accounts of events are united in the narratives of the Hexateuch. The further we push our inquiry the more clearly will this be seen. For the present a number of striking

instances will suffice to remove all doubt as to the true
character of the Hexateuch as a historical authority.

In the narratives which we owe to eye-witnesses or contemporaries, or which at any rate were written down
shortly after the events themselves, we find a unity and
mutual agreement qualified only by inevitable divergencies.
But in the case of later accounts, belonging to different
periods, and perhaps issuing from different circles, contradictions as to the main issues as well as the details must
inevitably appear. The historical reminiscences, orally preserved during a longer or shorter period, are constantly
taking up alien and not always identical matter into their
texture. When they come to be written down the legends
are worked up in one way by one writer and in another
by another, according to the point of view and purpose
of each respectively, so as often to be notably modified or
even completely transformed. That the narratives of the
Hexateuch have shared this fate appears in the first place
from their mutual contradictions. They often give us
[41] mutually excluding, or at any rate more or less widely diverg-
ing representations of one and the same event or individual.
We find these accounts either side by side or forced *quand
même* into a single whole. This phenomenon appears not
only in *Genesis*, i.e. in the narratives concerning the præ-
Mosaic time[11], but, just as unmistakably, in *Exodus, Numbers*[12], and *Joshua*[13]. A characteristic modification of the
same phenomenon appears in the historical reminiscences here
and there woven into *Deuteronomy*; on the one hand they
show acquaintance with the narratives which we possess in
Exodus and *Numbers*, but, on the other hand, their reproduction of them is extremely free[14].

[11] Here we find side by side
the two creation stories, *Gen.* i. 1—ii. 4[a], and ii. 4[b]-23. The division of
the work of creation into six days is entirely unknown to the second story.
Moreover, the order of creation is quite different in the second: first, the

man is created (*v.* 7), then trees and plants (*v.* 8 sq.), then animals (*v.* 19), and lastly the woman (*v.* 21, 22). Cf. the commentators, and H. Hupfeld, *Die Quellen der Genesis*, p. 109 sqq.; Bunsen's *Bibelwerk*, I. p. cxlii. sqq.;

two accounts of the destruction of Sodom and Gomorrah and Lot's escape, *Gen.* xviii. 1–xix. 28 and xix. 29;

two accounts of the origin of the name Beer-sheba, *Gen.* xxi. 31 and xxvi. 32, 33;

of the name Beth-el, *Gen.* xxviii. 10–19 and xxxv. 15;

of the name Israel, *Gen.* xxxii. 25–33 [24–32], and xxxv. 10;

of the names of Esau's wives, *Gen.* xxvi. 34; (xxvii. 46); xxviii. 9 and *Gen.* xxxvi. 2, 3;

of Esau's settlement in Seir, which took place, according to *Gen.* xxxii. 4 sqq.; xxxiii. 1 sqq., during Jacob's sojourn in Mesopotamia, and, according to *Gen.* xxxvi. 6, 7, after his return thence.

We have also the following cases of originally distinct narratives worked up together:—

two accounts of the deluge in *Gen.* vi.–ix.: 17. For (1) the corruption of mankind and the consequent displeasure of Yahwè are narrated and explained in vi. (1–4), 5–8, and again, but differently, in *v.* 9–13; (2) vi. 19, 20; vii. 8, 9, 14 sq. speak of one pair of every kind of animal being taken into the ark by Noah at God's command; while vii. 2, 3 distinguishes between clean and unclean beasts, and orders seven pairs each of the former to be preserved; (3) side by side with Yahwè's resolve that mankind shall not be destroyed again, viii. 20–22, stands God's covenant with Noah, and his promise that the deluge shall not be repeated, ix. 1–17;

two accounts of Joseph coming into Egypt, in *Gen.* xxxvii, xxxix, xl. According to one Joseph is thrown into a pit, at the advice of Reuben, but, while the brothers are eating bread, he is stolen by Midianitish merchants, carried away to Egypt and sold to Potiphar, a eunuch of Pharaoh's, who has charge of the prisoners as captain of the body-guard [42] (xxxvii. 1–25ᵃ, 28ᵃ, 29–36; xl. 1 sqq.). According to the other story Joseph, at the advice of Judah, is sold to Ishmaelites who carry him to Egypt and sell him to an Egyptian in whose house he enjoys prosperity at first, but is afterwards slandered by his master's wife; and only in consequence of this slander comes inside the prison house (xxxvii. 25ᵇ–27, 28ᵇ; xxxix, except a few words in *v.* 1).

The above absolutely irrefragable proofs of the composite character of the narratives of which Genesis is composed make it very probable that certain other narratives which strongly resemble each other, must also be regarded as doublets, i. e. as diverse renderings of a single tradition, or as variations on a single theme. Compare the following passages:—

Gen. xii. 10–20 and xx. 1–18: the author of the second account knows nothing of the first; the renewed recourse to the same deception after its first failure is too improbable psychologically for the same author to have ascribed both attempts to Abraham;

Gen. xvi. 4–14 and xxi. 8–21. See *Godgeleerde Bijdragen* for 1866, p. 467 sqq.;

Gen. xxi. 22–34 and xxvi. 26–33; observe the identity of the names Abimelech and Phicol, and the mutually excluding interpretations of the origin of Beer-sheba, xxi. 31 ; xxvi. 33, with which the stories respectively close.

[12] In these books we find two accounts side by side

of the revelation of the name Y a h w è , *Ex.* iii. 14, 15 and vi. 2 sq.;

of the name of Moses' father-in-law, R e ' u e l, *Ex.* ii. 18, 21 ; J e t h r o, *Ex.* iii. 1 ; iv. 18; xviii. 1 sqq. Cf. also *Num.* x. 29, where חתן משה may refer to Hobab (as in *Judges* iv. 11), but may also refer to Re'uel, as in *Ex.* ii. 18, 21 ;

of the lightening of Moses' task as judge and leader of his people, *Ex.* xviii. (appointment of judges over 1,000, 100, 50, and 10 families), and *Num.* xi. 11 sqq. (70 elders associated with Moses and inspired with his spirit). The two narratives diverge widely. But the latter betrays no trace of acquaintance with the former (see especially *v.* 14), and in *Deut.* i. 9–18 they are united into a single whole ;

of the manna and the quails, *Ex.* xvi. and *Num.* xi. : the latter chapter, when compared with the former, reveals a partial repetition accompanied by divergencies, e.g. concerning the manna ;

of the tabernacle : according to *Ex.* xxxiii. 7–11, it was pitched outside the camp, as is also assumed in *Num.* xi. 16, 26 ; xii. 4 ; *Deut.* xxxi. 14 sq., but the sanctuary described in *Ex.* xxv. sqq. ; xxxv. sqq. stands in the middle of the camp, in accordance with *Num.* ii. sqq.;

of the person and character of Balaam : in *Num.* xxii–xxiv. he is a prophet of Yahwè, whom Balak, king of Moab, tries to induce to curse Israel, but who, faithful to Yahwè's command, blesses the people and then returns home ; according to *Num.* xxxi. 8, 16 (cf. *Josh.* xiii. 22) Balaam sojourns amongst the Midianites, it is at his suggestion that the latter seduce Israel to idolatry, and accordingly he is slain together with them. With the former representation *Mic.* vi. 5 is completely in harmony, and *Deut.* xxiii. 4, 5 and *Josh.* xxiv. 9 at any rate substantially so.

The narratives in which heterogeneous elements are united into an often
[43] very ill connected whole need not be dissected here : we shall return to them presently. The composite character of the following passages is especially obvious : *Ex.* vii.–xi. ; xiv. (two representations of the passage of the Red Sea) ; xix. 1–xx. 21 and xxiv. (where an almost hopeless confusion results from the mingling of conflicting accounts), xxxi. 18–xxxiv. (where there is similar confusion—xxxii. 7–14, to name a single point, conflicting with *v.* 17 sqq., 30 sqq. ; and xxxii. 25–29 [where the punishment is actually inflicted] with *v.* 30–34 [where Moses prays that it may be averted]) ; *Num.* xiii., xiv. (cf. *Th. Tijdschrift*, xi. 545 sqq.); xvi., xvii. (ibid. xii. 139 sqq.) ; xxv. (according to the one account, Israel commits idolatry with the Moabitish, according to the other, with the Midianitish women ; cf. *De profeten en de profetie onder Israel*, ii. 134–136 [390–392]).

[13] A careful reading of *Joshua* constantly reveals the interweaving of divergent accounts. The dispatch of the spies (ii.) contradicts the date given in i. 10, 11, cf. iii. 2. Ch. iii. and iv. are full of repetitions which are inexplic-

able on the supposition of a single author. Ch. vi. 2–5 (where the sound
of the trumpet is the signal for the fall of Jericho) does not at all correspond
with *v.* 8 (where the whole procession round the city is continuously accompanied by the trumpets). In viii., *v.* 3 sqq. conflicts with *v.* 12 sqq. The
composite character of ix. is shown by *v.* 17–21, where the whole matter is
decided and the result made known to the Gibeonites, though in *v.* 22 sqq.
Joshua has still to inquire into it before pronouncing judgment; and also
by the two-fold representation of the destiny of the Gibeonites, as ' wood-
cutters and water-drawers for the community ' or as ' slaves of the house of
Yahwè ' (*v.* 21, 23 ; in which latter verse, in defiance of all grammar, the one
is combined with the other).

¹⁴ Cf. W. H. Kosters, *De historieheschouwing van den Deuteronomist, met
de berichten in* Gen.–Num. *vergeleken* (Leiden, 1868). We shall return to this
matter presently, and may confine ourselves here to a few examples. *Deut.* ix.,
x. sometimes reproduces *Ex.* xxxii. literally. *Deut.* i. 6 19 points clearly
enough to *Ex.* xviii. and *Num.* xi., weaving the two accounts into one (n. 12).
In *Deut.* i. 20–46 we recognise more than one expression from *Num.* xiii. sq.,
but we also find the statement, in *v.* 20–22, that Moses sent the spies at
the request of the Israelites. *Deut.* ii. 4–8 departs from *Num.* xx.
14–21. *Deut.* i. 37 ; iii. 26 ; iv. 21—where Yahwè is wroth with Moses
because of the Israelites—have nothing to correspond to them in
Numbers.

The clear indications of diversity of authorship furnished by these conflicting representations would lead us
a priori to expect linguistic evidence of a corresponding
nature. Nor is our expectation deceived : each of the divergent accounts has its distinctive language, and characteristic
turns of speech and style. Indeed the narratives differ so
widely in this respect, that without reference to their contents, and where, from the nature of the case, these contents
can give us no help, we are still able to place the diversity of
authorship above the reach of doubt by merely noting the
divergencies of form¹⁵. For our present purpose it will be [44]
enough simply to note this fact ; for characteristics of language and style serve not only to distinguish the narratives
of diverse origin, but, above all, to identify the passages due
to a single hand, and will therefore naturally present themselves for further consideration when we come to this portion
of our task.

¹⁵ It is almost superfluous to remark that the two creation stories, for example, and the two accounts of the flood (n. 11) differ widely in form as well as matter. Here, therefore, contents and language combine. The form alone is enough to stamp *Gen.* xvii., for instance, as due to some other hand than that which penned either *Gen.* xv. sq. or *Gen.* xviii.   *Gen.* xxiii. stands off with equal distinctness from what precedes and what follows it. But it is needless to go on; especially as the difference of language and style that we have established in the case of the legislative matter (§ 3, n. 9, 10) could not and does not fail to present itself here too, seeing how closely the laws and narratives are often connected.

The evidence furnished by the conflicting character of the narratives of the Hexateuch and their differences of form is confirmed by their contents, or the representation they give us of the course of the historical events, indicating that they are separated from the facts themselves by a very great lapse of time. The book of *Genesis* may here be left out of account, since the picture it contains of the age of the patriarchs gives us no unequivocal indications of the period at which it was produced¹⁶. It is otherwise with the description of the exodus from Egypt, the wandering in the desert, and the conquest and partition of Canaan, which the following books supply. Their representations, to put it in a word, are utterly unhistorical, and therefore cannot have been committed to writing until centuries after Moses and Joshua.

It cannot be denied, in the abstract, that we are justified in arguing from the character of the narratives to their chronological relation to the facts they record. It is true that our first endeavour must be to determine the age of the accounts, independently of their contents, by examining their mutual relations and their form, and thus gaining a clue to their historical value; but when this inquiry has been made and has led to a positive result, then the greater or smaller degree in which the historical character is stamped on the narratives themselves may, in its turn, be used as a help towards determining the interval that lies between their composition and the facts. Of course this [45] method can only be fruitfully employed upon one condition, viz. that the test is universally admitted as fair. Otherwise the inferences drawn will have no validity, at any rate in the eyes of those who object to the test selected. For this reason we must lay no stress in this connection upon the miracles of the Hexateuch, even now that we have learned something of its character as a historical authority: the question of miracles is too completely dominated by divergent personal convictions to supply materials for a unanimous conclusion. But there are requirements with which every story, whether miraculous or not, must comply, and from which, always and everywhere, narratives tend to depart in proportion as they recede from the times to which they refer and are less and less controlled by the reality or by the living tradition concerning it.

Amongst these requirements is a certain measure of fullness and clearness, never absent from a reflection of the actual facts, but on the other hand, often missed by those who have only realised them vaguely if at all. Now it cannot be denied that in the books of *Exodus–Joshua* incompleteness and indistinctness are far from rare; in particular the forty years' wandering in the desert is passed over almost in silence, and its main features are very imperfectly and divergently explained[17]. But since there is room for difference of opinion even here, let us apply another test which leads to absolutely incontrovertible results. The representations in the later books of the Hexateuch simply defy the conditions of space and time to which every event is subject, and by which, therefore, every narrative may be tested. The exodus, the wandering, the passage of the Jordan and the settlement in Canaan, as they are described in the Hexateuch, simply could not have happened. We strive in vain to conceive their occurrence

as long as we retain the data of the Hexateuch itself.
The more we go into detail the more clearly does this come
[46] out[18]. The fact is extremely important in determining the
character of the Hexateuch. All the more so since this
representation of the course of events is not sporadic, but
appears throughout, and is sometimes rounded into a complete system which at first produces the impression of an
accurate reflex of the facts, but, when we discover that it
cannot possibly be such, must be supposed to owe its origin
to the constructive imagination which works upon unhistorical premisses as readily as though they were facts[19].

This verdict on the character of the Hexateuch would
be forced upon us by the nature of its presentment of
the history even were we unable to explain it genetically.
But as a fact the explanation is quite easy. The mental
necessity of making the events of long past ages visibly,
and as it were tangibly present, makes tradition, elsewhere as well as in Palestine, concentrate the events of
a whole era within the narrow space of a few years and
the exploits of one or more successive generations within the
life of a single hero. That this took place in Israel with
regard to the great events recorded in *Exodus–Joshua* is not
only probable *a priori*, but is actually apparent from a number
of the accounts which we find in the books themselves[20].
They show the unmistakable traces of the condensing and
concentrating process that must have preceded their committal to writing; and this fresh confirmation of their later
origin serves at the same time to explain the unhistorical
presentation of the facts which we have noted, and which
could not but result from such a process of evolution[21].

[16] Cf. my essay on *De stamvaders van het Israëlietische volk* in *Th. Tijdschr.*,
v. 255-312. Many of my readers may think the facts there collected significant
enough. But since they can only lead indirectly to definite conclusions as to
the age of the narratives, they yield in importance to the phenomena which
are dealt with in n. 17-20.

[17] From the survey of contents (§ 1) we have seen that the announcement of the wandering, made in the second year after the exodus, occurs in *Num.* xiv. The place assigned to *Num.* xv.–xix. suggests that the laws there registered [47] were promulgated, and the revolt of Korah, Dathan, and Abiram took place, during this time of wandering; but there is no more specific indication of the date either of the laws or the events. Now follows *Num.* xx. 1: 'And the sons of Israel, the whole community, came into the desert of Çîn in the first month, and the people abode at Kadesh, and Miriam died there and there was she buried.' 'The first month'—of what year? If of the fortieth, then the intervening space of 38 years is filled by xv.–xix., with no other indication whatever; if of the third year, and if, accordingly, the events of *v.* 2–13 belong to this same year, then 37 years lie between *v.* 13 and *v.* 14–22 (embassy to the king of Edom) without a single word in the text to indicate it. But even this is not all. With regard to the wandering, the Hexateuch contradicts itself. It begins at Kadesh (or Kadesh Barnéa), according to *Deut.* i. 40 (cf. 19); ii. 1, 13, 14; *Josh.* xiv. 7; *Num.* xiii. 26 (קדשה), after the spies had been dispatched thence; and there is no mention in these passages of *Deuteronomy* of any return to Kadesh. But according to *Num.* xii. 16; xiii. 3, 26 (אל מדבר פארן) the desert of Pharan is the place from which the spies set out, and the arrival of the people at Kadesh falls much later, perhaps in the fortieth year (*Num.* xxxiii. 37; and probably xx. 1ᵃ also). Another version yet is found in *Deut.* i. 46: 'and ye abode in Kadesh many days, as long as ye abode there' (i.e. during a long period that the author does not venture to define); and any idea of twisting this representation into agreement with the two others, is dispelled by our finding it again elsewhere, viz. in *Judges* xi. 16, 17, and perhaps also in *Num.* xx. 1ᵇ ('and the people abode at Kadesh'). These phenomena really admit of but one explanation: when the stories of the Hexateuch were committed to writing Israel's abode in the desert belonged to a distant past, of which one had formed one idea and another another, but of which no one could give a consistent account. Why *Num.* xxxiii., in spite of *v.* 2, cannot modify our view of the case, will be seen hereafter (§ 6, n. 43 and § 16, n. 12).—Very fragmentary and obscure, too, is *Num.* xxi. 1–3 (cf. xxxiii. 40); and so is the description of the conquest of Canaan in general, extending, according to *Josh.* xxii. 3, over 'many days,' and according to xiii. 1, till Joshua had become an old man, whereas vi. sqq. would lead us to suppose that it was all accomplished in a very brief space of time. Other examples that do not lie so much on the surface will present themselves in great number as we go along.

[18] It is the great merit of the bishop of Natal, Dr. J. W. Colenso, to have recalled attention to this fact (which had been noted before, but was in danger of gradually falling into oblivion), and to have made it palpable to every one. See Part i. of his work referred to on p. 2. A single sub-section of the narrative, the passage of the Red Sea (*Ex.* xiv.), had already been submitted to similar criticism by H. S. Reimarus, in one of the fragments published by Lessing, and also included in Klose's (unfinished) edition of the *Schutzschrift für die vernünftigen Verehrer Gottes* (Zeitschrift für die

hist. Theol. 1852, p. 404–426). The number of Israelitish fighting men is
given in *Ex.* xii. 37; *Num.* xi. 21 as 600,000, with which *Num.* i. 46; ii. 32;
xxvi. 51 (cf. also *Ex.* xxxviii. 25 sq.) agree, and this gives a people of two and
a half million souls. This is the prevailing representation of the Hexa-
[48] teuch, and though some few texts conflict with it (cf. my *Godsdienst,* i. 174 sq.
[*Rel. Isr.* i. 172–176]), it must certainly be taken as the starting point of our
criticism. The herds of cattle were in proportion to the numbers of this huge
multitude (*Ex.* xii. 38); the enormous figures to which we must mount if we
accept as historical the accounts given in the Hexateuch of the regular celebration of the passover (*Ex.* xii.; *Num.* ix. 1–14; *Josh.* v. 10) have been shown by
Colenso (p. 57 sqq., 65 sqq.). Now consider what the migration of such a host
—including old and sick people, weaklings and little children—would be, the
inevitable confusion that would accompany it, the difficulties involved in the
people all living in tents, which they would have to carry with them, the
fodder that would be needed for all the cattle—and then read *Ex.* xii., xiv.
etc. Is it not obvious that the narrators had never once thought of all this
and regarded it as the simplest matter in the world to accomplish things
which, in point of fact, are absolutely impossible within the limits of
space and time which they themselves assign? Take, as specific instances,
the passage of the Red Sea in a single night (*Ex.* xiv. 20, 24, 27); the passage
of the Jordan, which, according to *Josh.* iii., iv., did not occupy more than
one day; the march of all the fighting men round Jericho, again accomplished
in a single day, nay, repeated as many as seven times on the seventh day
(*Josh.* vi.); finally, the march of all Israel—'both the stranger and the
native,' 'the whole assembly, and the women and the children and the
stranger, who went up in their midst'—out of the camp, through the midst
of the still unconquered land, to the mountains of Ebal and Gerizim, the presence of them all in the space between these two mountains and the reading
of the Tora in their hearing (*Josh.* viii. 30–35). It is not too much to say
that the representation of all this given in the Hexateuch is absurd. The
miraculous feeding of the people with manna and quails (*Ex.* xvi.; *Num.*
xi.), and the water from the rock (*Ex.* xvii. 1–7; *Num.* xx. 1–13), do not
remove a single one of these difficulties.

[10] By the side of these round numbers—*Ex.* xii. 37; *Num.* xi. 21—stand
the apparently very accurate figures of *Num.* i. 46; xxvi. 51, which are
obtained by adding up the numbers of the fighting men of the several tribes,
and in close connection with these, again, we find the detailed order of march
Num. ii., the minute regulation of the duties of the Levites and their position
in the camp, *Num.* iii., iv., and the description of the march out of the desert
of Sinai, *Num.* x. 11–28. Statements that go into such detail appear at
the first glance to rest upon personal observation, or at least upon very lively
reminiscences and contemporary data; and a corresponding verdict has, accordingly, often been passed upon them. But if it is established (cf. n. 18), that
the whole representation must be unhistorical, then we are forced to find
some other explanation. The round numbers then appear to be the earlier
ones, and the figures that pretend to greater accuracy, strike us as being based

upon the others, and worked out in such detail in order to leave nothing indeterminate or uncertain in the picture set before the reader. *A posteriori,* this view is supported by a whole series of phenomena, such as the extraordinary relation between the results of the census in *Num.* i. and in *Num.* xxvi. respectively (cf. my *Godsdienst,* ii. 74 [*Rel. Isr.* ii. 165 sq.]); the number of the male first-borns in Israel as given in *Num.* iii. 40–51 (cf. C o l. op. cit., p. 84–90); the description of the war against Midian, *Num.* xxxi. [49] (ibid. p. 139–146) etc. All these details, if t a k e n a s h i s t o r y, are beset with insuperable difficulties.—Other proofs of the later origin of the more elaborate narratives will be given below, § 15, n. 22.

[20] It seems advisable to begin by examining these special narratives, and then to proceed (n. 21) to develope and justify the general conclusions. Amongst the most striking examples are the following :—

a. *Num.* xxxii. 33, 39–42 ; *Deut.* iii. 12–16 ; iv. 43 ; xxix. 7 [8] ; *Josh.* xii. 6, and other passages in *Joshua,* where the settlement of half Manasseh as well as of Reuben and Gad appears as a disposition made by Moses. The case of Yaïr ben Manasseh comes expressly within this arrangement. Certain nomad villages in Gilead were called *Havvôth Yaïr* after him, and Moses himself declares (*Deut.* iii. 14) that the name has survived ' until this day ' (!). But in *Num.* xxxii. 1–32 a story is preserved in which Moses extends permission to remain beyond the Jordan to Reuben and Gad only, and in *v.* 33, 39–42 we detect the clearest proofs that half Manasseh was only added afterwards. Moreover, it appears from *Jud.* x. 3–5 that the eponymous Yaïr of the Havvôth belonged to the period of the Judges. Hence we conclude that the settlement of half Manasseh b y M o s e s is unhistorical, and that the story sprang from the tendency to ascribe to Moses everything that took place before the passage of the Jordan ; and this would include the dispositions made as to the settlement of the Transjordanic tribes. This is confirmed *a posteriori* by the fact that the writers of *Deut.* iii. 14 ; *Josh.* xiii. 30 make mistakes about the Havvôth Yaïr, placing them in Bashan instead of in Gilead, and confounding them with the sixty fortresses in the former region (in conflict with 1 *Kings* iv. 13 ; *Judges* x. 3, 4 ; 1 *Chron.* ii. 21–23). Cf. *Th. Tijdschr.,* xi. 478–482.

b. Hebron and Debîr are conquered by Caleb, the Kenizzite, and Othniel, his younger brother (*Josh.* xiv. 6–15 ; xv. 13–19). Since Caleb and his descendants were afterwards adopted into Judah there is no positive discrepancy in ascribing to that tribe the conquest, at any rate, of Hebron, *Jud.* i. 10. But elsewhere, in accordance with the theory that J o s h u a conquered the whole of Canaan, the capture of both cities is ascribed to him, *Josh.* x. 36 sq. (Hebron ; all the inhabitants destroyed) ; 38 sq. (Debîr ; treated in like manner) ; xi. 21, 22 (a l l the Anakim of Hebron, Debîr, Anab, and the whole mountain of Judah rooted out) cf. xii. 10, 13 (the kings of Hebron and Debîr enumerated amongst those whom Joshua slew).

c. According to *Jud.* i. 17 the tribe of Judah conquered Çephath after Joshua's death, and called the place Horma. But in *Josh.* xii. 14 the king of Horma is one of the princes overthrown by Joshua, and in *Num.* xxi. 1–3 the Israelites, under Moses, avenge themselves for the defeat inflicted upon them by the king of Arad, slay the Canaanites and call 'the place' Horma. The same name appears again in *Num.* xiv. 45 ; *Deut.* i. 44. Judah's exploit might be attributed in the later accounts either to Joshua or to Moses, since Horma was a frontier place, and might be considered as belonging to Canaan or to the desert indifferently.

   d. *Jud.* iv., v., distinctly show that the account of the conquest and devas-
[50] tation of Hazor in *Josh.* xi. 1, 10, 11, 13 is antedated. If Hazor had really been burned and all its inhabitants slaughtered by Joshua, how could it have become so powerful within the period of the Judges as to subdue the northern tribes and hold them in subjection for twenty years (*Jud.* iv. 2)?

   e. I have shown in *Nieuw en Oud*, 1868, p. 1–19, that the actual condition of the Gibeonites in Solomon's time (1 *Kings* ix. 20 sq.) is antedated and explained by an ordinance of Joshua's, in *Josh.* ix. On *v.* 21, 23, see above n. 13.

   [21] It is impossible to mistake the connection between the piling up of exploits on the era and the persons of Moses and Joshua, some examples of which have been given in n. 20, and the thoroughly unhistorical character of the general representations examined in n. 18, 19. Their common root is the antedating of the I s r a e l i t e n a t i o n, which in reality only came into existence under the monarchy and as a consequence of the struggles of the period of the Judges, whereas the Hexateuch represents it as already existing, issuing from Egypt, traversing the desert and settling in the Transjordanic region under Moses, and subsequently, under Joshua's lead, conquering and dividing Canaan at a single rush. Cf. my *Godsdienst*, i. 136 sqq. [*Rel. Isr.* i. 132 sqq.]. It was quite natural to think of this Israelite nation as very numerous and compact, collected into a single camp, constantly moved from place to place in the desert, but after the passage of the Jordan permanently pitched, first at Gilgal (*Josh.* iv. 19 sq. ; ix. 6 ; x. 6, 7, 9, 15, 43 ; xiv. 6), then at Shilo (*Josh.* xviii. 1, 9). Very judicious remarks on the historical reality that may lie at the basis of this will be found in K. H. G r a f, *Der Stamm Simeon* (1866), p. 9 sqq.; but the representations of the Hexateuch, as they stand, can only be regarded as the products of ages long after Moses and Joshua, when the true course of events was almost forgotten, and genuine historical reminiscences could only be preserved by having a place assigned them in a fictitious frame-work. Our further researches will make this still more plain. The main point, however, is already placed beyond the reach of question, and we are no longer in doubt as to the right point of view from which to regard the Hexateuch as a history.

The conclusion of this inquiry is identical with that of our provisional criticism of the legislation (§ 3). Although, as shown in § 1, it is impossible to deny a certain unity to the Hexateuch, yet we have seen (1) that elements of various origin may be distinguished in it ; (2) that most of them are

remote from the age of Moses and Joshua, and therefore, (3) that
the composition as a whole must be severed from the times to
which it refers by many centuries. The resolution of
the Hexateuch into its component parts, then, presents
the problem to the solution of which our efforts must now
be directed.

§ 5. *Points of departure in the resolution of the Hexateuch* [51]
*into its component parts: the collections of laws and the
designations of the Deity.*

In the critical analysis to which, having established its
right of existence, we must now proceed, everything depends
upon our securing fixed points of departure; and in
the light of the history of critical research, which has
now been zealously pursued for more than a century, we
cannot long remain in doubt where to look for them. The
mass of legislative matter spontaneously splits itself into
three groups or collections, while the characteristic employment of the divine names in *Genesis* and the opening chapters
of *Exodus* indicates the lines on which the narratives must be
united and severed respectively.

I. The division of the laws into three groups is raised
above all possibility of doubt by its distinct recognition in
the Tora itself, which compelled us to take some account of
it even in our initial survey in § 1. To begin with the
most obvious facts, then, we distinguish the following
groups :—

A. The laws in *Ex.* xx. 23–xxiii. 33. Their succession is
not always natural and regular. Some of the ordinances
break the context and suggest the idea that they may be
later insertions[1]. But on the whole the laws are a coherent
whole and form a code complete within the limits the author
seems to have imposed on himself[2] and closed by a hortatory

E

discourse in xxiii. 20–33. Accordingly we find the name סֵפֶר הַבְּרִית, the Book of the Covenant, applied to these laws in the narrative that immediately follows them (*Ex.* xxiv. 7)[3]. An introductory verse (xx. 22) brings them into direct connection with the words that Yahwè had spoken to Israel from heaven, i. e. the Decalogue (xx. 1–17); but there is no subsequent trace of this, and we may well doubt whether the connection was not established at a later date[4]. In one passage (xxiii. 15) reference is made to a previous command of Yahwè; probably the one contained in *Ex.* xiii. 3–10. But whether this reference is original, i.e. due to the author of the laws himself, may be [52] reasonably doubted[5]. We find no announcement in this collection of any laws to be drawn up subsequently.

[1] Ch. xx. 23–26 is related to xxii. 17 sqq. [18 sqq.] and to xxiii. 14 sqq., and would be more in place side by side with them than just before the ordinances relating to civil life in xxi. 1–xxii. 16 [18]. Ch. xxi. 16 disturbs the connection between *v.* 15 and 17, both of which deal with the relations of children to parents. Ch. xxiii. 4, 5 separates *v.* 1–3 and *v.* 6–8, which refer to the duties of judges and witnesses. Ch. xxiii. 9 is a mere repetition of xxii. 20 [21]. Ch. xxiii. 13 is thrust in amongst regulations concerning the holy seasons, *v.* 10–12 (sabbatical year and sabbath), and *v.* 14 sqq. (the three high festivals); the verse, moreover, contains a general exhortation which is premature. Finally, xxiii. 14–19 certainly seems to have been retouched, for *v.* 16 is but half grammatical after *v.* 15; *v.* 17 we should expect immediately after *v.* 14; and *v.* 19ᵃ repeats xxii. 28ᵃ [29ᵃ] in another form. Cf. Wellh. (xxi. : 559 sq.), who also raises doubts against certain other verses, e.g. xx. 23 ; xxii. 20ᵇ, 21 ; 24ᵇ; 30 [21ᵇ, 22; 25ᵇ; 31] ; xxiii. 9ᵇ, where the plural takes the place of the singular used elsewhere.

[2] What 'limits' I mean is obvious. The cultus is not regulated in detail ; the rights and duties of the priests are not determined at all. But in xxii. 28–30 [29–31] ; xxiii. 14 sqq. the lawgiver says all that he thinks necessary about the worship of Yahwè; and he might well refrain—as the author of *Deut.* xii. sqq. does, for example—from regulating matters which fell within the province of the priesthood. To call his code incomplete would be to judge it by an arbitrary standard.

[3] The unanimity with which xxiv. 3–8 is brought into immediate connection with xx. 23–xxiii., is only broken, as far as I know, by Colenso, who assumes (*Wellhausen on the Composition,* p. 27 sqq.), that xxiv. 3–8 is inserted into an older narrative, in which xx. 23–xxiii. (with the exception

of certain interpolated passages), and xxiv. 1, 2, 9–11 followed each other without a break. He therefore regards 'the Book of the Covenant' as a name of later origin than the code itself. He admits, however, that xxiv. 3–8 is intended by its author to refer to xx. 23–xxiii., which indeed is obvious. The distinction between 'words of Yahwè' and 'mishphatîm' (*v.* 3) accords with xxi. 1, but it is not apparent where these 'mishphatîm' end,—perhaps with xxii. 16 [17], up to and including which the ordinances generally take the conditional form (וְכִי), while the ethico-religious precepts and admonitions begin with *v.* 17 [18] (cf. n. 1).

⁴ We cannot fail to observe that in xxiv. 3–8, where the covenant between Yahwè and Israel is made, there is not the slightest mention of the Decalogue. It certainly was not included in the book written by Moses, and it was that book (*v.* 4, 7, 8) that formed the basis of the covenant. This can only be explained on the supposition that the Book of the Covenant itself and xxiv. 3–8 were not o r i g i n a l l y connected with the Decalogue, whence it would also follow that xx. 22ᵇ is a later addition serving to connect them; for it [53] is now generally admitted,—even by Colenso (*Pentateuch*, vii., Appendix, Synoptical Table, p. iii.), who formerly denied it (*Pentateuch*, vi. 149 sq.),—that the words 'ye have seen that I have spoken to you out of heaven,' refer to the proclamation of the Decalogue.

⁵ It occurs in the passage (xxiii. 14 sqq.), which, as already seen (n. 1), has been retouched, and moreover, in a verse that, in its present form, does not fit on to the one that precedes it. The analogy of xx. 22ᵇ (n. 4) strengthens the probability that the reference was inserted when the Book of the Covenant was incorporated into the account of the Sinaitic legislation.

B. The laws in *Deuteronomy.* It is impossible to doubt their independence of the laws in the other books. They stand in a setting of their own, and expressly assert themselves as a separate code (cf. § 1 and § 2, n. 4–7). The only questions are, (1) where the collection begins and ends, and (2) whether it has come down to us in its original form, or with later additions. If we follow the indications of the book itself we must begin by detaching *Deut.* i. 1–iv. 40; iv. 41–43 and xxvii. sqq. from the code of laws, and so reducing the latter to iv. 44–xxvi. (cf. § 1 and § 2, n. 4–7). Ch. v.–xi. may be regarded as an introduction,—whether from the hand of the law-giver himself or some other it would be premature to decide⁶. The collection of laws in the narrower sense, *Deut.* xii.–xxvi., strikes us as a single whole. The order of succession is not always what we might have expected, but

the supposition that the confusion is caused by later interpolations only seems to be admissible in a few exceptional
instances[7], and in any case the general character of this
second section remains unaffected by any such additions; it
is consistent throughout, and distinguishes these laws very
clearly from those of the Book of the Covenant on the one
hand and those which we have yet to consider on the other[8].

[6] *Deut.* v–xi. and xii–xxvi. are usually assigned to a single author. The
divergent opinion of W e l l h a u s e n (xxii. : 462 sq.) en J. J. P. V a l e t o n
(in his treatise : *Deuteronomium,* which appeared in Studien, Theologisch
Tijdschrift, vol. v. 169–206, 291–313 ; vi. 133–174, 303–321 ; vii. 39–56,
205–227) will be considered in § 7.

[7] Here and there the breach of continuity is obvious. Ch. xvi. 21, 22 ; xvii. 1
(against idolatrous practices and on the choice of sacrificial animals) have no
connection whatever with xvi. 18–20 (appointment of local judges) ; whereas
[54] xvii. 2–7 does stand in a kind of connection with it, and *v.* 8–13 directly continues it. The doubt, therefore, forces itself upon us whether xvi. 21–xvii. 1 (or
xvi. 21–xvii. 7) may not be misplaced. The succession of precepts in xxi.–xxv.
again, is sometimes suspicious ; but we shall see in § 7 that it can generally
be explained.

[8] On this point, also, see § 7. I may remark by anticipation that xvii. 2–7,
for instance, though somewhat strangely placed (n. 7), perfectly harmonises both
in language and spirit with other deuteronomic laws, such as xiii. 2–6, 7–12,
13–19 [1–5, 6–11, 12–18].

If we survey the laws that remain after removing the
Book of the Covenant and *Deut.* xii.–xxvi., we discover but
few of them (*Ex.* xii. 21–27 ; xiii. 1 sq., 3–10, 11–16 ; xxxiv.
10–27) which show any perceptible affinity with these two
collections[9]. This fact furnishes our first reason for constituting a third group—

C. comprising all the remaining laws of *Exodus–Numbers*[10].
The essential homogeneity of this group is confirmed on every
side. It is true that the laws in question do not form a closed
and ordered whole; indeed their arrangement leaves very much
to be desired; some of the ordinances or groups might be
removed without leaving any perceptible void; some of them
have every appearance of being n o v e l l a e ; and in some cases

they contradict each other[11]. But, in spite of all this, they form a single group which may best be characterised as the priestly legislation. By far the greater part of these laws concerns the cultus, the sanctuary and its servants, the sacrifices and festivals, ceremonial cleanness and purification, and vows; and even where other subjects are dealt with they are treated with reference to these great themes, or the rights and interests of the priests and Levites, or at any rate in the priestly spirit[12]. Add to this that cross references from one law to another are very frequent throughout the group and throw the mutual connection of the ordinances into clear relief[13]. We cannot hesitate, then, to mark them off from the Book of the Covenant and the deuteronomic code, but this conclusion must not prejudice our further investigation of certain phenomena that plead against the absolute unity and community of origin of the whole of this stratum of legislation. Neither must the recognition of the priestly [55] laws as a single group blind us to the close connection in which many of them stand with certain narratives[14]; on the contrary, we must note this attachment of the legislation to the history,—or, to put it in another way, this gradual transition from history to legislation—as one of the notes of the priestly passages that may throw light on their character.

[9] On these passages cf. Dillmann's commentary; Wellhausen (xxi. 543 sqq., 553 sqq.); Colenso, *Pentateuch*, vi. 142 sq.; and Appendix, p. 89 sqq.; and also § 9, n. 4.

[10] Group *C.* will therefore consist of *Ex.* xii. 1–20, 43–50; xxv.–xxxi. 17; xxxv.–xl.; all *Leviticus*; and all the laws in *Numbers*, viz. ii.–iv., v., vi., viii. 1–x. 10, xv., xviii., xix., xxvii. 1–14, xxviii.–xxx., xxxiv.–xxxvi., with the addition of certain passages half historical and half legislative in character, amongst which, indeed, we might have placed *Ex.* xxxv.–xl. Cf. below, n. 14.

[11] Our review of the contents of the Tora (§ 1) has furnished repeated confirmation of this fact. Unlike the Book of the Covenant and *Deuteronomy*, the laws of the third group have no exordium. *Lev.* xxvi. has all the appearance of a closing discourse, but is nevertheless followed by a whole series of laws, at the head of which *Lev.* xxvii. is very strangely placed, though not more so than *Lev.* xxiv. (v. 1–9 on the preparation of oil for the sacred lamp

and of the shew-bread; *v.* 10-23 on the punishment of the blasphemer and on punishments in general), between xxiii. (festivals) and xxv. (sabbatical year and year of jubilee). Note also the position of *Num.* v. 5-10 (trespass offering), *v.* 11-37 (offering of jealousy); viii. 1-4 (on lighting the golden lamp), etc., etc. Amongst the laws that might drop out without affecting the general structure may be mentioned *Lev.* xviii.-xx., and many detached ordinances in *Numbers*, which may likewise serve as examples of n o v e l l a e : *Num.* v. 5-10 (cf. *Lev.* v. 14-26 [v. 14-vi. 7]) ; xv. 22-31 (cf. *Lev.* iv. 13-21, 27-31) ; xxviii. sq. (cf. *Lev.* xxiii.) ; xxx. (cf. *Lev.* xxvii.).—We have already noted (§ 3, n. 20, 17) the contradictions between *Num.* viii. 24 and *Num.* iv. ; and between *Num.* xviii. 21-32) tithes of the fruits of the earth and of trees only) and *Lev.* xxvii. 32 sq. (tithes of cattle as well). Cf. also *Lev.* xix. 5-8 (thank-offerings must be consumed on the day on which they are offered, or the day following) and *Lev.* vii. 15-18 ; xxii. 29, 30 (praise-offerings—a *species* of the *genus* thank-offering—must always be eaten on the day itself), together with many other laws which will be reserved for consideration in § 6, inasmuch as their discrepancies do not lie so near the surface.

[12] In the great majority of cases the priestly character of the laws strikes us at once, e.g. in *Ex.* xxv.-xxxi. 17; *Lev.* i.-vii.; xvi.; xxi. sq.; xxiii., etc., etc. Nor is there any real doubt about it in the other cases. *Lev.* xi.-xv. treats of cleanness and cleansing, and perpetually refers the Israelite to the priest as the only person competent to distinguish between clean and unclean, and to cleanse, in the name of Yahwè, whatsoever has been polluted (cf. *Deut.* xxiv. 8; *Ez.* xliv. 23 ; *Hag.* ii. 11 sqq.). *Lev.* xviii.-xx. includes some purely ethical commandments, but the leading thought is the purity of the people consecrated to Yahwè, the Holy One ; and this fully accounts for the prominence given to the regulations of the sexual life. In all the priestly laws the day of rest is dwelt on with great emphasis (*Ex.* xxxi. 13-17 ; xxxv. 1-3 ; *Num.* xv. 32-36), and closely connected with this high reverence for the sabbath are the laws with respect to the sabbatical year and the year of jubilee (*Lev.* xxv.); the ideas as to the tenure of land, which are there enforced, reappear in *Num.* xxvii. 1-11 and xxxvi. ; devotion to the interest of the priests and Levites shines distinctly through *Lev.* xxv. 32-34. The treatment of vows in *Lev.* xxvii. ; *Num.* xxx. and vi. 1-21 is likewise thoroughly priestly. In fact there are really no exceptions to the rule laid down. Even *Num.* xv. 37-41, though at first sight we might think it would scarcely be out of place in *Deuteronomy* (cf. *Deut.* vi. 8, 9 ; xi. 18-20 ; xxii. 12 ; and further, *Ex.* xiii. 9, 16), has its own peculiarities which connect it with the preceding priestly laws. Observe the language of *v.* 38, and compare *v.* 40, 41 with *Lev.* xviii.-xx.

[13] Cf. § 1, especially n. 12, 14. The list of examples there given is not exhaustive. The fact that the Levites appear, for the first time, in the book of *Numbers* has sometimes been regarded as showing discrepancy between that book and the two that precede it ; but in reality it is an example of the consistency of *Exodus–Numbers* : the subordinate servants of the sanctuary and of the priesthood are not mentioned till the ô h e l m o' é d has been built, the priests consecrated, and the sacrifices and other elements of the cultus

[56]

regulated—and moreover, *Ex.* xxxviii. 21 and *Lev.* xxv. 32–34, which are exceptions to the rule, prove that the Levites are not unknown to *Exodus-Leviticus*, but are intentionally passed over in silence. Further, compare *Lev.* xxvii. 17 sq., 21, 23 sq. ; *Num.* xxxvi. 4 with *Lev.* xxv. ;—*Ex.* xxix. 38–42 with *Num.* xxviii. 3–8 ; *Lev.* vi. 1–6, etc. The minuter study of the priestly laws (§ 6 and 15), though revealing discrepancies, will at the same time establish far more numerous points of union.

[11] Cf. § 4, n. 1, 2. The connection between the historical and legislative passages is often so close that the line cannot be drawn between them, and many sections might be termed historical or legislative with equal propriety, e.g. *Lev.* x. ; *Num.* vii. (which is manifestly an example for imitation, if not a precept) ; ix. 1–14 ; xxxi.

We have seen that the division of the whole mass of laws into these three groups must ultimately influence our view of the narratives of the Hexateuch. This would come out still more clearly were we to start from this division of the laws, and, endeavouring to sift the historical pieces, were to affiliate to each group of laws the narratives that seemed akin to it. But before doing so we must review these narratives on their own merits, and, if possible, discover fixed points of departure for our critical analysis in them also.

II. Ever since the year 1753 A.D., in which Astruc gave [57] the world his *Conjectures* [15], the use of the divine names, and especially of Elohîm and Yahwè, in *Genesis* and the opening chapters of *Exodus*, has been the subject of diligent research and lively debate, which have not been barren of definite results. It is therefore unnecessary to arrive at and establish these results afresh, as though the question were a completely new one ; for we are at liberty to assume them as already made out, though not without indicating the grounds on which they rest and the way in which they were first obtained.

(1) The names Elohîm and Yahwè are by no means simple synonyms. Yahwè—probably derived from הוה=היה, but of doubtful signification [16]—is the proper name of Israel's god. Elohîm—derived from an obsolete stem אלה, to fear—was originally a true plural, signifying the objects

of men's fear, the higher beings; but it is generally used as a singular, in the sense of the higher power. It always retains its force as a *nomen appellativum* [17], and is accordingly applied to other gods as well as to Yahwè. In the books of the Old Testament, however, Elohîm, with or without the article, is very often applied to the only being whose full claim to the title the writers allowed, i.e. to Yahwè. To this extent it assumes the character of a *nomen proprium* [18].

(2) The original distinction between Yahwè and Elohîm very often accounts for the use of one of these appellations in preference to the other [19]. But this is not always the case. In *Genesis* and the opening chapters of *Exodus*, and elsewhere in the Old Testament, we find a number of passages in which the use of Elohîm or ha-Elohîm can be explained neither by the meaning of this word, as distinguished from Yahwè, nor by the love of variety [20]; so that we can only attribute it to subjective causes, i.e. we must suppose that the writers, for some reason or other, preferred the designation Elohîm or ha-Elohîm.

(3) Although elsewhere we can but guess at the motives concerned, the authors themselves explain them in the case [58] of *Genesis* and *Ex.* i.–vi. In *Ex.* vi. 2, 3 Elohîm declares that he had revealed himself to the patriarchs as El-Shaddai, and he reveals his name of Yahwè,—unquestionably for the first time, according to the writer,—to Moses [21]. Something similar is likewise to be found in *Ex.* iii. 13–15, in a narrative which cannot be due to the same author as *Ex.* vi. 2, 3 [22]. The writers who cherished this belief concerning the name Yahwè could not represent either God himself, in the præ-Mosaic times, or the people who were then living, as using this name; and in all probability they would themselves avoid it in the narratives that referred to this earlier period [23]. After the revelation to Moses there was no longer

any reason for their adhering to the name Elohîm, and we shall therefore no longer expect to find the narratives of these authors (supposing them to be preserved in the Hexateuch), characterised by this peculiarity. And, as a fact, the name Elohîm becomes much less frequent after *Ex.* vi. 2, 3, thereby showing that we were not deceived as to the influence which a belief in the Mosaic origin of the name Yahwè must exercise upon the usage of the authors[24].

(4) It is obvious at a glance that the exclusive use of Elohîm in the Book of *Genesis* is confined to certain portions, and that the name Yahwè is supposed to be known and is freely employed in others[25]. *Gen.* iv. 26[b] makes it very probable that this is connected with a different idea as to the antiquity of the name of Yahwè[26]; but, in any case, it furnishes a conclusive proof that *Genesis* is made up of narratives of various origin, for the writers whose opinions we learn from *Ex.* vi. 2, 3; iii. 13–15, may have composed the Elohîm-narratives or sections, but cannot have composed those in which Yahwè occurs.

(5) Although the two parallel accounts, in *Ex.* vi. 2, 3 and iii. 13–15, ought at once to have suggested the idea that more than one writer in *Genesis* studiously avoided the use of the name Yahwè, yet all the Elohîm-passages were at first ascribed to a single author. Further investigation showed that this position was untenable[27]. Some of the Elohîm-passages, evidently connected with *Ex.* vi. 2, 3, stand off very clearly and sharply from the Yahwè-sections with [59] which they are now united in *Genesis*; whereas others, which might be brought into connection with *Ex.* iii. 13–15, are closely allied to these same Yahwè-sections,—far more closely than to the former group of Elohîm-passages[28]. There is really nothing to surprise us in this. Authors who agreed in assigning a Mosaic origin to the name ' Yahwè,' and who therefore avoided its use in dealing with early times, may well

have differed in many other respects,—in date and in general tendencies for instance. The one characteristic which is common to both may be a specially obvious one, yet it is but one of the many marks which must be duly observed in tracing the origin and the mutual relations of the passages[29].

(6) Antecedent probability pleads that the authors of the narratives we have so far considered would deal with the sequel of the history, and that their accounts may be preserved in the Hexateuch[30]. And this turns out to be the case. We have already seen that the mutual relation of the narratives in *Exodus, Numbers,* and *Joshua,* is, on the whole, similar to that in *Genesis.* In the former, as in the latter, parallel and at the same time conflicting representations either stand side by side or have been worked up into a single whole (§ 4, n. 11–13, 15). Moreover, we can now recognise, without difficulty, the continuations of the groups of narratives which the use of the divine names enables us to distinguish in *Genesis*[31]. But, of course, the complete demonstration of all this must depend upon the results of our further investigations.

[15] *Conjectures sur les Mémoires originaux dont il paroit que Moyse s'est servi pour composer le livre de la Genèse* (Bruxelles, 1753). The very title shows how little Astruc questioned the Mosaic authorship of *Genesis.* On the development and modification of his hypothesis by Eichhorn and others see Merx in Tuch's *Genesis,* 2nd ed., p. lxxviii. sqq. ; de Wette-Schrader, *Einleitung in das A. T.,* p. 309–311 ; Bleek-Wellhausen, *Einleitung,* p. 56 sqq., and others.

[16] Cf. my *Godsdienst,* i. 397-401 [*Rel. Isr.* i. 398-403], Schrader, Article *Jahve* in Schenkel's *Bibel-Lexikon,* iii. 167-171, and my *Volksgodsdienst en Wereldgodsdienst,* p. 261-263 [*National Religions and Universal Religions* (Hibbert Lectures for 1882), p. 308–311].

[17] Cf. also Fleischer apud Delitzsch, *Die Genesis,* p. 25 sq., and in Levy's *Neuhebr. u. Chald. Wörterbuch,* ii. 445 *b.*

[60]   [18] The following examples from the book of *Judges* may be noted : iv. 23 ; vi. 36, 39, 40 ; viii. 3 ; ix. 7, 23, 56, 57 ; xv. 19 ; xviii. 10 ; xx. 27.

[19] When the god of Israel is placed over-against the gods of the heathen, the former is naturally described by the proper name, Yahwè (1 *Kings* xviii. 21, 36, 37 ; *Judges* xi. 24 ; *Ex.* xii. 12 ; xv. 11 ; xviii. 11). When heathens

are introduced as speaking, they use the word Elohîm (*Gen.* xli. 39 ; *Judges* i. 7, etc.), but this rule is often violated by an oversight, and the heathens are made to speak of Yahwè (*Gen.* xxvi. 28. 29 ; 1 *Sam.* xxix. 6 ; 1 *Kings* v. 21 [7] ; x. 9). So too the Israelites, when speaking to heathens, often use Elohîm, as Joseph does, for instance, to Potiphar's wife, *Gen.* xxxix. 9 ; to the butler and baker, *Gen.* xl. 8 ; and to Pharaoh, *Gen.* xli. 16, 25, 28, 32 (but also in *v.* 51, 52, where he is not addressing heathens, which makes us suspect that there may be some other reason for the preference of Elohîm) ; so too Abraham to Abimelech, *Gen.* xx. 13 (where Elohîm even takes the plural construction). —Where a contrast between the divine and the human is in the mind of the author, Elohîm is at any rate the more suitable word, e.g. *Judges* ix. 9, 13 ; *Gen.* iv. 25 ; xxxii, 28 ; *Ex.* viii. 15 ; xxxii. 16, etc.

[20] In a number of the Psalms, especially *Ps.* xlii. lxxxiv., Elohîm is prevailingly, but not exclusively, employed, and that too in phrases or connections in which Yahwè is exclusively used elsewhere, and also in cases where passages in all other respects parallel read Yahwè (e.g. *Ps.* liii. 3, 5–7 [2, 4–6] ; cf. xiv. 2, 4, 6, 7 ; *Ps.* lxviii. 8, 9 [7, 8] ; cf. *Judges* v. 4, 6). It is impossible to apply any of the principles of n. 19 to these cases, or to explain the use of Elohîm in *Gen.* i.–*Ex.* vi. by the signification of the word, as Hengstenberg, *Authentie*, i. 181–414 [i. 213–393] ; Keil, *über die Gottesnamen im Pentateuch* (Zeitschr. f. luth. Theol. u. Kirche, 1851, p. 215–280), and others try to do. These (mutually conflicting) attempts to find some grounds in the nature of the case for the use of Elohîm to the exclusion of Yahwè, or by its side, have simply failed, and need not be dealt with any more (cf. *Hist. krit. Ond.*, 1st ed., p. 64 sq., and in answer to Graetz, *Gesch. der Juden* ii. 1, p. 452 sqq., *Th. Tijdschrift*, x. 553 sqq.). Love of variety could only be pleaded if Elohîm and Yahwè generally occurred side by side, as in *Gen.* vii. 16 ; xxvii. 27, 28. But since, as a matter of fact, Elohîm occurs thirty-five times, for example, in *Gen.* i. 1–ii. 4ᵃ, and Yahwè nineteen times in *Gen.* xxiv., in either case to the complete exclusion of the other name, it is obvious that the motive in question did not come into play.

[21] The words of Elohîm (*v* 2ᵃ) run : 'I am Yahwè, and I appeared to Abraham, Isaac, and Jacob as (ב) El-Shaddai, but as to (or, by) my name Yahwè I was not known to them' (or, 'I did not make myself known to them') *v.* 2ᵇ, 3. Hengstenberg (*Authentie*, i. 262 sqq. [i. 274 sqq.]) and others attempt in vain to explain away the contrast between the patriarchal and Mosaic periods, so as to leave room for the acquaintance of the patriarchs with the name Yahwè. Cf. the Commentators, and Hupfeld, *Die Quellen der Genesis*, p. 87 sq.

[22] In the beginning of the narrative, as it now stands, the name Yahwè is repeatedly employed (*Ex.* iii. 2, 4, 7). But in *v.* 11 and 13 Moses addresses ha-Elohîm, and is answered by him in *v.* 12, 14, 15 (Elohîm, without the article, in *v.* 14, 15). So when Moses asks what he is to reply if the Israelites ask the name of Him who sent him, and therefore hears the name אהיה [61] (*v.* 14), for which יהוה is immediately substituted (*v.* 15), we can but suppose that this name had never been revealed previously, and was now for the first

time communicated to Moses, and by him to the people. *Ex.* iii. and vi. are therefore parallels, and are not from the same hand ; and accordingly they differ in detail though agreeing in their main idea. For example, the author of *Ex.* iii. does not mention El-Shaddai as the name of Elohîm in the patriarchal age.

[23] Passages such as *Gen.* xv. 7, in which God names himself Yahwè, or v. 29 ; xvi. 2, 5, 11, etc., in which others call him by this name, cannot possibly be assigned to the author of *Ex.* iii. 13–15 or of vi. 2, 3. But it is conceivable that when the writers are speaking of God in their own persons they may use the name of Yahwè, for, in any case, they were familiar with it themselves. Whether they actually did so or not cannot be determined *a priori* ; but, as a matter of fact, the texts themselves show that they use Elohîm throughout; and the rule is so precise that in the few passages in their narratives where Yahwè now stands we need not hesitate to ascribe it to the later manipulation or corruption of the text.

[24] The passages in which Elohîm occurs, as a *nomen proprium*, subsequently to the revelation of the name Yahwè, are the following : *Ex.* xiii. 17 (bis), 18, 19 ; xiv. 19 ; xviii. 1, 12, 15, 19 (bis) ; xx. 1, 19–21 ; xxiv. 11 ; *Num.* xxi. 5 ; xxii. 9, 10, 12, 20, 22, 38 ; xxiii. 4, 27 ; *Deut.* iv. 32 ; xxv. 18 ; *Josh.* xxii. 33 ; xxiv. 1, 26 ; exclusive of compound phrases such as ' spirit of Elohîm,' ' writing of Elohîm,' ' man of Elohîm,' ' finger of Elohîm,' which hardly come under the same category. Against these instances (about thirty in all) in the hundred and fifty-five chapters from *Ex.* vii. to *Josh.* xxiv. stand about one hundred and twenty such in the first fifty-six chapters of the Hexateuch.

[25] Delitzsch (op. cit., p. 56 sq.) divides *Gen.* i.–*Ex.* vi., in accordance with the use of the divine names, into *elohimische Abschnitte, jehovische Abschnitte, gemischte Abschnitte,* and *Abschnitte latenten Charaders* (in which no designations of God appear). To the second group he assigns, for instance, *Gen.* xii., xiii., xv., xvi., xviii., xix., xxiv., in which, as may be seen at a glance, Yahwè is extremely frequent.

[26] ' *At that time* (time of Enos) *they began* (לקרא בשם יהוה) *to call with the name,* or *by the name* (cf. Ges., § 138, anm. 3*) *of Jahve* = to address him in prayer (cf. Zeph. iii. 9 ; Jer. x. 25) and proclaim him (compare *Ex.* xxxiii. 19 ; xxxiv. 5 with xxxv. 30). . . . This passage [*Gen.* iv. 26ᵇ] is the first link in the chain, xii. 8 ; xiii. 4 ; xxi. 33 ; xxvi. 25. With Enos opened the formal and solemn worship of Jahve (or rather of God, as Jahve) with prayer and preaching and sacrifice ' (Delitzsch, op. cit., p. 179).

[27] As long ago as 1798 K. D. Ilgen (*Die Urkunden des ersten Buches Moses in ihrer Urgestalt,* Halle) distinguished two Elohists whom he called Eliel ha-rishôn and hassheni. But his opinion found little or no favour, and the Elohîm-passages were generally attributed to a single author until H. Hupfeld (*Die Quellen der Genesis und die Art ihrer Zusammensetzung,* Berlin, 1853) secured acceptance for the correct view.

[28] The two series of Elohîm-passages will presently be indicated and compared alike with each other and with the Yahwè-sections (§ 8 and § 13). At

present we have only to show that the anticipations raised by *Ex.* vi. 2, 3 and [62]
iii. 13–15 are confirmed by the perusal of *Genesis.* Observe that *Ex.* vi. 2, 3
is at any rate inseparably connected with *v.* 4–7; that *Gen.* xvii. and xxxv. 9–15
agree in the most striking manner both with each other and with *Ex.* vi.
2–7 (note Elohîm, *Gen.* xvii. 3, 15, 18, 19, 22, 23; xxxv. 9–11, 15; *Ex.* vi. 2;
El-Shaddai, *Gen.* xvii. 1; xxxv. 11; *Ex.* vi. 3; ארץ מגורים, *Gen.* xvii. 8; *Ex.*
vi. 4; הקים ברית, *Gen.* xvii. 7, 19, 21; *Ex.* vi. 4; the promise, *Gen.* xvii. 7,
8; *Ex.* vi. 7; the prediction, *Gen.* xvii. 6, 16; xxxv. 11[b]; פרה and רבה, *Gen.*
xvii. 6, 20; xxxv. 11; the changes of name, *Gen.* xvii. 5, 15; xxxv. 10); that
whereas the very characteristic style of these three connected pericopes reappears in a number of the Elohîm-passages of *Genesis* (e. g. i. 1–ii. 4[a]; ix. 1–
17; xxiii.; xxviii. 1–7, etc.) it is conspicuously absent from other narratives
which are none the less marked by the use of Elohîm, such as *Gen.* xx. 1–17;
xxi. 6–32, and the Elohistic portions of *Gen.* xxix.–xxxv.; that these latter
narratives not only differ in tone and character from the former, but even contradict them (compare *Gen.* xxi. 6–21, where Ishmael appears as a child carried
by his mother, with *Gen.* xvii. 25, where he is thirteen years old before the birth
of Isaac; Elohistic portions of *Gen.* xxix.–xxxv., which represent Jacob's
journey to Mesopotamia as a flight from Esau, with *Gen.* xxviii. 1–7, where it
is referred to other causes, etc.); and finally, that the Elohistic narratives of
the second group not unfrequently appear to be doublets of corresponding
Yahwè-passages or *vice versâ*, as the case may be (compare *Gen.* xx. 1–17 with
xii. 10–20, *Gen.* xxi. 6–21 with xvi.; *Gen.* xxi. 22–34 with xxvi. 26–33). All
this must be developed more clearly and precisely hereafter, and so must our
provisional assumption of the connection of the Elohîm-passages of the second
group with *Ex.* iii. 13–15. But the necessity of constituting the two groups
themselves and of severing the first group from the Yahwè-pericopes far more
sharply than the second is already obvious enough.

[29] The remark might seem superfluous; but the history of critical investigation has shown that far too much weight has often been laid on agreement in the use of the divine names—so much so that it has twice led the
critics wrong (cf. n. 27). It is well therefore to utter a warning against laying
an exaggerated stress on this one phenomenon.

[30] *Ex.* vi. 2–7 points forward as unmistakably as backward. The author
has obviously recorded the appearances of Elohîm to Abraham, Isaac, and
Jacob, and mentioned the covenant he entered into with them (*v.* 3, 4),
and it is equally obvious that he intends to describe the deliverance from
Egypt and the union of Yahwè with Israel (*v.* 5–7). *Ex.* iii. 15–17 likewise belongs to a greater whole, in which both Elohîm's relations to the fathers
and the redemption from Egypt and settlement in Canaan were mentioned
(cf. *v.* 8, 17). Now of course it is possible that these sequels are not to be found
in the Hexateuch, but the opposite is far more likely. Indeed there is no
conceivable reason for supposing that the two Elohîm documents were sud-
denly dropped at *Ex.* iii. and vi. respectively.

[31] The remarks made in n. 28 with regard to the Elohîm-passages in *Genesis*
are equally applicable here. At present we have only to show that what

[63] suggested itself as probable beforehand turns out, on reading the sequel, to be true. This becomes evident on considering the following points :—

(1) In *Ex.* vi. 2–7, *v.* 7 agrees with *Ex.* xxix. 45 ; *Lev.* xi. 45 ; xxii. 33 ; xxv. 38 ; and *Gen.* xvii.—the connection of which with *Ex.* vi. 2–7 was demonstrated in n. 28—agrees with the laws in *Ex.* xxv. sqq., *Leviticus*, and *Numbers*. This agreement is so obvious that it need not be established by the citation of single verses. All the characteristic formulæ of *Gen.* xvii. (ברית עולם, אחזת עולם, לדורות ; 'that soul shall be destroyed from out its people ;' בעצם היום הזה, etc.) reappear in the laws in question and the historical passages connected with them.

(2) With respect to *Ex.* iii. 15–17, a reference to *Ex.* xviii. must suffice for the present. The two agree as to Jethro, the father-in-law of Moses, the priest of Midian (iii. 1 ; xviii. 1, 2, 5), in the use of הר האלהים (iii. 1 ; xviii. 5) ; of 'the god of my (thy) father' (iii. 6 ; xviii. 4), and a number of other peculiarities which will be noticed hereafter.

The close connection between the laws and the narratives of the Hexateuch (§ 4, n. 1, 2) naturally suggests the question whether the separation of the narratives on the lines suggested by the use of the divine names in any way coincides with, or is related to, the division of the laws into three groups or collections. This question must be answered in the affirmative, for the following reasons :—

(1) The Elohîm-passages of the first group (n. 28) attach themselves spontaneously, so to speak, to the priestly or ritual legislation (n. 31).

(2) An unmistakable affinity exists between the Yahwè-sections and the second group of Elohîm-passages on the one hand, and the Book of the Covenant on the other [32].

(3) And further, historical passages of kindred form and contents are connected, as we have seen already (§ 4, n. 2), with the deuteronomic legislation [33].

This justifies the conclusion that three groups of narratives answer to the three collections of laws ; and there is no reason why we should not provisionally combine them thus, and so proceed to the study of each united group of laws and narratives ; but, of course, this must not prejudice the question as to their common origin, which is one of the very points we have to decide.

[32] Observe that we do not speak of their ascription to a single author. If we can show such a relationship between any one of our collections of laws and a certain group of narratives, as to exclude the possibility of their having [64] come into existence independently one of the other, that is enough for our present purpose. Now it cannot be denied that *Ex.* xxi.–xxiii. is connected alike with xix., xxiv., and with xxxii.–xxxiv., and therefore also with the narratives that introduce the former or grow out of the latter. And these are—speaking generally—not the Elohim-passages of the first group, but the Yahwè-passages together with the closely-related second group of Elohim-passages. See also § 8 and § 13, which must not be further anticipated here.

[33] This relationship is indicated rather than proved in § 4, n. 2. It is, however, generally admitted; and indeed many authorities go so far as to assign *Deut.* i. 1–iv. 40, and a number of passages in *Joshua* (e. g. i.; viii. 30–35; xxiii.) to the author of *Deut.* xii.–xxvi. himself. See, further, § 7 and § 14.

It would be very desirable to arrive at some general agreement as to the designations of the groups of laws and narratives indicated above, with corresponding abbreviations. As yet the practice of critics is far from uniform; but Wellhausen has proposed a system which does not in any way prejudge the mutual relations and relative antiquities of the different groups, and so might be accepted on all sides. We shall therefore follow it, though modifying and supplementing it in certain points. In explaining this system we shall sometimes have to assume the results of our further investigation (§ 6 sqq.).

The final editing of the Hexateuch which gave it its present form may be called the redaction. The redactor or redactors we shall call R, or R¹, R², etc., if it should prove necessary to distinguish different periods or stages of their work.

The whole priestly portion, including the ritual laws and any narratives which may be shown to be connected with them, will be indicated by the letter P. If any necessity should arise for distinguishing different strata, varying in date but all mutually related, we may use the abbreviations, P¹, P², etc.

In the same way all the laws and narratives written by the deuteronomic lawgiver, or in his spirit and under his [65] influence, may be indicated by the letter D; and here again we may distinguish, if necessary, between D¹, D², etc.

The analogy of these two designations would suggest that the remaining laws and narratives should be indicated by the initial letter of the Book of the Covenant. There are, however, valid objections to this. It will be better to designate them by J and E, in accordance with the use of Yahwè (Jahwè)* and Elohîm in *Genesis* and the opening chapters of *Exodus*, only we must remember that the Elohîm-passages shown to belong to the priestly laws and narratives have already been included under P, so that E will only embrace those Elohîm-narratives, with their continuations in the succeeding books, which do not belong to P, but are more nearly related to the Yahwè-sections. The mutual relation of J and E is one of the most vexed questions of the criticism of the Hexateuch, and the use of the symbols themselves must of course be affected by its solution; but, meanwhile, there can be no objection to our indicating all that is left in the Hexateuch after the withdrawal of R, P, and D, by the combination JE [34].

[34] Cf. Wellhausen, xxi. 392. His suggestion is (1) supplemented by distinguishing the stages or periods of R and D by means of the figures 1, 2, etc.; and (2) modified, as follows, with respect to the priestly elements: Wellhausen calls the great historico-legislative work that begins with the cosmogony in *Gen.* i. 1–ii. 4ᵃ and includes, amongst other passages, *Gen.* xvii.; *Ex.* xxv. sqq., etc., 'das Vierbundesbuch' because of the four covenants mentioned in it (*Gen.* i. 28–30; ix. 1–17; xvii.; *Ex.* vi. 2 sqq.), and indicates it by Q, from the Latin *quatuor*. The ritual laws, however, are in some cases not derived

* The continental J being the phonetic equivalent of the English Y and the Hebrew י, it is usual in Germany and Holland to write Jahve or Jahwe as the transliteration of יהוה. J, having thus become the accepted symbol of the work of the Yahwist, is preserved in this translation for the sake of uniformity.—Tr.

from Q, or only form a part of it in a secondary sense, so that Wellhausen has to distinguish ' der Priestercodex' (PC), which embraces all the priestly passages, from the special work Q. Against this it may be urged that the meaning of 'Q' is not sufficiently obvious—is, in fact, somewhat far-fetched (*Gen.* i. 28–30 is not really a covenant, but a blessing)—and that the relationship between Q and 'der Priestercodex' in its entirety is not reflected in their respective symbols. Both objections are removed by the use of P and the distinction between P¹, P², etc. It will presently be seen that Wellhausen's Q is my P².

No elaborate comparison of the system I have adopted with those of other writers is needed. I will only mention that Colenso indicates the Elohîm-passages of the first group (included under my P) by E ; those of the second group by *E* ; the Yahwè-sections by J ; the deuteronomic elements by D ; and the priestly laws and narratives by LL ('Later Legislation').

§ 6. *The Priestly elements of the Hexateuch* (P).   [66]

The various elements of the Hexateuch are now united into a single whole. The way in which this result was brought about we must leave, for the present, out of consideration ; but we must recognise the possibility of the later authors who worked over the older material, and the editors who combined independent laws and narratives, having made occasional omissions or modifications ; and this will naturally prevent our being able to clear up certain points until later on in our inquiry. The separation of the priestly elements, however, is least encumbered by this difficulty, and we will therefore undertake it first.

It was provisionally shown in § 5 that a connection exists between the priestly laws in *Exodus–Numbers*, and the Elohîm-passages of the first group in *Gen.* i.–*Ex.* vi. We will begin our investigation with the study of these latter passages, and on the strength of the connection indicated, will include them, by anticipation, under the letter P.

We have no difficulty in discovering in certain Elohîm-passages in *Genesis* the now scattered segments of a systematic work that begins with the creation in six days, followed by a genealogy from Adam to Noah, describes the deluge and the covenant of Elohîm with Noah and his posterity, passes by another genealogy (from Shem to Terah) on to the tribal fathers of Israel, Abram, Isaac, and Jacob, and continues their history down to the death of Jacob in Egypt. All this has come down to us nearly, but not quite, complete. There are some few verses and passages as to which we cannot yet determine whether they do or do not belong to the work; for it is only the study of the other elements of the Hexateuch and of the method of its redaction that can settle the point. But, generally speaking, the now scattered portions so obviously belong to each other and resemble each other so closely in language, style, and character, that there is no room for the smallest doubt as to [67] their common origin, so that, in point of fact, almost complete agreement reigns on the subject. This work, then, includes *Gen.* i.–ii. 4ᵃ; v. 1–28, 30–32; vi. 9–22; a number of verses and half verses in vii. and viii.; ix. 1–17, 28, 29; x. 1–7, 13–32 (in part); xi. 10–27, 31, 32; xii. 4ᵇ, 5; xiii. 6, 11ᵇ, 12ᵃ; xvi. 1, 3, 15, 16; xvii. (except יהוה in *v.* 1, which has taken the place of אלהים); xix. 29; xxi. 2ᵇ–5; xxiii.; xxv. 7–20 (except for slight additions), 26ᵇ; xxvi. 34, 35; xxvii. 46; xxviii. 1–9; xxxi. 18; xxxv. 9–15, 22ᵇ–29; xxxvi. 6–8, 40–43, and perhaps a few more verses; xxxvii. 1, 2ᵃ; xlvi. 6, 7; xlvii. 5, 6ᵃ (LXX.), 7–11, 27, 28; xlviii. 3–6; xlix. 29–33; l. 12, 13. In as far as this enumeration coincides with those of Nöldeke, Schrader, Colenso, Kayser, Dillmann, and Wellhausen, or at any rate the majority of them, its correctness need not be defended afresh. I shall only render the briefest possible account of those details as to which differences of opinion of more or less importance still exist[1].

---

[1] *Gen.* vi. 15, 16 is separated by Col. (*Pentateuch* iv. 30 sq.; vi. 535; *Wellhausen on the Composition*, etc., p. 95) from *v.* 9–14, 17–22, and assigned to J; but the language is that of P (cf. *Ex.* xxv. 10, 17, 23; xxx. 2; xxvii. 1), and

the two verses, so far from breaking the context, are essential to the description of the ark.—In vii., viii. two almost parallel narratives are combined into
a single whole, and consequently the analysis does not always yield very definite results. We find distinct traces of P in vii. 6, 7, 8, 9, 11, 13, 14, 15,
16ᵃ, 18–21, 22 ; viii. 1, 2ᵃ, 2–5, 13–19. But the verses have been worked
over by some later hand, for the distinction between clean and unclean
animals, vii. 8, belongs properly to the other narrative, in which it affects the
numbers taken into the ark (vii. 2). On the other hand, זכר ונקבה (vii. 3)
and רמש (vii. 23 ; and also vi. 7) remind us of P, in which these expressions
constantly recur (*Gen.* i. 27 ; v. 2 ; vi. 19 ; vii. 9, 16—i. 25, 26 ; vi. 20 ; vii.
14 ; viii. 17, 19 ; ix. 3). It is evident from these indications that when the
two texts were woven together a certain process of assimilation took place.—
On x. 1–7, 13–32, cf. Wellh. xxi. 395 sqq., according to whose careful study
(approved by Dillm., *Gen.*, p. 153 sqq., and K. Budde, *Die bibl. Urgeschichte
untersucht*, p. 219, and elsewhere), *v.* 1–5, 6, 7, 20, 22, 23, 31, 32 are taken
from P, and the remaining verses from JE. Such being the relations between
the two documents, it is easy to understand that x. (always excepting *v.* 8–12)
has been included in P by some critics and excluded from it by others. The
truth, in this particular case, lies between the two.—On xi. 28–32 cf. Wellh.
xxi., p. 398 ; Budde, op. cit., p. 415 sqq. *V.* 31, 32, unquestionably come from
P ; whereas *v.* 29 (cf. x. 21 ; xxii. 21 and xxii. 20, 23 ; xxiv. 15, 24, 27), and [68]
in all probability *v.* 28, 30 also, must be assigned to other sources (cf. xv. 7 ;
and xvi. 1ᵃ, the doublet in P of *v.* 30).—Ch. xxi. 2ᵇ–5 was of course preceded
in P by an account of Isaac's birth, which we probably still possess in *v.* 1, 2ᵃ,
though 'Elohim' has been changed to 'Yahwè' and לזקניו added from *v.* 7.—
Ch. xxv. 1–6 differs too much in form from the other genealogies in P (ילד for
הוליד) to have been taken from that document ; and its contents conflict with
the chronology of xxxiii. 1 ; xxiv. 7. Cf. Budde, op. cit., p.*216–225, on this
and other genealogies in *Genesis*. In the rest of the chapter, *v.* 7–11ᵃ, 12–17,
19, 20, certainly belong to P, and *v.* 11ᵇ and 18 are generally included also,
but see Wellh. xxi. 410, 417. The objections urged by Hupfeld (p. 59 sq.)
and Kayser (*Das vorex Buch d. Urgesch.*, p. 21 sq.) against the ascription of
v. 13–16ᵃ to P do not allow due weight to the formal evidence (בשמותם
בחצריהם ובטירותם, לתולדותם). *V.* 26ᵇ (cf. the chronology in the preceding sections of the work) shows that the birth of Isaac's sons was recorded
in P ; but *v.* 21–26ᵃ is from another source. Ch. xxvi. 34, 35 ; xxvii. 46 and
xxviii. 8, 9 (the last two verses presupposing *v.* 1–7, of which they are the
sequel) belong to each other, and cannot be united to xxvii. 1–45.—Ch. xxxi.
18 must of course have been preceded in P by an account of Jacob's abode in
Padan Aram, of his marriage and the birth of his children; but these accounts
—which analogy would lead us to suppose were short—are no longer to be
found in xxix.–xxxi. 17. Ch. xxxv. 22ᵇ–26 shows that P agreed with the other
narrators as to the names and the mothers of Jacob's children, but not as to
Benjamin's birth in Canaan.—Ch. xxxiv. (with the connected verse xxxv. 5)
is ascribed by many authorities, in whole or in part, to P, to which it really is
closely related in language and ideas ; see especially *v.* 1, 2, 5, 10, 13, 15, 17,

20, 22-24, 27-29, and cf. *Th. Tijdsch.*, xiv. 273 sqq. But on the other hand this chapter accords but ill with the sobriety and stateliness of the patriarchal history in P, and I have therefore omitted it from my enumeration. See, further, § 16, n. 12, on this point and on עוד in xxxv. 9 and on *v.* 14; xxxv. 9-15, as a whole, has already been dealt with in § 5, n. 28.—The contradiction between xxvi. 34, 35; xxviii. 8, 9 and xxxvi. 2-5, which has long perplexed the commentators, leads Wellh., xxi. 438-440, to the conclusion that the latter verses—together with *v.* 9-19, which depend upon them—must be excluded from P. Well-founded objections to *v.* 31-39 (the list of Edomite kings) and *v.* 20-30 (information about the Horites), as alien to the purpose and character of P, which never loses sight of the sacred line, had been urged by others. This only leaves *v.* 6-8 (cf. xiii. 6, 11ᵇ, 12ᵃ) and 40-43, —the discrepancy between the latter and *v.* 9-19 furnishing Wellhausen with another proof that he is right in rejecting *v.* 1-5, 9-19. All this is unanswerable; and yet the result is not quite satisfactory, for one would have expected more ample information concerning the Edomites than is contained in *v.* 40-43. Perhaps a list of Esau's descendants, which was given at this point in P, has been superseded by *v.* 1-5, 9-19.—It is universally [69] allowed that the elaborate history of Joseph, xxxvii. 2ᵇ-36; xxxix. sqq., is largely drawn from other sources. But it appears from the few fragments indicated above that P likewise contained an account of the emigration of Jacob and his family to Egypt, and ascribed it to Joseph's influence. This is obvious from xlvi. 6, 7, to which some would add *v.* 8-27. Against this latter passage, however, Kayser (p. 30-32, cf. Wellh., xxi. p. 441) has urged very weighty objections: the list constantly assumes details (see especially *v.* 12, 15, 18, 20, 25) which are mentioned in the other documents, but not in P; and moreover it betrays every sign (see especially *v.* 21) of being a very arbitrary piece of patch-work from other genealogies, especially *Num.* xxvi. In spite of *v.* 15, then, which is characterised by the linguistic peculiarities of P, the passage cannot be assigned to that document, but must be due to a compiler who knew *Genesis* in its present form, and, amongst other sources, *Num.* xxvi.—Ch. xlvii. 7-11, in which the language of P is unmistakable, seems nevertheless to be connected by *v.* 11ᵇ (' as Pharaoh had commanded') with what goes before (*v.* 5, 6, where a corresponding command of Pharaoh is given). It is usual, therefore, to consider *v.* 11ᵇ as an addition by R. But it is better to suppose with Wellh. xxi. 441 sq. and Dillm., p. 419 sq., that the LXX. has preserved the original text of *v.* 4 sqq., and that *v.* 5, 6ᵃ belongs to P. In that case *v.* 6ᵇ, preceded by the words εἶπε δὲ Φαραὼ τῷ Ἰωσήφ, contains the answer to the prayer of *v.* 4, and the text of P runs through thus, xlvi. 6, 7; [' and Jacob and his sons came to Egypt to Joseph, and Pharaoh said,' etc.]; xlvii. 5, 6ᵃ, 7-11, etc.—In xlviii., *v.* 7 is often assigned to P, as well as *v.* 3-6; and in that case of course xxxv. 16ᵃ, 19, 20 must also belong to it. But inasmuch as these latter verses are not in the style of P and are contradicted by xxxv. 22ᵇ-26, while *v.* 7 itself hangs on but very loosely to *v.* 3-6, it is better to regard this verse as a gloss, whether by R or by some later reader, who was of course acquainted with *Gen.* xxxv. 16 sqq. Cf.

Budde in *Zeitschr. f. a. t. Wissensch.* iii. 56–86. Observe that Ephraim and
Manasseh are here included amongst the sons of Jacob, i.e. amongst the
tribes. We shall refer to this again.—Before xlix. 29–33 we want the statement that Jacob's sons collected round him and were addressed by him. It
may possibly be still contained in *v.* 1ᵃ, 28ᵇ, and may originally have run thus :
' and Jacob called his sons and blessed them. Each one of them did he bless
with the blessing designed for him' (*dele* אשר, which makes the construction
needlessly strained). — In l., besides *v.* 12, 13, which join on immediately
to xlix. 29–33, the chronological data in *v.* 22, 26 may have been taken from
P, but as they now appear they are worked into the texture of other accounts.

In the opening chapters of *Exodus* we cannot fail to recognise the continuation of the work that we separated so easily
from the other narratives in *Genesis.* It embraces *Ex.* i. 1–7,
13, 14 ; ii. 23ᵇ–25, and the revelation of the name Yahwè to
Moses in *Ex.* vi. 2–7, which has already been dealt with
(§ 5, n. 21, 28). In P itself this revelation must have been [70]
preceded by some details concerning Moses, which have not
been able to hold their place by the side of the more elaborate
narrative of *Ex.* ii.–v. drawn from other sources. Now almost
all the critics take the revelation of the name Yahwè as the
opening of a new section of P, which may be traced through
Ex. vi.–xvi., and again in *Ex.* xxv. sqq.; but Colenso holds
that *Ex.* vi. 2–5 is the last passage preserved to us
of the book that begins with *Gen.* 1.–ii. 4ᵃ, while he ascribes
the passages that are usually regarded as its continuation to
a writer who lived many centuries later [2]. The grounds on
which this divergent opinion rests cannot for the most part
be examined till later on [3]. All we can say at present is
that it seems highly improbable that the sequel to *Ex.* vi.
2–5, which certainly existed once, should not have been
taken up into the Hexateuch, and that we can see no reason
whatever for ascribing to a far later follower the passages
which have always been regarded as forming that sequel [4]. We
recognise the continuation of our work, then, in *Ex.* vi. 8–12 [5] ;
vii. 1–7, and the five strikingly parallel accounts of the wonders performed by Moses and Aaron, vii. 8–13, *v.* 19 20 (21ᶜ?),

22 ; viii. 1–3, 11 ^b ; *v.* 12–15 [5–7, 15^b ; *v.* 16–19], and ix. 8–12
(35 ?), to which xi. 9, 10 belongs as an epilogue⁶. There can
be no doubt that xii. contains the sequel of this narrative, in
v. 1–20, 28, 40, 41, 43–51, which all hang together ; but the
legal prescriptions they contain, especially *v.* 14–20, 43–50, fit
very ill into the historical context. If the writer himself
placed them where they now stand his interest in the legislation made him forget the requirements of the narrative ; or if
not, then his account of the exodus must have been supplemented afterwards, in his own style and spirit, by the insertion of the connected laws⁷. We must further assign to P *Ex.*
(xiii. 20 ?) ; xiv. 1–4, 8, 9, 10 (in part), 15–18, 21 (in part),
22, 23, 26, 27 (in part), 28, 29⁸ ; xvi. (subsequently worked
over and expanded)⁹ ; (xvii. 1 ; xix. 2 ^a ?) ; xxiv. 15–18^{a 10}.

[71]　　² Cf. *Pentateuch*, vi. 130 sqq., 574 sqq. ; App., p. 116-144. Colenso
himself subsequently came to the conclusion that he had been at least to some
extent mistaken. Cf. R. Crompton Jones's communication to *The
Academy*, No. 583 (7 July, 1883), based on a letter from Colenso himself
(† 20 June, 1883).

³ Colenso affirms (1) that our document, from *Gen.* i. to *Ex.* vi., on
the one hand, and what I call its sequel, from *Ex.* vi. onwards, on the
other hand, stand in totally distinct relations to the matter by which
they are respectively surrounded in the Hexateuch ; and (2), that the
document itself must date from the time of Samuel, whereas the supposed
sequel (Colenso's LL) is exilian or post-exilian. This latter point is
obviously the more important. The date of our document being already fixed
by Colenso (*Pentateuch*, v., ch. viii., ix.), the question presented itself to him
thus : ' does the post-exilian origin of the priestly laws and narratives in
Exodus-Numbers and *Joshua* compel us to modify our previous conclusions
with respect to *Gen.* i.–*Ex.* vi. ? ' A negative answer involved the position—
which, as far as I know, Colenso alone defends—that LL is from another
and much later author than our document. The similarity between the two
is recognised (*Pentateuch*, vi. 576 sqq.), but is explained by imitation.—Now
the main supports of Colenso's opinion cannot be judged till later on. At
present we have only to inquire whether it is true, in contradiction with our
provisional results, that the narratives and laws announced, or at least fore-
shadowed in *Ex.* vi. 2–7, are not really to be found in the Hexateuch.

⁴ While referring to Dillmann, Nöldeke, Kayser, and Colenso himself for proof of the coincidence of language and style between the pericopes
before and after *Ex.* vi., I will only remark that at any rate in the passages

mentioned above there is nothing to indicate a different author. The high rank assigned to Aaron (*Ex.* vii. sqq.) has not become conspicuous till now, but there has not been any earlier opportunity for it. The affinity between *Gen.* xvii. and the laws in *Ex.* xii. is universally allowed. The vindication of the sabbath rest in *Ex.* xvi. recalls *Gen.* ii. 1–3. But the very fact that no critic has ever so much as suspected that an enormous interval lay between *Ex.* vi. 2–5 and *v.* 6–8, etc., when engaged on the analysis of *Exodus*, and that the idea was only suggested to Colenso himself by extraneous considerations, is quite enough to forbid our accepting the hypothesis at the present stage of our inquiry.

⁵ The verses 13–28 interrupt the progress of the narrative, and cannot possibly have been placed where they now are by the author of *v.* 2–12. When they were inserted—by R we may assume for the present—it became necessary to pick up the thread of *v.* 10–12 again; and this is actually done in *v.* 29, 30. And, when once we have seen R at work on his own account in this chapter, the question rises whether he has not been busy with the earlier verses also, especially *v.* 6–8 ? See below § 16, n. 12.

⁶ We must not fail to observe that the first four miracles are performed by Aaron, who also bears his part in the fifth ; that the wonders themselves are not so much of the nature of plagues as of demonstrations of Yahwè's might ; that all this is in perfect keeping with the idea of a match against Pharaoh's magicians, who come off worse and worse each time ; and finally that Moses and Aaron come forward from the first with the demand for the unconditional liberation of Israel (whereas in other accounts they merely demand temporary leave of absence, v. 1, 3; vii. 16, 26 [viii. 1]; viii. 16 [20]; ix. 1, 13; x. 3, 24–26; xii. 31).

⁷ We shall have to face this alternative ultimately, but may by that time [72] be in a position to make a choice which would be rash at present. The verses in question (14–20, 43–50) emphatically intrude upon the historical context, especially מקרא קדש (*v.* 16), and the regulations concerning the natives of the land and the strangers (*v.* 19, 45, 49, etc.). But on the other hand, *v.* 14–20, 43–50 are most closely related to *v.* 1–13, and are indispensable as the complement of the law contained in them. Wurster (*Zeitsch. f. a. t. Wissensch.*, iv. 112 sqq.) thinks these verses are shown to be a part of P by their very position in the framework of the history.—Kayser (p. 44 sq.) and Wellhausen (xxi. 542) do not assign *v.* 21–27 to our document, since the passage does not quite agree with *v.* 1–13. On the other hand, we cannot allow with Kayser (p. 45 sq.) that *v.* 11–13 belongs to the author of *v.* 21–27 ; for it is indispensable after *v.* 1–10, and is quite on the same lines.

⁸ So in the main Nöldeke, Kayser, Knobel-Dillmann, and others. Wellhausen (xxi. 545 sqq.) only derives *v.* 1, 2, 4 (in part), 8ᵇ, 9 (in part), 10 (in part), 15 (in part), 28 (?) from P, and the remaining verses from another source. His chief argument is that in *v.* 16, 21, 26 the magic staff is assigned not to Aaron (cf. *n.* 6), but to Moses. But this staff is only barely mentioned in *v.* 16 together with the outstretched hand, which supersedes it altogether in *v.* 21, 26, 27 (cf. vii. 5). We cannot be surprised at its being Moses

who performs this miracle, and indeed we could expect nothing else after
ix. 8–12. Moreover, P's representation of the miracle, according to our
analysis (the parting of the sea and the passage of Israel between two walls
of water, *v.* 21, 22, 26, 28), does not join on to any of the narratives fragments of which Wellhausen finds in xiv., and least of all to *v.* 19ᵃ, with its
'mal'ach Elohîm,' who would be quite superfluous in a narrative in which the
hand of Moses accomplishes everything.

⁹ So Nöldeke, p. 48 sq. On the divergent opinions of Kayser (p. 50 sqq.)
and Wellhausen (xxi. 547 sqq.) see *Th. Tijdsch.,* xiv. 281–302, and further
§ 16, n. 12.

¹⁰ The stations of the Israelites on their journey from Ramses to Sinai were
unquestionably mentioned in P. But whether the data in xiii. 20; xv. 22,
27; xvii. 1; xix. 1, 2ᵃ, come from thence must remain uncertain since they
are now worked into narratives taken from elsewhere. Ch. xvii. 1; xix. 1,
2ᵃ are, however, quite in P's style, so that the probability in their favour is
greater than that for the other verses.—On xxiv. 15–18ᵃ cf. Nöldeke,
p. 53 sq.; Kayser, p. 56, and Wellhausen, p. 566 sq.

Our right to speak of the verses and sections thus far
separated as the priestly elements of the Hexateuch
can no longer be doubted. Whenever the subject matter has
given the author of our document an opportunity of revealing
himself, he has displayed his lively interest in religious ceremonies and usages (*Gen.* ii. 1–3; ix. 4; xvii.; xxi. 4; *Ex.* xii.
1–20; 43–50; xvi. 4, 5, 22 sqq., 31 sqq.), and his great
reverence for Aaron the ancestor of the future priesthood
[73] (cf. n. 6 and *Ex.* xvi. 2 sqq.). But, as might have been
expected, the priestly character of his work comes out far
more distinctly when he goes on to describe, in *Ex.* xxv. sqq.,
the covenant between Yahwè and Israel which he had previously announced (*Ex.* vi. 7). For it can hardly be doubted
that these chapters are really the sequel of our document; the
language and style are the same ¹¹, and the ordinances put
forth with respect to the place of worship and the consecration
of Aaron and his sons as priests, answer completely to what
we should specially expect in the legislation of P. The
several ordinances of xxv.–xxix. follow each other in natural
and regular order, and may well have been arranged by the
author himself as they now stand ¹². In xxx. and xxxi. 1–17,

on the other hand, the connection is looser, or is altogether
wanting, and we find ordinances that diverge from what has
gone before, and are n o t assumed further on, where they would
naturally be referred to ; whence we gather that these two
chapters are later additions, constructed on the lines of
xxv.–xxix., but not drawn up by the author himself [13]. The
chapters that follow next in *Exodus*, xxxi. 18–xxxiv. 28, have
nothing in common with P, either in substance or form.
Ch. xxxiv. 29–35, though related to P, does not belong to it [14].
On the other hand, xxxv.–xl., and *Lev.* viii., are so completely dependent upon xxv.–xxxi., that their author must have
had these chapters in their entirety before him.   This in
itself is proof positive that the author of xxv.–xxix. cannot
have drawn them up.   Nay, they must even be later than
xxx.; xxxi. 1–17.   Just as xvi. was subsequently filled in and
expanded, so it would seem that a very short original account
of the execution of the commands of *Ex.* xxv. sqq. was
gradually elaborated, till at last it was brought almost into
the form of the instructions themselves.   The remarkable
divergencies of the Greek translation of *Ex.* xxxv.–xl. make
us suspect that the final redaction of these chapters was
hardly completed—if indeed completed—when that translation
was made, i. e. about 250 B. C. [15]

[11] Cf. Dillmann, *Ex. u. Lev.*, p. 262 ; Colenso, *Pentateuch*, vi. 576 sqq. Of [74]
course there are a number of technical terms in *Ex.* xxv. sqq. which occur nowhere else in the Old Testament, except in the corresponding passages in *Ex.*
xxxv. sqq., *Lev.* viii. sq., and are therefore not to be found in the sections
hitherto assigned to P.   But the only building instructions in *Genesis* which
are taken from P, viz. vi. 15, 16, strongly resemble *Ex.* xxv. sqq., and whenever P appears as a law-giver, i.e. in *Gen.* xvii. and *Ex.* xii., he uses the formulæ
which reappear in *Ex.* xxv. sqq. (לדרות with the pronominal suffix; 'that
soul shall be destroyed from amongst its people;' 'between the two evenings ;'
עולם preceded by the status constructus of ברית, חקה, כהנה, etc., etc.).

[12] The order of succession is as follows : *Ex.* xxv. 1–9, free-will offerings
for the establishment of the cultus ; *v.* 10–22, the ark of the covenant and the
Cherubim ; *v.* 23–30, the table of the shew-bread ; *v.* 31–38, the golden lamp-
stand ; *v.* 39, 40, postscript 'on all these utensils,' which, it will be observed,

pertain to the two divisions of the sanctuary proper; in xxvi. we come to the tabernacle itself, the construction of which is expounded in *v.* 1–30, and then (*v.* 31–37) follow the directions concerning the veil between the holy place and the holy of holies, followed by the indication of the position in the sanctuary of the utensils, the preparation of which was ordered in xxv. ; then we have xxvii. 1–8, the altar ; *v.* 9–19, the fore-court of the tabernacle ; *v.* 20, 21, the oil for the lamp; xxviii., the garments of Aaron and his sons ; *v.* 1–5, introduction; *v.* 6–14, the ephod; *v.* 15–30, the breast-plate ; *v.* 31–35, the mantle; *v.* 36–38, the frontlet; *v.* 39, the tunic, the turban, and the girdle ; *v.* 40–43, the garments of Aaron's sons ; with an anticipated injunction (*v.* 41, to which we shall return) to consecrate Aaron and his sons to the priestly office, as set forth in detail in xxix. 1–35 ; *v.* 36, 37, the purging and consecration of the altar; *v.* 38–42, the institution of the daily sacrifices for morning and evening, passing, in *v.* 43–46, into an epilogue : Yahwè will consecrate the sanctuary to himself and Aaron and his sons as priests, and so will dwell in the midst of Israel.

No further proof is needed that these five chapters, speaking generally, form a well arranged and rounded whole. A few points only demand further consideration. *a.* Moses receives the command to lay הָעֵדֻת in the ark (xxv. 16, 21 ; cf. xl. 20), i. e. the code of the ten words (*Ex.* xxxi. 18 ; xxxii. 15; xxxiv. 29) and not, as Knobel has it (*Ex. u. Lev.*, 1st ed., p. 263 sq.), the priestly code. How P can thus refer to *Ex.* xx. 1–17, which is not a part of his work, will be considered and explained in § 16, n. 12. *b.* P makes Moses ascend Mount Sinai, xxiv. 15–18ᵃ, and it is there, accordingly, that xxv. sqq. is revealed to him, cf. xxxi. 18 ; *Num.* iii. 1 ; xxviii. 6 (allusion to *Ex.* xxix. 38– 42). Ch. xxv. 9 and 40 are in harmony with this representation ; and if in xxvi. 30 and xxvii. 8 there seems to be a reference to what Yahwè 'had shown Moses on the mountain,' there is no reason why the *perfecta* in these verses should not be taken as *futura exacta* : when Moses has descended from the mountain he is to conform to what 'will have been revealed' to him. *c.* We shall see presently that in xxx., xxxi. later regulations have been added to the laws about the sanctuary and the garments and consecration of the priests. This makes us suspicious with respect to xxv.–xxix. also, which [75] would be no less liable to interpolation than to supplementing. We must therefore note that xxvii. 20, 21 occupies an unexpected place in a treatise so carefully arranged ; that xxviii. 41–43 really anticipates xxix., and moreover mentions that the sons of Aaron are to be anointed, which is not enjoined in xxix. ; that xxix. 36, 37—expiation for the altar and its purification, before it has been used,—hardly seems appropriate; and finally that the institution of the tamîd, *v.* 38–42, comes in strangely here. At present we confine ourselves to these remarks, but shall return to the subject hereafter.

¹³ Cf. Wellh., xxii. 410–414, and on some of the sections into which xxx. and xxxi. fall, Popper, *Der bibl. Bericht über die Stiftshütte*, p. 111 sqq., 194 sqq.; Graf, *Geschichtliche Bücher*, p. 63. The subsections are:—

Ch. xxx. 1–10, the altar of incense. If the author of xxv.–xxix. had been acquainted with this 'most holy' object (*v.* 10) he would have described it in xxv., and mentioned it in xxvi. 31–37; and in xxvii. 1–8 there would have been some indication that the altar there mentioned was not the only one. *Lev.* xvi. (*v.* 12, 18, 20, 33) likewise knows of but one altar, and does not mention the expiation prescribed in *Ex.* xxx. 10. On the other hand, it is urged that the golden altar, or altar of incense, appears repeatedly in P elsewhere (*Ex.* xxx. 27; xxxi. 8; xxxv. 15; xxxvii. 25; xxxix. 38; xl. 5 [cf. 10, 26]; *Lev.* iv. 7, 18; *Num.* iv. 11); that the altar of *Ex.* xxvii. 1–8; *Lev.* xvi. is often called, as if for distinction, the altar of burnt offering (*Ex.* xxx. 28; xxxi. 9; xxxv. 16; xxxviii. 1; xl. 6, 10, 29; *Lev.* iv. *passim*) or the brazen altar (*Ex.* xxxviii. 30; xxxix. 39), and that altars, in the plural, are mentioned (*Num.* iii. 31); further, that the altar of incense is known not only to the chronicler (1 *Chron.* vi. 49; xxviii. 18; 2 *Chron.* xxvi. 16, 19; cf. iv. 19) and to the authors of 1 *Macc.* (i. 21; iv. 49) and 2 *Macc.* (ii. 5), but to the writer of the books of Kings (1 *Kings* vii. 48; cf. vi. 20, 22; 'the brazen altar,' viii. 64; 2 *Kings* xvi. 14, 15): and probably also to Ezekiel, who speaks in ix. 2 of 'the brazen altar,' implying a knowledge of some other altar. All this evidence seems to Delitzsch, *Studien*, p. 113–121, and Dillmann, *Ex. u. Lev.*, p. 316 (cf. 264), to remove the doubts urged by Wellhausen against *Ex.* xxx. 1–10. But this cannot be allowed. The fact remains that the passage does not stand where the author of *Ex.* xxv.–xxix. must have placed it, and the natural inference that this author had in his mind a sanctuary without an altar of incense is commended *a posteriori* by Ezek. xli. 21, 22, and xliv. 16, which show that the prophet Ezekiel, likewise, left his proposed temple without any altar of incense distinct from the table of shew-bread, inasmuch as he identified the two. Such then was the intention of the author of *Ex.* xxv.–xxix. (and *Lev.* xvi.) likewise. *Ex.* xxx. 1–10 is a correction of this representation, as may be gathered from *v.* 10, for instance, which can only be regarded as a supplement to the rite prescribed in *Lev.* xvi.; cf. n. 23.— This conclusion would hold good even were it certain that the temple of Solomon had an altar of incense in it. But Stade (*Zeitsch. f. a. t. Wissensch.*, iii. 143 sqq., 168 sq.) has shown that this is at least doubtful.

Ex. xxx. 11–16, the poll-tax of half a shekel, to be paid at the census by all who had reached the age of twenty. The pericope would be out of place [76] anywhere amongst the directions for the construction of the tabernacle, and is most distinctly so when placed between *v.* 1–10 and 17–21. Moreover, it presupposes the command to number the people (*Num.* i.;—just as the yield of the tax itself, in *Ex.* xxxviii. 24–30, rests on the figures of *Num.* i.), whence it follows that it was written after *Num.* i., and therefore not by the author of *Ex.* xxv.–xxix. On *Neh.* x. 33 [32] see § 15, n. 30.

Ex. xxx. 17–21, the brazen laver, would have been mentioned in xxvii., if the writer of xxv.–xxix. had thought it necessary to speak of it.

Ex. xxx. 22–33, the holy oil of anointing. According to *Ex.* xxix. 7, 29, 30; *Lev.* viii. 12 Aaron only is anointed; and so too in *Lev.* iv. 3, 5, 16; vi. 13, 15 [20, 22]; xvi. 32; xxi. 10, 12; *Num.* xxxv. 25. In this pericope (*v.* 30), on the other hand, and in *Ex.* xxviii. 41 (cf. n. 12); xl. 15; *Lev.* vii. 36; x. 7; *Num.* iii. 3 the anointing is extended to the priests. This is, doubtless, the later representation, so that xxx. 22-33 appears to be a supplement, as we should have guessed from its position after xxix., not in it. In *v.* 27 the altar of incense is mentioned.

Ex. xxx. 34-38, on the incense, which belongs to *v.* 1-10, and is homogeneous with *v.* 22-33, must be regarded in the same light. On *v.* 17-21, 22-33, 34-38, consult, further, P o p p e r, p. 109, 197 sq.

Ex. xxxi. 1-11, the call of Bezaleël and his assistants, presupposes not only xxv.-xxix., but (*v.* 8, 9, 11) xxx. also, and must, accordingly, be one of the additions.

Ex. xxxi. 12-17, the sabbath ordinance, seems to be placed here (and repeated in xxxv. 1-3) to show that the preceding injunctions, though proceeding from Yahwè, did not override the regulations as to the seventh day. Hence P o p p e r, p. 109 sq., 198 sq., draws the very just inference that the pericope does not belong to the original document, but rose out of it upon subsequent reflection and was inserted with a subsidiary legislative intention. This comes out with special clearness in *Ex.* xxxv. 3, but the latter in its turn throws a similar light on this pericope also.

¹⁴ It is generally allowed that xxxi. 18—xxxiv. 35 takes up the narrative of *Ex.* xix.-xxiv., and is thrust in between xxv.-xxxi. and xxxv.-xl. in much the same way as xxv.-xxxi. itself is wedged in between it and xix.-xxiv. And indeed xxxiii. 7-11 diametrically contradicts P's representation.—The most we can ask is whether the name 'table of the testimony,' which appears in *Ex.* xxxi. 18 ; xxxii. 15 ; xxxiv. 29, may have arisen under the influence of P, whose usage it recalls ('ark of the testimony,' 'tent of the testimony,' etc.). In xxxiv. 29-35 W e l l h a u s e n (xxi. 566) sees a fragment of P, and no doubt we seem to detect his redundant style in *v.* 29, and are reminded of him by Aaron (*v.* 30, 31) and ' the princes in the congregation' (*v.* 31). I cannot, however, assign this pericope to him : it presupposes the existence of the sanctuary that, according to P, has still to be built, and seems to place it outside the camp (*v.* 34-35), in common with xxxiii. 7-11, which it also resembles, in point of form—especially in the use of the imperfect and perfect with ן in *v.* 34, 35. See below § 16, n. 12.

[77] ¹⁵ The question of the origin of *Ex.* xxxv.-xl. (cf. D i l l m. *Ex. u. Lev.*, p. 354 sqq.) is very difficult and involved. Before attempting to justify the conclusion I have reached, I will give a synopsis of the contents of these chapters, adding in a second and a third column references to the corresponding passages of the Greek translation and the parallels from *Ex.* xxv.-xxxi.

HEBREW TEXT.	GREEK TEXT.	Ex. xxv–xxxi.
	[References to Tischendorf's edition. In many editions the numbering of the verses is made to conform to the Hebrew.]	
xxxv. 1-3. Sabbath ordinance.	xxxv. 1-3.	xxxi. 12-17.
4-19. Moses exhorts the peo-	4-19 (*v.* 8 omitted ;	xv. 1-9.

HEBREW TEXT.	GREEK TEXT.	Ex. xxv–xxxi.
ple to free-will offerings, and enumerates the things they must provide.	*v.* 12 sqq. with trans- positions).	
20–29. The gifts are brought.	20–29.	
30–35. Moses announces the call of Bezaleël.	30–35.	xxxi. 1–11.
xxxvi. 1–7. The reception of gifts closed.	xxxvi. 1–7.	
8–19. The tapestries for the Tabernacle are made;	Cf. xxxvii. 1, 2.	xxvi. 1–12, 14.
20–34. the woodwork;	Cf. xxxviii. 18–21.	15–30.
35–38. the curtains;	xxxvii. 3–6.	31–33, 36, 37.
xxxvii. 1–9. the ark;	xxxviii. 1–8.	xxv. 10–21.
10–16. the table of the shew- bread;	9–12.	23–30.
17–24. the lamp-stand;	13–17.	31–40.
25–28. the altar of incense;	Wanting.	xxx. 1–6.
29. the oil of anointing and the incense;	xxxviii. 25.	Cf. xxx. 22–33, 34–38.
xxxviii. 1–7. the altar of burnt offering ;	Cf. xxxviii. 22–24.	xxvii. 1–8.
8. the brazen laver;	xxxviii. 26.	xxx. 17–19.
9–20. the fore-court;	xxxvii. 7–18.	xxvii. 9–19.
21–23. heading of the ac- counts of the gold, silver, and brass employed;	19–21.	
24–31. the accounts them- selves;	xxxix. 1–10.	Cf. xxx. 11–16.
xxxix. 1–31. the garments of the high priest and the priests are made;	xxxvi. 8ᵇ–4.	xxviii. 6–40.
32–43. the completed work is presented to Moses.	xxxix. 11, 14–23.	
xl. 1–16. Moses receives and executes the command to set up the sanctuary and consecrate the priests.	xl. 1–13 (*v.* 6–8 of the Hebrew partially, and *v.* 11 of Hebrew entirely omitted).	
17–33. The Tabernacle is erected, and the sacred utensils placed in it.	14–26; xxxviii. 27 ; xl. 27 (*v.* 28, 29ʰ of the Hebrew omitted).	
34–38. The pillar of cloud and fire.	28–32.	

I subjoin the following remarks. (1) The third column shows that *Ex.* [78] xxv.–xxviii., xxx., xxxi. are repeated, almost in their entirety, in xxxv.–xxxix. (while *Ex.* xxix. reappears in *Lev.* viii.). The omission of certain verses, e.g. *Ex.* xxv. 15, 16 ; 21, 22 ; 30 ; 40 ; xxvi. 12, 13 ; 30 ; 33, 34 ; xxviii. 29, 30 ; 35 ; xxx. 6–10 is no more than natural : they would be out of place in the account of the preparation of the sacred objects, and some of them actually appear in xl. 17–33, in the account of the erection of the tabernacle; just in the same way xxx. 18–21 is reproduced in xl. 30–32, and not after xxxviii. 8. On the other hand, we note the real omission of *Ex.* xxvii. 20, 21 (the equivalent of which does not appear till *Lev.* xxiv. 1–3) ; and the elaborate passage on the oil of anointing and the incense (xxx. 22-38) is but rapidly summarised in xxxvii. 29. (2) The order of the subsections in the Hebrew text of *Ex.* xxxv. sqq., though departing from that of *Ex.* xxv. sqq., is in itself unimpeachable. This is clear from the first column. The sabbath ordinance must now of course come first (cf. n.13); the call of Bezaleël, etc. is mentioned much earlier than in *Ex.* xxv. sqq. It is natural enough that in the actual order of manufacture the tent should come first, and the holy vessels afterwards, though the sacred character of the latter secured them the first place in xxv. sqq. The altar of incense and the laver, which figure in an appendix in xxv. sqq., take their proper place here (xxxvii. 25-29; xxxviii. 8). The accounts come in quite appropriately in xxxviii. 21-31, just after the construction of the metallic objects, and before the manufacture of the priestly garments, which follows that of the other articles both here (*Ex.* xxxix. 1-31), and in the o r i g i n a l (*Ex.* xxviii.). It is only in xl., taken in connection with *Lev.* viii., that the arrangement becomes somewhat strange. We shall return to this. (3) The Greek text is not so satisfactory. Its relation to the Hebrew may be gathered from a comparison of the first two columns. With regard to the opening, xxxv. 1–xxxvi. 7, and the close, xxxix. 32-xl. 38, passing over minor divergencies, there is no essential difference between the two texts. Ch. xxxvi. 8ᵃ (Hebrew and Greek) is immediately followed in the Greek text by the section on the priestly garments, so that xxxvi. 8ᵇ-40 in the Greek corresponds to xxxix. 1ᵇ-31 in the Hebrew. Then the rest of the description appears, but in a very strange order, and with very noticeable abbreviations. In the Greek xxxvii., we have in succession the Hebrew xxxvi. 8-19 (contracted into 2 verses); *v.* 35-38; xxxviii. 9-20; 21-23—and so on. The strangest of all is that the Hebrew xxxviii. 21-23 and 24-31—a single passage—is split into two, and the parts severed, in the Greek (xxxvii. 19-21 and xxxix. 1-10).

The added passages in *Ex.* xxx., xxxi. are throughout assumed in xxxv. sqq., so that these latter chapters cannot possibly be due to the author of xxv.-xxix. Nor can they even have a common origin or date with *Ex.* xxx., xxxi. This seems to me to be obvious alike from their contents and character and from their form. To give such a diffuse account of how Moses executed the commands of Yahwè, immediately after the commands themselves, and for the most part couched in identical terms, is an idea that would more readily occur [79] to later readers and manipulators than to the author of xxv.-xxxi., or of any portion of the ordinances themselves. The form, too, is very defective, especially when the writer ventures on anything beyond mere copying, e.g. xxxvi. 1-7. But we need not insist on these general impressions, for there are more definite proofs of later origin.

(1) According to xxxviii. 25-28 the 603,550 half shekels paid by the fighting men at the census are devoted to building the sanctuary. This conflicts with *Ex.* xxx. 11-16, where the poll-tax is assigned to 'the service of the ôhel mo'éd' (*v.* 16), i.e. defrays the expenses of the cultus, while the erection of the sanctuary is provided for by free gifts, including silver (*Ex.* xxv. 3; cf. xxxv. 5, 24). The writer of *Ex.* xxxviii. 24-31 was misled by the

position of *Ex*. xxx. 11–16, and misunderstood the passage.—When this is once established, other divergencies, especially the addition of *Ex*. xxxv. 2 (cf. xxxi. 12–17) and other small details, may fairly be taken as evidence of diversity of authorship. Cf. Wellh., xxii. 417 sq.

(2) A close comparison of *Ex*. xxv.–xxxi. and xxxv.–xl. reveals small grammatical divergencies, which seem inexplicable if the two sections are from one hand or period. Cf. Popper, p. 84–98, who shows that many of these peculiarities are identical in character with those that distinguish the Samaritan from the Masoretic text of the Pentateuch. Trifling as they are in themselves, this gives them a real evidential importance. What could have induced the author of *Ex*. xxv. sqq. to write אֶחָת אֶל־אֶחָת in xxxvi. 10, 12, 13, 22, instead of his own phrase, אִשָּׁה אֶל אֲחוֹתָהּ? The Samaritan editor, however, objects to this latter formula, when applied to lifeless objects, so strongly that he corrects or omits it even in the original section, xxvi. 3, 5, 6, 17.

(3) In the same connection it deserves notice that within the limits of *Ex*. xxxv.–xl., (and *Lev*. viii.) there are traces of more than one hand, leading us to suspect that the section was not written *uno tenore*, but successively. Ch. xl. 1–16 is altogether superfluous: the commands about erecting the sanctuary, placing the utensils in it, and clothing the priests, which have been given already in xxv., xxxi., are here repeated—apparently because they seemed to be wanting in xxxv.–xxxix., which is only concerned with the manufacture of the things themselves. The following section, xl. 17–33, now and then (*v*. 27, 29, 30ᵇ–32) anticipates the account of the consecration of the priests (*Lev*. viii.) and their first sacrifice (*Lev*. ix.); whereas if it had been from the same hand as these two chapters, even the semblance of inconsistency would have been avoided. Add that in xxxix. (*v*. 1, 5, 7, 21, 26, 29, 31, 42, 43), and a part of xl. (*v*. 16, 19, 21, 23, 25, 27, 29, 32) [cf. *Lev*. viii. 4, 5, 9, 13, 17, 21, 29, 36] the formula 'as Yahwè had commanded Moses' is constantly used, whereas in xxxv.–xxxviii. it never once occurs identically, and but seldom in a modified form (xxxvi. 1; xxxviii. 22).

(4) Finally, the Greek translation furnishes yet another proof of the late origin of the whole section,—a proof which is intimately connected with the indications of successive stratification just given. For, *a*. the difference [80] between the text and the translation is in itself evidence that the text was not fixed. Even suppose the translator had what we now read before him, in any case he did not feel bound to follow it, but considered himself at liberty to jump about in it as he chose. Why here more than elsewhere? It cannot be accidental. The translator must, for some reason, have regarded xxxv.–xl. and xxv.–xxxi. in different lights. *b*. This argument partly falls to the ground—but only to make way for a more weighty one—if we are justified in concluding (with Popper, p. 172–177) that the differences between *Ex*. xxv.–xxxi. and xxxv.–xl. in the Greek version indicate different translators. And in truth it is hard to see why the same translator should have translated בדים and בתים by ἀναφορεῖς (φορεῖς) and θῆκαι in the one section, and always chosen different words (διωστῆρες, μοχλοί and εὑρεῖς, ὥστε αἰρεῖν) in

the other. Other instances are equally striking. But would the translator
of xxv. sqq. have left xxxv. sqq. untranslated if he had found these latter
chapters in his text?

Popper, p. 142 sqq., draws further and more definite inferences from the
Greek version. The difference of form noted above (3) between *Ex.* xxxix.,
xl. (+ *Lev.* viii.) and xxxvi.–xxxviii. leads him to suspect that the former group
is earlier than the latter. In this connection he notes that in the Greek text
xxxix. 1^b–31 follows immediately after xxxvi. 8^a. Whence this phenomenon?
He answers: when the translator executed his task, xxxix., xl. (+ *Lev.* viii.)
were already written, and were therefore at once translated, with the rest.
The second stratum of the description (xxxvi. 8^b–xxxviii.) was not written till
later, was subsequently inserted by scraps into the Greek text, and was
naturally placed after xxxix. 1–31 (= xxxvi. 8^b–40).—This opinion, to which
I formerly inclined (cf. *Godsdienst*, ii. 266 [*Rel. Isr.* iii. 48, 49]) I am compelled, after repeated consideration, to reject ; a. because we should have to
suppose that the enumeration of the objects surrendered to Moses, xxxix. 32–
43, was written before the account of their fabrication, xxxvi.–xxxviii. ;
whereas the reverse order must be the real one ; and β. because the Greek
translation itself furnishes the proof that the priestly garments—in accordance
with the order observed in xxv.–xxviii—ought to occupy not the first, but the
last, or one of the last places. In the enumeration of xxxv. 9 sqq. (in the
Greek) the garments of Aaron and his sons come near the end, being followed
only by the sacred oil of anointing and the incense. So, too, in the list of the
articles delivered, xxxix. 14 sqq.: first the σκηνή and its utensils (*v.* 14–18
[*Hebr.* 33, 35, 38, 37, 36]) ; then the sacred garments of the priests (*v.* 19
[*Hebr.* 41]) ; and finally other portions of the tent and fore-court (*v.* 20, 21
[*Hebr.* 40, 34, 40]), which, in harmony with the natural order, preceded the
priestly garments in the Hebrew text (xxxix. 32 sqq.). It is true that the
translator mentions the garments before the σκηνή, in this last section (καὶ
ἤνεγκαν τὰς στολὰς πρὸς M. καὶ τὴν σκηνὴν κ.τ.λ.), but in so doing he betrays
himself, for in his own text, as we have seen, the στολαί appear later on.
And if we are thus driven to the conclusion that the translator transposed
the section on the priestly garments, thus showing that he considered
himself entitled to take such liberties when he saw occasion to do so, we
[81] can no longer allow Popper's inferences from the arrangement of the text.
I. e. we have no right to place the original Greek translator between the.
composition of *Ex.* xxxix., xl. (+ *Lev.* viii.) and the compilation of xxxvi.–
xxxviii.

My own inference as to the chronology of the passages may still seem
arbitrary, for it is conceivable that xxxv. sqq. was accidentally de-
ficient or defective in the MS. used by the Greek translator, and in that
case the confusion in the Greek text would of course prove nothing. But it
will spontaneously result from our further inquiries (§ 15) that the hypothesis
of an accident is unnecessary, and therefore inadmissible.

Exodus xl. does not complete the account of the carrying out of the ordinances concerning the institution of the cultus, for there still remains the consecration of Aaron and his sons as priests, which was commanded in *Ex.* xxix. The record of this act is contained in *Lev.* viii., which, as we have seen, is related to *Ex.* xxxv.–xl., and therefore belongs to a late stratum of P[16].

Between *Ex.* xl. and *Lev.* viii. there now stand the sacrificial ordinances of *Lev.* i–vii. In itself it is not surprising that these regulations should precede the first ritual performance in the tabernacle (*Lev.* ix.), and even the consecration of the priests, which itself involved certain sacrifices (*Lev.* viii.). But closer investigation shows that this position, however appropriate, was assigned to the section not by the author of *Ex.* xxv.–xxix., but by one of the later remodellers of his work. These chapters, though relatively speaking a single whole, are by no means due to a single hand. *Lev.* i.–v. [i–vi. 7], which strikes us as more original than vi., vii. [vi. 8–vii.], is itself the product of continuous redaction, shows some slight divergences from *Ex.* xxix., and betrays familiarity with *Ex.* xxx. 1–10, i. e. with a late stratum of P (cf. n. 13); *Lev.* vi., vii. [vi. 8–vii.] contains supplements to i. v. [i.–vi. 7], and in its turn was not written straight off, but was gradually accumulated[17]. The whole of *Lev.* i.–vii. may have existed as an independent collection, subsequently introduced, with a modified superscription (compare *Lev.* i. 1 with vii. 37, 38), into its present connection[18]. The possibility of accomplishing this union without any considerable disturbance of the unity of P is partly explained by the close original affinity of all the priestly narratives and laws, but partly by the [82] evident care with which they were brought into agreement and connection with each other at the time of compilation[19].

In *Lev.* ix., x. the historico-legislative work broken off after *Ex.* xxv.–xxix. is continued. After the insertion of *Ex.* xxxv.–xl. and *Lev.* viii., a connecting link was added to unite *Lev.* ix.

to this account of the execution of Yahwè's commands to
Moses[20]. In other respects, also, the original form of the
narratives has been altered. *Lev.* x. 6, 7; *v.* 8–11 ; *v.* 16–20
are evidently later expansions, the last of which presupposes
the incorporation of the sacrificial ordinances of *Lev.* i.–vii.,
and applies them to a certain detail in *Lev.* ix., the result of
which is a misconception of the latter and an unnecessary
attempt to justify it[21].

We do not find the direct continuation of *Lev.* x. 1–5 ;
12–15 till we come to *Lev.* xvi. (cf. *v.* 1). The intervening
chapters, *Lev.* xi.–xv., stand on the same footing as *Lev.* i.–vii.
They are not essential in the position they now occupy, but
are very appropriately inserted there. They come after the
consecration of the priests, whose functions concerning the
'clean' and the 'unclean' they regulate, and before the
law of the day of atonement on which the sanctuary is
cleansed from the pollutions caused by involuntary uncleanness of priests and people. *Lev.* xi.–xv. accordingly
belongs to P in the wider sense, though not assignable to
the author of *Ex.* xxv.–xxix., and *Lev.* ix. ; x. 1–5, 12–15.
The chapters further resemble *Lev.* i.–vii. in having risen
successively, and not in a single piece[22]. On the other hand,
Lev. xvi., which the author of *Ex.* xxx. 10 must have known,
is a single whole, in which the conception of the sanctuary
and its utensils which characterises *Ex.* xxv.–xxix. reappears[23].

---

[16] To what has been said on *Lev.* viii. in n. 15 we may here add that *v.* 2
assumes that the priestly garments have been handed over to Moses (*Ex.*
xxxix. 41); in *v.* 10, 11, 15 the altar—i.e. the altar of burnt offerings,
which appears to be the only one known to the writer—and other sacred
objects, including the laver and its pedestal (*Ex.* xxx. 17–21 ; cf. n. 13), are
[83] sprinkled and cleansed (cf. n. 12, near the end) ; in *v.* 16, 25, 26, compared
with *Ex.* xxix. 13, 22, 23, slight changes of expression occur which seem to
betray diversity of authorship (cf. Popper, p. 96 sq.) ; *v.* 30 differs in position from the corresponding *Ex.* xxix. 21, and mentions the oil of anointment
before the blood of the sacrifice,—in both which particulars it agrees with the
Samaritan text of *Ex.* xxix. (cf. Popper, p. 97 sq.); *v.* 31 (read צוית)

refers, not to *Lev.* vii. 29 sqq., but to *Ex.* xxix. 31; and finally, in *v.* 33, 34, if the text is sound, the original, *Ex.* xxix. 35-37, is very slavishly reproduced—assuredly not by the author himself.

[17] On *Lev.* i.–vii. consult *Th. Tijdschr.*, iv. 492–500, and the writers cited there. I must confine myself here to a brief defence of the position taken up in the text, which differs in some respects from my previous results.

a. Lev. i.–v. [i.–vi. 7] deals successively with the burnt offering (i.); the food offering (ii.); the thank offering (iii.); the trespass offering (iv., v. 1–13); the guilt offering (v. 14–26 [v. 14–vi. 7]). The fourth section is not from a single hand. Ch. v. 1–13 is an appendix, from the hand of a writer who, unlike the author of iv., thought it necessary to enumerate the several cases in which a trespass offering was required. He was acquainted with iv. and, on the whole, follows the same linguistic usage, though not without divergences (*v.* 1 ונשא עונו, cf. *v.* 17; vii. 18; *v.* 5 התודה; *v.* 6, 7, והביא את־אשמו). Neither is v. 14-26 [v. 14–vi. 7] a single whole: *v.* 14–16, 20–26 [vi. 1–7] give one and the same representation of the guilt offering, but *v.* 17–19 introduces confusion, and loses sight of the distinction between trespass and guilt offering; the opening (ואם) is inappropriate; ונשא עונו, as in *v.* 1, should be noted.

b. If vi., vii. [vi. 8–vii.] were from the same hand as i.–v. [i.–vi. 7], the succession of the several kinds of sacrifice would be identical; whereas in fact the trespass offering (vi. 17–23 [24–30]) and guilt offering (vii. 1–7) follow immediately after the burnt offering (vi. 1–6 [8–13]) and food offering (vi. 7–11 [14–18]), and the thank offering comes last (vii. 11–21). Moreover, one would expect the subject matter to be suitably divided between i. v. [i.–vi. 7] and vi., vii. [vi. 8–vii.]; and this is not the case, as Knobel rightly pointed out *Ex. u. Lev.*, p. 401. On the other hand, vi., vii. [vi. 8–vii.] did not come into existence independently of i.–v. [i.–vi. 7]; for the former presupposes the contents of the latter, and is not a complete sacrificial code in itself. It cannot, therefore, be regarded as more ancient than i.–v. [i. vi. 7]. The priority of iii. to vii. 11–21 is specially marked.

c. Ch. vi., vii. [vi. 8–vii.], again, is not written *uno tenore*. The sections vi. 1–6, 7–11, 17–23 [8–13, 14–18, 24–30]; vii. 1–7, 11–21 begin with זאת תורה, and run parallel to each other. Importations from another source, or later additions, appear in vi. 12–16 [19–23] (daily food offering of the High Priest; or, according to others, his offering of consecration: cf. *Th. Tijdschr.*, iv. 498 sq.); vii. 8–10 (additions concerning the priests' share in the burnt and food offerings, tacked on to *v.* 6, but out of place); vii. 22–27 (prohibition of fat and blood; cf. iii. 17); vii. 28–36 (express assignment of the breast and right shoulder of the thank offering to the priest).

d. The relation of *Lev.* i.–vii. to *Ex.* xxv.–xxix. is at once determined by the mention of the altar of incense (*Ex.* xxx. 1–10) in *Lev.* iv. (cf. n. 13). But besides this we note that in *Ex.* xxix. 10–14 (= *Lev.* viii. 14–17), in ordaining the trespass offering of Aaron and his sons, the burning of the victim's flesh is enjoined, but not the bringing of its blood into the sanctuary. It is other- [84] wise in *Lev.* iv. 5–7. Had this precept been incorporated by the author of *Ex.*

xxix. (and, *a fortiori*, if he himself had given it) he would not have departed
from it in *v.* 10–14. We must therefore regard *Lev.* iv. 3–12 as the description of the later and more developed practice. W e l l h a u s e n (xxii. 408 sq.)
draws the same conclusion from *Ex.* xxix. 15–18; 19–28; 31–34; 2, 3, 23, 24,
which regulate the burnt offering, thank offering, and food offering on occasion
of the consecration of the priests. Had the author of *Ex.* xxix., he argues,
intended to regulate the practice with regard to these kinds of offering, as is
done in *Lev.* i.–iii., he would not have described it so fully in these other
passages. But the validity of this reasoning is doubtful, for the description of
so exceptional a solemnity as the consecration of the first priests does not
make it superfluous to regulate the ordinary procedure. At any rate the
single discrepancy which W e l l h a u s e n notices proves more than the
many repetitions, especially in the case of a writer by no means distinguished
for conciseness.

    [18] Our point of departure is the subscription or colophon, vii. 37, 38. It
follows the order of vi., vii. [vi. 8–vii.], i. e. it places the thank offering last,
and moreover it presupposes vi. 12–16 [19–23], which it misunderstands as an
ordinance למלואים, i. e. concerning the High Priest's sacrifice of consecration. Now we read in *v.* 38 that Yahwè revealed these toras to Moses o n
M o u n t S i n a i. What I previously urged against the soundness of this
reading (*Godsdienst,* ii. 93 [*Rel. Isr.,* ii. 187]; *Th. Tijdschr.,* iv. 496) is
unfounded; for the concluding words, 'in the desert of Sinai,' mean that the
sacrificial cultus began there—to be continued, of course, afterwards. Thus,
if i.–vii. is derived, by the colophon, from a revelation on M o u n t S i n a i (cf.
Lev. xxv. 1; xxvi. 46), the statement in *Lev.* i. 1, that the laws were revealed
'from out the ôhel mo'éd' cannot be original, and must have received its
present form from the hand which inserted the whole collection here. And
indeed *Lev.* i. 1 shows evident signs of manipulation.—It is obvious from
n. 17 *d* that it cannot have been the author of *Ex.* xxv.–xxix. who incorporated
this group of laws.

    [19] We have seen already that *Lev.* vi., vii. [vi. 8–vii.] was written, or at
least collected, a s a s u p p l e m e n t to *Lev.* i.–v. [i.–vi. 7]. This is why,
for example, the ritual of the guilt offering is described (in vii. 1–7), and that
of the trespass offering not (in vi. 17–23 [24–30]). The latter had been completely handled by the author of *Lev.* iv., whereas the former had only been
dealt with by a reference to the trespass offering, *Lev.* v. 14–26 [v. 14–vi. 7].
From the precepts concerning the various trespass offerings in *Lev.* iv., a general
rule is deduced in vi. 23 [30].—But these are not the only passages in P with
which *Lev.* vi., vii. [vi. 8–vii.] stands in connection. Thus *Lev.* vi. 1–6 [8–13]
glances back at the institution of a morning and evening burnt offering in *Ex.*
xxix. 38–42 (*Num.* xxviii. 1–8), although, as we shall see (§ 15 n. 30), the
latter passage itself is not original. So, again, in *Lev.* vi. 12–16 [19–23] the
insertion of 'on the day that he is anointed' seems to be an attempt to give
another turn to the law about the d a i l y food offering of the High Priest
and to make it an injunction concerning the food offering of his c o n s e c r a-
t i o n (cf. vii. 37); for in its original form it was anterior to the ordinance

of a two-fold daily burnt offering, and was rightly perceived by the interpolator to be in contradiction with it. Subsequently the two laws were carried out side by side, and the interpolation was so explained as to lose its [85] force. Cf. Wellhausen, *Prolegomena*, p. 82, n. 2 [79, n. 2].—Finally, *Lev.* vii. 28–36 is expressly taken up into the *codex sacrificiorum* to emphasise an advance upon *Deut.* xviii. 3, the breast and the right shoulder being demanded as the priest's share. This demand seems to have been new when put forward in *Ex.* xxix. 27, 28, and is, therefore, repeated again in *Lev.* x. 14, 15 ; *Num.* xviii. 11, 18.

Dillmann, *Ex. u. Lev.*, p. 373 sqq., 438 sqq. takes an entirely different view of *Lev.* i.–v., vi. sq. [i.–vi. 7 ; vi. 8–vii.] from the one set forth in n. 17–19. In so far as his contention is not met by the facts indicated in n. 17–19, its consideration must be reserved till later on (§ 15, n. 6), since it is connected with views as to the priestly lawgiver's forerunners and sources which cannot be entered into here.

[20] 'The eighth day' of *Lev.* ix. 1 refers to the seven days' ceremony of consecration ordained in *Ex.* xxix. 35, but not described till *Lev.* viii. (*v.* 33–36). We have already remarked (p. 73) that *Ex.* xxxv.–xl. ; *Lev.* viii. has probably superseded a very short primitive notice of the execution of *Ex.* xxv. sqq. *Lev.* ix. originally stood in connection with this notice. See n. 21.

[21] According to the most natural meaning of *Lev.* x. 6, 7 the consecration of Aaron and his sons is still in progress ('for the oil of anointing of Yahwè is upon you '); whereas in *Lev.* ix. 1 it is already completed. The two former verses, therefore, are from another hand.—The general precept in *Lev.* x. 8–10 is tacked on to this insertion. It does not fit the historical context, and seems to be intended as a further preparation for the laws on uncleanness in *Lev.* xi.–xv.—*Lev.* x. 16–20 is admirably suited to throw light on the origin of the later amplifications. The trespass offering for the people is treated in *Lev.* ix. 15 exactly in the same way as that for the High Priest, *v.* 8–11, and this—as the personal presence of Moses would itself guarantee—was in perfect accordance with the law, closely conforming to the injunctions concerning the trespass offering at Aaron's consecration, *Ex.* xxix. 10–14 (*Lev.* viii. 14 17), and only including the sprinkling of the altar (of burnt offerings) and the burning of the flesh. But, judged by the standard of *Lev.* iv., this same performance was irregular, inasmuch as it omitted to bring the blood into the sanctuary, and to sprinkle the altar of incense. For this omission, therefore, the interpolator to whom we owe *Lev.* x. 16–20, and who occupied the stand-point of *Lev.* iv., might reasonably have blamed Aaron and his sons. But instead of that he assumes that they knew and followed *Lev.* iv., and therefore infers from the blood of the trespass offerings n o t being brought inside the sanctuary, that the flesh should not have been burnt either ; and that, this being so, the trespass offering for the people—though not the previous priestly one—ought to be eaten by the priests ; and he makes Moses rebuke them on this ground. It is true that this is not really in harmony with *Lev.* iv., but it is an easily explained inversion of the rule which was deduced from *Lev.* iv. in *Lev.* vi. 23 [30]. The writer of *Lev.* x. 16–20 acquiesced in it all

the more readily as it gave him an opportunity of explaining the motives of Aaron's (supposed) dereliction, and of making Moses tacitly accept them.

²² The successive filling in and amplification of the laws in *Lev.* xi.–xv. becomes manifest at once in *Lev.* xi. The colophon in *v.* 46, 47 shows that [86] this tora originally treated only of clean and unclean animals which respectively could and could not be eaten; *v.* 24–40, with the exception perhaps of *v.* 29, 30, is therefore a later addition. But *v.* 41 sqq. must also be regarded as a subsequent expansion; the parallel law in *Deut.* xiv. 3–20 is made up of three sections, *v.* 4–8; *v.* 9, 10; *v.* 11–20, answering to *Lev.* xi. 2–8, 9–12, 13–23, which makes it at least probable that the fourth section, *Lev.* xi. 41 sqq., was not committed to writing at the same time as the first three; and its position after *v.* 24–40, instead of after *v.* 13–23, strengthens the probability. —*Lev.* xii. 2 refers, as Wellhausen (xxii. 421) justly remarks, to xv. 19; and, therefore, xii. must be later than xv.—*Lev.* xiv. 33–53 (leprous houses) joins on to xiii. 47–59 (leprous garments), and would have immediately followed it had xiii., xiv. been written continuously. In the colophon, xiv. 55–57, the tora on the cleansing of the leper (xiv. 1–32) is not mentioned. Whether this pleads for the later origin of the section we will not stay to inquire.

From all that we have seen we should judge that *Lev.* xi.–xv. was a later insertion between x. and xvi. rather than a preexisting document incorporated by the author of these chapters; and we note further that xvi. 1 connects itself directly with x., and in no way suggests that such a mass of other laws has preceded the regulations for the day of atonement. The question is finally settled by the fact that in *Lev.* xi.–xv. the sacrificial precepts of *Lev.* i.–vii. are presupposed (e. g. in xii. 6–8; xiv. 12, etc.), whereas we have seen already that the author of *Lev.* ix.; x. 1–5; 12–15 was still unacquainted with them. See further § 15, n. 5.

²³ Starting from the position that the cleansing of the sanctuary and the atonement for the people are two distinct things, mixed up together in *Lev.* xvi. as it now stands, Oort, *Th. Tijdschr.*, x. 155–160, attempts to separate two elements, an original law to which *v.* 1–4, 11ᵇ–14, 16 (mostly), 18ᵃ, 19, 23, 24ᵃ, 25ᵃ, 29ᵃ belong, and the later expansions which include the remaining verses. In my opinion the cleansing of the sanctuary and that of the people—which surely belong to each other, since the uncleanness of the people pollutes the sanctuary (cf. *Ezek.* xlv. 18–20)—were alike dealt with by the original lawgiver himself. The attempt to separate the two has accordingly failed. *V.* 11ᵇ cannot follow immediately on *v.* 1–4; from *v.* 16, 19, it appears that the people had brought a trespass offering (which, however, is only mentioned in the verses which Oort cuts out, *v.* 5–11ᵃ, 15), whereas *v.* 24 tells us that there are likewise two burnt offerings, or, in other words, that *v.* 1–3 and *v.* 5 sqq. belong together. Nor is it possible to bring *v.* 29–34 into agreement with Oort's hypothesis.—The order of the ceremony in *Lev.* xvi. answers, *mutatis mutandis*, to *Lev.* ix.; while *Lev.* xiv. 6, 7, 52, 53 are analogous to *Lev.* xvi. 20ᵇ–22, the sending away of the goat 'for Azazel;' so that from this point of view likewise we find nothing to militate against the unity and originality of *Lev.* xvi.

Ex. xxx. 10 must be regarded as an amplification of *Lev.* xvi. ; or, if not, then it rests upon a misconception of the precepts contained in the latter ; for *Lev.* xvi. never mentions an altar of incense, even in *v.* 14, where it could not have been passed over if the author had known of it. The writer therefore occupies the position of *Ex.* xxv.–xxix., and t h e altar which he mentions is the altar of burnt offerings. Cf. n. 13.

The chapters we have next to consider, *Lev.* xvii.–xxvi., though [87] in general form and substance belonging to P, nevertheless differ considerably from the two priestly strata which we have discovered hitherto, and most recently in *Lev.* i.–xvi. The difference affects the language and general style, and, occasionally, the substance. It is not continuous, however, for here and there— either in whole sections or in detached verses and phrases, and especially in *Lev.* xvii., xxi. sq., xxiii.–xxv.—we recognise the peculiarities of the priestly passages already dealt with. All these phenomena are explained by the supposition that a n older stratum of priestly legislation lies at the basis of *Lev.* xvii.–xxvi., and that when it was introduced into its present connection it was fused together with more recent ordinances, similar in character to those of *Ex.* xxv.–xxxi., xxxv.–xl., and *Lev.* i.–xvi., or was worked over in their spirit. Indicating this older legislation by P^1, the historico-legislative work that begins with *Gen.* i.–ii. 4^a by P^2, and the later amplifications and recensions by P^3, P^4, we may say that in *Lev.* xvii.–xxvi. P^1 has been combined with fragments in the style of P^2 and his followers, or, at any rate, modified in that direction [24].

The complete proof of this hypothesis cannot be given till later on. But its general correctness is indicated, even at the present stage of our inquiry, by the following facts : —

(1) *Lev.* xxvi. 3–45 is clearly the conclusion of a code of priestly character, which the colophon in *v.* 46 declares to have been revealed to Moses by Yahwè 'on Mount Sinai' [25];

(2) the resemblances to *Lev.* xxvi. 3–45, in style and conception, which constantly recur in *Lev.* xvii. 1–xxvi. 2, render

it highly probable that the code of which we possess the conclusion in the first-named chapter (P¹) has been partially or
wholly preserved in those that precede it²⁶;

(3) in *Lev.* xvii. I–xxvi. 2 we occasionally find the char-
[88] acteristics of P², P³, etc., asserting themselves very distinctly
along side of the peculiarities of P¹, whether in independent
passages or in smaller additions to P¹ ²⁷;

(4) the mutual relations of P¹ on the one side, and of
P², P³, etc. on the other, hardly allow any other supposition than that P¹ represents an earlier stage of the
priestly legislation²⁸.

²⁴ The difference between *Lev.* xvii., xviii.–xx., xxvi. and the other priestly
formations was observed so long ago as by K n o b e l; and E w a l d and
N ö l d e k e explained it, at any rate as far as *Lev.* xvii.–xx. goes, from the
supposed use of older documents by the author of *Leviticus*; the hypothesis
put forward in the text is defended, though with differences of detail, by
G r a f (*Gesch. Büch.*, p. 75–83); myself (*Godsdienst*, ii. 58 sqq., 90 sqq. [*Rel.
Isr.*, ii. 151 sqq., 183 sqq.]); C o l e n s o (*Pentateuch*, vi. I sqq.); K a y s e r
(op. cit., p. 64–79, 176 sqq.), and W e l l h a u s e n (xxii. 421–444). The question
of the date and authorship of the legislation underlying *Lev.* xvii.–xxvi. will
be dealt with later on (§ 15), when we shall also have occasion to consider
D i l l m a n n 's hypothesis (*Ex. und Lev.*, p. 533 sqq.) concerning its origin.
At present we have only to show that *Lev.* xvii.–xxvi. b e l o n g s t o P,
and i n w h a t s e n s e it does so.

²⁵ The repeated mention of ' my ordinances, commandments, and statutes '
(*v.* 3, 15, 43), and on one occasion 'all t h e s e commandments' (*v.* 14),
can only be understood as referring to the preceding laws. Their priestly
character is evident from *v.* 11, 12 (Yahwè's dwelling, מִשְׁכָּן, conceived as
a portable tent, in the midst of Israel); *v.* 30, 31 (unlawful worship of
Yahwè, high value attached to sacrifice); *v.* 34, 35, 43 (disregard of 'my
sabbaths' one of Israel's chief sins). It is obvious how strongly analogy
pleads for this view of *Lev.* xxvi. 3–45; it would be very strange if this
discourse were not a concluding exhortation similar to *Ex.* xxiii. 20–33 and
Deut. xxviii. to which it bears a close resemblance, for instance, in its progress
from promises to threats. It is but natural, then, to regard *v.* 46 as the colophon of the code to which *Lev.* xxvi. 3–45 belongs (cf. *Deut.* xxviii. 69 [xxix. I]).
The revelation to Moses ' on Mount Sinai ' appears again in xxv. I, but as it
is likewise found in *Lev.* vii. 38 (n. 18) and xxvii. 34, this detail is not
decisive for the connection between xxv. and xxvi.

²⁶ It is probable *a priori* that something beyond the concluding exhortation of the code in question has been preserved; and the universally recog-

nised differences between *Lev.* xvii. sqq. and i.–xvi. at once suggest that we possess the remains of it in the first-named group of chapters; and the reality, at any rate in part, of the connection thus suggested, is demonstrated by the following points of agreement:

'I (am) Yahwè,' 'I Yahwè (am) your god,' and other more extended formulæ of like import occur in xviii. 2, 4–6, 21, 30; xix. 2–4, 10, 12, 14, 16, 18, 25, 28, 30–32, 34, 36, 37; xx. 7, 8, 24; xxi. 8, 12, 15, 23; xxii. 2, 3, 8, 9, 16, 30–33; xxiii. 22, 43; xxiv. 22; xxv. 17, 38, 55; xxvi. 1, 2, 13, 44, 45;

הלך בחקות xviii. 3; xx. 23; xxvi. 3;   [89]

עשה in conjunction with שמר, xviii. 4; xix. 37; xx. 8, 22; xxvi. 3;

חקותי ומשפטי, xviii. (4) 26; xix. 37; xx. 22; xxv. 18; xxvi. 15, 43;

נתן פניו, xvii. 10; xx. 3, 6; xxvi. 17;

והכרתי, xvii. 10; xx. 3, 5, 6; xxvi. 30;

'My,' or 'Yahwè's sabbaths,' 'its (the land's)' or 'your sabbaths,' xix. 3, 30; xxiii. 38; xxvi. 2, 34, 35, 43 (which last verses agree in c o n t e n t s likewise with xxv. 1–7, 18–22).

The chapters which are thus connected with *Lev.* xxvi. 3–45, and especially *Lev.* xviii.–xx., have a number of other words and expressions in common which are not met with elsewhere in the Pentateuch, and which therefore bear additional testimony to their separate origin; cf. D i l l m a n n, *Ex. u. Lev.*, p. 535, 540 sq.

[27] This is the case, for instance, in *Lev.* xvii. 4–6, 9, (where 'the entrance of the ôhel mo'éd,' at any rate in *v.* 4–6, is superfluous, not to say disturbing, and is apparently due to the influence of *Ex.* xxv. sqq.); in *Lev.* xix. 21, 22 (which obviously announces itself as a later addition to *v.* 20, in the spirit of *Lev.* v. 14–26 [v. 14–vi. 7], and is characterised by the 'entrance of the ôhel mo'éd'); in the texts which assume that the priesthood has been conferred on Aaron and his sons and that they have been consecrated to the office, such as *Lev.* xvii. 2 (introduction to the ordinances that follow); xxi. 1, 17, 21, 24; xxii. 2, 4, 18 (all which verses follow the uniform usage of *Ex.* xxv. sqq., whereas *Lev.* xxi. 10 ['the priest, who is great above his brethren'] departs from it, though agreeing with *Ex.* xxv. sqq.—as does *v.* 12 likewise—with respect to the anointing of the High Priest); in *Lev.* xxi. 23 (where 'the veil' is mentioned); in xxii. 29, 30 (where, as in *Lev.* vii. 15–18, the praise offerings must be eaten on the very day on which they are made, whereas in *Lev.* xix. 5, 8, the thank offerings—of which the praise offering is a species— may be consumed the following day); in *Lev.* xxiii. 1–8, 23–25, 26–32, 33– 38 (all which verses—except *v.* 3, which is shown by *v.* 38, 'beside the sabbaths of Yahwè,' to be a later addition—belong to each other and form a tolerably complete system of festivals, provided with a superscription *v.* 1, 2, and a colophon *v.* 37, 38 of its own, and agreeing in contents and terminology with the laws of phésach and maççôth in *Ex.* xii., and of the day of atonement in *Lev.* xvi., while standing off with some sharpness from the sections in *v.* 9–22 and 39–44, which latter clearly betrays its derivation from some other source by the very position it occupies after the colophon, *v.* 37, 38; see further, n. 28); in *Lev.* xxiv. 1–4, 5–9 (two passages which

appear to be strangely out of place and are manifestly connected with the ordinances of *Ex.* xxv.-xxxi. and the account of their execution); in *Lev.* xxiv. 10-23 (and especially in the framework of this passage, *v.* 10-14, 23, [cf. *Num.* ix. 6-14; xv. 32-36; xxvii. 1-11; xxxvi.], which is evidently not original, but derived from *v.* 16); in *Lev.* xxv. 8-17, 23-55 *passim* (most obviously in *v.* 9 'on the day of atonement,' and *v.* 23-34, the Levitical cities, cf. *Num.* xxxv. 1-8, but also in other verses, as will be shown more in detail in n. 28 and in § 15, n. 5).

[90]   28 The mutual relations between P¹ and P², P³, etc., are not always equally clear; in some cases there is room for more than one explanation, and in others—in *Lev.* xviii.-xx., for instance—parallel passages in P, which would enable us to form an opinion as to the relative antiquity of the different elements, are wanting. The following points, however, present no ambiguity:—

⊦ *a. Lev.* xvii. 3-7 ordains that all oxen and sheep which the Israelites desire to slaughter must be brought to the sanctuary and eaten there as thank offerings. The text of these verses is mixed (n. 27), but Kayser (*Jahrb. f. p. Theologie*, 1881, p. 541-544) attempts in vain so to emend them, by aid of the LXX., and so to analyse them into their two constituent elements as to get rid of the injunction to slaughter beasts nowhere but at the sanctuary. The great objection to his treatment of the passage is that he makes the amalgamation of two very ordinary precepts result, as if by accident, in the enunciation of a commandment which attaches itself to and developes the ancient usage of the people. The commandment in question was only possible of execution as long as the sanctuaries of Yahwè were so numerous that everyone could find one close at hand. But in this passage it is given in connection with the one only sanctuary—apparently by someone who was acquainted, at least by tradition, with the ancient practice, and desired to maintain it still. In P², etc., slaughtering is left entirely free (cf. *Gen.* ix. 3, 4; *Lev.* vii. 22-27), and the thank offering is implicitly ranked amongst the ordinary sacrifices by the assertion of the priest's right to a share in it. This latter conception is the more recent. See further, § 14, n. 6.

b. Lev. xix. 5-8 chronologically precedes *Lev.* vii. 15-18 (with which *Lev.* xxii. 29, 30 is parallel; cf. n. 27), for had the author of *Lev.* xix. been acquainted with the distinction drawn in *Lev.* vii. between the praise offerings and the other thank offerings he could not have issued his precept without qualification.

c. The festal code to which *Lev.* xxiii. 9-22, 39-44 belong, is earlier than the one with which they are now connected (cf. n. 27). In the latter, not only the month, but the day of the month on which the feast falls is determined (*v.* 5, 6, 27, 34), and the feast of tabernacles lasts eight days (*v.* 36). On the other hand, in *v.* 9-22 the sheaf of the first-fruits (and, seven weeks after, the sacrifice of the firstlings) is fixed for 'the day after the sabbath' (*v.* 11, 15, 16), i. e. the first day of the harvest week (*v.* 10), which of course would fall sometimes on one and sometimes on another day of the first month. Thus the feast still depends on the actual cultivation of the soil, which is certainly an earlier usage than its

fixed celebration on a given day ; but see further § 15, n. 8. So again
v. 39–44 originally contained the simple injunction that 'the feast of
Yahwè' (the old name of 'Tabernacles') should be celebrated 'in the
seventh month' (*v.* 41), 'when you have gathered in the produce of the
land' (*v.* 39). It was not till afterwards, when *v.* 39–44 was united
with P², or still later, that the fifteenth day of the seventh month was
inserted in *v.* 39. It is equally clear that the feast of tabernacles lasts
s e v e n days, according to the writer of *v.* 39–44 (see *v.* 39, 40, 41), and
that the eighth day, together with the sabbath observance on the first,
has been transferred by interpolation from *v.* 35, 36 into *v.* 39. In both
respects the priority belongs to *v.* 39–44, as will be further shown in
§ 15, n. 8.

   d. On the mutual relations of the elements of *Lev.* xxv., cf. K a y s e r,
op. cit. p. 75–77 ; W e l l h. xxii. 436–439. *V.* 1–7, on the sabbatical year, [91]
together with *v.* 18–22, on the same subject (out of place, therefore, since
v. 8–17 deals with the year of jubilee) certainly belongs to P¹. It would
be simplest to assign the w h o l e law on the year of jubilee, *v.* 8–17, 23–
55 to P², but we are prevented from doing so by traces of the language
and style of P¹ in *v.* 14–17, 35–38, and some other verses. It is probable,
therefore, that P¹ contained a law on 'the year of releasing' (שנת הדרור),
but it does not follow that it fell on the fiftieth year, and it may not have
differed from the seventh or sabbatical year ; see further, § 15, n. 4, 18.

   The regulations concerning the consecration of persons and
things in *Lev.* xxvii. presuppose the law of the year of
jubilee (*Lev.* xxv. 8–55), and are written with reference to
it. They do not belong to P¹, however, but to P³, or to
still later priestly formations. Their connection with *Lev.*
xxv. 8–55 may have been the occasion of their incorporation
in this context. The colophon, *v.* 34, is an imitation of
Lev. xxvi. 46 [29].

   There can be no question that *Num.* i.–x. 28 belongs to P.
In the historical sections (i.–iv., vii., viii. 5–26; ix. 15—x. 28)
the construction of the tabernacle and the consecration of
the priests are throughout assumed [30], and the laws in
v., vi., viii. 1–4 ; ix. 1–14, are closely connected with the
priestly ordinances we know already [31]. On the other hand,
it is clear that *Num.* i.–x. 28, as it stands, does not come
from P². The laws referred to above manifestly belong to
P³, or still later formations [32]. The narrative, too, has been

worked over, as viii. 5–26 shows beyond the possibility of
reasonable doubt [33]. How far this manipulation was carried
it is impossible to determine with certainty. Wellhausen
thinks we can only assign i. 1–16, 48–54; ii.; iii. 5–13;
ix. 15—x. 28 to P², inasmuch as the remaining sections
(i. 17–47; iii. 1–4, 14–51; iv.; vii.) contain repetitions
which elaborate and exaggerate the representations of P², and
must therefore be regarded as secondary, like *Num.* viii. 5–26,
in which the same phenomena appear [34]. But it is just the
question whether the author of P² is himself characterised by
any such sobriety as is here supposed, and whether, at any
[92] rate in *Num.* i. 17–47; iii. 14–51, and iv., it is not he
himself who has expanded his own ideas on the camp in
the desert and the service of the Levites beyond what was
strictly necessary [35]. In view of the results of our examination of P in *Exodus* and *Leviticus* we cannot be surprised
that we are unable to answer this question with certainty [36].

---

[29] Note the year of jubilee in *v.* 17, 18, 21, 23, 24; and the verb מוּך in
v. 8, only in *Lev.* xxv. 25, 35, 39, 47 besides. The later origin of the law is
shown by its whole contents : the idea of accurately determining the value of
persons (*v.* 3 sqq.) and things (*v.* 9 sqq.) is certainly of relatively late origin,
and is consequent upon difficulties that had arisen in practice. Moreover in
v. 32 tithes o f t h e c a t t l e are required—heightening the demand made in
Num. xviii. 21–32 (cf. § 15, n. 30 *c.*) On *v.* 34 cf. § 16, n. 15.

[30] Yahwè speaks to Moses ' in the ôhel mo'éd,' i. 1, the existence of which
is likewise constantly assumed in i. 49 sqq.; ii.–iv. *passim*; vii. etc. The
consecration of Aaron and his sons is referred to *passim*, and reference is
made to *Lev.* x. 1–5 in *Num.* iii. 1–4, and throughout the regulations concerning the work of the Levites.

[31] *Num.* v. 1–4, ejection of the leprous and unclean from the camp, is connected with *Lev.* xiii., xv.;—*Num.* v. 6–10, on the guilt offering, serves to
complete *Lev.* v. 14–26 [v. 14–vi. 7];—*Num.* v. 11–31, the law of the ordeal of
the wife suspected by her husband, presupposes (*v.* 15) the ordinance concerning the food offering, *Lev.* ii. etc.;—*Num.* vi. 1–21, on the Nazirite's vow, rests
on the general precepts as to sacrifices, *Lev.* i.–vii.;—*Num.* vi. 22–26, the
priestly blessing, is a more detailed account of one of the official duties of the
priests (cf. *Lev.* ix. 22);—*Num.* viii. 1–4, on the golden lamp-stand, supplements the laws as to the ôhel mo'éd and the sacred utensils;—*Num.* ix. 1–14,
celebration of the passover in the second month by those who are prevented

by uncleanness from taking part in the ordinary celebration, provides for a case not dealt with in the earlier laws on the subject (*Ex.* xii.; *Lev.* xxiii.); the language of the historical heading *v.* 1–5 quite agrees with that of the laws.

[32] This appears clearly enough, with respect to most of the laws, from the mere summary of their contents given in n. 31, and is thereby rendered probable with respect to the others too. Note, more especially, that *Num.* v. 1–4 is really nothing more than the application of *Lev.* xiii. and xv. (and perhaps we should add *Num.* xix.) to 'the camp,' the disposition of which was minutely described in *Num.* i.–iv.; that *v.* 5–10 deals with a question that might be raised by the law of the guilt offering, and decides it i n t h e i n t e r e s t o f t h e p r i e s t, who becomes the substitute of the injured man, when the latter is not forthcoming, and receives the compensation; that the strange position of *v.* 11–31 is perhaps best explained by the supposition that it once existed as an independent tora (cf. *v.* 29–31) and was subsequently incorporated here, together with the preceding and succeeding toras; that the second part, especially, of the law of the Nazirite's vow (vi. 9–12, 13–19), must be later than the ordinances in *Lev.* i.–vii., to which there is a very marked reference [93] in *v.* 20; that *Num.* viii. 1–4, both in position and contents, is closely parallel to *Lev.* xxiv. 1–4, 5–9 (cf. n. 27); that *Num.* ix. 1–14 does not quite fit the historical framework, since *v.* 1–5 places us on the fourteenth day of the f i r s t month, whereas in *Num.* i. 1 we had already reached the first day of the s e c o n d month; this departure from the chronology—which has doubtless caused the corruption of the text in *v.* 2, 3—indicates the later insertion of this passage, which is really nothing but an introduction to the *novella* on *Ex.* xii. contained in *v.* 6–14.—In considering all this we must remember that the laws which are presupposed and developed in *Num.* v., vi., viii. 1–4, ix. 1–14 have themselves been shown to be later additions to P², so that the result holds *a fortiori* of these appendices.

[33] We call attention to this passage first, because the results it yields are c e r t a i n. *Num.* viii. 23–26 directly contradicts *Num.* iv. 3, 23, 30, etc., and probably contains a l a t e r modification of that law (cf. § 3, n. 20) which may have been necessitated by the small number of the Levites. In 1 *Chron.* xxiii. 24 sqq. David is made to fix the beginning of their time of service at a still earlier age. Now, though *Num.* viii. 5–22 is not directly connected with *v.* 23–26, yet it falls under the same judgment. It is an insipid repetition and exaggeration of the account of the separation of the Levites for the service of the sanctuary in *Num.* iii. and iv. If the author of these last-named chapters had supposed that the Levites, before entering on their duties, had to be purified, and presented to Yahwè by תנופה, like a sacrifice, he would not have passed it over in silence; for he represents them in iii. and iv. as already entrusted with the task which in that case they would only have become qualified to undertake in viii. 5–22. This pericope, then, must be a later addition, as we might have supposed from its setting, viii. 1–4, 23–26. Its author observed that a formal consecration of the Levites, analogous to that of the priests (*Lev.* viii.), was not recorded, though it seemed to be neither unsuitable nor superfluous. This defect he supplied.

[34] Cf. Wellhausen, xxii. 413, 448–451. His objections, the relative weight of which I am far from denying, are enumerated in n. 35, together with what may be said against them.

[35] It is urged against i. 17–47 that it may be borrowed from ii., including *v.* 44, 46 (cf. ii. 32) and *v.* 47 (cf. ii. 33); that the order of the tribes does not agree with i. 5–16, but with ii., and that *v.* 48–54 ought not to follow the census, but, as its contents show, to precede it. On the other hand, it is not unnatural that the order in which the tribes encamped should be followed by anticipation even in i., that i. 46, 47 should be repeated after the description of the encampment, or that *v.* 48–54 should be placed after the census, since strict logic would otherwise have required that it should precede *v.* 5–16 also (no head of the tribe of Levi being mentioned). We cannot be surprised that in a f i c t i t i o u s narrative the succession of details should be open to criticism. Moreover—and this is the chief argument in support of i. 17–47—if i. 48–ii. 34 followed immediately upon i. 1–16 then there would be no account at all of t h e c e n s u s i t s e l f, for in ii. it is assumed.

[94] With regard to iii. 1–4 Wellhausen observes (xxii. 413) that *v.* 3 extends the process of anointing to the sons of Aaron, in contradiction with *Ex.* xxix. (cf. n. 12, 13). In iii. 5–iv. 49 he considers iii. 5–13 alone to be primitive; iv. 1–33 is a repetition, in slightly modified order and with much exaggeration, of the precautions of iii. 14–39 against the contact of the Levites with the sacred vessels. In iv. 34–49 we have another census of the three Levitical clans, which may likewise have been manufactured out of iii. 14–39. In iii. 14–39 itself (and the connected *v.* 40–51) we have the elaboration of the main idea of iii. 5–13, which was all that the original author (P²) had given ; the earliest interpolator r e p e a t s, in iii. 14 sqq., the command that had been given once already in *v.* 5 sqq., and thereby betrays himself. Add to this that (as Wellhausen had previously noted) iii. 31 ; iv. 11 mention the golden altar of incense, and iv. 16 mentions the incense and oil of anointing (cf. *Ex.* xxx. 1–10 ; 22–33 ; 34–38, and n. 13).—Against this may be urged that iii. 5–13 contains a commandment simply, and no kind of record of its execution, and that it would be more than strange if P² had given the numbers of the other tribes, but not those of the Levites, and had omitted to give any more detailed account of the duties of the latter. The objections to iii. 14–iv. 49, a s w e n o w h a v e t h e m, are not imaginary, especially in the case of iv. But this does not justify us in simply erasing them, for what would then remain cannot be the complete narrative of P².

W e l l h a u s e n ' s objections to the originality of *Num.* vii., which I simply endorse, are drawn from *v.* 1, 10, 84, 88, where the gifts of the heads of tribes are brought into connection with the consecration of the altar, i. e. with an event which preceded *Num.* i. 1 in order of time. *Num.* vii., then, is out of place, and must consequently be attributed—not to the author of the precepts in *Ex.* xxv. sqq., but—to a later priestly writer, who desired to introduce the heads of the tribes, mentioned in *Num.* i. 5–16, as models of liberality towards the sanctuary which his own contemporaries would do well to copy. Moreover P² is never quite so monotonous and wearisome as the author of *Num.* vii.

[36] We must bear in mind (1) that we no longer hold the thread of P² in our hands, for in *Lev.* xvii.–xxvi. we have found P¹ welded together with P² and later priestly fragments, and are unable to say what position was occupied in P² by the law of festivals and of the year of jubilee, fragments of which we have discovered respectively in *Lev.* xxiii. and *Lev.* xxv.; whence results an uncertainty that prevents our drawing any inferences from the plan of P²; (2) that, even in *Exodus* and *Leviticus*, P² is not only s u p p l e m e n t e d by, but also w e l d e d   t o g e t h e r with, or s u p p l a n t e d by, P³, P⁴, etc. In other words P² has been not only interpolated but recast again and again. It is really no more than natural, therefore, that in *Num.* i. 1–x. 28 we should come upon passages which can neither be granted nor denied to P². The relation is too complicated to admit of so simple a statement, and from its very nature it is sometimes impossible to disentangle.

The wanderings of Israel in the desert are treated very briefly in P, as in the other strata of the Pentateuch. To P² we owe one of the two accounts of the despatch of the [95] spies and its consequences, which are now welded together in *Num.* xiii., xiv., and an account of the revolt of Korah and his party against Moses and Aaron, which was subsequently united into a single whole with a story of Dathan's and Abiram's revolt against Moses, in *Num.* xvi. [xvi. 1–35]. This story of Korah is continued—still from P²—in *Num.* xvii. [xvi. 36—xvii.], and followed in *Num.* xviii. by a law concerning the revenues of the priests and Levites. In *Num.* xiii. xiv., as well as in xvi. xvii., P²—whether before or after its fusion with the narratives now united to it—has been expanded by later priestly writers [37].

By the side of these historical or historico-legislative passages we find a few detached laws in *Num.* xv. and xix., which seem to stand on the same footing as the other priestly ordinances which form the more recent strata of P—those in *Num.* v. and vi. for instance [38].

[37] Cf. *Th. Tijdschr.*, xi. 545–566 ; xii. 139–162, where the following results are obtained: *Num.* xiii. 1–17ᵃ, 21, 25, 26ᵃ, 32 ; xiv. 1ᵃ, 2ᵃ, 3, 5–7, 10, 26–38, and again *Num.* xvi. 1 (in part), 2 (in part), 3–11, 13–15ᵃ, 16–24, 27ᵃ, 35, belong to P. All this is, in the main, from P², but his narrative has been expanded in *Num.* xiv. 26–38, though quite in his own spirit ; and one of his followers (P³ or P⁴) has so far modified his representation of Korah's revolt, in

Num. xvi. 1, 8–11, 16–18, as to make Korah and his two hundred and fifty associates into L e v i t e s who covet an equality of priestly functions with Aaron and his sons. *Num.* xvii. 1–5 [xvi. 36–40] is likewise from the hand of this later writer, whereas the rest of xvii. [xvi. 41–xvii. 13] and the whole of xviii. belong to P². The proofs of these statements are given in the essay referred to. Further, cf. § 16, n. 12.

³⁸ The passages in question contain the following regulations :—

Num. xv. 1–16, on the measure of the food offerings that must respectively accompany the various burnt and thank offerings,—evidently a *novella* to *Lev.* ii., intended to regulate what was there left to the free will of the sacrificer or to usage. The heading, *v.* 2, coincides with *Lev.* xix. 23 ; xxiii. 10 ; xxv. 2 ; and *v.* 14–16 extends the precept to the גרים (cf. *Lev.* xvii. 8, 10, 13 ; xxiv. 22).

V. 17–21, offering to Yahwè of first-fruits of barley meal. *V.* 18 coincides with *v.* 2 and indicates a common origin of the two laws.

V. 22–31 on the trespass offering of the community and the individual. This law differs from *Lev.* iv. in demanding, for the involuntary trespasses of the community, an ox for a burnt offering and a goat for a trespass offering, instead of an ox for a trespass offering (*Lev.* iv. 13–21), and perhaps we should add, in containing no separate regulations concerning the high priest and the [96] nasi (*Lev.* iv. 3–13, 22–26). The tone of *v.* 31, too, differs from that of the laws in *Lev.* i.–vii. and reminds us of P¹ in *Lev.* xvii.–xxvi.

V. 32–36, stoning the sabbath-breaker. This passage shows its kinship to the framework in *Lev.* xxiv. 10-14, 23 (cf. n. 27) by the use of such words as משמר and פרש. Like *Ex.* xxxi. 12–17 ; xxxv. 1–3, it is a *novella* on the observance of the sabbath.

V. 37–41, the çiçîth on the garment as a reminder of the commands of Yahwè ; cf. above, § 5, n. 12.

W e l l h a u s e n ' s conjecture (xxii. 447) that these ordinances were collected and incorporated by the same hand that worked over P¹, in *Lev.* xvii.–xxvi., and inserted it in its present place, is strongly supported by the phenomena indicated above.

. *Num.* xix. 1–13, 14–22, the ashes of the red heifer, and their use as a means of purification. See W e l l h a u s e n, xxii. 447 sq. He rightly regards *v.* 14–22 (with the heading זאת התורה) as an appendix to *v.* 1–13, and further notes the peculiarity of form and contents of the law. It can only be taken as a later modification of the original demand that the restoration of the un-clean must be accompanied with a trespass offering (cf. *Lev.* v. 2, 3). If the author of *Lev.* v. 1–13 or xv. had been acquainted with *Num.* xix. he would have referred to it, or inserted it after his own ordinance. The present position of *Num.* xix.—as of *Num.* xv.—out of all connection with what precedes and follows, is enough in itself to rouse the suspicion that n e i t h e r chapter is taken from P² ; for the latter follows a regular plan in which each law has its proper motive, as is once more illustrated in the last of the sections assigned to P² in the text, viz. *Num.* xviii. (introduced by xvi. 27 sq. [12 sq.]).

In the remaining chapters of Numbers (xx.–xxxvi.), which transport us to the fortieth year after the exodus (§ 4, n. 17), we find in the first place a number of laws which must certainly be assigned to P. Such are xxviii., xxix. (on the festival offerings); xxx. (on the vows of married and unmarried women); xxxiv. 1–15, 16–29 (on the boundaries of Canaan, and the partition of the land, to which the section xxxiii. 50–56 belongs as an introduction); xxxv. 1–8 (on the Levitical cities); xxxv. 9–34 (on the cities of refuge and on unintentional homicide). Again, the half narrative, half legislative pieces xxvii. 1–11; xxxvi. (the daughters of Çelophechad and the inheritance of daughters), and xxxi. (the war against Midian, the division of booty, and the preservation of cleanness during war) likewise belong to P. We reckon xxvii. 1–11; xxxiii. 50—xxxvi., amongst the original components of P² [39], while the other passages are later additions, as appears from position, contents, or character, as [97] the case may be [40].

It is *a priori* probable that, in the second place, the historical framework into which these laws fit, and to which they refer, has been preserved in *Num.* xx. sqq. And in point of fact we at once recognise in xx. 22–29; xxi. 10, 11; xxii. 1; xxv. 6–19 [6–18]; xxvi. and xxvii. 12–23, pieces of P², here and there, especially in xxv. 6–19 and xxvi. (*v.* 9–11), not quite untampered with, but elsewhere preserved in their original form [41]. Moreover, we gather from references in *Num.* xx. 24; xxvii. 14 (*Deut.* xxxii. 51), that P² contained an account of the rebelliousness of Moses and Aaron at Kadesh; and xxxiv. 13–15; xxxv. 14, assume a previous statement concerning the settlement of Reuben, Gad, and half Manasseh in the Transjordanic district. The former is preserved in *Num.* xx. 1–13, and the latter in *Num.* xxxii., but it is not easy to separate them from the other narratives with which they are now welded [42].

H

Ch. xxxiii. 1–49, the list of stations in the journey through the desert, which, according to *v.* 2, was written down by Moses himself (§ 2, n. 2), presupposes the accounts in P², but it also assumes the other accounts of Israel's abode in the desert, and can only have been drawn up and inserted by R⁴³.

The account in P² of the death of Moses, for which *Num.* xxvii. 12–23 prepares us, is not now to be found in the book of *Numbers*, but is preserved in *Deut.* xxxii. 48–52, and xxxiv., though united with matter drawn from other sources⁴⁴. Originally these pericopes followed immediately after *Num.* xxxvi., so that the whole of *Deuteronomy* must be considered with reference to P² as an interpolation. The colophon in *Num.* xxxvi. 13 may be contemporaneous with the incorporation of *Deuteronomy*⁴⁵.

---

[39] All these laws share the obvious characteristic of fitting into a historical context. In *Num.* xxvii. 1–11 the daughters of Çelophechad (cf. xxvi. 33) come to Moses and Eleazar (cf. xx. 22–29), and speak of Korah's rebellion, their account of which agrees with that of P² in *Num.* xvi. [xvi. 1–35] (cf. n. 37); and the decision promulgated in connection with their application rests [98] on the same motive as the year of the jubilee, viz. the retention of the ownership of the soil in the family of the original proprietor.—*Num.* xxxvi. 1–12 serves as a supplement to the law just mentioned, and restricts the marriage of heiress daughters to their own tribe; in *v.* 4 the year of jubilee is expressly mentioned. This supplement might, of course, be due to a later legislator; but the two laws are so completely in harmony with each other that there is nothing to prevent our assigning them to the same author.— The ordinances in *Num.* xxxiii. 50–xxxv. all stand in immediate connection with the approaching settlement in Canaan and join on to laws and narratives which have been (or will shortly be) assigned to P². Note Eleazar and Joshua (xxxiv. 17; cf. xx. 22–29; xxvii. 12–23); Caleb as nasi of Judah (xxxiv. 19; cf. xiii. 6); the recognition of the special position of the Levites and the provision for their support to which xxxv. 1–8 bears testimony; the exalted rank in the state and over his brethren taken by the High Priest, xxxv. 25, 28, 32, 'who is anointed with the sacred oil' (cf. n. 13). To all this must be added the linguistic usage in these laws, which in no way departs from that of P²—unless it be in xxxiii. 50–56, and especially *v.* 52, 55, 56, which remind us of *Lev.* xvii.–xxvi. (cf. מסכה משכית‎, במה‎, in *v.* 52, and the tone and style of *v.* 55, 56). But inasmuch as P¹ precedes P², the latter—to whom *v.* 54, for instance, is certainly due—may in this passage have conformed to his predecessor's usage. See, however, § 16, n. 12.

[40] That *Num.* xxviii. sq. and xxx. stand in no kind of connection with the progress of events is obvious. They would be in their place after *Lev.* xxiii. and xxvii. As regards *Num.* xxviii. sq., in particular, note that the author of this catalogue of festivals presupposes the law of P[2] which is now welded together with another law, from P[1], in *Lev.* xxiii. (cf. n. 27). He goes beyond P[2], however, for he fixes the amount of every festal offering—which P[2] had left to the liberality of the community or to usage—with such minuteness as to prescribe a special sacrifice for each day of the feast of tabernacles (*Num.* xxix. 12–39). We gather, then, that he is later than the author of this other law, in *Lev.* xxiii. In complete harmony with this view we find him beginning with a precept as to the tamîd, *Num.* xxviii. 3–8, taken from *Ex.* xxix. 38–42, to which he refers in *v.* 6. Such an attempt to deal exhaustively with the subject of the communal sacrifices betrays the lateness of the passage. —I have rested nothing on the relation of *Num.* xxviii. 27–29 to *Lev.* xxiii. 18–20; for it is almost certain that the latter text has been interpolated from the former, and originally simply enjoined a thank offering of two lambs and an אשה, not further defined (cf. *Lev.* xxiii. 8, 25, 27, 36); when the interpolation was made, or still later, 'an ox, two rams' was accidentally or designedly altered into 'two oxen, a ram.' Cf. especially Dillm. *Ex. u. Lev.*, p. 591.

Num. xxx. (except *v.* 1 [xxix. 40], which seems to belong to xxviii. sq.) serves to supply an omission in the laws concerning vows (*Lev.* xxvii.; cf. *Num.* vi. 1–21) which, in all probability, had only been discovered by experience. Hence it would follow that this ordinance, together with the preceding one, belongs to the class of *novellæ*.

On the position of *Num.* xxxi., W e l l h a u s e n (xxi. 582) should be consulted. It appears from *v.* 2 that the author was acquainted with *Num.* xxvii. 12–23, [99] and intended his narrative for the place it now occupies. But the writer of *Num.* xxvii. 12–23 himself cannot have meant to make the punishment of the Midianites precede the death of Moses; and had he mentioned it at all he would have brought it in after xxv., and would have placed the announcement of the death of Moses later (on xxv. 16–19 [16–18] see n. 41). The suspicion thus roused that *Num.* xxxi. is the work of one of the followers of P[2], seems to me to be fully justified by its contents. The peculiarities of P[2] are much exaggerated, for example, in *v.* 19 sqq. (the purification of the executioners), and in *v.* 25 sqq. (the very minute regulations concerning the division of booty). The chapter is parallel with *Num.* vii., for example, (n. 35).

[41] In *Num.* xx. 22–29; xxvii. 12–23, which, moreover, are closely connected with each other, all the characteristics of P[2] appear in unison. On the language cf. K n o b e l. There are references to *Ex.* xxviii. in *Num.* xx. 26, 28; xxvii. 21.

Num. xxv. is not a single whole. *V.* 1–5 deals with the apostasy of the Israelites to Baal-Peor, to which they are seduced by t h e d a u g h t e r s of M o a b, and for which, by the order of Moses, they are punished by t h e i r j u d g e s (or, strictly, *are to be* punished, for the execution of the sentence is not recorded). In this story there is nothing to suggest P. On the other hand, in *v.* 6–15 connections between **Midianitish** women and **Israelites** are mentioned, in consequence of which **Yahwè sends a plague,** which is checked by Eleazar's bold deed when twenty-four thousand men have already perished. Eleazar's zeal is rewarded by the promise that the priesthood shall be hereditary in his family. This narrative—unquestionably belonging to P², cf. אהל מועד, עדה מגפה, עדה כהנת עולם, כפר, etc.—is not complete: the beginning, in which the trespass itself and the breaking out of the plague were described (cf. *Num.* xxxi. 16), was omitted when the story was united to the other, of which, in its turn, we now possess the beginning, but not the end. But what are we to say to *v.* 16–19 [xxv. 16–xxvi. 1ᵃ], or rather—since *v.* 19 [xxvi. 1ᵃ] belongs to xxvi.—to *v.* 16–18? It prepares the way for *Num.* xxxi., and would necessarily incline us to assign this latter to P², if it belonged to P² itself. But this is very doubtful : the verses are clumsy in form, and the combination of 'the affair of Peor'—which is mentioned in *v.* 1–5, but not in *v.* 6–15—with 'the affair of Cozbi,' makes it very probable that they were written after the union of *v.* 1–5 and *v.* 6–15, and must be attributed either to the author of *Num.* xxxi. (cf. n. 40), or to R. More on this in § 16, n. 12.

Num. xxvi., the account of the second census, appears to belong to P², with the exception of *v.* 9–11, which refers to *Num.* xvi. [xvi. 1–35], in its present form, and is therefore a later addition (n. 37). The coupling of 'Moses and Eleazar' (*v.* 1, 3, 63) is in harmony with *Num.* xx. 22–29 ; *v.* 65 agrees with P² in *Num.* xiii., xiv. (n. 37) ; *v.* 52–56 proves that the census is in its place here, and is part of the preparation for the approaching settlement in Canaan (cf. *Num.* xxxiv.). Wellhausen (xxii. 454 sq.) considers *v.* 57–62 (genealogy of the Levites) primary, and *Ex.* vi. 13–28 ; *Num.* iii. 14 sqq. ; *Gen.* xlvi. 8–27, all of them secondary. He can therefore see no reason against assigning *v.* [100] 57–62 to P². But the relation of *Num.* xxvi., as a whole, to *Num.* i., ii. causes him difficulties. In the heading of *Num.* xxvi., he urges, there is no reference to the former census, and indeed in *v.* 3, 4 the population now numbered is described as 'the children of Israel, who had come out of Egypt,' and it is not till *v.* 63–65 that this census is clearly distinguished from the previous one. In my opinion this objection is unfounded. *V.* 3 (to whom does אתם refer?) and 4 (the beginning of which is wanting, so that we cannot tell whether the second part is or is not a superscription) are corrupt, and do not warrant any certain conclusion ; but besides this, the distinction which Wellhausen misses is found in the mention of Eleazar together with Moses (*v.* 1, 3), which, it is true, is not explained till *v.* 63–65, but which indicates the fortieth year after the exodus clearly enough from the first.

⁴² With regard to *Num.* xx. 1–13 opinions differ much. The portions assigned to P² are as follows :—by Colenso (*Pentateuch*, vi. 76 sq. and Appendix, p. 25), *v.* 2–13 ; by Schrader, *v.* 1ᵃ, 2, 3ᵇ–13 ; by Nöldeke (op. cit., p. 83 sq.), *v.* 1 (in part), 2, 3–5 (in part), 6–11, 12 (in part), 13 ; by Kayser, *v.* 2, 3ᵇ, 6, 8ᵃ, 9, 10ᵃ, . . . 12, 13 ; by Wellhausen (xxi. 576 sq.), 1ᵃ, 2, 3ᵇ, 6, 9 (in part), 12 (probably) ; by Knobel (op. cit., p. 101), *v.* 1ᵃ, 2, 6. This divergence of opinion is quite explicable. The whole pericope looks like a doublet

of *Ex.* xvii. 1–7, which latter does not belong to P²; and this inclines us to
think (with Colenso, etc.) that our passage is from P². But against this may
be urged : (1) that *v.* 4, 5, 9 (at the end), 11 (at the end), depart from the
linguistic usage of P², and that although the staff preserved in the sanctuary
is mentioned in *v.* 8, 9 (cf. *Num.* xvii. 25, 26 [10, 11]), in *v.* 11, on the contrary, it is the staff of Moses that is spoken of; (2) that the version of what
took place at Kadesh referred to by P² in *Num.* xx. 24, xxvii. 14 (*Deut.* xxxii.
51) differs from that of *Num.* xx. 1–13. In the passages cited we read that
Moses and Aaron had been contumacious (מרה) or had dealt faithlessly (מעל)
with Yahwè. Now in *Num.* xx. it is not clear what the sin of Moses and
Aaron is, but it certainly is not contumacy or breach of faith. It is the
Israelites that are called (*v.* 10) 'stubborn.' And although the further contents of *Num.* xxvii. 14 and *Deut.* xxxii. 51 show that, in spite of the difference
noted, it is one and the same event which is referred to in these passages and
in *Num.* xx., yet the story in P² must have undergone v e r y i m p o r t a n t
m o d i f i c a t i o n s when incorporated in *Numbers* or at some later date, and
these modifications may in their turn have influenced the text of *Num.* xxvii.
14 and *Deut.* xxxii. 51, the integrity of which I gravely suspect. The question, then, seems more than usually involved, for the welding of P² with
another account was accompanied by a recasting of P² itself. Such being the
state of the case, I should prefer to abstain from any decisive opinion on the
details.

That P² told of the settlement of the two and a half tribes in the Transjordanic district is raised above all doubt by *Num.* xxxiv. 14–16 ; xxxv. 14 (and
also by *Josh.* xiii., of which more hereafter). It is equally clear that *Num.*
xxxii., as we now have it, cannot be identified with P²'s account. Here—to
take a single point—we find that in *v.* 1–32 Gad and Reuben (Reuben and
Gad in *v.* 1 only) appear on the stage without half Manasseh, and when the
latter has been included, without warning given or reason assigned, in *v.* 33,
he is then called Machir in *v.* 39, 40 ; but according to P² (*Num.* xxvi. 29–34)
Machir is Manasseh's only son, and cannot therefore signify the more eastern
of the two sections of the tribe only. And yet it is equally impossible to deny
the connection between P² and *Num.* xxxii. *V.* 6–15 is an extremely late [101]
addition (*Th. Tijdschr.*, xi. 559–562) and need not be further considered. But
in *v.* 1–5, 16–32 the characteristics of P² are here and there unmistakable,
especially (but not exclusively) in *v.* 2 (Eleazar and the princes of the
community), 18 (התנחל, *Lev.* xxv. 46 ; *Num.* xxxiv. 13), 19 (נחל), 22 (כבש,
אחזה), 24 (היצא מפיכם, *Num.* xxx. 3 [2], cf. 13 [12]), 25, 27 (אדני, *Num.*
xxxvi. 2), 27 (חלוץ צבא, *Num.* xxxi. 5 ; *Josh.* iv. 13), 28 (Eleazar, Joshua,
and the heads of the tribes), 29 (cf. 22), 30 (נאחזו, cf. *Josh.* xxii. 9, 19 ;
Gen. xxxiv. 10; xlvii. 27). It is not clear how we are to explain this
priestly colouring of a narrative which, for the reasons already given, cannot
be assigned to P². Perhaps we must assume that the author of *Num.* xxxii.
1–5, 16 sqq., on this occasion, departed from his usual practice of simply
weaving his two authorities together, and made up an account of his own
from them. In this case the characteristics of either source might reappear

indifferently in his narrative. Possibly the original narrative of P² dealt separately with Reuben and Gad on the one hand and half Manasseh on the other, and the redactor, for some unknown reason, thought good to omit his account of the latter. Here, as in the case of *Num.* xx. 1–13, I must leave the question undecided.

⁴³ Cf. Kayser, op. cit., p. 97–99; Wellh. (xxii. 453 sq.). The agreement of *Num.* xxxiii. 1–49 in language and contents with P² is generally allowed (cf. Knobel and others), and the passage has therefore usually been assigned to that work. But this is inconsistent with the references to events related elsewhere (compare *v.* 8 with *Ex.* xv. 22; *v.* 9 with *Ex.* xv. 27; *v.* 14 with *Ex.* xvii. 1 sqq.; *v.* 16. with *Num.* xi. 34; *v.* 17 with *Num.* xi. 35; *v.* 40 with *Num.* xxi. 1–3); and since the comparison of *Num.* xxxiii. 1–49 with the parallel passages leaves no room to doubt the priority of the latter, the only hypothesis left is the one put forward in the text, viz. that *Num.* xxxiii. 1–49 is compiled from various sources, including the narratives of our Pentateuch. What value attaches to those geographical names that must have been derived from other sources it is impossible to say.

⁴⁴ As to *Deut.* xxxii. 48–52 there is no room for doubt : *Num.* xxvii. 12–14 is taken up again and repeated because the moment there foretold has now arrived. Inasmuch as *Num.* xxviii.–xxxi., xxxiii. are derived from other sources (n. 39–43) so that, in P², only *Num.* xxxii. (in its original form) and xxxiv.–xxxvi. intervened between *Num.* xxvii. 12 sqq. and *Deut.* xxxii. 48–52, it is p o s s i b l e that ' this same day,' in *v.* 48, may mean the day on which Moses received the prediction of his death. It is more probable, however, that some later day is meant, which was clearly indicated in a portion of P² that had to be omitted when *Deuteronomy* was incorporated into it.—It cannot be precisely determined how much of *Deut.* xxxiv. is taken from P². Certainly *v.* 8, 9, cf. *Num.* xx. 29 ; xxvii. 18–23 ; probably also *v.* 1ᵃ (cf. *Deut.* xxxii. 49) and *v.* 7ᵃ (in accordance with P²'s frequent practice of giving ages); but see *Deut.* xxxi. 2. The rest of the chapter is without the obvious characteristics of P², and may very well be taken from other sources. Nothing is more natural than that when the materials were worked into a single whole details identically given in the various sources should be dropped now from one and now from the other.

[102]   ⁴⁵ The qualification ' with reference to P² ' is necessary. If we regard *Deuteronomy* as the continuation of the non-priestly passages in *Exodus* and *Numbers* then we should rather speak of P as an interpolation. We shall not be able to choose between these alternatives till later on.—*Num.* xxxvi. 13 seems to include the laws that we have seen reason to deny to P² (*Num.* xxviii. sqq.), and if this be so it can hardly be earlier than the union of the priestly and non-priestly passages in a single work.

The death of Moses did not bring the writers whom we have indicated by P to their goal. The settlement of Israel in Canaan unquestionably lay within the limits of the task they had undertaken [46]. And the book of Joshua furnishes the proof that they actually went on to describe this settlement, and, specifically, that P^2's statements on this subject have not been lost [47].

We must leave it doubtful whether the account of the conquest in P^2 went into detail. The fragments still preserved in *Josh.* i.–xii. are insufficient for its reconstruction as a whole. They are *Josh.* iv. (13?), 19; v. 10–12; ix. 15[b], 17–21, 27[a]; and it is only the last of these passages that suggests anything approaching to an elaborate account of Joshua's victories [48].

In the second half of the book of Joshua (xiii.–xxiv.), the remains of P^2 are much more extensive. They appear in combination or alternation with materials drawn from other sources, which must likewise have described the division of the land and the territory of each tribe [49]. In xiii., xv., xviii. 11—xix. 48, especially, it is often difficult to determine how to divide the geographical data between P^2 and these other sources; in some cases the lists of cities may equally well have been taken from the former or the latter, and perhaps were almost identical in them from the first [50]. We will therefore leave the point undecided, and will likewise defer the inquiry into the mode in which the two sets of materials were woven together. Without anticipating, however, we may at once assign the following passages to P^2, on the strength of their form and contents : xiii. 14[b] (LXX.), 15, 23[b], 24, 28, 29 (in part), 31 (in part), 32 ; xiv. 1–5 ; xv. 1, 20 ; xvi. 4–8 ; xvii. 1[a], 3–6 ; xviii. 1, 11[a], 20[b], 28[b]; xix. 1 (in part), [103] 8[b], 16, 23, 24, 31, 32 (in part), 39, 40, 48, 51 ; xx. (according to the text of the LXX.) ; xxi. 1–40 [51].

Two remarks must here be made :—

(1) These passages evidently have not come down to us in all cases in their original form and order: differences between the representation of P^2 and that of the other

sources may well have necessitated transposition or modification [52].

(2) As in all parts of the Pentateuch, so here and there in *Josh.* xiii.–xxiv., we come upon passages side by side with those from P² which may more properly be assigned to his later followers than to himself. This is the case, specifically, with *Josh.* xiii. 21ᵇ, 22 ; xxii. 9–34 [53].

[46] For proof of this we need only go back to *Num.* xxxiii. 50–xxxv. It is hardly conceivable that the author who wrote down these precepts would not record their execution. So too *Num.* xxvii. 15–23 makes us expect to hear more of Joshua as the leader of the people.

[47] A single glance at *Josh.* xiv. 1–5 ; xx. ; xxi. 1–40, compared with the chapters in *Numbers* cited in n. 46 is enough to establish this. But see the following notes also.

[48] On *Josh.* iv. 13 cf. Colenso, *Pentateuch*, vi. App. p. 51 : חלוצי הצבא, as in *Num.* xxxi. 5 ; xxxii. 27 ; לפני יהוה, as in *Num.* xxxii. 20, 21, 27, 29, 32 (with למלחמה in *v.* 20); ערבות יריחו, as in *Josh.* v. 10. But note that in *Num.* xxvi. the fighting strength of the two and a half tribes is far above 40,000, so that if P² gives this figure he is inconsistent with himself. Hence the hesitation with which I assign *v.* 13 to P². On the other hand, *v.* 19 is certainly his, as shown by the careful definition of time and the form of its expression (cf. *Ex.* xii. 3, 6, 18 ; xvi. 1ᵇ, etc., etc.). The connection is very close between this last verse and *v.* 10–12 ; for the language of which cf. iv. 13, 19 ; *Num.* xxxiii. 3 ; *Ex.* xii. 17, 41 ; *Lev.* xxiii. 21, 28–30 ; *Deut.* xxxii. 48 ; and for *v.* 12 *Ex.* xvi. 35.—In *Josh.* ix., *v.* 17–21 and 22 sqq. are evidently doublets, the latter taking up again what had been dealt with in the former. We can identify P² in *v.* 15ᵇ and 17–21 by the mention of 'the congregation' and its 'princes' (*v.* 15ᵇ, 18, 19, 21), and from the use of נלוֹן (*v.* 18 cf. *Ex.* xvi. 2 ; *Num.* xvii. 6 [xvi. 41]) and קצף (*v.* 20 cf. *Num.* i. 53 ; xvii. 11 [xvi. 46] ; xviii. 5, etc.) In *v.* 21 the princes decree that the Gibeonites shall be 'wood-cutters and water-carriers for the congregation.' *V.* 23ᵇ originally ran ולא יכרת מכם עבד לבית אלהי ; the rest of what we now read is interpolated from *v.* 21, as is sufficiently shown by the singular יכרת before וחמבי, etc. So in *v.* 27 the two descriptions ('wood-cutters and water-carriers of the congregation' and '(slaves) of the altar of Yahwè') stand side by side, and here again the former is taken from P².—Thus it appears that in P² the treaty with the Gibeonites was [104] related at length. It would be natural to infer that the whole story of the conquest was given in detail were it not that the priestly author may have had a special interest in describing the position of the Gibeonites more accurately than he felt had been done in *v.* 23, 27 ('slaves of the house' or 'of the altar of Yahwè'). It is possible, then, that P² may exceptionally have treated this one event in detail.

Elsewhere, too, in *Josh.* i.–xii. some critics have thought they detected traces of P². Nöldeke (*Untersuchungen*, p. 95-98) marks, though not without hesitation, iii. 1; vi. 20, 24; vii. 1, 14, 16, 17, 24, 25ᵇ; x. 27; 28-43; xi., xii. (these last sections recast); Colenso (*Pentateuch*, vii. Appendix, Synoptical Table, p. v.) assigns the following to P², in addition to what I have given him; iv. 12; vi. 19, 24ᵇ; vii. 1, 18 (in part), 25ᵇ; ix. 14; x. 27ᵇ. My reasons for not being able to follow these scholars are obvious: conclusive signs of P² are absent. If it were known that the conquest of Jericho, the death of Achan, etc., were really narrated in P², such minute indications as are found in these verses might be allowed to weigh. But this is not the case.

⁴⁹ Such passages as xiii. 1-7; xiv. 6-15; xv. 13-19; xvii. 14-18; xviii. 2-10, which certainly do n o t belong to P²—since they either contradict it or have nothing in common with it—prove that the narrators from whom the greater part of *Josh.* i.-xii. was borrowed also described the settlement of the tribes in their territories.

⁵⁰ It is obvious at once that the list of passages from P², to be given immediately, includes a number of verses and half verses which are nothing more than superscriptions and colophons, and as such are parts of a f r a m e w o r k, which must, of course, have had c o n t e n t s in the document to which it belonged. This I am as far as possible from denying. But we must admit (cf. n. 49) that the geographical details m a y have been taken from other documents. I am therefore unable expressly to assign them to P². In most cases, fortunately, it is of little consequence to which source the names of the cities are ascribed, for the reason, amongst others, that the geographical material, as already said, was presumably identical in the sources themselves, whether it was that one borrowed from the other or that the two were alike dependent on a common authority.

⁵¹ Cf. *Th. Tijdschr.*, xi. 484-496 [criticised by Colenso, *Wellhausen on the composition*, p. 86-95], where several points which can only be touched upon here, are treated more in detail. I there assume that it was P² who brought *Josh.* xiii.-xxiv. into its present form; but I cannot now pronounce so decidedly. If the accounts of P² and of other sources were welded together by a third hand, the process is more involved than I once supposed, but my judgment as to the ultimate sources of the sections and verses themselves remains unaffected.

The heading of the description of the Transjordanic region, that has fallen out of the Hebrew text of *Josh.* xiii., but is preserved in the LXX. in *v.* 14, is certainly genuine, as shown *inter alia* by its agreement with *v.* 32. Of a similar character are the headings and colophons in *v.* 15, 23ᵇ, 24, 28, 29 (emended after the LXX.) They must all be assigned to P² on account of the agreement between *v.* 14ᵇ [LXX.], 32 and xiv. 1; xix. 51, and the use of מטה throughout. In *v.* 31 the last words ('t o h a l f the sons of Machir after their [105] families') are a correction of what precedes ('to the sons of Machir'), made to harmonise it with P², who knows of no son of Manasseh except Machir (*Num.* xxvi. 29-34), and can therefore only locate a portion of Machir's descendants in the Transjordanic region.—Ch. xiv. 1-5 rests so completely upon *Num.* xxxiv. sq. that no doubt can be entertained as to its origin. It

shows that P² contained an account of the inheritance of the nine and a half
tribes, of which we have the colophon in xix. 51. It is therefore highly
probable that the verses out of xv., xviii., xix. indicated above—in which ממה
repeatedly occurs, and which are parallel in many other respects to the superscriptions and colophons in xiii.—likewise belong to P². Ch. xvi. and xvii.
remain for special notice. In xvi. 1–3 (cf. xvii. 14) 'the sons of Joseph'
receive one lot. These verses, therefore, are n o t from P ², for he expressly
says that the sons of Joseph were t w o t r i b e s (xiv. 4; *Gen.* xlviii. 3–6
and elsewhere). The latter conception reappears in xvi. 4, which we
therefore assign to P², together with *v.* 5–8 that cannot well be from the
author of *v.* 1–3. So, too, xvii. 1ª is from P², who elsewhere (xiv. 4; xvi. 4),
gives the precedence to Manasseh as the elder. *V.* 1ᵇ, 2, on the contrary
(Manasseh's sons in the plural, and Machir dwelling in the Transjordanic
district) is at variance with P²(see above), and is accordingly contradicted
by *v.* 3–6, in which latter we at once recognise the author of *Num.* xxvii.
1–11; xxxvi., that is to say, P².—The ascription of xviii. 1 to P² needs no
justification (נכבש ,אהל מועד ,כל־עדת בני־ישׂראל), while the ascription of
v. 2–10 to some other source is equally certain, for we find neither Eleazar
nor the princes, nor the 'ôhel mo'éd' in them, but שבט throughout, בית יוסף
in *v.* 5, in harmony with xvi. 1–3; xvii. 14–18, and Levi (not Aaron and his
sons) called to the priesthood in *v.* 7. Such divergences put beyond all reach
of doubt the division of *Josh.* xiii. sqq. between P² and other sources.—With
respect to xx. (on the text of which cf. *Th. Tijdschr.*, xi. 467–478) and xxi. 1–40
(or 1–42 if we count in the verses on Reuben which have dropped out after *v.*
35) there can be no two opinions; taken together they correspond to the two
parts of *Num.* xxxv., and moreover, xxi. 1–42 was announced as early as in
xiv. 4.—Ch. xxiv. 33 is generally assigned to P², since Phinchas only appears
elsewhere in priestly passages (amongst which *Jud.* xx. 27ᵇ, 28ª must be
reckoned). But xxi. 10 sqq. assigns cities i n J u d a e a to the priests, the sons
of Aaron, and the 'hill of Phinehas' in the mountains of Ephraim does not
agree very well with this. Probably, therefore, xxiv. 33 stands on the same
footing as *Deut.* x. 6 (cf. § 7, n. 6).

⁵² It follows from xiv. 4; xvi. 4; xvii. 1ª (' for he was Joseph's first-born')
that in P² Manasseh preceded Ephraim; whereas in *Josh.* xvi., xvii. Ephraim
is dealt with before Manasseh.—According to W e l l h a u s e n 's acute conjecture (xxi. 596 sqq.) xviii. 1 preceded xiv. 1–5 in P², so that the w h o l e of
the land was divided at S h i l o h. This is supported by the close of xviii. 1,
' and the land was subdued before their face,' which sounds much more like
an introduction to the account of the w h o l e division than the announcement
[106] of the second half of the work; and again in xiv. 1–5 the ascription of the land
by lot to the nine and a half tribes is treated as a single act; and finally in xix.
51, 'the tribes of the children of Israel'—not seven of these tribes only—are
said to have received their inheritance at S h i l o h. All this can hardly be
denied. But W e l l h a u s e n 's conjecture is too closely connected with xiii.
1–7 to be finally pronounced upon at this stage of our inquiry. See below,
§ 7, n. 27; 16, n. 12.

[53] On *Josh.* xiii. 21[b], 22—borrowed from *Num.* xxxi. 8—cf. *Th. Tijdschr.*, xi. 495 sq.—*Josh.* xxii. 9–34 (to which v. 7, 8 perhaps belongs, but certainly not v. 1–6) does not appear to me to be composite. Knobel (*Num.–Josh.*, p. 475 sq.) distinguishes two elements: viz. v. 9–11, 13–15, 21, 30–33[a], from P[2], and v. 12, 16–20, 22–29, 33[b], 34, from the 'Kriegsbuch.' Kayser (op. cit., p. 106 sqq.) divides the passage otherwise: v. 9 (in part), 10 (in part), 11, 12 (in part), 13, 14, portions of v. 15, 16, 19, 20 (?), 21, 23–26, all v. 29, parts of v. 31, 32 from P[2]; the rest from a Yahwistic narrative in which the Transjordanic tribes are taxed with apostasy from Yahwè, whereas in P[2] the accusation is that they wish to withdraw from the one sanctuary at Shiloh. The unity of the narrative is defended with perfect justice by Colenso (*Pentateuch*, vi., App. p. 66, 67), Wellhausen (xxi. 601), and others: the contrast between v. 26, 29 (P[2]) and v. 22, 27, 28, 34 (another source) which Kayser attempts to establish does not exist, and Knobel's division is purely arbitrary. I cannot, however, allow Wellhausen's assertion that 'the conceptions and expressions are altogether those of Q (= P[2]).' Note שׁבט in v. 9–11, 13, 15, 21 (מטה in v. 14 only), and still more the agreement in tone and style with *Num.* xxxi. and xxxii. 6–15 (see above, n. 40, 42), i.e. with the later additions to P[2]. The contents also plead for a later origin: the narrative is an absolutely unhistorical invention framed to defend the doctrine of a unique sanctuary which it represents as completely established and assimilated by the popular consciousness. In harmony with this, too, is the silence concerning Joshua, who is still the chief personage in v. 1–8, and the *rôle* assigned to Phinehas.

§ 7. *The deuteronomic elements of the Hexateuch* (D).

The study of the deuteronomic elements of the Hexateuch must start from the collection of laws in *Deut.* xii.–xxvi., which, as already seen (§ 5, n. 6–8), is led up to by i.–iv. and v.–xi., and presupposed in xxvii. sqq., and has accordingly been universally accepted as the kernel of the deuteronomic literature.

Deut. xii.–xxvi. is a single whole. Here and there the order of the precepts leaves something to be desired, and occasionally the suspicion of later interpolations is provoked[1]; but in spite of this it remains quite unmistakable that these chapters as a whole come from one author, and constitute a single book of law. 'The tora of Yahwè' which they [107] promulgate is intended by the writer to embrace all the demands that Yahwè makes from his people, and accordingly

it regulates not only the worship—which must be offered
to Yahwè alone and in his one sanctuary,—but also the
political, civic, and domestic life of the people consecrated
to him, and the moral duties of the individual Israelite [2].
This unity of conception is, of course, perfectly compatible
with the use of existing materials, whether detached laws
or collections; and in all probability the use of such materials furnishes the true explanation of the differences we
detect on comparing xxi.–xxv. with the rest of the code [3].
But even these chapters are not without traces of the
characteristic language of the deuteronomic lawgiver,
which comes out much more distinctly in xii.–xx. and xxvi.,
and pleads so powerfully for the unity of the whole collection [4].

[1] To these digressions I shall return in § 14, n. 1. Even those who lay
most stress upon them regard them as exceptions to the rule, and do not
hesitate to accept the unity of the law-book in the relative sense which will
be more closely defined in n. 2.

[2] The following survey of the contents of *Deut.* xii.–xxvi. may serve to confirm the statement in the text. The code opens with an emphatic warning
against the religious practices of the Canaanites, especially against sacrificing
in more than one place, the use of blood, etc. (xii. [xii. 1–31]). Then, after
a parenthetical exhortation to faithful and complete observance of all the
commandments (xiii. 1 [xii. 32]), follow laws concerning the prophet (*v.* 2–6
[1–5]) or the near and dear one (*v.* 7–12 [6–11]) who tempts to idolatry, and
the curse upon the apostate city (*v.* 13–19 [12–18]). Let Israel consecrate
himself to Yahwè and shrink from everything unclean (xiv. 1–21). Let tithes
of the fruits of the field, and the firstlings of cattle be consecrated to Yahwè
(*v.* 22–29). The shemitta must be observed in the seventh, or sabbatical year
(xv. 1–11); and the Hebrew slave, male or female, released after seven years'
service (*v.* 12–18). A more precise injunction (cf. xiv. 23) as to the consecration of the firstlings (*v.* 19–23) is followed by the deuteronomic calendar of
festivals (xvi. 1–17 : passover and maççôth, feast of weeks, and feast of
tabernacles). Precepts concerning the judges (xvi. 18–20), the supreme court
in the city of the sanctuary (xvii. 8–13), the king (*v.* 14–20), the priests (xviii.
1–8), and the prophets (*v.* 9–22) are broken, somewhat abruptly, by the prohibition of ashéras and maççébas (xvi. 21, 22), by the command to offer beasts
without blemish to Yahwè (xvii. 1), and by a law on stoning the idolater (*v.*
2–7), which latter is brought into a certain connection with the precepts on the
administration of justice by its definition of the duties of the two witnesses
(*v.* 6, 7). The law of the cities of refuge (xix. 1–13) and the regulations about

witnesses (*v.* 15 and 16–21)—the latter preceded by the prohibition of the [108]
removal of land-marks (*v.* 14)—are likewise connected with the administration of justice. Ch. xx. deals with war; *v.* 1–9 with relief from military
service; *v.* 10–18 with the fate of conquered cities; *v.* 19, 20 with the fruit
trees near a besieged city. Then follow, generally speaking, shorter laws:
the steps needed to purify the land when the body of a slaughtered man is
found in the open field (xxi. 1–9); marriage with a female captive of war
(*v.* 10–14); rights of first-born sons (*v.* 15–17); punishment of the contumacious son (*v.* 18–21); removal of the body from the gibbet before evening (*v.* 22,
23, related to *v.* 1–9); preservation and restitution of discovered property (xxii.
1–3); helping up a neighbour's beast of burden that has fallen (*v.* 4);
against change of garments between men and women (*v.* 5); on taking bird-
nests (*v.* 6. 7); on making a parapet round the open roof (v. 8); against
mixing unlike sorts in sowing seed, in using beasts, or in making clothes
(*v.* 9–11); tassels on the four corners of the garment (*v.* 12); punishment of
the man who slanders his bride (*v.* 13–19); but also of the woman who has
committed fornication before her marriage (*v.* 20, 21); kindred regulations
against adultery, under various circumstances (*v.* 22, *v.* 23 sq., *v.* 25–27, *v.* 28
sq.); prohibition of a man's marriage with his father's wife (xxiii. 1 [xxii.
30]); qualifications for admission into the assembly of Yahwè (*v.* 2–9 [1–8]);
precautions to secure the cleanness of the camp (*v.* 10–15 [9–14]); against
surrender of run-away slaves (*v.* 16 sq. [15 sq.]); prohibition of prostitution
in honour of the deity, and the dedication of the hire to Yahwè (*v.* 18 sq.
[17 sq.]); against usury (*v.* 20 sq. [19 sq.]); against neglecting to perform a
vow (22–24 [21–23]); the use of a neighbour's vineyard and corn-field and
its limits (*v.* 25 sq. [24 sq.]); on divorce (xxiv. 1–4); the first year of marriage (*v.* 5); against taking a mill-stone in pledge (*v.* 6); prohibition of kid-
napping (*v.* 7); on leprosy (*v.* 8 sq.); mercifulness in taking pledges (*v.* 10–
13); justice to the day-labourer (*v.* 14 sq.); limitation of the punishment to
the culprit himself (*v.* 16); regulations in favour of foreigners, widows, and
orphans (*v.* 17–22); scourging as a punishment (xxv. 1–3); provision for the
ox that treads the corn (*v.* 4); marriage with a deceased brother's wife (*v.* 5–10);
observance of decencies when two men are at blows (*v.* 11 sq.); against dis-
honesty in trade (*v.* 13–16); on rooting out the Amalekites (*v.* 17–19). The
Israelite is to bring his first-fruits to the sanctuary of Yahwè and to testify
his gratitude to him (*v.* 1–11); after giving up the tithes of the third year he
is solemnly to declare that he has fulfilled his obligation, and is to implore
Yahwè's blessing (*v.* 12–15). Israel is to pledge himself to observe ' these
institutions and statutes ' and to belong to Yahwè, who on his side will bless
and exalt Israel (*v.* 16–19).

If I call *Deut.* xii.–xxvi. ' a single book of law' it is in no small degree on
the strength of xxvi. In xxi.–xxv. the precepts are often defectively arranged;
kindred matter is not always treated together, and no fixed plan seems
to be followed. But in xxvi. the lawgiver returns to the subjects he had
placed in the fore-front—the one sanctuary, the first-fruits, the tithes, the
Levitical priests—and follows them up with a covenant (*v.* 16–19) between

[109] Yahwè and Israel based on the laws and ordinances now set forth at length. In xxi.–xxv. he seemed to lose himself in all kinds of details, but in xxvi. he recovers himself and shows that he is the same man at the end that he was at the beginning.

³ P. Kleinert, *Das Deut. u. der Deuteronomiker* (1872), defends the position (p. 124–135 and elsewhere) that *Deut.* xii.–xxvi.—and indeed the whole of *Deut.* v.–xxvi.—should be regarded as the 'codification' of older (Mosaic) laws, which are in some cases simply adopted, in others worked up and expanded, and in yet others enforced by more or less elaborate exhortations, so that *Deut.* xii.–xxvi. may be regarded as a series of paraphrases and discourses on Mosaic texts. But this description does not correspond with the facts. We shall indeed see presently that even in the earlier chapters, e.g. xiv. 1–21 ; xv. 1–11 ; 12–18 ; xvi. 1–17, D has assimilated older laws ; but it is a veritable assimilation, and in the process he moulds his material into his own forms and nowhere betrays dependence. So he proceeds up to the end of xx. ; it is the author himself that is speaking throughout, and we can never distinguish between a text and a commentary. Ch. xxvi. resembles xii.–xx. in this respect. It is only in xxi.–xxv. that the relations are such as Kleinert describes. Here, for the most part, the writer seems to confine himself to adopting precepts or lessons, expounding their motive, and exhorting his readers to observe them. See xxi. 21ᵇ, 23ᵇ ; xxii. 5 ᵇ, 7 ᵇ, 21ᵇ, 22ᵇ, 24ᵇ ; xxiii. 6, 8 ᵇ, 21ᵇ [5, 7 ᵇ, 20ᵇ] ; xxiv. 4ᵇ, 7 ᵇ, 9, 13ᵇ, 19ᵇ ; xxv. 12 ᵇ, 15 ᵇ, 16, 19. We shall see from the following note that these verses contain their full share of the linguistic peculiarities of xii.–xx., xxvi.

⁴ On the characteristics of the deuteronomic language—though not of xii.–xxvi. only, but of v.–xxvi., or the whole book of *Deuteronomy*—compare Knobel (*Num. Josh.*, p. 586–589) ; Colenso (*Pentateuch*, iii. 402–405 and elsewhere), and above all Kleinert (op. cit., p. 214–235). With a view, *inter alia*, to the question we shall have to discuss presently as to the relations between xii.–xxvi. and v.–xi., i.–iv., xxvii. sqq., I here subjoin a list of the principal expressions and turns of language which constantly recur in xii.–xxvi., and which, in almost every case, either do not appear at all or appear comparatively rarely, except in the deuteronomic literature. I need hardly say that such a list as this, even were it far more complete, could never adequately characterise the style of the author, a true impression of which cannot really be gained except by repeated perusal of his work :—

1. אהב, אהבה (nominal infinitive), of Yahwè to Israel and *vice versa*, xix. 9 ; xxiii. 6 [5] ; xiii. 4 [3].

2. אכל, 'to eat before Yahwè's face,' xii. 7, 18 ; xiv. 23, 26 ; xv. 20.

3. אלהים אחרים, '(go after, serve) other gods,' xiii. 3, 7, 14 [2, 6, 13] ; xvii. 3 ; xviii. 20.

4. אלהים with pronominal suffix, preceded by יהוה, especially ' Yahwè, your God,' *passim* throughout Deuteronomy. (307 times according to Colenso, *Pentateuch*, iii. 405.)

5. ארך in Hiphil with ימים, xvii. 20 ; xxii. 7 ; cf. xxv. 15.

6. בחר, in the formula : '(the place) that Yahwè shall choose,' xii. 5, 11,

14, 18, 26; xiv. 23–25; xv. 20; xvi. 2, 6, 7, 11, 15, 16; xvii. 8, 10, 15; xxvi. 2.

7. בער, 'to root out (the evil thing),' xiii. 6 [5]; xvii. 7, 12; xix. 13, 19; [110] xxi. 9, 21; xxii. 21, 22, 24; xxiv. 7.

8. ברך, in Piel, '(that) Yahwè may bless you,' etc., xiv. 24, 29; xv. 4, 10; xvi. 10, 15; xxiii. 21 [20]; xxiv. 19.

9. גר, 'stranger, orphan, and widow,' xxiv. 17, 19, 21; coupled with 'the Levite,' xiv. 29; xvi. 11, 14; xxvi. 12, 13.

10. הלך, 'after Yahwè,' xiii. 5 [4]; 'in Yahwè's ways,' xix. 9; xxvi. 17.

11. זכור, 'that ye were slaves,' etc. xv. 15; xvi. 12; xxiv. 18, 22.

12. חוס, 'let not your eye pity,' xiii. 9 [8]; xix. 13. 21; xxv. 12.

13. חקים (never in the singular), united with 'statutes,' 'testimonies,' 'law,' 'command' or 'commands,' *passim* throughout Deuteronomy.

14. ידע, in the formula: 'gods whom ye have not known (nor your fathers),' xiii. 3, 7, 14 [2, 6, 13].

15. יום, 'all the days,' xii. 1; xiv. 23; xviii. 5; xix. 9.

16. יטב, 'that it may be well with thee,' xii. 25, 28; xxii. 7.

17. יטב, inf. Hiph. as an adverb, xiii. 15 [14]; xvii. 4; xix. 18.

18. ירא, in the form ליראה, xiv. 23; xvii. 19.

19. ירש, of the acquisition of Canaan, xii. 29; xvi. 20; xvii. 4; xix. 1; xxvi. 1; especially לרשת, xii. 1, 29; xv. 4; xix. 2; xxi. 1; xxiii. 21 [20]; xxv. 19.

20. לב, only in iv. 11; xxviii. 65; xxix. 3, 18 [4, 19]; everywhere else in *Deuteronomy* לבב.

21. למד, Kal xiv. 23; xvii. 19 (xviii. 9); Piel xx. 18.

22. נדח, Kal xx. 19; Hiphil xiii. 6, 11, 14 [5, 10, 13]; Niphal xix. 5; xxii. 1.

23. נחל in Hiphil xii. 10; xix. 3; xxi. 16.

24. נחלה, of Canaan (never אחזה), xii. 9, 12; xiv. 27, 29; xv. 4; xviii. 1, 2; xix. 10; xx. 16; xxi. 23; xxiv. 4; xxv. 19; xxvi. 1.

25. סקל with באבנים, xiii. 11 [10]; xvii. 5; xxii. 21, 24.

26. עבט, Hiphil, and עבוט, xv. 6, 8; xxiv. 10–13.

27. עשה, in the formula מעשה ידים, xiv. 29; xvi. 15; xxiv. 19.

28. פדה, redeem, i.e. release from Egypt, xiii. 6 [5]; xv. 15; xxi. 8; xxiv. 18.

29. צוה, Piel, in the phrase: 'which I command thee,' xii. 11, 14, 21; xiii. 1, 19 [xii. 32; xiii. 18]; xv. 5, 11, 15; xix. 7, 9; xxiv. 18, 22.

30. המצוה, collective, xv. 5; xvii. 20; xix. 9; xxvi. 13.

31. שמח, with לפני יהוה, xii. 7, 12, 18; xiv. 26; xvi. 11 (14; xxvi. 11).

32. שבע, Niphal; of the oath of Yahwè to the fathers, xiii. 18 [17]; xix. 8; xxvi. 3, 15.

33. שכן, Piel, in the formula: 'Yahwè makes his name dwell, etc.,' xii. 11 (cf. 5); xiv. 23; xvi. 2, 6, 11; xxvi. 2.

34. שלח, in משלח ידים, xii. 7; xv. 10; xxiii. 21 [20].

35. שמע, hearken to, obey, with אל and בקול, xiii. 4, 5, 9, 19 [3, 4, 8, 18]; xv. 5; xvii. 12; xviii. 14, 15, 19; xxi. 18, 20; xxiii. 6 [5]; xxvi. 14.

36. שׁמע, in the phrases 'they shall hear (the whole people, or Israel, shall hear) and be afraid,' xiii. 12 [11]; xvii. 13; xix. 20; xxi. 21.

37. שׁמר with המצוה or one of its synonyms as object, xiii. 5, 19 [4, 18]; [111] xvii. 19; xix. 9; in conjunction with לעשׂות, xii. 1; xiii. 1 [xii. 32]; xv. 5; xvi. 12; xvii. 10; xxiv. 8.

38. שׁמר, Niphal, taking לְ before a pronoun, xii. 13, 19, 30; xv. 9; xxiv. 8.

39. שׁער, 'in thy gates (=cities),' xii. 12, 15, 17, 18, 21; xiv. 21, 27–29; xv. 7, 22; xvi. 5, 11, 14, 18; xvii. 2, 5, 8; xviii. 6; xxiii. 17 [16]; xxiv. 14; xxvi. 12.

40. תעב: תעבה and תועבת יהוה, xii. 31; xiii. 15 [14]; xiv. 3; xvii. 1, 4; xviii. 12; xxii. 5; xxiii. 19 [18]; xxiv. 4; xxv. 16.

See further, n. 10, 16, 26.

The collection of *Deut.* xii.–xxvi. has no heading. It is Moses who proclaims the laws to Israel (xviii. 15, 17, etc.), but there is no express declaration to that effect at the beginning. This is no omission, however, for in *Deuteronomy* the code is the second portion of a discourse delivered by Moses which begins at v. 1, and is introduced by the superscription in iv. 45–49. It is obvious that v.–xi. is intended as an introduction to xii.–xxvi., and that on the whole it is not inappropriate as such [5]. Now this does not in itself prove that the former is from the same hand as the latter, and that the collection of xii.–xxvi. was from the first put into the mouth of Moses, addressing Israel after the conquest of the Transjordanic district; but the objections to the unity of authorship, which have been urged most recently by Wellhausen and Valeton [6] are not convincing. The position occupied by the author of xii.–xxvi. is faithfully indicated in the superscription iv. 45–49 [7]. The hortatory character and diffuseness of v.–xi. by no means compel us to ascribe it to another author [8]. In details v.–xi. and xii.–xxvi. completely and yet spontaneously agree [9]. Finally, in language and style they present just that degree of agreement and difference which we should be justified in expecting on the hypothesis of a common origin [10]. Any difficulties that may still remain fall away if we accept the very natural supposition that the author of xii.–xxvi. composed the introduction (v.–xi.) subsequently, with his eye upon the laws that he had already collected [11].

[5] The contents of v.–xi. shall be described in **W e l l h a u s e n**'s words [112] (xxii. 462 sq.) ; for they contain a forecast of the reasons that prevent him from attributing these chapters to the author of xii.–xxvi., and will therefore enable us to summarise his further objections the more briefly in n. 6. 'The laws do not begin till xii., up to which point Moses is always c o m i n g but never c o m e s to business. In v. 1, he announces the institutions and statutes which the people are to observe in the land of Canaan, but immediately involves himself in a historical presentation of the occasion on which they were communicated to himself on Horeb forty years ago, when the people begged him to interpose as mediator. At the beginning of vi. he again appears to be coming to the communication of the ordinances and statutes, but turns off into a plea for obedience to the laws, based on love of the lawgiver. And in similar ways our patience is yet further tried in the following chapters. The discourse always turns upon the o r d i n a n c e s a n d s t a t u t e s w h i c h I s h a l l g i v e y o u t h i s d a y, but we are never told what they are. In vii. and viii. an attempt is made to disarm by anticipation all manner of threatening dangers which might lead to their neglect after the conquest of Canaan. Yahwè's grace—which the Israelites might think they could dispense with when they were out of the wilderness—will always be needed, and his wrath will always be terrible. This gives occasion to a long digression on the golden calf ; and it is not till x. 12 sqq. that we return to the enforcement of the commandments ; while xi. once more insists that Yahwè's past care for Israel demands both gratitude and obedience, but that his future care will not be rendered superfluous by the possession of the land, since its fruitfulness depends upon the grace of heaven.' On V a l e t o n see the following note.

[6] After giving his survey of the contents (cf. n. 5) W e l l h a u s e n goes on to say that the reason why the author of v.–xi. so constantly mentioned ' the ordinances and statutes ' was that they actually lay before him in a w r i t t e n w o r k to which he was composing a preface. How else can we explain xi. 26 sqq., setting forth the blessing and the curse attendant on the observance or neglect of the laws which are not yet so much as issued ? And if the author of v.–xi. e d i t e d the code of xii.–xxvi. with a preface, we may suppose that at the same time he introduced a modification here and there. Ch. xvii. 14–20 (in which xxxi. 9, 26 are assumed) may have been inserted by him, as well as xxiii. 5–7 [4–6], which places us in the fortieth year after the exodus. For xxvi. 17, 18 seems to be parallel to *Ex.* xix., xxiv. ' Deuteronomy originally presented itself as an enlarged edition of the old Book of the Covenant. It did not make Moses carry about with him for forty years the laws and statutes he had received on Horeb, but made him publish them to the people at once ' (xxii. 464).

V a l e t o n (*Studiën*, vi. 157–174) agrees with W e l l h a u s e n in denying the exhortations of v.–xi. to the author of xii.–xxvi., but differs from him in thinking he can trace a definite plan in them. The author is diffusive and sometimes falls into repetitions, but does not lose sight of his object ; which is an appeal for the faithful observance of the tora contained in xii.–xxvi.,—an appeal based on the decalogue and drawn in part from the dangers Israel must expect in Canaan, and in part from the experiences of the wilderness. If he [113] seems now and then to wander from his subject, it is because his discourse has been largely interpolated ; v. 5 ; vii. 17–26 ; ix. 18–20, 22–25 ; x. 1–10ᵃ, 18–20 ; xi. 13–21 (or at any rate *v.* 16, 18–20) ; 26–28 (but see *Studiën,* vii. 44 n.) ; 29–31 are all later additions.—As far as this view coincides with W e l l h a u - s e n 's it will be criticised in n. 7–10.—As for the supposed interpolations, I may say at once that it seems to me extremely difficult to determine whether it is the author himself who indulges in these digressions, or deviations, or whether they are due to some other hand. It must be admitted that they might well be dispensed with, and sometimes disturb the context. But the author himself is indicated in general by the style and language of the suspected sections, which agree with D even in minutiæ. Ch. vii. 17–26, for instance, is a string of deuteronomic expressions. Even where the writer keeps closest to *Ex.* xxiii. 20–33—though, for that matter, no closer than the author of *v.* 1–16—he still uses deuteronomic formulæ ; *v.* 21 ערץ מפני (cf. n. 16) ; *v.* 22 נשׁל (*Deut.* vii. 1 ; xxviii. 40) ; *v.* 23 שׁמד Niphal (*Deut.* xii. 30 ; xxviii. 20, 24, 45, 51, 61 ; iv. 26), etc. But I need not examine the interpolations severally. A decision upon them, though a necessary part of any future commentary on *Deuteronomy,* would have no decisive influence on our views concerning *Deut.* v.–xi. as a whole. An exception must be made, however, in the case of x. 1–10ᵃ, since the authenticity of these verses is far from a matter of indifference to the criticism of the Hexateuch. On *v.* 1–5 cf. *Th. Tijdschr.,* xv. 204–207, where it is shown that at any rate the verses in question should not be denied to D without very grave reason. But no such reason is forthcoming. *V.* 1–5 is a digression, it is true, but a perfectly appropriate and— after mention of the tables of the covenant in v. 19 [22] ; ix. 11, 17—a far from superfluous one. Then *v.* 8, 9 are most closely connected with the preceding verses ; it is on account of the ark that the election of the Levites is mentioned here—in purely deuteronomic phrase, cf. xviii. 5 ; xxi. 5—and, accordingly, we see that the duty of carrying this ark is the first to be mentioned (*v.* 8). *V.* 6 and 7, again, belong to *v.* 8, 9, to which they are introductory. Unquestionably they are borrowed from some such source as the work to which *Num.* xxi. 12 sqq. belongs. But the writer of *v.* (1–5) 8, 9 himself may have taken them thence, for they record a circumstance connected with the service of Yahwè (*v.* 6) and bring us to the place, Yotba, at which the Levites were set aside for it (*v.* 7). In *v.* 10ᵃ the speaker returns from this digression to the point from which he had started (ix. 26–29). I admit that this is a strange style of composition, but I cannot think that we are justified in saying that it is impossible, and so regarding as an interpolation a passage which bears the author's stamp so clearly upon it. See, further, *Th. Tijdschr.,* xv. 200 sq.

⁷ Consider the following points, taken in their mutual connection :—In

xii.-xxvi. Moses is the speaker; see xviii. 15, 17, 18; xxiv. 18, 22, and also xii. 8, where the lawgiver reveals himself as one of the people. He is speaking at a definite point of time, 'this day,' xii. 8; xiii. 19 [18]; xv. 5, 15; xix. 9; xxvi. 17, 18 (cf. 'here,' xii. 8). The passage of the Jordan is mentioned, apparently as imminent, xii. 10, and also, repeatedly, the seizure of Canaan, the rooting out of its inhabitants, etc., xii. 1, 2, 29; xv. 4; xvi. 20; [114] xvii. 14; xviii. 9, 12, 14; xix. 1, 2, 14; xx. 16-18; xxi. 1. 23; xxiii. 21 [20]; xxiv. 4; xxv. 19; xxvi. 1. And on the other hand there is nowhere so much as a word of reference to any future wanderings in the desert. Ch. xxiii. 5-7 [4-6] is written as if in the fortieth year after the exodus (and is therefore withheld from the author of xii.-xxvi. by Wellhausen; cf. n. 6). The same may be said of xxiv. 9, which presupposes not only Miriam's leprosy, *Num.* xii., but even her death, *Num.* xx. 1; and likewise of xxv. 17-19, where it is evident that Amalek's former misdeeds are recalled to mind, and the sentence provoked by them repeated, in view of the approaching conquest. In xviii. 16-20, finally, a glance is thrown back upon the sojourn at Horeb and the 'day of assembly' (cf. n. 9) as upon long past events.

[8] In the nature of the case the tone of xii. sqq. must differ from that of v. sqq. We have only to ask whether, if the author of xii.-xxvi. had wished to insist on the faithful observance of his precepts, he would have been likely to do so in the style of v.-xi. Unquestionably he would; for even in the code itself he does not avoid repetitions (xii., etc.), and easily drops into the hortatory tone (e. g. xii. 28; xv. 4-6, 15; xvi. 20; xviii. 9 sqq.; xxvi. 1 sqq.). Cf. also the list of Deuteronomic phrases in n. 4 and in n. 10 below.

[9] Especially noteworthy, I think, is the resemblance between xviii. 16-20 and the hortatory introduction. In *v.* 16 בחרב, as in v. 2; ix. 8; ביום הקהל, as in ix. 10; x, 4, cf. v. 19 [??]; לא אסף, cf. v. 22 [25]; 'this great fire,' as in v. 22 [25], cf. v. 4, 23 [26]; ix. 10; x. 4; ולא אמות, cf. v. 22 [25]; in *v.* 17 הימיר as in v. 25 [28]. Yet it cannot be said that the author of v.-xi. is simply borrowing from xviii. 16 sqq., for he moves quite freely, and never touches upon the thesis of the last-named passage about prophecy as a substitute for Yahwè's immediate revelation. It is the same author who describes the assembly at Horeb in v., mentions it incidentally in ix., x., and makes an independent use of it in xviii.

Again, compare, xxvi. 5 (גוי גדול עצום ורב; במתי מעט) with x. 22 and vii. 1; ix. 1, 14; xi. 23.

xxvi. 8, display of might and miracles at the exodus, with v. 15; vi. 21, 22; vii. 8, 19; ix. 26; xi. 2-4 (the agreement extends to the phraseology);

xviii. 1-8, on the Levitical priests, with x. 8, 9: agreement in substance, again, without servile imitation;

xii. 3 with vii. 5.

See, further, the following note.

[10] Of the forty expressions registered in n. 4 we find the following in v.-xi. **1.** v. 10; vi. 5; vii. 13; xi. 1.—**3.** v. 7; vi. 14; vii. 4; viii. 19; xi. 16, 28.— **4.** *passim.*—**5.** v. 30 [33]; xi. 9, cf. v. 16; vi. 2.—**9.** x. 18.—**10.** vi. 14; viii. 19;

xi. 28 ('go after other gods') ; v. 30 [33] ; viii. 6 ; x. 12 ; xi. 22 ('on Yahwè's path' or 'paths').—**11**. v. 15 (a verse which does not appear in the other recension of the Decalogue).—**12**. vii. 16.—**13**. *passim*.—**14**. xi. 28.—**15**. v. 26 [29] ;

[115] vi. 24 ; xi. 1.—**16**. v. 16 (למען ייטב) does not occur in *Ex.* xx. 12), 26 [29] ; vi. 3, 18.—**17**. ix. 21.—**18**. v. 26 [29] ; vi. 24 ; viii. 6 ; x. 12.—**19**. vi. 18 ; viii. 1 ; xi. 8, 23, 31.—**20**. likewise occurs in v.-xi.—**21**. v. 1, and in Piel v. 28 [31] ; vi. 1 ; xi. 19.—**24**. x. 9 ; cf. ix. 26, 29.—**28**. vii. 8 ; ix. 26.—**29**. vi. 2, 6 ; vii. 11 ; viii. 1, 11 ; x. 13 ; xi. 8, 13, 22, 27, 28.—**30**. v. 28, [31] ; vi. 1, 25 ; vii. 11 ; viii. 1 ; xi. 8, 22.—**32**. vi. 10, 18, 23 ; vii. 8, 12, 13 ; viii. 1, 18 ; ix. 5 ; x. 11 ; xi. 9, 21.—**35**. viii. 20 ; ix. 19, 23 ; x. 10 ; xi. 13, 27, 28 ; —**37**. v. 10, 26 [29] ; vi. 2, 17 ; vii. (8), 9, 11 ; viii. 2, 6, 11 ; x. 13 ; xi. 1, 8, 22 ; together with לעטות, v. 1, 29 [32] ; vi. 3, 25 (vii. 12) ; viii. 1 ; xi. 32. —**38**. vi. 12 ; viii. 11, xi. 16.—**39**. v. 14 ; vi. 9 ; xi. 20.—**40**. vii. 25, 26 ; the Piel of תעב, which occurs twice in the latter verse, and also occurs twice in xxiii. 8 [7].

Twenty-seven out of the forty phrases occur, then, in v.-xi., and we must add that from the nature of the case **2, 6, 7, 25, 26, 31, 33, 36** c o u l d n o t occur, so that really only five out of a list of thirty-two are wanting. —The following parallels may now be added :

41. אכל, in the phrase 'eat and be filled,' vi. 11 ; viii. 10, 12 ; xi. 15 ; xiv. 29 ; xxvi. 12.

42. אמה, v. 14, 18 [21] ; xii. 12, 18 ; xv. 17 ; xvi. 14. The synonym שפחה does not occur in *Deuteronomy* except in xxviii. 68.

43. בית עבדים, v. 6 ; vi. 12 ; vii. 8 ; viii. 14 ; xiii. 6, 11 [5, 10].

44. דבק, 'cleave to (Yahwè),' x. 20 ; xi. 22 ; xiii. 5 [4].

45. דגן, in the formula : 'corn, new wine, and oil,' vii. 13 ; xi. 14 ; xiv. 23 ; xviii. 4.

46. נתן לפנים, vii. 2, 23 ; xxiii. 15 [14].

47. סגלה, in the phrase, 'to be to him a people of his own,' vii. 6 ; xiv. 2 ; xxvi. 18.

48. שכח, in the connection, 'to forget Yahwè,' vi. 12 ; viii. 11, 14, 19 ; ix. 7 ; xxvi. 13.

49. שמאל, in the formula, '(to depart) to the right hand or to the left,' v. 29 [32] ; xvii. 11, 20.

50. שמע, in the formula, 'Hear, O Israel !' v. 1 ; vi. 4 ; ix. 1 ; xx. 3.

All this seems amply to justify the opinion expressed in the text. In v.-xi. the legislative terminology does not occur, but otherwise the formal agreement with xii.-xxvi. is as great as it well could be, while there is not the faintest trace of servile imitation.

[11] On this supposition *Deut.* xii.-xxvi. was never p u b l i s h e d without the heading and introduction (iv. 45-49 and v.-xi. respectively), but these latter may have been w r i t t e n at a longer or shorter interval after the code. The only objection, so far as I can see, which can be urged against this view is that the preliminary work is incomplete. The author who thus introduces Moses as the speaker could hardly omit to tell us further how the discourse had been preserved and could now be published in writing. But this he has

really done, for we shall see presently that the account of how 'this tora' was written down (xxxi. 9-13) is from the same hand as v.-xi., xii.-xxvi. This will also remove the difficulty presented, according to Wellhausen, by xvii. 18 (cf. n. 6), and we shall not be obliged to withhold the ordinance in [116] v. 14-20, to which it belongs, from the author of xii.-xxvi., in whose code it is quite in its place—is indeed indispensable—and whose language is stamped upon almost every word of it.

The chapters which precede v.-xxvi. in the book of *Deuteronomy* must now be submitted to a closer examination, with a special view to the question whether they are due to the author of the great legislative discourse (D^1) or not.

Deut. i. 1-iv. 40, and the postscript *v.* 41-43 cannot be assigned to D^1. This appears from their very position before the heading, iv. 45-49, and from their relation to it [12]. And it is confirmed by their contents, which are at any rate in part foreign to the hortatory and legislative purpose of v.-xxvi. Obviously i. 1-iv. 40 was composed by a writer whose spirit responded to that of D^1, and whose interest in history and archæology made him feel the absence of all mention of the historical antecedents of the legislative discourse of v.-xxvi. He therefore supplied the defect through the mouth of Moses himself, and took the opportunity of laying upon his lips fresh exhortations to observe the tora [13]. That he made use of narratives which we still possess in *Exodus* and *Numbers* is unquestionable [14]; but that he intended his historical introduction to link the Deuteronomic legislation to the older narrative cannot be proved and is not likely [15].

This hypothesis excludes the supposition, which many scholars still regard as admissible, that D^1 himself subsequently added this introduction to his work. The language of i.-iv. seems at first sight to plead for unity of authorship, but it really tells against it; and the great similarity must be explained as the result of imitation [16]. The question is settled by the fact that in certain details i.-iv. contradicts

D¹, and in such a way as to exclude any idea that D¹ intended to correct himself [17]. These chapters, then, are the work of one of the followers of D¹, whom we may designate provisionally as D².

[117] [12] Were i.-iv. and v.-xxvi. from a single hand there would be no necessity for a fresh superscription to v. If the promulgation of the laws began here it would be another matter, but v.-xi., though not quite homogeneous with i.-iv., is just as much introductory, as a comparison, more especially, of iv. with v. sqq. will show us. But even if we grant the necessity of separating v.-xxvi. from i.-iv. by a fresh inscription, still there was no need to define the time and place of the discourse with such minuteness as characterises iv. 46-48, since everything noted there has been told and retold to the reader of ii. and iii. already. In other words, the heading in iv. 45-49 is due to a writer who was not acquainted with the introduction to v.-xxvi. contained in i.-iv. These chapters, then, were added later, and not by the author of v.-xxvi., who would surely have taken sufficient pains with the completion of his own work to have perceived that the heading in iv. 45-49 had become superfluous, and must therefore be withdrawn, or at least shortened.— V. 44 is a connecting link, probably inserted when i.-iv. 43 was joined on to v.-xxvi.

[13] Let us begin by forming an idea of the contents of i. 1-iv. 40; 41-43. Ch. i. 1-5 is a lengthy but far from lucid heading ; in which the connection of v. 1, 2 with the definitions of time and place in v. 3-5 remains obscure. In v. 6 Moses begins to speak. He first tells of Yahwè's command to depart from Horeb (v. 6-8); then of the appointment of judges and officers, who were to assist him in guiding the people (v. 9-18) ; then of the journey through the desert, the arrival at Kadesh-Barné'a (v. 19), and the despatch of the spies with its consequences (v. 20-45). After a brief mention of the stay at Kadesh (v. 46) and the circuit of Mount Seir (ii. 1), he describes the march through the territory of Edom and the rules observed on that occasion at Yahwè's command (v. 2-8ᵃ) ; then he speaks of Israel's arrival on the Moabite frontier, the integrity of which was respected—again at the command of Yahwè (8ᵇ, 9). [At this point there is a note on the earlier inhabitants of the lands of Moab and Seir (v. 10-12)]. Israel arrives at the brook Zared, thirty-eight years after leaving Kadesh ; Yahwè's sentence on the recalcitrants is accomplished (v. 13-16). Ammon's territory is not violated (v. 17-19). [Here again a note on the successive inhabitants of Canaan and the neighbouring lands (v. 20-23)]. Sihon, on the other hand,—so Moses proceeds,—the king of the Amorites at Heshbon, was slain, in accordance with Yahwè's prediction and decree, and his land was conquered by Israel (v. 24-37), after which Og, king of Bashan, met the same fate, and the territory of these two princes was assigned to Reuben, Gad, and half Manasseh (iii. 1-17). [In this passage also there are two notes, on the name of Mount Hermon (v. 9) and on the iron bed of king Og (v. 11) respectively]. The tribes just

named are exhorted to help in the conquest of Canaan (*v.* 18 20), while Joshua is encouraged by an appeal to the display of Yahwè's might which he has now experienced (*v.* 21, 22). For it was Joshua who should lead the people to their destination, not Moses himself, whose repeated prayer to be allowed to cross the Jordan had been rejected (*v.* 23–29). Here the historical reminiscences cease, and the discourse of Moses takes a more hortatory character. He insists, in general, upon the strict observance of the precepts he is about to issue (iv. 1–4), and specially points to the privilege which Israel enjoys above [118] other peoples in this revelation of Yahwè's will (*v.* 5–8), to the theophany at Horeb and, in connection therewith, to the duty of eschewing idolatry and star-worship (*v.* 9–20). Soon Moses himself will be dead and the people will be settled in Canaan (*v.* 21–23); but let them not on that account forget Yahwè and draw his punishment upon their heads, so as to experience his wrath before they turn and seek his mercy (*v.* 24–31); rather let the thought of Yahwè's unique and unheard-of tokens of favour lead them to fidelity towards him (*v.* 32–40)!

The postscript *v.* 41–43 mentions the selection of three cities of refuge in the Transjordanic district. Their function is described in *v.* 42, in expressions which we meet with again in *Deut.* xix. 4, 6. In *v.* 41 הבדיל, as in *Deut.* xix. 2, 7. See below, n. 17.

The characterisation of the author of these chapters given in the text hardly needs any further justification after this review of his work. The notes, glosses as it were on the discourse, which he himself puts into the mouth of Moses, are the clearest proofs of his interest in antiquities; but the discourse of Moses itself is also drawn up mainly with a h i s t o r i c a l purpose, though the tone of warning and exhortation is not wanting. Note, especially, *Deut.* ii., iii. 1–17, evidently written to throw light upon Israel's relations to his neighbours and to explain the settlement in the Transjordanic region. When the author passes, in iv. 1 sqq., from history to admonition, he anticipates the points which D¹ impressed upon his readers in v. sqq., and, like him, though with a somewhat different intention (cf. n. 17), makes use of the events at Horeb for the purpose. Characteristic of his historical sense, in this connection, is his comparison of Israel with other peoples (iv. 6–8; 32–34). His affinities with D¹ are as unmistakable as the difference that parts him from him.

See, further, V a l e t o n, *Studiën*, vi. 304–320, who describes the character and tendency of the historical introduction, i.–iv., very justly. But his contention that this discourse, as well as v.–xi. (n. 6), has been subjected to interpolation cannot be accepted. No doubt the verses which he regards as later additions, viz. ii. 10–12, 20–23; iii. 9, 10ᵇ, 11, 13ᵇ–17; iv. 21, 22 (23–31? cf. *Studiën*, vii. 225, n. 3), really are, for the most part, notes on the discourse of Moses—but they are notes from the hand of the same author that put the discourse into his mouth. His language betrays him, and the parenthetical communication of these historical and geographical details is in perfect harmony with the general character of i.–iv.

¹⁴ Dr. W. H. K o s t e r s, *De historie-beschouwing van den Deuteronomist*,

p. 32–85, shows this by a comparison of *Deut.* i. 6–19 with *Ex.* xviii. 13–27 ; *Num.* xi. ; of *Deut.* i. 20–45 with *Num.* xiii., xiv. ; of *Deut.* ii. 2–23 with *Num.* xx. 14–23 and xxi. ; of *Deut.* ii. 24–iii. 11 with *Num.* xxi. 21–35 ; of *Deut.* iii. 12–20 with (parts of) *Num.* xxxii. The agreement, in matter and form, is too great to allow of the supposition that the parallel narratives rose up independently of each other ; the departures in *Deut.* i.–iii. from the parallel passages may be severally explained on the supposition that the author freely reproduced or intentionally modified the other accounts.

[119]   15 We leave it undecided, for the present, what the character of this older narrative was ; but in any case it embraced the events of the fortieth year, so that the discourse of Moses in v.–xxvi. would directly connect itself with it. No bridge from one to the other was needed, and in no case could it have been furnished by a sometimes rather widely divergent representation of those very events that had just been recorded in the older narrative. No doubt i.–iii. is a recapitulation, but it was intended for readers not acquainted with the older narratives, which certainly were not placed in their hands together with it.

The case is different with i. 1–5. Whether K n o b e l is right in taking *v.* 1, 2 to refer to the p r e c e d i n g discourses of Moses in *Exodus—Numbers* I will not undertake to say, for the two verses seem to me unintelligible. But in *v.* 3, 4 we really have the link that joins *Deuteronomy* to a narrative of the exodus and the events of the fortieth year. Observe that the month in which Moses speaks is here specified as the eleventh—by a number, that is, not a name. This usage is not found elsewhere in *Deuteronomy* (see xvi. 1), but is characteristic of P (*Ex.* xii. 2, etc.), from whom it is doubtless borrowed here. In all probability, therefore, we must attribute *v.* 3, 4 to R, and may perhaps assume that they were thrust in between the beginning (*v.* 1, 2) and the end (*v.* 5) of the heading of i.–iv., and that on that occasion the text of *v.* 1, 2 was marred—not entirely by accident. V a l e t o n takes a rather different view (*Studiën*, vi. 304 sq.) ; he makes the original heading of the historical discourse consist of *v.* 1ᵃ, 5 ('These are the words which Moses spoke to all Israel. On the other side of the Jordan, in the land of Moab, Moses began, etc.') ; *v.* 1ᵇ–4 he attributes to R.

16 In characterising the language of i.–iv. I shall again make use of the list in n. 4 and 10. We meet in these chapters with the following :—**1.** iv. 37.— **4.** here too *passim.*—**5.** iv. 26, 40.—**13.** here too *passim.*—**15.** iv. 40.—**16.** iv. 40.—**18.** iv. 10.—**19.** iii. 12, 20 ; iv. 1, 22 and לרשת, ii. 31 ; iii. 18 ; iv. 5, 14, 26.—**20.** holds equally for i.–iv.—**21.** Kal iv. 10 ; Piel iv. 1, 5, 14.—**22.** iv. 19.—**23.** i. 38 ; iii. 28.—**24.** iv. 21, 38.—**27.** ii. 7.—**29.** iv. 2, 40.—**32.** i. 8, 35 ; ii. 14 ; iv. 31.—**35.** i. 45 ; iii. 26 ; iv. 1, 30.—**37.** iv. 2, 40 ; with עשה, iv. 6. —**38.** iv. 9, 23 (cf. 15 ; and without ל, ii. 4).—**46.** i. 8, 21 ; ii. 31, 33, 36.— **48.** iv. 9, 23, 31.—**49.** ii. 27. In proportion to the extent of the section, i.–iv., and considering the subject of i.–iii., the number of these words and phrases is high ; and it might be raised still further. With **44**, the verb רבק, compare iv. 4, הדבקים. The following supplement should also be duly considered :—

51. הארץ, in conjunction with הטובה, i. (25), 35; iii. 25; iv. 21, 22; vi. 18; viii. (7), 10; ix. 6; xi. 17.

52. האש (מותך), iv. 12, 15, 33, 36; v. 4, 21, 23 [24, 26]; ix. 10; x. 4.

53. יד, in the formula, 'with mighty hand and outstretched arm,' iv. 34; v. 15; vii. 19; xi. 2; xxvi. 8.

54. כיום (הזה), ii. 30; iv. 20; vi. 24; viii. 18; x. 15.

55. כעס, Hiphil iv. 25; ix. 18 (and xxxi. 29; cf. xxxii. 16).

56. לבב, in the phrase, 'with all your heart and with all your soul,' iv. 29; vi. 5; x. 12; xxvi. 16.

57. מרה, Hiphil i. 26, 43; ix. 7, 23, 24 (and xxxi. 27).   [120]

58. נסה, and the subst. מסות, iv. 34; vi. 16; vii. 19.

59. עבר, in such phrases as, 'which ye pass over, to etc.,' iii. 21 (sing.); iv. 14, 22, 26; vi. 1; xi. 8, 11, 31.

60. ערץ, fear, i. 29; vii. 21; xx. 3.

It is not surprising that a great number of scholars, including K n o b e l, G r a f, K o s t e r s, C o l e n s o, and K l e i n e r t, should have assigned i.–iv. to the author of v.–xxvi., chiefly on the strength of the linguistic evidence. At present only K l o s t e r m a n n (*Stud. u. Krit.*, 1871, p. 253 sqq.); H o l l e n b e r g (*ibid.*, 1874, p. 467–470); W e l l h a u s e n (xxii. 460 sqq.) and V a l e t o n (op. cit.) stand on the other side. In my opinion these scholars are right in not allowing themselves to be led away by the language of i.–iv. from the opinion they have formed, on other grounds, as to its origin. The resemblance which is especially marked in iv.—is not of a kind to exclude the hypothesis of imitation; and is accompanied by divergences. It is only in i.–iv. that we find יְרֻשָּׁה, ii. 5, 9 (bis), 12, 19 (bis); iii. 20; the forms התגרה, התחנן, התעבר (ii. 5, 9, 19, 24; iii. 23; iii. 26) [התאנף is not peculiar to i. 37; iv. 21, but occurs in ix. 8, 20 also]; the expression כור חברזל, for Egypt, iv. 20; the formula עם נחלה, iv. 20, in place of עם סגלה (cf. **47** in n. 10). The use of האמרי in i. 7, 19, 20, 27, 44; iii. 9 differs from that in vii. 1; xx. 17 (and approximates to the use of this name in *Josh.* xxiv. 8, 12 [LXX.], 15, 18). More of a like kind might be added; but I attach greater weight to the different general impression left by the perusal of iv. and of the exhortations of v. sqq. The redundancy observable even in the latter degenerates into diffuseness, repetitions, and the piling up of stock phrases and exhortations in the former. I think, therefore, that, although the strength of the proof lies in the phenomena pointed out in n. 12, 13, 17, yet the language itself also pleads against the unity of authorship.

[17] It is but natural that the author of i.–iv. should for the most part agree even in details with v. sqq., which he had completely assimilated and which was always in his mind. This makes the following points of difference all the more significant.

a. In *Deut.* xxiii. 4–7 [3–6] a very unfavourable judgment is passed on Moab and Ammon, on the ground, amongst others, that they had refused bread and water to the Israelites; whereas the Edomites are regarded as brothers (*v.* 8 [7]). But in ii. 29 we are told that the Edomites and the Moabites alike—who are therefore placed on the same footing here and in *v.* 4 sqq. 9,—granted the request for food and drink, that was addressed in vain to Sihon.—This contradiction, which cannot be got rid of, is decisive if we accept the authenticity of *Deut.* xxiii. 2–9 [1–8]. On this point see § 14, n. 1.

b. The passage relating to the covenant at Horeb, iv. 11 sqq., rests upon v. 1 sqq., xviii. 16–19, and has much in common with them. But there are points of difference too. In iv. 11 the mountain burns ‘even into the heart [לב] of heaven.’ In *v.* 12 the Israelites are reminded that they saw no form (תמונה), and then in *v.* 15–18 and again in *v.* 23 sqq. this circumstance is made the occasion of an emphatic warning against worshipping images. Exaggeration may explain the former point, but the latter specifically distinguishes this author from D¹, who makes no such use of the events at Horeb either in v. or in xviii., and indeed never displays such zeal against image-worship as does our writer.

[121]

c. In v.–xi. stress is laid on the Israelites whom Moses is addressing having witnessed the miracles of Yahwè at the exodus and in the desert, and being the same generation with which Yahwè had made a covenant at Horeb (v. 2, 3 ; xi. 2–7). The writer of i.–iv., on the contrary, brings it out very clearly that all the Israelites who had shown their contumacy at Kadesh-Barnéa had died in the desert (ii. 14–16). I find no actual and conscious contradiction in this. Klostermann (p. 254) and Hollenberg (p. 468) express themselves too strongly when they say that *Deut.* v.–xxvi. lacks all ‘chronological moorings’ and that Moses speaks ‘as though his hearers had themselves come out of Egypt and were themselves in the very act of entering Canaan.’ The author of v.–xi. knows of the wandering in the desert for forty years (viii. 2, 15 ; xi. 5), and of the rebelliousness of the Israelites after the despatch of the spies (ix. 23). He evidently knows that the recipients of the deuteronomic legislation were not really identical with the witnesses of the theophany at Horeb, but nevertheless he wishes to identify them with them. But the author of i.–iv. is particularly anxious to distinguish them. Is it not clear that he cannot be D¹ himself? What could move the latter thus to correct himself?

d. According to Klostermann (p. 258 sq.) and Hollenberg (p. 468) the postscript iv. 41–43 is meant to remove the contradiction between *Num.* xxxv. 9–34 (three + three cities of refuge) and *Deut.* xix (three cities of refuge, and when Israel’s territory has received its ultimate extension, three more) by showing that when Moses delivered *Deut.* xix. he had already assigned the three Transjordanic cities of refuge, and had therefore only now to mention the three (ultimately six) Canaanite ones.—This is not correct. There is not the least evidence that the writer of *Deut.* iv. 41–43 was acquainted with the law of *Num.* xxxv. 9–34. Nor could the design of harmonising *Deut.* xix. with it be attributed to him in any case, for it is just by making Moses assign these three cities that he comes into conflict with *Num.* xxxv. and its sequel *Josh.* xx., in both of which the selection is made later, after the conquest of Canaan and by Joshua. *Num.* xxxv., therefore, must be left wholly out of consideration. Either D¹ assumes the account in *Deut.* iv. 41–43, and therefore only speaks, in xix., of the cities of refuge in Canaan, or else he omitted to mention the Transjordanic cities, together with the others, in xix., because his legislation is throughout conceived as intended for the people settled in Canaan proper ; and in this case iv. 41–43 is intended to make good the omission and (in accordance with the actual facts) to give due recognition to the rights of asylum of the Transjordanic cities also.   Probability pleads for the second alternative, for iv. 41–43 was written by someone who knew *Deut.* xix. and followed it (n. 13).   This cannot have been D[1] himself, for had he observed his own omission he would have removed it by a modification of *Deut.* xix.

e. The historical background of the exhortation in iv. 23–31 seems not to be the same as that of D[1] in v.–xi.   More on this in n. 22, under (4).

With respect to the last chapters of *Deuteronomy* various [122] questions arise which are too closely connected with the redaction of the Hexateuch to admit of being answered at present.   As to their relations or want of relations with D[1], the following points should be noted :—

(1) Ch. xxxii. 48–52, and certain verses of xxxiv., have already been assigned to P[2] and his followers (§ 6, n. 44).

(2) ' The blessing wherewith Moses, the man of God, blessed the children of Israel, before he died,' xxxiii., stands in no sort of connection with what goes before, and was doubtless inserted here simply because the death of Moses is recorded in xxxiv. ; no traces of D[1] or his followers can be discovered in it [18].

(3) Neither is ' the song of Moses,' xxxii. 1–44, deuteronomic itself [19], though it is brought into connection with the deuteronomic passages by an introduction, xxxi. 14-30, and a short postscript, xxxii. 45–47.   This setting itself is composite.   Ch. xxxi. 16–22 constitutes the real introduction, and *v.* 14, 15, 23 ; xxxii. 44, prove that the song itself was once a portion of a historical composition that dealt with the times of Moses.   Now whether the song, together with the introduction, was incorporated in *Deuteronomy*, or whether it was subsequently united to it, together with, and as a part of, the historical writing to which it belonged, must

be left for the present undecided. Probability favours the latter alternative, which involves the ascription of the second introduction, xxxi. 24–30, and the postscript, xxxii. 45–47, to a redactor, who must however, as shown by his language, be reckoned amongst the followers of D^1 [20].

(4) Amongst the passages that remain after the removal of these non-deuteronomic elements (xxvii. 1–xxxi. 13, and xxxiv. in part), there are some which, it seems, we must ascribe to D^1, viz. xxvii. 9, 10; xxviii., which form the conclusion of the great legislative discourse of v.–xxvi.; and xxxi. 9–13, in which Moses is said to have committed it to writing and given the necessary orders for its preservation and public reading. The objections urged against the ascription of these [123] passages to D^1 fall to the ground if we suppose that he added them, like v.–xi., when he issued his code xii.–xxvi [21].

(5) On the other hand, xxvii. 1–8; 11–13; 14–26; xxix.; xxx.; xxxi. 1–8, and the deuteronomic verses of xxxiv., must be looked upon as later additions and elaborations in the style of i.–iv. Ch. xxvii. 1–8 is a deuteronomic recasting of an earlier original, and is, in that respect, parallel with xxxi. 14–30. It breaks the context, and for that, if for no other reason, must be regarded as a later addition; *v.* 11–13 rests on a misunderstanding of xi. 29–32, and so betrays its later origin at once; *v.* 14–26 is a still later interpolation provoked by *v.* 11–13, with which, however, it no more agrees than it does with xii.–xxvi. Ch. xxix. and xxx., in so far as they run parallel with xxviii., are superfluous and out of place; and moreover a different historical stand-point from that of D^1 may be detected in them. Ch. xxxi. 1–8 belongs to i.–iv. and therefore cannot be attributed to D^1. Finally, the deuteronomic parts of xxxiv. seem to be a recasting and expansion of some older narrative and therefore appear to stand on the same footing as xxvii. 1–8; xxxi. 14–30 (see above, under (3)) [22].

The inquiry we have instituted shows that the tora of D^1

called a literature into existence that held very closely to the form and contents of its prototype. This conclusion may be used all the more boldly in the sequel inasmuch as it perfectly harmonises with what we should have expected *a priori* [23].

[18] It is now admitted on all hands that *Deut.* xxxiii. is not by the same author as the rest of the book, and it is pretty generally allowed that the blessing is the earlier. According to K. H. Graf, *Der Segen Mose's*, p. 79 sqq., it dates from the time of Jeroboam II. C o l e n s o, who was at first disposed to regard D¹ as its author (*Pentateuch*, iii. 570 sqq.), subsequently admitted that it was otherwise (*Pentateuch*, vii., Appendix, Synoptical table, p. iv.)

[19] The opposite view is taken by C o l e n s o, *Pentateuch*, iii. 563 sqq. vii. Appendix, Synoptical table, p. iv., and, of course, by the defenders of the Mosaic authorship, such as F. W. S c h u l t z, *Das Deut. erklärt*, p. 649 sqq.; K e i l, *Lev. Num. Deut.*, p. 537 sq. [iii. 466]. The real points of linguistic similarity to D¹ and his followers are but few, especially if xxxi. [124] 14–30, which has naturally borrowed much from the song, is excluded from the comparison; and if any explanation of those that remain were needed, it might be found in the supposition that the song was known to D¹, etc. With *v.* 3, גדל, compare (*Num.* xiv. 19) *Deut.* iii. 24; v. 21 [24]; ix. 26; xi. 2; with *v.* 17, 'gods whom they did not know, whom their fathers feared not,' compare *Deut.* xi. 28; xiii. 3, 7, 14 [2, 6, 13]; xxviii. 64; xxix. 25 [26]; with 16, 19, 21 (bis), 27, כעס, *verb* and *subst.*, compare *Deut.* iv. 25; ix. 18; with *v.* 13, צור חלמיש, compare viii. 15 (in reversed order); and with the appeal to heaven and earth in *v.* 1, compare *Deut.* iv. 26; xxx. 19 (and xxxi. 28). The other similarities alleged have no evidential value.

[20] On this point consult K l o s t e r m a n n's interesting study, *Das Lied Mose u. das Deuteronomium* (*Stud. u. Krit.*, 1871, p. 249–294). The hypothesis from which K l o s t e r m a n n starts with reference to the book of *Numbers* within which *Deuteronomy* was included, I regard as untenable. But he seems to have p r o v e d, partly with and partly against K n o b e l (*Num., Deut., Josh.*, p. 320 sq.), (1) that xxxi. 16–22 is the real introduction to the song; (2) that the song itself, together with the introduction, once formed part of a composition on the Mosaic age from which xxxi. 14, 15, 23; xxxii. 44 are also taken; (3) that xxxi. 24–30; xxxii. 45–47 are deuteronomic, and probably from the hand that united the work just referred to with the deuteronomic passages in which it is now embedded. Passing over the questions of redaction I may here note the main proofs of these three points.

(1) Ch. xxxi. 16–22 is an independent piece, not from the same hand as *v.* 14, 15, 23. In *v.* 16 there is a new opening; there is not a trace of Joshua in the whole passage, כתבו in *v.* 19 being addressed to the Israelites. It is n o t deuteronomic; it does not contain one of the usual turns and expressions, and on the contrary has a number of words and phrases foreign to *Deuteronomy* : נאץ; חיה לעד ;פנה אל ;רעות ;הסתיר פנים ;הפר ברית ;אלהי נכר ;זנה אחרי

עשׂה יצר; בטרם. Its connection with the song to which it now forms the introduction is evident in every line and needs no further proof.

(2) *V.* 14, 15 again are n o t deuteronomic, cf. אהל מועד; קרב למות. Klostermann is of opinion that the author of these verses incorporated the song and the introduction (*v.* 16–22) into his own narrative, and in order to make them fit in placed the introduction between *v.* 14, 15 (Moses and Joshua in the ôhel mo'éd) and *v.* 23 (Yahwè's command to Joshua). Thus the song would be revealed to Joshua also, and he might share the command to promulgate it, which accords with xxxii. 44 (from the same hand as xxxi. 14, 15, 23).—Nothing can be urged against this view in itself, but it is not, as Klostermann thinks, the only possible one. If it should appear that the song and introduction are later than xxxi. 14, 15, 23, we might then suppose that the author of the introduction had woven both introduction and song into his account of Joshua's consecration to his office, and that xxxii. 44 was likewise inserted by the same author. Whether this hypothesis is actually preferable to the other cannot be decided yet. Cf. § 8, n. 15, and § 13, n. 30.

(3) Ch. xxxi. 24–30; xxxii. 45–47 are deuteronomic in the first place, (cf. Klostermann, p. 266–270, 275 sq., whose proof covers the verses, xxxi. [125] 24, 25, 30, which Knobel derives from another source), and in the second place their special purpose is to bring the preceding section, *v.* 14–23, and the song itself, xxxii. 1–43, 44, into connection with the inditing and depositing of the deuteronomic tora. The author follows *v.* 14–23, but without ceasing to depend on D¹.

[21] On the subject of this and the following notes, cf. *Th. Tijdschr.*, xii. 2 ? 7– 323, where the propositions laid down in the text as to xxvii. are expressly worked out. I will not now dwell on the verses I have denied to D¹ (cf. n. 22), but will briefly note the reasons for assigning the passages indicated above to him.

(1) Ch. xxvii. 9, 10. The tora does not come to an end with xxvi.; the closing discourse (parallel to *Ex.* xxiii. 20–33; *Lev.* xxvi. 3–45) and the colophon have still to be supplied; and accordingly they appear in xxviii. 1–68 and xxviii. 69 [xxix. 1] respectively. Now, although we can imagine these passages joining on immediately to xxvi., yet xxvii. 9, 10 forms an admirable connection between them, suited to the weight of the denunciation in xxviii. There is nothing, then, to prevent our following the linguistic evidence of these verses and assigning them to D¹ (cf. **4, 29, 35, 50** in n. 4, 10).

(2) The warp and weft of xxviii. are so obviously spun out of deuteronomic material, that the only question left is whether it is possible to explain the fact as resulting from imitation rather than from unity of authorship. Wellhausen (xxii. 461 sq.) points out that in *Deut.* xxviii. 58, 61, 'the words of this tora, written in this book' and 'the book of this tora' are mentioned, and hence he concludes that the author of the blessing and the curse had the work of D¹ before him, and therefore was not D¹ himself. But here the remarks on xvii. 18, 19, made in n. 11, are again applicable; if D¹ himself (xxxi. 9–13) records the writing down of 'this tora' by Moses, he

might well drop into the mention of ' the book of this tora,' especially in a subsequent addition to his work—and such in any case we must hold xxviii. no less than v.–xi. (cf. n. 11), to have been. So much is certain, that the position taken up by the author of xxviii. is precisely that of D^1. Like him (xi. 13 sqq., xxvi. sqq.) he sets the blessing and the curse over against each other and leaves the free choice between the two open to Israel. His description of the blessing (*v.* 1–14) is briefer than that of the curse (*v.* 15–68), but this lies in the nature of the case. Amongst the many disasters which are to ensue on Israel's disobedience, deportation to a foreign land occurs (*v.* 36, 37, 41, 63–68), but it is merely one out of numberless afflictions, and the first mention of it is followed by the enumeration of other penalties which are to fall upon Israel in his own land (*v.* 38–40, 42 sqq.). The deportation is to the author a simple possibility—and one out of many such—so that he never follows it up, in the whole of his long discourse, or says anything of its consequences or its fruits. In *v.* 63–68, likewise, the threatened captivity closes the scene, and the threat 'you shall offer yourselves for sale there (in Egypt) to your enemies, and no one shall bid for you,' is the last word. All this is in marked contrast (cf. n. 22) with iv. 26 sqq.; xxix. [xxix. 2–29], xxx., so that the limited outlook of our passage cannot be regarded as accidental. Add that the colophon xxviii. 69 [xxix. 1] answers to the exordium v. 2 sqq. There is really no reason, then, to depart from the usual opinion concerning xxviii., which is also defended by G r a f, K l o s t e r m a n n, and H o l l e n b e r g. The last-named scholar, however, holds, with good reason, [126] that the distinction between xxix. sq. [xxix. 2–xxx.] and xxviii. [xxviii.–xxix. 1] is more certain than the unity of v.–xxvi. and xxviii. K l e i n e r t ' s opinion (op. cit., p. 196 sqq.), that xxviii. 28–37, 49–57 are interpolations, many centuries later than the rest, stands or falls with the antiquity he assigns to the original discourse, cf. § 12, n. 1–7. V a l e t o n (*Studiën,* vii. 44 sq.) only allows *v.* 1–6, 15–19 to the author of the hortatory discourse (v.–xi.) and regards all the rest as later expansion. He points out the connection of these verses with xxvi. 16–19, and the beautiful parallelism between the blessing and the curse which marks them. Undoubtedly the denunciation would have gained in force if the author had restrained himself within the limits supposed, but does this give us any right to deny that the elaborate development of the antitheses is his? In *v.* 7–14, 20–68, I cannot discover a single indication of diverse authorship, and the language and style of D^1 are obvious throughout—in *v.* 47–68, which K a y s e r (*Jahrb. f. p. Theologie,* 1881, p. 530 sq.) denies to the original author, as well as elsewhere. But after all it must be admitted that a discourse such as this courted interpolation, so to speak, and we cannot therefore guarantee the authenticity of every word.

(3) Ch. xxxi. 9–13 may easily be detached from *v.* 1–8, to which it in no way refers, and may be regarded as the continuation of xxviii. The language is that of D^1 without a single departure (with *v.* 9 compare x. 8; with *v.* 10 compare xv. 1–6; xvi. 13–16; with *v.* 11 compare the passages under **6** in n. 4; with *v.* 12 compare ibid. **39, 18, 21, 37, 4**; with *v.* 13 compare ibid. **21,**

18, 15, and xii. 1 [but also iv. 10]). A main argument for assigning these verses to D^1 is that they not only harmonise with the setting he has chosen, but are a necessary part of it. He could not send forth the legislative discourse in v.–xxvi. without at the same time answering the question how it had been preserved—preserved as we shall presently see, § 12, for many centuries ! This is why he states that Moses himself provided for its being written down and perpetuated. Add to this the evidence of xvii. 19 (see above, n. 11).

The limits I assign to the original 'book of the tora' coincide exactly with those laid down by C o l e n s o (*Pentateuch*, vii., Appendix Syn. table, p. iv.), except that he puts iv. 44, instead of iv. 45–49, at the head of the book. In this I would gladly follow him if iv. 44 contained any indication of the time and place of the discourse of Moses ; but we find none such till we come to *v.* 45–49, and since something of the kind is really indispensable we are forced to lay hold of these verses and claim them, or some shorter heading of similar purport, for D^1.

[22] In brief, the reasons are as follows :—

(1) Ch. xxvii. 1–8. Here an older injunction, *v.* 5–7 [a] (sacrificial feast on Ebal), is taken up by a writer who knows and copies D^1, and the feast is made a means of enforcing 'this tora' (*v.* 3, 8). That the author is not D^1 appears less from his language (compare באר, *v.* 8, with i. 5, however), than from the position of the passage and from its character, passing as it does beyond the lines of D^1.

(2) *V.* 11–13 is unconnected with *v.* 1–8, and is certainly from another hand. It is placed here because of Ebal, in *v.* 4, but it really refers back to [127] xi. 29–32. In this latter passage, however, nothing is said of dividing the people into two sections. The idea, in D^1, is to 'lay the blessing on Gerizim and the curse on Ebal,' where they will both lie ready to hand, and will one or the other fall upon the people, when settled in Canaan, according to their deeds. The misconception in xxvii. 11–13 betrays the later writer.

(3) *V.* 14–26 is only in appearance the continuation of *v.* 11–13. Levi takes a different *rôle* in the second passage; and it was unknown to the writer of *Josh.* viii. 30–35, who was acquainted with xxvii. 1–8, 11–13. The writer of *v.* 14–26 intended his addition to stand where we now find it (*v.* 26, 'the words of this tora'), and attaches himself indifferently to D^1 (compare *v.* 17 with xix. 14; *v.* 19 with xxiv. 17; *v.* 20 with xxiii. 1 [xxii. 30]), and to P^1 in *Lev.* xviii.–xx. (compare *v.* 18 with *Lev.* xix. 14; *v.* 21 with *Lev.* xviii. 23; *v.* 23 with *Lev.* xviii. 8, etc.). These verses are not—as they would have been had D^1 been their author—an epitome of *Deut.* xii.–xxvi. For all these reasons we must regard this passage as a late interpolation. Cf. K a y s e r, op. cit., p. 101 sq.; *Th. Tijdschr.*, xii. 306–309 and below, § 16, n. 12.

(4) Ch. xxix [xxix. 2–29], xxx. is a single whole. K l e i n e r t ' s supposition that xxix. 21–27 [22–28]; xxx. 1–10 are interpolations, comes under the same judgment as his views concerning xxviii. (n. 21 (2)). In xxix. 1 [2] we have a fresh opening, which, when taken in connection with xxviii. 69 [xxix. 1], at once challenges the suspicion that the discourse so introduced is a later addition. The only real question is whether this interpolation was made by D^1 (K n o b e l,

G r a f, and others), or by one of his followers. The linguistic evidence is not conclusive ; deuteronomic words and phrases abound, but there is also much that is special, e.g. אלה (xxix. 11, 13, 18–20 [12, 14, 19–21] ; xxx. 7), and in general the phraseology of xxix. 3 [4], 9 [10] (נצב), 10 [11] (wood-cutters and water-carriers), 11 [12] (עבר בבריה), 16 [17] (גלולים), שקוצים, 17, 18, [18,19], 21 [22] (תחלאים, חלה), 22 [23], 25 [26] (ולא חלק להם, cf. iv. 19), 27 [28] (נתש), xxx. 3 (שב שבות), 6 (circumcision of the heart), 11–14, 15 (cf. 19 bis, 20, pregnant use of חיים, blessed life). But the contents forbid us to ascribe the two chapters to D¹. It is true that the author observes the conditions imposed by the historical situation so far as to treat the lot of Israel after the settlement in Canaan as still uncertain and dependent upon his atti-tude towards the tora. But this is merely a matter of form, for it is obvious throughout that to the writer's mind the punishment has already actually fallen upon the people in the specific form of banishment, and the blessing can only be earned after and in consequence of it. 'The realisation of the curse is taken for granted, and is the point of departure for the hopes of conversion and blessing in the future' (W e l l h a u s e n). See especially xxx. 1 sqq.; at first it seems as though the realisation of ' all these words,' including blessing and curse alike, were to be spoken of, but the writer falls at once into a dis-course exclusively concerned with the curse, and with the exiles, their repent-ance, and the blessedness that will follow it. T h i s h a s n o p a r a l l e l i n D¹, either in xxviii. or elsewhere ; but only in iv. 25 sqq. Here, too, the opening is hypothetical, ' i f you beget children and grand-children . . . and do what is evil in Yahwè's eyes,' etc. (*v.* 25), t h e n ye shall not live long in the land, etc. (*v.* 26 sqq.). But instead of any notice of the alternative possibility [128] we find a promise (*v.* 29 sqq.) to the exiles who seek Yahwè that they shall be restored and shall enjoy the tokens of his favour undisturbed. This resem-blance to i.–iv., taken in connection with n. 12 sqq., is an additional reason for assigning xxix. [xxix. 2–29], xxx. to one of the followers of D¹ rather than to himself.

(5) Ch. xxxi. 1–8. This is a fragment of a history of the Mosaic period, standing in no direct connection with ' this tora.' The contents are essentially the same as those of *v.* 14, 15, 23, which we have assigned above (n. 20) to an older narrator : what Yahwè says to Joshua in *v.* 23, Moses says to him in *v.* 7 (read תביא) and 8. Our passage, then, is the expanded deuteronomic parallel of the older account, which was itself afterwards appended—of course by another hand—to the deuteronomic pericope that had been built upon it (thus reversing the process by which *Deut.* i.–iv. was appended to the narra-tives of *Exodus* and *Numbers*, of which it was itself the deuteronomic epitome ; cf. n. 14, 15). The agreement of xxxi. 1–8 with i.–iv. appears (*a*) from the references in *v.* 2 to iii. 27 (i. 37) ; and in *v.* 3ᵇ to iii. 28 (i. 38 ; iii. 21 sq.); (*b*) from the language, which bears the common deuteronomic stamp, יהוה נחיל; אלהיד; השמיד; ירש; נתי לפניו; כל-המצוה; the oath to the fathers ; הנחיל, but agrees more particularly with i.–iv. Observe the combination of חזק with אמץ, original in xxxi. 23 and adopted thence in *v.* 6, 7 ; iii. 28, cf. i. 28 (*Josh.* i. 6, 7, 9, 18 ; x. 25) ; הרפה, iv. 31 ; xxxi. 6, 8 (with עזב here as in *Josh.*

K

i. 5); אל תיראו ולא תחת, xxxi. 8 (cf. *v.* 6 ואל תערצו ואל תיראו); i. 21 (*Josh.*
i. 9; viii. 1; x. 25). On the parallel passages in *Joshua* more hereafter; at
present we need only state our conclusion that i.–iv. and xxxi. 1–8 belong to
a single work by one of the followers of D[1].

(6) Ch. xxxiv. Cf. § 6, n. 44. Traces of deuteronomic language and
conceptions in *v.* 4 (the oath to the fathers; שמה לא תעבר), 6 (מול)
פעור, cf. iii. 29), 7[a] (? cf. xxxi. 2[a]), 11, 12. But by their side—not counting P[2]
in *v.* 1[a], 8, 9—are expressions that point to other sources: *v.* 7[b] does not
agree with xxxi. 2[b]; *v.* 10, פנים אל־פנים, as in *Gen.* xxxii. 31 [30]; *Ex.* xxxiii.
11 (but פ״ בפ in *Deut.* v. 4). The case is therefore identical with that of
xxxi. 14–30 and not unlike that of xxvii. 1–8; xxxi. 1–8.

[23] D[1] is well aware that he conceives and regulates the relation between
Yahwè and Israel in a manner special to himself, and the very form which
he adopts emphasizes the importance and novelty of his tora. How fully he
was justified in this belief will appear presently (§ 12). It is, therefore, perfectly natural that a portion of the prophetic literature should show signs of
his influence, and that men should rise to carry on his work, and, specifically,
to write the history of the Mosaic and subsequent ages in his spirit. The
book of *Joshua* at once supplies the proof that this is what actually took
place.

Just as the close of *Numbers*, from the hand of P[2], raises the
expectation of a narrative of the conquest and division of
Canaan from the same source, and just as we actually find
the narrative we expect, mingled with other documents, in
[129] the book of *Joshua* (§ 6, n. 46–53), so we are likewise prepared,
by the closing chapters of *Deuteronomy*, for further information
from the same hand, or from the same school, concerning the
doings of Joshua as the successor of Moses[24]. Nor do we
search the book of *Joshua* in vain in this case either.

Joshua i.–xii. is by no means deuteronomic as a whole. We
cannot even detect and separate any connected deuteronomic
narrative in it. And yet these chapters contain turns and
conceptions so characteristically deuteronomic, that when taken
in their mutual connection and with reference to their context
they justify the conclusion that *Joshua* i.–xii.—apart from the
fragments of P[2] embraced therein (§ 6, n. 48)[25]—contains
the *deuteronomic expansion and recasting* of an older history.
The line cannot always be drawn with certainty between this

original narrative and the modifications introduced into it.
But it is highly probable that the following passages and
verses should be regarded as inserted, or at least recast, in the
deuteronomic recension :—i. (almost entirely); ii. 10, 11; iii.
3, 7 ; iv. 14, 21–24 ; v. 2 (שוב and שנית), 4–7 ; viii. 1,
2[b], 27, 29(?)[b], 30–35 ; ix. 24, 25, 27[b] ; x. 8, 25, 27(?), 40–42 ;
xi. 10–20, 23[b] ; xii., largely [26].

In the second portion of the book of *Joshua* (xiii.–xxiv.)
the deuteronomic recension has likewise left distinct traces,
amongst which we include xiii. 1[b]–6, 8–12, 14, 33 ; xiv. 6–
15 ; xviii. 7 ; xxi. 41–43 [43–45] ; xxii. 4, 5 ; xxiii. ; xxiv. 1,
9, 13, 31 [27]. All these are additions, not to P[2], but to the
accounts which we have already (§ 6, n. 49–53) seen are now
united with his in *Joshua* xiii.–xxiv [28]. Ch. xx. would be an
exception to this rule were the deuteronomic phrases that occur
in it (*v.* 3 (in part), 4, 5, 6[b]) allowed to rank with those indicated above. But the text of the LXX. proves that they were
not inserted in the priestly account of the selection of the cities
of refuge until after the final redaction of the whole book [29].

Our previous investigations (n. 12 sqq.) at once suggest the
question whether these passages and verses are from D[1], or [130]
from one or more of his followers. The latter hypothesis,
which Hollenberg has conclusively defended, has antecedent
probability on its side also, and completely harmonises with
the conclusions we have reached in regard to *Deut.* i.–iv.,
xxvii., xxix.–xxxiv [30]. It seems hardly possible, however, to
ascribe the deuteronomic recension to a single author ; nor is
there anything against our supposing several hands to have
been at work on the same lines [31].

---

[24] Cf. *Deut.* xxvii. 1–8 ; xxxi. 3–6, 7, 8, 23, as well as passages that come so
early in the book as i. 38; iii. 21, 22, 28.

[25] The question whether the deuteronomic editor had these fragments of
P[2] before him, or, in other words, whether they were a constituent part of the
narrative into which he inserted matter of his own, cannot be solved by the

evidence of i.–xii.; but xiii.–xxiv. yields a negative answer (n. 27, 28), which, when once we have obtained it, we may extend to i.–xii. likewise.

²⁶ We will first enumerate the deuteronomic terms and expressions in the book of *Joshua*, a s a w h o l e, referring to the list in n. 4, 10, 16; and we will then proceed to the more detailed statement and defence of the conclusions they warrant.

In *Joshua*, then, we recognise, **1**. xxii. 5; xxiii. 11.—**3**. xxiv. 2, 16.—**4**. Yahwè, followed by אלהים with pronominal suffix, *passim*, e. g. i. 9, 11, 13, 15, 17; ii. 11; ix. 9, 24, etc., etc. In narrative always 'Yahwè, the god of Israel,' vii. 13, 19, 20; viii. 30; ix. 18, 19; x. 40, 42; xiii. 14, 33; xiv. 14; xxii. 24; xxiv. 2, 23, a formula which does not appear in the Pentateuch except in *Ex.* v. 1; xxxii. 27.—**5**. cf. xxiv. 31.—**6**. ix. 27ᵇ.—**10**. xxii. 5.—**13**. xxii. 5.—**15**. iv. 24.—**19**. i. 15; xxiii. 5; רשׁת, i. 11; xiii. 1; xviii. 3; xxiv. 4. —**23**. i. 6.—**24**. נחלה, xiii. 6, 7, 14, 33; xxiii. 4 (also occurs in P², xiv. 3; xvii. 4, 6; xix. 49).—**25**. vii. 25.—**30**. xxii. 5.—**32**. i. 6; v. 6; xxi. 41, 42 [43, 44].— **35**. i. 17; v. 6; xxiv. 24.—**37**. שׁמר, xxii. 3 (with משׁמרת, very common in P², etc., but also occurring in *Deut.* xi. 1; *Gen.* xxvi. 5), 5; with לעשׂות, i. 7, 8; xxii. 5. —**38**. נשׁמר, with מאד, xxii. 5, and with personal pronoun, preceded by ל, xxiii. 11; cf. *Deut.* ii. 4; iv. 9, 15.—**43**. xxiv. 17.—**44**. xxii. 5; xxiii. 8.—**46**. x. 12; xi. 6.—**49**. i. 7; xxiii. 6.—**51**. xxiii. 16 (cf. האדמה הטובה, v. 13, 15).—**53**. iv. 24.—**56**. xxii. 5.—**57**. i. 18.—**60**. i. 9.

This list is enough in itself to show that deuteronomic phrases occur with special frequency in the passages and verses indicated above; and the impression is confirmed by the parallel passages collected in n. 22, and also by the following supplement.

61. יום, in the formula 'many days,' xi. 18; xxiii. 1; xxiv. 7, cf. *Deut.* i. 46; ii. 1; xx. 19.

62. לחם, in 'Yahwè fights for Israel,' x. 14, 42; xxiii. 3, 10, cf. *Deut.* iii. 22.

63. נוח in Hiphil, i. 13, 15; xxii. 4; xxiii. 1, cf. *Deut.* iii. 20; xii. 10; xxv. 19.

64. כל־נשׁמה, x. 40; xi. 11, 14, cf. *Deut.* xx. 16.

65. שׁמד in Hiphil, ix. 24; xi. 14, 20; xxiii. 15; xxiv. 8, cf. *Deut.* ii. 22, 23, and elsewhere.

On the deuteronomic recension of *Josh.* i.–xii., in particular, consult H o l - l e n b e r g 's careful investigations in *Stud. u. Krit.*, 1874, p. 472–506, and note the following points :—

Ch. i. With *v.* 3–5ᵃ compare *Deut.* xi. 24, 25ᵃ (see below, n. 30). In *v.* 8, ' this book of the law' as in *Deut.* xxix. 20 [21]; xxx. 10. The שׁטרים, *v.* 10, appear in *Deut.* xvi. 18; xx. 5, 8, 9; xxix. 9 [10]; xxxi. 28, but also in *Ex.* v. 6, 10, 14, 15, 19; *Num.* xi. 16; the editor may therefore have found them in the original, from which he certainly took the c o n t e n t s of *v.* 1, 2, 10, 11, though not without running them into his own mould. With *v.* 12–15 compare *Deut.* iii. 18–20; the answer of the Transjordanic tribes, *v.* 16–18, which is replete with deuteronomic phrases, is evidently a homiletic addition.

Ch. ii. 10, החרים, of Sihon and Og, as in *Deut.* ii. 34; iii. 6. With *v.* 11ᵇ compare *Deut.* iv. 39.—H o l l e n b e r g (p. 490 sq.) believes *v.* 9, 24 also to bo deuteronomic additions ; but they do not contain the characteristic phrases (cf. *Deut.* ii. 25) and may have been borrowed from *Ex.* xv. 15, 16, by the earlier author himself; in which case *v.* 10, 11 is a development of the theme given in *v.* 9.

Ch. iii. 2–iv. 24 remains a compound narrative (§ 4, n. 13) even when the deuteronomic additions have been thrown out. The latter are easily detected by their language : iii. 3 (הכהנים הלוים) as in *Deut.* xvii. 9, 18 ; xviii. 1 ; xxiv. 8 ; xxvii. 9) ; 7 (cf. i. 5, and *Deut.* ii. 25) ; iv. 14 (refers back to iii. 7) ; 21–24 (paraphrase and expansion, addressed to all Irsael, of what was said to the twelve men in *v.* 6, 7, though referring there to the heap of stones in t h e b e d o f t h e r i v e r). It might be asked whether ' the priests bearing the ark' (iii. 6, 8, 13–15, 17 ; iv. 9, 10, 16, cf. *Deut.* xxxi. 9) are not also deut- eronomic, and, if so, whether one of the two accounts of the passage of the Jordan must not be placed in its entirety amongst the deuteronomic additions. But these verses do not display the usual characteristics of the editor, so that we had better attribute no more than iii. 3, 7 ; iv. 14, 21–24 to him.

Ch. v. 2, 3, 8, 9 are very properly regarded by H o l l e n b e r g (p. 193 sq.) and, independently of him, by W e l l h a u s e n (*Geschichte*, 1st ed., i. 365) as an old account of the i n t r o d u c t i o n of circumcision, which is represented as an E g y p t i a n practice, the application of which to the Israelites will remove the reproach of uncleanness hurled at them by the Egyptians. *V.* 4–7 serves to bring this account, which could not but offend the editor, into at least the semblance of agreement with the current belief as to the origin of circum- cision. These verses betray their dependence upon *Deuteronomy*, not only by the parallels already cited, but by their agreement with *Deut.* i. 34, 35, and the resemblance of the heading (וזה הדבר) to *Deut.* xv. 2 ; xix. 4. But see below, § 16, n. 12. It obviously follows that, in *v.* 2, שוב and שנית— which are quite beside the mark, since Joshua had performed circumcision on no previous occasion were added by the author of *n.* 4–7.   [132]

On the ark of Yahwè, borne by the priests, vi. 6 sqq., see above on iii., iv.

In viii. 1, perhaps the first words only (cf. n. 22) are a deuteronomic addition. *V.* 29 agrees with *Deut.* xxi. 23 in substance, but not in words, so that its deuteronomic character must remain doubtful.—The destination of the booty of Ai, *v.* 2b, 27, is midway between the deuteronomic ordinances concerning non-Canaanite and Canaanite cities respectively (*Deut.* xx. 12–14 ; 16–18). The meaning is that Israel was allowed to take possession of the property of the men of Ai a s a n e x c e p t i o n; and *v.* 2b, 27 must therefore be regarded as dependent on *Deut.* xx.—*V.* 30–35 assumes *Deut.* xxvii. 1–8, 11–13 through- out. See further, n. 30.

Ch. ix. 27b is evidently of deuteronomic origin. According to H o l l e n- b e r g (p. 496 sq.) the same may be said of *v.* 22–27 as a whole. But W e l l h a u s e n rightly contests this (xxi. 593 sq.); *v.* 22 and 23 are the indispensable sequel of *v.* 16 and are continued, in their turn, in *v.* 26, 27ᵃ (which has passed through the hand of the redactor however, cf. § 6, n.

134   *The Hexateuch.*   [§ 7.

48). *V.* 24, 25, on the other hand, looks like a subsequent addition and re-minds us of D¹ and his followers.

On x. cf. H o l l e n b e r g (p. 497 sqq.) and W e l l h a u s e n (xxi. 594 sqq.). As to *v.* 8—an obvious insertion—no doubt can exist. The same may be said of *v.* 25. For *v.* 27 cf. note on viii. 29. H o l l e n b e r g regards *v.* 12–15 as a deuteronomic addition also, but in spite of נתן לפני (*v.* 12) and יהוה נלחם לישראל (*v.* 14), I hold, with W e l l h a u s e n, that this is very doubtful; the style is not the same. As to *v.* 28–39, 43 I am not clear. W e l l h a u s e n assigns them, together with *v.* 40–42, to the deuteronomic writer; and it certainly harmonises with the latter's spirit thus to extend the area of Joshua's victories, and then allow him the free disposal of the land whose inhabitants have been slaughtered. Nevertheless the discrepancy between *v.* 37 (ואת־מלכה) and *v.* 23 (את־מלך הברון) makes it probable that a story lay at the basis of *v.* 28–39, 43, whose author was unacquainted with *v.* 16–27. If so, this story was taken up by the deuteronomic writer and reproduced in *v.* 40–42.

In xi. the deuteronomic recension is clearly traceable, perhaps even in *v.* 2, 3 (where the four kings of *v.* 1 are increased by an indefinite number of others), but certainly in *v.* 10–20, which is due in its entirety to the deutero-nomic editor, save for a few details in *v.* 10, 11. *V.* 23ᵇ (cf. xiv. 15) must likewise be attributed to him. But *v.* 21, 22 (inconsistent with xiv. 6–15) and *v.* 23ᵃ (that comes too soon ; see below on xiii. sqq.) are not his. In all probability they are a still later addition, in which Joshua's conquests were yet further expanded in defiance of the fixed tradition about Caleb as the conqueror of the Anakites.

Ch. xii. 1–6 recalls—without any real appropriateness—the conquest of Sihon's and Og's territory. It is closely related to *Deut.* iii. 9–12, 14–17 and presumably comes from the same hand or the same school. The title (*v.* 7, 8,) of the list that now follows resembles xi. 17 ; it uses ירשה, cf. *v.* 6 ; i. 15 ; *Deut.* ii. 5, 9, 12, 19 ; iii. 20, and generalizes Joshua's victories, cf. x. 28 sqq. ; xi. 10–20. It may therefore be assigned to the deuteronomic editor, and in that case the list itself, *v.* 9–24, must also have been drawn up by him. [133] It is quite in harmony with this that the original authors of vi. sqq. and xxiv. appear not to have known of the thirty-one kings defeated by Joshua.

²⁷ We have already seen from § 6, n. 49–53, that *Josh.* xiii.–xxiv. presents a most complicated problem for solution. In order to arrive, if possible, at some trustworthy conclusion as to the nature and extent of the deuteronomic recension of these chapters, we must take xxiii. as our point of departure, for the language of this chapter (n. 26) proves it to be deuteronomic in its entirety. Against K n o b e l (p. 480 sqq.) who divides it between the 'Kriegsbuch,' the Jehovist, and Deuteronomist, see amongst others, C o l e n s o, W e l l h a u s e n, and especially H o l l e n b e r g (p. 481–485). Now in Joshua's discourse the defeat of the Canaanites is an accomplished fact (*v.* 3, etc.) ; the tribes have a heritage assigned them, still partially in the possession of the old inhabitants (*v.* 4) ; t h e i r s e t t l e m e n t i n t h a t h e r i t a g e i s s t i l l t o c o m e (*v.* 5 sqq.) ; and Joshua utters his admonitions and warnings in view of it.

The meaning of *v.* 1 is, 'After many days (cf. xxii. 3) when Yahwè had given rest,' etc. (and not, 'many days after Yahwè,' etc.). In a word, just as the Transjordanic tribes are dismissed to their homes in xxii. 1 sqq., so here the rest of the Israelites are d i s b a n d e d by Joshua when the conquest and the partition of the land have been completed (cf. xxiv. 28).—We infer from xxiii., therefore, that the deuteronomic editor conceived the partition of the land to be an act of Joshua's, so far forming a complete and single whole that the settlement itself, likewise regarded as a single act, could follow in due course upon it. But this is not the only view we find in *Josh.* xiii. sqq. According to xviii. 2 sqq. Judah and Joseph established themselves first (see especially *v.* 5^b), and then the remaining seven tribes had their heritage assigned them at Shiloh—by lot in their case, but, it would seem, n o t s o in the case of Judah and Joseph, otherwise Joshua would not have reproached the tribes (*v.* 3 sqq.), but would have borne the blame of the delay himself. Ch. xvii. 14–18 agrees with xviii. 2 sqq. The independent settlement of Judah and Joseph, however, is not further described in xiii. sqq.; the account of it which the original author of xvii. 14–18; xviii. 2 sqq. must have left, has certainly been omitted. It is not difficult to guess why. The deuteronomic editor makes a point of showing that all the tribes had their heritage assigned them by Joshua, and that too in one and the same manner, namely, by lot. He could therefore only retain so much of the older accounts as seemed capable of being reconciled in some sort with this conception; and could not retain the heading which definitely excluded it. This throws some light on the obscure verses xiii. 1–7. *V.* 1 probably belonged to xviii. 2 sqq., originally, but was transferred to its present place by the deuteronomic writer. The words (*v.* 1^b), 'there yet remains exceeding much land to be taken and possessed,' which originally referred to the whole of Canaan except the territory occupied by Judah and Joseph, are now taken in another sense and applied to the districts which still remained in the possession of the old inhabitants (*v.* 2–6, where this explanation is, oddly enough, put into the mouth of Yahwè himself). The command to divide the remaining territory (amongst the seven tribes, to wit) that must also have belonged originally to xviii. 2 sqq., is now made to embrace t h e n i n e a n d a h a l f t r i b e s, and is transplanted together with the rest (*v.* 7), without the writer's taking the trouble to bring [134] it into any connection with his own words (*v.* 2–6). This hypothesis also throws light on the almost verbal coincidence of xiii. 1 with xxiii. 1^b, 2^b, and of xiii. 6^b with xxiii. 4^a.

Having thus modified the account of the partition of the land the deuteronomic editor added certain details of his own. In the first place the concise description of the Transjordanic land, xiii. 8–12, which sometimes agrees verbally with xii. 1–6 (cf. n. 26); then the remark as to Levi, xiii. 14 (cf. *Deut.* xviii. 1, 2), repeated in *v.* 33—though the text of the LXX. indicates the hand of a later copyist here; then the passage xiv. 6–15, the relation of which to *Deut.* i. 19–36 is extremely close (cf. *Th. Tijdschr.*, xi. 551 sq., 558 sq., where it is also shown that וְעַל־אֲדוֹתִיק, *v.* 6, is a gloss); and finally xviii. 7 (=xiii. 14).

Linguistic evidence shows that xxi. 41–43 [43–45] likewise is an addition by the deuteronomic writer, as well as xxii. (3 ?), 4, 5, if, indeed, the whole pericope xxii. 1–6 is not from his hand, or at least recast by him (*v.* 7, 8 I regard as a very late addition, intended to explain the ויברכם of *v.* 6 more fully; *v.* 7ᵃ is quite superfluous and interrupting).—On the other hand, xxiv. 1–27 is certainly not of deuteronomic origin; cf. Hollenberg (p. 485–488), and Wellhausen (xxi. 601 sq.); but a comparison of *v.* 1ᵇ with xxiii. 2; of *v.* 13 with *Deut.* vi. 10; and of *v.* 31 with the passages collected under 5 in n. 4 and *Deut.* xi. 7, makes it probable that these verses were recast or inserted by the deuteronomic editor. There are, likewise, traces of the deuteronomic usage in *v.* 2 (עבד אלהים אחרים), 4 (לרשת אותו), 7 (cf. n. 26, **61**), 16 (cf. 2), 17ᵇ (cf. *Deut.* xxix. 15 [16]), 24 (cf. n. 4, **35**), but they are not distinct enough to lead to any definite conclusion; *v.* 9 and 10 certainly resemble *Deut.* xxiii. 5 and 6, but they also differ from, and therefore are not dependent on, them.

²⁸ With respect to most of the texts dealt with in n. 27, this is obvious at a glance. In xiv. 6–15 we find Joshua at Gilgal (*v.* 6), whereas it is highly probable, to say the least, that P² makes the whole partition of the land take place at Shiloh (§ 6, n. 52). Ch. xviii. 7 occurs in a connection (*v.* 2–10) that has nothing in common with P². Ch. xxi. 41–43 [43–45], though it now follows the list of priestly and Levitical cities (from P²) is in no way whatever connected with it; but attaches itself to xxii. 1–6, which does not belong to P². Neither in xxiii., nor in the deuteronomic additions to xxiv., nor in the original text of that chapter, is the smallest knowledge of xxii. 9–34 (P³ or P⁴) betrayed.

²⁹ Cf. Hollenberg, *Der Charakter der alex. Uebersetzung des B. Josua,* p. 15, and *Th. Tijdschr.,* xi. 467–478.

³⁰ See *Stud. u. Krit.,* 1874, p. 462–506. Hollenberg clearly shows that the deuteronomic passages in *Joshua,* while resembling *Deut.* v.–xxvi. in language, are in far closer agreement yet with *Deut.* i.–iv., xxvii., xxix.–xxxi., etc. He also points out that *Deut.* xi. 24, 25 is cited in *Josh.* i. 3–5ᵃ as a word of Yahwè to Moses—a mistake of which the writer of *Deut.* xi. could hardly have been guilty. I cannot allow, with Hollenberg (p. 479 sq.), that *Deut.* xxvii. 1 sqq. has been misunderstood by the author of *Josh.* viii. 30–35, or, in other words, that the latter identifies the plastered stones with the rough stones of the altar; but I agree with him that the original writer to whom we owe *v.* 30–32, 34 (except 'the blessing and the curse') and 35, was himself one [135] of the followers of D¹, inasmuch as *Deut.* xxvii. 1–8 was either composed by him or lay before him as he wrote (cf. n. 22 under (1)); *a fortiori,* then, the same may be said of the man who added *v.* 33 and 'the blessing and the curse' in *v.* 34, in accordance with *Deut.* xxvii. 11–13 (cf. n. 22, under (4)). The outlook into the future at the close of the discourse in xxiii. (*v.* 12–16), is the same as in *Deut.* xxix.; xxx.; iv. 26 sqq. (cf. n. 22).

³¹ I have shown in *Th. Tijdschr.,* xii. 315–322 that *Josh.* viii. 30–35 is the work of two deuteronomic redactors (cf. n. 30). But apart from this it seems difficult to believe that the deuteronomic passages dealt with in n. 26, 27 are

all from the same hand. Ch. xxi. 41–43 [43–45] and the passages related to it, viz. xxii. 1–6 ; x. 40–42 ; xi. 10–20 differ in purport from xxiii. ; xiii. 2–6. Now it is perfectly true that D^1 himself is not always consistent. For example, he insists, according to the changing needs of his admonitions, now upon the greatness (*Deut.* x. 22 ; xxvi. 5) and now upon the smallness (vii. 7, cf. 1, 17, 22; ix. 1 ; xi. 23) of Israel's numbers. But this is not exactly parallel to the inconsistency we should have to ascribe to the deuteronomic editor of *Joshua*, if he had allowed xxi. 41–43 [43–45] and xxiii. to follow one upon the other. We may further ask whether *Josh.* i. 8 is not later than *v.* 7 ? whether x. 36, 37 can have been taken into his history by the author of xiv. 6–15 ? and, finally, whether xi. 21–23ᵃ—on which consult n. 26—does not give additional evidence of the r e p e a t e d recasting of the historical narra- tive in a deuteronomic sense ? Cf. § 16, n. 12.

The results yielded by the analysis of *Joshua* suggest the question whether the deuteronomic recension was confined to that book alone, or whether it embraced *Genesis—Numbers* also. The latter hypothesis cannot be rejected or even pronounced improbable *a priori*. As a matter of fact C o l e n s o believes he has recognised the hand of the Deuteronomist in *Genesis, Exodus, and Numbers,* and assigns to this source no inconsider able portion of the laws and narratives they contain—four hundred and twelve Masoretic verses in all [32]. He would not stand alone—or almost alone [33]—in his opinion, if any evidence for it lay on the surface of the texts. Whether a closer examination, especially of the non-priestly portions, will con- firm his position, can only appear hereafter (§ 8, 13).

[32] So in *Pentateuch,* vii., Synopt. table, p. i.–vi., and *App.,* p. 145 sqq. In the previous volumes of his work C o l e n s o had already found numerous traces of D in *Genesis, Exodus,* and *Numbers,* but had not represented his influence as so extended. The deuteronomic verses in *Genesis* he now puts at 117, those in *Exodus* at 138½, those in *Numbers* at 156½.

[33] There are points of contact between C o l e n s o's opinion and that of Stähelin, who (most recently in his *Specielle Einleitung,* p. 22 sqq.) identifies the Deuteronomist with the Jehovist, i.e. the author of *Genesis—Numbers* [136] after the withdrawal of P ; but the difference between him and C o l e n s o is far greater than their agreement. W e l l h a u s e n approaches more nearly to C o l e n s o's position when, from time to time (xxi. 543 sq., 549, 555, 564, 584), he notes a relationship between JE, i. e. the redactor of the two works J and E, and the book of *Deuteronomy,* and even asks whether JE may not have been revised by a deuteronomic redactor. A d . J ü l i c h e r (see § 8, n. 10) goes

further and asserts that this actually was so. But the assumption of a deuteronomic recension of this kind falls notably short of C o l e n s o's contention.

§ 8. *The 'prophetic' elements of the Hexateuch (JE).*

The designation of 'prophetic,' which is here applied to all that remains of the Hexateuch when the priestly and the deuteronomic elements are removed, must be regarded as altogether provisional. It rests upon the indisputable relationship between s o m e of the passages in question and the writings of the prophets of the eighth and seventh centuries before Christ, but in no way prejudges the question whether these passages were actually written by prophets; and still less does it imply any decision concerning the origin of the passages in which this relationship cannot be traced. The possibility, for instance, that priests of Yahwè may also have had a hand in the work is by no means excluded by our nomenclature. What we want is simply a common title for all that does not belong to P or D, and the name selected does not seem inappropriate when we consider the phenomenon already noticed and remember the width of the connotation of prophecy in Israel [1].

[1] See further § 13.

The examination to which these 'prophetic' elements are submitted in the present § is exclusively concerned with their mutual relations and the connection in which they stand to the rest of the Hexateuch. The results to which it leads us, therefore, must necessarily be incomplete; and will be supplemented in the following §§.

Nothing is clearer than that the 'prophetic' elements do not form a literary whole. The usual indications of the union of different accounts—repetition, discrepancies, differences of language—force themselves repeatedly and un-

mistakably upon us. But it is no less obvious that some [137]
of the narratives and pericopes have a common origin : they
presuppose one another, and agree in language and style [2].
The ultimate goal of the critic, therefore, must be the complete indication of the connected works—and the detached
narratives and laws, if there are any—which lie at the basis
of the 'prophetic' portions of the Hexateuch, and the explanation of the method in which they have been interwoven on
the one hand, or welded together and recast on the other. But
this remains at present an unattained ideal. As the analysis
has been carried gradually further it has become increasingly
evident that the critical question is far more difficult and
involved than was at first supposed, and the solutions which
seemed to have been secured have been in whole or in part
brought into question again. The present position is, in its
main outlines, as follows :—

The phenomena which present themselves in the 'prophetic'
elements of *Gen.* i.–xi. leave room for more than one hypothesis.
These chapters undoubtedly contain divergent accounts of the
earliest generations of men and their distribution over the
earth, which cannot possibly be due to one and the same
author. Nevertheless we now find them united together, and
it is not immediately obvious whether the fragments which
we may suppose to be the earliest have been incorporated by
a later author into his own work, or whether they have been
welded with the more recent pericopes by a third hand [3].
The first half of Abraham's history, in *Gen.* xii.–xix., even
when the passages taken from P have been removed, again
shows the clearest traces alike of complexity of origin and of
successive recensions. For example, the whole of xiv. is
derived from a different source from that which precedes and
follows. But the study of these chapters still fails to yield
any definite results [4]. From *Gen.* xx. onwards, however, the
general character of the 'prophetic' elements becomes much

clearer; for at this point a writer appears who, widely as he differs from P in other respects, resembles him in avoiding the name Y a h w è, and employing E l o h î m or H a -
[138] e l o h î m instead. In the rest of *Genesis* this use of E l o h î m, even in non-priestly passages, constantly recurs, and the same conceptions and the same style that we note in *Gen.* xx. reappear with it. Now these sections do not form a well connected whole; they are but fragments, and, moreover, in spite of all that they have in common, they do not always breathe the same spirit. But notwithstanding this we must regard them as portions of a single work, which, on account of its use of E l o h î m, we may call the elohistic document, and may indicate by the letter E[5]. Side by side with these passages we also find in *Genesis*, from xx. onwards, another set of narratives or pericopes, which are connected together, and which often run parallel with E in matter, though departing from it in details and language. This group must also be derived from a single work which we may call the Y a h w i s t i c document, inasmuch as it is distinguished from E by the use of Yahwè (Jahvè), and which we may indicate by the letter J*. It is no more complete than E[6]. This J is also the chief, though not the only source from which the earlier chapters of *Genesis* draw, alike in i.–xi. and xii.–xix[7]. On the other hand it is not strictly demonstrable that E has contributed anything to the first half of Abraham's history (*Gen.* xii.–xix.), and there is no reason whatever to assign any portion of *Gen.* i.–xi. to him[8].

It is probable *a priori* that neither E nor J would confine himself to the patriarchal period. Both alike would have something to say of the release of Israel from Egypt and the settlement of the tribes in Canaan[9]. And as a fact in *Exodus*, *Numbers*, and *Joshua* we here and there detect just

---

* See translator's note on p. 64.

such a parallelism between E and J as we have seen in *Genesis*. But here it is sporadic, and by no means so clear as in *Genesis*. Traces of E appear in *Ex.* i. and ii., and in *Ex.* iii. 1–15 the same document comes very distinctly into view, though not without foreign admixture. This pericope is the 'prophetic' counterpart of the priestly passage, *Ex.* vi. 2 sqq., and it explains the use of E l o h î m in the accounts of the præ-Mosaic age which are drawn from E[10]. We should naturally expect that this particular characteristic of E would now disappear, but the facts do not confirm our expectation : E l o h î m and H a - e l o h î m still characterise the document, even after *Ex.* iii. 15, though we cannot follow its [139] traces at all easily. It is only here and there that we can detect it with certainty amongst the 'prophetic' elements of *Ex.* iii. 16–xii[11]. Subsequently it reappears in *Ex.* xiii. 17–19, 21, 22 ; xiv. 19[a] (and 19[b] (?)) ; xv. 22–26 ; xvii. 1[b]–7, 8–16 ; xviii. ; and then again in *Ex.* xix. 9[a], 10 17 ; xx. 18–21, 1–17 ; xxiv. 12–14, 18[a], but we also find it in certain other sections of *Ex.* xix.–xxiv., which seem to contradict the representation of the Sinaitic legislation given in E, and therefore, it would seem, cannot be assigned to that document, i.e. in *Ex.* xxiv. 1, 2, 9–11, and in the Book of the Covenant, with the appended narrative of the covenant itself, *Ex.* xx. 22–xxiii. and xxiv. 3–8. The solution of this riddle cannot be attempted till later on[12]. The story of Israel's apostasy at Sinai, which is preserved in an expanded form and combined with other narratives in *Ex.* xxxii.–xxxiv. also belonged originally to E[13]. We may further ascribe the following passages, with more or less probability, to the same document : *Num.* x. 33–36 ; xi. 1–3 ; one of the strands out of which xi. 4–35 is twisted ; xii. ; the 'prophetic' portion of xiii., xiv., and of xvi. ; xx. 1–13 in part, 14–21 ; xxi. 4[b]–9, 12–20, 21–32 ; and xxii. 2–xxiv., with the exception of a certain amount of matter which must have

been borrowed from elsewhere [14]. In *Deut.* xxxi. 14–23 again
we find traces of E [15]. Finally, it is obvious from *Josh.* xxiv.,
which must be largely drawn from E, that this document
related the conquest of Canaan by Joshua, but we can no
longer detect its accounts with any certainty in *Josh.* i.–xii [16].

Still more scanty and indefinite are the results of the
critical analysis of *Exodus—Joshua* with respect to J. In
Ex. i.–xv. we can, no doubt, detect the narrative of J, running
parallel with that of E, as in *Genesis*, but it appears in far less
distinctness and purity than before [17]. On the other hand, it
is doubtful whether J has contributed anything to the
accounts of the Sinaitic legislation and the apostasy of the
people (*Ex.* xix.–xxiv. and xxxii.–xxxiv). The specific assign-
[140] ment of the Book of the Covenant (*Ex.* xx. 22–xxiii. and xxiv.
3–8) to J is emphatically to be rejected [18]. As to the rest of
the Hexateuch, J may apparently be discovered in *Num.* x.
29–32 ; in the story of the quails that lies at the bottom
of *Num.* xi. 4–35, and in *Num.* xxi. 1–3 [19]. A part of *Josh.*
i.–xii., with a few stray sections in xiii. sqq., especially xvii.
14–18, may perhaps belong to our document, but conclusive
proof of the fact is not forthcoming [20].

[2] Specimens of discrepancies within the limits of the 'prophetic' matter may
be found amongst the examples in § 4, n. 11 sqq. Many more will be added
in the course of this section. The mutual harmony of many of the narratives,
both in matter and form, is allowed on all hands, and need not be demonstrated till the facts brought out in n. 3 sqq. spontaneously develope it.

[3] On these chapters cf. the Commentaries and monographs cited by D i l l -
m a n n, *Genesis*, p. 14 sq., 49 sq., and elsewhere, to which must now be added
K. B u d d e, *Die bibl. Urgeschichte untersucht* (Giessen, 1883) and my review
of it in *Th. Tijdschr.*, xviii. 121–171. B u d d e rightly judges, in agreement
with W e l l h a u s e n (xxi. 398 sqq.) and to some extent with E w a l d and
D i l l m a n n, that *Gen.* iv. 16[b]–24; and xi. 1–9 know nothing of the deluge, and
derive the present race of men from Cain, in unbroken descent ; and also that
a story lies at the basis of *Gen.* ix. 20–27 which represents Noah as the father
of Shem, Japheth, and Canaan, and is therefore irreconcileable with the conception that runs through *Gen.* vi. sqq. elsewhere, making Noah the father of
Shem, Ham, and Japhet, and through them the ancestor of a new humanity.
Gen. vi. 1–4, again, though not exactly in conflict with its surroundings, like

the three passages just named, strikes us as a detached fragment. At any rate, it is connected neither with what goes before it, i.e. *Gen.* iv., nor yet with what follows. But on the other side, we must observe that *Gen.* iv. 16ᵇ–24 is led up to by *v.* 1–16ᵃ, and is assumed in *v.* 25, 26; that *Gen.* ix. 20–27 is crudely harmonised with *Gen.* vi. sqq. by the insertion of the words 'Ham, the father of' in *v.* 22ᵃ (cf. *v.* 18ᵇ), and that *Gen.* xi. 1–9 is anticipated by x. 25 (the explanation of the name Peleg). We may explain all this either, with B u d d e, as the work of a redactor who interwove the materials supplied by two independent documents, or as due to the method of the latest of the 'prophetic' writers, who appropriated fragments from one or more predecessors, and incorporated them in his own work. I incline to the latter hypothesis, but it would be rash to determine the question at this stage of the inquiry, and at present we have simply to note the phenomena of *Gen.* i.–xi. as they stand.

⁴ The most remarkable instance is *Gen.* xiv. The story is in its proper place, for it pre-supposes Lot's separation from Abram, and his settlement in Sodom (xiii. 5, 7–11ᵃ, 12ᵇ, 13). But it does not contain the least hint of the wickedness of the men of Sodom, and conversely the author of *Gen.* xviii., xix. knows nothing whatever of the conquest of the five cities, or the rescue of their inhabitants by Abram. *Gen.* xiv., then, must be due to a different [141] author, and in point of fact it is distinguished from the other chapters by marked linguistic peculiarities.—The evidence borne by *Gen.* xv. is of another character: here two accounts are united into a badly fitting whole, and then further supplemented by elements foreign to both. *V.* 5, 6 places us in the middle of the night; *v.* 12 (continuation of *v.* 7–11) and 17 (continued in *v.* 18) describe the afternoon and approaching evening. In *v.* 2–4 the question is who shall be Abram's heir, and elsewhere (e.g. *v.* 7 sqq., 17 sq.) it is what his posterity shall inherit. The prediction in *v.* 13–16, which is itself composite, breaks the connection between *v.* 12 and 17. Finally, the curious list given in *v.* 19–21 is without parallel in the 'prophetic' passages, and is certainly not part of the original story.—But the other chapters also yield unmistakable evidence of composite origin, and of recension. The author of *Gen.* xii. 10–20 does not think of Abram as accompanied by Lot, and therefore cannot be the same as the writer of *v.* 1–4ᵃ, 6–9; xiii. 5, etc. (though the gloss 'and Lot with him,' xiii. 1ᵇ, attempts to harmonise the two). Or if we decline to accept this inference we must suppose that *Gen.* xii. 10–20 is misplaced. (Cf. W e l l h a u s e n, xxi. 413 sq.; D i l l m a n n, *Gen.* p. 211 sq.).—*Gen.* xiii. 14–17 and xv. 5, 18 are variations on one theme. Cf. W e l l h. xxi. 414. and on *Gen.* xvi. 8–10, ibid. p. 410.—According to W e l l h a u s e n (xxi. 415 sqq.), *Gen.* xviii. and xix. have also been recast; he regards xviii. 22ᵇ–33ᵃ and *v.* 17–19 which leads up to it, as later additions; he likewise thinks that 'the two angels' who appear in xix. 1 sqq., and are distinguished from Yahwè, are later than 'the three men' of xviii. 2 sqq. 22, who represent Yahwè. This view, on which more hereafter, § 13, n. 21, is not refuted by D i l l m a n n, *Genesis*, p. 248 sq.; but even those who cannot accept it must admit that more than sufficient proof has already been given of the thesis that the 'prophetic' sections of *Gen.* xii.–xix. are not all taken from the same source.

⁵ Cf. de Wette - Schrader, p. 274 sqq.; Dillmann, *Genesis*, passim; Wellhausen, xxi. 405 sqq.; Colenso, *Wellhausen on the Composition*, p. 95–132; *Pentateuch*, vii., App., p. 145 sqq.; cf. v., Crit. Anal., p. 77 sqq. Though these scholars fall notably short of c o m p l e t e agreement, yet they are so far at one as to leave no room for doubt that we are treading upon firm ground in our identifications of E. On the other hand, it must be admitted (1) that the resemblance between E and the narratives or pericopes now united with it is sometimes bewilderingly close, so that when the use of E l o h î m does not put us on the track, we are almost at a loss for means of carrying the analysis through; (2) that the accounts which we assign to E on the strength of their language and mutual connection sometimes develope internal differences, which force us to ask whether all that we rank, and cannot choose but rank, under E can really be from one and the same hand. With the reservations implied in these remarks I would assign the following passages to E : *Gen.* xx. 1–17; xxi. 6 (?), 7 (?), 8–31; xxii. 1–13, 19; probably a part of xxvii. ; xxviii. 10–12, 17–22; a part both of xxix. and of xxx.; nearly all xxxi. ; xxxii. 1–3, 14ᵇ–22 [xxxi. 55–xxxii. 2; xxxii. 13ᵇ–21] and perhaps a few more verses of xxxii. and some verses of xxxiii. 1–17; further, xxxiii., 18–20, in great part; xxxv. 1–4, 6–8; xxxvii. 2ᵇ–14, 21, 22, 28–30, 32 (in part), 34 (in part), 35 (in part), 36, and some other verses; xl.–xlii.
[142] (except for slight modifications, and, it would seem, further expansions of E's text by a later hand) ; xlv. 1–5 (modified here and there), 6–28 (in great part) ; xlvi. 1–5ᵃ ; xlviii. 1, 2, 8–22 (save for the later addition of *v.* 13, 14, 17–19) ; l. 15–26. I must be content with referring to my predecessors, enumerated above, and with very short comments on the results set forth. In xx. 1–17 E l o h î m or H a - e l o h î m occurs six times, whereas in the parallel xii. 10–20 Y a h w è is used throughout. *V.* 18, in which Y a h w è occurs, is evidently a gloss on *v.* 17, due to another hand, for it misrepresents the meaning : Abimilech too had been sick ; whence וילדו instead of ותלדנה.—On xxi. 6, 7 cf. B u d d e, op. cit., p. 215, 224, *v.* 8–31, beyond all doubt is of common origin with xx. 1–17 ; not so *v.* 32–34 : witness Y a h w è, in *v.* 33, against E l o h î m nine times in *v.* 6–31 ; 'land of the Philistines,' in *v.* 32, 34, at variance with xx. 2.—Ch. xxii. 1–13, 19 is E's, except for the change of E l o h î m *v.* 11 (cf. xxi. 17), to Y a h w è; whereas in *v.* 14–18 we have an addition, dependent on xii. 1–3, and agreeing with it in the use of Y a h w è (*v.* 14 bis, 15, 16, against E l o h î m five or six times in *v.* 1–13). On the purpose of *v.* 14–18, and on 'the land of Moriah,' in *v.* 2, cf. W e l l h a u s e n, xxi. 409 sq. and § 13, n. 29. The heading of the section, *v.* 20–24 (cf. *v.* 1) seems to indicate E as its source ; but see B u d d e, p. 220 sqq.—On xxvii., cf. W e l l h a u s e n, xxi. 422 sqq. ; D i l l m a n n, *Genesis*, p. 309. It appears from the sequel of E in *Gen.* xxxii., xxxiii., that in this document, as well as others, Jacob was represented as sinning against Esau and fleeing to Haran ; an account of his trespass, therefore, must have occurred in E and, as a matter of fact, *Gen.* xxvii. betrays itself clearly enough as composite ; the contributions of E, however, cannot be identified with certainty.—Ch. xxviii. 10–22 is evidently two-fold : *v.* 10–12, Jacob's dream, should be followed

immediately by *v.* 17 (perhaps preceded by וייקץ from *v.* 16); Jacob understands, by the ladder, that Bethel is a place at which heaven and earth
communicate. In the interpolated passage, *v.* 13–16, note Y a h w è (*v.* 13,
16), against E l o h î m in the other story (*v.* 12, 17, 20, 22), for the single
appearance of Yahwè in the latter (*v.* 21) can hardly be original ; see further
n. 6.—The analysis of xxix., xxx. yields no complete result. Ch. xxix. 31–35
(Y a h w è four times), and xxx. 25–43 (contradicting xxxi.) are certainly not
E's; whereas he is indicated in xxx. 6, 8, 17, 18, 20, 22, 23, by E l o h î m,
note especially *v.* 23, of which *v.* 24 (Yahwè) is the doublet. Cf. further,
W e l l h a u s e n, xxi. 425 sq. and D i l l m a n n, *Gen.*, p. 319 sq.—With
regard to xxxi. there is remarkable harmony amongst the critics. E is
credited by S c h r a d e r with *v.* 1, 2, 4–17ª, 19–47, 51–54; by C o l e n s o
with *v.* 2, 4–9, 14–17, 19–48ª, 50–54; by D i l l m a n n with *v.* 2, 4–17, 19,
20, 21 (in part), 22–24, 26, 28–45, 47, 51–54; by W e l l h a u s e n (xxi.
430 sqq.) with almost the same verses. *V.* 18 has already been assigned to
P². The rest of the chapter has received some additions, such as *v.* 1 (doublet
of 2), 3 (uses Y a h w è, and is ignored in *v.* 4 sqq.), 23ᵇ (doublet of 25ª) and
others, especially in *v.* 45–54, W e l l h a u s e n ' s masterly treatment of which
should be consulted ; but it is impossible not to see that, with these exceptions,
it is a single whole, conflicting with xxx. 25–43 and agreeing in substance and
in language with the passages taken from E.—Ch. xxxii. 1–3 [xxxi. 55–xxxii. 2] [143]
is certainly from E, in which document השכים בבקר, נשק with ל, פגע with
ב and מלאכי אלהים repeatedly occur. On xxxii. 4 [3]–xxxiii. 17, on the other
hand, W e l l h a u s e n, xxi. 433 sqq., and D i l l m a n n, *Gen.*, p. 340 sq.
differ somewhat. Both scholars hold that xxxii. 14ᵇ–22 [13ᵇ–21] and certain
details in xxxiii. 1–17 (E l o h î m in *v.* 5, 10, 11) are taken from E, but xxxii.
25–33 [24–32] is derived by D i l l m a n n from the same source, and by
W e l l h a u s e n from J (cf. n. 6). In this case E l o h î m, *v.* 29, 31 [28, 30]
is no sufficient evidence, for in *v.* 29 [28] it is appellative (cf. *Judges* ix. 9, 13),
and *v.* 31 [30] is dependent on 29 [28]. Nor is the linguistic evidence of the
passage conclusive in other respects. The decision must, therefore, be made
upon other grounds, which cannot be considered till later on ; cf. § 13, n. 23.
At present we can only say that in the E-sections, after *Gen.* xxxii., the
patriarch is g e n e r a l l y called ' Jacob,' whereas the J-passages g e n e r a l l y
speak of Israel : this pleads for the derivation of *Gen.* xxxii. 25–33 from J, but
it is not conclusive, since i n o u r m o n g r e l t e x t o f *G e n e s i s* numerous
exceptions to the rule occur.—Ch. xxxiii. 18–20 may be derived in the main
from E, but the language of P² has influenced the form of *v.* 18. W e l l h a u-
s e n ' s objection (p. 438, but compare p. 602) to the derivation of *v.* 19 from E
cannot be maintained. It is true that the verse contradicts xxxiv., but neither
this chapter, nor xxxv. 5, which builds upon it, can be assigned to E. The
latter does not harmonise with xxxv. 4, and is quite superfluous. For the
rest, xxxv. 1–8 is rightly assigned to E by the great majority of critics ;
C o l e n s o ' s objections with respect to *v.* 2–4 (*Pentateuch*, vi., App., p. 111)
are not made good by the parallel passages he cites.—On the history
of J o s e p h, xxxvii. and xxxix.-l., W e l l h a u s e n (xxii., p. 442 sqq.) and

Dillmann (*Gen.*, p. 372 sqq., 382 sqq.) may be profitably compared with each other. The narrative of E is distinguished from another with which it is now united, by the following points, amongst others: Reuben, not Judah, takes the lead amongst Joseph's brothers (xxxvii. 21, 22, 29, 30; xlii. 22, 37); Joseph is kidnapped by Midianites, without the knowledge of his brothers, not sold by his brothers to Ishmaelites, and is carried off to Egypt, where he becomes the slave of Potiphar, Pharaoh's eunuch, captain of the body-guard, and keeper of the prison, not of a married Egyptian, whose wife slanders him and has him thrown into prison (xxxvii. 28ª, 36, cf. xxxix. 1ª; xl. 15ª; xli. 12, cf. xl. 3, 4, 7; xli. 10). If this is the general relation in which the two stories stand to each other, then the three chapters, xl.–xlii., together with a part of xxxvii., belong to E. As we now have them, the chapters have not only been retouched here and there to harmonise them with the other story, but are characterised, like xxxix., by a redundancy not usually observed in E. On the presumable cause of this, cf. § 16, n. 12. As for xxxix., we must follow Dillmann and dissent from Wellhausen in denying it to E, in spite of the linguistic suggestions of *v.* 6, 7, 9, 14: Pharaoh's eunuch cannot have been married, and E does not make Joseph a prisoner, but a slave of the prison-keeper. It seems natural, at first, to see the continuation of xl.–xlii. in xliii., xliv., which, on the whole, take the same view of the [144] course of events. But they diverge in details (cf. Wellhausen and Dillmann), and Elohîm in xliii. 29; xliv. 16 is no evidence for E, since Joseph speaks and is spoken to as a heathen until xlv. It is only in xlv. that E reappears: observe Elohîm in *v.* 5, 7–9; xlvi. 2; and the notable departures in xlv. 2ᵇ, 16 sqq. from xlvi. 28–xlvii. 6. In *v.* 4, 5 (Joseph sold by his brothers) E's representation (xl. 15ª and parallel passages) is combined with that of the other story.—On xlvii. 12–26 the critics are at variance, but there are no conclusive reasons for assigning the verses to E. In xlviii. 1, 2, 8–22, on the other hand, the characteristics of E come out distinctly: note Elohîm in *v.* 9, 11, 15, 20, 21, and other points of linguistic agreement (cf. Wellhausen, xxi. 449 and Dillmann). The passage, however, is not from a single hand, as Budde, after Dillmann, has clearly shown (*Zeitschr. f. a. t. Wissenschaft.*, 1883, p. 57–62). The two scholars are not at one in defining E's share. In my opinion it consists of *v.* 1, 2, 8–12, 15, 16, 20–22; while Ephraim's promotion (*v.* 20) is elaborated in *v.* 13, 14, 17–19, which must therefore be regarded as interpolations, not as remnants of another narrative. Ch. xlviii. 22 presents difficulties in connection—not with xxxiv., with which E has nothing to do, but—with xxxiii. 19, which by no means prepares us for a conquest of Shechem by Jacob, and with *Josh.* xxiv. 32 (also belonging to E), where this conquest is likewise ignored. Cf. *Th. Tijdschr.*, xiv. 272 sq.—On l. 15–26 there is hardly room for diversity of opinion: note Elohîm, not only in *v.* 19, where it is unavoidable, but in *v.* 20, 24, 25 also. Cf. further Dillmann, *Genesis*, p. 453.

Colenso(*Pentateuch*, vii., App. and Synop. table) differs from Dillmann and Wellhausen in only assigning the following passages of *Gen.* xxxvii., xxxix.-l. to E: xl. 2, 3ª, 4, 5ª, 6–23; xli. 1–30, 32–34, 36–39, 44 45, 47, 56,

57; xlii. 5, 6ª, 7ª; xlv. 16–18, 21ª; l. 22, 23, 25. The composite character
of *Gen.* xxxvii. is here overlooked; and moreover the inadmissible hypothesis
is embraced that the writer who generally speaks of Y a h w è now and then
(xlv. 5, 7–9; xlvi. 2; xlviii. 9 sqq.) uses E l o h î m.

⁶ The 'prophetic' passages still left in *Gen.* xx.–l., when E has been
removed, agree in the use of Y a h w è, but are not otherwise homogeneous.
They are i n p a r t parallel with E, independent of it, and generally more or
less divergent from it, and i n p a r t dependent on E, and apparently intended
to supplement or expand it. We have already (n. 5), brought xx. 18; xxii.
14–18 under the latter category. What further passages should be embraced
in it rather than in the other group is sometimes doubtful; or at any rate we
cannot decide the question at this stage of our inquiry. The following list of
passages t a k e n f r o m t h e d o c u m e n t J, with the remarks appended,
must therefore be regarded as merely provisional; cf. throughout W e l l -
h a u s e n, D i l l m a n n, and n. 5. The independent J-sections, then, are
Gen. xxiv. (on *v.* 61ᵇ–67, cf. W e l l h. xxi. 418, and on the other side D i l l m.
Gen. p. 289 sq.); xxv. 1–6 (cf. B u d d e, p. 220 sqq.); 21–34 (with the
exception of 26ᵇ, from P²; D i l l m a n n, p. 299, finds traces of E also, in
this passage, but see B u d d e, p. 217, n. 2); xxvi. 1–33 in part (*v.* 1–5
departs considerably from J's style, and has, at any rate, been worked over;
v. 15 and 18 are manifest interpolations, dependent upon xxi. 22–31); xxvii. [145]
1–45, in part (cf. n. 5); according to W e l l h a u s e n, xxi. 410 sqq., D i l l -
m a n n, p. 316, and others, xxviii. 13 16, together with certain touches in *v.*
17–22; but I think it highly improbable that these are fragments of an independent account, by J, of a revelation at Bethel; *Gen.* xii. 3ᵇ, it is true, is
repeated almost to the letter in *v.* 14, but the same follower of J who notably
modified this promise elsewhere (xviii. 17–19), xxii. 15–18; xxvi. 4, may have
reproduced it here without alteration; there is no reference to the theophany
at Bethel anywhere in the sequel of J, and we may gather from *Gen.* xii. 8
(cf. xiii. 3) where the place is mentioned, that J carried back its consecration to Abraham rather than to Jacob; xxviii. 13–16 must, therefore, be
regarded as homogeneous with xxii. 14–18, and as due to the same hand that
modified the text of E in *v.* 21ᵇ;—xxix. xxxiii., in part (cf. n. 5); certain
verses of xxxiv., in which Simeon and Levi avenge their sister (including *v.*
11, 12, 19, 25, 26, 30, 31; cf. *Th. Tijdschr.*, xiv. 257–281, and on the other
side D i l l m. *Genesis*, p. 348 sqq.; also cf. § 16, n. 12; perhaps xxxv. 22ª
(but see remarks on xlix.), and some touches in *v.* 16–21; a part of
xxxvii. (cf. n. 5), but not *v.* 12–18, for the flocks pasturing at S h e c h e m
can hardly be reconciled with xxxiv.; the whole of xxxviii.; xxxix. in
part (cf. n. 5; but the wordy style and constant repetitions by which
this chapter is unfavourably distinguished from the other J-pericopes, justify
some doubts; cf. § 13, n. 26 and 16, n. 12); a few touches in xl.–xlii.;
almost the whole of xliii., xliv. (cf. n. 5); xlvi. 28–xlvii. 5ª, 29–31; according
to most of the critics xlix. 1ᵇ–28ª, the blessing of Jacob, adopted though not
composed by J, and in this case we must add xxxv. 22ª, a note by J to
explain and justify xlix. 3, 4; but this very note raises my suspicions; it is

too slight for J, who always enters more into details, and seems rather to indicate a later collector, to whom, in that case, we must likewise attribute the preservation of Jacob's blessing ; the sentence on Simeon and Levi, *v.* 5–7, is illustrated by the portion of xxxiv. borrowed from J, but the latter was not written for this purpose, and has, therefore, no bearing on our question ;— finally l. 1–11, 14 (at any rate in great part, cf. D i l l m . p. 453).

[7] With regard to the main 'prophetic' narrative of *Gen.* xii.–xix., no doubt exists ; it is the beginning of J's account of the lives of the patriarchs, the continuation and conclusion of which we have provisionally gathered up in n. 6. The passages agree in the use of Yahwè throughout, and, more generally, in language and style ; and the contents of the former series are constantly assumed in the latter. The original narrative has been subject to later additions and modifications, as shown in n. 4, but the very fact that these can be detected as they can serves to bring out the unity of what remains all the more clearly. Cf. further the Commentaries, especially D i l l m a n n .—*Gen.* i.–xi. presents a more complicated problem. Is J, in *Gen.* xii.–l., the continuation of *Gen.* [ii. 4 b–iii.] iv. 17–24 ; xi. 1–9, which k n o w n o t h i n g o f a d e l u g e, or of *Gen.* vi.–viii., x., containing the account of the flood and all that depends upon it (cf. n. 3) ? It is hard to decide, for the two 'prophetic' elements of *Gen.* i.–xi. have not only been woven together, as we have remarked already, but were closely related to one another from the first. And the language of J in
[146] *Gen.* xii. sqq. has points of affinity with either group. (Compare, for example, *Gen.* xiii. 10, יהוה גי, with ii. 8, etc., and *Gen.* xii. 7, and the parallel passages, with viii. 20.) We must, therefore, reserve our judgment on this point, but the presumption seems already to favour the connection of the main narrative of *Gen.* xii. sqq. with the e a r l i e r 'prophetic' passages in *Gen.* i.–xi. ; for the expansion and modification of xii. sqq. will then be parallel to the introduction of a later stratum into i.–xi., whereas, on the other supposition, it will have no analogy in these earlier chapters.

[8] Schrader (op. cit.) ascribes the following to E : *Gen.* iv. 23, 24 (?) vi. 1 (in part), 2, 3 ; x. 1–7, 13, 18^a, 19, 20, 22–24, 26–32 ; xii. 6^{a-c}, 8$^{a b}$, 9 ; xiii. 2, 3, 5, 7^{a-c}, 8–10$^{a b e}$, 11^a, 12^c, 18$^{a b}$; xiv. (except *v.* 22 in part). D i l l - m a n n detects the same document in *Gen.* iv. 17–24 ; vi. 1–4 ; ix. 20–27 ; xiv. ; xv. 1, 2, 4, 8, 9–11, 17, 18 (cf. *Genesis*, p. 86 sq., 111 sq., 147 sq., 218 sq., 230 sq., where it will be seen that he does not pronounce with equal decisiveness in every case). Now it is perfectly true that *Gen.* xx is the continuation, not the beginning, of a history, and must therefore have been preceded in the document itself by other statements about Abraham. But it does not follow that any of these have been preserved in *Gen.* xii.–xix. If, as we should gather from *Josh.* xxiv. 2, 3 (E), they dwelt upon the idolatry of Abraham's relatives, their omission is extremely natural. We should, however, be quite prepared to recognise E-passages in *Gen.* xii.–xix. were there any clear traces of such. But this is not the case, either in *Gen.* xiv., which is quite long enough to furnish material for the identification of the writer, or in *Gen.* xv. The latter is certainly composite (cf. n. 4), but it cannot be shown that E is one of its sources. The linguistic evidence is so far from conclusive as to

allow B u d d e (p. 416, n. 1), in contrast with D i l l m a n n (as above), to assign nothing to E but *v.* 1 (in part), 2ᵇ, 3ª, 5, and to refer 1 (in part), 2ª, 3ᵇ, 4, 6–11, 17, 18 to J.—The supposition that E likewise contained an 'Urgeschichte' is altogether arbitrary. We have certainly no right to assume it *a priori*, and there is no positive evidence that any single passage in *Gen.* i.–xi. belongs to E. This being the state of the case, it is not surprising that C o l e n s o, amongst others, should find no trace of E before *Gen.* xx., and that W e l l-h a u s e n, agreeing with him as to *Gen.* i.–xi. (xxi. 419), should only point out the influence of E here and there, and even that with hesitation, in *Gen.* xii.–xix., especially in xv. (p. 411 sq.). B u d d e, likewise, is unable to assign any portion of *Gen.* i.–xi. to E (op. cit., p. 6 sqq., 216 sqq., 381 sq., 414 sqq.).

⁹ Texts such as *Gen.* xlvi. 1–5 ; xlviii. 8–22 ; l. 24, 25 (E) and *Gen.* xii. 7 ; xxiv. 7 ; xxvii. 28, 29 (J) make it as good as certain that in both documents the narratives about the patriarchs formed an introduction to the history of the exodus and the settlement in Canaan. We are therefore justified, on every ground, in looking for the continuation of both in *Exodus–Joshua.*

¹⁰ On *Ex.* i. sqq. cf., in addition to W e l l h a u s e n (xxi. 538 sqq.) and Dillmann, *Exodus u. Leviticus,* A d. J ü l i c h e r, *Die Quellen von Ex.* i.–vii. 7 (Halle, 1880), and *Die Quellen von Ex.* vii. 8–xxiv. 11 (*Jahrb. f. protest. Theo-logie,* viii. 79–127, 272–315), to which essays I shall refer in this and the [147] following notes as J ü l i c h e r A and J ü l i c h e r B.—In *Ex.* i. 17, 20, 21 Elohîm occurs ; and accordingly *v.* 15–21, to which *v.* 8–12 seems to belong, is pretty unanimously assigned to E. On the origin of *Ex.* ii. 1–23ª there is more difference of opinion : according to J ü l i c h e r (A, 9 sqq.), *v.* 1–22 is borrowed from E ; according to Dillmann, *v.* 1–14 from E, and 15–23ª from J ; W e l l h a u s e n (xxi. 539) regards the narrative throughout as a patchwork of J and E. In *Ex.* iii. 1–15, on the contrary, E is quite unmistakable : Elohîm or Ha-elohîm in *v.* 1ᵇ, 4ᵇ, 6, 11–15 ; *v.* 4ᵇ from the same hand as *Gen.* xxii. 11 ; xlvi. 2, cf. xxii. 1, 7 ; xxxi. 11 ; xxxvii. 13 ; *v.* 12, 'I will be with you,' as in *Gen.* xxviii. 20 ; xxxv. 3, etc. To this narrative—in which Y a h w è could not possibly be used before *v.* 14, 15—another account is now welded (or detached verses added) in which that name occurs (*v.* 4ª, 7) ; whence the repetition in *v.* 9, cf. *v.* 7, 8. All this tends to obscure the unquestionable fact that E has now reached a turning point, inasmuch as the E-portion of *Ex.* iii. 1–15 is parallel with *Ex.* vi. 2 sqq. (P²), and in direct contradiction with *Gen.* iv. 26 (J).—On the use of Elohîm for Yahwè after *Ex.* iii. 15, cf. § 5, n. 24. It will be shown, in n. 11 sqq., that the pericopes and verses in which it occurs may be referred with great probability to E.

¹¹ After the removal of P (cf. § 6, n. 6) we still have a composite narrative left in *Ex.* vi. 2–xii. ; and it is yet more obvious, even to the most superficial inspection, that *Ex.* iii. 16–vi. 1, though entirely 'prophetic,' is far from forming a single whole. It is true that in *Ex.* vii. 8–xi. the plagues are usually announced in the same terms, identical phrases constantly recur, and a certain gradation in the negotiations between Moses and Pharaoh is obvious. Cf., for example, (v. 3) ; vii. 16 ; ix. 1, 13 ; x. 3 ('the god of the Hebrews') ; (iv. 23 ;

v. 1); vii. 16, 26 [viii. 1] ; viii. 16 [20] ; ix. 1 ; x. 3, 7 ('let my people go out, that they may serve me [celebrate a feast in my honour],' sometimes with the addition 'in the desert') ; (iv. 23); vii. 14, 27 [viii. 2] ; ix. 2 ; x. 3, 4; (מאן, of Pharaoh); viii. 4, 5, 24, 25 [8, 9, 28, 29] ; ix. 28 ; x. 17 (עתר in Hiphil; viii. 26 [30]; x. 18 in Kal (?)); viii. 18 [22] ; ix. 4 ; xi. 7 (הפלה; cf. also ix. 26, parallel in substance); viii. 4, 21 [8, 25]; ix. 27 ; x. 8, 16 (xii. 31), (Moses and Aaron summoned by Pharaoh); vii. 14; viii. 11, 28 [15, 32] ; ix. 7, 34 ; x. 1 [כבד, הכביד, Pharaoh's heart, or Pharaoh . . . his heart]; ix. 18, 24 ; x. 6, 14 ; xi. 6 (such plagues had never been before, and should never be again) ; viii. 21 [25]; x. 9-11, 24 (rising concessions of Pharaoh) ; (iii. 21, 22) ; xi. 2, 3 (xii. 35, 36) (spoiling the Egyptians). But alongside of these proofs of relative unity there is the clearest evidence of diversity of sources. Ch. x. 28, 29, if not immediately followed by xi. 4-8, is wholly irreconcileable with it, for the discourse in the latter passage is addressed, according to v. 8, to Pharaoh himself. Sometimes it is the staff of Moses that works the miracles (vii. (15), 17, 20 ; ix. 23 ; x. 13, as well as x. 21-27, in which it is understood, though not mentioned), but in the great majority of cases this staff is not, and hardly could be, mentioned, for the plagues are simply a n n o u n c e d in Yahwè's name, often a day in advance (viii. 19 [23] ; ix. 5, 6, 18 ; x. 4, cf. viii. 6, 25 [10, 29]). In iii. 16-vi. 1 we meet with the [148] following contradictions. After iv. 10-12, where Yahwè promises to teach Moses what he shall say, we hardly expect the complaint of v. 10 to be met, in v. 14-16, by the association with Moses of Aaron as a mouth-piece ; and moreover it is clear from vii. 8-xi., where Moses is constantly the speaker, that Aaron did not figure as Moses' prophet in all the narratives of the exodus, and it is even a question whether he was mentioned at all in some of them ; so much is certain, that in the compound narrative of vii. 8-xi.—always assuming the withdrawal of P²—Aaron only appears to disappear again, so that W e l l h a u s e n, D i l l m a n n, and J ü l i c h e r (B) unanimously assume that in viii. 4, 8, 21 [8, 12, 25] ; ix. 12, 27 ; x. 3, 8, 16 the original author only spoke of Moses.—Ch. iv. 19 sounds strange indeed after v. 18, and, in general, after all that has preceded it in iii., iv.—Ch. iv. 21-23, especially the command to threaten Pharaoh with the death of his first-born from the begin- ning, harmonises ill with iii. 18-20 and with the action of Moses in vii. sqq.—Ch. iv. 24-26, Yahwè's attack on Moses by night, is enigmatical in its present con- nection.—In *Ex.* iii. 16-xii., then, we may find abundant points of support for a critical analysis ; but here we cannot separate two distinct documents, as we have done in Jacob's biography and elsewhere, and assign its share to each with confidence. The most we can hope for is to determine whether it is E or J that l i e s a t t h e b a s i s of the narrative; and sometimes even this is doubtful. 'The staff of E l o h î m,' iv. 20ᵇ, and consequently the command in v. 17, must come from E, and this carries with it the passages indicated above, in which the plagues are brought about by the waving of this staff. From this it would follow that the divergent accounts in which Yahwè himself sends the plagues and makes Moses announce them, come from J, though per- haps in a more primitive form than they have now assumed. And, accordingly, this is the view now dominant, though the scholars who agree in accepting it differ from each other in detail (Dillmann, Jülicher), or shrink from any decisive utterance (Wellhausen).   As a specimen I may cite the results arrived at by Dillmann and Jülicher with respect to E's contributions.   Dillmann enumerates iii. 16–22 mostly; iv. 17, 20^b, 18, 21; v. mostly; vii. 15, 16, 17^b, 20^b, 21^a, 23 in part, 24; viii. 16^a, 21–24^a, 25^b; ix. 22, 23^a, 24^a, 25^b (?), 31, 32, 35; x. 8–13^a, 14 in part, 15 in part, 20; x. 21–27; xi. 1–3; xii. 31–33, 37^b, 38.—Jülicher (A and B): iv. 17, 18, 20^b; v. 1, 2, 5; vii. 17 in part, 18, 20 in part, 21, 24, 25^a; viii. 21^b, 22, 23; ix. 22, 23^a, 24 and 28 in part, 35; x. 7, 8–11, 12, 13^a, 14^a, 15^a, 20; 21–27; 28, 29; xi. 1–3; xii. 32, 35–38.   Here we find enough agreement to show that criticism is not following imaginary tracks, but enough disagreement to prove that again and again the tracks are obliterated.   It appears that in *Ex.* i. sqq. the simple interweaving of the authorities with the retention of the special characteristics of each, gave way to their free use, and their intimate blending and recasting.

[12] It is obvious that the first group of passages here mentioned is not a connected whole.   But in indicating the verses that may be derived with some confidence from E—and that is our only concern at present—we need not trouble ourselves about their connection.   Here again the chief characteristics [149] of E which appear in the passages may be indicated.   In *Ex.* xiii. 17–19 Elohîm occurs three times; *v.* 19 is obviously from the same hand as *Gen.* l. 25.   Our conclusion as to *v.* 21, 22 must depend very much on what we think of xiv. 19^b.   Now xiv. 19^a is from E; cf. מלאך האʼ, *Gen.* xxii. 11 (above, n. 5); xxxi. 11, 13; xlviii. 15, 16 (also xxviii. 12; xxxii. 2).   Hence Wellhausen (xxi. p. 546), Dillmann, and Jülicher conclude that *v.* 19^b is taken from another narrative.   But is not this account of the column of cloud and fire really the indispensable explanation of the statement about 'the angel of Elohîm' in *v.* 19^a?   What is the meaning of his changing his place from before to behind the camp of Israel, if not that the column placed itself between the two camps, giving light to the one and leaving the other in darkness (*v.* 20)?   If *v.* 19^a had meant anything else some kind of explanation would at least have been indicated.   'The angel,' then, must be identified with 'the column,' and in that case *v.* 19^b, 20 as well as *v.* 19^a must be referred to E.   It will also follow that xiii. 21, 22 belongs to E, and the use of מוש (cf. xxxiii. 11; *Num.* xiv. 44) confirms this conclusion.—*Ex.* xv. 23–25^a presents no special characteristics of E, but *v.* 25^b, from which the passage cannot be separated, is from the same hand as *Josh.* xxiv. 25 (cf. n. 16); and the concluding words remind us of *Gen.* xxii. 1.   *V.* 26 contains more than one deuteronomic turn of expression (יהישר בעיניו, יהוה אלהיך מצוה and חקים, שמר), and we may therefore suppose that it has been recast (cf. § 13, n. 31); but compare xviii. 16, 20, and for רפא *Gen.* xx. 17; *Num.* xii. 13.—The derivation of *Ex.* xvii. 2–7, 8–16 from E is supported by the proximity of xviii., the staff in Moses' hand, which is called 'the staff of Elohîm' in *v.* 9, the mention of Joshua, who takes an important place elsewhere in E, and the use of גבר (*v.* 11) and חלש (*v.* 13), cf. xxxii. 18.   In *v.* 2–7, however,

foreign elements have been incorporated, and *v.* 8–16 also seems to have been worked over. Cf. W e l l h a u s e n (p. 549 sq.); D i l l m a n n (*Ex. u. Lev.* 178) and J ü l i c h e r (B, 276 sqq.), the last of whom does not duly appreciate the traces of E in *v.* 8–16.—On the origin of *Ex.* xviii. the critics are almost unanimous. Observe E l o h î m in *v.* 1ᵃ, 5, 12 (bis), 15, 16, 19 (ter), 21, 23; אכל לחם in *v.* 12 as in *Gen.* xxxi. 54; xxxvii. 25; the agreement of *v.* 16, 20 with xv. 26; חזה in *v.* 21, like ראה in *Gen.* xxii. 8. But *v.* 1 sqq. has been worked over, as W e l l h a u s e n (xxi. 550 sq.), D i l l m a n n (p. 184 sqq.), and J ü l i c h e r (B, 294 sq.) have shown in detail.

On *Ex.* xix.–xxiv. see *Th. Tijdschr.*, xv. 175–223, where I showed that *Ex.* xx. 18–21 originally stood before *v.* 1–17, as J ü l i c h e r (B, 312 sqq.) was maintaining at the very same time. It is further shown in the same article that the account of the delivery of the Decalogue originally contained nothing about a Covenant-Book or the establishment of a covenant (*Ex.* xxiv. 3–8), and that *Ex.* xxiv. 12 in its primitive form contained the command to ascend the mountain and there to receive both the tables written by God a n d the revelation of the laws and commandments destined for Israel. Now this decalogue-story may be referred with high probability to E. Not reckoning the Decalogue itself—on which more in § 13, n. 20—it contains the following traces of E's usage: E l o h î m xix. 17; xx. 1, 19–21; xxiv. 13; נשמר followed by לְ xix. 12, as in *Gen.* xxxi. 24, 29; נסה in Piel, xx. 20 as in *Gen.* xxii. 1; *Ex.* xv. 25; the mention of Joshua, משרת of Moses, xxiv. 13, as in xxxiii. 11; of Aaron and Hur, xxiv. 14, as in xvii. 10, 12; of Moses' office of [150] Judge, xxiv. 14, as in xviii. 13 sqq. The following expressions are likewise quite in harmony with E's style: התיצב, xix. 17, as in *Num.* xxiii. 3, 15; *Josh.* xxiv. 1; בזה, xxiv. 14, as in *Gen.* xlviii. 9; *Num.* xxii. 19; xxiii. 1, 29 (but also in *Gen.* xxxviii. 21, 22, J).—Now it is very remarkable, and at first sight most perplexing, that certain passages are found for which there is no room in this decalogue-story, and which nevertheless conform, or at least approximate, to the linguistic usage of E. This holds good (*a*) of *Ex.* xxiv. 1, 2, 9–11 (on the connection of which, in point of m a t t e r, with xix. 13ᵇ, 20–25, cf. *Th. Tijdschr.*, xv. 214–220); observe h a - e l o h î m in *v.* 11, and the agreement of this verse with xviii. 12; (*b*) of the Book of the Covenant, *Ex.* xx. 23–xxiii. 33, and the narrative in *Ex.* xxiv. 3–8 that belongs to it. The numerous points of contact with E had already been pointed out by K n o b e l (*Ex. u. Lev.* 1st ed., p. 183 sq., cf. *Num.-Josh.* p. 532 sqq.) and have quite recently been elaborately treated by J ü l i c h e r (B, 305). Specially worthy of note is the use of H a - e l o h î m or E l o h î m in xxi. 6, 13; xxii. 7, 8, 27, [8, 9, 28], (making it probable that E l o h î m originally stood in xxii. 10, [11] also), of אמה in xxi. 7, 20, 26, 27; xxiii. 12; of השכים בבקר in xxiv. 4, and, in the same verse, the mention of the twelve maççébas (cf. *Gen.* xxviii. 18; xxxi. 52; and also xxxiii. 20, in which read מצבה and לה). These phenomena must not induce us, with K n o b e l and D i l l m a n n, to regard the Decalogue and the Book of the Covenant as parts of one and the same narrative, nor, with J ü l i c h e r (B, 312 sqq.), to regard the Decalogue as the original introduction to the Book of the

Covenant, explaining its proclamation f r o m   h e a v e n as a later modification of E's account. These views are opposed by *Ex.* xxiv. 3-8 (where
the Decalogue is n o t mentioned) ; *v.* 12 (where, on the one hand, ' the stone
tables,' which were destined for the Decalogue alone, are mentioned,
and on the other hand the revelation of further laws and commandments
is represented as still to come; so at least in the genuine and original text,
now recast); and also by the absolute silence alike of *Ex.* xxxii.-xxxiv.,
and of *Deuteronomy* concerning the Book of the Covenant and its acceptance by all the people. But this relationship with E must none the less
be taken into account, and we shall therefore revert to it hereafter, § 13,
n. 32.

[13] On the repeated manipulation and expansion of *Ex.* xxxi. 18-xxxiv. cf.
the essay in *Th. Tijdschr.,* xv. already mentioned. I refer the following passages to the original narrative : *Ex.* xxxii. 1-6 ; 15-20 (21-24 ?); fragments
of xxxii. 30-xxxiii. 6 ; xxxiii. 7-11 entirely; xxxiv. 1, 4, 28ᵇ. The relationship of these verses to E is unmistakable. The use of E l o h î m in (xxxi. 18),
xxxii. 16 proves little *in casu,* for it is almost appellative (' divine work, or
writing '). But we must note נזמי זהב, xxxii. 2, 3, cf. *Gen.* xxxv. 4 ;—השכים
xxxii. 6, and the agreement of the whole verse with xxiv. 11 ;—xxxii. 18, cf.
xvii. 11, 13 ;—xxxiii. 6, הר חורב, cf. iii. 1 ; xvii. 6 ;—xxxiii. 9, 10, cf. n. 12 on
Ex. xiii. 21, 22 ;—xxxiii. 11, פנים אל-פנים, cf. *Num.* xii. 8 ; xiv. 14; *Deut.*
xxxiv. 10 ; also Joshua, משרת of Moses, as in xxiv. 13 ; xxxii. 17, and מוש
as in xiii. 22 ; *Num.* xiv. 44 ;—and finally, xxxiv. 4 השכים בבקר.

[14] A few remarks on these passages must suffice. *Num.* x. 33-36 is of
uncertain origin; *Num.* xiv. 40-45 runs in many respects parallel with it,
and would therefore suggest E as its source, and so also would *Deut.* i. 33, inasmuch as *Deut.* i.-iv. shows an obvious dependence upon E throughout; no
inference can be drawn from *v.* 33ᵃ; for *v.* 33ᵇ 36, which embodies a general
rule, does not belong to it; perhaps *v.* 33ᵃ goes with xi. 1-3. This brief [151]
narrative recalls E by the intercessory prayer of Moses in *v.* 2, cf. *Gen.* xx. 7,
17 ; *Num.* xxi. 7; and by צעק followed by אל, as in *Ex.* xv. 25 ; xvii. 4 ; *Num.*
xii. 13 ; xx. 16, etc.—On *Num.* xi. 4-35 see n. 19.—The ascription of *Num.* xii.
to E is supported by על-אדות, *v.* 1, as in *Gen.* xxi. 11, 25; *Ex.* xviii. 8; *Num.* xiii,
24 (*Josh.* xiv. 6) ; האיש משה, *v.* 3, as in *Ex.* xi. 3 ; אהל מועד, *v.* 4, cf. *Ex.*
xxxiii. 7; *v.* 5, cf. *Ex.* xxxiii. 9 ; *Deut.* xxxi. 15, and also *Num.* xi. 25; *v.* 6,
התודע, as in *Gen.* xlv. 1 ; and likewise by the dream as a means of revelation,
cf. E *passim* ; *v.* 8, cf. *Ex.* xxxiii. 11.—The verses that remain in *Num.* xiii. sq.
when P is withdrawn (xiii. 17ᵇ-20, 22-24, 26ᵇ, 27-31 ; xiv. 1ᵇ, 2ᵇ, 4, 8, 9,
11-25, 39-45), contain, in my opinion, a narrative from E, but recast and
expanded by another hand, which has dealt very drastically with xiv. 11-25,
especially. According to W e l l h a u s e n (xxi. 571 sq.) and E. M e y e r (*Kritik
der Berichte über die Eroberung Palaestinas,* in *Zeitschr. f. alttest. Wissenschaft,*
i. 117-146, especially p. 124, 139 sq.), this remoulder of the story had
another account at his service as well. Be this as it may, we trace the
linguistic usage of E in xiii. 20 (התחזק, as in *Gen.* xlviii. 2); *v.* 24.
על-אדות, as in *Num.* xii. 1, etc.; xiv. 1 (נתן קול), cf. *Gen.* xxi. 16); *v.* 14

(pillar of cloud and fire, as in *Ex.* xiii. 21, etc.) ; *v.* 40 (בבקר השכים, as in *Ex.* xxxiv. 4, etc. ; הננו, as in *Ex.* iii. 4 ᵇ, etc.) ; *v.* 42 (Yahwè in the midst of Israel, as in *Deut.* xxxi. 17, though elsewhere too, *Ex.* xvii. 7, etc.) ; *v.* 44 (מוש, as in *Ex.* xiii. 22 ; xxxiii. 11).—It would likewise appear that E lies at the basis of the story of Dathan and Abiram (*Num.* xvi. 1 in part, 12–14, 15 ᵇ, 25, 26, 27 ᵇ–32 ᵃ, 33, 34 [?]). Cf. *v.* 12 (קרא followed by ל, as in *Num.* xxii. 5, 20) ; 14 (שדה וכרם, as in *Num.* xx. 17 ; xxi. 22) ; *v.* 25 (the elders of Israel, repeatedly in E) ; *v.* 27 (נצב followed by פתח אהל, just as in *Ex.* xxxiii. 8) ; *v.* 28 (מלבי, as in *Num.* xxiv. 13). But the original has been largely remodelled, especially *v.* 13, 14, 28 sqq., and was further altered when fused with P².—On *Num.* xx. 1–13 cf. § 6, n. 42. The narrative welded with that of P² seems to be derived from E. Compare *v.* 4, 8, 11, בעיר, with *Gen.* xlv. 17 ; *Ex.* xxii. 4 ; *v.* 5 in general with *Num.* xvi. 13, 14 ; *v.* 8 (המטה) and *v.* 11 (מטהו)—wherewith *v.* 9 מלפני יהוה is only half in accord—with *Ex.* iv. 20 ᵇ, and the parallel passages.—*Num.* xx. 14–21 ; xxi. 21–31 are referred to J rather than E by W e l l h a u s e n (xxi. 577), on account of 'the remarkable use of names of peoples as singulars ' (cf. *Ex.* xiv.). But this is a weak argument, for the use of the singular in xx. 14 sqq. is explained by the very natural opening ' thy brother Israel ; ' and the plural occurs also (*v.* 15–17, 19 ᵃ) ; in xxi. 21 sqq. אעברה, *v.* 22, is the only singular. The two pericopes are from the same hand, as may be seen by comparing xxi. 21 sq. with xx. 14, 17, and xxi. 23 with xx. 18, 20. Their derivation from E is supported by xx. 14 (תלאה followed by מצא, as in *Ex.* xviii. 8) ; the מלאך in *v.* 16 ; נתן, ' grant,' in xx. 21 ; xxi. 23, as in *Gen.* xx. 6. Compare, further, צעק, xx. 16 with *Ex.* xv. 25 ; xvii. 4 ; *Num.* xii. 13 ; *Josh.* xxiv. 7 (but elsewhere also). M e y e r, too, detects E in this passage (p. 118).—From the same document comes *Num.* xxi. 4 ᵇ–9, attached by *v.* 4 ᵃ to xx. 22–29 (P²). In *v.* 5 occurs Elohim (replaced by Yahwè in *v.* 6–8) ; *v.* 5, 7, דבר followed by ב as in *Num.* xii. 1 ; [152] in *v.* 7, התפלל followed by אל and בעד, as in *Num.* xi. 2 and the parallel passages. On the other hand, there is a similarity of idea, though not of words, between הלחם הקלקל, *v.* 5, and *Num.* xi. 6 (J, cf. n. 19), but this only proves that E and J shared an idea of the manna which differs from that of P² in *Ex.* xvi.—V. 12–20 and *v.* 21–31 do not quite agree together : the embassy to Sihon does not start from ' the field of Moab ' (*v.* 20), but from a previous station, probably from the Arnon (*v.* 13). This would incline us to derive *v.* 12–20, in whole or in part, from some other source than that of *v.* 21–31. But the author of the latter (E) is quite in agreement with 13 ᵇ as to the facts, and the quotations in *v.* 14, 15, *v.* 17, 18 ᵃ, and *v.* 27–30 are evidently all of them due to the same hand. We must therefore suppose that E prefaced his own narrative (*v.* 21–31) by a passage from an older *itinerarium*— whence perhaps *Deut.* x. 6, 7 is likewise taken—and illustrated certain points by poetical citations (*v.* 13 ᵇ–15 ; *v.* 17, 18 ᵃ), just as he did with the main feature of his own narrative also (*v.* 26, 27–30). Cf. my essay in *Th. Tijdschr.*, xviii. 497 sqq., and below, § 13, n. 12 ; 16, n. 12, both on this passage and on *Num.* xxii. 2–xxiv. This latter section is referred to E by K n o b e l in its entirety, and by S c h r a d e r with the exception of xxii. 22–35 ; xxiv. 20–24 ;

while **Wellhausen** (p. 578 sqq.) divides it between E and J, and **Colenso** between E and D.

[15] *Deut.* xxxi. 14–23, xxxii. 44, belongs to xxxii. 1–43, cf. § 7, n. 20. The language of this frame-work has been influenced by 'the song of Moses' itself, but independently of this it is very peculiar, and here and there approaches the usage of P[1]. The following list of parallel passages will bring this out, and at the same time will show the relationship to E which is here and there unmistakable.

Ch. xxxi. 14, קרבו ימיך למות, *Gen.* xlvii. 29; התיצב, occurs *passim* in the 'prophetic' passages, and is found in *Ex.* xix. 17; *Josh.* xxiv. 1 (E); אהל מועד, cf. *Ex.* xxxiii. 7–11; *Num.* xi. 16, 17 (E).

V. 15, עמוד ענן repeatedly in E (*Ex.* xiii. 21, 22; xiv. 19; xxxiii. 9, 10; *Num.* xii. 5).

V. 16, שכב עם־אבותיך, *Gen.* xlvii. 30.—זנה followed by אחרי, of idolatry, *Ex.* xxxiv. 15, 16, and *Lev.* xvii. 7; xx. 5, 6; *Num.* xv. 39 (P).—אלהי נכר, *Deut.* xxxii. 12 and *Gen.* xxxv. 2, 4; *Josh.* xxiv. 20, 23 (E).—עזב, with Yahwè as its object, *Josh.* xxiv. 16, 20, and elsewhere.—הפר ברית, *v.* 20 and *Lev.* xxvi. 15, 44, cf. *Num.* xv. 31 (P).

V. 17, חרה אף, *Num.* xi. 33 and elsewhere.—הסתיר פנים, *v.* 18, taken from xxxii 20.—מצא, 'befall,' as in *Ex.* xviii. 8; *Num.* xx. 14 (E).—רעות, *v.* 21, taken from xxxii. 23.—בקרב, Yahwè in the midst of Israel, as in *Num.* xiv. 42 (E), but elsewhere also.

V. 18, פנה אל, in the religious sense, *v.* 20, *Lev.* xix. 4, 31; xx. 6—אלהים אחרים, *v.* 20, fifteen times in *Deut.*, and also in *Ex.* xx. 3 (*Deut.* v. 7) (E); xxiii. 13; xxxiv. 14, and *Josh.* xxiv. 2, 16 (E).

V. 19, שים בפי, as in *Num.* xxiii. 5 (where Yahwè is the subject, however).—היה לעד, as in *Josh.* xxiv. 22 (E), cf. *Gen.* xxxi. 52 (E).

V. 20, הביא אל־האדמה, found nowhere else.—The oath to the fathers, *v.* 23; in *Deut.* passim; further in *Gen.* xv.; xxii. 16; xxiv. 7; xxvi. 3; l. 24, (E); *Ex.* xiii. 5, 11; xxxii. 13; xxxiii. 1[b]; *Num.* xi. 12[b]; xiv. 16, 23.— 'flowing with milk and honey,' five times in *Deut.*; further in *Ex.* iii. 8, 17; [153] xiii. 5; xxxiii. 3; *Num.* xiii. 27; xiv. 8; xvi. 13, 14, and *Lev.* xx. 24 (P).— אכל ושבע, a deuteronomic phrase (*Deut.* vi. 11; viii. 10, 12; xi. 15; xiv. 29; xxvi. 12).—דשן, the same idea as in xxxii. 15.—נאץ, as in *Num.* xiv. 11, 23; xvi. 30.

V. 21, ענה, *Gen.* xxx. 33 (followed by ב); with עד, *Ex.* xx. 16.—יצר, as in *Gen.* vi. 5; viii. 21.—בטרם, *Gen.* xxvii. 4, 33; xxxvii. 18; xli. 50; xlv. 28; *Ex.* i. 19, and *Lev.* xiv. 36 (P).

V. 23, חזק ואמץ, a deuteronomic formula (*Deut.* iii. 28; xxxi. 6, 7; *Josh.* i. 6, 7, 9, 18; x. 25).—'I will be with you,' not uncommon elsewhere, and occurs in *Gen.* xxviii. 15, 20; xxxv. 3; xlviii. 21 (E).

How these phenomena are to be explained we shall inquire in § 13, n. 30.

[16] *Josh.* xxiv. is full of references to earlier narratives and consequently has most important bearings upon the criticism of the Pentateuch. It is, therefore, much to be regretted that no agreement has yet been reached as to the origin of this chapter. Against **Knobel**, **Nöldeke** (*Untersuchungen,*

p. 105), Hollenberg (*Studien u. Kritiken*, 1874, p. 485–488) and Wellhausen (xxi. 601 sq.), who derive it, at any rate in great part, from E, we must set Schrader, who refers it to his 'prophetischer Erzähler' (i. e. J, or—since this narrator is also the redactor—JE), and Colenso, who assigns it—with the exception of *v.* 28-30, 33 (JE) and *v.* 26, 27, 33 (P)—to D, i. e. the deuteronomic editor of the 'prophetic' elements of the Hexateuch (*Pentateuch*, vi., app. p. 70–73; *Wellhausen on the Composition*, p. 83 sqq.). We have already observed (§ 7, n. 27) that the chapter has not escaped a deuteronomic recension, but even so it retains such marked peculiarities of form and contents, and stands off so sharply from xxiii., that we cannot possibly attribute it to the author of the latter, viz. D. There is more to be said in support of Schrader's opinion, but the following list will show that the characteristics of E preponderate. How we are to explain the presence of elements foreign to that document must be considered hereafter.

V. 1, התיצב, see above on *Deut.* xxxi. 14.—לפני האלהים האלהים, as in *Ex.* xviii. 12 (E).—*V.* 2, 16, אלהים אחרים, see on *Deut.* xxxi. 18. The circumstance is not mentioned in *Gen.*—*V.* 3, הרבה followed by זרע, *Gen.* xvi. 10; xxii. 17, etc. (not in E).—*V.* 5, נגף, also in *Ex.* xii. 23, 27; xxxii. 35, etc.—*V.* 6, וברכב ובפרשים, not only in *Ex.* xiv. 9, 17, 18, 26, but in *Ex.* xv. 19 also.— *V.* 7, צעק אל־יהוה, see above on *Num.* xx. 16.   כסה not only in *Ex.* xiv. 28, but in *Ex.* xv. 5, 10.—*V.* 8, 12, 15, 18, 'the Amorite,' as a generic name for the inhabitants of Canaan, not only in *Deut.* i. 7, 20, 27; iii. 9; *Josh.* v. 1; vii. 7; x. 5, 6, but also in *Gen.* xv. 16 and xlviii. 22 (E). (The end of *v.* 8, ואשמידם מפניכם is perhaps an addition by D; cf. § 7, n. 26 under **65**).— *V.* 9, 10, though related to *Deut.* xxiii. 5, 6 (קלל and אבה), has a character of its own; Balak's war against Israel, and Israel's 'deliverance out of his hand,' do not appear elsewhere, though this phrase itself is common enough in E (*Gen.* xxxvii. 22; *Ex.* iii. 8; xviii. 9, 10; but also in *Gen.* xxxii. 12 [11]; *Deut.* xxxii. 39; *Josh.* ix. 26, etc.).—*V.* 11, the names of the seven peoples are evidently a gloss; the war of 'the lords of Jericho' with Israel was not mentioned in vi. —*V.* 12, (to be emended after the LXX, with Hollenberg, *Die alex. Uebers. d. B. Josua*, p. 16), the expulsion of 'the twelve kings of the Amorite' appears here only, and is a de- [154] parture from *Josh.* xii. The concluding words 'not with thy sword, nor with thy bow' occur in *Gen.* xlviii. 22 (E).—*V.* 14, 15, 18, 19, 21, 24, עבד את־יהוה, as in *Deut.*, but joined in *v.* 14 with בתמים ובאמת, a phrase unknown to D. On הסיר see under *v.* 23.—*V.* 16, חלילה followed by ל, as in *Gen.* xviii. 25; xliv. 7, 17; *Josh.* xxii. 29, never in E.—*V.* 17, בית עברים, *Ex.* xiii. 3, 14, but also xx. 2 (E).   שמר בדרך, as in *Ex.* xxiii. 20, but also in *Gen.* xxviii. 20 (E).— *V.* 18, את־כל־העמים is a later addition, parallel to the one in *v.* 11.—*V.* 19, אל־קנוא, cf. *Ex.* xx. 5.—נשא לפשע, *Ex.* xxiii. 21, but also *Gen.* l. 17 (E).—*V.* 20, 23, אלהי נכר; see under *Deut.* xxxi. 16; united with הסיר (cf. *v.* 14), in *Gen.* xxxv. 2 (E), and elsewhere.—*V.* 25, שים חק ומשפט, *Ex.* xv. 25 (E); the task here assigned to Joshua is special to this chapter; in xxiii. he constantly refers to the book of law left him by Moses.—*V.* 26, a reference to some other 'book of law,' than the one we know; 'Elohim,' as in *v.* 1; the rearing of a stone, as in *Gen.* xxviii. and elsewhere in E.—*V.* 27 again is very peculiar; תהיה־בנו לצדה, much as in *Deut.* xxxi. 19; cf. especially *Gen.* xxxi. 44 sqq. (E; coincidence both in matter and form).—*V.* 29, אחרי הדברים האלה, very frequent in E.—*V.* 32ª = *Gen.* l. 25; *Ex.* xiii. 19 (E); *v.* 32ᵇ = *Gen.* xxxiii. 19 (E). If the concluding words of *v.* 32, which give no sense, may be emended after the LXX. (ויתנה ליוסף לנחלה), then the statement of *Gen.* xxxiii. 19 is not only accepted but expanded, probably by its author himself, in *Josh.* xxiv. 32ᵇ; cf. *Gen.* xlviii. 22.

Now it is obvious that the representation of the conquest of Canaan given in *Josh.* i.-xii. does not coincide with that which underlies *Josh.* xxiv. 11-13. According to the latter passage the Israelites cross the Jordan and are attacked by the men of Jericho, whom God gives into their hand; after which he sends the hornet before them and expels the twelve kings of the Amorites, whereupon they become masters of the whole land without striking a blow. The document in which this conception—merely referred to in *v.* 11-13—was duly developed, may have been used in the composition of *Josh.* i.-xii., but it cannot be precipitated from it. We must therefore decline to accompany Knobel, followed by Schrader, in his attempt to identify E's narrative in the following passages : ii.; iii. 1, 7-17; iv. 1ª, 4-7; 14, 18, 20-24; v. 1, 2-9, 13-15; viii. 12, 13 (and *v.* 30-35 in part); x. 12-15; and further, xiv. 6-15; xv. 14-19; xvii. 14-18; xxii. 7, 8 (to which Schrader adds *v.* 12, 16ᶜ, 18ᵇ, 19ᵇ, 22-29, 33ᵇ); neither this particular resolution of the narratives, nor the assigning of the above pericopes to E, can be justified or rendered probable. Cf. Hollenberg in *Stud. u. Krit.*, 1874, p. 492 sqq.; Wellhausen, xxi. 585-596, and below, n. 20; § 13, n. 29.

[17] Cf. n. 10-12, whence we may easily infer how the case stands with J's contributions to *Ex.* i.-xv. Note also that according to E's representation Moses' wife and sons stay behind in Midian, when he himself returns to Egypt (*Ex.* xviii. 1 sqq.; אחר שלוחיה in *v.* 2 is evidently a harmonising addition). It follows that *Ex.* iv. 20ª, 24-26 cannot be taken from E, and we may attribute it with high probability to J.

[18] Cf. n. 12 and 13. Wellhausen (p. 551 sqq.) and Dillmann (*Exodus u. Leviticus*, p. 190 sqq.) evidently start from the assumption that J described the events at Sinai and that we must possess at any rate some remains of his [155] account. Jülicher (B, 295 sqq.) takes the same view as far as *Ex.* xix.-xxiv. 11 is concerned. But their conclusions as to J's actual contributions are widely divergent. Wellhausen finds them in *Ex.* xix. 20-25 . . . .; xx. 23-26; xxi.-xxiii.; xxiv. 3-8;—Dillmann in xix. 9ª, 20-25; (xx. 1-17; perhaps in another form); xxiv. 1, 2; xxxiv. 10-27; fragments in xxiv. 3-8; *v.* 9-11, 12 in part, 18ᵇ; xxxii. 1-14, 19ᵇ-24, 30-34; fragments in xxxiii. 1-6; *v.* 12, 13, 18-23; xxxiv. 1-9 : xxxiii. 14-17;—Jülicher (B), finally, in *Ex.* xix. 9ª, 11 (12, 13ª in part), 15, 16ª, 18, 20-22, 25; but not in xx.-xxiv. 11, at which latter verse Jülicher's investigation closes. Clearly all is uncertainty. The cause is not far to seek; the Sinai stories have passed through many phases before reaching their present form, and no small part of the original contents of the documents has been lost in the process (§ 13, n.

32). The fact that the so-called Words of the Covenant, *Ex.* xxxiv. 10-27, show traces of some other code in addition to the Decalogue and the Book of the Covenant—which are derived from, or at least related to, E—naturally suggests that this other legislation was supplied by J. But as soon as we try to test the hypothesis we are met by the difficulty that the Words of the Covenant have undergone more than one recension (§ 13, n. 21, 32). The ten short commandments, which W e l l h a u s e n (xxi. 554, n. 2), following other scholars, detects in these 'Words,' may really have come from J, but there is no clear proof of it.

[19] *Num.* x. 29-32 is a very curious passage, in which the human aspects of the matter are dwelt on, as elsewhere in J ; cf. n. 5. on *Gen.* xxix.-xxxi.—In *Num.* xi. 4-35 I think three elements must be distinguished, (*a*) the story of the quails and the origin of the name Kibrôth-hattaäva, that lies at the basis, (*v.* 4-13, 15, 31-33, perhaps in an earlier form, 34, 35); (*b*) later expansions and embellishments (*v.*18-24ª, perhaps 31-33 in part); (*c*) an independent story of how Moses' complaint that his task was too heavy was met by the gift of the spirit of prophecy to seventy elders (*v.* 14, 16, 17, 24ᵇ-30). Probably (*a*) belongs to J ; cf. the more sober conception of the manna in *v.* 6-9 ; (*c*) on the contrary comes from E, compare *v.* 25 with *Ex.* xxxiii. 9 ; *Num.* xii. 5 ; *Deut.* xxxi. 15 ; *v.* 28 with *Ex.* xxiv. 13 ; xxxii. 17 ; xxxiii. 11; *v.* 30, אֹסֵף, with *Num.* xii. 14, 15 ; on the difficulty which *Ex.* xviii. seems to present to the derivation of (*c*) from E, cf. infr. § 13, n. 25 ; and on the origin of (*b*) ibid. n. 29.—Ch. xxi. 1-3 is certainly not from the same hand as xiv. 45, where Horma occurs as the name of a place already known ; it is not from E, therefore, and there is no reason why we should not assign it to J. On xxii. 2-xxiv. ; xxv. 1-5, cf. the essay referred to at the end of n. 14. The 'prophetic' elements of xxxii. cannot belong either to E or J ; for more, see § 13, n. 29.

[20] In *Josh.* i.-xii. we found (§ 7, n. 26) a historical narrative, recast and expanded by D², in which (according to § 6, n. 48) a few fragments of P² are incorporated, but which otherwise belongs to 'the prophetic stratum.' This 'prophetic history'—to which we must assign ii. 1-9, 12-iii. 2, 4-6, 8-iv ; 12, 13 (?), 15-18 ; 20 ; v. 1, 2 (recast by D²), 3, 8, 9 ; 13-vii. 26; viii. 2ª, 3-26, 28, 29 (?): ix. 1-15ª, 16, 22, 23, 26; x. 1-7, 9-24, 26, 27 (?), 28-39; xi. 1-9, 21-23ª—though clearly betraying its composite origin, has evidently been worked up systematically into a single whole, as appears, especially, from the anticipatory and retrospective notices in vi. 17, 22, 25, cf. (ii.) ; ii. 10 (cf. iv. 23); vi. 18 (cf. vii. especially *v.* 26); ix. (which assumes vi. viii.); x. (which assumes vi., viii., ix.); xi. 19 (cf. ix.). The one pericope, viii. 30-35, which might be removed without injury to the context, is added by D² (§ 7, n. 26, 30). This systematic plan makes it probable *a priori* that the written accounts were not taken as they stood and placed side by side, but freely worked up, or, in other words, that they simply furnished the writer with materials, which he used in his own way and from his own point of view. Investigation shows that this is actually the case, especially in vi. sqq. In ii.-v. the two narratives may still be severed to some extent : between i. 11

[156]

and iii. 2 there is no room for what is recorded in ii., so that this chapter cannot be from the same hand as iii. 2 sqq.; in iii. 2–iv. (when P² and D² have been withdrawn), iii. 12, 15 in part, 16 in part; iv. 4–7, 9, 10, 11ª, 15–18 (raising a heap of stones in the bed of the Jordan), must differ in origin from the rest, wherein the stones are piled up at Gilgal; in v. the connection of *v.* 13–15 with what precedes (as well as with what follows) is unsatisfactory. But from vi. onwards the indications of various accounts lie far less near the surface. Wellhausen (xxi. 589 sq.) has succeeded in showing the traces of a story in vi. in which the priests and the ark are not mentioned, but the people, after compassing Jericho on six days in succession, raise the war cry and blow the trumpet on the seventh, whereupon the walls fall; and likewise (p. 594, cf. Hollenberg, op. cit., p. 596) in tracing the remains of a narrative in ix. in which the negociations with the Gibeonites were conducted by 'the men of Israel,' and not by Joshua. Again, in viii. 1–29,—which certainly was not written *uno tenore*, cf. § 4, n. 13—Wellhausen finds in *v.* 3ª, 12, 13, 14ᵇ, 18, 20 in part, 26, fragments of a widely divergent representation of the course of events. Throughout these chapters the earlier account is continually asserting itself in spite of the author, who endeavours to supplant it by his own representation. Such being the state of the case it is more than difficult to indicate the original sources from which the earlier narratives must have been derived. On E's share cf. n. 16. The inferences there drawn from *Josh.* xxiv. 11–13 seem to carry with them the conclusion that the fundamental lines of i.–xii. were drawn by or copied from some other hand than E's; and, as far as I can see, it may very well have been J's. But this rests on considerations that cannot be presented and estimated till later on. See § 13, n. 14.

Josh. xiii. sqq. also rests, as shown in § 6, n. 49–53; 7, n. 27, on a 'prophetic' account of the partition of the land; but the only remaining portions of it, which contain anything but lists of cities, are xvii. 14–18; xviii. 2–6, 8–10. Ch. xvii. 14 18 is a very remarkable passage, which gives a different and, as we see at once, an older representation of the settlement of the tribes than the one based on a partition by Joshua which underlies xiii. sqq. elsewhere. The pericope therefore stands upon the same footing as the more antique fragments in i.–xii., of which we spoke just now, and may therefore be assigned to J. Ch. xviii. 2–6, 8–10, on the other hand, rests on the current con- [157] ception in its most developed form—that of a partition by lot. See more in § 13, n. 29.

We have now arrived at a stage of our investigation of the 'prophetic' strata at which we must consider the relation in which they stand to the rest of the Pentateuch, especially to P.

It was long thought that a satisfactory answer to this question was supplied by the so-called 'Ergänzungshypothese' (or 'filling-in hypothesis'), which suggested itself in the study of *Genesis* and was then applied to the other books of the Hexateuch as well. The upholders of this hypothesis found the original stratum or ground-work of the Hexateuch in the whole body of Elohistic passages (P^2, E), which they assigned to a single author, while regarding the Yahwistic and deuteronomic laws and narratives as later additions, intended to fill in the original [21].

The theory cannot now be defended in its primitive form. It fell to the ground as soon as it had been shown that all the Elohîm-pericopes could not possibly be derived from one and the same document; and this was shown by K. D. Ilgen first, and then yet more conclusively by H. Hupfeld. Moreover these same scholars further demonstrated that the passages supposed to have been written merely as supplements and expansions were for the most part complete and intelligible by themselves, and departed so widely from the supposed 'Urschrift' or 'Grundschrift,' even when they did not diametrically contradict it, that they were strangely unsuited to 'fill it in,' and could never have been intended to do so [22].

This latter difficulty also applies to the more recent Ergänzungshypothese which Knobel, Schrader, and Colenso defend in various forms [23]. Widely as these forms may differ, they all of them imply the gross improbability of the supposed later author having designed or adduced his narratives to fill in an account into which they did not fit and which they often contradicted. We might perhaps suppose him to have been unconscious of the disagreement occasionally; but we really cannot allow that he could have overlooked or disregarded it throughout [24].

[158] If we acknowledge, then, that the 'prophetic' elements are independent of the priestly ones, and call in a redactor to unite the two, we have still to inquire into the mutual

relations of the prophetic elements themselves. Nöldeke's supposition that E was incorporated by J, and H. Schultz's opposite theory that E built upon and expanded J [25], seem equally inadmissible, for the following reasons:—

(1) Neither hypothesis agrees with the contents of J and E. Though the two documents differ far less from each other than from P, yet they are too widely discrepant to allow their combination to be ascribed to the author of either of them. It must be the work of a third hand [26];

(2) This conclusion is confirmed by the fact that some of the 'prophetic' passages cannot be derived either from E or J, and must therefore have been taken from elsewhere; and this process of supplementation appears in the Hexateuch in such a form as to make it difficult—sometimes impossible—to ascribe it to either of the two main authors [27];

(3) There is still room for much inquiry concerning the literary process by which the 'prophetic' elements acquired their present form. But we may safely say that it was highly intricate in its nature. The redaction was sometimes scrupulously conservative in regard to the documents, sometimes harmonising, sometimes independent and free. Its character is incompatible with the idea that it was the work of one of the authors themselves [28].

We have still to ask whether this redaction of the 'prophetic' elements coincides with that of the Hexateuch in general (Dillmann), or whether it preceded it in point of time, so that this stratum, compressed into a single whole, lay before the final redactor amongst his other documents (Wellhausen). The outcome of our further studies as to the respective antiquities of the great strata of the Hexateuch will be one of the hinges on which our definite choice between these two opinions must turn, but we are already in a position [159] to pronounce Wellhausen's the more probable. We may

M

note especially that the deuteronomic recension and expansion of *Joshua* affect the prophetic elements alone (§ 7, n. 28), and this fact is irreconcilable with Dillmann's theory [29].

[21] This 'Ergänzungshypothese' was defended by F. Tuch (*Commentar über die Genesis*, 1838; 2nd ed. 1871, p. xxxix. sqq.); F. Bleek (*Einleitung in das A. T.*); Stähelin (*Krit. Untersuchungen über die Genesis*, 1830; *Krit. Unt. über den Pent., die Bücher Jos. Richt. Sam. u. der Könige*, 1843; *Spezielle Einleitung in das A. T.*, 1862, p. 22 sqq.); C. von Lengerke; de Wette (in the later editions of his *Einl. in das A. T.*), and others. Stähelin, who identifies the Deuteronomist with the Jehovist, assumes but one supplementation of the 'Grundschrift;' the others regard the Jehovist as the author of *Gen.–Num.*, and of *Josh.* in its original form, and believe that his work was again 'filled in' by the Deuteronomist. It is the former 'filling in' with which we are here concerned.

[22] Cf. K. D. Ilgen, *Die Urkunden des Jerus. Tempelarchivs in ihrer Urgestalt*, i. Halle, 1798); H. Hupfeld, *Die Quellen der Genesis u. die Art ihrer Zusammensetzung* (Berlin, 1853). The former scholar divides *Genesis* between three writers, two Elohists (Sopher Eliël harishon and hassheni) and one Yahwist (Sopher Elijah harishon). Just and discriminating remarks on their mutual distinctions are not wanting, but Ilgen is often unfortunate in his analysis, especially in his separation of the two Elohists, which—perhaps partly in consequence of his ill success—fell more and more into discredit, until at last Hupfeld completely rehabilitated it, by establishing the distinction between P and E, p. 38 sqq., 167 sqq.; and the independence of J, p. 101 sqq.; and, finally, by furnishing the compact demonstration that the combination of these three documents must be the work of a redactor, p. 195 sqq. Hupfeld's main argument is embodied in the text and seems to require no further development: it is indeed a complete misconception of the character and the mutual relations of the narratives to suppose that E and J were intended to fill in P—*Gen.* ii. 4^b–iii., for instance, to fill in *Gen.* i. 1–ii. 4^a; and the stories about Esau and Jacob in E and J to fill in the completely heterogeneous representation of P^2 (§ 6, n. 1), etc.

[23] Knobel retains the name 'Grundschrift' for P; he holds that it was filled in by the Jehovist, who made use of two documents, 'das Rechtsbuch' (=E; the name being taken from *Josh.* x. 13) and 'das Kriegsbuch' (the name from *Num.* xxi. 14), but also made independent contributions himself, especially in *Genesis*, which is largely his work, whereas in *Exodus* sqq. he generally confines himself to making excerpts from his two documents.

Schrader (de Wette's *Einleitung*, 8th edition) makes the 'annalistic narrator' (=P) and the 'theocratic narrator' (=E) compose their works in complete independence of each other; the 'prophetic narrator' weaves them together, but at the same time fills them in by narratives of his own; his [160] additions—answering to Knobel's 'Kriegsbuch' and 'Jehovist'—are of very considerable extent in *Genesis, Exodus, Numbers*, and *Joshua*. In Schrader's hands, therefore, the 'Ergänzungshypothese' undergoes an important modification: for it is no longer P, but P + E that is 'filled in.' Schrader's P + E, however, answers very much to the 'Grundschrift' of Tuch, Stähelin, etc.

The form under which Colenso defended the 'Ergänzungshypothese' is very peculiar. It will be remembered that he makes the 'Grundschrift' of Tuch and the rest end with *Ex.* vi. 2–5; and refers what is usually regarded as its continuation (P in *Ex.* vi.–*Josh.* xxiv.) to the most recent of all the elements of the Hexateuch, viz., LL ('Later' or 'Levitical Legislation'). The 'Grundschrift' (Colenso's E) is therefore filled in from *Gen.* i. to *Ex.* vi., and continued from *Ex.* vi. onward, first by E (=our E, Knobel's 'Rechtsbuch,' Schrader's 'theocratic narrator'), and then by J, who in his turn exchanges the character of supplementer for that of continuator after *Num.* xxii.–xxiv., where E comes to an end. Thus we have two successive layers of supplement and continuation, though we must bear in mind that E and J are very closely related, if they are not one and the same person. ('The second Elohist, E, perhaps merely the Jahvist in an early stage of his literary activity,' *Pentateuch*, vii. *App.* p. 136, 139 and elsewhere.) The work that rose under the successive labours of E, E, and J, is, according to Colenso, 'the Original Story' (O. S.), which—centuries after its completion—was interpolated and expanded by the Deuteronomist or by more than one deuteronomic redactor, and into which the partially historical but chiefly legislative passages indicated by the letters LL were inserted at a still later date.

[24] Cf. n. 22. The remarks by which Colenso (*Pentateuch*, vii. *App.* p. 129 sqq.) once more attempts to establish the supplemental character of the contributions of E and J are anything but conclusive. No doubt there are stories in E and J which do, as a matter of fact, serve to fill in the data of P in our present book of *Genesis. Gen.* v. 29, for instance, supplements *v.* 28; in *Gen.* xvi. 4 (J) 'Hagar' takes us back to *v.* 1, 3 (P), etc. But even if these examples were far more numerous than they really are, they would not prove the point in support of which they are alleged, viz. that E and J were written with a view to filling in P. It is perfectly obvious that they were not. The story of the flood in J has not so much as the distant semblance of a supplement to the one in P; nor does the representation of the plagues of Egypt in 'the prophetic passages' stand in any such relation to that in P. *Et sic in ceteris.* The point of agreement between the hypotheses of Knobel, Schrader, and Colenso, viz. that all alike rob one (or even more) of the original authors of the Hexateuch of his independent activity and force him to do duty as a redactor, involves so gross an improbability that we could only accept it if it were supported by unequivocal evidence; whereas, as a fact, all the phenomena appealed to in its support may be as well, if not better, explained in other ways.

[25] Cf. Nöldeke, *Untersuchungen*, etc., p. 3 sq.; H. Schultz, *Alttestamentliche Theologie* (2nd ed. 1878), p. 85–88. Nöldeke believes the 'Ergänzungshypothese' to have been 'completely refuted' by Hupfeld and others; the combination of P, and 'the prophetic elements' must be the work of a

redactor; E and J are, he thinks, correctly determined in general by Hup-
[161] feld, but incorrectly regarded as independent of each other: 'the writer who
has most genius of all the pentateuchal authors, the Jehovist, made use of
this Elohist as one of his chief authorities. . . . He borrowed long passages
from him, but in such an independent manner that we cannot always quite
distinguish what belongs to the Jehovist himself from what he has taken
from the Elohist, especially in the middle books of the Pentateuch.'
Schultz is also a pronounced opponent of the filling-in hypothesis (p. 86) and
distinguishes between J and E (whom he calls B and C). After stating that
C is generally regarded as earlier than B he adds, ' I am convinced, on the
contrary, that C is later than B, was acquainted with the latter's work and
expanded it, more especially enriching it from sources derived from Northern
Israel.' Schultz appeals in confirmation of this view, (1) to the fact that C
does not appear till well on in Abraham's history (*Gen.* xx.); (2) to the resemblance of his style and vocabulary to B's ; (3) to the fusion of the two accounts,
especially in the stories of Jacob and Joseph ; (4) to the fact that where C and
B run parallel it is the former whose representations are heightened and
betray a conscious purpose, e.g. in *Gen.* xx. compared with xii. 10–20 and
xxvi.

²⁶ When E and J can be distinctly identified, so as to bring out their relations to each other clearly, e. g. in *Gen.* xx. sqq., xxviii. sqq., xxxvii., xxxix. sqq.,
we see that the idea of one having taken up and elaborated the other is
altogether inadmissible. To take a single example: in *Gen.* xxxvii., how
could the writer who says that Joseph was sold to Ishmaelites have
incorporated in his narrative the story that he was kidnapped by Midianites, or *vice versa* ?—It is urged on the other side (1) that E and J are too
much alike to have been written independently of each other. (But no one
denies that J may have known and imitated E, or *vice versa*. What we do
deny is that either of these authors marred his own work by combining it
with that of the other) ; (2) that here and there one of the two authors, and
specifically J, obviously takes the *rôle* of commentator or harmonist. (But
this harmonist, though he too uses the name Yahwè, must certainly be distinguished from J. Cf. n. 28.)

²⁷ The hypothesis that E was filled in by J, or *vice versa*, both with original
matter and with fragments drawn from other sources, is no doubt admissible
in the abstract; but as soon as we trace out the supposed process in specific
cases it breaks down. In *Ex.* xix.–xxiv. and xxxii.–xxxiv. we find three conceptions of the Sinaitic legislation side by side. There is nothing to indicate
that they were woven together by any one of their three authors, and we have
therefore no right to assume that they were, since *a priori* the supposition has
everything against it.—If *Gen.* xiv. had been incorporated by J in his narrative, some trace of it would surely appear in xviii., xix., whereas as a fact there
is not the least trace in these chapters of what, according to xiv., had just
befallen Sodom and the other cities, and Lot. *Et sic in ceteris.*

²⁸ The proofs of this assertion as to the character of the redaction lie
scattered through n. 4 sqq. Its scrupulous conservatism is proclaimed loudly

enough by the presence of so many doublets (compare *Gen.* xx. with xii. 10–20 ; *Gen.* xvi. with xxi. ; *Gen.* xxix. sqq., etc.) It is harmonising in *Gen.* [162] xxvi. 15, 18, for instance, and (in another way) in *Gen.* xxii. 14–18 ; xxviii. 13–16 ; and (in yet another way) in the little additions to E and J in *Gen.* xl. sqq., which are evidently intended to smooth down the inequalities that must necessarily arise when fragments now of one, now of the other narrative are successively taken up. The best examples of the free use of the two sources have been supplied by the prophetic portions of *Ex.* vii.–xii. and *Josh.* vi.–xii. But see more below, in § 13 and 16, where we shall show that the redaction has penetrated far deeper than has yet appeared, and that more than one stage must be distinguished in it.

[29] Consult the inquiry into the age of the various documents in § 9 sqq., and on the special questions of the redaction of J E and of the whole Hexateuch respectively, see § 13 and 16.

§ 9. *Provisional determination of the chronological order of the constituent elements of the Hexateuch.*

It has hardly been possible to trace out and dissect the various constituents of the Hexateuch, as we have tried to do in § 6–8, without now and then touching on the question of their chronological relations to each other. The results already obtained, or flowing directly from the investigations conducted, may now be gathered up, before we proceed to examine the evidence of the literature and history of Israel as to the genesis of the Hexateuch (§ 10 and 11). These results cannot, in the nature of the case, be complete ; but since they are yielded by the Hexateuch itself, however fragmentary or negative they may be, they deserve to be collected and set forth independently, for comparison with anything we may learn hereafter from other sources. They may be summed up in the four theses that follow.

I. The 'prophetic' narratives of the Hexateuch (JE) were not written to fill in or elaborate the priestly accounts (P), and therefore need not necessarily be subsequent to them [1].

[1] Cf. § 8, n. 21–24. Schrader (*Einl.*, p. 313, n. *a*) still asserts that 'the prophetic passages take account of the work of the annalistic narrator (P).'

But not one of the examples he cites has any real evidential value: either the references are imaginary, or they occur in verses which belong not to JE but to R.

[163]   II. The deuteronomic laws are later than the ordinances incorporated in the 'prophetic' portions, and, in particular, later than the laws of the Book of the Covenant. In *Deut.* v. 6–18 [6–21], when compared with *Ex.* xx. 2–17, this relation would appear still more clearly than it does, were it not that in the latter text subsequent insertions have been made, and some clerical errors have slipped in; but even now the matter is beyond dispute[2]. The parallels between *Ex.* xx. 23–xxiii. 33 and *Deuteronomy* are very numerous, especially in *Deut.* xii.–xx., and are of such a character as to leave no doubt as to the priority of the former collection; here, at any rate, the few exceptions confirm the rule[3]. The relation of *Deuteronomy* to *Ex.* xiii. 1, 2; 3–10; 11–16, to the kindred passage *Ex.* xii. 21–27, and to the Words of the Covenant, *Ex.* xxxiv. 10–27, is not so easy to determine, and accordingly various conceptions of it are current. It seems well therefore to leave it an open question for the present[4].

---

[2] D's version is distinctly marked as the later of the two by the insertion 'as Yahwè, your god, has commanded you,' *v.* 12, 16, 'and that it may be well with you,' *v.* 16 (cf. § 7, n. 4, **16**); 'and thy ox and thy ass,' *v.* 14; 'and his field,' *v.* 18 [21]; and by the substitution of לֹא־תִתְאַוֶּה for the second לֹא־תַחְמֹד, *v.* 18, together with the inversion of the order of אִשָּׁה and בַּיִת, whereby the latter term receives the narrower signification of 'dwelling,' whereas in *Ex.* xx. 17 it is the whole establishment, the several parts of which are then enumerated with the repetition of לֹא־תַחְמֹד. On the other hand וְכָל־תְּמוּנָה, *Ex.* xx. 4, is a corruption of כָּל־תְּמוּנָה, *Deut.* v. 8, and עַד־שֶׁקֶר, *Ex.* xx. 16, is an explanation of עֵד־שָׁוְא, in *Deut.* v. 18 [20], (cf. *Deut.* v. 11; *Ex.* xx. 7). But there is no reason why we should not lay these readings to the charge of the copyists. A more important fact is the occurrence in the Decalogue, even in *Ex.* xx., of deuteronomic formulæ: 'thy stranger that is within thy gates' (*v.* 10); 'that thy days may be prolonged' (*v.* 12); 'in the land which Yahwè thy god giveth thee' (*v.* 12), [cf. § 7, n. 4]. But if it seems improbable that D found these expressions in the Decalogue and appropriated them to himself, we are still at liberty to suppose that

they were transferred from the deuteronomic recension to that of *Ex.* xx.: nothing is commoner than for parallel passages to be brought into closer agreement by redactors or copyists. The most important of the differences between the two recensions, that between *Ex.* xx. 11 and *Deut.* v. 14^b (from לְמַעַן, onwards) 15, admits of more than one explanation. *Deut.* v. 14^b, 15, is quite in the style of D, and is certainly from his hand. But it is not probable that he substituted these grounds of the observance for the reference to the creation story in *Ex.* xx. 11; for elsewhere in the Decalogue he expands, but never omits. We must therefore look upon *Deut.* v. 14^b, 15, as an addition, not a substitution; and in that case *Ex.* xx. 11 must be a later and independ- [164] ent amplification of the text which D had before him. See further, § 16, n. 12.

³ The relation of D to the Book of the Covenant is not uniform throughout, but it is always that of a later to an earlier legislator. The permission to build altars, *Ex.* xx. 24–26, is repealed in *Deut.* xii., etc.; the law of the feasts, *Ex.* xxiii. 14–18 (cf. xiii. 3–10; xxxiv. 18, 22, 23), is very notably modified by the introduction of the one only sanctuary; but the three great feasts are retained, and more than one special expression reappears; the ordinance of the sabbatical year, *Ex.* xxiii. 10, 11, is superseded by another, *Deut.* xv. 1 sqq., in which שָׁמַט, *Ex.* xxiii. 11, is used in a modified sense, *Deut.* xv. 1–3, 9; xxxi. 10. Elsewhere D simply adopts the older law, omitting what is no longer appropriate, and amplifying certain details. Thus in Deut. xv. 12–18, compared with *Ex.* xxi. 1–11, the symbolical action at the sanctuary drops out, since D only recognises one such sanctuary, and the present to the released slave is added.—And again, in *Deut.* xix. 1–13 compared with *Ex.* xxi. 12–14, the specially determined cities of refuge take the place of the many altars of Yahwè.—*Deut.* xix. 19–21 paraphrases the rule of *Ex.* xxi. 23, 24. *Deut.* x. 19; xiv. 29, etc., are quite in the spirit of *Ex.* xxii. 20–23 [21–24]; xxiii. 9; but the positive 'support' takes the place throughout of the negative 'not oppress.'—*Deut.* xvi. 19 further illustrates *Ex.* xxiii. 8.—*Deut.* xv. 7–11 elaborates *Ex.* xxii. 24 [25]; and in the same way *Ex.* xxii. 28, 29 [29, 30]; xxiii. 19^a (cf. xiii. 11–16; xxxiv. 19, 20, 26^a) are worked out more fully in *Deut.* xv. 19–23 (cf. xiv. 22–29); and *Ex.* xxii. 30 [31], in *Deut.* xiv. 1–21^a. The precept so oddly placed in *Deut.* xiv. 21^b, is certainly taken from *Ex.* xxiii. 19^b (cf. xxxiv. 26^b). The hortatory conclusion, *Ex.* xxiii. 20–33, also lay before D, at any rate in part; in vii. 20^a, 22 he adopts *v.* 28, 29 almost literally from it, though the passage squares but ill with his own representation of the numbers of the Israelites (x. 22) and the conquest of the land (ix. 3).

In *Deut.* xxi.–xxv. some of the precepts and exhortations agree in substance with those of the Book of the Covenant, though there is no evidence of borrowing. Compare *Ex.* xxi. 16 with *Deut.* xxiv. 7; *Ex.* xxii. 20–23 [21–24] with *Deut.* xxiv. 14, 15; *Ex.* xxii. 24 [25] with *Deut.* xxiii. 20; *Ex.* xxii. 25, 26 [26, 27] with *Deut.* xxiv. 6, 10–13. The same may be said of *Ex.* xxiii. 4, 5 compared with *Deut.* xxii. 1, 4, though in this case the Book of the Covenant, which speaks of the ox and the ass of 'thine enemy' ('thy hater') seems to be less primitive than D, which has 'thy brother.' But this furnishes no proof of the priority of D, since the expressions are independent, and moreover *Ex.* xxiii. 4, 5 breaks the context and is a later addition (§ 5, n. 1).

⁴ The following points must be considered in determining the relation of these passages to *Deuteronomy*, (*a*) *Ex.* xiii. 2 is a very short and general precept, parallel in substance with *Ex.* xxii. 28ᵇ, 29 [29ᵇ, 30]; xxxiv. 19, 20ᵃᵇ, elaborated in *Ex.* xiii. 11-16, on which see below, under (*c*); (*b*) *Ex.* xiii. 3-10, the tora on eating maççôth, is referred to in *Ex.* xxiii. 15; xxxiv. 18; the reference, however, is not due to the authors of the regulations in *Ex.* xxiii. and xxxiv. themselves, but rather to the redactor (R) who placed these latter regulations after *Ex.* xiii., though they are really older, and are themselves elaborated in *Ex.* xiii. 3-10, not *vice versa*. *Deut.* xvi. 1-8 agrees in contents with our tora; compare *v.* 3ᵃ, 3ᵇ, 4ᵃ, 8 with *Ex.* xiii. 6ᵃ, 8 sq. 7, 6ᵇ, but D seems to be the less original alike in combining maççôth with phésach, [165] in the reasons assigned in *v.* 3 (לחם עני, בחפזון), and in *v.* 8 compared with *Ex.* xiii. 6ᵇ. With *Ex.* xiii. 8 (=*v.* 14, 15; *Ex.* xii. 25-27) cf. *Deut.* vi. 7, 20 sqq.; xi. 19; *Josh.* iv. 6 sqq., 21 sqq.; with *v.* 9 (=*v.* 16) compare *Deut.* vi. 8; xi. 18—a remarkable group of parallels which gives great likelihood to the conjecture that *Ex.* xiii. 3-10 rose in the circles whence *Deuteronomy* issued; (*c*) *Ex.* xiii. 11-16, the consecration of the first-born, is likewise related to *Deuteronomy*, as shown by the parallel passages already cited. Compare, further, *Ex.* xiii. 12 (שגר) with *Deut.* vii. 13; xxviii. 4, 18, 51; *Ex.* xiii. 13; xxxiv. 20 (ערף) with *Deut.* xxi. 4, 6. But the consecration of the human first-born to Yahwè is not enjoined in *Deuteronomy* either in xv. 19-22 or elsewhere; the relation, therefore, is not one of complete agreement in this case; (*d*) on *Ex.* xii. 21-27, see § 6, n. 7. The coincidence between *v.* 24-27 and *Ex.* xiii. 8, 14, 15 and the parallel passages has already been pointed out. The preceding verses, *v.* 21-23, though not written by P², are in his style and spirit. In *Deut.* xvi. 1-8 there is not a trace of the practices here enjoined as עד־עולם חק, *v.* 24, nor indeed is there any room for them. This would lead to the conclusion that *Ex.* xii. 21-23 is later than *Deuteronomy*; (*e*) in *Ex.* xxxiv. 10-27 we must distinguish between the original ritual decalogue, and the two-fold recension which it has undergone. We shall learn presently that the second reviser, at any rate, was dependent upon *Deuteronomy*; the precepts which D shares with the original (compare *v.* 18 with *Deut.* xvi. 1, 3; *v.* 23 with *Deut.* xvi. 16; *v.* 25ᵇ with *Deut.* xvi. 4; *v.* 26ᵇ with *Deut.* xiv. 21ᵇ), occur elsewhere too (*Ex.* xxiii. 14, 15, 18ᵇ, 19ᵇ) and therefore need not have been taken by D from ' the words of the Covenant;' it does not appear that D was acquainted with the first recension of the original. But see, further, § 8, n. 18; 13, n. 21, 29, 32.

III. The deuteronomic history consists in part of recensions and amplifications of 'prophetic' narratives, necessarily involving the priority of the latter; in part of more independent compositions,

which, however, still run parallel, in almost every
case, with JE, and are dependent on it. In the nature
of the case this relation cannot be equally obvious everywhere ; but generally speaking it is unmistakable, even where
the Deuteronomist or his followers depart pretty widely from
JE in their accounts of what took place [5].

[5] Cf. Graf, *Gesch. Bücher*, p. 9–19 ; W.H. Kosters, *De Historiebeschouwing
van den Deuteronomist* ; Kayser, op. cit., p. 141–146 ; Wellhausen, xxii.
465–473 ; and, on the narratives and pericopes recast by D^2 and D^3, § 7, n.
20 (on *Deut.* xxxi.) ; n. 22 (on *Deut.* xxvii., xxxiv.) ; n. 25, 27, 28 (on *Josh.*
i.–xii., xiii.–xxiv.) There is really no difference of opinion as to the relation
here asserted between D and JE. It is only on the question whether D
presupposes historical portions of P also, and works them up in his own
characteristic style, that opinions differ.   See n. 6.   I may therefore confine
myself here to pointing out D's parallels with JE, and the chief indications of [166]
the dependence of the former. In *Deut.* i. 6–19 use is made alike of *Ex.* xviii. 13–
27 and of *Num.* xi. 11–17, 24–29.   *Deut.* i. 20–45 is taken from JE in *Num.*
xiii., xiv. (§ 8, n. 14) ; *v.* 39, emended after the LXX., is no exception to the rule ;
on *v.* 23 see n. 9 ; *v.* 22 and others contain embellishments and amplifications by
D himself.   *Deut.* ii. 2–23 is a free recension of *Num.* xx. 14–23 ; xxi. 1 sqq. ; and
Deut. ii. 24–iii. 11 of *Num.* xxi. 21–35 ; beneath iii. 12–20 lies the same conception of the settlement in the Transjordanic district which we find in *Num.* xxxii.,
but the formulæ of P^2 (§ 6, n. 42) do not occur in *Deut.* iii. With regard to the
events at Sinai, *Deut.* v., ix., x. (cf. iv. and xviii. 16 sqq.) reproduce the representation of *Ex.* xix.–xxiv., xxxii.–xxxiv. ; the agreement is sometimes verbal
(compare, especially, *Deut.* ix. 9 with *Ex.* xxiv. 18, xxxiv. 28 ; *Deut.* ix. 10 with
Ex. xxxi. 18 ; xxxii. 16 ; *Deut.* ix. 12–14 with *Ex.* xxxii. 7–10 ; see, also, the
writers cited above). D's silence as to the revelation and promulgation of
the Book of the Covenant—which he knows and makes use of, n. 3—may be
explained as a deliberate and intentional avoidance of all reference to a legislation which his own was intended to supersede, or may be taken as an
indication that the Book of the Covenant and the striking of the covenant
itself (*Ex.* xx. 23–xxiii. ; xxiv. 3–8) had not yet been taken up into the cycle
of Sinai-stories when D handled it. The same may be said, *mutatis mutandis*,
of 'the Words of the Covenant,' with the reservations that flow from n. 4.
Cf. *Th. Tijdschr.*, xv. 179 sqq., 191 sqq. and below § 13, n. 32.—In *Deut.* vi.
16 ; ix. 22 mention is made of ' Massa,' which appears, along with Meriba,
in *Ex.* xvii. 2–7 ; cf. *Num.* xx. 1–13 ; but whether D was acquainted with either
of these narratives cannot be determined ; the mention of Tab'era and
Kibrôth-hattaäva points to *Num.* xi. 1–3, 4 sqq.—In *Deut.* viii. 3, 5, 16 ;
xxix. 5 [6] the representation of the manna given in JE (*Num.* xi. 6–
9 ; xxi. 4, 5) is adopted and turned to purposes of edification. Cf. *Th. Tijdschr.*,
xiv. 287 sq.—*Deut.* viii. 15 looks like an allusion to *Num.* xxi. 4–9—*Deut.* xi.

6 presupposes the story about Dathan and Abiram in JE, which we now have in combination with P's story of Korah in *Num.* xvi. [xvi. 1-35]—*Deut.* xxiii. 5, 6 [4, 5] brings Balaam into connection with (the Ammonites and) the Moabites, as in *Num.* xxii.-xxiv.; so that this or a similar story, in marked divergence from *Num.* xxv. 6 sqq.; xxxi. (P), is implied by D.—So too *Deut.* xxiv. 9 implies a story of Miriam's leprosy (*Num.* xii.) and xxv. 17-19 an account of Amalek's onset (*Ex.* xvii. 8-16; Amalek's treachery may be regarded as D's exaggeration).

IV. There is no evidence that the Deuteronomist and his followers were acquainted with the priestly laws and narratives. The texts that are commonly cited as references to a written priestly tora demand another interpretation [6]. The deuteronomic legislation never depends on the priestly ordinances as it does on those incorporated in JE [7]. Not a single one of the narratives that we possess in a deuteronomic recension is borrowed from P (§ 7, n. 20, [167] 22, 25, 27, 28). As a rule the historical accounts of P are neither adopted nor contradicted by D, but are simply treated as non-existent [8]. Parallels which, considered alone, might lead to an opposite conclusion, must of necessity be otherwise explained when we consider the relations in which D and P stand to one another as wholes [9].

[6] In *Deut.* x. 9 and xviii. 2 alike, the statement that Levi is to have no territory assigned to him because 'Yahwè is his heritage' is followed by the words 'as he said to him.' When? Naturally at the moment when Levi was separated for the divine service, i. e. when Israel was encamped at Yotba (*Deut.* x. 7). There is no reference, then, to any earlier law, and least of all to *Num.* xviii. (*v.* 20), where the qualifications and revenues of Levi are regulated quite otherwise than in *Deut.* xviii. 1-8.—In *Deut.* xxiv. 8 the Israelites receive the exhortation 'do according to all that the Levite-priests shall teach (יורו) you; as I commanded them, so ye shall observe to do.' Here the oral tora of the priests on cleanness and uncleanness is referred to, and the conviction is expressed that in delivering this tora they are the organs of Yahwè (cf. *Deut.* xxxiii. 10ᵃ and the parallel passages; and below, § 10, n. 4). Had the writer been thinking of the toras on leprosy and its treatment now found in *Lev.* xiii., xiv., he would have expressed himself otherwise.

[7] The only laws with respect to which one might be disposed to question this assertion are *Deut.* xiv. 3-21 and *Lev.* xi. 2-47: the former might be regarded as an excerpt from the latter, with the language of which (that of P)

it certainly agrees. And so Riehm, in common with most of the commentators, actually takes it, *Stud. u. Krit.*, 1868, p. 358 sqq. His view is combated in my *Godsdienst*, i. 502-504 [*Rel. Isr.*, ii. 94 sqq.] and below, § 14, n. 5.—The other examples alleged by Riehm, op. cit., will be considered elsewhere. They do not furnish so much as the semblance of a proof of D's dependence upon P.

⁸ We have seen already (n. 5) that in general D follows JE in his representation of the past. This phenomenon is coupled with the complete ignoring of P, and, more specifically, of P's Sinaitic legislation, to which there is not the remotest reference in *Deut.* v. sqq. In other words, *Ex.* xxv.–xxxi., the account of the building of the tabernacle, etc. in *Ex.* xxxv.–xl., and the whole systematising of the ritual in *Lev.* i.–*Num.* x., are for the author of *Deut.* v. sqq. as though they were not. If any doubt as to the significance of this silence were left it would be removed by *Deut.* xii. 8, 9, for it is here assumed that in the fortieth year after the Exodus freedom to sacrifice in more than one place still existed, whereas according to P the one sanctuary had been in use from Sinai onwards. And, accordingly, D never once mentions the tabernacle of *Ex.* xxv. sqq. Ch. xxxi. 14, 15 is not from his hand, and moreover the ôhel mo'éd there mentioned is that of *Ex.* xxxiii. 7–11 ; *Num.* xi. 24 sqq.; xii. 4 (JE).— Add to this that D knows nothing of Joshua as a faithful spy (*Deut.* i. 36; *Josh.* xiv. 6–15 ; on the words 'and concerning thee' in *v.* 6 see § 7, n. 27) ; that he makes the spies start from Kadesh Barnéa and not from the desert of [168] Pharan (*Deut.* i. 19 sqq.) ; that he gives an account of the manna differing from P's version in *Ex.* xvi. (*Deut.* viii. 3, 5, 16) ; makes Aaron die at Mosera, not on Mount Hor (*Deut.* x. 6) ; knows nothing of Korah (*Deut.* xi. 6), and shows no acquaintance with P's representation of the events in the field of Moab and the part which Balaam played in them (*Deut.* xxiii. 5, 6 [4, 5], cf. iv. 3, as against *Num.* xxxi. 8, 16 ; *Josh.* xiii. 22, cf. *Num.* xxv. 6 sqq.). Amongst the details which D never mentions, though they are recorded in P, there is scarcely one which could have presented any difficulties to him ; the supposition that he was unacquainted with P is the only satisfactory explanation of his silence.

⁹ See the writers cited in n. 5, and likewise Nöldeke's remarks on Kayser's arguments in *Jahrb. f. prot. Theologie*, i. 348–351, and my answer in *Th. Tijdschrift*, ix. 533–536, compared with Wellhausen's, op. cit.—Nöldeke appeals in the first place to *Deut.* iv. 41–43 ; xix. 2–7, compared with *Num.* xxxv. 9–34 ; *Josh.* xx.; but see § 7, n. 17, 29. In the next place he points to the following passages :—

Deut. i. 23 compared with *Num.* xiii. 1–16. But D was not acquainted with these names, or at any rate did not adopt them, for he does not count Joshua amongst the spies. The agreement is therefore confined to the number being twelve, which circumstance P may equally well have taken from D, unless it was in JE already, as may well have been the case, for the redactor of *Num.* xiii., xiv. could hardly have preserved JE's statement of the number while adopting P's list of the names.

Deut. x. 3 (ארון עצי שׁטׁים), cf. *Ex.* xxv. 10 sqq. But the ark of *Ex.* xxv. 10

sqq. was not made by Moses, but by Bezaleel and his associates; and when completed it could hardly be called 'an ark of shittim wood' any longer, for it was overlaid with gold and surmounted by Cherubim ; the command to make it, in *Ex.* xxv. sqq., stands in quite a different connection from that of *Deut.* x. 1-5. Moreover JE is acquainted with the ark (*Num.* x. 33-36 ; xiv. 44) and the ôhel mo'éd in which it was kept (*Ex.* xxxiii. 7-11 and parallel passages). We are therefore fully justified in supposing that JE likewise contained an account of its construction, which D adopted with or without modifications. When *Ex.* xxv. 10 sqq. was taken up by the redactor, this account in JE had of course to be omitted.

Deut. x. 6 sq. compared with *Num.* xx. 22-29 and the other texts of P which mention Eleazar as the son and successor of Aaron. But D disagrees with *Num.* xx. as to the place in which Aaron died and was succeeded by Eleazar, so that he cannot have drawn his information thence, nor need he have done so, for Eleazar ben Aaron appeared in JE also (*Josh.* xxiv. 33).

Deut. i. 38 ; iii. 28, etc. compared with *Josh.* xiv. sqq., where Joshua actually does divide Canaan by lot. But it is doubtful whether this is the meaning of הנחיל (without בגורל), and suppose D and P really do agree in this conception of the partition (cf. § 7, n. 27), even then there is no special reason for giving P the priority.

Deut. xxxii. 48-52 ; xxxiv. regarded as an amplification of the account in the 'Grundschrift,' almost the very words of which it still preserves. But *Deut.* xxxii. 48-52 is simply a fragment of P, and in *Deut.* xxxiv. we find JE, the additions of D, and P, all welded together by a redactor. Cf. § 7, n. 22, under (6).

Josh. ix. 27[b], considered as an addition by D to *v.* 27[a] (P). But see § 6, n. 48 ; 7, n. 26.

[169]   *Josh.* xviii. 3 sqq. as an addition by D to *v.* 1, 2 (P). But see § 6, n. 52 ; 7, n. 27.

Josh. xxii., as a deuteronomic recension of a narrative from P. But see § 6, n. 53 ; 7, n. 27.

Deut. x. 22 compared with *Gen.* xlvi. 8-27 ; *Ex.* i. 5. But see *Th. Tijdschr.*, ix. 533 sq. 'Which is the earlier, the round figure of 600,000 in *Ex.* xii. 37 and the parallel passages, or the elaborate genealogical lists in *Num.* i. and xxvi.? Nöldeke himself has taught us that the latter form an artificial superstructure raised on the basis of the former. Just so the figure 70 in *Deut.* x. 22 is far more ancient than the list of Jacob's descendants in *Gen.* xlvi. 8-27, which *v.* 21 alone would at once betray as a "Machwerk" of a very late date.'

These parallels, extremely doubtful and insignificant in themselves, are of course wholly insufficient to disarm the unmistakable results of n. 8.

There is nothing in theses I. and IV. to determine the relative antiquity of P with respect to JE and D : P may be later than D and *a fortiori* than JE, but it may also be contemporary with one or the other, or it may even be earlier than JE and *a fortiori* than D, provided only that for some reason or other it remained unknown to both.   The definitive choice between these several possibilities will depend, amongst other things, on the evidence of the Israelitish literature and history (§ 10 and 11).   But now that we have drawn the boundaries between the three Hexateuchal groups we are in a position, without further delay, to estimate the probable historical value of each, and thence infer what result to expect from our continued investigations.   Amongst the passages formerly cited (§ 4, n. 17 sqq.) in proof of the unhistorical character of the Hexateuch, we now perceive that the most striking examples come from P[10].   Wherever we can compare its accounts with those of JE and D they seem to depart further from the reality[11].   In all probability, then, P's narratives are the latest[12].

[10] See especially § 4, n. 19. the genealogies there referred to all belong to P.   It is in P, too, that the absolutely unhistorical representation of Israel's settlement in the Transjordanic district and of the division of Canaan by lot is most fully developed (§ 4, n. 20 ; 6, n. 52).

[11] It is not easy to determine the limits we must observe for such a comparison to retain its full demonstrative force.   I will therefore confine myself to a few examples, and can do so the more readily as we shall have to return to this matter again (§ 15).   When P, evidently with the ritual institutions of Moses in view, scrupulously avoids the mention either of sacrifices or altars in his narratives of the patriarchs, and when he gives an account of Jacob and Esau (*Gen.* xxxv. 27–29; xxxvi. 6–8), which excludes those hostile relations that occupy so important a place in JE's account of the brothers, he shows little concern with the reality, and [170] subordinates historical probability to considerations of quite another order. In distinction from JE he makes Moses and Aaron demand the complete release of Israel, and represents the plagues of Egypt as a contest between them and Pharaoh's magicians (§ 6, n. 6); he purges the exodus of its character of a hasty flight (*Ex.* xii. 1–20, 28, 40, 41 as against *v.* 29–39); describes the passage of the Red Sea as walking on dry land between the waters heaped up on either hand (§ 6, n. 8); and sees in the manna no meagre and distasteful food, but bread from heaven, wherewith Israel was sated (*Th. Tijdschr.*, xiv. 287 sqq.).   Can it be denied that his representations in all these cases are less probable and therefore later than those of JE?

[12] See further, § 15.

§ 10. *The Hexateuch and the other books of the Old Testament.*

To determine the antiquity of the whole Hexateuch and of its several elements, it is of the utmost importance to compare *Genesis–Joshua* with the other books of the Old Testament; and also with the history of the Israelitish people and their religion, which we gather from these books. The literary comparison must take the precedence, for we must assume its results in our investigation of the historical position occupied by the laws of the Hexateuch. This comparison must deal alike with actual quotations from the Hexateuch and with passages so similar in form and contents as to indicate dependence, or at least relationship. It need hardly be said that all the alternative explanations of each parallel must be duly considered, that in many cases no decisive choice can be made amongst them, and that our judgment on the ambiguous phenomena must conform to the results arrived at in cases which admit of but one interpretation.

The prophetic writings must be taken before the historical and those again before the poetical books, for the antiquity of the first is least doubtful or contested, and that of the last most so. Within each of these three groups the latest books will as far as possible be taken first, since this procedure will again secure our advancing, as far as may be, from the known to the doubtful or unknown.

[171]

A. The Prophets.

We must consider separately, (1) the attitude of the prophets towards the Tora generally ; (2) any passages we may find in their writings which present specific parallels to laws or narratives of the Hexateuch.

(1) The book of *Daniel* (ix. 11, 13) and Malachi (iii. 22 [iv. 4] cf. iii. 7) mention Moses as a law-giver, but he does

not appear in this capacity in the older prophets. Deutero-Isaiah (lxiii. 11, 12) knows of him as Israel's leader at the passage of the Red Sea and in the desert ; Jeremiah (xv. 1) places him by the side of Samuel, as a prophet, Micah (vi. 4) by the side of Aaron and Miriam as Israel's deliverer from Egypt, and finally Hosea evidently refers to him when (xii. 14 [13]) he ascribes the deliverance from Egypt and the subsequent guidance of the people to 'a prophet'[1].

But did the prophets before Malachi refer to the Law, though without naming Moses as the law-giver? So much is obvious, that they did not regard it as the divinely sanctioned code to which they and the whole people of Israel were subject. Not a single trace of any such view is to be found[2]. Least of all did they recognise the authority of the ceremonial injunctions, for, if we except Ezekiel and certain utterances relative to the sabbath (*Isaiah* lvi. 1–8 ; lviii. 13 ; *Jeremiah* xvii. 19–27), they show complete indifference towards them, or even declare that they do not include them amongst the commands of Yahwè. This is conspicuously the case with Jeremiah (vii. 21–23), Isaiah (i. 11–15), Micah (vi. 6), and Amos (iv. 4, 5 ; v. 21–27)[3]. What they mean by the tora (or teaching) of Yahwè is not a book of law at all, but the commandments and exhortations which Yahwè has previously given or still gives to his people by his interpreters, the priests and prophets. In most cases we are to think of oral teaching, but the existence of written 'tora' also is expressly asserted in one passage (*Hosea* viii. 12), and rendered highly probable by the context in others (*Amos* ii. 4 ; *Jeremiah* xliv. 10, 23, etc. ; *Ezekiel* v. 6, 7 ; xi. 12, 20, etc.)[4]. The covenant between Yahwè and [172] Israel is also mentioned now and then by some of the prophets, and specifically by Jeremiah, in a manner evidently implying that a written statement of its conditions was present to the mind of the speaker[5].

¹ The text of *Isaiah* lxiii. 11 is corrupt, משׁה probably being a later insertion; but *v.* 12 still remains.

².At least five centuries had elapsed since the time of Moses, when those prophets flourished whose writings we still possess. A Mosaic law-book, rendered venerable by its origin and its high antiquity, and itself laying claim to a quite exceptional authority (e. g. *Deut.* iv. 2; xiii. 1 [xii. 32]), must have been constantly cited and upheld against the people by any teachers who recognised it. But there is not a trace to be found in our prophets of the 'it is written' style. Even if they show any knowledge of written laws (cf. n. 4) they mention them but very rarely—especially the pre-exilian prophets—and even then not at all in the spirit of unconditional submission with which a complete Mosaic code must have inspired them. In considering this matter, we must of course allow for the prophets' consciousness of being themselves the trusted ones of Yahwè (*Amos* iii. 7), the 'men of the spirit' (*Hosea* ix. 7), but this is not enough by itself to explain their independence; if 'the tora of Yahwè' had been codified in their time they could not have advocated and enforced the service of Yahwè without in some way defining their relation to it.

³ On the sabbath in the prophetic writings cf. § 11, n. 22; on Ezekiel see below, n. 10-12 and § 11, *passim*. Here we may confine ourselves to those of the passages cited above which refer to the sacrifices and feasts in honour of Yahwè. We must not assert that the prophets reject the cultus unconditionally. On the contrary they too share the belief, for instance, that sacrifice is an essential element of true worship (*Isaiah* lvi. 7; *Zech.* xiv. 16-19; *Mic.* iv. 1 sqq.; *Isaiah* ii. 1 sq.; xviii. 7; xix. 19 sqq., etc., etc.). The context always shows that what they really protest against is the idea that it is enough to take part in the cultus, that there is no inconsistency in devotional zeal coupled with neglect of Yahwè's moral demands, and that as long as his altars smoke and his sanctuaries are frequented his favour is sure (cf. *Jer.* vii. 8 sqq., etc., etc.). But it is also clear from the manner in which the prophets give utterance to this ethical conviction, and maintain it against the people, that they are far from regarding the cultus as in like manner and in like degree an ordinance of Yahwè, or as resulting from a positive divine command insisted on with as much emphasis as the other. And this would have been the case had the Mosaic tora, as we know it, existed and been recognised in their day. Only consider, from this point of view, the texts just now cited. Jeremiah's contemporaries could have met his assertion in vii. 22 ('for I spoke not to your fathers nor gave them commandments, on the day that I led them out of Egypt, concerning burnt offering and sacrifice') with a direct denial, if they had known the laws in P, such as *Lev.* i.–vii. To Isaiah's question: 'when ye come to see my face (read לראות), who has [173] required this of you, to tread my forecourts flat?' (i. 12), the answer must have been: 'Yahwè himself!' Amos is especially unequivocal. His strong expressions in v. 21, 22 are inexplicable if the feasts, the burnt offerings and the gifts had been ordained by Yahwè himself. To the question

which he adds (*v.* 25): 'did ye offer me sacrifice and food-offering in the desert forty years long, O house of Israel?' he expects a negative answer, whereas the laws and narratives of P allow of nothing but an affirmative one. Equally clear is iv. 4, 5. Here Amos ironically exhorts his hearers to make their (yearly) sacrifices every day and to bring their tithes (due every third year) every third day, to consume their praise-offerings on leavened bread and to proclaim free-will offerings, 'for,' he adds, 'this you delight in,' or, 'this is your fancy.' Could he have spoken thus if the Israelites had only been showing their obedience to Yahwè's command, and, at worst, merely displaying a somewhat exaggerated zeal?—Cf. on the other side the essay by K. Marti in *Jahrb. f. prot. Theologie*, 1880, p. 308–323. Marti generally interprets the prophetic texts on sacrifice fairly enough, but he uniformly misconceives, and so contrives to escape, the inferences with respect to the priestly tora to which they lead. Our thesis, that the polemic of the prophets against the religion of their contemporaries would necessarily have differed in form had they known and recognised a ritual legislation, is untouched by Marti.

⁴ The original meaning of תורה is the pointing out of what is to be done in some special case. Hence Smend, in his essay *Über die von den Propheten des* viii. *Jahrh. vorausgesetzte Entwickelungsstufe der isr. Religion* (Stud. u. Krit., 1876, p. 599–664), correctly infers that tora primitively signified the instruction given by the priest, who pronounced in Yahwè's name, not only on cleanness and uncleanness, but also—and this is our special point just now—on right and wrong. It is thus that our oldest witnesses use the word, viz. Amos (ii. 4, on which more presently) and Hosea (iv. 6, where the priest appears as the bearer of the tora, identified by Hosea with the true knowledge of Yahwè; viii. 1, where sinning against Yahwè's tora stands in parallelism with violating his command; *v.* 12, which must be interpreted, like *v.* 1, in accordance with iv. 6; see below). Nor did later writers lose consciousness of this original connection between 'priest' and 'tora;' tora always remains the *vox propria* for the priestly decisions, especially in the administration of justice. Cf. *Deut.* xxxiii. 10 (from the period of Jeroboam II.; Levi is the subject; the תורה stands in parallelism with 'the statutes' (משפטים) of Yahwè): *Mic.* iii. 11 (the priests 'point out,' give tora, for hire): *Zeph.* iii. 4 (המסו תורה, of the priests); *Jeremiah* ii. 8 (the priests תפשי התורה); xviii. 18 ('tora and priest' go together, like 'counsel and sage,' 'word and prophet': all the more interesting inasmuch as Jeremiah is here reproducing the *vox populi*); perhaps other passages of Jeremiah, which will be discussed presently, might be added; *Hab.* i. 4 (parallel to משפט); *Ezek.* vii. 26 (=*Jer.* xviii. 18, with slight modifications, but 'tora and priest' are retained unaltered); xxii. 26; xliv. 23, 24; *Hagg.* ii. 11 ('ask tora of the priests'— on cleanness and uncleanness, *v.* 12, 13); *Malachi* ii. 6–9 (a very remarkable passage, to be compared with *Deut.* xxxiii. 8–11).—Meanwhile the word 'tora' was not confined to the activity of the priest as the interpreter of Yahwè's will: the prophet not only rebukes the sins which have been or are being [174] committed, but points out what ought to be done; so that his preaching

N

likewise may be called ' tora of Yahwè.' So the prophet Isaiah, with his
high position and influence, may be said to use the formula habitually (i. 10;
ii. 3 [= *Mic.* iv. 2]; v. 24; viii. 16, 20, cf. *v.* 1 sqq.; xxx. 9), while he calls the
prophets the teachers ('moreh') of Jerusalem's citizens (xxx. 20). Nothing
is more natural than that his usage should have been followed by others,
e.g. *Jeremiah* vi. 19 (in parallelism to 'my words'); xxvi. 4 (cf. *v.* 5),
perhaps also ix. 12 [13]; xvi. 11; xxxii. 23 (in which places, however, the
written law may be included, for it was not unknown to the prophet; see
below); further, Deutero-Isaiah, xlii. 4 (of the preaching of the servant of
Yahwè); perhaps also xlii. 21, 24 ; li. 4, 7 ; and Zechariah vii. 12 (where
התורה is followed by 'and the words which Yahwè has sent by his spirit, by
the hand of the former prophets;' cf. i. 2–6).

With the prophets, then, ' the tora of Yahwè ' is by no means a closed and
completed whole, handed down from antiquity, but the continuous and ever
renewed indication to Israel of Yahwè's will. There was of course nothing
to prevent this 'pointing out' from being committed to writing. And it is to
this that a reference is found as early as in Hosea, viii. 12, where Yahwè
says, ' I write (or, if I write) for him (Israel) ten thousand of my toras, they
are counted as those of a stranger.' The text is doubtful, the reading I have
translated is Hitzig's (רִבּוֹ־תּוֹרָתִי), which is recommended by its close
adherence to the traditional text, but militated against by the use of רִבּוּ,
which occurs nowhere else except in much later writers, and by the displeasing
hyperbole of the ' ten thousand' which is quite unjustified by the context.
The Keri רֻבֵּי, ' the multitudes,' is no better. Perhaps we must make up our
minds with Graetz (*Gesch. d. Juden*, ii. 1. p. 469 sq.) simply to read
דִּבְרֵי־תּוֹרָתִי 'if I write for him the words of my tora, they are,' etc. Now
although this utterance of Hosea's is hypothetical (not כתבתי, but אכתב),
yet it proves that the idea of committing the tora to writing was not strange
to him, whence we may presume that it actually took place, or had taken
place, from time to time. Ch. viii. 1 agrees with this; ' violating the covenant' with Yahwè may at any rate be understood without violence as
breaking an act of covenant drawn up by Yahwè. It is the priests that we
must think of as the guardians, if not the authors, of such documents (iv. 1–10),
but, in Hosea's opinion, they did not stand any the higher themselves, nor
exercise any the more influence over the people, on that account.—Thus prepared by Hosea we recognise some such written tora, at any rate
with a high degree of probability, even in the earlier Amos (ii. 4), who
reproaches the men of Judah with having ' despised the tora of Yahwè and
broken his statutes, חֻקִּים;' but חֻקִּים may be taken, in case of need,
to indicate the hallowed usage, so that תורה would refer to the oral
teaching of priests and prophets, though the first interpretation is the more
probable. Why the phrase should compel us to deny *v.* 4 to Amos (Duhm,
Wellhausen, Oort), I cannot see.—Two centuries after Amos, in the time
of Jeremiah, a written tora had evidently become a current conception.
Yahwè laments, 'They have not walked after my tora and after my ordinances, which I laid upon them and their fathers.' (*Jer.* xliv. 10, cf. *v.* 23 where

besides the חקות, we have the עדות of Yahwè), and with this (written) tora in his mind the prophet declares his faith that in time to come Yahwè will set his tora in the inward parts and write it in the hearts of his people (xxxi. 33). The priests and prophets, against whom he is contending, likewise make use of writing, as a means of influencing the people, whence he complains of 'the lying pen of the writers,' viii. 8.—Ezekiel too must surely be thinking, at any rate in part, of written laws, when he mentions Yahwè's חקות and משפטים, in a way which generally implies their existence long ago, and in xx. (*v.* 11, 13, 6, 19, 21, 24, 25) involves their having been given in the desert. Finally, see *Isaiah* xxiv. 5.

[5] On Hosea viii. 1, to which vi. 7 is parallel, cf. n. 4. Jeremiah's use of ברית does not always suggest a written document (xiv. 21 ; xxii. 9 ; xxxii. 40 ; cf. xxxiii. 21, the covenants with David and with Levi) ; but it certainly does so in xi. (*v.* 2, 3, 6, 8, 10, where the words of the covenant are constantly referred to) ; in xxxiv. 13, 18 (where a specific commandment is a part of the covenant) ; in a certain sense also in xxxi. 31–33 (since the tora written in the heart is coordinate with the new covenant). Ezekiel's usage (xvi. 8, 59 sq., 61 sq. ; xx. 37 ; xxx. 5 ; xxxiv. 25 ; xxxvii. 26 ; xliv. 7) is identical with Jeremiah's. In Deutero-Isaiah ברית is used throughout of the future union between Yahwè and Israel (liv. 10; lv. 3; lix. 21; lxi. 8), only in lvi. 4, 6, of a former covenant to which the Sabbath ordinance, amongst others, belonged. In *Isaiah* xxiv. 5 we find ברית along with תורה and חק.

(2) The author of the book of *Daniel*, and Malachi, who mention the ' tora of Moses,' also show the actual acquaintance with it that might have been expected. The small number of the parallels presented by the first-named book is not surprising. In *Malachi* they are more numerous and are borrowed from various parts of the tora [6]. In the book of *Jonah* and in Joel, which may probably be placed about the time of Malachi, the agreement with the Hexateuch is confined to a few texts of JE, to which, in the case of Joel, a reminiscence of D must perhaps be added [7]. Haggai and Zechariah (i.–viii.) perhaps show points of contact with D, but certainly not with P [8]. In the prophecies uttered shortly before and immediately after the return from the Babylonian captivity the influence of D is again distinctly perceptible, here and there, as well as an acquaintance with the narratives of JE. The allusions to details in P, which some have traced in a few passages, are, to say the least, very doubtful [9].

[176] Ezekiel's connection with the Hexateuch is far closer than that of any of these prophets. He shares with them the use of JE and D^{10}. But, in addition to this, he manifests, (1) a great resemblance in conception and style to the priestly passages which we indicated by P^1 in § 6^{11}, and (2) striking parallels with P^2, together with some of his characteristic words and formulæ[12]. This relationship with P at once establishes a marked distinction between Ezekiel and his immediate predecessors, the prophets of the closing period of the kingdom of Judah. Obadiah, Habakkuk, *Zech.* xii.–xiv., Nahum, and Zephaniah afford certain points of comparison with JE and D; and, considering the narrow limits and the subject-matter of these prophecies, we cannot expect much more ; but there is not a trace of P in any of them [13]. From the nature of the case, we learn more from Jeremiah, who began his preaching in 626 B.C., and committed it to writing in 604 B.C., and subsequently. We might call him, in one word, the deuteronomic prophet. He has a great number of peculiar words and turns of expression in common with D^1 and his followers—so much so indeed that some have thought they recognised him as the author of *Deuteronomy*, though in taking up this idea they have allowed the really remarkable agreement to blind them to no less important differences [14]. The few points of contact with P must not pass unnoticed, but they cannot for a moment be accepted as proofs of acquaintance with the priestly laws and narratives [15].

Ascending from the seventh to the eighth century we completely lose sight of *Deuteronomy :* the traces of the book that have sometimes been seen in Micah and Isaiah or their predecessors *Zech.* ix.–xi., Hosea, and Amos are not really there[16]. Nor is there any evidence of acquaintance with P in these prophets; for what commonly does duty as a proof to the contrary is hardly worthy of attention[17]. On the other hand, they yield us more or less distinct parallels to the narratives in JE, though in some cases it remains doubtful whether we should explain them as evidence that the prophets had read the stories, or in some other way[18].

[6] The subject to which the rest of this § is devoted is dealt with by Dr. [177] H. Gelbe, *Beitrag zur Einl. in das A. T.* (Leipzig, 1866), *passim*, and more expressly by Colenso, *Pentateuch*, vii. p. 85–482, as well as in the general introductions to the Hexateuch. A subsection of it is treated by K. Marti, *Die Spuren der sogenannten Grundschrift des Hexateuchs in den vorex. Proph. des A. T.* (*Jahrb. f. prot. Theologie*, 1880, p. 127–161, 308–354). The points raised in this and the following notes must constantly be compared with the facts discussed in § 11, from which the present § may often be supplemented, for it is not always possible to draw a clear line between them.

The points of contact between *Daniel* and the Hexateuch are, from the nature of the case, few in number, though unequivocal in character. Acquaintance with the Hexateuch is shown not only in ix. 4 sqq., but by the use of התמיד (viii. 11–13; xi. 31; xii. 11) and of קדש קדשׁים (ix. 24), both of them terms borrowed from P. Again, compare i. 8 with the dietary laws in *Lev.* xi. and *Deut.* xiv. —Malachi attaches himself to D in iii. 22 [iv. 4] (Horeb); iii. 3 (the sons of Levi as priests); ii. 4 sqq. (the covenant with Levi), and in this last passage specifically to *Deut.* xxxiii. 8–11; further compare iii. 17 (סגלה) with *Deut.* vii. 6; xiv. 2; xxvi. 18; *Ex.* xix. 5. But the denunciation in i. 8 sqq. presupposes (not only *Deut.* xvii. 1, but also) *Lev.* xxii. 20–25, and the requirement to bring 'all the tithes' into the treasury of the temple cannot be based on D, but must rest on *Num.* xviii. 21 sqq.

[7] Compare *Jonah* iv. 2 with *Ex.* xxxiv. 6, 7; and perhaps i. 14 with *Deut.* xxi. 8, though the coincidence here may be accidental; further *Joel* ii. 13 with the above cited *Ex.* xxxiv. 6, 7; *Joel* ii. 3 with *Gen.* ii.; xiii. 10; *Joel* ii. 2 with *Ex.* x. 14; *Joel* ii. 12 with *Deut.* vi. 5; *Joel* ii. 23 with *Deut.* xi. 14. It will be seen that these parallels are unimportant, and moreover Joel's date is so much contested that his evidence has little value.

[8] Compare *Haggai* ii. 17 with *Deut.* xxviii. 22, though it does not follow that this passage was in the prophet's mind. *Zech.* i. 2–6; vii., viii., i. e. Zechariah's discourses as distinguished from his visions, recall Jeremiah, and consequently D, in tone and in style, but they show no traces of imitation.—As to P, if Haggai had been acquainted with a written priestly law, he would have appealed to it (in ii. 11–13), and especially to *Num.* xix. 11, instead of leaving it to the priests to decide the ritual question which he took as the point of departure for his exhortation. I cannot discover (with Colenso, vii. 291) a reference to *Ex.* xxix. 45, 46, in *Hag.* ii. 5. Zechariah, as appears from vii. 5; viii. 19, knows of no other fast in the seventh month than the one in commemoration of Gedaliah's death (2 Kings xxv. 25), which he calls 'the fast of the seventh month.' In other words, he knew nothing of the great day of atonement of *Lev.* xvi., etc. On the other hand, *Zech.* iv. 2 shows agreement with *Ex.* xxv. 31 sqq., but it does not extend to the expression, and

only consists in the representation of the lamp-stand (which Zechariah may have seen in Zerubbabel's temple) as having seven lights, in opposition to 1 *Kings* vii. 49. Cf. Graf, *Geschichtliche Bücher*, p. 62.

[9] The influence of D is less perceptible in the style than in the conceptions of Deutero-Isaiah. In vindicating the unity of Yahwè (xliii. 10–12; xliv. [178] 6, 8, 24; xlv. 5, 6, etc.), the prophet advances along the path opened by D (vi. 4, etc.) Cf. also *Isaiah* liii. 10 (ימים הֶאֱרִיךְ); lxiii. 17 (יהוה דרכי; Israel Yahwè's (נחלה); li. 13 (שׁכח), etc.—Parallels with JE may be detected at once in *Isaiah* li. 2 ; 3 (גַּן־יְהוָה and עֵדֶן); 10; lii. 4; 12 (בחפזון, cf. *Deut.* xvi. 3); lxiii. 11–13.—I think we should also add liv. 9, for *Gen.* viii. 21, 22 underlies it. Others, however (e.g. Colenso, vii. 290 sq.), find a citation of *Gen.* ix. 11 or 15 here, but in neither of the passages in *Genesis* is an oath of Elohîm (Yahwè) mentioned, and עבר followed by עַל is equally remote from שחת and from הכות. No conclusive proof of the use of P can be found, then, in *Isaiah* liv. 9. Still less can such a proof be derived from xxxiv. 11 (קֹו־תֹהוּ וְאַבְנֵי־בֹהוּ) compared with *Gen.* i. 2 (for *tohu-wabohu* was, beyond doubt, a current expression for chaos), or from xiii. 19 compared with *Gen.* xix. 29 (for הפך is the fixed expression, occurring in *Gen.* xix. 21, 25 also, for the lot that fell upon Sodom and Gomorrah—which two cities P never mentions at all!—and 'Elohîm' added to מַהְפֵּכָה expresses the idea that these cities were destroyed in a supernatural manner, by the higher powers).

[10] The combination of חום with עַיִן (*Ezek.* v. 11; vii. 4, 9; viii. 18; ix. 5, 10; xvi. 5; xx. 17) is certainly borrowed from D (vii. 16; xiii. 9; xix. 13, 21; xxv. 12); as also כעס *Ezek.* viii. 17; xvi. 26; המרה, *Ezek.* v. 6; xx. 8, 13, 21; שׁמר לעשות, *Ezek.* xviii. 9; xx. 21; שֵׂעִירִים, *Ezek.* xxi. 20 [15]. For parallels with *Deut.* xxviii. and xxxii. see Colenso, *Pentateuch*, vi., App., p. 4. Moreover, we shall presently see that Ezekiel's ordinances for the future are based upon the laws of D, and presuppose them throughout (§ 15, n. 12 sqq.) Acquaintance with JE shines through in *Ezek.* xxxiii. 24; xxviii. 13; (xxxi. 8, 9, 16, 18; xxxvi. 35), xx. 6 ('flowing with milk and honey'), etc.

[11] I shall return to this resemblance in § 15, n. 10. Here I need only point out that it is sufficiently striking to have induced Graf, and after him Colenso, Kayser, Horst (*Lev.* xviii.–xxvi. *und Ezekiel*) and others, to find in Ezekiel the author or redactor of *Lev.* xvii. sqq.

[12] Ezekiel and P[2] agree in the use of the following words and idioms:—

אֶרֶץ מְגוּרִים, *Ezek.* xx. 38; *Gen.* xvii. 8; xxviii. 4; xxxvi. 7; xxxvii. 1 (xlvii. 9); *Ex.* vi. 4.

עֶצֶם הַיּוֹם הַזֶּה, *Ezek.* ii. 3; xxiv. 2; xl. 1; *Gen.* vii. 13; xvii. 23, 26, etc. (also *Lev.* xxiii. 14, 21, 28–30).

רָקִיע, *Ezek.* i. 22 sq., 25 sq.; x. 1; *Gen.* i. 6–8, etc.

מִין, *Ezek.* xlvii. 10; *Gen.* i. 11, etc.; vi. 20; vii. 14; *Lev.* xi. 14–16, etc. (*Deut.* xiv. 13–15, 18).

צִפּוֹר כָּל־כָּנָף (כֹּל), *Ezek.* xvii. 23; xxxix. 4, 17; *Gen.* vii. 14.

אֲחֻזָּה, *Ezek.* xlv. 5, 7, 8, etc.; *Gen.* xvii. 8, etc.

בִּמְאֹד מְאֹד, *Ezek.* ix. 9; xvi. 13; *Gen.* xvii. 2, 6, 20; *Ex.* i. 7.

קדש קדשים, *Ezek.* xli. 4; xlii. 13; xliii. 12; xliv. 13; xlv. 3; xlviii. 12; *Ex.* xxvi. 33 sq., etc., etc. (in 1 *Kings* vi. 16; vii. 50; viii. 6, it is probably a gloss).

עשה שפטים, *Ezek.* v. 10, 15, etc.; *Ex.* xii. 12; *Num.* xxxiii. 4.

נשא יד (in taking an oath), *Ezek.* xx. 6, 15, 23, 28, 42; xlvii. 14; *Ex.* vi. 8; *Num.* xiv. 30.

חברת אשה אל־אחותה, *Ezek.* i. 9, cf. 11; *Ex.* xxvi. 3, etc.

תבנית, *Ezek.* viii. 3, 10; x. 8; *Ex.* xxv. 9, 40.

But the Concordances should also be consulted on עולם (preceded by ברית, חקת, חק); נשא followed by עון; זרק; נסך; תמיד; תרומה; שקץ (*Ezek.* viii. 10; *Lev.* xi. passim; but also *Deut.* vii. 26); כפר as a sacrificial term; אורה (ריח ניחוח; לרצון; מושבות (*Ezek.* xlvii. 22; *Ex.* xii. 19, 48 sq., etc.), נשיא, and a number of other terms collected by Smend, p. xxvii. sq.

There are striking parallels in *Ezek.* iv. 6 and *Num.* xiv. 34; *Ezek.* xxxvi. 3, 13 and *Num.* xiii. 32; *Ezek.* xx. 42 and *Ex.* vi. 8; *Ezek.* xxviii. 13 and *Ex.* xxviii. 17 sqq. (xxxix. 10 sqq.); *Ezek.* xx. 12 and *Ex.* xxxi. 13.

These phenomena certainly demand an explanation, and they will receive it in § 15, n. 11 sqq. Here I must content myself with noting that the supposition that Ezekiel imitated P² is only one of several possible explanations. Why should not P² have imitated Ezekiel, for example, or both have drawn their style and language from some common source?

[13] Compare *Hab.* iii. 3 with *Deut.* xxxiii. 2; *Hab.* iii. 6 with *Gen.* xlix. 26; *Deut.* xxxiii. 15; *Hab.* iii. 19 with *Deut.* xxxiii. 29;—*Zech.* xiii. 3 with *Deut.* xviii. 20; *Zech.* xiv. 5 with *Deut.* xxxiii. 2;—*Nahum* i. 3ª with *Ex.* xxxiv. 6, 7; *Num.* xiv. 18;—*Zeph.* iii. 3 with *Gen.* xlix. 27; *Zeph.* iii. 5 with *Deut.* xxxii. 4. Even Marti can discover no traces of P in these prophets.

[14] The latest exposition of the striking agreement in language and style between Jeremiah and D is due to Colenso (*Pentateuch*, vii., App., p. 85–110), who collects no less than two hundred words and formulæ, common to the prophet with D, or common to D with the redactor of *Judges*, *Samuel*, and *Kings*. Cf. also Kleinert's survey of D's language compared with the parallel passages in other books (op. cit., p. 214–235), which has the advantage of including the terms and phrases in D which do not occur in Jeremiah. It is needless to enumerate the many parallel passages once more, since the fact to which they bear testimony is unchallenged. The only question would be whether it justifies the conclusion that Jeremiah and D are identical. For us, however, the question does not exist in this form, for we have recognised (§ 7, n. 12 sqq.) more than one writer in *Deuteronomy*; and which of these should we identify with Jeremiah? D² and D³ have at least as good a claim as D¹, if we are to take what appears to me the wholly mistaken course of resting the decision on the question of formal agreement and taking nothing else into consideration, when in point of fact there is a m a t e r i a l difference amounting to nothing less than a divergence in the very conception of religion. Cf. Duhm, *Die Theologie der Propheten*, p. 194 sqq., and especially p. 240 sqq. There is not a trace in Jeremiah of D's zeal for the one only sanctuary, of his interest in the cultus,

[179]

or his devotion to the Levitical priesthood. Ch. xxxiii. 17–26 is in all probability not from Jeremiah's hand; and in vii. (cf. xxvi.) he takes up a definite position against the deuteronomic conception.

[15] The points of contact referred to appear in

Jer. ii. 3, where it is assumed that any (unqualified) person who eats קדש is rendered guilty (אשם), cf. *Lev.* xxii. 10, 16. But there is nothing to show [180] that this assumption rests on *Lev.* xxii. It was doubtless an article of the popular creed, whence Jeremiah may have taken it direct.

Jer. iii. 16 (xxiii. 3), where פרה and רבה (in the opposite order in iii.) stand close together as in *Gen.* i. 22, 28; viii. 17, and in eight other places in P. But what is to prevent our adopting the reverse supposition that P borrowed this formula from Jeremiah, or that it was current in the priestly circles in which both alike moved?

Jer. iv. 23, תהו ובהו, as in *Gen.* i. 2. But see n. 9 on *Isaiah* xxxiv. 11.

Jer. vi. 28; ix. 3, הלך רכיל, as in *Lev.* xix. 16. But there is not the least proof that the prophet is referring precisely to this law.

In *Jer.* xi. 4; xxiv. 7; xxx. 22; xxxi. 1, 33; xxxii. 38, the phrase occurs 'ye shall be to me for a people, and I will be to you for Elohim,' which is derived by C o l e n s o (*Pentateuch*, vii., App., p. 133). from *Gen.* xvii. 7, 8. But in this passage (as in *Ex.* xxix. 45) it only appears in half, whereas in *Deut.* xxix. 12 [13] it occurs in full. And in no case can anything be urged for the priority of *Gen.* xvii. rather than Jeremiah.

Jer. xxx. 21, והקרבתיו ונגש אלי, cf. *Ex.* xix. 22; *Lev.* x.. 21; *Num.* xvi. 5, 9. But נגש אל was, beyond doubt, the *vox propria* for the priest's drawing near to Yahwè, and as such was at any rate known to Jeremiah; he agrees with *Num.* xvi. in the use of הקריב, but surely he need not have borrowed the word from this or that specific document.

Jer. xxxii. 27, cf. *Num.* xvi. 22; xxvii. 16; but it is precisely the characteristic רוחת before כל־בשר that is not found in Jeremiah.

[16] Supposed parallels have been discovered in the following passages: *Isaiah* xxx. 9 and *Deut.* xxxii. 6, 10; but the resemblance is extremely slight; *Isaiah* xxx. 17 and *Deut.* xxxii. 30 (*Lev.* xxvi. 8) which do really resemble each other, but so far from there being anything to indicate that Isaiah is the imitator, the elaboration of the idea in *Deuteronomy* and *Leviticus* suggests the contrary; *Micah* v. 6 [7] and *Deut.* xxxii. 2, but if there is anything more than an accidental coincidence of imagery—with wide divergency of application —where does the priority lie? *Micah* vi. 8 and *Deut.* x. 12, 13, but the contents of Yahwè's demand differ completely in *Micah* and in *Deuteronomy* (cf. R o o r d a, *Comm. in vat. Mich.*, p. 120); *Micah* vi. 14, 15 and *Deut.* xxviii. 39, 40, but in the latter passage the vine and olive bear no fruit, in the former the fruits are gathered in and prepared, but not enjoyed; *Amos* iv. 9, 10 and *Deut.* xxviii. 22, 38 sqq. (*Lev.* xxvi. 25), but the prophet had no need to learn the disasters which visited Canaan from D; *Amos* ix. 8 and *Deut.* vi. 15 agree in the use of the words השמיד מעל־פני האדמה, but D may just as well have taken them from Amos as *vice versa*; *Hos.* ii. 10 [8] and *Deut.* vii. 13; xi. 14, in both which passages 'corn, wine, and oil' are mentioned (!); *Hos.*

iii. 1 and *Deut.* vii. 8; xxxi. 18, with a number of other parallels of equal
weight (Haevernick's *Einl.* i. 2, p. 545 sqq. [418 sqq.]), which collectively
indicate a certain relationship between D and Hosea, but throw no light on
the question of priority until combined with other considerations—which
decide it in Hosea's favour. Cf. § 12, n. 5.

[17] Marti (op. cit., p. 325 sqq.) gives the following as parallels : *Amos* vii.
4 (*Isaiah* li. 10; *Psalm* xxxvi. 7 [6]), תהום רבה, from *Gen.* vii. 11; but why
should not P², on the contrary, have borrowed the words from the impressive [181]
and poetical style of language with which he was familiar in his predecessors?
Gen. xix. 29, underlying *Amos* iv. 11 (*Deut.* xxix. 22 [23]; *Isaiah* xiii. 19),
but see above, n. 9, on the last named passage. *Gen.* xxxv. 9–15, known to
Hosea, see xii. 5ᵇ [4ᵇ], who makes the theophany at Bethel follow Jacob's
wrestling (*Gen.* xxxii. 25–33). Now it is true that the book of *Genesis*, as we
possess it, contains an account of this theophany taken from P² (*Gen.* xxxv.
9–15), but E also makes Jacob go to Bethel and build an altar there (*v.* 1–4,
6–8); and *Gen.* xxviii. 10–12, 17–22 makes it extremely probable that this
document, in its unmutilated form, recorded a theophany there likewise, a
trace of which has perhaps been preserved in *Gen.* xxxv. 14 by R, who took
v. 9 sqq. from P². But see § 13, n. 4.—No one is likely to follow Marti
(p. 338 sq.) in tracing the influence of *Ex.* vi. 7, and the parallel passages, in
Hos. i. 9; ii. 25 [23]. The only proof alleged that Isaiah (x. 24, 26; xi. 15,
cf. lxiii. 12) makes use of P² (*Ex.* xiv.) is the word בקע—which, however, only
occurs in Deutero-Isaiah, and need not have been borrowed from P² even by
him. Is it not more probable that the representation of the passage of the
Red Sea in P² is based on a literal acceptation of the poetical בקע? Nor can
one see why *Ex.* xl. 34–38 (cf. *Num.* ix. 15, 16) must be the original of *Isaiah*
vi. 4 (*Ezek.* x. 3, 4) and iv. 5, for E likewise knows of the column of cloud
and fire (*Ex.* xiii. 21 sq.), and, what is more, knows of it specifically as resting
on the tent in which Yahwè revealed himself to Moses (*Ex.* xxxiii. 9, 10;
Num. xii. 5; *Deut.* xxxi. 15) : why may not Isaiah have followed this document? For *Isaiah* vi. 4 we surely need not seek any source at all. Nor
should *Lev.* vi. 6 [13] be cited in explanation of *Isaiah* vi. 6, for the prophet
says nothing of an ever-burning fire, and even had he done so he might have
known of it in other ways.—It does not follow that Amos had read the law of
the Nazirite's vow in *Num.* vi. 1–21 because he speaks of the Nazirites and
their abstinence in ii. 11 sq. To make *Num.* xvi. 8, 9 the original of *Isaiah*
vii. 13, and to see a reference to *Num.* xxviii. 11 in *Hos.* ii. 13 [11] is strange
indeed !

[18] Compare *Isaiah* i. 9; iii. 9 with *Gen.* xix., especially with *v.* 4. 5; *Isaiah*
xi. 11, 15, 16; xii. 2; xxx. 29 with *Ex.* xiv. and with xv., as a whole, but
especially *v.* 2ª; *Mic.* vi. 5 with *Num.* xxii.-xxiv.; *Mic.* vi. 4; vii. 15, 20
with JE on the patriarchs and the exodus (though no proper citations occur);
Hos. xii. 4, 5 with *Gen.* xxv. 26ª; xxxii. 25–33 [24–32] (on *Hos.* xii. 5ᵇ [4ᵇ]
see n. 17); *Hos.* xii. 13 [12] with *Gen.* xxvii. 43; xxix. 18 sqq.; *Hos.* ix. 10
with *Num.* xxv. 1 sqq.; *Amos* ii. 9, 10; v. 25 (forty years' wandering) with
the representation in JE, which lies, for instance, at the basis of *Deut.* ii. 7 ;

viii. 2. On the other hand, the agreement between *Amos* ii. 9, 10 and *Num.* xiii. 27–33 is unimportant.

B. The Historical Books.

The book of *Esther* may be passed over in silence here. The Chronicles, beyond all doubt, presuppose the Hexateuch in its present form. The genealogical section with [182] which they open (1 *Chron.* i. 1–ix. 34) makes use of its different elements and borrows all that fits into the author's plan[19]. In the second section (1 *Chron.* ix. 35– 2 *Chron.* xxxvi.) the references to the tora are very numerous, and it serves the author throughout as the standard by which to judge the past. It is specifically the ordinances of P, including the points in which they differ from D, that stand before his eyes and which he conceives as having been in force in earlier as well as later times[20]. The redactor of the books of Ezra and Nehemiah can hardly be any other than the Chronicler himself; or, at any rate, he adopts exactly his attitude towards the tora[21]. The passages he incorporates from the memoirs of Ezra and Nehemiah attach themselves more closely to D, though the relationship with P may be detected even in them[22]. *Neh.* viii.–x. will be best treated in another connection (§ 12, n. 12, 13). The only book of the fifth century B.C. that remains is Ruth, in which the line of Judah's descendants conforms with P (compare *Ruth* iv. 18–22 with *Ex.* vi. 23; *Num.* ii. 3; vii. 12; xxvi. 19–21), but which is by no means dependent on the tora in other respects,—as to the levirate marriage, for instance iv. 1–12. The character of the book, however, forbids us to argue hence that its author was unacquainted with the tora[23].

In the books of Kings repeated reference is made to 'the tora of Moses' or 'of Yahwè' (1 *Kings* ii. 3; 2 *Kings* x. 31; xiv. 6 [cf. *Deut.* xxiv. 16]; xvii. 13, 34, 37; xxi. 8; xxiii. 25). There can be no doubt that what is meant is the tora which

Deuteronomy represents Moses as delivering in the Trans-jordanic region and subsequently committing to writing: the references themselves prove it, and moreover the redactor of *Kings* occupies the position and uses the language of D[1] and his followers [24]. There is no evidence of acquaintance with P, unless it be in 1 *Kings* xviii. 31[b] (cf. *Gen.* xxxv. 10) and viii. 1–11, the latter of which passages has evidently passed through a later recension [25].—In the books of Samuel the Mosaic tora is not mentioned and is but very seldom made use of; when it is we see that the writer is dependent on D [26]. —The redactor of Judges also attaches himself to D and [183] follows his linguistic usage [27]. The connection with Joshua is effected (ii. 6–10) by the repetition of a few verses belonging to the prophetic portion of that book which D had worked over (xxiv. 28–31) and in which we likewise find certain details which reappear in the introduction to Judges (i. 1–ii. 5) [28]. Of the two appendices (xvii. sq. and xix.–xxi.) the first shows a remarkable independence with respect to the Hexateuch, whereas the other betrays some points of contact alike with D and P [29].

[19] It is generally allowed that 1 *Chron.* i. 1–ii. 2 is borrowed from *Gen.* v.; x.; xi. 10–32; xxv. 1–4: 12–16; xxxv. 23 26; xxxvi. In the sequel the writer avails himself, for instance, of the list of priestly and Levitical cities in *Josh.* xxi. 10–39 (see 1 *Chron.* vi. 39–66) of *Gen.* xlvi., *Ex.* vi., and *Num.* xxvi. (see *Chronicles* passim). Cf. Bertheau's commentary.

[20] See 1 *Chron.* xvi. 40; 2 *Chron.* xii. 1; xiv. 3; xvii. 7 sqq.; xxiii. 18; xxv. 4 (= 2 *Kings* xiv. 6, cf. *Deut.* xxiv. 16); xxx. 16; xxxi. 3, 4, 21; xxxiii. 8; xxxiv. 19; xxxv. 26. Most of these references leave no room to doubt that the ritual law, amongst and indeed above the rest, stood before the writer's mind. His accounts of the observance of its special precepts will be enumerated and discussed in § 11. In proof of his adhesion to P, even where the latter departs from D, I need only mention the following examples: the constant distinction between priests and Levites; the account of Solomon's eight day celebration of the feast of tabernacles (2 *Chron.* vii. 8, 9), in accordance with Lev. xxiii. 36, 39, and in conflict with 1 *Kings* viii. 65 sq.; and the statement that tithes, including tithes of cattle, were brought to the Levites (2 *Chron.* xxxi. 5, 6). It is generally acknowledged that the writer also adopted the language of P, and we need therefore cite no texts to prove it.

[21] Cf. *Ezra* iii. 2 ; vi. 18 ; vii. 6 ; *Neh.* xiii. 1. Here too we note adherence to the precepts which distinguish P from the other legislators, e. g. the distinction between the priests and the Levites (*passim*), and the destination of tithes of the fruits of field and tree (*Neh.* xii. 44-47 ; xiii. 5).

[22] See especially *Ezr.* ix. 10-12, to be compared with *Deut.* vii. 1-3 ; xxiii. 7, but also with *Lev.* xviii. 24, 25 ; all these passages are cited in a free form by Ezra, and—which is highly remarkable—cited as utterances of Yahwè, 'by the hand of his servants the prophets.' Further, *Neh.* i. 8, 9, a free citation, again, of *Deut.* xxx. 1-5. That we are justified, however, in assuming acquaintance with P also on the part of Ezra and Nehemiah, appears from *Neh.* xiii. 10-13 (tithes of the fruits of field and tree for the Levites); 14-22 (strict enforcement of the Sabbath rest).

[23] Cf. Bleek-Wellhausen, *Einl.*, p. 204 sq., where the post-exilian origin of the genealogy and its dependence upon P are alike made clear. On iv. [184] 1-12 see § 11, n. 33, and, on the attitude of the book of *Ruth* towards the measures taken by Ezra and Nehemiah against the foreign wives see my *Godsdienst*, ii. 148 sqq. [*Rel. Isr.*, ii. 242 sqq.]. This polemical purpose, and the interest in ancient customs to which iv. 1-12 bears witness, alike forbid us to receive the writer's evidence in the cause we are now trying as altogether unbiassed. In no other writer would the silence with which *Deut.* xxv. 5-10 is passed over possess so little significance.

[24] The deuteronomic tora is the standard by which the redactor of *Kings* judges Solomon and his successors at Jerusalem (1 *Kings* iii. 2, 3 ; xiv. 23 ; xv. 14 ; 2 *Kings* xii. 3 ; xiv. 4 ; xv. 4, 35 ; xvi. 4) together with the kings of Israel (1 *Kings* xv. 26, 34 ; xvi. 26, 31 ; xxii. 53 [52] ; 2 *Kings* iii. 3 ; xiii. 2, 11 ; xiv. 24 ; xv. 9, 18, 24, 28) ; and the praise he awards to Hezekiah (2 *Kings* xviii. 3 sqq.), the blame he lays on Manasseh for returning to the worship on ' the high-places ' (xxi. 3) and his delight in Josiah's reformation (xxii. sq.) all rest on the same tora. So far there is really no difference of opinion. It is only when we add to the assertion that the writer knows and constantly presupposes D, the further statement that he knows nothing of the laws and narratives of P (n. 25) that we meet with contradiction. It is needless therefore to expatiate further on the adhesion of the redactor of *Kings* to D, or to show expressly that the pericopes which he wrote, or at any rate recast (2 *Kings* xvii. 7-23, 34-41; further, 1 *Kings* ii. 3,4 ; iii. 5-15[a]; viii. 12-61; ix. 1-9; xi. 1 sqq., etc.) agree with D[1], and still more with his successors, in the choice of language and in style. The agreement is so great that Colenso, in the wake of others, has thought he could recognise D himself, whom he believes to be the prophet Jeremiah, in the redactor of *Kings*—(*Pentateuch*, vii. p. 4 sqq., App., p. 85 sqq.)—an opinion which seems to me wholly inadmissible, but which I mention here because it could never have been maintained in former times, and could not have come up again now, had not the connection with D been extremely close.

[25] On 1 *Kings* viii. 1-11 cf. Bleek-Wellhausen, *Einl.*, p. 233-235, and Colenso, *Pentateuch*, vii. p. 27 sqq., 158 sq. The main proof is that the writer of *Kings* cannot have written, ' the priests and the Levites ' (*v.* 4). In the

first place he mentions the priests alone in *v.* 3, 6, 10, 11, and in the next place he regards all the Levites as qualified for the priesthood (1 *Kings* xii. 31), and therefore could not distinguish between them and the priests. This led me formerly to suppose (*Godsdienst*, ii. 208 [*Rel. Isr.*, ii. 301]) that 'the Levitical priests' originally stood in *v.* 4, as in the parallel passage 2 *Chron.* v. 5; and further that the 'ôhel mo'éd' of *v.* 4 was the tent pitched upon Zion by David (2 *Sam.* vi. 17; 1 *Kings* i. 39; ii. 28–30), and not the Mosaic tabernacle (*Ex.* xxv. sqq.); for the author never mentions the latter, and therefore does not place it, as the Chronicler does (cf. § 11), at Gibeon (see 1 *Kings* iii. 4). But I must now grant to Wellhausen and Colenso that 'ôhel mo'éd' never signifies the tent of David, and does not occur at all in the older historical books (1 *Sam.* ii. 22ᵇ is an interpolation, cf. the LXX.); that 'all the holy vessels which were in the ôhel' recalls the Mosaic tabernacle; that *v.* 4 is wholly superfluous after *v.* 3 and before *v.* 6, and departs from the linguistic usage of *v.* 3, 6 in employing the phrase יהוה ארון, for all which reasons it must be denied to the author of *Kings* and assigned to a later interpolator, who was acquainted with P, and who therefore very naturally missed the 'ohel mo'éd' and its holy vessels at this point. In that case *v.* 5 (כל-עדת ישראל) [185] and נועד, as in P) is a later insertion also. This supposition is the less hazardous inasmuch as we are forced to recognise interpolations in *v.* 1, 2 ('this is the seventh month') and *v.* 6 ('to the holy of holies'), which are to some extent subsequent even to the text translated by the LXX.—And since it thus appears that the only passage which obviously depends upon P has passed through a later recension, it is highly probable that 1 *Kings* xviii. 31ᵇ, a literal citation of *Gen.* xxxv. 10, must be explained in the same way: in its contents it is parallel to 2 *Kings* xvii. 34ᵇ (from the hand of the redactor), and we may well suppose that the reference to the change of the name of Jacob into Israel was inserted here by an ancient reader. It is worth noticing that most of the MSS. of the LXX., including the best, read Ἰσραήλ for בני-יעקב, which may be a trace of another attempt to bring the verse into agreement with the usual and more acceptable phraseology, before the second half had been added.

²⁶ The agreement with D comes out especially in 1 *Sam.* vii.; viii.; x. 17 27; xii.; 2 *Sam.* vii., on which chapters cf. Thenius, and also Bleek-Wellhausen, *Einl.*, p. 209 sqq.; Colenso, *Pentateuch*, vii. p. 56 sqq., 107 sqq. It is, therefore, restricted to a few chapters, which are, moreover, clearly distinguished from the body of the work in other respects as well. The—altogether negative—relation to P will come out of itself in § 11.

²⁷ The general scheme or programme of the book of *Judges*, ii. 10–iii. 6, and the stereotyped opening of the accounts of the several judges so nearly related to it (iii. 7; iv. 1; vi. 1, 7–10, etc.), bear a close resemblance to the retrospective survey in 2 *Kings* xvii. 7–23, 34–41, and therefore to D also. Cf. Bleek-Wellhausen, *Einl.*, p. 183 sqq.; Colenso, *Pentateuch*, vii. p. 56 sqq., 85 sqq. In the stories which the redactor fits into his framework we no longer trace this resemblance.

²⁸ On the origin of *Josh.* xxiv. 28–31 see above, § 7, n. 27; 8, n. 16. P's

hand cannot be traced in these verses, so the supposition that the redactor of *Judges* adopted them is not at all inconsistent with his adhesion to D (n. 27). There are further parallels between *Judges* i. 10-15 and *Josh.* xv. 13-19; *Judges* i. 21 and *Josh.* xv. 63; *Judges* i. 27, 28 and *Josh.* xvii. 12, 13; *Judges* i. 29 and *Josh.* xvi. 10.   On the source of these passages in *Josh.* xiv. sqq. cf § 6, n. 49.   Here again the redactor of *Judges* shows complete literary independence of P.

[29] On *Judges* xvii. sq. cf. § 11; on xix.–xxi. Bleek-Wellhausen, *Einl.,* p. 199–203; Graetz, *Geschichte d. Juden,* i. 351 sqq.   The source and character of this narrative are not yet fully made out; but it certainly has not so high an antiquity as Graetz gives it.   *Jud.* xx. 13 (נבערה רעה מישׂראל) recalls *Deut.* xiii. 6 [5]; xvii. 12 : xxii. 22; *Jud.* xxi. 11, 12 (זכר) and (משׁכב ז') recalls *Num.* xxxi. 17, 18, 35; זמה (*Jud.* xx. 6) frequently occurs in P and in Ezekiel, but also in *Hosea* vi. 9; *Jud.* xx. 1 (ותקהל הערה) is parallel with *Lev.* viii. 4; *Num.* xvii. 7 [xvi. 42].   *Jud.* xx. 27[b], 28[a] (cf. *Num.* xxv. 6 sqq.; *Josh.* xxii. 9–34) would also have to be considered were it not that these words break the context and are evidently a later insertion.

[186]

C. The Poetical Books.

The antiquity of the poetical books, and of the several poems embraced in one of them, namely the book of Psalms, is the subject of so much controversy that their evidence concerning the Hexateuch and its constituent parts cannot throw much weight into the scale.   The assertion that the Psalms of David, and the Proverbs of Solomon,—to which some have added the book of Job—demonstrate the existence of the tora before the division of the kingdom, is in any case incapable of proof[30].   Those poetical compositions as to the date of which comparative agreement has been reached, confirm in general the inferences drawn from the prophetic and historical writings contemporary with them.   Ecclesiastes and the Song of Solomon may be passed over.   We notice the repeated mention of the tora and a varied use of the sacred history it contains in those Psalms which are put down by common consent as the latest[31].   The epic of Job, from the nature of the case, yields scanty results.   Its author knew ' the ten words,' and probably also *Deuteronomy*[32].   Nor are the parallels in Proverbs numerous; i.–ix. shows a certain relationship to *Deuteronomy*; and references to *Gen.* ii., iii. are found both within this section (iii. 18) and beyond it (xi. 30; xiii. 12; xv. 4)[33]. Finally, the Lamentations resemble Jeremiah, to whom tradition assigns them, in their dependence upon *Deuteronomy*. We seek in vain for any traces of P in them[34].

[30] This assertion was formerly made by Delitzsch, *Die Genesis*, 2nd ed., p. 13 sq. No one can seriously maintain, (1) that the literature of the century of David and Solomon is proved to be authentic, and (2) that its evidence covers the whole tora. And yet both points must be established before that century can be fixed as the *terminus ad quem* of the composition of the tora.

[31] The later poems here referred to include the following, amongst others: *Ps.* i., xix. 8–15 [7–14], lxxvii., lxxviii., xcv., cv., cvi., cxiv., cxix., cxxxv., cxxxvi., etc.

[32] Compare especially *Job* xxxi. 9–12, 26–28 (עָוֹן פְּלִילִים) with *Ex.* xx. 2, 14; perhaps there is also a reference to *Deut.* xxii. 22; xvii. 2–7. In weighing the evidence of the Jobeid we must not forget that the hero lives outside [187] Canaan and in the patriarchal age. The poet would have violated the form he had selected had he cited or obviously followed the tora.

[33] Compare *Prov.* vii. 3 with *Deut.* vi. 8; *Prov.* iii. 12 with *Deut.* viii. 5, etc. But it is more important to note the hortatory tone of *Prov.* i. sqq., which recalls both Jeremiah and D; and also the affinity of *Prov.* iii. 9, 10 with the tendency of *Deuteronomy*, and again the affinity of *Deut.* iv. 5–8 with the tendency of the book of Proverbs as a whole, but more especially of i.–ix.

[34] Compare *Lamentations* i. 10 with *Deut.* xxiii. 3 (a formal reference); *Lam.* i. 9 with *Deut.* xxxii. 29; *Lam.* i. 20 with *Deut.* xxxii. 25; *Lam.* ii. 20; iv. 10 with *Deut.* xxviii. 53–57; *Lam.* iii. 64; iv. 2 with *Deut.* ii. 7; iv. 28, etc.

In drawing our conclusions from the facts we have now collected we must not forget that chance may have had its share in them. The Israelite writers were not aware that they would sometime be forced to give direct or indirect evidence of their attitude towards the Hexateuch; and their silence therefore is no absolute proof that they were unacquainted with the whole or with any special part of the collection, and still less that it did not exist. But when two or more contemporaries represent one and the same attitude, positive or negative, then the hypothesis of mere accident becomes more and more improbable and at last wholly in-

admissible. We are therefore fully justified in concluding
from the survey made in this §, (1) that *Deuteronomy* was
not known before the last quarter of the seventh century
B.C., and (2) that the priestly laws and narratives were still in
the nascent stage in Ezekiel's time (592–570 B.C.) and did not
exist, in the form in which we now have them in the Hexateuch, before the time of Ezra and Nehemiah [35].

[35] Note, in illustration of (1), that not one of the prophets of the eighth
century is dependent on D (n. 16). The impossibility of ascribing the fact
to chance is emphasized by the persistency with which D asserts itself, shining
more or less distinctly through all the subsequent literature, as soon as once
its influence appears. As to (2), on the other hand, note that Ezekiel at first
stands alone in his affinities of style and spirit with P. Deutero-Isaiah and his
contemporaries, Haggai and Zechariah (i.–viii.), have no knowledge of him. It
is not till about 450 B.C. that the priestly document comes definitively forward,
never to be lost sight of again. This in itself leads up to the view of the
genesis of P set forth in the text. Moreover Ezekiel, for all his affinity with P,
does not follow him, as we shall presently see in § 11. This confirms the
[188] idea that the later writers, up to the middle of the fifth century, do not
ignore P by accident, as it were, but that his historico-legislative work did
not really exist in their day. See further, § 11 sqq.

§ 11. *The Hexateuch and the political and religious history of Israel.*

Our previous investigations have shown us in the first
place that the book of *Joshua* is most intimately connected
with the Pentateuch and presupposes its laws and narratives
(§ 1, cf. § 7–9); and in the second place that the representation of the Mosaic times and of the settlement in
Canaan which the Hexateuch gives us is, as a whole, contradicted by the veritable history (§ 4, n. 16–21). The former
result forbids us to admit the book of *Joshua* as an independent witness to the Mosaic origin or the high antiquity of
the Pentateuch ; but the latter by no means absolves us from
the duty of going on to compare the Hexateuch with the
history alike of Israel and of the Israelitish religion,—and

this with especial reference to the laws and to the accounts of their observance in Joshua's time. This comparison may not only define the purely negative results already obtained more closely, but may throw light on the chronological succession of the several elements of the Hexateuch.

The rules we must follow rise out of the very nature of the case, and therefore need no express defence. They are the following :

(1) None but firmly established historical facts or doings can be allowed as evidence of the existence of any legal ordinance they may imply. The historian's own conviction on the subject can be taken as direct evidence only concerning the time at which he himself lived, and must be confirmed independently before it can be trusted as regards the period of which he wrote and from which he may have been separated by many centuries. The possible influence of his very conviction upon his account of the past must never be lost sight of ; and in proportion as we discover it to have been greater or smaller, our confidence in his records will fall or rise.

(2) Proceedings at variance with the tora must not be [189] accepted without more ado as proofs that it did not exist or was not held binding. This is only justified when the desire of those concerned to comply with Yahwè's demands is above all doubt, and when the repeated occurrence of the act in question, or some other such circumstance, precludes the idea of accident.

(3) On the other hand, actions that harmonise with the precepts of the tora cannot be accepted as proving its existence, unless it is clear that they were done not in obedience to the custom out of which the tora itself was developed, but in view of the positive legal prescription [1].

---

[1] On this subject, in its whole scope or in some of its branches, the following works, amongst others, may be consulted with advantage : De Wette, *Über den Zustand des Religionscultus der Israeliten in Hinsicht auf die Gesetzgebung*

des Pentateuchs (Beiträge zur Einl. in das A. T., i. 223–265); Gramberg, *Krit. Gesch. der Religionsideen des A. T.* (2 Bände, 1829–30), *passim;* Hengstenberg, *Der Pent. u. die Zeit der Richter (Beitr. zur Einl. in das A. T.,* iii. 1–148 [ii. 1–121]); Haevernick, *Einl.,* i. 2. p. 493–540 [367–437]; Wellhausen, *Prolegomena,* 17–174 [17–167] *(Ordinances of Worship);* Colenso, *Pentateuch,* vii. *passim.*

From the accounts of Ezra and Nehemiah *(Ezr.* vii.–*Neh.* xiii.) we learn that about the middle of the fifth century B.C. the Mosaic tora was in existence, and that its precepts, more specifically, concerning the cultus, the priests, the Levites, their revenues, and so forth, were then put into practice through the influence of these two men, and, when necessary, maintained against the opposition they encountered in certain quarters. To this rule, however, which is supported by a relatively large number of texts[2], there are some few exceptions. From *Ezra* ix. 4 we must conclude that when Ezra arrived at Jerusalem a food offering was made every evening in the temple, but not a burnt offering *(Ex.* xxix. 38–42 ; *Num.* xxviii. 3–8) ; from *Neh.* x. 33 [32], that the ordinance of a yearly contribution of half a shekkel for the sanctuary *(Ex.* xxx. 11–16) was not found in Ezra's and Nehemiah's tora ; and, finally, from *Neh.* x. 38–40 [37–39] ; xii. 44–47 ; xiii. 5, 12 that this tora claimed for the Levites tithes of the fruits of field and tree, but not of cattle (cf. *Lev.* xxvii. 32, [190] 33)[3]. How these phenomena are to be explained cannot appear till later.

The first half of the book of *Ezra* (i.–vi.) has been omitted from this survey, partly because it deals with an earlier period, the return from the Babylonian captivity and the first experiences of the community in Judæa, but chiefly because its accounts of the Mosaic tora and the observance of its precepts are essentially homogeneous with the passages in the books of Chronicles which deal with the pre-exilian period. According to these accounts, then, the tora, and particularly its ritual portions, had been established from the earliest times,

and specially since the reign of David, as the universally
recognised standard, which all well-disposed persons,
whether kings or people, observed and maintained. Thus,
in obedience to the precepts of the tora (*Ex.* xxv. sqq.), the
ôhel mo'éd remained the only legitimate place of offering till
Solomon's temple was completed (1 *Chron.* vi. 17, 34 [32, 49];
xvi. 39, 40; xxi. 28–30; 2 *Chron.* i. 3, 5 sq.; v. 5); the
priesthood was hereditary in Aaron's family (1 *Chron.* vi. 34
[49] and *passim*); the high-priestly office was filled by the
descendants of Eleazar ben Aaron (1 *Chron.* v. 30–41 [vi. 4–
15], etc.); the exclusive qualification of the priests to offer
sacrifice was jealously guarded (2 *Chron.* xxvi. 16–21); the
Levites were always distinguished from the priests and confined to those lower offices about the sanctuary with which
they were specially entrusted (1 *Chron.* xii. 26 sq.; xiii. 2; xv.
4 sqq.; xxiii. 3 sqq., 28–32 and *passim*), while all non-Levites
were excluded from the sanctuary (2 *Chron.* xxiii. 6 sqq.).
The priests and Levites, again in accordance with the requirements of the tora, were in possession from the first of
their forty-eight cities with the surrounding pastures (1 *Chron.*
vi. 39–66 [54–81]; xiii. 2; 2 *Chron.* xi. 14; xxxi. 19), and
the people brought to the sanctuary and its servants all
that was enjoined in the tora, including tithes of oxen and
sheep (2 *Chron.* xxxi. 4–6) and the yearly temple-tax of half a
shekkel (2 *Chron.* xxiv. 6, 9). In the temple the worship was
carried on, from the time of Solomon downwards, in perfect
accordance with the law (2 *Chron.* ii. 4; viii. 12, 13; xiii. 11;
xxxi. 3; *Ezr.* iii. 3–5; vi. 16 sqq.); the morning and evening [191]
burnt offerings were performed in the tabernacle at Gibeon
even before the temple was built, and were continued thenceforth (1 *Chron.* xvi. 40; *Ezr.* iii. 3); and as early as in the
days of Solomon the eight days of the feast of tabernacles were observed (2 *Chron.* vii. 9). The temple music was
organized by David (1 *Chron.* xxv., etc.), but the sacred

trumpets of the priests were still kept in use (1 *Chron.* xv. 24;
xvi. 6 ; 2 *Chron.* xiii. 12), in accordance with the Mosaic
precept (*Num.* x. 1–10). Real departures from this rule
never appear in the Chronicles and *Ezr.* i.–vi. : what
might at first appear to be in conflict with the tora, or at
least with the ordinances of P, is really in harmony with them
or is a further development of them. There was nothing to
prevent the Chronicler from now and again using the (deuteronomic) designation of ' Levitical priests ' (2 *Chron.* v. 5 ; xxiii.
18 ; xxx. 27), inasmuch as he too regarded the Aaronites—and
it is to them alone that he refers—as belonging to the tribe of
Levi (1 *Chron.* v. 27 sqq. [vi. 1 sqq.] ; vi. 1 sqq. [16 sqq.], etc.).
David's ordinance as to the age at which the Levites were to
enter upon their service (1 *Chron.* xxiii. 24, 27) is but a continued movement in the direction of the prescriptions of the
priestly tora upon which it rests (*Num.* iv. 3, 23, 30, 35, 39,
43, 47 ; viii. 24). The other departures from the tora—if
not explained by the author himself (1 *Chron.* xxi. 28–30),—
may be ascribed to the effect of tradition in heightening the
written law and rendering it more precise (1 *Chron.* xxiii. 31 ;
2 *Chron.* xxix. 34, cf. xxx. 3 ; xxx. 2 sqq. ; xxxv. 6, 11) [4].

[2] The redactor of *Ezra* and *Nehemiah* has dealt with his authorities,
amongst which were the memoirs of Ezra and Nehemiah themselves, in
varying style. Sometimes he has taken them up unaltered, and sometimes he
has excerpted and recast them more or less freely. The deviations from the tora
to be noticed in n. 3 occur in the chapters which he has taken direct from his
sources ; but side by side with them we may trace even here dependence
upon the tora ; and it appears undiluted wherever the redactor himself is
speaking. Priests and Levites are distinguished throughout, in both books ;
starting with the list of the returning exiles, *Ezr.* ii. (*Neh.* vii.), and on
through *Ezr.* vii. 13, 24 ; viii. 15 sqq., 29, 30, 33 ; ix. 1 ; x. 5, 18–23 ; *Neh.*
iii. 17 ; viii. 7 ; x. 1, 9, 10, 29 [ix. 38 ; x. 8, 9, 28] ; xi., *passim* ; xii. 1 sqq.,
8 sqq., 22 sqq., 27, 30, 44 ; xiii. 13, 29, 30. The priestly trumpets (*Num.* x.
1–10) are mentioned in *Neh.* xii. 35. The eighth day of the feast of tabernacles
[192] (*Lev.* xxiii. 36, 39) appears in *Neh.* viii. 18. As to the things to be tithed a
deviation from P may be observed (n. 3), but in the main point, viz. the payment of tithes to the Levites, and by the Levites themselves to the priests,
Neh. x. 38–40 [37–39] ; xii. 47 ; xiii. 5, 12 agree with *Num.* xviii. 21–28 ; and

so too *Neh.* x. 37 [36] (firstlings) with *Num.* xviii. 15–18; and *Neh.* x. 34 [33] with P's regulation of the cultus in general.

³ *Neh.* x. 34 [33] is perhaps in harmony with *Ezr.* ix. 4, inasmuch as it mentions the perpetual mincha by the side of the perpetual burnt offering. But see more on the deductions warranted by these and the other texts, and on *Neh.* viii. 1 sqq. compared with *Lev.* xvi. and the parallel passages, in § 15, n. 30, 32.

⁴ Elaborate comment on the numerous parallels with P would be super-fluous, for there can be no difference of opinion as to their significance. And yet we cannot pass them by unnoticed, partly because, as we shall presently see, the Chronicler deviates from the older narrative of *Kings*, and sometimes diametrically contradicts it (n. 5 sqq.), when he thus runs parallel with P; and partly because these parallels are of no small weight in determining whether the Chronicler's deviations from P are of the same character as those we observe in the books of *Judges–Kings* and the prophets. The remarks in the text upon this subject are directed against Ives Curtiss (*The Levitical Priests,* p. 110–120, and *De Aaron. sacerdotii atque thorœ eloh. orig.,* p. 32–40), supported by Marti (op. cit., p. 134 sqq.) Their reasoning is subtle, but sophistical. According to Curtiss himself (p. 114, n. 6) priests and Levites stand side by side twenty-three times in the books of *Chronicles, Ezra,* and *Nehemiah*; and the number must be raised if we include 1 *Chron.* ix. 2; *Ezr.* x. 5; *Neh.* x. 29, 35 [28, 34]; xi. 20, where the ו between לוים and כהנים is wanting, but must certainly be either supplied mentally or (*Neh.* xi. 20) actually inserted. Now what is the meaning, in the presence of this fact, of the use of the deuteronomic formula in the three texts mentioned above? The idea that the writer changes his position is absurd and perfectly gratuitous, for this ancient formula does not contradict his own belief even in semblance— though his belief, on the other hand, does contradict the ancient formula, when used, as it is in D, to express the sole qualification of birth which the priests must possess. Had the Chronicler perceived all that D asserted and denied in his הכהנים הלוים, he would unquestionably have avoided the expression; but in the third century B.C. all this had long passed into oblivion.—The remaining texts hardly need illustration. The comparison of the mutually discrepant regulations of the age of service for the Levites (*Num.* iv., viii., 1 *Chron.* xxiii.) renders it highly probable that their scanty numbers (cf. *Ezr.* ii., viii. 15 sqq.) made it necessary to admit them to their duties at an ever earlier age, and that the successive regulations on the subject were ascribed in part to Moses and in part to David. Cf. § 6, n. 33; 15, n. 15, 28.—The note on David's sacrifice at Arauna's threshing-floor, 1 *Chron.* xxi. 28–30, is rendered all the more significant by its absence from the parallel narrative (2 *Sam.* xxiv.) For the celebration of the passover on the wrong month, 2 *Chron.* xxx. 2 sqq., cf. *Num.* ix. 6–14: Hezekiah, while not applying this law, yet acts on it by analogy. The slaughter of the pascal lambs by the Levites is explained in 2 *Chron.* [193] xxx. 17 as due to the uncleanness of the fathers of families, to whose duty it really fell (*Ex.* xii. 6). But we gather from 2 *Chron.* xxxv. 6, 10; *Ezr.* vi. 20

that, apart from accidental causes, the task was usually entrusted to the Levites; nor is this actually forbidden by the Tora, though in this particular the written law is more liberal towards the laity than the later practice.—A similar judgment must be passed on 2 *Chron.* xxix. 34 (cf. xxx. 3, 15, 24). According to *Lev.* i. 1–6; iii. 1 sq., 6–8, the burnt and thank offerings are to be slaughtered and flayed by the worshipper who makes them. The Chronicler assumes that the flaying at any rate is part of the priestly task, and goes on to show that under certain circumstances it may be committed to the Levites (cf. 1 *Chron.* xxiii. 31). Obviously the established practice of his day was more stringent than the legal regulation out of which it had been gradually developed.—Curtiss also refers (*The Levit. Priests*, p. 117 sq.) to 2 *Chron.* xi. 13, 14; xxix. 5; xxxi. 2, as texts which might be cited in proof that the Chronicler does not draw a uniformly sharp distinction between priests and Levites. But since he himself admits that ' there is not the slightest doubt in regard to the interpretation of the foregoing passages, because they are abundantly explained by the connection ;' and that only when ' isolated ' could they seem to imply a deviation from the writer's representations elsewhere, we really must ask him to abstain from ' isolating ' them, and in that case they may n o t be cited for his purpose.

We get a very different impression of the attitude in which the centuries before Ezra stood to the Mosaic tora if we consult the other historical books and the prophetic literature.

According to 2 *Kings* xxii., xxiii., 'the book of the law of Moses' was the foundation and norm of the reformation in Josiah's eighteenth year (621 B.C.). The relation between this book and the whole Tora, as to which we have already gained some light (§ 10, n. 35), will be established more expressly hereafter (§ 12 and 14). No accounts can be discovered of the previous recognition of the whole Tora or of any portion of it as a binding authority : 2 *Kings* xi. 12 (2 *Chron.* xxiii. 11) furnishes no proof whatever of the existence of the Decalogue at the time of the crowning of Joash ben Ahaziah [5].

On comparing the accounts contained in the writings referred to above with the several regulations of the Tora, we arrive at the following conclusions with reference (I) to holy places; (II) to holy persons; (III) to holy seasons; (IV) to

religious acts and usages; and (V) to the political and civic
life :—

I. There is not a trace in *Judges–Kings* of the Mosaic [194]
ôhel mo'éd (*Ex.* xxv. sqq.), afterwards set up, according
to *Josh.* xviii. 1; xix. 51, at Shiloh; for 1 *Sam.* ii. 22[b] is an
interpolation, and 1 *Kings* viii. 4 does not belong to the
original account of the building of the temple by Solomon
(§ 10, n. 25). The repeated declaration of the Chronicler that
the ôhel mo'éd was pitched at Gibeon in David's time is
never confirmed by the books of *Samuel*, and is contradicted
by 1 *Kings* iii. 4 [6].

The restriction of worship to the one sanctuary was never
so much as thought of, as far as we can tell, before Hezekiah.
In the period of the Judges there was a temple of Yahwè at
Shiloh (1 *Sam.* i. 9; iii. 3, 15; cf. *Judges* xxi. 19; xix. 18);
Mica had a sanctuary in Mount Ephraim, and the tribe of
Dan afterwards erected one in the city of their own name
(*Judges* xvii. sq.); while altars were raised and sacrifices made
at Bochim (ii. 5), at Ophra (vi. 24 sqq.; viii. 27), at Çor'a
(xiii. 19), at Miçpha (xx. 1), and at Bethel (xx. 23, 26–28;
xxi. 2, 4). Samuel sacrifices at Miçpha (1 *Sam.* vii. 9), builds
an altar at Rama (*v.* 17), and celebrates a feast there (ix. 12)
on a high place (במה), as he subsequently does at Bethlehem
(xvi. 4 sqq.). And so again, in Samuel's presence (xi. 15), or
at his express command, Saul sacrifices at Gilgal (x. 8; xiii. 9).
It is recorded in praise of Saul that he built an altar to
Yahwè (xiv. 35). In his reign the clan to which David
belonged held a sacrificial feast at Bethlehem (xx. 29), and this
was obviously nothing exceptional. Absolom asks and obtains
leave from his father David to attend a similar feast at Hebron (2 *Sam.* xv. 7 sqq.). David himself makes sacrifices
wherever the ark halts between Kiryath-Ye'arîm and Jerusalem, as well as on the hill of Zion (vi.) and on the threshing-
floor of Arauna (xxiv.); and there was a place near the

capital where it was his custom to pray, and assuredly to sacrifice also (xv. 32). Solomon held a great sacrificial feast ' on
the high place' at Gibeon (1 *Kings* iii. 4) [7]. After the erection
[195] of the temple at Jerusalem the same freedom still prevailed
for centuries, not only in Ephraim (xviii. 20 sqq.), but in
Judah too, whose kings, Asa (xv. 14), Jehoshaphat (xxii. 44
[43]), Joash (2 *Kings* xii. 3), Amaziah (xiv. 4), Uzziah (xv.
4), Jotham (*v.* 34), and Ahaz (xvi. 4), are all reported to have
maintained the bamôth. The writer of *Kings* registers this as
a transgression (ibid.), but it does not appear that either the
monarchs themselves or their contemporaries regarded it as
such. At any rate, not one of the prophets of the eighth century champions the exclusive claims of Jerusalem [8]; and as this
is true of Isaiah as well as the rest, it must remain doubtful
whether Hezekiah really attempted the complete suppression
of the worship in the high places attributed to him in 2 *Kings*
xviii. 4 (cf. *v.* 22 ; *Isaiah* xxxvi. 7). In any case, his reformation was but a preliminary effort followed by a reaction under
Manasseh (2 *Kings* xxi. 3) [9]. It was Josiah who first succeeded in making the temple the one only sanctuary of
Yahwè, in accordance with the requirements of the book of
law found by Hilkiah (xxii. sq.). Whether it retained this
position under his successors is doubtful (cf. xxiv.). But in
the captivity Ezekiel, to whom the bamôth are an abomina-
tion (xx. 27 sqq.), ordains a single sanctuary for the future,
quite in the spirit of Josiah's reformation (xl. sqq.), and such
was the undisputed position, so far as we know, of Zerubbabel's temple after the return [10].

[5] In the Pentateuch הָעֵדוּת is the Decalogue (*Ex.* xxxi. 18; xxxii. 15;
xxxiv. 29; xl. 20 ; whence אֲרוֹן הָעֵ׳, אֹהֶל, מִשְׁכָּן, פָּרֹכֶת), but exclusively in P,
or (as in *Ex.* xxxii.–xxxiv.) in R. There is nothing to show that this name
was adopted in ordinary usage ; for though such an inference might follow
from 2 *Kings* xi. 12, were it certain or even probable that a collection of laws
is referred to in the passage at all, yet as a matter of fact, when we read that
Jehoiada ' brought out the royal child and laid or placed upon him (עַל נָתַן)

the crown and עֵדוּת,' it is anything but natural to understand (with Thenius, Bertheau, etc.) that a collection of laws is meant. Indeed, the 'laying' or 'placing upon' seems absolutely to exclude this interpretation. Presumably עֵדוּת is synonymous with עֲדִי, and means, in this passage, the royal insignia—perhaps a mantle or other such adornment.

[6] The absence of 1 *Sam.* ii. 22 [b] from the LXX. in itself renders its authenticity doubtful. But besides this, the clause is inconsistent with the rest of the narrative: neither ii. 11 sqq., 23 sq., nor the prophetic discourse in *v.* 27–36, refers to this crime of Eli's sons. *V.* 22 [b] is a haggadic addition by some one [196] who had read *Ex.* xxxviii. 8.—The Chronicler's accounts of the tabernacle at Gibeon have already (p. 195) been cited. The author who explains Solomon's sacrificial feast at Gibeon by the words ' for this was the great bama' (1 *Kings* iii. 4), knows nothing of an ôhel mo'éd erected there. And again, this presumably later writer, who both disapproves of and excuses Solomon's sacrificing on the high places (*v.* 2, 3), would have been surprised to hear that the one lawful sanctuary was at that very time reared at Gibeon itself!

[7] The evidence referring to the period before the completion of the temple hardly requires any comment. Samuel's offerings fall in the period during which the ark of Yahwè was in the hands of the Philistines, or was lying unnoticed at Kiryath-Ye'arim (1 *Sam.* iv. 11 ; vi.; vii. 1, 2), and therefore, according to Hengstenberg (op. cit., p. 48 sqq. [39 sqq.]) they are no proof that the tora ordaining the one only sanctuary was not in existence. But this contention overlooks the facts (1) that taking the ark to the scene of battle (see the passages already cited and 2 *Sam.* xi. 11 ; xv. 25 sqq.) is 'inconsistent alike with the letter and the spirit of the law,' both of D and of P (cf. my *Godsdienst*, i. 231 sq., 255 sqq. [*Rel. Isr.*, i. 231 sqq., 256 sqq.]); and (2) that if the ark had been indispensable for the legality of sacrifice, and if Samuel had recognised it as being so, he would either have gone to Kiryath-Ye'arim or abstained from all sacrifice : there is not the smallest connection between his supposed motive and his actual conduct.—The subterfuges by the aid of which an attempt has been made to disarm the remaining items of evidence are, if possible, still more wretched, and may, therefore, be passed over.

David's sacrifices on the way to Jerusalem (2 *Sam.* vi. 13) I have of course only included for the sake of completeness. They are recorded in 1 *Chron.* xv. 26 also, and indeed are quite unexceptionable in themselves. David's sacrifice by the ark on Zion shortly afterwards (2 *Sam.* vi. 17 ; 1 *Chron.* xvi. 1) may also be defended, though only as an exception; and in this light accordingly it is represented—by the Chronicler (1 *Chron.* xvi. 37–43). Parallel to this is the excuse made for David's sacrifice in 1 *Chron.* xxi. 28–30.

[8] The Chronicler, like his predecessor, mentions the maintenance of the bamôth under Asa (2 *Chron.* xv. 17), Jehoshaphat (xx. 33), Joram (xxi. 11), and Ahaz (xxviii. 4, 25), their abolition by Hezekiah (xxxi. 1 ; cf. xxxii. 12), and Josiah (xxxiv. 3), and their restoration by Manasseh (xxxiii. 3, 17, 19). But he also records their suppression by the pious kings Asa (xiv. 2, 4 [3, 5]) and Jehoshaphat (xvii. 6). This cannot be historical, for it is contradicted by *Kings* and in the passages cited above from the Chronicler himself. We

must therefore suppose that since Asa and Jehoshaphat both did what was
right in the eyes of Yahwè (xiv. 1 [2]; xvii. 1–4), the Chronicler ascribed to
them the deeds which he regarded as immediately involved in their piety, and
which they really would have performed if they had been acquainted
with the Tora.—The assertion that none of the prophets of the eighth century
condemns the worship of Yahwè on the high places seems to be in conflict
with *Mic.* i. 5, 'For the transgression of Jacob is all this, and for the sin of
the house of Israel. What is the transgression of Jacob? Verily Samaria.
And what the bamôth of Judah? Verily Jerusalem.' The 'bamôth,' it has
[197] been argued, would not be used as a parallel to 'transgression' (פֶּשַׁע), unless
such abominations were committed at them as to lead the prophet utterly
to condemn the worship conducted there. But in that case how could Micah
call Jerusalem 'the bamôth of Judah'? The very thing characteristic of the
bamôth was that they were found all over the kingdom, and those at Jerusalem (2 *Kings* xxiii. 8) were no more numerous, and were certainly no more
objectionable, than those elsewhere. *V.* 5ᵃ shows us that the true reading
must certainly be הַמֹּאת, 'and what the sin of Judah? Verily Jerusalem.'
And so it actually stands in the LXX. Cf. R o o r d a, *Comment. in Mich. vat.*,
p. 12 sqq.; C h e y n e, *Micah* (in *Cambridge Bible for Schools*), p. 18 sq. My
position, then, is unassailed by Micah, and Isaiah strengthens it. The latter
prophet condemns most sternly the way in which Yahwè is served in the
temples of the bamôth, and especially the use of images (ii. 8; xvii. 8;
xxxi. 7); and he regards a reformation as a crying need. But it will consist
in flinging away the gold and silver images, not in suppressing the bamôth
(ii. 18–20; xxx. 22).

⁹ W e l l h a u s e n (*Prolegomena*, i. 26, 48 sqq. [25 sq., 46 sqq.]) seems inclined
to reject the account of Hezekiah's suppression of the bamôth altogether.
If 2 *Kings* xviii. 4 stood alone I should agree with him. But in *v.* 22 (*Isaiah*
xxxvi. 7; 2 *Chron.* xxxii. 12) the account receives a confirmation at once so remarkable and so unsought, that I cannot put it altogether on one side. We may
well suppose, however, that Hezekiah did not carry through his reformation;
he contemplated the centralisation of worship, but did not bring it about.
Hence Josiah's measures, which were far more drastic than his, and were separated from them too by a space of nearly a hundred years, appeared to contemporaries altogether novel. Cf. my *Hibbert Lectures* for 1882, p. 149, n. 2 [*Volksgodsdienst en wereldgodsdienst*, p. 126, n. 1].

¹⁰ What we hear in 2 *Kings* xxiv. of Josiah's successors makes it doubtful
whether they maintained his reformation of the cultus. We need not wonder,
therefore, that Jeremiah laments over the number of altars in Judah and
Jerusalem (ii. 26–28: xi. 13)—at which sacrifice was undoubtedly offered to
Yahwè as well as to Baal. For the rest, the quite exceptional sanctity of the
temple of Jerusalem had become an article of faith even amongst the prophet's
opponents (vii. 4), and this was certainly in some degree the consequence of
Josiah's measures and of their rigid enforcement till the end of his reign. We
cannot wonder that Ezekiel, who had formerly done priestly service in the
temple himself, should take the same view, or that the returning exiles should

have kept up the tradition (*Ezra* iii. 1 sqq.).   Haggai (*passim*) and Zechariah
(e. g. iv. 8 sqq.; vi. 9 sqq.) likewise used their influence in the same direction.
Cf. also Wellhausen, *Prolegomena*, i. 28 sq. [27 sq.].

II. The regulations of the Tora conferring the exclusive
qualification for offering sacrifice and doing the other priestly
duties on the single tribe of Levi, or a single family within
that tribe, were not observed by Gideon (*Judges* vi. 26),
Manoa (xiii. 19), Mica (xvii. 5), the citizens of Beth-
shemesh (1 *Sam.* vi. 14, 15), Samuel (vii. 9, 10, etc.), Saul
(xiii. 9), David (2 *Sam.* vi. 17, 18; viii. 18; xx. 26; xxiv. [198]
18 sqq.), Solomon (1 *Kings* iii. 4; iv. 5; viii. 62–64), and
Jeroboam I. (xii. 32 sq.; xiii. 1). Almost all the accounts
are irreconcileable with the supposition that the precepts in
question nevertheless existed[11]. From *Judges* xvii. 7–13 we
can infer no more than that the Levites were considered better
suited for the priestly office than others. According to
Ezekiel xliv. 6–9, even foreigners were admitted to the service
of the sanctuary before the captivity[12].

The distinction between priests and Levites—so emphatically
enforced by P (§ 3, n. 16)—only appears once in the whole pre-
exilian and exilian literature. It is in 1 *Kings* viii. 4, and the
passage, both on this and on other accounts, lies under suspicion
(cf. n. 6 and § 10, n. 25). Of Aaron, as the ancestor of the
legitimate priesthood, no writer before Ezra knows anything.
From the end of the seventh century we find the priesthood
assigned to the tribe of Levi as a whole, just as it is in *Deuteronomy*[13]. Ezekiel confirms this, but ordains that in the
future only one Levitical family, that of Çadok, shall exercise the priesthood, while the other Levites are to occupy
themselves in the lower services connected with the cultus
(xliv. 10–16; cf. xl. 46; xliii. 19; xlviii. 11)[14].

The notices of the organization of the priesthood in the
temple of Jerusalem are in the nature of the case too fragmentary and incomplete to furnish any adequate conceptions.

So much, however, is clear, that they partly conflicted with
the regulations of P, and were partly independent of them [15].

With respect to the revenues of the priests, again, we are
but imperfectly informed. What can be gathered from 1 *Sam.*
ii. 13–16 ; 2 *Kings* xii. 4 sqq., differs totally from the regulations of the Tora [16]. Nor do Ezekiel's ordinances on the
subject agree with them any better [17]. No mention is anywhere found of the priests' right to tithes of the fruits of
field and tree and of cattle, or of the priestly and Levitical
cities [18].

[199]   [11] Some of these texts require annotation. 1 *Sam.* vi. 14, 15 is cited on
the supposition that 15ᵃ is a gloss intended to remove the scandal of the
sacrifice by the men of Beth-shemesh. Had the writer himself known anything of the Levites he would have mentioned them at once in *v.* 14, and not
after the sacrifice.—Samuel, who appears in 1 *Sam.* i. sqq. as a servant of the
sanctuary and constantly acts as a priest in vii. sqq., is made a descendant
of Kehath ben Levi by the Chronicler (1 *Chron.* vi. 7–13, 18–23 [22–28, 33–
38]), but according to 1 *Sam.* i. 1 he was an Ephraimite.—In 2 *Sam.* viii. 18
it is said of David's sons: כהנים היו, i.e. they were made or appointed
p r i e s t s. T h e n i u s and B e r t h e a u, following 1 *Chron.* xviii. 17, where
these words are replaced by הראשנים ליד המלך, take כהן as designating some
other high office filled by David's sons. But it is highly improbable, in fact
inconceivable, that so common a word should be used in such a double sense.
The writer can only mean that David's sons acted as p r i e s t s—perhaps on
special occasions, such as household and family sacrifices. The Chronicler
could not but regard this as an incredible statement, so he altered the text.
This view is confirmed by 2 *Sam.* xx. 26 : after mentioning Çadok and Abiathar as priests in *v.* 25, the writer goes on ' and also Ira, the Yairite, became
(היה) David's priest.' Note both the qualifying ' David's,' and the opening וגם,
which excludes any other interpretation. In 1 *Kings* iv. 5ᵇ is a similar statement : after Çadok and Abiathar (*v.* 4) follows another priest, Zabûd ben
Nathan, who was also 'the king's friend' (cf. 2 *Sam.* xv. 37 ; xvi. 16), and
as such well suited to support him on occasion of his domestic sacrifices. I
have not cited 1 *Kings* iv. 2, for הכהן is probably a gloss (cf. the LXX.), and
in any case it is not a title of Azaria ben Çadok—unless we are to suppose
that כהן is used in t h r e e senses, and that too in an official list of high
functionaries!—Amongst all the witnesses we have now summoned against
the existence of the Tora there are only two to whom objection might be
taken, viz. Mica and Jeroboam I. In my opinion even they would have
b e e n c o m p e l l e d to conform to the Tora, if it had really limited the
right of sacrificing in their day; and of all the others we may add that they
would have d e s i r e d to comply with it, h a d i t e x i s t e d.

[12] The evidence given by the prophet, however amazing from the point of view of the Tora, is quite unequivocal, and is indirectly confirmed by *Josh.* ix. 23, 27 (cf. § 6, n. 48), and by 2 *Sam.* vi. 10, 11, where the ark is deposited in the dwelling of Obed-Edom of Gath. The Chronicler himself tells us that this man and his descendants remained in the service of the sanctuary (1 *Chron.* xv. 18, 24 sq.; xvi. 38; xxvi. 4, 8, 15), though he endeavours to remove the scandal by finding room for Obed-Edom amongst the descendants of Levi, in defiance alike of his name and of the epithet הגתי, which stamps him as a Philistine.

[13] The state of things to which *Judges* xvii. 7–13; xix. 1, 18, bear witness indicates a l e a d i n g up to the exclusive exaltation of Levi to the priesthood, and the exclusive claim is a s s u m e d as established in *Jer.* xxxiii. 17–22 (probably later than Jeremiah); *Isaiah* lxvi. 21 (read לכהנים לוים); [200] 1 *Kings* xii. 31 (where the redactor tells us how Jeroboam ought to have acted, according to the Law: he should have appointed L e v i t e s—not 'sons of Aaron'—as priests). The recognition of Levi as the priestly tribe also underlies *Zech.* xii. 13[a] and the gloss in 1 *Sam.* vi. 15[a] (cf. n. 11). 2 *Sam.* xv. 24 is corrupt: it appears from 24[b], 27–29, that Abiathar should have been mentioned immediately after Çadok; but his place is now taken by 'and all the Levites with him,' while ויעל אביתר is wholly out of place. When we consider that the Levites are represented here as 'bearing the ark,' and that it is this task which the Chronicler, in conformity with P, always assigns to them (1 *Chron.* xv. 2, 13, 15; 2 *Chron.* v. 4; xxxv. 3), it strikes us as more than probable that this verse has been purposely altered in order to bring it into harmony with the demands of the Tora. On *v.* 27 see n. 15.

[14] Cf. S m e n d ' s Commentary. The attempts to explain Ezekiel's utterances in some other way do not merit refutation. Every effort to bring them into harmony with P is wrecked upon the undeniable fact that Ezekiel regards the exclusion of the Levites from the priestly office as something new, as a degradation, as the punishment of the idolatry they practised and fostered while they were yet priests of the bamôth. Commentators who are pledged not to admit this really deserve our pity. See further, § 15, n. 15.

[15] In David's reign Çadok and Abiathar stand side by side as priests (2 *Sam.* viii. 17; xx. 25; cf. also 1 *Kings* iv. 4)—a position wholly unrecognised by the Tora. The former of the two is called הכהן הראש in 2 *Sam.* xv. 27 (cf. W e l l h., *Text der Bücher Sam.*, p. 198), but this is only a post-exilian gloss. Solomon's action with respect to Abiathar (1 *Kings* ii. 26 sq., 35) implies that the king could dispose of the priesthood as he chose, which is again incompatible with P.—The chief of the Jerusalem priests is called הכהן הגדול; כהן הראש, in 2 *Kings* xii. 11 [10]; xxii. 4, 8; xxiii. 4 (xxv. 18 [=*Jer.* lii. 24]). Whether this t i t l e was employed as early as the time of Joash I will not decide; elsewhere (2 *Kings* xvi. 10 sqq.; *Isaiah* viii. 2, etc.) we find 'the priest' in its place, and this is perhaps the older designation; but there can be no doubt as to t h e f a c t of a primacy. 'The priest,' κατ' ἐξοχήν, had a deputy, כ' המשנה (2 *Kings* xxiii. 4 [read כהן]; xxv. 18). Under him stood three threshold-watchers, שמרי הסף (2 *Kings* xii. 10 [9];

xxii. 4; xxiii. 4; xxv. 18 [*=Jer.* lii. 24]), who were evidently high officials. According to Jehoiada's ordinance (2 *Kings* xi. 18; xii. 12 [11]; *Jer.* xxix. 26) another priest commanded the temple police, which itself no doubt consisted of priests (*Jer.* xx. 1). In 2 *Kings* xix. 2 we read of 'the elders of the priests;' and in *Isaiah* xliii. 28 of 'the princes of the sanctuary;' cf. also 1 *Chron.* xxiv. 5; 2 *Chron.* xxxvi. 14.—The regulation of the temple service by the Chronicler deviates widely from this. Cf. *Th. Tijdschr.*, iii. 469–472.

[16] Cf. W e l l h., *Prolegomena*, 160 [154]. It is mentioned in 1 *Sam.* ii., as a proof of the coarse greed of Eli's sons, that they sent their servants to demand a portion of the cooked or even the raw flesh of the sacrifice; the meaning evidently being that they should have waited for anything the sacrificer might choose to give them. Neither *Deut.* xviii. 3 nor *Lev.* vii. 34, therefore, can have [201] been known in their time, or even to the author of this narrative. Characteristic, too, and quite outside the range of the Tora is the usage to which 2 *Kings* xii. 4 sqq. bears evidence; that of making money offerings to the priests, out of which the latter had to pay for repairs to the temple.

[17] Cf. *Ezek.* xliv. 28–30; xlv. 4, 5; xlviii. 10–14; and further, xlv. 24; xlvi. 5, 7, 11, 14; and on the relation of these regulations to *Deut.* xviii. 1 sqq. and *Num.* xviii. 8 sqq. see S m e n d, *Ezekiel*, p. 367.

[18] *Amos* iv. 4 is no exception, cf. § 10, n. 3. The prophet assumes that the Israelites brought tithes to the sanctuary every three years. For the priests? He never says so; and the presumption is that they were devoted to sacrificial feasts. The third year is still called 'the year of tithes' in *Deut.* xxvi. 12, though, for that matter, D's own ordinance is that the tithes are to be ceded to the poor in the third year and eaten at the sanctuary the other two (xiv. 22–29); so that Amos is at variance with him too.—In 1 *Sam.* viii. 14, 17 the tithes are mentioned again. But there it is the king who adds to his other extortions a demand for tithes from corn-land, vineyard, and sheep-fold, to enrich his favourites. Whatever else these verses prove they certainly do not show that the Israelites were accustomed to paying tithes to the servants of the sanctuary.—As to the priestly and Levitical cities, the texts in the Chronicles which mention them stand alone. There are no parallels even in Ezekiel, though he uses (xxxvi. 5 [?]; xlv. 2; xlviii. 15, 17) the characteristic word מִגְרָשׁ, which is applied in *Num.* xxxv. 1–8; *Josh.* xxi. to the territory of these cities. Ezekiel's equivalent for this institution of P appears in the texts cited in n. 17. On the presumable origin of P's regulations see § 15, n. 16.

III. The celebration of feasts in honour of Yahwè might be taken for granted even if it were not expressly mentioned; but the notices we can collect do not lend themselves to the supposition that the precepts of the Tora were known. With regard to the three high festivals, if we pass over a doubtful allusion in Isaiah (xxx. 29), Josiah's passover is the first

celebration of which we possess historical assurance (2 *Kings*
xxiii. 21–23). The feast of first-fruits or weeks is never
mentioned at all, even by Ezekiel. The feast of ingathering
or tabernacles, on the other hand, is frequently mentioned,
and appears as the feast κατ᾽ ἐξοχήν. It was probably for a
long time the only feast celebrated by the whole people, or
at least by the population of a whole district, at one
of the greater sanctuaries (1 *Kings* viii. 65; xii. 32; *Hos.*
xii. 10 [9]; *Zech.* xiv. 16–19; *Ezek.* xlv. 25; cf. *Judges*
xxi. 19; 1 *Sam.* i. 3, 21; ii. 19). But although this remained the chief festival up to the captivity, we also hear of [202]
'feasts' in the plural as early as in the eighth century (*Am.*
v. 21; viii. 10; *Hos.* ii. 13 [11]); and in Isaiah they seem to
be spoken of as held at Jerusalem (xxix. 1; xxxii. 9 sqq.; cf.
xxxiii. 20)[19].

As to the other holy seasons we should note the following
points: *a.* the great day of atonement (*Lev.* xvi. and the
parallel passages) is never mentioned, and was unknown
even to Ezekiel (xlv. 18–20)[20]; *b.* the feast of the new
moon was observed from the earliest times (1 *Sam.* xx. 5, 6;
2 *Kings* iv. 23; *Am.* viii. 5; *Hos.* ii. 13 [11]; *Isaiah* i. 13),
but this cannot be regarded as due to the enactments of the
priestly tora (*Num.* xxviii. 11–15), and accordingly there is
not a trace of the 'day of blowing the trumpets' at new moon
(*Lev.* xxiii. 23–25; *Num.* xxix. 1–6)[21]; *c.* the sabbath also
appears to be a very ancient institution (2 *Kings* iv. 23; *Am.*
viii. 5; *Hos.* ii. 13 [11]; *Isaiah* i. 13), though it was only in
the Babylonian captivity and afterwards that it came to be so
deeply reverenced, and to be regarded as a main item in the
covenant between Yahwè and Israel (*Jer.* xvii. 19–27; *Isaiah*
lvi. 2; lviii. 13; *Ezek.* xx. 16; xxii. 26, etc.)[22]; *d.* the
sabbatical year (*Lev.* xxv. 1–7) was not observed before
the captivity, as we see not only by the silence of the prophets and historians as to its observance, but from positive

statements that it was neglected (*Lev.* xxvi. 34 sq., 43; 2 *Chron.* xxxvi. 21)²³; *e.* the year of release (*Deut.* xv. 1–11) appears to be mentioned once by Ezekiel (xlvi. 17), but the year of jubilee (*Lev.* xxv. 8 sqq.) never at all, not even, as has been supposed, by Jeremiah, in xxxiv. 9–20, for the law that underlies this passage is the ordinance concerning the release of the Israelitish slaves after six years' service (*Deut.* xv. 12–18)²⁴.

¹⁹ Note, in illustration, that *Isaiah* ix. 2 [3] (כשׂמחת בקציר), and *Hos.* ix. 1, justify the inference that reaping and threshing were accompanied by festivities, which doubtless bore a religious character, but which seem, at any rate as far as these passages show, to have been confined to the field and the threshing-floor, or in other words—like the sheep-shearing—to have had no connection with the public or general cultus;—and further, that the designation of 'the feast,' 1 *Kings* viii. 65, etc., admits of no other interpretation than [203] the one given in the text, for Jeroboam I. could hardly have confined himself to changing the time of the feast of the seventh month, if the two others had taken equal rank with it. And in *Judges* xxi. 19, in like manner, we read 'the feast of Yahwè,' not 'a feast in honour of Yahwè;'—and, again, note that *Isaiah* xxix. 1, which seems from xxxii. 9 sqq. to have been uttered at the great autumn festival, mentions a cycle of feasts, which must have been closed every year by the autumn festival and could hardly have been treated as a single whole unless the feasts of which it consisted had all been celebrated in one place, viz. the temple.

²⁰ In this passage Ezekiel ordains a cleansing of the sanctuary, necessitated by the involuntary trespasses of the people, on the first day of the first and seventh months (on the text of *v.* 20, cf. Smend). *Lev.* xvi. would have rendered this completely superfluous, and must therefore have been unknown to him.

²¹ The passages cited speak for themselves. 2 *Kings* iv. 23 deserves attention as indicating that the day of the new moon (like the sabbath) was withdrawn from ordinary work, and might, for instance, be employed in paying visits—perhaps to the priest or prophet. Cf. *Amos* viii. 5.

²² According to Geiger, *Urschr. u. Uebersetzungen,* p. 95 sq., and Rowland Williams, *Hebrew Prophets,* ii. 155 sq., *Jer.* xvii. 19–27 is an interpolation dating from after the captivity (cf. *Neh.* xiii. 15–22). Cf. my *Profeten,* ii. 74–76 [*Prophets and Prophecy in Israel,* p. 339 sq.]. So much at least is certain, that this prophecy is without parallel either in Jeremiah himself or any of his contemporaries, and that if it is really from his hand we must suppose that he was enunciating something new in insisting on the high importance of rest on the seventh day as such.

²³ On the mutual relation of *Ex.* xxiii. 11, 12 and *Lev.* xxv. 1–7, see Hup-

feld, *De primit. fest. apud Hebr. rat.*, ii. 10 sq. Letting all the fields lie fallow in the seventh year is such an important circumstance in the life of a people that it must have been mentioned in the prophetic and historical books had it really been observed, and accordingly in the post-exilian period, when the Tora was actually carried out, we do find it referred to more than once (1 *Macc.* vi. 49, 53, and in Josephus). The *argumentum e silentio* has great force in this instance. But *Lev.* xxvi. 34 sq., 43, is still more unequivocal. Even D (*Deut.* xv, 1–11) had already substituted another ordinance for *Ex.* xxiii. 11 sq. Cf. Wellh., *Prolegomena*, i. 123 sqq. [114 sqq.].

[24] Here Ezekiel ordains that the territories granted by the prince to his servants shall remain in their possession till 'the year of release' (שְׁנַת הַדְּרוֹר), and shall then revert to him. This is usually taken to refer to the year of jubilee, to which the word דְּרוֹר is no doubt applied in *Lev.* xxv. 10. The argument is weak, however, and in the absence of any proof that Ezekiel was acquainted with *Lev.* xxv. 8 sqq., no weight can be attached to it. Nor is it likely, in the abstract, that a temporary grant would hold good for—in some cases—over forty years. But there is more. Jeremiah—with whose writings Ezekiel was unquestionably familiar—uses the word דְּרוֹר of the liberation of slaves after six years' service (xxxiv. 8, 15, 17). Accordingly Ezekiel's שְׁנַת הַדְּרוֹר would probably be the seventh year, which D (*Deut.* xv. 1 sqq.), following *Ex.* xxiii. 11 sq., calls שׁ׳ הַשְּׁמִטָּה. The regulation in *Ezek.* [204] xlvi. 17 is in perfect keeping with the character of this seventh year, and at the same time it may be regarded as the germ which the (later) law of the year of jubilee, *Lev.* xxv. 8 sqq., brought to full development.—As to *Jer.* xxxiv. 8–22 itself, it points (v. 14) unmistakably to *Deut.* xv. 12. It is true that this tora, like *Ex.* xxi. 1 sqq., lays it down that every Israelitish slave is to be released after six years' service. But Jeremiah himself says (v. 15, 16), that this precept of the Law had long been neglected. The manumission, therefore, which would otherwise have been an individual matter, had to be carried out by all the nobles at once, and after a solemn pledge. Cf. Graf, *Jeremia*, p. 430 sqq.

IV. The sacred actions recorded deviate in more respects than one from the precepts in P. This is at once exemplified by the sacrifices, which, as might have been expected, are frequently mentioned in the prophetic and historical books. Deviations may be noted in the sacrificial rites, but still more in the estimate of the ritual and of the sundry kinds of sacrifice. Whereas P regulates the sacrificial procedure down to the minutest details, and ranks the burnt-offering, and still more the trespass-offering, above the thank-offering, it is this latter that appears most prominently in the historical notices; and it is obvious that no importance is

P

attached in any case to the method in which the sacrifice is made [25]. The trespass-offering is not unknown, but, at any rate before the captivity, there is no trace of the distinction drawn in *Lev.* iv. sqq. between the trespass and the guilt-offering [26]. Again, we find traces and examples in the historians and prophets of human sacrifices made to Yahwè (*Judges* xi. 30–40; 1 *Sam.* xv. 32 sq.; 2 *Sam.* xxi. 1–14; *Mic.* vi. 7[b]; *Ezek.* xx. 25 sq.), whereas the only human sacrifices known to the Tora are those in honour of strange gods (*Deut.* xii. 31; xviii. 10; *Lev.* xviii. 21; xx. 2–5) [27].

The chief difference between the Nazirite's vow in *Judges* xiii.; and 1 *Sam.* i. (cf. *Amos* ii. 11 sq.), and that of the Tora (*Num.* vi. 1–21), is that the latter is temporary and the former permanent. The permanent form of the vow is unquestionably the earlier [28]. The application of the cherem to the Amalekites (1 *Sam.* xv.) and to the tribe of Benjamin (*Judges* xx.) leaves it an open question whether the custom was legally [205] regulated or not [29]. According to *Am.* viii. 10; *Isaiah* iii. 24; xxii. 12; *Mic.* i. 16; *Jer.* xvi. 6; xli. 5, the Israelites employed forms of mourning which the Tora condemns (*Deut.* xiv. 1; *Lev.* xix. 27 sq.) [30]. Circumcision appears to have been regularly practised, but is never represented —as it is in *Gen.* xvii.—as the distinguishing mark of the Israelite [31]. Finally, the distinction between things clean and unclean exists, but betrays no clear traces of the influence either of the deuteronomic or of the priestly Tora [32].

---

[25] Cf. especially Wellh., *Prolegomena*, 54–85 [52–82]. I must be content with touching upon the main points. Thank-offerings of slaughtered beasts, accompanied by sacrificial feasts, occur in 1 *Sam.* i. 3 sqq.; xx. 29; 2 *Sam.* vi. 18; xv. 7 sqq., 12; 1 *Kings* viii. 62 sqq.; *Isaiah* i. 11; xix. 21, etc. They are also the most frequent class in D (*Deut.* xii. 7 and the parallel passages), though burnt-offerings are also mentioned alike by D and by our other witnesses. Of this latter kind we find a very remarkable description in *Judges* vi. 19–21. We see from 1 *Sam.* xiv. 34; 1 *Kings* xix. 21, what short work was sometimes made of sacrificial formalities, and 2 *Kings* v. 17 tells in the same direction, inasmuch as no kind of prescriptions are given to the foreigner Naaman as to

the way in which he is to make his sacrifices; offering them in honour of Yahwè is the chief and indeed the only point.

²⁶ Cf. *Hos.* iv. 8. But this passage does not mean that the priests ate the trespass-offerings of the people—which, according to the Tora, they had a right to do—but (cf. viii. 11) that they traded on the zeal for the cultus displayed by the people, instead of guiding them, as they should have done, to the true ethical knowledge of God (iv. 1 sqq.). Hosea's words, therefore, give but a very faint, if any, indication of the existence of sacrifices of atonement. —In 2 *Kings* xii. 17 [16], on the other hand, we even find אשם and חטאת side by side, but they are preceded by כסף, and must therefore mean the money fines which the Israelite had to pay in the case of certain trespasses, and which, as we learn from this passage, fell to the priests. There is a certain connection between this usage and the regulation of trespass and guilt-offerings in *Lev.* iv. sqq., but that the former sprang from the latter by no means appears. In Ezekiel we find the two-fold offerings of atonement, as we should have expected, xl. 39; xlii. 13; xliii. 19; xliv. 29; xlvi. 20; they are amongst the many verbal and substantial coincidences between him and P.

²⁷ Perhaps 1 *Sam.* xv. 32 sq. ought not to be included in the list, since Agag fell a victim to the cherem which had been launched upon all Amalek (*v.* 3); but it deserves note that Samuel hews him in pieces 'before the face of Yahwè.' In *Mic.* vi. 7ᵇ פשעי and נפשי חטאת are parallel: "חטאת therefore is not a sin-offering, but the sin itself, which the questioner supposes may be made good or expiated by the sacrifice of one of his children. This seems to [206] imply that human sacrifices were not altogether unknown in the worship of Yahwè, and were not regarded as wholly irreconcileable with it. The law-givers, however, do not attack this error (though E, in *Gen.* xxii. 1–19, does so, at least indirectly).

²⁸ Many scholars have seen in the life-long Nazirite's vow an extension or exaggeration of the tora in *Num.* vi. But *Amos* ii. 11 sq. and the example of the Rechabites (*Jer.* xxxv.) do not favour this idea, and moreover it is clear as a matter of history that the specific Judaism was disposed to restrain rather than to stimulate the Nazirite's vow. It is but natural to explain the difference between *Num.* vi. and the pre-exilian practice as produced by the same tendency.

²⁹ The trustworthiness of *Judges* xx. is doubtful (§ 10, n. 29); and 1 *Sam.* xv. is a late narrative. But, in any case, the two chapters can hardly be cited as indicating that the tora of *Deut.* xx. 16–18 (cf. vii. 1 sqq.; xiii. 13–19 [12–18]), was recognised as binding; for these ordinances regulate the application of the cherem to the Cananites and to Israelitish idolaters, and therefore do not run parallel with *Judges* xx. and 1 *Sam.* xv.; and moreover the laws assume a practical acquaintance with the cherem itself, which, in point of fact, was not introduced by the tora but adopted and regulated by it.

³⁰ D, in *Deut.* xiv. 1, uses exactly the same words (קרחה and התגדד) that the prophets employ to describe the ordinary mourning customs. Could Amos have made Yahwè threaten to 'bring baldness upon every head,' if Yahwè's own tora, with an appeal to Israel's consecration to himself, had forbidden

'the making of a bald place between the eyes for the dead'? It is remarkable, but not inexplicable, that even Jeremiah does not condemn the popular
usage; he is not D himself (§ 10, n. 14), and there was no reason why he
should submit to the latter's authority in a matter well-nigh indifferent.

[31] The uncircumcised are the Philistines (2 *Sam.* i. 20; *Judges* xiv. 3;
xv. 18; 1 *Sam.* xiv. 6; xvii. 26, 36; xxxi. 4; cf. xviii. 25; 2 *Sam.* iii. 14), not
the Canaanites or the surrounding tribes in general. It is not till near the
captivity (*Jer.* ix. 24 sq. [25 sq.]), or in its actual course (*Ezek.* xliv. 7, 9),
that the foreskin becomes the sign of distinction between the Israelite on the
one hand, and his neighbours or the stranger in general on the other; and this
is the state of things reflected in the conception of the circumcision found in
Gen. xvii.

[32] Cf. *Amos* vii. 17; *Hos.* ix. 3; *Isaiah* vi. 5. But the agreement between
Hos. ix. 4 and *Deut.* xxvi. 14 is remarkable. Both the prophet and the law-
giver here adopt the current popular conception.

V. There are comparatively few facts that testify for or
against the existence of the Mosaic ordinances concerning the
political and civic life. The proceeding described in
Ruth iv. 1–12 lies outside the laws of *Lev.* xxv. 25; *Deut.* xxv.
5–10 [33]. The account of Saul's election as king in 1 *Sam.* viii.;
[207] x. 17–27, is subject to grave suspicion; but if it be accepted
as history it shows that Samuel was unacquainted with the
law of the monarchy in *Deut.* xvii. 14–20 [34]. In 1 *Sam.* xxx.
21–25 David regulates the partition of the spoil in a way
that cannot be harmonised with *Num.* xxxi [35]. His answer to
Nathan's parable, 2 *Sam.* xii. 5, 6, can hardly be looked upon
as an application of *Ex.* xxi. 37 [xxii. 1]—a precept from
which *Prov.* vi. 31 also deviates [36]. In the conversation
between David and the woman of Teko'a (2 *Sam.* xiv. 4–17)
it is obvious that no legal regulations of blood-avenging (cf.
Deut. xix. 1–13; *Num.* xxxv. 9–34) are present to the mind
of either interlocutor [37]. The judicial murder of Naboth
(1 *Kings* xxi.) cannot be regarded as perpetrated in outward
conformity with the Tora known to us [38]. In 2 *Kings* xiv. 6
(2 *Chron.* xxv. 4) it is not Amaziah who is speaking, but the
historian,—who was, as we know, perfectly well acquainted
with *Deuteronomy* (xxiv. 16). Other points of contact with

the laws regulating the civil life have sometimes been discovered in the Old Testament, but they are not really
there [39].

[33] See above, § 10, n. 23. *Deut.* xxv. 5–10 only lays the brothers of
the deceased under obligation to marry his widow, and has therefore no application to the case in point. Accordingly the passage is never appealed to in the
transactions between the go'él and Boaz. The symbolical act mentioned in
Ruth iv. 7 has no connection with *Deut.* xxv. 9, 10, and has nothing beyond
the fundamental idea in common with *Lev.* xxv. 25.

[34] Hengstenberg's attempted demonstration (op. cit., iii. 246–261 [ii.
201–213]), 'that the transaction presupposes the existence of the Pentateuch in
general and especially of the law of the monarchy,' no longer needs refutation.

[35] In *Num.* xxxi.—which forms, as a whole, a very sharp contrast to the
accounts of David's wars—we have specially to consider *v.* 27–30. The עדה
to whom these verses assign half the booty is not once thought of by David.
Neither does he give the priests any share.

[36] The four-fold restitution of *Ex.* xxi. 37 [xxii. 1]—which *Prov.* vi. 31
makes seven-fold—occurs again in 2 *Sam.* xii. 5 sq., but had David been
thinking of the Tora, he would not have added, in violation of its precepts, a
sentence of death as well.

[37] Both laws agree in requiring that wilful murder shall be punished by
death (*Deut.* xix. 11–13; *Num.* xxxv. 16–21), and this is just what David's
sentence remits (2 *Sam.* xiv. 8–11).

[38] Keil (on the passage) thinks that Naboth refused to sell his heritage in
obedience to *Lev.* xxv. 23–28; *Num.* xxxvi. 7 sqq.—as though these laws
forbade such a sale, instead of presupposing it in the very fact of restricting
its validity to the year of jubilee.—On 1 *Kings* xxi. 9, 10, he cites not only [208]
Deut. xvii. 6 sq.; xix. 15; *Num.* xxxv. 30 (which are more or less to the purpose, as they require the testimony of at least two witnesses, though this
requirement seems to be determined by the nature of the case), but
also *Ex.* xxii. 27 and *Deut.* xiii. 11 [10]; xvii. 5, 'in which idolatry,
as the practical denial of God, is punished by stoning.' But Naboth
is not accused of denying Yahwè, and so of idolatry, but of a political
offence—and that is why his inheritance falls to the king without
more ado, though no such provision comes within the scope of the Tora.

[39] Marti does not merit refutation, when he asserts (op. cit., p. 333 sq.)
that *Jer.* xxii. 17; xxvi. 15; *Ezek.* xvi. 38; xxxiii. 6, 8 sq.; iii. 18, 20, must
necessarily rest upon *Gen.* ix. 5, 6, or (p. 352) that *Jer.* xliv. 19 presupposes the law as to the validity of a married woman's vow, *Num.* xxx. 4 sqq.;
or (*ibid.*) that *Num.* xxxv. 33 underlies *Mic.* iv. 11 and *Ezek.* xxxvi. 17. For
whose benefit such parallels are cited it is not easy to imagine.

§ 12. *The origin and antiquity of the constituent parts of the Hexateuch.* A. *The reformations of Josiah and Ezra as starting-points for determining the chronology of the legislation, and of the evolution of the Hexateuch.*

Having now ascertained that the Mosaic law was not in force in Israel from the first, and further that it consists of heterogeneous elements, it is natural that we should next inquire when and how the legislation as a whole, or any portion of it, was actually drawn up and enforced. *A priori* it seems probable that events of such profound significance must have left some traces behind them in the historical records of the people, and as a matter of fact we do not look for them in vain. In the accounts of the period of the Judges and the Kings down to Josiah (639–608 B.C.) there is not a single word about the introduction of the Law or its acceptance by the people or its leaders. The assertion that the legislation of *Exodus–Numbers*, or even the whole Tetrateuch, was published under Ahaz, is not even indirectly supported by the narratives concerning him [1]. The oldest accounts of Hezekiah's reformation (2 *Kings* xviii. 4) say nothing whatever of its being founded on a written law [2]. On the other hand, we are told in 2 *Kings* xxii., xxiii. that Josiah's [2c9] reformation in the eighteenth year of his reign (621 B.C.) was based upon the book of law found in the temple by Hilkiah. The names applied to it, and all the particulars given as to its contents, lead us to identify it with the laws and exhortations that make up the kernel of the book of Deuteronomy (v.–xxvi., xxviii) [3]. This does not in itself prove that the book which was now made known and promulgated was also composed about the same time. But the evidence derived from the literature of Israel, both before and after Josiah's reformation, makes it extremely probable that this was the case [4], and the probability is raised almost to certainty by a minute consideration of the contents of the deuteronomic legislation[5]. And if this be so, then there is no room to doubt that the book was written with a view to the use that Hilkiah made of it. It was not by accident, but in accordance with the writer's deliberate purpose, that it became the foundation and the norm of Josiah's reformation[6].

[1] The supposition is made by Graetz, *Gesch. der Juden*, II. i., p. 149 sqq., 160 sqq. He believes that the promulgation of *Genesis-Numbers* under Ahaz had been preceded by the public reading of special narratives and laws, e.g. of *Ex.* xxxiii. 12–17 on occasion of the coronation of Joash; of *Ex.* xxv. sqq. when the temple was restored under the same king; of *Num.* xvi.–xviii. under Uzziah (p. 56, 61, 102 sq., 470 sq.). Graetz distinguishes between this public reading and the original composition, whether of the special narratives and laws or of the whole Tetrateuch. This latter he places far earlier, though assigning no external influence to it, inasmuch as he believes the priests to have kept the written Tora to themselves at first while giving their decisions by word of mouth (p. 56 and elsewhere). See the refutation of this highly arbitrary and unsatisfactory theory in *Th. Tijdschr.*, x. 549–576. I must content myself here with remarking that 2 *Kings* xvi., while mentioning the interest taken by Ahaz in the temple service, does not say a word of such an important fact as the promulgation of the Tetrateuch would have been; nor is any trace of it to be found in 2 *Chron.* xxviii. The same may be said of the records of Joash and Uzziah (2 *Kings* xi.; xii.; xv. 1–7; 2 *Chron.* xxiii.; xxiv.; xxvi.). Indeed all that Graetz attempts to show is that the reading out alike of these special passages and of the whole Tetrateuch was specially needful and suitable at the particular moments he indicates—as though this alone proved anything, or could have any significance except to those who are convinced already that the Tetrateuch was in existence!

[2] Cf. § 11, n. 9. It is very remarkable that the author of *Kings*, who is himself acquainted with the deuteronomic code, and ascribes it to Moses, declares (2 *Kings* xviii. 6) that Hezekiah observed the commandments of Yahwè, which he had commanded Moses, but yet does not venture to repre- [210] sent his reformation as the carrying out of these commandments. Cf. 2 *Kings* xviii. 22, where the suppression of the bamôth is represented as an arbitrary measure of Hezekiah's own, and the writer himself does not protest against such a view of it. Even in 2 *Chron.* xxix.–xxxii., though it is completely dominated in other respects by the Chronicler's view of the Law (§ 11, n. 4), this peculiarity of the older narrative is not quite obliterated.

[3] So (amongst others) De Wette (*Beitr. zur Einl.*, i. 168 sqq.), Bleek, Ewald, Riehm, Colenso, Reuss, Graf, etc., and also Wellhausen (xxii. 458 sq.; *Prolegomena*, 426 sqq. [402 sqq.]) and Valeton (*Studien*, vii. 210 sqq.), allowing for their special views on the limits of the original *Deuteronomy* (§ 7, n. 5–10). Hilkiah's book is called 'the book of law' (2 *Kings* xxii. 8;

cf. 11 and xxiii. 24, 25), or 'the book of the covenant' (xxiii. 2, 3, 21). In
the books of Kings the former designation can hardly mean anything but the
deuteronomic code, the only one with which the author is acquainted (§ 10,
n. 24, 25); the second is applicable to more than one collection (cf. *Ex.* xxiv. 7),
but is, at any rate, perfectly appropriate to *Deuteronomy* (xxviii. 69 [xxix. 1];
cf. v. 3). The length of the book was such as to allow of its being read aloud
to the king by Shaphan (2 *Kings* xxii. 10), and by the king in his turn to
the people, in the temple (xxiii. 2); and this prevents our thinking of the
whole Pentateuch, but falls in well enough with the supposition that the
kernel of *Deuteronomy*, or a still smaller collection, is intended. Hilkiah's
book contained precepts about the pascal feast (2 *Kings* xxiii. 21; cf. *Deut.* xvi.
1 sqq.), and terrible denunciations against those who should transgress its ordinances (2 *Kings* xxii. 13 sqq.; cf., inter alia, *Deut.* xi. 13 sqq.; xxviii.) Finally,
it occasions a reformation of the cultus, aiming at the complete extirpation of
idolatry and the suppression of the bamôth, i. e. the centralisation of the
sacrifices and festivals at the temple of Jerusalem; and such passages as *Deut.*
vii.; xiii. 1–6 [xii. 32–xiii. 5], 7–12 [6–11], 13–18 [12–17], etc.; xii. *passim*;
xiv. 23–25; xv. 20; xvi. 2, 6, 7, 11, 15, 16; xvii. 8, 10; xviii. 6; xxvi. 2,
show how completely this tendency is embodied in the deuteronomic tora
also.

The objections urged against these proofs of the identity of Hilkiah's book
of law with the deuteronomic tora are very weak. S e i n e c k e (*Geschichte d.V.
Israel*, i. 386 sq.) appeals to Jeremiah's silence concerning the covenant to
which Josiah pledged his people (2 *Kings* xxiii. 1 sqq.), but does not notice *Jer.*
xi. 1 sqq., which confirms both the main contents of 2 *Kings* xxii. sq., and the
view we have taken as to Hilkiah's book. He is further of the opinion that
the threat of punishment which made so deep an impression on Josiah (2 *Kings*
xxii. 11 sqq.) must have been u n c o n d i t i o n a l, and therefore cannot be
identified with that in *Deuteronomy*, which is still dependent on the attitude
of the people towards the law, and is balanced by promises conditional on
submission to its precepts. But this assumes, in the first place, that the
ipsissima verba of Josiah and Huldah are preserved in 2 *Kings* xxii. 11 sqq.,
though the author wrote when the actual catastrophe had shown that the
punishment was inevitable; and, in the second place, it overlooks the circumstance that even in this long subsequent redaction of Josiah's and Huldah's
[211] words, emphatic stress is laid on the fact that the precepts of the book have
already been transgressed by the fathers and up to the present moment (*v.* 13,
16 sq.), so that the (originally conditional) penalty has already been incurred
and can no longer be averted.—V a t k e's objections (*Bibl. Theol.*, i. 504 sqq.,
511, n. 5) are better supported. He maintains that Hilkiah's book of
law coincides substantially with the older laws in *Ex.* xx.–xxiv., together
with certain other ordinances now incorporated in *Deuteronomy*, and certain
denunciations which were appended to them, while *Deuteronomy* itself he regards as the outcome, rather than the basis of Josiah's reformation, i.e. as the
codification of the measures taken. But V a t k e fails to observe that Josiah's
violent measures against idolatry and the bamôth immediately follow upon

the solemn acceptance of Hilkiah's book of law (xxiii. 1 sqq.), and would unquestionably have been resisted had they not been justified by it. A perfectly valid appeal against the centralisation of the cultus might have been made to *Ex.* xx. 24, etc. And moreover, *Deut.* xii. 8 was written when the bamôth were still in existence.—K l e i n e r t objects not so much to the identification of Hilkiah's book of law with *Deuteronomy* (see op. cit., p. 79–82), as to fixing the date of its composition so late as in Josiah's reign. We shall, therefore, reserve his remarks for n. 5.

[4] Cf. § 10, n. 16, 13, 35. To reconcile the belief that *Deuteronomy* existed in the eighth century B. C., or still earlier, with the absence of all reference to it in the older prophets, it has been supposed that it was kept concealed from the people in prophetic or priestly circles. But this contradicts the spirit of *Deuteronomy* itself, which is essentially addressed to the people, and is an appeal to their zeal for Yahwè. Neither the legislation proper (xii. sqq.), nor the exhortations (v. sqq.), can have been written as a mere literary essay; both alike are meant in dire earnest, and would, therefore, be brought to the knowledge of the people on the very first opportunity.

[5] The composition of *Deuteronomy* in the seventh century B.C. (whether under Manasseh or under Josiah will be discussed in n. 6) is supported, (1) by a number of the special exhortations and precepts, and (2) by its relation to the religious development of Israel as a whole.

(1) In the many passages referring to the one sanctuary of Yahwè (*Deut.* xii. 5, 11, 14, 18, 21, 26; xiv. 23–25; xv. 20; xvi. 2, 6 sq., 11, 15 sq.; xvii. 8, 10; xviii. 6; xxvi. 2; cf. xxxi. 11) *Deuteronomy* presupposes the existence of the temple of Jerusalem. It is true that the usual formula runs, 'the place which Yahwè s h a l l c h o o s e,' but this is only because the laws are put into the mouth of Moses. The real author had an actual sanctuary in his mind, as we see from the texts themselves, and especially from xii. 5 (out of all your tribes), 14 (in one of your tribes); and also from xii. 5, 21; xiv. 24; xxvi. 2, which imply a fixed abode of Yahwè rather than a moveable tent.

The law of the monarchy (*Deut.* xvii. 14–20) was written after Solomon's time and with the express purpose of averting errors such as his. This is especially obvious in *v.* 17, alike from the use of נשים by itself (unintelligible, in connection with what follows, unless we mentally supply נכריות from Solomon's history), and from ולא יסור לבבו (evidently written by some one acquainted with the consequences of Solomon's polygamy). How much more probable this is than that Solomon should not only have transgressed the law, [212] but gone on to justify its apprehensions by his own example!

The ordinance of *Deut.* xvii. 8–13 presupposes the existence of a high court of appeal at Jerusalem under a two-fold presidency, spiritual and civil. Such a court was surely not the creation of the early years of the monarchy. The Chronicler says that it was instituted by Jehoshaphat (2 *Chron.* xix. 8–11), and his statement may deserve credit; but if the long period that lies between his own date and ± 900 B.C. makes us question his authority, we shall suppose that he antedates the institution rather than the reverse. This would throw the deuteronomic ordinance, which implies that this court of appeal had been long established, so much the later.

The inference drawn from the absence of all mention of *Deuteronomy* in 2 *Kings* xviii. 4 (n. 2), is strengthened by the warning in *Deuteronomy* against worshipping ' the host of heaven' (xvii. 3; cf. iv. 9). The prophets of the eighth century never mention this form of idolatry, but Jeremiah (viii. 2; xix. 13; cf. xxxiii. 22) and Zephaniah (i. 5) do. The author of *Kings* tells us that it was introduced by Manasseh and abolished by Josiah (2 *Kings* xxi. 3, 5; xxiii. 4, 5). This argument would be conclusive as to the date of the deuteronomic law were it not that the same author attributes this form of idolatry to the ten tribes also (2 *Kings* xvii. 16). But this is in a general survey of a long-vanished past which is characterised by anything but pre-cision; nor is it supported by the evidence of Amos and Hosea, for example, or by any statements of the author himself concerning the introduction or patronage of this special idolatry by the kings of Ephraim. We can therefore attach no value to this statement, and cannot allow it to invalidate the con-clusions drawn from his precise and positive data as to Manasseh and Josiah. For the opposite view, see K l e i n e r t (op. cit., p. 105–112).

(2) Cf. D u h m, *Die Theol. der Propheten*, p. 194–202. *Deuteronomy* rests, on the one hand, on Hosea, who laid such stress on the e x c l u s i v e character of Israel's relation to Yahwè, and in connection therewith fostered the dis-positions to which D so fervently appeals; and on the other hand, on Isaiah's preaching of the inviolability of Jerusalem as the seat of Yahwè and on its rati-fication by the events, which alone could justify the intrinsically monstrous and unnatural demand that the worship of Yahwè should be confined to the one single temple.—And again, *Deuteronomy* presupposes Hezekiah's partial reformation (2 *Kings* xviii. 4; cf. n. 2), for the incomplete and partially defeated practice usually precedes the theory, and not *vice versâ*; and it also presupposes the reaction under Manasseh (2 *Kings* xxi.), which would serve to draw those who sympathised with Isaiah more closely together, and to direct their thoughts towards such changes in the religious condition of the country as would best answer to the purpose of Hezekiah and Isaiah, and make such apostasy as had taken place under Manasseh impossible. *Deuteronomy* is the programme of a drastic reformation of this kind which would guarantee its own permanence.

As against the arguments ranged under (1) and (2) K l e i n e r t ' s objections to the composition of *Deuteronomy* under Manasseh or Josiah are of very little weight. They are drawn, *a.* from the command to exterminate the [213] Canaanites (*Deut.* vii.; xx. 16 sqq., etc.), as unnecessary and inappro-priate in Josiah's days; *b.* from the military laws (*Deut.* xx. 1–15; xxi. 10–14; and also xxv. 17–19), as presupposing a very different and much earlier condition of things than obtained under Josiah; *c.* from the precepts concerning the one sanctuary (cited under (1) above) and the prohibition contained in *Deut.* xvi. 21 sq., as directed against Canaanite abuses, and not against the errors of the seventh century B.C., when the high places of Y a h w è had long been abolished for ever (2 *Kings* xviii. 4) and the mingling

of the worship of Yahwè with heathen rites and symbols was a thing of
the past; *d.* from the numerous references to Egypt (*Deut.* xxiii. 8 sq.
[7 sq.]; v. 15; vi. 21, etc.; and also xvii. 16), as equally strange and
purposeless under Josiah; *e.* from *Deut.* xii. 8, as compelling us to place
Deuteronomy nearer to the time of Moses.—Amongst these objections there is
one—that under *c.*—which is wholly false; for we know nothing of a permanent suppression of the bamôth by Hezekiah, but on the contrary read
(2 *Kings* xxi. 3ᵃ) that Manasseh rebuilt the high places that his
father had destroyed; we also learn (xxiii. 8, 9) that Yahwè was
worshipped at the bamôth which Josiah abolished; and thus the attempt
to show that *Deut.* xvi. 21 sq. would have been superfluous in his time breaks
down completely. The other objections fall to the ground when we take
into consideration the form in which D thought fit to present his exhortations,
and his obvious dependence, which Kleinert himself admits, upon
earlier collections of laws. In xii. sqq., as well as in v.-xi. (§ 7, n. 7), D
selects the moment immediately before the conquest of Canaan, and preaches
the ideal that stood before his own mind through the lips of Moses. In spite
of this the period in which he actually lived may well be expected to shine
through here and there, and so it does (see under (1) and (2) above). But
Kleinert seems to demand that he should always forget his part.
Why should he not give utterance to his horror of idolatry, and his ideal of a
people consecrated to Yahwè, under the form of a command to exterminate
the Canaanites? How completely subservient this command is to the expression of an idea, and how little it is intended for practice, we learn especially
from vii., where *v.* 20 sqq. (borrowed from *Ex.* xxiii. 28–30) conflicts with the
precepts and representations of D himself (x. 22). The reproduction of older
laws or conceptions is likewise ignored by Kleinert. *Deut.* xxv. 17-19 was
doubtless impossible to carry out in Josiah's time, but does it follow that it
was out of place in a Mosaic book of law drawn up in his reign with the help
of earlier documents? To produce such a work as D at all it was necessary
to keep the past and its institutions as steadily in view as the demands of
the present. If we cannot believe in the possibility of such a compromise we
must take up the position (from which Kleinert shrinks) that what we have
called the dress of the book is the simple expression of the historic truth.
On the other hand, if once we have relinquished its authenticity, we must
thenceforth take due account of all that a literary fiction necessarily involves.

⁶ The opinion that D wrote under Manasseh—upheld by Ewald, Bleek,
Riehm (in 1854; though he subsequently declared in favour of Hezekiah's
reign), Valeton, and others—seems at first to have an advantage in preserving
the complete good faith of Hilkiah, Shaphan, and Huldah, who take the
leading parts in 2 *Kings* xxii. A book of law that was some decades old in [214]
621 B.C., however it happened that it strayed into the temple and was discovered there, may have been regarded as really Mosaic, and may have been
presented as such to Josiah. But this is open to the great, and in my opinion
fatal, objection that it makes the actual reformation the work of those who

had not planned it but were blind tools in the service of the unknown projector. Analogy is against the supposition. And the *rôle* assigned to D himself is almost equally improbable ; for he is made to commit his aspirations to writing, urge their realisation with intensest fervour—and leave the rest to chance. How much more probable that he and other kindred spirits planned the means which should lead to the end they had in view ! Experience had shown, under Hezekiah and Manasseh alike, that much, if not all, depended on the disposition o f t h e k i n g ; and the problem therefore was how to secure Josiah for the plans of the reformers. Its solution is recorded in 2 *Kings* xxii. If this be so, then D himself must have been near to Josiah and must have worked in his reign. Cf. *Nieuw en Oud*, viii. 207–221.

V a l e t o n ' s treatment of the question upon which we are engaged deserves special notice. He does not deny that the book of law found by Hilkiah and enforced by Josiah is the same as the original *Deuteronomy*, but he will not allow that it is rightly regarded as the programme of a so-called Mosaic party, or that it was drawn up as the standard of a reformation such as Josiah accomplished. *Deuteronomy*, he contends, is simply what it is called in 2 *Kings* xxii. sq., ספר התורה, i. e. the codified expression of Yahwè's demands, which the writer believed had been in force from the first, and might therefore be properly laid upon the lips of Moses. In this case there would be nothing strange in the supposition that it had been written for some considerable time before it excited attention, was recognised by Josiah as the expression of Yahwè's will, and accordingly accepted and carried out (*Studien*, vii. 212 sqq.).—V a l e t o n ' s characterisation of *Deuteronomy* is incomplete rather than unjust (cf. § 7, n. 2). It overlooks alike the great significance of the command to worship Yahwè alone, in the one only sanctuary, and the sharp contrast between this command and the actual condition of affairs, which was so completely at variance with it that its introduction amounted to a revolution. We see as clearly as possible from 2 *Kings* xxiii. what it was that Josiah and his coadjutors regarded as the essential matter. Is it likely that they mistook the real purport of *Deuteronomy*, and that it was only by accident that they attached the greatest importance to one out of its many groups of precepts and proceeded immediately to put it into practice ? The supposition is improbability itself. What the law-book accomplished was what it intended to accomplish. Our conception of its origin then is fully justified. There is certainly nothing capricious in illustrating its special tendencies by reference to the events of Hezekiah's and Manasseh's reigns (n. 5, under (2)), and thence inferring that the centralisation of the cultus was still opposed to the popular convictions when the book was composed. It follows that *Deuteronomy*—not in all its commands, but in this one central principle and everything that flows from it—expressed the conviction of a m i n o r i t y ; and whether we call it ' the Mosaic party ' or anything else, the essential fact remains that it was a [215] minority, and that its triumph in 621 B.C. cannot reasonably be ascribed to chance.

The preceding argument involves the thesis that in Josiah's eighteenth year the priestly legislation had not yet been introduced, and was not introduced in company with the deuteronomic code. The evidence alike of the Israelitish literature and of the history of the people, together with its religious development, is in perfect harmony with this position[7]. And this being so, the importance of the deviations of the priestly code from the standard of *Deuteronomy* becomes the measure of our confidence that the former, when its turn came, cannot have been introduced by a side wind, but must have been proclaimed to the people and accepted by them no less than the other. Now this did not happen before the Babylonian captivity; or at any rate, there is not a trace of it to be found either in Jeremiah and his contemporaries or in the annals of the years 621–586 B.C. That it should have taken place during the captivity is in itself highly improbable, and is contradicted by the literature of the period, and especially by the prophecies of Ezekiel[8]. The accounts of the early years after the return from Babylon (536 B.C.) are, in like manner, absolutely silent as to the introduction of the priestly law, while the writings of Haggai and Zechariah (i.–viii.) bear evidence of its non-existence[9]. It is not till we come to *Neh.* viii.–x. (in which Ezra and Nehemiah both appear upon the stage, and which must therefore refer to 444 B.C. or one of the years immediately following), that we find what we want. The law which the narrative represents as read out and ultimately (x. 1 sqq.) accepted by the representatives of the people, is no other than the priestly legislation. As to this there cannot be a moment's doubt[10]. But we have still to determine whether the legislation in question had reached its present dimensions at that period, and also whether, when Ezra read it, it was already united with the deuteronomic code and the still earlier prophetic matter. Certain traits in the narrative itself, together with other historical notices, lead us to answer both questions, but the first with the greater confidence, in the negative[11].

The trustworthiness of *Neh.* viii.–x., which is here assumed, [216] has recently been called in question, chiefly on the ground that we owe the narrative to the Chronicler, who goes to work with the utmost freedom and is very untrustworthy, more especially when, as here, he is describing religious assemblies and ceremonies[12]. But although the books of *Ezra* and *Nehemiah,* including *Neh.* viii.–x., were doubtless brought into their present form by the Chronicler, he commanded older materials for his compilation, some of which were accounts contemporary with the events themselves. Such an account he must have followed throughout, and generally reproduced literally, in *Neh.* viii.–x. The supposition that he composed these chapters independently, or actually invented the scenes they sketch, is in violent opposition to their contents[13].

[7] Cf. § 10, n. 15, 17, where it is shown that neither the prophets of the eighth century, nor even Jeremiah and his contemporaries, were acquainted with the priestly laws and narratives; n. 24, 25, from which it appears that the author of *Kings* had no knowledge of P, and cannot therefore have included it within his meaning in 2 *Kings* xxii. sq.; § 11, *passim*, where we have seen that the existence of P's precepts, especially where they deviate from D, is unsupported by a single fact of history in the pre-exilian ages. When combined with the arguments for identifying Hilkiah's book of law with D, and with nothing else (n. 3–6), all these facts make it perfectly evident that in 621 B.C. the introduction of the priestly law was still in the future.

[8] Cf. § 10, n. 10–12. However simple it may seem to explain Ezekiel's affinity with P[1] and P[2] by making the prophet dependent upon the priestly authors, we find that in point of fact this view is utterly untenable, and we are forced to deny all knowledge of their laws and narratives to him. For it is only so that we can understand his setting down, in xl.–xlviii., his own regulations of the very matters which the priestly legislators also deal with—the arrangements of the sanctuary, the sacred utensils, the qualifications for assuming the priestly office, the privileges and duties of the priests, the festivals, the partition of the land, the territory of the sanctuary and its servants. Were his ordinances capable of being interpreted as a modification of the precepts in P, in view of the altered circumstances, they might be considered in some degree intelligible, however strange. But this is not really the case. See, provisionally, § 11, n. 12, 14, 17, 20, 24, and further, § 15.

[9] Cf. § 10, n. 8 (on Haggai and Zechariah i.–viii.). The fortunes of the

returned exiles are but imperfectly known to us. But *Ezr.* i. sqq., and the description of their religious condition in *Ezr.* vii. sqq., give us anything but the impression that a new era of legislation had broken during the years 536–458 B.C. The Jewish community was evidently feeding in the old pastures—and finding no support for zeal and inspiration in them.

¹⁰ The precepts on the celebration of the feast of tabernacles, which, accord- [217] ing to *Neh.* viii. 13–18, were first made known by Ezra, and were subsequently observed by the people, are found in *Lev.* xxiii. 40 43 ; and the extension of the festal period to eight days, deviating from *Deut.* xvi. 13–15, appears in *Lev.* xxiii. 39 (cf. *Neh.* viii. 18). The obligations undertaken by the signatories of the act of covenant in *Neh.* x. 30–40 [29–39] are those imposed by P. This is specially noteworthy with respect to the observance of the sabbath rest and the sabbatical year (*v.* 32 [31]); the contributions to meet the cost of the shew-bread and the daily and other sacrifices (*v.* 34 [33]) ; the offering of the firstlings, including the first-born of man and beast, and tithes of the produce of the land, to the Levites, who are to yield a tithe in their turn to the priests (*v.* 36–40 [35–39]). The occasional deviations from the priestly law in its present form (§ 11, n. 3 ; 15, n. 30) certainly demand an explanation, but they do not prejudice the general agreement. This agreement is most conspicuous in *v.* 36–40 [35–39], which deviates from *Deut.* xviii. 1 sqq.; xiv. 22–29; xv. 19–23, while agreeing with *Num.* xviii. On *v.* 31 [30], where all marriages with heathens are condemned, cf. Smend, *Die Listen der Bücher Esra und Nehemia,* p. 5 sq. The prohibition of *connubium* with the Canaanites, to which Ezra and Nehemiah must have appealed in justification of their exclusive policy, occurred in the older laws (*Ex.* xxxiv. 12–16; *Deut.* vii. 1 sqq.), and is both assumed and repeated in P (*Num.* xxxiii. 51–56 ; *Lev.* xviii., xx.).

¹¹ See § 11, n. 3, and especially § 15, n. 30. Our further inquiry will embrace the question whether P had been welded with the older laws and narratives when Ezra read out the Tora (§ 15, n. 25). It is answered in the affirmative in my *Godsdienst,* ii. 134 sqq. [*Rel. Isr.*, ii. 229 sqq.]; and in the negative by Reuss, *L'histoire sainte et la Loi,* Introduction, p. 256 sqq.

¹² In my *Godsdienst,* ii. 198–201 [*Rel. Isr.*, ii. 286–291], I tried to correct the one-sided and partially erroneous view of *Neh.* viii.–x., which I had myself advanced in the first edition of this work (i. 347–352). Since then the trustworthiness of this passage has been attacked by Colenso, *Pentateuch,* vii. 423–430, and defended by Wellhausen in Bleek's *Einl.,* p. 268, n. 1 ; and *Geschichte,* 1st ed. i. 433.

¹³ *Neh.* viii.–x. deserves special treatment on its own account, but I must content myself at present with showing that the chapters cannot be regarded as the free composition of the Chronicler, but must have been derived by him from some older and, on the whole, trustworthy document. This seems obvious at the outset from the fact pointed out in § 11, n. 2–4 (cf. n. 10, above), that agreement with P, which is unqualified in the Chronicler, is accompanied by deviations in *Neh.* viii.–x., as in other passages borrowed by the Chronicler from his sources. The force of this argument will come out more clearly if we illustrate a few branches of it separately. Can we suppose that the writer

who shows his acquaintance with *Ex.* xxx. 11–16 in 2 *Chron.* xxiv. 6, 9, would
ignore the precept in *Neh.* x. 33 [32], and substitute a voluntary engagement
on the part of the people to contribute a smaller yearly sum ? or that the
author of 2 *Chron.* xxxi. 5, 6 (where tithes of cattle are paid), should mention
[218] tithes of corn, new wine and oil alone in *Neh.* x. 36–40 [35–39] ? Add to this
that the writer (unquestionably the Chronicler himself), who tells us, in *Ezr.*
iii. 4, that the exiles, on their return to Judæa, immediately 'celebrated the
feast of tabernacles a c c o r d i n g t o w h a t i s w r i t t e n,' can hardly be identical
with the author of *Neh.* viii. 13–17 ; and that the distinction between Levites
on the one hand, and singers and porters on the other, which appears in *Neh.*
x. 40 [39], is not only foreign to the Chronicler's ideas, but is expressly denied
by him in his picture of David's regulation of the cultus (1 *Chron.* xxii. sqq.).
—Against this C o l e n s o (*ibid.*, and Appendix, p. 74–77) urges the l a n g u a g e
of *Neh.* viii.–x., which seems to him to indicate the Chronicler as author. But
this is a mistake. No doubt there is a comparatively close agreement in
vocabulary and style between the two writers, but this is adequately explained
by the short space of time that separated them, and also by the freedom
which the Chronicler may occasionally have allowed himself in reproducing
the work of his predecessor. The agreement itself, however, is far from continuous or complete. In purity of language and Hebrew construction, *Neh.*
viii.–x. appears to me to be far superior to the passages invented and composed
by the Chronicler himself.

W e l l h a u s e n (*ibid.*) bases his proof that the Chronicler borrowed *Neh.*
viii.–x. from some other source exclusively upon a comparison between *Ezr.*
ii., iii. 1, and *Neh.* vii., viii. 1[a]. The Chronicler takes the list of returning
exiles in the former passage from *Neh.* vii., and lets the beginning of the narrative in *Neh.* viii.–x. follow immediately upon it (*Ezr.* iii. 1 = *Neh.* vii. 73[b] ;
viii. 1[a]) ; in the work that lay before him, therefore, he must have found *Neh.*
(i.–vi.) vii. and viii.–x. in their present order, and therefore he cannot himself have been the author of viii.–x. This is perfectly sound, and retains its
force even if W e l l h a u s e n' s conjecture as to the character and antiquity
of the document in question be regarded as inadmissible or as too hazardous.

Taken in connection with our previous investigation of the
chronological succession of the several elements of the Hexateuch (§ 9), these accounts of Josiah's and Ezra's reformations
lead to the following results :

The 'prophetic' elements, as we have already seen, are in
general pre-deuteronomic, and we now perceive that this
involves their being earlier than 621 B. C. It is highly
probable, on various grounds, that their union with D had
taken place before the further incorporation of P could in any
way be contemplated[14]. Though we have not discovered

when this union (JE + D) took place, we have seen that it cannot be the work of D¹ himself (§ 7, n. 13 sqq.). The 'prophetic' passages, then, remained independent during a longer or shorter period subsequent to 621 B.C., and we cannot be sure that they underwent no expansion or modification [219] in the course of it. We must keep this in mind in the sequel of our inquiry (§ 13).

The length of the deuteronomic period, which begins in the year 621 B.C., and which called the additions to D¹ into existence, cannot yet be determined. All we can say is that it extended beyond the beginning of the Babylonian captivity (§ 7, n. 13 sqq.). This period covers not only the activity of D¹'s successors, but the combination of *Deuteronomy*, as expanded by them, with the 'prophetic' elements (§ 14).

In the year of Ezra's reformation, 444 B.C. or shortly afterwards, the priestly code,—accompanied of course by the historical framework from which it cannot be severed,—existed a s a b o o k o f l a w. Its history therefore naturally falls into two periods. During the first, from . . . to 444 B.C., Ezra's law-book was being prepared and put into the form in which he read it. The second period, from 444 to . . . B.C., covers the further recension and expansion of the book. The union of this work with the deuteronomico-prophetic elements that had already been welded into a single whole is placed in the first period by some, and in the second by others (cf. n. 11). In the natural course of our investigation of the history of P we shall see which hypothesis is the more probable (§ 15). The way in which this union was effected and our present Hexateuch brought into existence will still remain as the subject of further inquiry (§ 16).

[14] The long period that separates D¹ and his successors from Ezra leaves time enough and to spare for a process of amalgamation, which the form of *Deuteronomy* itself seemed to challenge. But besides this, we have already

seen that the deuteronomic recension of the Hexateuch only extends to the prophetic elements (§ 7, n. 28), which is a direct indication that D and JE were once united, without P. We shall meet, in the course of our investigation, with still further proofs that P was incorporated into or interwoven with a combined D + JE.

[220] § 13. Continuation. B. *The origin and compilation of the 'prophetic' elements of the Hexateuch.*

Speaking generally, and without prejudice to the possibility of a partial expansion at a later date,—perhaps on a considerable scale,—the 'prophetic' elements are prae-deuteronomic, i.e. earlier than the year 621 B.C. (§ 12). The *terminus a quo* of their origin is the ninth century before our era, and, more closely yet, the second half of that century. The prophetic literature, in the narrower sense, does not begin before the eighth century ; and it would seem probable at the outset that the historiography, if older at all, is at any rate not much older[1]. The literary characteristics of the ' prophetic ' passages point to the same period. The poetical treatment of Israel's history is already behind them, and the germs of historical research are apparent[2]. But the chief consideration that forbids us to assign a higher antiquity to the ' prophetic ' narratives is based on their contents. The sagas about the patriarchs, the exodus, and the conquest, presuppose the unity of the people (which only came into existence with and by means of the monarchy) as a long-accomplished fact which had come to dominate the whole conception of the past completely[3].

[1] I assume that we possess no more ancient prophecies than those of Amos, the contemporary of Jeroboam II., and that *Isaiah* xv., xvi. must be referred to the same reign. The fact that the earlier prophets, as far as we can tell, did not appeal to writing, finds its most natural explanation in the supposition that in their time Israelitish literature was in its infancy, if it existed at all.

[2] Cf. § 4, n. 4–7. The references there discussed occur in ' prophetic ' narratives, in which are also imbedded the poetical fragments of which no

sources are indicated, such as *Gen.* iv. 23, 24; xlix. 1–27; *Ex.* xv. 1–19; *Num.* xxi. 17, 18, 27–29; *Deut.* xxxii. 1–43; xxxiii. No doubt some of these narratives might have been contemporary with the songs, or at least with collections such as 'Sepher milchamôth Yahwè' and 'Sepher hayyashár;' but this is not probable *a priori*, and is contradicted by the contents of the narratives themselves, of which more will be said in n. 3.

³ Cf. § 4, n. 16–21, where the narratives of the Hexateuch are dealt with as a whole; but with the needful restrictions, the remarks are applicable to the 'prophetic' passages also; for they too start from the unhistorical assumption of Israel's national unity at the time of the deliver- [221] ance from Egypt and the settlement in Canaan, and so cannot have been written till the facts upon which this conception was based had not only occurred but had *settled*, as it were, so as to be able to bear a superstructure. This necessitates the lapse of at least two centuries from the union of the tribes. The same may be said of the stories of the patriarchs. The succession of Abraham, Isaac, Jacob-Israel, and his twelve sons, is completely established, and the authors agree even as to the side branches, Lot (Moab and Ammon), Ishmael, and Esau-Edom; cf. *Genesis* and *Num.* xx. 14–21; xxi. 13 sqq. The several sagas were probably of local origin. For example, Isaac belongs originally to Beërshéba, and Jacob to Bethel. The welding process cannot have begun till the national unity was established; and it must have reached its ultimate completeness when the stories out of which *Gen.* xii. sqq. is worked up and compiled were written. The same conclusion is indicated by the details further discussed in n. 15.

To determine the date of the writings from which, as we have seen (§ 8), the 'prophetic' elements of the Hexateuch are largely drawn, is a task beset with no small difficulties. The facts we have to go upon are comparatively few and are often ambiguous. And sometimes, too, it is doubtful whether the evidence refers to the original narratives themselves or to the more or less modified form in which they have come down to us. We must therefore be on our guard against too hasty conclusions, and must be content, when the circumstances require it, with a more or less vague result.

The external evidence of the date of the 'prophetic' elements—excluding *Deuteronomy*, to which we shall return— is scanty and inconclusive. Positive proof that A m o s was acquainted with the narratives of E and J is not forthcoming. The particulars referred to by H o s e a occur in narratives derived from J (*Hos.* ix. 10; xii. 4, 5, 13 [3, 4, 12]).

Isaiah (x. 24–26; xi. 11, 15 sq.; xii.) presupposes some such account of Israel's deliverance from Egypt as we possess in *Ex.* i. sqq.; and elsewhere (iii. 9), it would seem, the Yahwistic account of the fall of Sodom (*Gen.* xix. 4 sq.). [222] The author of *Mic.* vi. 4 sq. was acquainted with *Num.* xxii. 2 –xxiv., presumably in nearly the present form. Later citations only confirm what is established on other grounds, and may therefore be passed over here. There are large portions of the Hexateuch which are never cited at all, or only cited in works dating from the exile [4].

[4] A summary of the results previously obtained (§ 10, n. 18) will secure us against neglecting any of them in the present §. *Am.* i. 11 is not necessarily dependent on *Gen.* xxvii. 40, and 'the Amorite' in ii. 9, 10 is the dweller in Canaan, not in the Transjordanic district, so the passage cannot be taken as referring to *Num.* xxi. The agreement of Amos (ii. 10; v. 25) with E (*Num.* xiii. sq.) as to the forty-years' wandering is equally far from proving his dependence on this document.—The passages in Hosea are clear. The least conclusive is ix. 10, compared with *Num.* xxv. 1–5, for the expressions used differ. That xii. 4 sq., 13 [3 sq., 12], depend upon *Gen.* xxv. 26[a]; xxvii. 43; xxix. 18 sqq.; xxxii. 25–33 [24–32], is all but certain. The words (xii. 5 [b] [4 [b]]), 'at Bethel he (Yahwè) found him (Jacob) and there spoke he with him' (read עִמּוֹ), point to an account of a theophany at Bethel after Jacob's return from Aram. Strictly speaking, the only such narrative we possess is from P[2], in *Gen.* xxxv. 9 sqq. But we have already observed, § 10, n. 17, that material foreign to P[2] is embedded in this passage, especially in *v.* 14, for P[2] nowhere else mentions the maççéba, or the libation by which it is here consecrated. Apparently, then, P[2]'s account is expanded here by R, not with original matter, however, but with extracts from JE, in which latter surely something more was said of Jacob's second stay at Bethel than simply that he built an altar there (xxxv. 7; cf. xxviii. 10–22; xxxv. 1–4). We may now gather from *Hos.* xii. 5 [b] [4 [b]] that this further account was originally contained in that same document which the prophet follows elsewhere, viz. J. —The texts of Isaiah and the passage *Mic.* vi. 4, 5 (in the opinion of many scholars not from Micah, but from a later prophet, contemporary with Manasseh) need no comment. On the evidence from the last half-century of the kingdom of Judah, cf. § 10, n. 13, 14. This survey has brought out the fact that the prophets of this and of a still later period are wholly silent concerning Joseph, for example, and concerning Joshua's military operations. Noah and the flood are not mentioned by any prophets before Ezekiel (xiv. 14, 20) and Deutero-Isaiah (liv. 9).

It is but natural that many of the 'prophetic' narratives

should give no clue to their n a t i v e s o i l. But by far
the greater number of those which do furnish more or less
explicit indications on the subject had their origin, and were
probably committed to writing, in Northern Israel. J a c o b -
I s r a e l, who appears in *Genesis* as the ancestor of the whole
people, was originally the personification of the tribes which
ranged themselves round Ephraim[5]. In the stories about [223]
him, in *Gen.* xxvii.–l., J o s e p h, the father of Manasseh
and Ephraim, is the chief personage, and he is presented
to us, with unmistakable sympathy, as the favourite of
Yahwè, and as a model of wisdom, power, and generosity ;
while all this is rendered the more conspicuous by the freedom
with which the writers dwell on the less praiseworthy conduct
of his brothers, alike in their relations to him, and in other
respects (*Gen.* xxxiv. ; xxxv. 22 ; xxxvii. ; xxxviii. ; xlix. 2–
4, 5–7, 14 sq.). The connection between this conception of
Joseph and the mutual relations of the tribes comes out
with special clearness in *Gen.* xlviii. 8–22[6]. The accounts
of the exodus and the journey through the desert betray
no special sympathy with any one section of united Israel,
but in the narrative of the conquest it is the Ephraimite,
J o s h u a,—whose part has not been without importance,
even in the days of Moses (*Ex.* xvii. 8–13 ; xxiv. 13 ;
xxxii. 17 sqq. ; xxxiii. 11 ; *Num.* xi. 28 sqq.),—who steps
to the front (*Deut.* xxxi. 14, 15, 23 ; *Josh.* i. sqq. ; xvii. 14–
18 ; xviii. 1 sqq.; xxiv.). The localities that have derived
a consecration from the heroes or events of the olden time are
likewise situated in Northern Israel, as Bethel (*Gen.* xii. 8 ;
xiii. 3, 4 ; xxviii. 10–22 ; xxxv. 1–4, 6–8); Shechem (*Gen.* xii.
6, 7 ; xxxiii. 18–20 ; xlviii. 22 ; *Josh.* xxiv. 1 sqq., 32) ;
Gilgal (*Josh.* iv. 3, 8, 20–24 ; v. 9, 13–15); Ebal (*Deut.* xxvii.
5–7 ; *Josh.* viii. 30) ; the burial places of Joshua (*Josh.* xxiv.
30), of Eleazar (*v.* 33), of Deborah and Rachel (*Gen.* xxxv. 8,
16–20); Machanaïm, Penuel, and other Transjordanic places

(*Gen.* xxxi. 47, 49 ; xxxii. 3, 31 [2, 30] ; xxxiii. 17 ; l. 10, 11) ; or are connected with Northern Israel, like Beërshéba (*Gen.* xxi. 14, 31-33 ; xxii. 19 ; xxvi. 23, 33 ; xxviii. 10 ; xlvi. 1-5 ; cf. *Amos* v. 5 ; viii. 14). The only exception to this rule is Hebron, the place where Abraham settles (*Gen.* xiii. 18 ; cf. xiv. 13 ; xviii. 1), and where Jacob also dwells (*Gen.* xxxvii. 14) ; but the authenticity of this latter notice is much suspected [7]. The mere mention of these places would of course determine nothing as to the fatherland of the writers. But what they have to tell us about them is in most cases [224] obviously intended to consecrate and strengthen the worship of Yahwè of which they were the seats ; and this we should only expect from men who took an interest in the sanctuaries or were in the habit of visiting them, i. e. from Northern Israelites [8]. Now this rule would make the author of the texts referring to Hebron (i. e. J) a Judæan ; and many scholars have accepted the inference as sound and have found support for it in *Gen.* xxxvii. 26 sq. ; xxxviii. ; xliii. 3 sqq. ; xliv. 14-34 ; xlvi. 28 ; xlix. 8-12. But these passages are not conclusive ; for such ideas and language concerning Hebron and Judah might well arise in Northern Israel, and the texts previously cited, not a few of which belong to J, plead for the supposition that he was a Northerner [9].

[5] The juxtaposition ' Israel and Judah,' or ' Judah and Israel,' which occurs in the Old Testament *passim,* ought not to be regarded as an inaccurate expression, involving a combination of or a contrast between the whole and one of the parts. It is a reflection of the original fact. It was only in relatively later times that Judah, which is not mentioned in *Judges* v., was incorporated into Israel, thus extending the meaning of this latter name. The idea found favour in Judah itself, but it is more than probable that the narratives in which it was expressed, and by which it was perpetuated, had their origin in Ephraim and not in Judah. On *Gen.* xxxvii. 14, the solitary ' prophetic ' text which makes Jacob dwell at Hebron, see n. 7.

[6] It would be incorrect to assert that the narrators in *Genesis* exalt Joseph at the expense of his brothers, and are unfriendly to Judah. This would contradict their ever-present idea that all the tribes have sprung from a single father and on the strength of this common descent are a single people. And

moreover, both Judah (*Gen.* xxxvii. 26 sq.) and Reuben (*v.* 22, 29 sq.) attempt to rescue Joseph, and the spirit, for instance, of *Gen.* xlii. 21 sq.; xliv. 14–34; l. 15 sqq., is anything but unfriendly to the brothers. See also n. 9. Nevertheless, it remains true that Joseph alone, 'crowned of his brethren' (*Gen.* xlix. 22–26), is represented as without spot or blemish, and receives the homage of all the rest (*Gen.* xxxvii. 5–11, 19 sq.; xlii. 6, 9; l. 15 sqq.).

[7] Perhaps the mountain on which Abraham stood, prepared to offer up Isaac (*Gen.* xxii. 1 sqq.), should be added to the list of places in Northern Israel. See below, n. 29.—With respect to Beërshéba, note that although it is assigned to Judah in *Josh.* xv. 28, it properly belonged to Simeon, *Josh.* xix. 2; 1 *Chron.* iv. 28. Amos, as cited above, condemns the worship at Beër-shéba, but it is obvious from his own words that participation in it was far from exceptional amongst his contemporaries.—While J, in the texts cited above, makes Hebron Abraham's dwelling-place, E places him at Beërshéba [225] (*Gen.* xxi. 14, 33; xxii. 19), where J and E unite in fixing Isaac's abode (*Gen.* xxvi. 23 sqq.; xxviii. 10). In weighing these accounts, for our present purpose, we must remember that the writers were not free to choose whatever spots they liked. Hebron was Abraham's 'territorial cradle,' and Beërshéba Isaac's. It needs no explanation or justification, therefore, when they make the two patriarchs dwell respectively in these two places, but we have to give some account of why Abraham is transplanted to Beërshéba. See n. 9. —Jacob's dwelling at Hebron, *Gen.* xxxvii. 14 (E), is extremely strange. Shechem and Bethel, according to *Gen.* xxxiii. 18–20; xxxv. 1 sqq.; xlviii. 21 sq., are his proper homes, and in the same district we must look for his grave, *Gen.* xlvii. 29–31; l. 4 sq. (not to be confounded with P² in *Gen.* xlix. 29–33; l. 12 sq.). He might, however—in narratives of the same origin —sojourn at Beërshéba, whence he is made to spring (*Gen.* xxviii. 10); so that *Gen.* xlvi. 1–5 (E) need not surprise us, though the passage would seem more natural if Jacob did not come to Beërshéba (whence?), but was dwelling there already. The sacrificial feast and the theophany would be more appropriate at the beginning of his journey to Egypt, than at one of his halting-stations. Possibly *v.* 1 has been altered with a view to P²'s representation to be mentioned immediately. But we should not expect to find Jacob at Hebron either in E or in J. In P², on the other hand, it would seem quite natural, for there Hebron is very emphatically described as the abode of Abraham and Isaac (*Gen.* xxxv. 27), and Jacob is said to have dwelt 'in the land of his father's sojourning' (*Gen.* xxxvii. 1), while all three patriarchs are buried in the cave of Macphela at Hebron (*Gen.* xxiii.; xxv. 9, 10; xxxv. 29; xlix. 29–33; l. 12 sq.). It is natural, therefore, to suspect that in *Gen.* xxxvii. 14 the name of Hebron has been substituted for some other, under the influence of P².

[8] In this connection, note specially *Gen.* xii. 6 sq., 8; xiii. 3 sq., 18; xxi. 31, 33; xxvi. 23–25; xxviii. 18, 20–22; xxxi. 45 sqq.; xxxii. 2, 30 [1, 29]; xxxiii. 20 (on the reading cf. § 8, n. 12, p. 152); xxxv. 7; xlvi. 1–4; *Deut.* xxvii. 5–7; *Josh.* iv. 3, 8; v. 9, 13–15; viii. 30; xxiv. 26 sq. On the stage of religious development to which these passages testify, see n. 19.

9 **Dillmann** (*Genesis*, p. xii. and elsewhere) and **Stade** (*Geschichte d. V. Israel*, p. 57 sq.) agree in regarding Judæa as J's fatherland; and **Wellhausen** (*Geschichte*, 1st ed., i. p. 373 sq., and elsewhere), though less confident, adopts the same view. On the other side are de **Wette-Schrader** (p. 321 sq.) and **Reuss** (*Geschichte der heil. Schrift. A. T*s, p. 249 sqq.), and their opinion seems to me preferable. We have already noted (n. 6) that neither J nor E takes sides with any one of the tribes, or, specifically, for or against Joseph or Judah ; for both alike occupy the **Israelite** position, in the widest sense of the word. And, from that position, J, though an Ephraimite, might very well mention Hebron as Abraham's dwelling-place—for in fact he had hardly any choice in the matter, cf. n. 7—and might present Judah in a favourable or, at any rate, half favourable light. This would not prove his prepossession in Judah's favour, or his Judæan origin, unless we knew (as **Dillmann** thinks we may) that J was later than E, and was acquainted [226] with his work. In that case he must have **substituted** Hebron for Beërshéba, and, in the history of Joseph, Judah for Reuben, which could hardly be attributed to any motive but patriotism. But if, on the other hand, J is the earlier narrator (cf. infr., n. 10 sqq.), then the texts on Judah and Hebron prove nothing.—On *Gen.* xxxviii., to which these remarks do not apply, opinions differ widely. **Schrader** (p. 321) finds ' an unfavourable aspect of Judah ' displayed in it; **Reuss** (p. 250) thinks that Judah is treated with ' bitter scorn ' in the narrative; but most other scholars find a friendly disposition towards Judah in it. If I had to choose I should accept the latter view, for *v.* 26 is enough by itself to prove that the writer had not the least intention of reviling Judah. The fact simply is that he took a lively interest in this tribe, and was acquainted with the sagas in which its history and the jealousies of its very heterogeneous elements were reflected. But this is as easy to understand in a Northern Israelite, possibly a neighbour of Judah, as in a Judæan. *Gen.* xxxviii., therefore, breaks down, like the other passages, when appealed to in proof of the Judæan origin of J's work. The phenomena, then, which plead for Northern Israel retain their full significance ; and we must add that the literary merit of J's narratives, and the freedom and robustness of spirit which they indicate, suit Israel far better than Judah. See more on this in n. 23.—As to E's fatherland there is hardly any difference of opinion. Almost everything combines to stamp him as an Ephraimite, and all that appears to weigh in the other scale admits, as we shall see (n. 25 sq.), of an explanation that removes all serious difficulty. If E is really later than J (n. 10 sqq.), then the removal of Abraham from Hebron to Beërshéba, and the substitution of Reuben for Judah (*Gen.* xxxvii. 22, 29 sq.; xlii. 21 sq., 37), are additional proofs of his sympathies with Northern Israel.

In attempting to determine the r e l a t i v e a n t i q u i t y of the ' prophetic ' narratives we may pursue three methods. We may (1) compare the more or less closely parallel narratives, and endeavour to discover which are the earlier ; (2)

examine and weigh the references to historical events which
occur in some of the narratives ; (3) test the religious and
moral ideas reflected in the stories by those of the prophets
whose dates we know. In the nature of the case we shall find
that the three lines of research sometimes converge, and that
in a great many cases no one of them leads to any certainty.

(1) M u t u a l c o m p a r i s o n often yields no definite
solution of the question of priority ; for the points of difference are sometimes unimportant or susceptible of more than
one explanation. This is the case, for instance, with the
parallel accounts of Joseph and his brothers (*Gen.* xxxvii., [227]
xxxix. sqq.) and the release from Egyptian slavery (*Ex.*
i. sqq.) [10]. On the other hand, strong probability, if not
certainty, supports the originality of *Gen.* ii. 4^b–iii. ; iv. 16^b–
24 ; xi. 1–9, as against vi. 5–viii. and x. ; of *Gen.* ix. 20–27,
as against the same vi. 5–viii. and x. ; of *Gen.* xvi. 2, 4–14,
as against xxi. 9 19 ; of *Gen.* xxvi. 6–12, as against xx. and
xii. 10–20 ; of *Gen.* xxvi. 25^b–33, as against xxi. 22–31 ; of
Gen. xxx. 14–16, as against *v.* 17, 18, and 21–23 ; of *Gen.*
xxx. 28–43, as against xxxi. 4–13 [11]. In *Num.* xxii. 2–xxiv.
we have not two stories running parallel ; but xxii. 22–34
preserves a fragment of an account of Balaam that appears to
be older than the redaction we now possess, and may therefore
be regarded as its original. Similar fragments of earlier and
more original narratives may also be traced here and there in
the book of J o s h u a, especially in vi., viii., and ix [12]. The
far sharper contrast which some scholars have discovered
between two representations of the conquest of the Transjordanic district, now woven together in *Num.* xxi. sqq., is not
really there [13]. Nor can it be allowed that the accounts of
Joshua as leader of the people at the conquest of Canaan are
balanced by another representation, in another document of the
Hexateuch, in which Joshua does not appear [14].

[10] On the points of difference between E and J in *Gen.* xxxvii., xxxix. sqq.,

see § 8, n. 5. The priority of neither can really be established. We may ask, however, whether the round-about way in which the author of xxxix. brings Joseph into prison does not mark him as later than the writer of xxxvii. 36, especially since the chapter serves to throw Joseph's virtue and the favour in which he stood with Yahwè into so strong a light. Cf. n. 26.—The comparison of E and J in *Ex.* i sqq. likewise leaves the question of priority open. The essential agreement of the two becomes all the more striking when we note the divergence between them and P² (which appears to be later) with reference alike to the demands made by Moses and to the plagues (§ 9, n. 11).

¹¹ On the whole subject-matter of this note, cf. Wellhausen, *Geschichte*, 1st ed., p. 370 sqq., with whom I agree in many points. My reasons in each case for regarding the one parallel passage as more original than the other are briefly as follows :—

[228]   *Gen.* ii. 4ᵇ-iii. ; iv. 16ᵇ-24; xi. 1-9, belong to each other, and differ from *Gen.* vi. 5-viii. in knowing nothing of a flood. They must therefore be much older than the last-named narrative, the contents of which could not have been either unknown or intentionally ignored, had it existed. As a matter of fact, *Gen.* vi. 5-viii. follows the Assyrio-Babylonian saga, which must of course have become known in Israel at some definite period, so that the earlier writer may very well have been ignorant of it. It agrees with this view that we find the geographical knowledge of the author of the story of Paradise, *Gen.* ii. 10-14, extremely primitive, whereas the horizon of the author of the table of nations, *Gen.* x., who is also the writer of *Gen.* vi. 5-viii., is notably wider. In the same way iv. 1-16ᵃ, 25, 26, which lead up to the account of the flood or are connected with it, are later than ii. 4ᵇ-iii. ; iv. 16ᵇ-24, and thus confirm the conclusion to which we have been led. Cf. Budde, *Die bibl. Urgeschichte*, passim ; and below, n. 26.

Gen. ix. 20-27. The triad, Shem, Japheth, Canaan, which characterised this pericope in its original form, must assuredly be older than the received Shem, Ham, and Japheth, which a later editor introduces by means of חם אבי (*v.* 22, cf. also *v.* 18ᵇ). For the latter triad, which is connected with Noah, the ancestor of the new race of man, may easily have been developed out of the former, whereas it is impossible to imagine how Canaan could have been made into one of the three sons of this tribe-father.

Gen. xvi. 1-14 (except *v.* 1, 3, which are P²'s) and xxi. 9-19 are doublets, in spite of the difference in the circumstances. The names of Hagar and Ishmael are the immediate occasion of the legend, and in this respect xvi. keeps closest to the source, not only in *v.* 11, but in making Hagar take flight instead of being expelled. Ch. xvi., then, is nearest the origin. Moreover, Abraham is much gentler and nobler in xxi. 11, 12 than in xvi. 6 ; the angelophany in xxi. 17 ('out of heaven') is not so naïvely materialistic as in xvi. 7 ('and the angel of Yahwè found her,' etc.), and, finally, the well, only introduced in xvi. 7 for the sake of the name to be given it in *v.* 14, has become an essential part of the narrative in xxi.

Gen. xxvi. 6-12, xx., and xii. 10-20, betray dependence on one side or the other, even in the choice of words and the forms of expression. Cf. המקום,

xxvi. 7; xx. 11; אחותי הוא, xxvi. 7; xx. 5; xii. 19; הרג, xxvi. 7; xx. 4; xii. 12; מה־זאת עשית לנו, xxvi. 10; xx. 9; xii. 18; compare also the description of Isaac's wealth, xxvi. 14, with xx. 14; xii. 16; and further, note גור in xx. 1; xii. 10 (xxvi. 3); and compare מובת־מראה, xxvi. 7, with יפת־מ', xii. 11. But no inferences as to priority can be drawn from these parallels. Nor do the contents of the three narratives force any conclusion upon us. Ch. xii. 10-20 has least claim to rank as the original; for the Pharaoh is evidently a super-lative form of the king of Gerar, and the representation of Abram's conduct and Yahwè's intervention (*v.* 13, 16, 17) is a far from pleasing exaggeration of the corresponding features of the other two stories. It is harder to decide between xxvi. 6-12 and xx. The last-named has a special and antique flavour, in *v.* 3-7, 16, for example. But on the other hand it is made to serve for Abraham's glorification, and that too in his character of prophet (*v.* 7, 17), [229] and may easily be taken as an elaboration of the theme supplied by xxvi., whereas one does not see how the reverse process could have produced the far simpler representation of xxvi. out of xx. It is easier to suppose that a threatening danger developed into an actual one, averted by divine inter-vention, than that the latter shrank down into the former. The play on the name of Isaac, too, xxvi. 8, seems to be an original trait.

Gen. xxvi. 25ᵇ-33 and xxi. 22-31, again, have certain expressions in common; compare xxvi. 28 with xxi. 22, 27; xxvi. 29 with xxi. 23; xxvi. 32 with xxi. 30. In this case there can be no question as to the original identity of the two stories. Now xxvi. is far simpler than xxi. In the latter the covenant extends to the posterity of either party (*v.* 23), the oath is considered as an oath of purgation (*v.* 25 sqq.), and, to complete the explanation of the name Beërshéba, the seven lambs are introduced (*v.* 28 sqq.). What could have induced the author of xxvi. to drop this trait? On the other hand, what more natural than to add it? Isaac, not Abraham, as the protagonist, pleads for the originality of xxvi. 25ᵇ-33, and also for that of xxvi. 6-12 as against xx.; for Beërshéba is Isaac's 'cradle,' and the principle, 'to him that hath shall be given,' would easily explain the transference to Abraham of sagas concerning him.

Gen. xxx. 14-16 explains Rachel's pregnancy (and Joseph's birth) by Reuben's dudaïm, and the name of Issachar by Leah's cession of the dudaïm to Rachel. In comparison with this, *v.* 17 sq. (another and less offensive etymo-logy of Issachar) and *v.* 22 sq. (Joseph a gift of Elohîm) are less spontaneous and further removed from the popular beliefs.

Gen. xxx. 28-43 and xxxi. 4-13 explain Jacob's great wealth by his own cunning and by the care of Elohîm respectively. The former is in perfect harmony with the uniform representation of Jacob's character. Can the latter be anything but an ethico-religious improvement upon it? For observe that the mutual agreement of the two passages forbids us to regard them as inde-pendent, so that one must in any case be a transformation of the other.

¹² On *Num.* xxii. 2-xxiv. see § 8, n. 14, p. 154, and the essay there referred to. That xxii. 22-34 gives us a fragment of an older Balaam-legend is not susceptible of rigorous demonstration, but it is highly probable: the Balaam

who sets out without consulting Yahwè, or perhaps against his orders, and is
then opposed by the angel, seems to me to have an antique flavour, in keeping
with the introduction of the speaking ass, and to be more primitive than the
Balaam who is determined from the first to submit to God's command (xxii. 8),
in spite of his wish to comply with Balak's proposal.—On *Josh.* vi., viii., ix.
see § 8, n. 20. The higher antiquity of the very fragmentary narratives preserved in these chapters, as compared with the accounts into which they are
woven, appears clearly enough from their greater simplicity. This argument is
specially conclusive in vi. The priests, the continuous trumpet-blast, and the
seven circuits on the seventh day can only be later improvements and
embellishments.

[230]   [13] The opinion here rejected is upheld by M e y e r in the essay referred to in
§ 8, n. 14, and by S t a d e, *Geschichte d. V. Israel*, p. 113 sqq., and is combated in *Th. Tijdschr.*, xviii. 516–532. According to M e y e r and S t a d e, E's
narrative in *Num.* xxi. 21–31 is a later invention, written with a purpose;
the older accounts knowing nothing of an A m o r i t e kingdom in the Transjordanic district, while in *Num.* xxi. 18^b–20 it is the M o a b i t e territory
into which Israel forces his way, and in *Num.* xxv. 1–5 he dwells at Shittim
with M o a b i t e s; the same version of the facts reappearing in one of the component elements of *Num.* xxii. 2–xxiv. But all this cannot be allowed. On
the relation of *Num.* xxi. 21–31 to *v.* 12–20, see above, § 8, n. 14. If the view
there taken be correct, then it does not follow from *v.* 18^b–20 that the author
knew of no Amorite kingdom; for, his *itinerarium* being a mere list of the
places of encampment, he would have no occasion to mention it in any case.
Thus in *Num.* xxxiii. 1–49, the later origin of which is unquestioned by M e y e r
and S t a d e, no mention is made of Sihon. The names שדה מואב and
"מ ערבות, by which Israel's place of encampment beyond the Jordan is indicated, simply show that this district was originally Moabitish territory, and do
not exclude the supposition that it was ruled by an Amorite king at the time;
and accordingly these designations are used by D and P, who certainly knew
all about the Amorite kingdom across the Jordan. Nor is *Num.* xxv. 1–5
inconsistent with the existence of that kingdom, for we are not to suppose
that the Amorite invaders expelled or exterminated the people of the land
they conquered. On *Num.* xxii. 2–xxiv., in connection with this controversy,
see *Th. Tijdschr.*, xviii. 528-532.—M e y e r's proofs, as we have seen, turn
out to be inconclusive; and the objections to his view are overwhelming.
First of all comes the ancient poem in *Num.* xxi. 27–30. M e y e r is compelled to strike out the words למלך אמרי סיחון (*v.* 29^b) as a gloss, in spite
of their poetical form, and to content himself with a very unsatisfactory explanation of the whole fragment (p. 130 sq.); whereas the poem as it stands is
admirably suited to confirm the main fact in E's account, which is further
supported by the numerous parallel passages mentioning the defeat of Sihon,
king of the Amorites. Small evidential value can be assigned to the passages
of D and P, for they are entirely dependent on *Num.* xxi. 21 sqq. *Judges*
(x. 8) xi. 12–28 is of relatively ancient date (*v.* 24) and has rather more
significance, for though it presupposes *Num.* xxi. yet it adds some traits of its

own (*v.* 16, 17, 25), and is therefore something more than a mere copy. But I lay chief stress on 1 *Kings* iv. 19, where 'the land of Gilead' is described as 'the land of Sihon, king of the Amorites, and of Og, king of Bashan.' Even if we felt compelled to read 'King of Heshbon' with the LXX., the epithet, which is very different from 'King of Moab,' would still prove that when the list of Solomon's officers, *v.* 7-19, was drawn up, it was an accepted fact that the Transjordanic region had been conquered from a non-Moabite prince. The idea, then, cannot have been a late invention directed against the Moabites—with whom, moreover, Israel surely never waged a paper war. It is one thing to make apologetic use of such a fact as Israel's respect of Moab's frontier, and quite another thing to invent it for polemical purposes.—There is no proof, therefore, that J's representation of the events in the Trans-jordanic district was remote from that of E and much more historical and ancient.

[14] Meyer's assertion 'that the Yahwist (=J) knows nothing of Joshua' [231] (p. 133 sqq.) is in my opinion rash and unsubstantiated. He finds the yahwistic account of the conquest in *Judges* i.; ii. 1-5, when purged of later additions. Between the conquest of Jericho (assumed in i. 16), and the exploits of the tribes narrated in i., he thinks it probable that the treaty with the Gibeonites stood, and finds a few fragments of J's account of it in *Josh.* ix. (cf. § 8, n. 20), whereas in all the rest of the book of Joshua he believes there is not a single letter taken from J. From this it would follow that the person and work of Joshua are pure inventions, since nothing else could explain J's silence. But this result is wholly inadmissible. The Joshua of the book that bears his name, the leader of the united Israel, the conqueror and divider of all Canaan is certainly not a historical character, but neither is he a pure creation out of nothing. The accounts of him show that in tradition and literature his work gradually assumed grander dimensions and his person greater significance. The deuteronomic redactor goes further than his predecessors. *Josh.* xxiv. is simpler than i.–xii.; and in *Josh.* xvii. 14-18 far more is ascribed to the initiative and efforts of the several tribes than elsewhere in the book. The analogy of these phenomena might naturally lead us to expect a narrative in which Joshua appeared simply as an Ephraimite hero, but does not give the least suggestion that in the earliest narratives he did not appear at all. Yet it is this expectation that dominates Meyer's criticism. Remove it and there is no reason left for denying all share in the book of *Joshua* to J, or assuming a contrast here between J and E far sharper than they display elsewhere in the Hexateuch.

(2) References to historical facts, such as might give a clue to the dates of composition, are extremely rare in the 'prophetic' narratives of the Hexateuch. In *Gen.* ix. 20–27 the subjection of the Canaanites to Israel, i. e. the reign of Solomon, is presupposed. The author of *Gen.* xxvii. 29,

39 sq. is not only familiar with David's victories over the
Edomites, but also with the rebellion of the latter under
Solomon and their revolt against Jehoram ben Jehoshaphat.
The writer of *Gen.* xxxi. 44 sqq. in all probability had in
view the wars of the Aramæans and Israelites for the possession of the Transjordanic district. *Ex.* xv. 17[b] was written
some considerable time after the building of Solomon's
temple; *Num.* xxiv. 7 after the institution of the monarchy;
v. 17 sq. after David's successful wars against Israel's neighbours; *v.* 22–24 in the Assyrian period, presumably not
[232] earlier than the seventh century B.C. Finally, *Josh.* vi. 26
cannot have been written till the rebuilding of the walls
of Jericho, in Ahab's reign, had long been a thing of the
past [15].

The poetic passages, some of which have been mentioned
already, give pretty clear indications as a rule of the period in
which they arose. 'The blessing of Jacob,' *Gen.* xlix. 1–27,
combines elements of different dates, some of which cannot
have been written until after the establishment of the
monarchy, or even till after the beginning of the wars between
the Aramæans and the kingdom of Ephraim. 'The blessing
of Moses,' *Deut.* xxxiii., is later than *Gen.* xlix. 1–27, and
cannot have been written till sometime in the reign of
Jeroboam II., at earliest. 'The song of Moses,' *Deut.* xxxii.
1–43, appears to belong to the Chaldæan period [16]. But the
value of these chronological indications is impaired by our
uncertainty as to the history of the i n c o r p o r a t i o n of
these poems into the Hexateuch. The supposition that they
were not inserted till long after their composition, though not
always likely, may well be defended in some cases [17].

---

[15] The date assigned to *Gen.* ix. 20–27 is elaborately defended by B u d d e
(op. cit., p. 506 sqq.), who very justly takes 1 *Kings* ix. 20 sq. as his point of
departure, and at the same time shows that the slavery of the Gibeonites,
which is ascribed to an ordinance of Joshua in *Josh.* ix. 21 sqq., did not really

begin till the time of Solomon. In Saul's day they were still independent (2 *Sam.* xxi. 1-14), and it must have been long after Solomon that the idea sprang up of their having been slaves of the temple from the beginning.— Israel's supremacy over Edom dates from the events recorded in 2 *Sam.* viii. 13, 14, for 1 *Sam.* xiv. 47 is too vague to be built upon. An attempt was made to throw off the yoke under Solomon (1 *Kings* xi. 14-16); it was successfully repeated under Jehoram (2 *Kings* viii. 20-22); and it was not punished till the time of Amaziah (2 *Kings* xiv. 7, 10). Knowing what we do of the date of the 'prophetic' narratives, we shall not hesitate to regard the events under Jehoram at any rate as already known to the author of *Gen.* xxvii. 40. —The inference from *Gen.* xxxi. 44 sqq. speaks for itself, when once we have learned that the relations of tribes and peoples are presented to us in *Genesis* in the form of family history. Note especially *v.* 51 sq. The wars with Aram for the possession of the Transjordanic district began, so far as we know, under Ahab (1 *Kings* xx., xxii.), and were carried on thenceforth almost without intermission.—Since the settlement of Israel in Canaan is assumed throughout *Ex.* xv. 1-18 (*v.* 13, 16, 17), the ascription of the song to Moses in *v.* 1 ª cannot be accepted. Equally unequivocal is *v.* 17 ᵇ: 'the sanctuary of the Lord, established by your hands' can be no other than the temple of Jerusalem; nor would it rise immediately after its foundation to the commanding position it occupies here. It is possible, however, with Wellhausen, *Prolegomena*, [233] p. 23 n. [22 n.], to take *v.* 17 ᵇ as a later addition, an incorrect explanation and limitation of 'the holy dwelling-place' (*v.* 13) and 'the mount of thine inheritance, the place which Yahwè has made his dwelling' (*v.* 17ª), by which the poet may have intended the holy land in general. In that case *v.* 17 ᵇ would not indicate a later origin for the whole poem. But the question remains whether it would be possible, on other grounds, to assign a high antiquity to it. Wellhausen himself (*Prolegomena*, p. 374, n. 1 [352, n. 1]) answers in the negative, and we cannot but allow, with him and Jülicher, B, p. 125 sq., that *Ex.* xv. 20 sq. renders the preceding account of a song sung by Moses and the sons of Israel improbable, if it does not positively exclude it; and on the other hand that the tone and style of the song itself by no means support its reference to a high antiquity. Isaiah adopts *v.* 2 ª in xii. 2 ᵇ, and xii. 5 reflects *v.* 1 ᵇ. But apart from the doubts affecting the authenticity of *Isaiah* xii. (Ewald, *Propheten d. A. Bundes*, i. 459 [ii. 239 sq.]) this citation of the opening words (cf. *v.* 21) cannot pass as a conclusive proof of the existence of the whole poem.—*Num.* xxiv. 7 would be anticipated by xxiii. 21, were it clear that the 'royal shout' refers to the earthly monarchy; but the parallelism seems to show that the king in whose honour the shout is raised is the national deity Yahwè. But *Num.* xxiv. 7 is unequivocal, and *v.* 17, 18 must certainly be taken as referring to David's victories (2 *Sam.* viii. 2; x.; on 1 *Sam.* xiv. 47 see above). The much-discussed verses 22-24, which announce the deportation of the Kenites by the Assyrians and the humiliation of the latter by foes who 'come from the coast of Chittim,' transplant us to the Assyrian period, and, it would seem, to the second half of the seventh century B.C. Cf. M. M. Kalisch, *Bible Studies*, i.

285 sq., 291 sqq., and *Th. Tijdschr.*, xviii. 538 sqq.—The author of 1 *Kings* xvi. 34 was acquainted with *Josh.* vi. 26, to which he refers. Both writers regard the deaths of Hiël's sons as a judgment from Yahwè on the violation of the cherem. It is generally assumed that Hiël lost his sons during the rebuilding of Jericho, and that this, being understood as a judgment, caused the prediction to be put into Joshua's mouth. But this makes everything hang on the mere accidental coincidence of these deaths with the rebuilding of the walls of Jericho; and moreover it does not really satisfy the expressions 'lay the foundations on his first-born' and 'rear the gates on his youngest son.' Hiël, assuredly, sacrificed his two sons to avert the wrath of the deity whose possession he violated, and *Josh.* vi. 26, as it now stands, was not written till the real significance of the fact was forgotten and another explanation had to be found. Hence it follows that a considerable period must have elapsed between the rebuilding of Jericho and the date of *Josh.* vi. 26.

   16 The hypothesis that *Gen.* xlix. is a collection of proverbs, judgments, and aspirations of various dates concerning the tribes, worked up into a single whole, was first enunciated by E. Renan (*Hist. Génér. des Langues Sémitiques*, p. 111 sqq.), and was further developed by J. P. N. Land (*Disp. de carm. Jacobi*, L. B. 1857). It still appears to me to give the best account of the [234] phenomena presented by 'the blessing.' The settlement of the tribes in Canaan is presupposed throughout. But while some of the apophthegms point to the period of the Judges (*v.* 5-7, *v.* 14 sq., *v.* 16 sq.), others transplant us to a later time. Whatever interpretation be adopted of the difficult verse 10, the words on Judah, *v.* 9-12, can in any case hardly date from before David. And would Joseph be called 'the crowned of his brethren' (*v.* 26) before a king had risen from his ranks, i.e. before the foundation of the Ephraimite kingdom? If we accept the natural inference, *v.* 23 sq. must in all probability be referred to the attacks of the Aramæans and their repulse; for the words do not suit the personal fortunes of Joseph, and in any case the analogy of all the other sayings and the contents of *v.* 22, 25 would oppose any such explanation. Finally we may ask whether the division of the people into twelve tribes, or rather the union of the twelve tribes into the single Israel, is not enough in itself to prevent our making 'the blessing' older than the tenth or ninth century B.C.? Cf. also Wellhausen, *Geschichte*, 1st ed., p. 375, n. 1; Stade, *Geschichte d. V. Israel*, p. 145-173.

   On *Deut.* xxxiii. cf. K. H. Graf, *Der Segen Mose's erklärt* (1857). The monarchy has long been established, *v.* 5. Judah is separated from Israel, and aspirations towards a reunion are cherished, *v.* 7. In *v.* 17 a warlike and victorious king, sprung from Joseph,—in all probability Jeroboam II.—is referred to. The verses on Levi, *v.* 8-11, indicate a high estimate of the spiritual privileges of the tribe; even if, as we may well suspect, it was a Levite who uttered them, still we cannot place them earlier than the eighth century B.C.; and, indeed, if it were not that they are thrown into such an original form and must be judged in connection with the other sayings, they might even lead us to look for the poet in the same circles from which the Deuteronomist issued. Cf. Stade, op. cit., on this point also.

Deut. xxxii. 1–43 will be best discussed in connection with the introduction, xxxi. 16–22. See n. 30.

[17] On *Ex.* xv. 1–17 see n. 15, whence we may gather that the incorporation of this poem should not be referred to the writer of *v.* 20 sq., but to a hand which worked over both this and the other ancient accounts of the passage of the Red Sea, that is to say to JE; cf. n. 29; and in this case it throws no light on the date either of E or J.—It is uncertain to whom we owe the preservation of *Gen.* xlix. 1–27 (§ 8, n. 6). *Deut.* xxxiii. is completely detached, and might very well have been incorporated even after the final redaction of the Hexateuch, but its date gives no support or countenance to such a supposition (cf. n. 16). *Deut.* xxxii. 1–43, on the other hand, is made an integral portion of the present Hexateuch by the two-fold introduction, xxxi. 16–22, 25–30, and the postscript, xxxii. 44; and it is therefore as important in its bearing on the question of the composition of the Hexateuch as *Num.* xxii. 2–xxiv., for instance, which cannot be torn out of the context in which it occurs. See further, n. 29.

(3) Judged by the ethico-religious conceptions they [235] reflect, the 'prophetic' elements of the Hexateuch are by no means all on the same level. In the first place, we find certain passages distinguished by their close adhesion to the primitive popular beliefs, by their crudely anthropomorphic representations of the deity, and by the *naïveté* with which they bring out Israel's attitude towards the earlier inhabitants of Canaan, or give expression to Israel's national pride,—in a word, by the absence, or at any rate the feeble manifestation, of the ethico-religious spirit that breathes through the written prophecies of the eighth century [18]. In the second place, a somewhat analogous attitude towards the popular religion characterises a second series of narratives. So far from being hostile, they were evidently intended alike to purify this popular religion from the heathen practices that went along with it, and to impress it upon the hearts of their original readers [19]. In the third place, we have yet another group of narratives and laws in which the conceptions of the prophets of the eighth century B.C. are so distinctly reflected that it seems no more than natural to refer them to their age and their school [20]. And finally, there are also passages that seem rather to belong to the seventh

R

century, parallels to which, at any rate, we seek in vain in the earlier prophets [21].

Deuteronomic ideas, and the terms and expressions inseparable from them, are comparatively rare in the 'prophetic' portions of the Hexateuch. They are not altogether wanting, however, and they demand an explanation. At the close of our whole survey we shall return to them [22].

[18] Peculiar difficulties beset the comparison we are about to institute in this and the following notes. We can only make use of passages that bear unequivocal evidence of their own date, i.e. such passages as definitely fit a certain period and would really be unintelligible if referred either to an earlier or to a later epoch. Their number cannot, from the nature of the case, be great, and the impression they make on the reader, which cannot always be analysed objectively, must play an important part in their identification. In each case I shall begin by enumerating the passages in the successive books which appear to me to reflect the spirit of some definite period, and shall then touch on the chief points upon which my judgment is founded. In the first group, then, I place the following :—

[236] *Gen.* ii. 4ᵇ–iii.; iv. 1–16ᵃ, 16ᵇ–24; vi. 1–4; ix. 20–27; xi. 1–9; xviii. 1– xix. 28 (but cf. § 8, n. 4, and below, n. 21); *v.* 30–38; xxv. 21–34; xxvii. 1–45; xxxii. 25–32 [24–31]; xxxiv. (cf. § 8, n. 6); xxxviii.; *Ex.* iv. 24–26; xxiv. 1, 2, 9–11; *Num.* x. 29–32, 33–36; *Josh.* v. 2 sq., 8 sq. The passages betray themselves as præ-prophetic, or at least as unaffected by the spirit of canonical prophecy, by the anthropomorphisms of *Gen.* iii. 8, 22; iv. 14, 16ᵃ; xi. 5, 6; xviii. 20, 21; *Ex.* xxiv. 9–11; by the mythological elements in *Gen.* vi. 1–4; xxxii. 25–32 [24–31] (cf. also Studer in *Jahrb. f. prot. Theologie,* 1875, p. 536–545); *Ex.* iv. 24–26; by the identification of Yahwè with the ark in *Num.* x. 33–36; by the *naïveté* with which hatred of Moab and Ammon is expressed in *Gen.* xix. 30–38, and jealousy of Edom in *Gen.* xxv. 21–34; xxvii. 1–45, without any feeling, apparently, that the preference given to Jacob needs justification to the moral as well as to the national consciousness of the reader (cf. *Gen.* xxx. 28–43, and, in contrast, xxxi. 4–13; see above, n. 11); by their attitude towards the Canaanites, especially the condemnation of Simeon's and Levi's deed of violence and exclusiveness in the 'prophetic' factor of *Gen.* xxxiv., the juxtaposition of Shem (Israel) and Japheth (the Phœnicians? cf. Budde, op. cit., p. 338 sqq.) as the joint masters of Canaan (the original population of the inland parts) in *Gen.* ix. 20–27, the unconcerned recognition of Judah's half-Canaanitish origin in *Gen.* xxxviii.—a chapter which is marked throughout by its realism, and the absence of the ethical factor from the author's judgments no less than from the doings of his heroes; by the secular and historical interest, so to speak, which betrays itself especially in *Gen.* iv. 16ᵇ–24 (explanation of the different modes of life and the arts); *Num.* x. 29–32 (the Kenites Israel's guides during the wanderings in

the desert) ; *Josh.* v. 2 sq., 8 sq. (recognition of the Egyptian origin of circumcision and of Israel's duty to conform to the judgment of the Egyptians with respect to uncircumcision).

[19] The passages that fall under this head have already been indicated in n. 8. The constantly recurring statements that at this or that place in Canaan one of the patriarchs built an altar, planted a tree, or reared a stone,—and that, too, in honour of Yahwè,—can have no other purpose than the one suggested in the text. The authors who chronicle these particulars are warm upholders of Yahwism, but they are not puritans like Amos, for instance (cf. *Am.* iii. 14; iv. 4; v. 5; viii. 14, against Bethel, Gilgal, Beërshéba and Dan) or Hosea (iv. 15; ix. 15; x. 5, 15, against Bethel and Gilgal). Their attitude towards the maççebas (see the passages cited) deserves special notice. They do not share the superstition originally associated with them. In their eyes they are memorials of Yahwè's presence or help, or of a sacrificial feast held in his honour. But when thus regarded they appear harmless to them; just as Hosea (iii. 4; x. 1, 2) and Isaiah (xix. 19) mention them without express condemnation. In the subsequent laws, on the other hand, the maççebas are forbidden without any reservation (not only in *Ex.* xxiii. 24; xxxiv. 13; *Deut.* xii. 3, which deal specifically with the destruction of the maççebas of the Canaanites, but in *Deut.* xvi. 22 ; *Lev.* xxvi. 1, which are directed against the use of maççebas in the Yahwè-worship).

There is yet another indication that at any rate some of the ' prophetic ' writers are not altogether in line with Amos, Hosea, etc. They not only [237] tell of sacrifices and festivals held in honour of Yahwè, but also enjoin their observance; for the ' words of the covenant,' which are preserved in a later version in *Ex.* xxxiv. 10–26 (cf. n. 21), all refer to the cultus of Yahwè, and in the Book of the Covenant we find, side by side with ' the ordinances ' and the moral exhortations, certain regulations of the cultus also (*Ex.* xxii. 28–30 [29–31]; xxiii. 12, 14–19, though these last verses are under suspicion of being borrowed from *Ex.* xxxiv.). *Ex.* xiii. 3–9, 10–16 on maççôth and the consecration of the first-born, and the kindred precept in *Ex.* xii. 21–27, must also be referred to this category. Now although we have seen (§ 10, n. 3) that Amos and his successors must not be represented as condemning all sacrifices and feasts, yet they would not themselves have either regulated or enforced them ; and there is therefore a real difference in this respect between them and the writers who incorporate these ordinances.

A somewhat different view of *Gen.* xxviii. 10-22, and consequently of all the texts now under review, is put forward by Oort, *Th. Tijdschr.*, xviii. 299–301. He thinks it conceivable, not to say probable, that the legends about the sacred spots were committed to writing at a time when their claims were assailed; that is to say, not before 722 B.C., but after Hezekiah, when the idea of centralization began gradually to gain ground. But I think Beth-el and the other sanctuaries are not so much defended and maintained as exalted and commended by the writers in *Genesis*, and this might be done when the kingdom of Ephraim was still flourishing, and indeed rather then than later.

The writers, as far as we can see, never thought of the centralising policy
either way.

[20] Under the reservations expressed at the beginning of n. 18, I reckon
amongst the passages completely in their place in the eighth century, *Gen.*
xx.; xxii.; xxxv. 2–4; *Ex.* iii. 1–15; xix. 10 sqq.; xx. 1–17; xx. 23–xxiii.;
xxxii. 1 sqq.; *Num.* xxi. 4[b]–9; xxii. 2–xxiv. 19; *Josh.* xxiv—of course excluding the verses already indicated (§ 8) which were not united with or
incorporated into these pericopes till later. The following considerations support the date assigned:—

In *Gen.* xx. 7, 17 Abraham is styled 'nabi,' and great power is ascribed
to his intercession, indicating the century in which the prophets had undertaken the spiritual guidance of their people and were reverenced as Yahwè's
trusted servants. *Gen.* xviii. 17 is to some extent parallel (cf. *Amos* iii. 7),
but see n. 21.

Gen. xxii. shows how Elohim, though having the right to demand the sacrifice of children, does not actually require it, but is content with the willingness
to make it. Cf. *Mic.* vi. 6, 7.

Gen. xxxv. 2–4 makes the appearance of Elohim dependent alike on the expulsion of strange gods and on ceremonial bodily cleanness. The former
condition is developed in *Josh.* xxiv. and elaborately supported by an appeal
to Yahwè's 'holiness' and 'jealousy' (קַנָּא); the latter we come upon again
in *Ex.* xix. 10 sqq. These passages serve, in their way, the great object
pursued by the prophets from the eighth century onwards, viz. the complete
consecration of all Israel to the worship of Yahwè alone.

Ex. iii. 1–15 and, in connection therewith, the use of Elohim by the writer
[238] (E) from whom this pericope is largely derived, bear witness to reflections on
the historical development of religion which contrast rather sharply with the
unconcerned manner in which J uses the name of Yahwè from the beginning,
and even puts it upon the lips of non-Israelites. I think this indicates a period
at any rate not earlier than the eighth century. Cf. also n. 26 on *Gen.*
iv. 25 sq.

Ex. xx. 1–17. This redaction of the Decalogue has been interpolated alike
from D and from P² (§ 9, n. 2; 16, n. 12); nor is it possible now to determine
its original form with certainty, whence its date must also remain doubtful.
Now *Ex.* (xxiv. 12–14;) xxxii. 1 sqq. assumes the proclamation of some Decalogue, which might, accordingly, be assigned, together with *Ex.* xxxii. 1 sqq.,
to the eighth century, or might be brought down (together with the narrative
again), to the seventh century (vid. infra). But was this Decalogue essentially identical with the one we possess in *Ex.* xx. 1–17? If the original has
been merely expanded and in other respects left as it was, the choice between
the eighth and seventh centuries still remains perplexing, for most of the
'words' fit equally well into either. If we are to regard the writer who summarised Yahwè's commands in the Decalogue as an original and creative
author, we must place him in the eighth century; but if we are to suppose
that he merely resumed what the prophets of Yahwè had already uttered, we
must make him a contemporary of Manasseh. His ethical conception of the

service of Yahwè finds its closest analogue in *Mic.* vi. 1–vii. 6, which is in all probability a product of this latter period.

Ex. xx. 23–xxiii. In comparing the Book of the Covenant with the prophetic literature our thoughts naturally turn, not to the mishphatìm, with which the prophets hardly ever come into contact, but to the moral exhortations, some of which, however, seem to be later incorporations (§ 5, n. 1). The most important are *Ex.* xxii. 20-23 [21–24] (against the oppression of strangers, widows, and orphans) ; 24–26 [25–27] (justice and mercy to the needy); xxiii. 1–3 (against false witness and false judgment); 6–8 (against unjust sentences and bribery) ; 9 (as in xxii. 20 [21]) ; 10–12 (the sabbatical year and the sabbath, enforced on behalf of the poor and the bond-servants). Now we note at once that by far the greater number of these precepts can be paralleled from the prophets of the eighth century, especially Amos (e.g. iv. 1 sqq. ; vi. 3–6 ; viii. 4–6) and Micah (e.g. ii. 1 sq., 8 sq. ; iii. 1 sq., 9–11, and also vi. 10–12). But at the same time we must confess that they would not be the least out of place either earlier or later. The errors against which they are directed existed before the eighth century, and had still to be rebuked by Jeremiah and his contemporaries.

Ex. xxxii. 1 sqq. can only be understood as a condemnation of the established religion of Northern Israel, and at the same time of the priests connected with it, who probably traced their descent from Aaron. This condemnation is quite in the spirit of Amos (iv. 4 ; v. 5 ; viii. 14) and still more of Hosea (viii. 4–6; x. 5, 6, 15 ; xiv. 4 [3]), with whom, I need not say, Isaiah and Micah are completely at one. The command given to Moses to lead the people into Canaan (*v.* 34[b]) is followed by the words, 'and in the day of my visitation I will visit their sin upon them.' We must not ignore the possibility that the [239] writer is only expressing an expectation, but it is more natural to see in his words a reference to a punishment that had already fallen, viz. the deportation of Northern Israel in 722 B.C. According to this view the author will have lived in the reign of Hezekiah or soon after. Cf. Oort, *Th. Tijdschr.*, xviii. 295, 312 sq.

Num. xxi. 4[b]-9 must be brought into connection with 2 *Kings* xviii. 4[h]. The author of this latter was acquainted with the story in Numbers, as we see from his words ' the brazen serpent, which Moses made.' But it is very doubtful whether Hezekiah and his advisers likewise knew it. The breaking of the Nehustán seems rather to indicate that they regarded it not as a venerable and ancient symbol, but as an idol, or at any rate an image of Yahwè, on which it was their duty to execute the sentence pronounced by Isaiah (ii. 8, 19 sq. ; xxx. 22 ; xxxi. 7). To that extent the writer of *Num.* xxi. 4[b]-9 and Isaiah differ, but on the main issue they are at one, since even the former does not defend the idol or Yahwè-image, and only rescues the brazen serpent by making it an innocent symbol of Yahwè's healing power, just as the maççebas are elsewhere incorporated into Yahwism (cf. n. 19). He would scarcely have written thus after Hezekiah's treatment of the Nehustán, so that we may regard him as a precursor of Isaiah's, with whom however the latter was unacquainted or whom at any rate he declined to follow slavishly.

Num. xxii. 2–xxiv. 19. We have already seen that Balaam's blessing presupposes alike the establishment of the monarchy and the victories of David (n. 15). And we may now add that the political and military tone of the description of Israel's might and prosperity places us in the eighth century B.C., either in the reign of the second Jeroboam himself (cf. 2 *Kings* xiv. 23–29 ; xiii. 5), or in the period which still retained the memory of his warlike fame. Cf. *Th. Tijdschr.*, xviii. 537 sq. We need not be surprised, therefore, to find thoughts put into the mouth of Balaam, which we also meet with in the prophets of the eighth century. Compare *Num.* xxiii. 19 with *Hos.* xi. 9[b] (1 *Sam.* xv. 29) ; *Num.* xxiii. 23[b] with *Am.* iii. 7 (2 *Kings* xiv. 25). And moreover, the whole conception of 'the prophet' (illustrated in Balaam's person) as Yahwè's organ, bound to announce his will whether he would or no (*Num.* xxii. 8, 13, 18, 20, 38 ; xxiii. 3, 12, 26 ; xxiv. 1, 12, 13), is completely in the spirit of these same prophets. Cf. *Am.* iii. 8, and the reproaches hurled against their opponents by Micah, ii. 11 ; iii. 5–7 ; and Isaiah, xxx. 10 sq., etc.

[21] Under the same reservation as in n. 20 I should now refer the following passages to the seventh century B.C.; *Gen.* xv. 5, 6 ; xviii. 17–19, 22[b]–33[a] ; *Ex.* xix. 3–8 ; xxiii. 20–33 in part ; the recension of *Ex.* xxxii.–xxxiv. ; (especially xxxii. 7–14 ; 25–29, the revelation of Yahwè's glory to Moses, xxxiii. 12[b], 13, 17–23 ; xxxiv. 2[b], 6–8, and the expansion of the Words of the Covenant in *Ex.* xxxiv. 10–28[a]) ; *Num.* xi. 14, 16, 17, 24[b]–30 ; xii. ; *Deut.* xxxi. 14–23 ; *Josh.* v. 13–15.

The later recension and expansion of the stories in E and J, indicated in § 8, n. 3 sqq., drop down into the seventh century as a natural consequence [240] of the results we have obtained (n. 18–20) ; but this conclusion must now be submitted to independent verification. From the nature of the case, however, it is impossible to establish the correctness of our chronology separately for each one of the added passages, either by comparison with the prophetic literature or by any other method. Nor is this necessary, for we have every right to extend the judgment passed on the few verses or pericopes mentioned above to the passages connected with them or obviously of common origin with them. As to the passages in *Genesis*, note that xii. 3 (xxviii. 14), where 'the families of the land' are mentioned, is certainly more primitive than xviii. 18 ; xxii. 18 ; xxvi. 4, where 'the peoples of the earth' are substituted. The latter formula stands, in *Gen.* xviii. 17–19, in a context that sounds almost deuteronomic, and may therefore be brought down with high probability to the seventh century (cf. *Jer.* iii. 17 ; iv. 2 ; xii. 15–17 ; xxxiii. 9). In the immediate neighbourhood of these verses stands the pericope *v.* 22[b]–33[a], the theme of which, viz. the righteousness of Yahwè in connection with the lot of individuals, appears again to point to the seventh century, in which at all events it was dealt with by the Deuteronomist (vii. 9, 10 ; xxiv. 16), Jeremiah (xvii. 14–18 ; xviii. 19–23 ; xxxi. 29 sq. [30 sq.]), and Habakkuk (i. 12 sqq.).—While the passage testifies to continued theological reflection, its soteriology finds an echo in *Gen.* xv. 5, 6, which is parallel not with *Isaiah* vii. 9[b], but with *Hab.* ii. 4[b].

In *Ex.* xix. 3–8—or perhaps it would be more accurate to say 3[b]–8, taking

3ᵃ as continued in 10ᵇ, and *v.* 3ᵇ–8, as a later insertion—we are struck by the strong assertion of Yahwè's unity and supremacy in *v.* 5 and the highly idealistic conception of Israel's relation to the peoples in *v.* 6. No parallels are to be found earlier than in *Deuteronomy*, where the characteristic סגלה (*v.* 5) also recurs (vii. 6; xiv. 2; xxvi. 18), as well as the opening phrase of *v.* 5, 'if ye will listen obediently,' etc. (*Deut.* xv. 5; xxviii. 1; also in *Ex.* xv. 26; xxiii. 22).

On *Ex.* xxiii. 20–33, see below, n. 32.

With regard to *Ex.* xxxii.–xxxiv. I would call attention to the following points : (1) *Ex.* xxxii. 7–14 on the one hand clearly does not belong to the original, as appears from its inconsistency with *v.* 17 sqq., and yet on the other hand it was known to D, who adopts these verses in ix. 12 sqq., sometimes verbally, though bringing them into conformity with his special style and usage. This in itself defines their date pretty closely, and so far from there being anything in their contents to forbid our bringing them to the seventh century, we may compare *v.* 12, 14 (והנחם על־הרעה) with *Jer.* xxvi. 18 sq.; xlii. 10 (*Joel* ii. 13; *Jonah* iv. 2); and the appeal to Abraham, Isaac, and Israel, *v.* 13 (cf. xxxiii. 1 ; *Num.* xxxii. 11), with *Jer.* xxxiii. 26; *Deut.* i. 8, and elsewhere ; (2) *Ex.* xxxii. 25–29 is best explained as a translation of *Deut.* xxxiii. 9 into a visible act and at the same time as a preparation for the deuteronomic representation of the election of Levi as the priestly tribe—so that we shall have to bring down this interpolation (for such it is) to the seventh century likewise ; (3) the verses on the revelation of Yahwè's glory to Moses (*Ex.* xxxiii. 12ᵇ, 13, 17–23; xxxiv. 2ᵇ, 6–8), now interwoven with the plea by which Moses strove to induce Yahwè still to accompany Israel, represent a later stage of religious development than that of the prophets of the eighth century; they testify to continued reflection upon Yahwè's being and attributes, and contain the germs of a doctrinal belief; [241] we must add that xxxiv. 7 rests on the Decalogue; (4) the 'Words of the Covenant' appear to have been expanded twice, *a.* when they were still isolated (*v.* 14ᵇ–16, 19ᵇ, 20, 21ᵇ, 22) ; *b.* when taken up into the connection in which they now appear (*v.* 9, 10–13, 24). On this last extension see below, n. 32. The first, though showing no sign of the influence of D, is dependent on the Decalogue (cf. *v.* 14ᵇ with xx. 5), and, especially in *v.* 15, 16, adopts a later style of language, so that we cannot concede any higher antiquity to it than to the other interpolations in *Ex.* xxxii.–xxxiv.—From this result it follows that *Num.* xiv. 11–25, in its present form, must likewise date from the seventh century. The pericope is older than *Deut.* i.–iv., as a comparison of *v.* 22–24 with *Deut.* i. 35, 36 shows beyond dispute ; but on the other hand *v.* 17, 18 proves that it is either dependent upon *Ex.* xxxiv. 6, 7 or of identical origin with it. Compare, further, *v.* 11–16 with *Ex.* xxxii. 9–14 and *v.* 21 with *Isaiah* vi. 3, which the writer has followed.

Num. xi. 14, 16, 17, 24ᵇ–30 and xii. are mutually connected 'studies of prophecy,' in which the spirit of prophecy is recognised as indispensable for Israel's guidance and its extension to every Israelite is aspired after, while at the same time it is placed on a lower level than the immediate and unbroken inter-

course with Yahwè (xi. 17, 29 ; xii. 6–8). The man who drew these sketches
may have started from certain touches in the earlier prophets (*Am.* iii. 7, 8 ;
Isaiah xxxii. 15 sq.), but the development of prophecy in the eighth century
lay behind him, and his aspirations are most nearly paralleled by *Jer.* xxxi. 31–
34 ; *Ezek.* xi. 19 sq., and the still later prediction of *Joel* iii. 1 sq. [ii. 28 sq.].
On *Deut.* xxxi. 14–23, cf. § 8, n. 15, and below, n. 30.

Josh. v. 13–15—perhaps continued in vi. 2 sqq. (vi. 1 being a parenthesis),
though it is Yahwè himself that is the speaker there—is related to *Ex.* iii. 1
sqq., as we see especially from a comparison of *v.* 15 with *Ex.* iii. 5. But 'the
prince of the host of Yahwè' has taken the place of the Mal'ach Yahwè, who
speaks as Yahwè himself. The formula יהוה צבא is itself late (*Ps.* ciii. 21 ;
cxlviii. 2 ; cf. 1 *Kings* xxii. 19), and hence it would seem to follow that the
idea of a captain of that host must be late likewise. And in fact it has no
real parallel either in Ezekiel or in *Zech.* i.–viii., but only in Daniel (x. 12
sqq.). We cannot be accused of rashness, then, in placing *Josh.* v. 13–15
among the later pericopes.

²² The deuteronomic tone of *Ex.* xix. 3ᵇ–8 ; xxxiv. 10–13, 24 has been indicated by anticipation in n. 21. But see further, n. 31, 32.

The phenomena to which attention has now been directed
(p. 232–348) lead up to the following hypothesis with regard
to the origin and subsequent fortunes of J and E:—

The yahwistic document (J) was composed in the
north-Israelite kingdom within the ninth or quite at the
beginning of the eighth century B.C.²³ The elohistic
[242] document (E) was written, in the same kingdom, by an
author who was acquainted with J, and who must have lived
about 750 B.C.²⁴ Both works were known and well received
in Judah also. But they could not permanently satisfy the
existing and gradually unfolding requirements of the latter
kingdom. Accordingly both alike were so expanded and recast
that in the second half of the seventh century distinctively
Judæan editions of J and E had come into existence²⁵. This
supposition, so natural in itself, is supported by the facts
already indicated (n. 20, 21), as well as by certain other
phenomena presented by the yahwistic and elohistic passages
of the Hexateuch²⁶.

At some period later than 650 B.C. the documents J and E,
thus supplemented and worked over, were combined into

a single whole. The moment at which this took place,
giving rise to J E, cannot be determined with certainty, but
we may place it with high probability at the close of the
seventh or the opening of the sixth century. For it does not
appear that the Deuteronomist himself, i. e. the author of
Deut. v. sqq., had J E before him as a whole[27]. His followers, on the other hand, made use of it in *Deut.* i.–iv. and
in *Joshua*[28]. This leads to the supposition that the harmonist
of J and E accomplished his task after the year 621 b.c. and
before the beginning of the Babylonian captivity. This is in
harmony with the fact that though not directly dependent
on the Deuteronomist (cf. n. 31, 32), he has nevertheless
a close affinity to him, and incorporates at any rate some few
fragments that issued from deuteronomic circles[29]. Moreover
there is at least one positive reason for bringing down J E as
late as this, for if he incorporated the so-called 'Song of
Moses,' *Deut.* xxxii. 1–43, and wrote the introduction to it,
Deut. xxxi. 14–23, his work cannot be much earlier than
the date we have assigned. To give it a higher antiquity
would involve the assumption that the Song and its introduction had no place in it, but were inserted later, though
still before the Babylonian captivity. And this assumption
has nothing to support it[30].

[23] The northern origin of J, pronounced probable in n. 9, is supported by
the use which Hosea makes of this document specifically, and also by its
general character. As long as the northern kingdom existed it was the centre [243]
of the life of Israel, spiritual and literary, as well as material; and it is
there, rather than in Judah, that we should be inclined to look for an author
such as J, thoroughly devoted to Yahwism, but free from any touch of scrupu-
losity and marked by such freshness, originality and graphic power.—The date
assigned rests on the following considerations :—According to n. 11, 12, J is
the earlier of the two documents. Of the passages described as 'præ-prophetic'
in n. 18 by far the greater number belong to J; the only exceptions
being *Ex.* xxiv. 1, 2, 9–11 and *Num.* x. 33–36, which we have assigned to E
(§ 8, n. 12, 14). The conclusion that J himself lived before the close of the
era the characteristics of which he reflects so clearly, is certainly not rash.
And now it becomes obvious why we assigned *Gen.* xxxii. 25–33 [24–32] to J

rather than E in § 8, n. 5. It falls in far better with the former's than with the latter's tone of thought. The inferences justified by all these considerations are defined still further by n. 3 and 4. J cannot be earlier than the second half of the ninth century, nor later than Hosea, who is acquainted with his narratives, including *Gen.* xxxii. 25–33 [24–32].

[24] On E's fatherland, see n. 9. In support of the date here proposed, note, (1) that we have seen E to be later than J (n. 11, 12); (2) that the ethico-religious ideas expressed in a number of his narratives and in his laws take us right into the atmosphere of the eighth century prophecy (n. 20); (3) that his representation of events and style of narrative give corresponding evidence of reflection and research, and are inexplicable unless referred to this, or a still later, period. Note, specifically, the studied use of Elohîm (n. 20); the careful avoidance, as a general rule, of anthropomorphic descriptions of God's revelations; and the use of poetical citations, in *Num.* xxi. 14, 27, to support historical statements.—If these considerations forbid us to mount higher than about 750 B.C., on the other hand we cannot come down much lower. For, (1) E is an Ephraimite, and therefore earlier than 722 B.C. No doubt some portion of the people remained in the land after that year, and the literary life of northern Israel might conceivably have been prolonged. But there is no positive evidence that it was so, and it hardly seems probable (cf. 2 *Kings* xvii. 24 sqq.); and moreover the passages in E concerning Ephraim contain no allusions to the catastrophe which would have been a thing of the past had the document been composed after 722 B.C.; (2) E's attitude towards the sacred places, of which details were given in n. 19, implies that they were still in existence and were frequented by the worshippers of Yahwè; (3) none of the passages on which we can confidently reckon as fragments of the original E give the smallest indication of a later date. Anyone may convince himself of this by reading them. The very fact that Nöldeke, Schrader, and Dillmann have been able to regard E as the earlier of the two writers shows, at any rate, that no clear marks of the seventh century, for instance, can be found in the document. We have already observed, in n. 20, that the composition of *Num.* xxii. 2–xxiv. 19, for example, cannot be brought down as late as the seventh century; and such anthropomorphisms as appear in xxii. 9, 20 add their testimony in favour of the earlier date. So too with *Ex.* xxiv. 1, 2, 9–11 and *Num.* x. 33–36, the contents of which show that they belong in spirit to the 'præ-prophetic' passages of n. 18.

[244]   [25] What I have said of J and E in n. 23, 24 does not refer to these documents in their present form, but to their older and original elements; the necessity of separating which from the later additions follows immediately from the phenomena pointed out on p. 241 sqq. Now it is generally assumed that these additions came from the pen of the harmonist who made a single whole of the two documents (n. 27–30). But by far the greater number of them have not the remotest connection with the process of fusion; they have no harmonising purpose, but serve to continue, expand or improve upon the special document, be it J or E, in which they are incorporated. Moreover they have no such internal affinities with each other,

either in form or contents, as to be suitably referred to a single hand. I
have therefore given the preference to the hypothesis of a Judæan edition
alike of J and of E, though I must not be understood to deny the possibility that some of the additions may be due to a hand no earlier than
that of the redactor of the 'prophetic' elements; for though his chief concern was unquestionably the combination of J and E, it does not follow
that he always confined himself to harmonising, or rather that he was never
led by the very nature of the harmonising task itself to overstep its strict
limits.

It appears from n. 21 that *Gen.* xviii. 17-19, 22ᵇ-33ᵃ must be referred to the
Judæan edition of J. See, further, n. 26.—But the expansion and elaboration
more especially of E must have been very important and extensive. Some
of the later passages pointed out in n. 21 should probably be referred to
the harmonist, and will therefore come under discussion shortly (n. 29);
but others, viz. *Num.* xi. 14, 16, 17, 24ᵇ-30; xii.; xiv. 11-25,—belong to
the Judæan recension of E, together with *Num.* xxiv. 20-24 (cf. n. 15). The
objection to assigning the former group to E, which seemed to flow from *Ex.*
xviii., has now disappeared. It is not improbable that the author of *Ex.*
xviii. himself, after relating the appointment of judges over 10, 50, 100
and 1000 families, should have mentioned the selection of seventy elders,
filled with the spirit of prophecy, without so much as a word of allusion
in the latter narrative to the contents of the former; but there was no reason
why the Judæan editor of E, who was more interested in vindicating its
true place for prophecy than in illustrating the Mosaic age, should be restrained from inserting his own sketch by the existence of an imperfect
parallel in his predecessor.—Still more important than these additions were
the modifications introduced by the Judæan editor into the Sinai-records
of E, which must indeed have undergone several successive recensions.
In n. 20 we saw that the Decalogue and the account of its proclamation
(*Ex.* xix. 3ᵃ, 10ᵇ-19; xx. 18-21, 1-17, cf. § 8, n. 12) together with the associated story of the worship of the golden calf (*Ex.* xxiv. 12-14; xxxii.
1-6, 15 sqq.), were probably not incorporated till at least as late as Hezekiah's reign. According to n. 21, *Ex.* xxxii. 7-14 and other additions
in *Ex.* xix., xxxii.-xxxiv. are later still; but some of them are shown by
their deuteronomic tinge not to belong to the Judæan recension on which
we are now engaged (cf. n. 22). Here it may well be objected that criticism, so freely applied, positively eliminates the subject on which it is
operating! What remains for the original narrative of E when all these
additions are removed? Not much except xxxiii. 7-11, it must be con- [245]
fessed. And this passage itself is incomplete, for the ark, of which the
ôhel mo'êd must surely have been the receptacle from the first, is not mentioned in it. But this result, however strange at first sight, is really
quite natural. In E's primitive account, the journey of the children of
Israel to 'the mountain of Elohîm' can hardly have had any other purpose
than to give them the occasion for receiving 'the ark of Elohîm' which
was to accompany them on their further journey towards Canaan. On

the one hand it is certain that E mentioned this ark (*Num.* x. 33–36;
xiv. 44), and must therefore have given an account of its origin ; and on
the other hand the texts just cited prove that he must have regarded its
possession as a privilege and represented its acquisition as a sign of the
favour of Elohîm. In other words, the connection in which the ôhel mo'éd,
the receptacle of the ark, now occurs, is not original ; and *Ex.* xxxiii. 7–11
can only be a fragment. In *Ex.* xxiv. 1, 2, 9–11 another fragment of like
nature is perhaps preserved. See further, n. 32.

[26] (1) The character of the Judæan recension of J comes out most clearly
in *Gen.* i.–xi. We have already recognised *Gen.* ii. 4[b]–iii.; iv. 1, 2[b], 16[b]–24;
vi. 1–4; ix. 20–27; xi. 1–9 as the more ancient elements of J's 'history of
origins' (cf. n. 18, and § 8, n. 3). The question was then left open, whether
these older passages were taken up and recast by a later hand, or whether
they were amalgamated with an independent 'history of origins' by a redactor;
but it may now be decided in favour of the former hypothesis. The supposition of a Judæan edition of J not only accounts for the facts, but commends
itself by its simplicity. The original narrative was first supplemented by the
incorporation of *Gen.* iv. 2[a], 3–16[a], a comparatively ancient notice (cf. n. 18),
derived from the same circle of ideas to which the story of Paradise and the
family tree of Cain belong (cf. *Th. Tijdschr.*, xviii. 153 sqq.). A later writer,
to whose knowledge the Assyrio-Babylonian legend of the flood had come,
thought good to incorporate it, recast in the Israelitish spirit, into J's 'history
of origins,' and to make Noah (whom he took from *Gen.* ix. 20–27) the rescued
survivor from the flood and the ancestor of the new race of men. But the
saga required this Noah to be the tenth from Adam, and since he could not be
a descendant of the fratricide Cain, the original list of Cainites was recast and
expanded into a genealogy of ten generations of Sethites, of which we possess
the heading only in *Gen.* iv. 25, 26 and a fragment in *Gen.* v. 29, the rest having
made way for the similar list of P[2] (*Gen.* v. 1–28, 30–32). After this the
editor placed the story of the flood, important fragments of which we possess
in *Gen.* vi. 5–viii. Contents and style combine to show that it is not older
than the seventh century (*Th. Tijdschr.*, xviii. 164 sqq.; to the ideas and expressions of a later date there collected we may add Yahwè's repentance in
Gen. vi. 6, 7, which only appears in writings of this or a still later period,—
if we except the not quite similar utterance of Amos, vii. 3, 6). After *Gen.* ix.
20–27 the editor inserted a table of nations of which again we possess mere fragments (*Gen.* x.; cf. § 6, n. 1 ; 8, n. 7); but what we have—especially *Gen.* x.
[246] 8–12—harmonises perfectly with the date we have assumed.—We shall have
no difficulty now in recognising the hand of the Judæan editor here and there
in the other portions of *Genesis.* For instance, in xii. 10–20 (cf. § 8, n. 4),
where a saga of which Isaac was originally the subject is transferred, in imitation of E (xx), to Abram; in *Gen.* xv. (on *v.* 5, 6, see n. 21), though the chapter
has been worked over more than once and must therefore come under consideration again (§ 16, n. 12) ; also, it seems, in *Gen.* xxxix., which we have already seen cause to assign to a later form of the Joseph-saga (n. 10), and
which sinks below the undoubted J-passages in point of form, while distin-

guished from them by its pronounced ethical tone.—It is almost certain
that in *Exodus, Numbers,* and *Joshua,* likewise, J has been subject to recension, but in these books the harmonist has been more drastic in his
treatment of J and E than in *Genesis,* so that it is often impossible now
to distinguish between the earlier and later elements of his sources. Cf.
n. 27–30.

(2) Most of the additions to E have been dealt with already in n. 25,
and the presumable expansions of his narrative in *Ex.* i. sqq., *Josh.* i. sqq.,
have just been mentioned under (1). It remains to note *Num.* xxi. 32–35
—which is evidently a later addition, rounding off the conception of the conquest of the whole Transjordanic district as the work of Moses. In xxxii.,
likewise, the half-tribe of Manasseh, that takes possession of the kingdom
of Og, is inserted (*v.* 33 in part, 39–42) into a narrative that only mentioned Reuben and Gad and their settlement. This might suggest that
the original story, together with *Num.* xxi. 21–31, is E's, and the later additions (*Num.* xxxii. 33, in part, 39–42), together with *Num.* xxi. 32–35,
the Judæan editor's. But we shall see in n. 29 that another hypothesis
deserves the preference.

[27] Cf. § 9, n. 5. Anyone who ascribes the whole mass of later ' prophetic '
additions to the harmonist JE, must without question place his date
earlier than the year 621 B.C., for D¹ had most certainly read *Ex.* xxxii.
7–14, *Num.* xiv. 11–25, not to mention any other passages (n. 21). But
if we assign these, and certain other additions, to the Judæan edition of
E, we need only suppose that D¹ had this edition before him; for the combined documents, or in other words JE as a whole, cannot be traced with
certainty in the historical allusions of D¹. An exception would have to be
made in the case of the story of the quails in *Num.* xi. 4 sqq., did D¹ really
allude to it (ix. 22); but he may have found the story in J before its
combination with E. On the other hand Dathan and Abiram (xi. 6) belong
to E (§ 8, n. 14), and therefore the reference to them is not an exception to
the rule, as Meyer thinks it is (*Zeitschr. f. alttest. Wissenschaft,* i. 123).
The *argumentum e silentio* has more than its usual force in this instance, since
not a few of the narratives in J (*Gen.* vi. 5–viii.; xviii., xix., etc.) would
have served D¹'s purpose admirably, and would surely have been used by him
had they lain before him in the very same document in which he read the
stories of E which he so generally followed.

[28] The strongest evidence is furnished by the deuteronomic recension of
Joshua, which extends to all the 'prophetic' elements and of which, therefore,
nothing short of JE can have been the subject.—But even *Deut.* i.–iv., xxix.
sqq. betray acquaintance not only with J and E, but with JE also. Compare
Deut. iv. 3 with *Num.* xxv. 1–5; *Deut.* xxix. 23 with *Gen.* xviii. sq.; x. 19;
Deut. i. 9 sqq., both with *Ex.* xviii. and *Num.* xi. 4–34, which latter story was [247]
only brought into its present shape by JE (n. 29). It would be possible to
argue that these passages only prove an acquaintance with the Judæan edition
of E side by side with the occasional consultation of J. But the ' prophetic '
portion of *Num.* xxxii., which is closely followed for the most part in *Deut.* iii.

12–20, must in all probability be referred to JE (n. 29), and in that case we have positive proof that *Deut.* i.–iv. stands on the same footing as the recension of *Joshua*.

²⁹ We will begin by pointing out the sections and verses which must be assigned to JE, and which may serve to characterise the method he followed. The minor harmonising additions and modifications, inseparable from the attempt to weave two works into one, may be passed over in silence. *Gen.* xvi. 8–10 (to be assigned—with Wellh. xxi. 410, and against Dillmann, *Genesis*, p. 237 sqq.—to JE, who makes Hagar return to her master's house, because of *Gen.* xxi. 9 sqq., whereas in the original story she brought her son into the world in the desert);—xx. 18 (an incorrect explanation of *v.* 17, marked as JE's by 'Yahwè,' § 8, n. 5);—xxii. 15–18 (where the yahwistic promise to Abraham in *Gen.* xii. 3; xviii. 18 is incorporated into a story of E's. But JE did not confine himself to this expansion. He has likewise been busy with *v.* 11, 14, and Wellhausen, xxi. 409 sq.; Dillmann, *Genesis*, p. 273 sqq., and others, rightly judge that he substituted 'Moria' in *v.* 2 for the name of some place in Ephraim, with the express purpose of transplanting Abraham's deed of faith to Jerusalem—whence it also follows that we are not to look for JE in Northern Israel);—xxvi. 15, 18 (remarkable harmonising glosses, dictated by *Gen.* xxi. 22 sqq., inserted into J's narrative);—xxviii. 13–16 (which I take to be a complete parallel to xxii. 15–18; cf. § 8, n. 6);—*Ex.* i.–xi. (where the 'prophetic' narrative, in its present form, is due to JE, who did not simply interweave his documents, in this case, but made their statements the groundwork of a narrative of his own, especially in iv.–xi., cf. § 8, n. 10, 11; leading us to infer that the emphasis laid upon the miraculous character of the plagues and the contrast between the lot of Israel and that of the Egyptians are due to him or at least were heightened by him);—xiii. 1 sq., 3–10, 11–16 (mutually connected ordinances on maççôth and the consecration of the first-born to Yahwè. We have seen, § 9, n. 4, that these ordinances are not dependent upon *Deuteronomy*, though they have a strong affinity with it; they stand in no connection with the documents that underlie *Ex.* xii., xiii.; and we may probably assume that they were inserted here by JE, though not written by him; on *Ex.* xii. 21–27 see § 16, n. 12);—xv. 1–19 (likewise lashed in by JE, cf. n. 15);—xviii. 1 sqq. (recast by JE, in order to harmonise J's representation, in iv. 24–26, that Moses took his wife and one son to Egypt, with E's idea that the wife and two sons staid behind with the father);—*Num.* xi. 4–34 (a combination of E² on the seventy elders, *v.* 14, 16, 17, 24ᵇ–30, with J on the feeding with quails, the latter story being expanded and embellished, especially in *v.* 18–24ᵃ, 31, 32; Wellhausen, xxi. 568 sqq., distinguishes between two quail stories, but their existence cannot be proved, and the recension of J by JE, including the insertion of 'the [248] elders,' completely accounts for the narrative as it now stands);—*Num.* xxxii. (i.e. the 'prophetic' account of the settlement of Reuben, Gad, and half Manasseh in the Transjordanic district, which is welded together with a parallel story from P² in that chapter. We have already seen, in § 6, n. 42, that it is impossible accurately to assign its own to each of the main documents,

whence again it follows that the pedigree of the 'prophetic' narrative cannot be determined with certainty. A hypothesis was suggested in n. 26 which seemed very probable. But I cannot accept it as definitive for the following reason : the 'prophetic' narrative in *Num.* xxxii. asserted not only that Reuben and Gad received the Transjordanic district as their heritage, but also that their armed men crossed the Jordan and took part in the conquest of Canaan. Now this latter trait is a remote *corollary* of the wholly unhistorical conception of the unity of Israel in the time of Moses, and the conquest of Canaan as an act accomplished *simul et semel*. But this corollary cannot be shown to rest on any premises supplied either by J or by E. It only emerges among the followers of D¹, in *Deut.* iii. 12–20; *Josh.* i. 12–15; iv. 12; xxii. 1–6; in P², if *Josh.* iv. 13 is from his hand, § 6, n. 48, and in the very late author of *Josh.* xxii. 7, 8, 9–34, § 6, n. 53. This being so I think the ' prophetic' portion of *Num.* xxxii. must be referred to the very last recension, i. e. to JE. It is probable enough that the 'prophetic' redactor had an older account, of E's, before him, which would explain the omission of half Manasseh in *v.* 1–32 even now. But in that case the older account was completely recast by JE in *v.* 1–32 and supplemented in *v.* 33, 39–42 by the introduction of Manasseh. All that remains of it, then, has passed through the hand of JE, and must be regarded as his work) ;—*Josh.* i.–xii. (which, according to § 8, n. 16, 20, must be regarded in the same light as *Ex.* i. sqq., and must therefore be referred to JE,—with the exception of the deuteronomic additions and the few verses inserted from P². Cf. also § 16, n. 12) ;— xiii. sqq. (also JE's redaction,—though with the same reserve as before, which in this case covers a good deal, cf. § 6, n. 46 sqq. and § 7, n. 26 sqq. The 'prophetic' redactor's hand is most obvious in xviii. 2–6 [*v.* 7 is a deuteronomic addition], 8–10. These verses embody the idea that an inheritance was assigned to the seven lesser tribes, though not to Judah and Joseph, by lot. D¹ does not know, or at any rate does not accept it, § 9, n. 9 ; whereas P² extends it to all the tribes on this side the Jordan, xiv. 1–5. In JE the partition is made by Joshua, without Eleazar, who is first introduced by P², ibid. The section, therefore, cannot be assigned to the final redactor, who adheres to P, § 16. But it is unquestionably late ; for even this qualified division by lot, preceded, observe, by a plan and survey of Canaan, as though it were an uninhabited land, is an advanced deduction from the unhistorical conception of Israel's settlement, and would be out of place either in J or E. The language, too, is far from antique. Compare *v.* 3, עַד־אָנָה, with *Ex.* xvi. 28 ; *Num.* xiv. 11 ; *v.* 4, לְפִי, with *Jer.* xxix. 10 ; *Gen.* xlvii. 12, and a number of other passages in P ; *v.* 5, 6, 9, חֵלֶק, with *v.* 7 ; xiv. 4, and other texts of D and P. All this agrees perfectly with the supposition that JE is the author).

The consideration of JE's work shows us in the first place that he certainly does not belong, as has sometimes been supposed, to the eighth century B.C. [249] The mingled reverence and freedom, so strange sometimes to our ideas, with which he treats his documents, is quite out of keeping with the age in which the narratives themselves arose, or were supplemented from the still living springs of the popular saga, and is thoroughly characteristic of the later student, collecting and recasting, making it his first object to preserve, and even when he attempts something more never quitting the beaten tracks. I can hardly think that Reuss would have supported the date mentioned above (*Geschichte d. Alt. Test.*, § 213–216), if he had examined JE's method in detail.—We have already glanced at the relation in which JE stands to *Deuteronomy*, which is important in determining his date more closely. It comes out clearly, for example, in his incorporation of *Ex.* xiii. 1, 2, 3–10, 11–16, and in *Josh.* xviii. 2–6, 8–10. But his linguistic usage also testifies to JE's close affinity with D¹ and his followers. This is exemplified by the way in which he speaks of the inhabitants of Canaan. E, it would seem, uniformly employed the general term 'the Amorite' (*Gen.* xlviii. 22; *Josh.* vii. 7; x. 5, 6, 12; xxiv. 12, 15, 18, perhaps also in the now expanded verse *Josh.* v. 1), which D² subsequently adopted from him (*Deut.* i. 19, 20, 27, 44; cf. also *Gen.* xv. 16). J, on the other hand, called the native population 'the Canaanite' (*Gen.* xii. 6; xxiv. 3, 37; l. 11), or 'the Canaanite and the Perizzite' (*Gen.* xiii. 7; xxxiv. 30; cf. xxxviii. 2), and his usage also was adopted by later writers (not only *Judges* i. 1, 3–5, 9, 10, 17, 27–30, 32, 33, but *Ex.* xiii. 11; *Deut.* xi. 30; *Gen.* xlvi. 10; *Ex.* vi. 15). JE—in agreement with *Deuteronomy* (xx. 17 six peoples, vii. 1 seven peoples)—preferred the resonant enumeration of six peoples, and constantly inserted them into the periods he adopted or recast. See *Ex.* iii. 8, 17; xiii. 5 (where the Hivvites are wanting in the Masoretic text); xxiii. 23; xxxiii. 2; *Josh.* ix. 1; xii. 8. To some of these texts, however, a deuteronomic origin may be assigned with equal probability, and such is undoubtedly the source of *Ex.* xxxiv. 11 (six peoples); *Josh.* iii. 10; xxiv. 11 (seven peoples); *Judges* iii. 5 (six peoples). This insertion is more than once coupled with the description of Canaan as 'a land flowing with milk and honey,' *Ex.* iii. 8, 17; xiii. 5; xxxiii. 3; cf. *Num.* xiii. 27; xiv. 8; xvi. 13; which expression may be borrowed either from J or from E, but if so was adopted and constantly employed alike by JE and by D¹ (vi. 3; xi. 9; xxvi. 9, 15; xxvii. 3; cf. xxxi. 20; *Josh.* v. 6), and afterwards by others (*Jer.* xi. 5; xxxii. 22; *Ezek.* xx. 6, 15; *Lev.* xx. 24). This single example will suffice to show how natural it is that there should still be some want of agreement whether certain verses should be assigned to JE or to one of the followers of D¹. Cf. n. 31.

³⁹ 'The song of Moses' was found ready to hand, not composed, by the author of the introduction, *Deut.* xxxi. 14–23. Had he written it himself, he would have made it answer the intention with which he inserted it better. He would have sung in the person of Moses, and would have brought the close of the song into harmony with his purpose. The first question, then, is: What is the date of the song itself? Knobel (*Num., Deut. u. Josh.*, p. 324 sq.) and Schrader (De Wette's *Einleitung*, p. 322) are wrong in assigning it to the Syrian period, about 900 B.C. The 'no-people,' the 'foolish (godless) [250] nation,' of *v.* 21, must of necessity refer either to the Assyrians or to the Chaldæans. But the latter supposition is really the most natural, for *Isaiah* v. 26, 27; xiv. 31; xxxiii. 19, are not nearly such close parallels as *Jer.* v. 15, 16; vi. 22, 23, and above all *Hab.* i. 6 sqq. How the poet could signify the

Aramæans by these names I cannot see. Now *v.* 21 is not a prediction, but a description of what Yahwè had declared he would do (*v.* 20) and has now accordingly done. For from *v.* 29 onwards the poet deals with the consequences of the (now accomplished) chastisement, and expresses the hope that Israel will humble himself in consequence, and that so the. worst may be averted. This is the position either of an Ephraimite poet of about 740 B.C., or of a Judæan contemporary of Jeremiah. Now the style and language of the song plead for the second alternative. The opening (*v.* 1–3), which is not free from inflation, is imitated but likewise exaggerated from *Isaiah* i. 2, and has affinities with *Ps.* xlix. 2–4 [1–3]. Expressions constantly recur which we seek in vain in the writers of the eighth century, e.g. *v.* 4, עול ; 16, הכעיס and תועכה ; 17, שׂער ;18, חולל ; 20, תהפכות ; 21, הבל ; 22, קרח, להם ; 24, לחם, eat ; 30, מכר ; 33, אכזר ; 35, מוש, איד ; 42, שׁביה ; 43, הרנין ; linguistically the song may be classed with Jeremiah and Ezekiel. More than this cannot in my opinion be inferred from the parallel passages in D¹ (cf. § 7, n. 19) and in Jeremiah. On this last point, cf. Kamphausen, *Das Lied Mose's*, p. 295 sqq., where the following parallels are specially pointed out: *v.* 1, 43 (*Jer.* ii. 12 ; vi. 18, 19); *v.* 4ᶜ, 21ᵇ (*Jer.* ii. 5) ; *v.* 5 (*Jer.* ii. 31) ; *v.* 6ᵇ (*Jer.* iv. 22 ; v. 21) ; *v.* 6ᶜ, 18 (*Jer.* ii. 26–28 ; iii. 19) ; *v.* 15 (*Jer.* ii. 20 ; v. 7, 28) ; *v.* 18, 19 (*Jer.* vi. 19, 30) ; *v.* 21 (*Jer.* ii. 11, 12) ; *v.* 25 (*Jer.* vi. 11) ; *v.* 30 (*Jer.* iii. 14) ; *v.* 35 (*Jer.* vi. 15) ; *v.* 37, 38 (*Jer.* ii. 26–28). To these we may add *v.* 22 (*Jer.* xv. 14 ; xvii. 4) ; *v.* 13 (*Lam.* iv. 9). Kamphausen does not doubt the priority of *Deut.* xxxii., but it is really very questionable. Jeremiah follows his originals closely and on a large scale when he follows at all, as in xlvi. sqq. for example ; and as for *Deut.* xxxii. being one of his models, it is out of the question. His points of agreement with it are no greater than are usual between contemporaries of kindred spirit. 'The song of Moses' may have been composed about 630 B.C., but may equally well be twenty or thirty years later.—The introduction, xxxi. 14–23, presents no difficulties to this date. We have already (§ 8, n. 15) found traces of E's language, and affinities with *Josh.* xxiv. in it. But points of difference are not wanting, either in the language (here and there related to P¹), or in the historical stand-point, for the writer lives in the midst of the 'many disasters and distresses' which he makes Moses announce, and he therefore does not take the song as a warning against apostasy, but as evidence that Israel's humiliation is the consequence of his sin, and as such is a dispensation of Yahwè. The author of *Josh.* xxiv. does not take so gloomy a view. His Joshua is deeply concerned as to Israel's future, but is by no means sure that it will be as gloomy as it is painted in *Deut.* xxxi. by Moses. *Josh.* xxiv., then, need not prevent our placing the introduction to the Song somewhere between 597 and 586 B.C., for example ; though it might, for that matter, be still later, i. e. exilian. The short time allowed between the composition of the song and that of the introduction presents no difficulty ; for it need not have prevented the author of the latter from believing the song to be really Mosaic ; and, moreover, it is by no means certain that he did believe this ; for the hortatory purpose which it served would doubtless have seemed [251]

S

to him a complete justification of its ascription to Moses.—On xxxi. 24-30, cf. § 7, n. 20. These verses, which presuppose the introduction, are due to an exilian writer, and therefore present no difficulty to the date we have assigned. The only question that remains, then, is whether to ascribe the introduction—together, of course, with the incorporation of the song—to JE himself, or to one of the earliest readers of his work. Such an interpolation is not altogether impossible, but it is very improbable. It must have preceded the amalgamation of JE with D, which would bring it nearly back to the date of JE himself. And, moreover, there is no positive evidence for it of any kind. On the contrary, the introduction is so interwoven with the account, borrowed from E, of Joshua's consecration to his task (*v.* 14, 15, 23) as to form a fairly consistent whole with it. We cannot suppose, then, that the union was affected by any other hand than that of JE himself.

Had JE's work been preserved in its original form, our inquiry might close at this point. As it is, we have still to inquire what influence the amalgamation with D[1] and his followers had upon JE (cf. § 14). We have already seen that the deuteronomic redactor who reduced the two works to one recast the account of Israel's settlement in Canaan in his own spirit (§ 7, n. 26–31). But it was only the book of Joshua and the accounts of the last activities and death of Moses (*Deut.* xxvii., xxxi., xxxiv.) leading up to it, that underwent such drastic treatment. In the preceding books the redactor confined himself to adding a few deuteronomic touches, which show, by the comparative ease with which we can separate them, that the contents of JE have remained otherwise unaltered[31]. On one point only did the redactor allow himself rather more freedom. He very considerably expanded the Sinaitic legislation, which embraced nothing but the Decalogue in JE, by transposing both the Book of the Covenant (*Ex.* xx. 22–xxiii.) and the Words of the Covenant (*Ex.* xxxiv. 10–28) from the place which they occupied in JE to the account of the legislation of Sinai. Positive evidence or proof of this thesis cannot be given, but the indirect indications which support it from various sides give it a high degree of probability[32].

[252] [31] Colenso's contention, mentioned but not criticised in § 7, n. 32, 33,

has not been confirmed by our further researches, including those of the present §. Moreover, when examined closely it is inadmissible in itself. The sections attributed by Colenso to D, i. e. to the Deuteronomist himself or to one or more redactors working upon his lines, have little indeed in common, and they often conflict with the known purport of D's laws. It is hard to conceive of a writer or a school that could enrich *Genesis*, for example, with the following verses and sections :—vi. 4; x. 8-12; xi. 28-30; xii. 1-1ᵃ, 6-20; xiii. 1-5, 7ᵇ, 14-17; xv. 1-21; xvi. 10; xviii. 13-19, 22ᵇ-33; xix. 27, 28; xxii. 14-18; xxiv. 4-8, 38-41, 59, 60; xxvi. 2-5, 24, 25ᵃ; xxviii. 13-15, 20-22, etc. We look in vain for any connection between such heterogeneous passages, and we wonder how D, of all men, came to embellish the theophany at Bethel in *Gen.* xxviii. 10 sqq., by the insertion of *v.* 13-15, and even to supplement it by a vow to found a temple there, *v.* 20-22. Truly this *farrago* is wanting in all internal unity, and is only held together in appearance by a few words and formulæ that recur from time to time, but which, though employed by D¹ and his followers amongst others, are by no means their characteristic or favourite expressions.

Reserving *Ex.* xix.-xxiv., xxxii.-xxxiv., for special treatment in n. 32, we observe clear traces of D's influence in *Gen.* xxvi. 5 (the synonyms משמרת, מצות, חקות, and תורת side by side; *v.* 4 is practically identical with xxii. 17, 18 (JE) to which *v.* 3ᵇ refers, cf. xxii. 16; and *v.* 1ᵃ presupposes a certain passage of J², viz. *Gen.* xii. 10-20, so that there too either JE or a later redactor is at work. We must therefore either refer *v.* 1ᵃ, 3ᵇ, 4 to JE and *v.* 5 to D, or give *v.* 1ᵃ, 3ᵇ 5 to D. The latter hypothesis is preferable as being the simpler); *Ex.* xv. 26 (cf. § 8, n. 12; the deuteronomic colouring is not to be mistaken; the poetic האזין, too, occurs in *Deut.* i. 45). —No other deuteronomic phrases can be pointed out with equal certainty. But we must grant, with Jülicher, that a number of verses in *Ex.* iv. sqq. suggest the question whether JE's narrative has not been retouched by a deuteronomic redactor. The supposition is far from unnatural, for *Ex.* i. sqq., like *Josh.* i. sqq., must have invited expansion and supplement. But I imagine that—partly because JE and D are separated by so short a period—an intimate deuteronomic recension is incapable of being strictly proved, and I shall therefore content myself with enumerating the passages that might be referred to it, and indicating the pages on which Jülicher deals with them :—*Ex.* iv. 21-23 (?) (A, p. 24 sq.); viii. 18ᵇ (?); ix. 14ᵇ, 16, 29ᵇ; x. 1ᵇ, 2 (B, p. 90, 92, 97); xii. 42 (B, p. 116). I have already dealt with *Ex.* xii. 21-27; xiii. 1-16, 17ᵃ; xv. 25ᵇ, 26; xvii. 14ᵇ, 16 (B, p. 110 sq., 117 sq., 119, 275 sqq., 272 sq.).

³² I shall here describe in detail the process by which, after repeated attempts in another direction (cf. *Th. Tijdschr.*, xv. 164-223), I was led to this hypothesis, for I think this will be my best way of supporting it.

(1) D¹ is acquainted with the Book of the Covenant and makes diligent use of it (§ 9, n. 3), but he never mentions that it was submitted to the [253] people and accepted by them at Sinai. He does speak of revelations received by Moses on the mountain (*Deut.* v. 27, 28), but the proclamation

of their contents is, according to him, still in the future at the moment at which he introduces Moses as speaking, and therefore it did not take place at Sinai. Nor is there any room for the Words of the Covenant, *Ex.* xxxiv. 10–27, in D¹'s representation of the events at Sinai. The Sinaitic legislation, according to him, embraced the Decalogue, and nothing else. And such was still the view of his follower, the author of *Deut.* i.–iv., as appears from iv. 10–15.

(2) These facts are fully explained by either of the two following suppositions: *a.* D¹ found the Book of the Covenant and the Words of the Covenant in the Sinai-story that he had before him, but intentionally passed them over in silence because he wished to supersede them by his own legislation; *b.* the documents in question were not embodied in the Sinai-stories known to D¹. The agreement of *Deut.* iv. 10–15 with D¹ is an argument, though not a conclusive one, against *a.*; while *b.* finds a powerful support in the fact that neither the Book of the Covenant (together of course with the conclusion of the covenant itself, *Ex.* xxiv. 3–8), nor the Words of the Covenant fit into the Sinai-stories; or rather, in the fact that they are excluded by them. In *Ex.* xxxii.–xxxiv. the conclusion of the covenant on the basis of the Book of the Covenant is by no means assumed; nor yet in *Ex.* xxiv. 12–14, where, on the contrary, the revelation of Yahwè's will is still a thing of the future. Conversely, there is no allusion in *Ex.* xxiv. 3–8 to the proclamation of the Decalogue. The articulation of the Book of the Covenant to the Decalogue (*Ex.* xx. 22) is defective and evidently not original. The Words of the Covenant likewise stand in a connection which they do not fit. In matter they have nothing to do with Israel's apostasy in *Ex.* xxxii., and in form they are very clumsily attached to the preceding theophany by *Ex.* xxxiv. 9. This being so we must conclude that when D¹ and the author of *Deut.* i.–iv. wrote, the Book and the Words of the Covenant had not yet been incorporated into the 'prophetic' Sinai-stories, or, in other words, that they were not a part of JE's account of the events at Sinai. Cf. the fuller development of (1) and (2) in *Th. Tijdschr.*, xv. 179–183, 191–197.

(3) On the other hand, the Book of the Covenant and the conclusion of the covenant itself belong to E (§ 8, n. 12), and we may consider it probable, at any rate, that the Words of the Covenant, in their original form, are very ancient and were once part of a narrative of the foundation of Israel's national existence, possibly due to J (§ 8, n. 18). Both alike, therefore, must have been contained in JE.

(4) This forces the suspicion upon us that the Book and the Words of the Covenant occupied a different place in JE, and that that place was the very one now taken by the deuteronomic law itself, so that their promulgation by Moses and acceptance by the people immediately preceded the passage of the Jordan. Kadesh, 'the well of right' (*Gen.* xiv. 7), would not be inappropriate as the scene of this drama (*Num.* xx. 1; *Deut.* i. 46; xxxiii. 2); but if we suppose that 'the field of Moab' was represented in JE as the scene of the legislation, which, be it always remembered, was destined for Canaan,

then we understand alike why D[1] locates the legislative activity of Moses
there, and why the amalgamation of D and JE forced the Book and the [254]
Words of the Covenant to make way for D's laws and find some other place.
The fact is that *Deut.* xii.–xxvi. is really a new edition of the Book of the
Covenant, though very greatly amplified and modified, and the idea that its
place in history was prescribed beforehand by that Book seems extremely
natural; and equally natural, in that case, is the transference both of the Book
and of the Words of the Covenant to Sinai, where, according to D itself, the
revelation of Yahwè's will had had a beginning in the proclamation of the
Decalogue.

(5) *A posteriori* this suspicion is confirmed p a r t l y by the strange massing
of laws in *Ex.* xix.–xxiv. and xxxii.–xxxiv. and the loose connection in which
they stand to each other and to the Sinai-stories (see under (2)), but c h i e f l y
by the numerous and distinct traces of a deuteronomic recension o
these chapters. These traces are found, *a.* in *Ex.* xix. 3[b]–8; see above, n.
21; *b.* in the Decalogue itself, *Ex.* xx. 1–17; see above, § 9, n. 2; *c.* in
Ex. xx. 22[b], 23; cf. *Deut.* iv. 13, 36; *Ex.* xix. 4 and observe the difference
of form between *v.* 23 (2 pers. plur.) and 24 (2 pers. sing.) which shows
at any rate that *v.* 23 is from another hand; *d.* in *Ex.* xxiii. 30–33. The
Book of the Covenant, even in its earliest form, no doubt closed with a
hortatory address, but its present conclusion is not all from one hand.
Wellhausen (xxi. 560), Dillmann (*Ex. u. Lev.,* p. 251 sqq.), and
Meyer (*Zeitschr. f. alttest. Wissenschaft,* i. 138) find its kernel in *v.* 20–
22[a], 25[b]–31[a], and later amplifications in *v.* 22[b]–25[a], 31[b]–33. With regard
to *v.* 23, 24 and again *v.* 31[b]–33, it is impossible not to agree with them.
The verses interrupt the progress of the discourse or introduce foreign
matter into it. Whether *v.* 22[b] and 25[a] are later additions I dare not
decide. But it does seem clear to me, that the reviser, who may have
retouched the kernel of the discourse itself here and there, was under the
influence of D. Compare *v.* 22[a] with *Ex.* xv. 26 (D); *Deut.* xv. 5; xxviii.
1, etc.; *v.* 23, the six peoples of Canaan, with *Deut.* xx. 17 (see n. 29); *v.*
24[a], to bow down and serve, with *Deut.* iv. 19; v. 9; viii. 19; xi. 16;
xvii. 3; xxix. 25 [26]; xxx. 17; *v.* 24[b] with *Deut.* xii. 30; vii. 5; xii. 3;
v. 32 with *Deut.* vii. 2; *Ex.* xxxiv. 12, 15; *v.* 33 with *Deut.* vii. 16.
When taken in connection with the fact that the heading of the Book of
the Covenant, *Ex.* xx. 22[b], 23, likewise contains deuteronomic turns of
expression, these parallels at any rate rouse the suspicion that the same
redactor who gave this tinge to the heading has revised the concluding
discourse also. Jülicher (B, p. 299 sqq.) finds traces of his hand still
earlier, in *Ex.* xxii. 19, 20–23 [21–24], 24–26 [25–27]; xxiii. 1 sqq.; *e.* in
Ex. xxxiv. 10-13, 24; for it seems, in the first place, that *v.* 11–13 anticipates
v. 15, 16, and has been placed before it by a later editor; nor is the
joining on of *v.* 14 to *v.* 11–13 by כִּי original; and in the second place, it
is obvious that in *v.* 10–13, 24 the deuteronomic formulæ are comparatively numerous. Compare *v.* 10, יהוה מעשׂה, with *Deut.* xi. 7, *Josh.* xxiv.
31; נורא, with *Deut.* i. 19; vii. 21, etc.; *v.* 11, 'that which I command

you this day,' with D *passim* ; cf. also *Deut.* xii. 28 ; *v.* 12, נשׁמר followed by ל, מוקשׁ, בקרב found in *Deuteronomy* ; *v.* 13 with *Deut.* vii. 5 (which verse, however, might in its turn be regarded as an amplification of *v.* 13 and *Ex.* xxiii. 24) ; *v.* 24, הורישׁ מפני, with *Deut.* iv. 38 ; ix. 4, 5 ; xi. 23 ; xviii. 12 ; *Josh.* xxiii. 9, 13 ; הרחיב גבול, with *Deut.* xii. 20 ; xix. 8.—Taken together *a.–e.* surely make it highly probable that *Ex.* xix.–xxiv. and xxxii.–

[255] xxxiv. were brought into their present form by a **deuteronomic reviser**, and more specifically yet that it was this reviser who lashed the Book and the Words of the Covenant into their present connection.

(6) From the nature of the case this hypothesis, even if accepted, still leaves many questions unanswered. The repeated recensions of the Sinai-stories (cf. n. 21, 25) could not but result in an ill-fitting whole, and conversely nothing is more natural than that we should be unable to reascend, through all the successive modifications, from the final outcome to the original source. All that can fairly be required is that the hypothesis I have framed to account for the present form of the story should be found not to conflict with those phenomena upon which it is not based, but with which it comes into contact. And this requirement it meets. The Words of the Covenant, in their primitive form and as they appeared in JE (cf. n. 21), contain nothing whatever that would compel us to regard them as having been Sinaitic from the first. The same may be said of the Book of the Covenant. Even the concluding dis-course, xxiii. 20–33—in its entirety with no great violence, and in its kernel (see under (5)) quite naturally—might originally have been laid upon the lips of Moses as he stood upon the border-land of Canaan. In the account of the conclusion of the covenant, *Ex.* xxiv. 3–8, there is just one trait that points to Sinai, viz. 'under the mountain,' in *v.* 4. But we are certainly no rash in ascribing the addition of these two words to the redactor who incor-porated the account into the Sinai-stories with a clear knowledge of what he was about. In *Ex.* xxxii. sqq., again, there is nothing to conflict with my hypothesis. These chapters were part of JE, and were used by the deutero-nomic redactor, without alteration, for the frame-work of the Words of the Covenant. *Ex.* xxxiv. 9 is the clumsy articulation of his insertion with the narrative into which he inserted it, and *v.* 28 that really belongs to *v.* 1, 4, now has to do second duty as the conclusion of the passage immediately preceding it, *v.* 10–27, though it does not really stand in any connection with it, and is not even in harmony with it. Finally, on *v.* 29–35, see § 16, n. 12.

§ 14. Continuation. C. *The Deuteronomist, his precursors and his followers.*

The character of the deuteronomic elements of the Hexa-teuch enabled us, from the outset, to reach pretty firm results both as to their mutual relations (§ 7) and their relative (§ 9) and absolute antiquity (§ 12). But it does not seem super-

fluous once more to review the results of our previous researches, on the one hand to draw them to a focus, and on the
other hand further to support and supplement them.

Whereas the sacred history is the centre of interest to the
prophetic writers in the Hexateuch, it is the legislation of
Deut. xii.–xxvi. that makes the kernel of the deuteronomic
portions, while all the rest exists only in connection with this [256]
and for its sake. It is therefore of the utmost importance
that we should form as complete and correct a conception as
possible of this legislation, and of its origin and date. The
question whether our point of departure is to be *Deut.* xii.–
xxvi. (and xxvii. 9, 10, cf. § 7, n. 21) in its present extent
must be answered in the affirmative. The few sections which
possibly did not belong to it originally are in no way out of
keeping with the whole, and were perhaps incorporated in
his book of law by the author himself in a subsequent
revision. This will apply, for instance, to xv. 4, 5; xvii.
14–20; xx., and also to xxiii. 2–9 [1–8] [1]. Deviations from
the natural order in the sub-sections must likewise be explained as due to interpolation by the author himself, or
must be attributed to the copyists [2]. With the reservations
necessarily involved in what has been said, the arrangement
of the book of law can be perfectly understood and justified,
if we bear in mind that the writer, though working with
a special end in view, was not altogether independent. In
deploying the duties of the people consecrated to Yahwè
alone, he not only takes the long-established customs
into account but also uses written sources. It has been
shown already that he was acquainted with the Book of the
Covenant, and that he borrowed many ordinances from it,
generally modifying them more or less [3]. But in addition to
this collection it is highly probable that he had command
of another, perhaps of more than one other, of which he made
special use for xxi.–xxv. [4] Not a single trace of acquaintance

with the priestly legislation can be found. *Lev.* xi. is not
the original of *Deut.* xiv. 3–21, but rather a later and
amplified edition of those priestly decisions on clean and unclean animals which the deuteronomist adopted[5]. Nor can
Lev. xvii.–xx., with which he sometimes agrees in substance,
have been amongst his sources[6]. From this side, then, no
objections can be urged against the supposition already defended (§ 12, n. 1–6), that *Deut.* xii.–xxvi. dates from Josiah's
reign. In so far as the language and style can be taken in
[257] evidence, they completely harmonise with this conclusion[7].

[1] It cannot be denied that xv. 4, 5 conflicts with *v.* 7, and that *v.* 6 joins on
to *v.* 3 even better than to *v.* 5. On the other hand, the verses are completely
deuteronomic both in form and contents, and it is therefore probable that they
were inserted by the writer himself when it occurred to him that the poverty
of some of the Israelites, which is assumed in *v.* 3, 7 sqq., would never exist
at all if Yahwè's demands were complied with perfectly.—On xvii. 14–20 see
§ 7, n. 11.—Wellhausen (xxii. 463 sq.) questions whether xx. belongs to the
original work, inasmuch as *v.* 5–8 more especially is quite unpractical, and
was presumably written when the kingdom of Judah no longer existed. But
the lawgiver's idealism comes into conflict with the reality elsewhere too,
and in *v.* 5–8 he is by no means inconsistent with himself. Cf. Valeton,
Studien, vi. 133 sqq. The last named scholar has also urged objections to
xiv. 2, which he regards as an amplification by the second hand (*Studien*, vii.
40, n. 2); against xviii. 16–22, where Yahwè himself is the speaker, in violation of the rule elsewhere observed, and where the language of v.–xi. (cf. v.
25; ix. 9; x. 4) is followed (*Studien*, vi. 161, n. 1); against xix. 7–10 as
breaking the connection between *v.* 4–6 and 11–13, and probably referring to
the conquest of the Transjordanic district, with which event the writer of xii.–
xxvi. does not elsewhere concern himself (*Studien*, v. 308 sq.). But these
objections proceed on the assumption that xii.–xxvi. and v.–xi. are not from
the same hand, and they have no weight for those who think otherwise (§ 7,
n. 5–11).

Ch. xxiii. 2–9 [1–8] demands a special investigation. Wellhausen (xxii.
464) and Valeton (*Studien*, vi. 143 sq.) find difficulties in *v.* 5–7 [4–6], the
former because these verses presuppose the events of the fortieth year after
the exodus, in conflict with xxvi. 18 sq., which places us at Sinai; the latter
on the same grounds, and also because they give a reason for the exclusion of
Moab and Ammon other than their unclean origin (*v.* 2–4 [1–3]). These
objections cannot be allowed. Against the first, see § 7, n. 7; as to the
second, note that *v.* 4 [3] need not be taken as an application of the general
rule of *v.* 3 [2], and that the historical justification contained in *v.* 5–7 [4–6]
is parallel with that of *v.* 8 [7]. If the one is in its place, so is the other.—

The objections urged by Geiger (*Urschrift*, p. 88–91) against the genuineness of the whole section are more weighty. The formula קְהַל יְ״ (*v.* 2, 3 bis, 4 bis, 9 [1, 2 bis, 3 bis, 8]) occurs nowhere else in *Deuteronomy* and recalls *Ezr.* x. 8. The hostility towards Moab and Ammon and the first reason given for it (*v.* 5 [4]) conflict with *Deut.* ii. 9 sqq., 19–21. The episode of Balaam is referred to here (*v.* 5ᵇ–7 [4ᵇ–6]), but nowhere else in *Deuteronomy*; nor does it fit into the frame-work of the book which makes Moses promulgate his tora in the fields of Moab, and find his grave there (xxxiv. 5, 6). The phrase לאֹ־תִדְרֹשׁ שְׁלוֹמָם וְגוּ has some resemblance to *Jer.* xxix. 7; xxxviii. 4, but does not occur in its entirety until after the captivity (*Ezr.* ix. 12; *Neh.* xiii. 1; *Esth.* x. 3). It is only in this latter period that the whole passage really finds its place, for the problem as to who should and who should not be admitted into the community was then a burning question, [258] whereas it can hardly be said to have existed before the exile.—The coincidence of so many at first sight remarkable phenomena cannot fail to make some impression; but Geiger's argument will not really bear examination. The external evidence for the authenticity of xxiii. 2–9 [1–8] is very strong. Not only *Ezr.* ix. 12 and *Neh.* xiii. 1 sq., but even *Lam.* i. 10 alludes to it. The conflict with ii. 9 sqq., 19–21 is real, but proves nothing; for i.-iv. is from another hand. The parallels to *v.* 7 [6] are citations or imitations of the verse itself. The formula קְהַל יְ״, which occurs not only in *Num.* xvi. 3; xx. 4 (P²), but as early as *Mic.* ii. 5, is not found elsewhere in D, but this is probably because it is borrowed from the collection of laws whence the materials of xxi.-xxv. are derived. The objection against *v.* 5ᵇ–7 [4ᵇ 6] has just been met; so that nothing remains but the general drift of the passage. Now in judging of this Geiger fails to notice that 8ᵃ [7ᵃ] would be wholly inexplicable, and 8ᵇ [7ᵇ] very surprising in a post-exilian passage. The ideas then entertained about Edom may be learnt from *Obad.* *v.* 11 sqq.; *Ezek.* xxv. 12; xxxv. 5 sqq.; *Isaiah* xxxiv.; *Mal.* i. 2–5; *Psalm* cxxxvii. 7. The events of which the memory lives in all these passages, were evidently unknown to the author of *Deut.* xxiii. 8ᵃ [7ᵃ], that is to say, they were subsequent to his date.

² The arrangement of the precepts in *Deut.* xii. sqq. is examined with special care by Valeton, *Studien*, v. 169 sqq., 291 sqq.; vi. 133 sqq. He holds that xvi. 21–xvii. 1 is misplaced (not xvii. 2–7, which concerns the administration of justice regulated in xvi. 18–20, xvii. 8–13); also xix. 14 (that ought rather to come after xxiv. 5 [?]); xx. (that may once have stood between xxi. 9 and xxi. 10, with which latter verse its opening words coincide); and lastly xxii. 1–10, which has nothing to do with the ordinances concerning domestic life before and after it, and which might perhaps be added to xxiii. 16 [15]–xxv. This latter group, however, presents us with no orderly succession of precepts, and is only a whole in so far as it reflects the humane spirit of the legislator and his effort to secure fairness. This last remark of Valeton's is undeniably true, but that very fact forbids our making too severe demands on the logical arrangement of the commandments. It is only exceptionally that we have any right to attribute the want of order to the copyists.

[3] See § 9, n. 3, and cf. Valeton's treatise, cited in n. 2, which embraces a survey of these parallels.

[4] Note 2 has already shown us that xxiii. 2–9 [1–8] was probably borrowed from some such collection. Elsewhere too the language gives evidence of D's dependence on a predecessor, e. g. in xxi. 4, 6 (the verb ערף, elsewhere only in *Ex.* xiii. 13; xxxiv. 20, and even there not of such an action as that in xxi. 1–9, which is quasi-sacrificial, though quite *sui generis*); or again xxiii. 18, 19 [17, 18] (בית יי, not to be found elsewhere in *Deuteronomy*, though occurring in *Ex.* xxiii. 19); also xxiv. 5 (where the same expressions are not used for the same subject as in xx. 7). Attention has already been directed, in § 7, n. 3, to the deuteronomic additions to ordinances obviously taken from elsewhere.

[5] Cf. § 6, n. 22. The relation of *Lev.* xi. to *Deut.* xiv. 1–21, indicated in the text, is quite unmistakable, even apart from the additional proof furnished by [259] *Lev.* xi. 41–45. Observe that the popular enumeration of the mammalia that may be eaten (*Deut.* xiv. 4, 5) is omitted in *Lev.* xi., in which their general characteristics only are mentioned; that *Lev.* xi. 9–12 strikes us as a paraphrase of *Deut.* xiv. 9, 10; and that *Deut.* xiv. 19 is worked out more accurately in *Lev.* xi. 20–23. A comparison of *Deut.* xiv. 21[a] with *Lev.* xi. 39, 40 gives equally clear results. The prohibition in *Deuteronomy* is absolute, but not so in *Leviticus*, where it is expressly added that the uncleanness consequent on the transgression lasts 'till the evening,' and may be removed by washing the clothes. The distinction between the Israelite and 'the stranger within your gates and the foreigner,' which appears in *Deut.* xiv. 21[a], has vanished without a trace in *Lev.* xi.; and in *Lev.* xvii. 15, 16, in the treatment of the same subject, the two are expressly placed on the same footing. In both respects the priority of *Deuteronomy* is undeniable. On the other hand, it must be admitted that the language of *Deut.* xiv. 3–20 departs from that of D and resembles that of P. Note למין in *v.* 13–15, 18; שרץ in *v.* 19. But this may easily be explained on the supposition that D, who knew of 'the Levitical priests,' who was in communication with them (xvii. 18; xxxi. 9), and who elsewhere, too, shows that he attached value to their teaching (xxiv. 8), adopted this tora on 'things clean and unclean' from them, either by word of mouth or from the written notes of one of them. In either case it is highly natural that traces should be found in *Deut.* xiv. 3–20 of the same style which reappears in a more advanced stage of development in P.

[6] D (xii. 16, 23, 27; xv. 23) has in common with *Lev.* xvii. 10–14 the prohibition of blood, which occurs elsewhere in P also (*Gen.* ix. 4; *Lev.* iii. 17; vii. 26, 27; xix. 26). But there is nothing to indicate indebtedness to P. The belief that Yahwè condemned the eating of blood was primeval (1 *Sam.* xiv. 32–34), and was simply accepted by D, whereas in *Lev.* xvii. it was brought into connection with the more recent theory of atonement on which it was made to rest.—There is much more difficulty in deciding the relation of D to *Lev.* xvii. 3–7, which forbids the slaughter of oxen and sheep except as thank-offerings, and to *v.* 8, 9, which confines sacrificing to the ôhel mo'éd. *V.* 3–7 conflicts with *Deut.* xii. 15, 20–22, where express permission

is given to slaughter, elsewhere than at the sanctuary, for private use; *v.* 8, 9, on the other hand, centralises the worship, as does D *passim.* Then did D appropriate and confirm the one precept and cancel the other? In that case we should expect him to allude to *Lev.* xvii., or at least to have some few expressions in common with it. But neither the one nor the other is the case. And, what is more, *Deut.* xii. 8 absolutely excludes this hypothesis. The command to worship Yahwè in one single place could not have been put forward as something new and as a command for the future only had D known that Moses had already laid it down as the rule in the desert, which would certainly imply that it had been regularly practised under his own eye. It is certain, therefore, that D was not acquainted with *Lev.* xvii. 3–7, 8 sq. in the present form. Neither can we suppose that he knew the original precept of P^1, which is now embodied in these verses of *Lev.* xvii., together with traits borrowed from P^2 (§ 6, n. 27; 15, n. 5); for in its original form it was identical in purport with the present recension. Against this it is urged that *v.* 3–7 fits closely to the ancient popular usage, which really held slaughtering [260] to be a religious rite, and therefore only allowed its performance at the sanctuary, i. e. at the nearest bama (*Hos.* ix. 4). But before we can assert that *v.* 3–7 upholds this practice we must strike out everything that refers to the one sanctuary. And Diestel, cited by Kittel in *Theol. Stud. aus Würtemberg,* ii. 44 sqq., actually attempts to do this. But his analysis is extremely arbitrary, and really amounts to the manufacture of a law to meet the demand. 'The dwelling of Yahwè' (*v.* 4), the camp (*v.* 3), and 'the priest' who does service at the dwelling of Yahwè (*v.* 5, 6) can no more be got rid of from *v.* 3–7 than the 'se'irim,' which only appear in later writers (*Isaiah* xiii. 21; xxxiv. 14; 2 *Chron.* xi. 15) can be expunged from *v.* 7. The question how P^1 could make such a demand as that all oxen and sheep should be slaughtered at the one only sanctuary, has already been answered in § 6, n. 28. Anyone who finds the answer unsatisfactory may note that in this passage the command to slaughter 'by the dwelling of Yahwè' is given by Moses to the Israelites in the desert, and may suppose that by throwing his ordinance into this form P^1 intended to show what Yahwè really might demand, even though he should not intend to insist upon rigorously maintaining it under quite altered circumstances.

The passages parallel with *Lev.* xviii. xix., taken in the order of the chapters in *Deuteronomy,* are the following (cf. Kayser in *Jahrbuch. f. prot. Theologie,* 1881, p. 656 sqq.):—

Deut. xii. 16, 23; xv. 23 = *Lev.* xix. 26 and the parallel passages (just dealt with);

Deut. xiv. 1 = *Lev.* xix. 28 (terminology differs, showing that the two precepts were independently formulated);

Deut. xvi. 19, 20 = *Lev.* xix. 15, 16 (but far more closely parallel with *Ex.* xxiii. 2, 3, 6–8; there is no evidence that D was acquainted with the passage in *Leviticus* also);

Deut. xviii. 10^a = *Lev.* xviii. 21; xx. 2–5 (agree in subject-matter only);

Deut. xviii. 10^b, 11 = *Lev.* xix. 26^b, 31 (the same);

Deut. xxii. 5, 9–11 = *Lev.* xix. 19 (in spite of all resemblances there is great difference here. *Deuteronomy* adds the prohibition of change of clothes between man and woman, and of ploughing with an ox and an ass; and *Leviticus* the prohibition of crossing different animals. The use of mules, which conflicts with this, is mentioned in David's time (2 *Sam.* xiii. 29; xviii. 9; 1 *Kings* i. 33, 38, 44) and later (1 *Kings* x. 25; xviii. 5, etc.), whence Dillmann infers (*Ex. u. Lev.*, p. 554) that the prohibition had already been forgotten by that time; but what the texts really show is that no such prohibition had as yet been thought of, and that we must regard it as the last deduction from the theory that underlies *Deut.* xxii. and *Lev.* xix. alike. *Lev.* xix., then, is certainly not older than *Deut.* xxii.);

Deut. xxii. 22 = *Lev.* xviii. 20 (here again the resemblance is only in the contents);

Deut. xxiii. 1 [xxii. 30] = *Lev.* xviii. 8 (resemblance only in contents; and, moreover, it must be observed that in *Lev.* xviii., xx. this one prohibition is followed by a whole series of analogous regulations which D could not have passed over in silence had he known them. It is only in *Leviticus* that the *locus* of the forbidden degrees is fully developed. *Deut.* xxvii. 22, 23 is not considered here, inasmuch as it does not belong to D, but is a later interpolation. Cf. § 7, n. 22);

[261]   *Deut.* xxiii. 18 = *Lev.* xix. 29 (no trace of dependence on either side);

Deut. xxiv. 14, 15 = *Lev.* xix. 13, 14 (but also = *Ex.* xxii. 22–24; there is no evidence that D was acquainted with the passage in *Leviticus* also);

Deut. xxiv. 19–22 = *Lev.* xix. 9, 10, cf. xxiii. 22 (the two writers formulate the same precept independently);

Deut. xxv. 13–16 = *Lev.* xix. 35, 36 (agree only in contents; the more systematic formulating of *Leviticus* is certainly not earlier that that of D).

In this connection we must also consider *Deut.* xxv. 5–10, in connection with *Lev.* xviii. 16; xx. 21. The levirate marriage rests on a primeval usage (*Gen.* xxxviii.), but is recognised by D (*ibid.*) and even insisted on as a stern duty. According to Dillmann (p. 546), it must be regarded as an exception to the rule which is laid down in the parallel passages of *Leviticus*, and which was followed whenever the union with the first brother had had issue. But in that case how comes it that D never alludes to the rule itself and that the exception to it is never mentioned in *Leviticus*? To me it seems obvious that D cannot have been acquainted with *Lev.* xviii. and xx., and that the prohibition of marriage with the brother's wife in these latter passages is a corollary of the priestly theory of cleanness, directed against the ancient usage and the tora that sanctioned it.

[7] The extant Israelitish literature is too limited in extent to enable us to determine the age of any work with certainty from mere considerations of language and style. Moreover, *Deuteronomy* rather set than followed the style of the age in which it was written. Nevertheless, it is undeniable that, in general terms, Deuteronomy and Jeremiah, not Deuteronomy and Isaiah, Hosea or Amos, go together (cf. § 10, n. 14, 16). This is an indirect confirmation of the arguments which plead for the reign

of Josiah. The passage in *Mic.* vi. 1–8 points in the same direction. It is not dependent on Deuteronomy, and yet it is more deuteronomic in tone and style than any other passage of the old prophetic literature, and is marked by the same intense earnestness that distinguishes D's exhortations; compare *Mic.* vi. 8 with *Deut.* x. 12. The author of this passage might be called a precursor of D. This remark holds true if the words are ascribed to Micah, but it gains a still higher significance if we are to attribute them, with Ewald and others, to a contemporary of Manasseh.

Our previous investigation led us to the conclusion that the book of *Deuteronomy* contained a number of passages, besides the legislation of xii.–xxvi. (xxvii. 9, 10), which must be ascribed to the same author; viz. the hortatory introduction, v.–xi.; the closing discourse, xxviii.; and the very brief historical notice, xxxi. 9–13 (§ 7, n. 5–11, 21). All this had been combined with the book of law probably before the latter came to the knowledge of Josiah and was put into force by him, certainly before it was copied out and published. Presumably this publication took place shortly after the [262] reformation in the eighteenth year of Josiah's reign. At any rate the enlarged edition contains nothing which could prevent our assigning this date to it [8].

[8] To what has been said already in support of this view, in § 7, especially n. 21, I may now add that an edition of Deuteronomy without the Decalogue must be considered highly improbable. If the Decalogue really possessed the authority that D assigns to it when he makes Yahwè himself utter it, what could be more obvious than to attach his own legislation to it and put it forward as the fuller elaboration of the principles laid down therein? And this is what he actually does in v. 1 sqq., 24 sqq. [27 sqq.]. On xxviii. and xxxi. 9–13, see § 7, n. 21, where it also appears that the præ-exilian position is maintained both here and in v.–xxvi.

The subsequent history of the deuteronomic book of law may be divided, generally, into two periods. Throughout the former it stood by itself, at the beginning of the latter it was united into a single whole with the 'prophetic' elements. In the first period, beyond all doubt, we must place the addition of the historical introduction, i. 1–iv. 40, to which xxxi. 1–8 belongs; and perhaps also the tacking on of xxix., xxx.[9] All else that bears the deuteronomic stamp must be referred to the second period. Some sections, viz. *Deut.* xxvii. 1–8; xxxi. 24–30; xxxii. 44, 45–47; xxxiv. 4, 6, 7[a], 11, 12, and the original deuteronomic recension of the historical narrative in Joshua, may be due to the redactor who inserted the deuteronomic tora into the ' prophetic' sacred history[10]. On the contrary, *Deut.* xxvii. 11–13, 14–26, a portion of *Josh.* viii. 30–35, and certain other deuteronomic sections in *Joshua*, which cannot be indicated with absolute certainty, must be regarded as later interpolations[11].

Deut. i. 1–iv. 40; xxxi. 1–8; xxix., xxx., were written after the beginning of the Babylonian captivity, i. e. at the earliest after Jehoiakim was carried away captive in the year 597 B.C. (§ 7, n. 22, under (4), (5)). At that time *Deuteronomy* had not been welded with the prophetic history. The moment at which this union took place can no more be determined than [263] the exact dates of the sections which were subsequently woven in. But when the Jewish exiles returned to their fatherland (536 B.C.) the deuteronomico-prophetic book may have existed in the same form in which it was united with the priestly codex some century later[12].

[9] Cf. § 7, n. 12–17, 22 under (4), a glance at which will explain the distinction drawn in the text between i. 1–iv. 40; xxxi. 1–8 and xxix. sq. It is very certain that i. sqq. is not intended to link v. sqq. to the preceding history; and it is equally certain that, when it was added, v. sqq. still stood alone. After the union with JE it would have been, to a great extent, superfluous, and could hardly have been incorporated. On the contrary it is quite possible that xxix. sq. was inserted when the amalgamation with JE had already taken place. But even so these two chapters still remain essentially an addition not to the united deuteronomico-prophetic work (DJE), but to the deuteronomic legislation and exhortations, and are in fact a modified edition of the closing discourse of xxviii.

[10] Cf. § 7, n. 22 under (1), (6); n. 20 under (3); n. 25–31. What is there said will quite explain why the sections mentioned in the text are assigned to the redactor of D + JE. *Deut.* xxvii. 5–7[a]; xxxi. 14–23; xxxii. 1–43; xxxiv. 1[b]–3, 5, 7[b], 10, as well as the original account of the conquest and partition of the land in *Joshua*, are fragments of JE; and inasmuch as they now appear combined with or incorporated in passages of deuteronomic tone, some

of which are obviously intended to connect them with the deuteronomic tora, we can hardly attribute these latter passages to any other hand than that of the redactor. Consider, more especially, the way in which *Deut.* xxvii. 5–7ª is amplified and framed-in, *v.* 1–8; and also *Deut.* xxxi. 24–30, where 'this tora' and 'this song' are spoken of and commended to the love of the Israelite. *Deut.* xxxii. 44, 45–47, too, serves in its way the purposes of the redaction of D + JE, and the deuteronomic additions to JE in *Joshua* really are additions, written with JE in view and intended from the first to supplement it and bring it, as far as necessary, into agreement with the deuteronomic tora.

[11] Cf. § 7, n. 22 under (2), (3) and n. 30, 31. If, as shown in these notes, *Deut.* xxvii. 11–13 rests on a misunderstanding of xi. 29–32, and was inserted here on the strength of the mention of Ebal in *v.* 4, then it must be attributed to a later interpolator. In that case, the same hand must have expanded *Josh.* viii. 30–35 by adding *v.* 33 and the words 'the blessing and the curse' in *v.* 34; unless indeed these additions were made, in view of *Deut.* xxvii. 11–13, by a still later interpolator (cf. § 16, n. 12). Neither the writer nor the reviser of *Josh.* viii. 30–35 shows any knowledge of *Deut.* xxvii. 14–26, which section, accordingly, must be regarded as of still later origin. With respect to the two-fold deuteronomic recension of JE in *Joshua*, we can get no further than the recognition of its reality and more or less probable guesses as to the mutual relations of the two strata. Cf. § 7, n. 31.

[12] On the historical background of *Deut.* i. 1–iv. 40; xxix. sq., see § 7, n. [264] 22 under (4). Now that we know D¹ to have been a contemporary of Josiah, we cannot be surprised to find that his followers, the authors of i.–iv. and xxix. sq., had the beginning of the captivity behind them, whether we think of the year 597 or the year 586 B.C. This date is in perfect harmony with the view of history taken in i.–iv. and the antiquarian glosses with which the author illustrates the discourse of Moses (§ 7, n. 13).— The amalgamation of JE with D, therefore, must be exilian at least, if not post-exilian. But the date at which it was accomplished can no more be defined with precision than the antiquity of the later interpolations indicated above (n. 11). Meanwhile it is intrinsically probable that JE and D did not long exist separately. D seemed to court attachment to JE from the first; the historical introduction, i. 1–iv. 40, though borrowed from JE, did not render the more elaborate narratives of the latter superfluous; and the necessity of a deuteronomic amplification of JE in *Joshua* must have made itself early felt. For all these reasons we may well suppose that the origin of JE + D falls within the period of the exile, in which indeed it seems more in place than in the years that followed 536 B.C. And if we may suppose that the returning exiles brought JE + D out of Babylon with them, then the redaction of the Hexateuch as a whole, on which more in § 16, becomes perfectly comprehensible in its turn.

§ 15. Continuation. D. *History of the priestly legislation and historiography.*

With regard to the priestly legislation, we arrived at the provisional conclusion in § 12 that it was introduced in Judæa by Ezra and Nehemiah in the year 444 B.C., or shortly afterwards, and had been reduced to writing not long before. The closer examination of the priestly elements of the Hexateuch, to which we shall now proceed, must show us whether this conclusion is shaken by the objections urged against it, how it is related to the critical analysis in § 6, and whether, in connection with that analysis, we can make it more precise.

It is an established fact that from primeval times the priests of Yahwè uttered tora orally, i. e. declared the will of Yahwè to the people that came to consult them or invoked their intercession. The priestly tora was naturally concerned, in the first instance, with the worship of Yahwè (2 *Kings* xvii. 27, 28), but it also covered the whole field of administrative justice, and therefore the personal and social relations of the [265] Israelites [1]. Naturally the local judges also had an interest in knowing the rules which underlay the priestly sentences on these latter subjects. It is therefore anything but surprising that when, in about the eighth century B.C., an Israelitish literature arose, the rules of justice and the closely associated ethical injunctions, including exhortations to observe the religious duties, should have been written down. That this really happened we learn from Hosea (viii. 12), and even apart from his evidence we should have known it from the Book of the Covenant, from the Deuteronomist's other sources, and from the deuteronomic law itself, all which can hardly have been committed to writing without the assistance of priests of Yahwè; and in any case they rested on the tradition preserved by them [2]. The priestly laws, in the narrower sense, which we find in the Pentateuch, likewise include regulations which would not have been misplaced in the collections just named, and which may have been written down, in their present or in some earlier form, before Josiah's reformation [3]. But a written regulation of the cultus did not exist in the præ-deuteronomic times. Even were this otherwise, in no case could any such high antiquity be ascribed to the special regulation of the cultus which lies before us in *Exodus–Numbers*. Its existence before the Babylonian captivity is excluded by the evidence of the Israelitish literature, and is, moreover, irreconcilable with its relation to *Deuteronomy*, with which it cannot be contemporary and which it cannot chronologically precede [4].

[1] Cf. § 10, n. 4. To the texts from the writings of the prophets there cited I would now add 2 *Kings* xvii. 27, 28, where the 'teaching' of the priests is brought into immediate connection with the question 'how they'—the Assyrian colonists—'should fear (or serve) Yahwè.' We rightly distinguish between public worship and the administration of justice, but we must not forget that the two are far from forming an absolute contrast. Hence the collections of laws to be mentioned in n. 2, though they do not regulate the worship of Yahwè, nevertheless contain precepts which bear upon it inasmuch as they define the duties of the Israelite towards Yahwè and his sanctuary as well as in other matters. See, for example, *Ex.* xxii. 19, 28–30 [20, 29–31]; xxiii. 13, 14–19; *Deut.* passim.

[2] Whether the authors of law were themselves priests can- [266] not be determined. But it is obvious from *Deut.* xxiv. 8, and still more from xvii. 18, xxxi. 9, that the Deuteronomist had relations with the priesthood of Jerusalem. In xiv. 3–21 he even incorporates a priestly tora on clean and unclean animals into his book of law (§ 14, n. 5).

[3] Cf. the parallel passages in *Deuteronomy* and *Lev.* xviii.–xx., in § 14, n. 6. Besides these there are other precepts or admonitions in the priestly laws that bear the same character: *Lev.* xix. 3, 4, 11, 12, 14, 16–18, 20; xx. 9; xxiv. 10–23; xxv. 17, 35–38. If Dillmann's assertion (*Ex. u. Lev.*, p. 373 sqq., 533 sqq.), that 'a Sinaitic law-book of hoary antiquity' underlies *Lev.* xvii.–xxvi., especially, were accepted with the needful sobriety and confined to such ordinances as are quoted above, it might at least be discussed. The priestly laws of this kind, which are embodied in P, might conceivably be as old, for instance, as the precepts of the Book of the Covenant. Whether they really were written down so early must form the subject of a special inquiry, in which their surroundings must also be duly considered. See below, n. 8.

[4] I am now building upon the results obtained in § 10, 11. It was there shown that even the later prophets and historians, but more especially and emphatically those that lived before the exile, were unacquainted with any

ritual legislation, and specifically with that which has come down to us. See especially § 10, n. 3, 13, 15, 17, 25; § 11, i.-iv., p. 199-212. In perfect agreement with this we find D and his followers either assuming or expanding and recasting in their own spirit the narratives and laws of JE, but never those of P² (§ 9, n. 6-9); and also that the representation of historical facts in P² is less worthy of credit, and therefore later, than that of JE, with which D agrees (§ 9, n. 11). It is true that most of these arguments are negative and rest on the silence observed concerning the ritual legislation and the narratives associated with it, but in spite of this their complete convergence gives them a high degree of evidential value. Moreover, they are confirmed by a number of considerations of a positive character, which will be discussed successively in this §. Here, where we are concerned with the question whether the priestly legislation can or cannot be præ-exilian, its relation to *Deuteronomy* is the decisive consideration. Now we know something of this relation already from the comparison between the deuteronomic and the priestly laws instituted in § 3, n. 14-19, 21. But there we only proved that the laws were inconsistent with each other and could not be contemporaneous. The investigations of § 11, however, amply justify the conviction that there is not a single instance in which the deuteronomic law can be taken as a later modification of the priestly law, whereas the latter always can and sometimes must be regarded as the development and rectification of the former. For—

a. (§ 3, n. 14). The laws in which the one only sanctuary is presupposed are later than those which introduce it as something new (*Deut.* xii. 8) and urge with unmistakable emphasis the duty of frequenting it. Even the single priestly law that insists on the centralisation of worship (*Lev.* xvii. 1-9) and thus forms an exception to the rule, stands in the same relation to *Deuteronomy* as the rest (§ 14, n. 6).

b. (§ 3, n. 15). The hypothesis that the priestly regulation of the festivals is earlier than that of Deuteronomy would make the silence of the latter concerning the day of atonement utterly inexplicable; but the priestly cycle of [267] seven holy seasons may very well have been developed out of the deuteronomic triad, and the (sacred) number of seven itself, in connection with the heterogeneous character of the festivals included, pleads directly in favour of such an origin. But see more below, n. 8 and 17.

c. (§ 3, n. 16). One has only to read the priestly regulations about the priests and Levites, and their respective privileges and duties, to convince oneself that D¹ could not have ignored them, had he known them. On the other hand, the limitation to a single family of the hereditary qualification which had originally been allowed to others also, is not at all surprising. And moreover it can be shown *in casu* what the historical occasion of the change was, and how it was brought about. See below, n. 15.

d. (§ 3, n. 17). If we have fairly stated the case with respect to the distinction between priests and Levites, then a similar judgment must be passed on the assignment of tithes to the latter. It is later than the deuteronomic ordinance which destined the tithes for sacrificial feasts. Even apart from this consideration we must regard the consecration of the tithes to Yahwè as the original, and their assignment to the servants of the sanctuary as a later modification. To arrange these two precepts in the reverse order is against all analogy. See more below, n. 16.

e. (§ 3, n. 18). For the same reason we must regard the priestly laws on the firstlings of cattle as later than those in Deuteronomy. This is confirmed by a comparison between *Ex.* xiii. 13[a]; xxxiv. 20[a] and *Num.* xviii. 15 sq.; *Lev.* xxvii. 27 (the firstlings of unclean animals), which shows quite unmistakeably that in Israel, as elsewhere, the priests had an eye to their own revenues, and made the legislation serve to increase them.

f. (§ 3, n. 19). It is hardly possible to conceive that the law on the priestly and Levitical cities, *Num.* xxxv. 1–8, should first have been carried out, as we are told it was in *Josh.* xxi. 1–40, and then allowed to lapse. On the other hand, if we regard such a law as demanded in the interests of the temple servants, then the necessity for a change in the position of the Levites revealed by *Deuteronomy* makes it all the more natural. In this case it stands in line with Ezekiel's ordinances, on which more in n. 16.

g. (§ 3, n. 21). The mutual relation of (*Ex.* xxi. 1–6) *Deut.* xv. 12–18 and *Lev.* xxv. 39–43 can only be matter of dispute as long as the two laws are considered by themselves. When we reflect that the year of jubilee is never mentioned except in P[2] (cf. § 11, n. 24), and further that the law which refers to it speaks of the Levitical cities (*Lev.* xxv. 32–34), and strikes us on the one hand as a relaxation of the ordinance in *Ex.* xxi. 1–6; *Deut.* xv. 12–18, which, as we see from *Jer.* xxxiv. 8–22, cf. § 11, n. 24, encountered practical difficulties, and on the other hand as the remotest of the deductions from the sabbatical commandment—a theoretical completion, unsuited for practice— then we shall no longer hesitate to pronounce *Lev.* xxv. 39–43 later than *Deut.* xv. 12 18. Cf. also n. 18.

From this point forwards our inquiry must proceed on the facts brought to light by our analysis of the priestly elements, in § 6. We discovered, there, that the passages in question were due neither to a single hand nor a single period. The legislation, fragments of which are preserved in *Lev.* xvii.– xxvi., is clearly distinguished from the great mass of priestly [268] laws and associated narratives. And with this we must begin, inasmuch as we have provisionally shown (§ 6, n. 24–28) that it is older than the matter that surrounds it either in *Lev.* xvii.–xxvi. or elsewhere. Although we cannot always separate out the fragments of this legislation (P[1]) from their present setting with adequate certainty, yet the incontestable remains of it are sufficiently numerous to enable us to determine its character and antiquity[5]. It was not written *uno tenore*, but is a collection of ordinances,—closely related to each other doubtless,—brought together by a redactor who fitted it into a frame-work of his own[6]. The idea of holiness comes even more prominently into the foreground in this collection than it does in the other priestly laws, so that it has been not inappropriately styled 'the legislation of sanctity[7].' In determining its antiquity we must begin by considering its relation to *Deuteronomy*, to which it is evidently subsequent, though not so remote from it as the laws of P[2] are. This comes out most clearly in the legislation concerning the feasts. Other indications, though less unequivocal, plead for the same relationship[8]. In the next place the legislation itself gives evidence of the date of its origin, and those data which justify a positive inference point to the Babylonian captivity[9]. Finally the comparison with Ezekiel enables us to fix the date still more closely. The points of contact between this prophet and P[1] are so numerous and striking that K. H. Graf, and after him certain other scholars, have regarded Ezekiel himself as the author or as the redactor of the collection. But this is a mistake. The hypothesis gives no account of the difference that accompanies the resemblance, nor is the difficulty met by suggesting that some interval elapsed between Ezekiel's prophecies, especially xl.–xlviii., and the laws he drew up, either earlier or later. In as far as the agreement between Ezekiel and P[1] really requires an explanation, it [269] may be found in the supposition that P[1] was acquainted with the priest-prophet, imitated him and worked on in his spirit. From this it would follow that the 'legislation of sanctity' arose in the second half of the Babylonian captivity, presumably shortly before its close; and there is not a single valid objection to this date[10].

[5] Cf. § 6, n. 26, 27 and L. Horst, *Lev. xvii.–xxvi. und Hesekiel; Ein Beitrag zur Pentateuchkritik* (Colmar, 1881). In identifying the fragments of

P[1] criticism avails itself of a two-fold criterion. We may assign to P[1] with high probability, (*a*) the sections which obviously are not a part of P[2] or its later amplifications, and (*b*) those that are related in form and substance to the concluding discourse in *Lev.* xxvi. 3–45. We therefore recognise P[1] without hesitation in *Lev.* xviii.; in xix., except *v.* 2[a] (where "כל־עדת בני י points to P[2]) and *v.* 21, 22 (which forms an addition to *v.* 20, and shows traces of P[2]'s language); in xx. (except 'and of the stranger who sojourns in Israel,' in *v.* 2, which is taken from P[2]); and in xxvi. 1, 2 (verses which, it must be confessed, have no connection with what precedes or follows, but which manifest all the characteristics of P[1]). As to these chapters and verses there is great unanimity amongst the critics. Kayser (*Das vorexil. Buch*, p. 69) and Horst (op. cit., p. 19), it is true, deny *Lev.* xix. 5–8 to P[1], and regard *v.* 6–8 as an interpolation from *Lev.* vii. 17, 18, but in doing so they fail to observe that a distinction between praise-offerings and ordinary thank-offerings is made in *Lev.* vii. 15–18, which is not observed in *Lev.* xix. 5–8, and must, therefore, have been unknown to the author of these latter verses. They do not depend upon *Lev.* vii. 17, 18 then; and their formal agreement therewith shows rather that the author of *Lev.* vii. knew and adopted them, but at the same time supplemented them. Cf. § 6, n. 28 *b*.—It is not such a simple matter to separate P[1] out of *Lev.* xvii., xxi.–xxv. On *Lev.* xvii. cf. § 6, n. 28 *a*, Dillmann (p. 535) and Horst (p. 14–17). The last-named scholar assigns to P[1] the prohibition of sacrifices elsewhere than at Yahwè's dwelling (*v.* 3–7 in part), of offerings to other gods than Yahwè (*v.* 8 sq.), and of eating blood (*v.* 10–14); to P[2] the prohibition of slaughtering cattle and sheep elsewhere than at the ôhel mo'éd (*v.* 3–7 in part), and of eating terépha and nebéla (*v.* 15 sq.). But his splitting up of *v.* 3–7 cannot be pronounced successful, and traits of P[2] are as obvious in *v.* 8 sq. and 10–14 (Israelites and gérim on the same footing; the entrance into ôhel mo'éd) as traces of P[1] are in *v.* 15 sq. (נשא עונו). When two texts are so completely amalgamated as is here the case, it is impossible to arrive at any certainty as to the original form of either. —In *Lev.* xxi., xxii. I think we must assign the following passages to P[1]:— xxi. 1[b]–9, 10[a] (as far as מאחיו), 11, 12 (in part), 13–15, 16, 17[b]–20, 21 (except 'from the seed of Aaron, the priest'), 22 (the words 'the bread of his god shall he eat' only), 23 (except 'to the veil he shall not draw nigh'); xxii. 8, 9, 10–14 (the last verse perhaps revised after P[2]); 15, 16, 26–28, 31–33; in xxii. 1–7 I can find but a few traces of this legislation; all the rest has been added from or in imitation of P[2], especially the repeated mention of Aaron and his sons, as appears, for instance, from the order of the words in xxi. 17, 21; the regulations concerning temporary uncleanness in xxii. 1–7, the passage [270] xxii. 17–25, which is in formal and substantial harmony with P[2] and *v.* 29, 30 (= *Lev.* vii. 15, 16, deviating from *Lev.* xix. 5–8; see above). Cf. Horst, p. 20–24, with whom I here agree almost throughout.—*Lev.* xxiii. 9–22, 39–43 can only be ascribed to P[1] in a qualified sense, for the characteristic representations and expressions of the rest of the chapter (from P[2]) reappear here also. Note עצם היום הזה (*v.* 14, 21); מלאכת עברה,מקרא קרש, etc. (*v.* 21). Moreover *v.* 18–20 seems to be interpolated from *Num.* xxviii. 27, 29, and *v.* 39–43

likewise appears not to have come down to us in its original form. Cf. § 6,
n. 28, and below, n. 8.—In *Lev.* xxiv. 15–22 we recognise P[1] with ease (*v.* 15,
נשׂא חטאו; *v.* 19,עמית ; *v.* 22, אני יהוה אלהיכם), though even in this section
certain touches appear to have been added from or after P[2] (*v.* 16, 22, where
the gérîm and the Israelites are put on the same footing).—Finally, in *Lev.*
xxv. there can be no doubt that *v.* 1–7 and 18–22 belong to P[1]; in the rest of
the chapter the usual characteristics of the 'legislation of sanctity' only appear
sporadically, especially in *v.* 14, 17, 39[b], 40[a], 43, 46[b], 53, 55 (cf. Horst, p.
27–30). See § 6, n. 28, and below, n. 18.

Nothing could be more natural than that the remains of P[1] should immediately precede the closing discourse *Lev.* xxvi. 3–45, which belongs to them,
that is to say, should be collected in *Lev.* xvii–xxvi. Nevertheless it remains
possible, and indeed is far from improbable *a priori*, that fragments of P[1]
may appear elsewhere also. And as a fact some scholars, relying especially
on linguistic evidence, have thought they could identify such scattered fragments in *Ex.* xxix. 38–46 (or at any rate *v.* 45, 46); xxxi. 12–14[a]; *Lev.* v. 21,
22 [vi. 2, 3] (according to Dillmann elsewhere also, in *Lev.* ii.; *v.* 1–7, 21–26
[vi. 2–7]; vi. [vi. 8–30]; vii.; see below, n. 6); x. 9–11; xi. 1–23, 41–47; xiii.
2–44, 47–58; xiv. 34–45, 48; *Num.* iii. 11–13; x. 9, 10; xv. 37–41; and yet
further in *Ex.* vi. 6–8; xii. 12[b]; and in some other priestly narratives. Cf.
Horst, p. 32–36, and the writers he cites. It is quite true that some of these
passages bear a certain resemblance to P[1] in language. Thus, 'I am Yahwè,'
or 'I, Yahwè, am thy god' (*Ex.* xxix. 46; xxxi. 13; *Lev.* xi. 44, 45; *Num.* iii.
13; x. 10; xv. 41; *Ex.* vi. 6–8; xii. 12[b]) is one of P[1]'s formulæ, though not
peculiar to him (cf. *Ex.* xx. 2; *Deut.* v. 6.) The word עמית, *Lev.* v. 21 [vi. 2],
is likewise one of his terms (*Lev.* xviii. 20 [19]; xix. 11, 15, 17; xxv. 14, 15, 17).
It must also be conceded that the demand for sanctity, which is one of the
most striking characteristics of P[1] (cf. n. 7), is advanced in some of the above-
named passages (*Ex.* xxix. 44; xxxi. 13; *Lev.* xi. 44, 45; *Num.* xv. 40). But
it remains a question whether these phenomena justify us in assigning the
passages to P[1]. An alternative explanation is that their authors knew and
imitated P[1] (cf. n. 12 sqq.). It is only where the several indications combine
and where the context also points to borrowing that the derivation from P[1]
gains more probability. Now this is the case with *Lev.* xi. 44, 45 (with which
v. 1–23, 41–43, 46, 47 are connected) and with *Num.* xv. 37–41. The former
tora might be regarded as announced in *Lev.* xx. 25, and the latter stands off
sharply from the ordinances in *Num.* xv. 1–36, and certainly has not a common origin with them.

[271]   P. Wurster's opinion, *Zur Charakteristik des Priestercodex und Heilig-
keitsgesetzes* (*Zeitschr. f. alttest. Wissensch.*, 1884, p. 112-133), deserves
special mention. He attempts to show that even in *Lev.* xi.-xv., which is
only separated from xvii. sqq. by the single chapter xvi., the oldest elements,
afterwards revised and amplified, were drawn from P[1], viz. *Lev.* xi. 1-7, 9-23,
41, 42, 46, 47; xiii. 1-46[a]; xiv. 1-8[a]; and he discovers the same author
again in *Num.* v. 11-31; vi. 2-8. Vid. op. cit., p. 123-127; and on the addition
of *Num.* vi. 9-12, 13-21, p. 129-133. It is true that these are separate

torôth, adopted and not written by P[2] and his followers. Nor is a certain affinity to P[1] wanting. But it is only in *Lev.* xi. that this affinity is so marked as to make it probable, as we have already seen, that the kernel of the chapter is derived from P[1]. The division of *Num.* vi. 1–21 between two authors is in my opinion impossible : even in *v.* 2–8 it is assumed that the Nazirite's vow is temporary (*v.* 4–6, 8).

[6] It seems rash at first to pronounce so positively on a collection of laws which we only possess in fragments, but in reality nothing is more natural than that Wellhausen, Kayser, Horst and others should agree in the matter. Graf (*Geschichtliche Bücher*, p. 76 sq.) had already remarked, with justice, that *Lev.* xviii. and xx. could not be from one and the same hand ; the current opinion that the latter chapter defines the punishment of the acts forbidden in the former, is not correct. It is a case of two independent, though substantially parallel torôth on the same subject. When we have recognised the mutual relation of these two chapters, we shall be ready to perceive that *Lev.* xxi., xxii. is not by the author (for instance) of xix. It is far soberer and more monotonous than would have been the case had the writer of xix. handled its subject-matter. Nor are the introductory or epitomising exhortations in *Lev.* xviii. 1–5, 24–30 ; xix. 37 ; xx. 22–27 ; xxii. 31–33 ; xxv. 18–22 so closely connected with the precepts that precede or follow them as necessarily to have a common origin with them. It is far more natural to ascribe them to the author of the discourse in *Lev.* xxvi. 3–45, which they strongly resemble in purport and language. Cf. § 6, n. 26, and compare *Lev.* xxv. 19, 22 with xxvi. 4, 10, 20.

All this involves the rejection of Dillmann's hypothesis as to the origin of *Lev.* xvii. sqq. That hypothesis is, in substance, that there existed in Israel a Sinaitic law-book of extreme antiquity—which may be indicated by the letter S—which was drawn upon by later but still præ-exilian authors, including D, and before his time P[2] and J (I use my own designations to avoid confusion). S, adopted and recast by P[2] (say SP[2]), lies at the basis of *Lev.* ii. ; v. 1–7, 21–26 ; vi., vii. ; and, in the recension of another and later lawgiver, of *Lev.* iv. (*Ex. u. Lev.*, p. 373 sqq.). In *Lev.* xi. two recensions of S were employed by R, namely SP[2] and J's recension (say SJ), from the latter of which *v.* 41–44[a] and *v.* 1–23 are largely drawn, whereas *v.* 24–40 and 44[b]–47 are chiefly from SP[2] (p. 480 sq.). A similar origin is assigned to *Lev.* xvii. sqq., which was adopted by R partly from SP[2], partly from SJ. *Lev.* xvii. rests upon SP[2], but in *v.* 4–7 on SJ also (p. 535 sqq.) ; *Lev.* xviii. on SP[2] again (p. 541 sq.) ; *Lev.* xix. 20–22, 30–36 likewise on SP[2], while the [272] rest of this chapter, together with *Lev.* xx. (a few touches from SP[2] excepted) comes from SJ (p. 550, 560). In *Lev.* xxi., xxii., in like manner, R followed SJ for the most part in xxi. 1–15, 16–24, and SP[2] throughout xxii. (p. 563 sqq.). *Lev.* xxiii., xxiv., on the contrary, is taken in its entirety from P[2], but the latter had appropriated regulations from S in xxiii. 9–22, 39 43 ; xxiv. 15–22 (p. 575 sq., 596 sq.). The case is almost the same with *Lev.* xxv. ; xxvi. 1, 2, though here R took a few verses (xxv. 18–22 ; xxvi. 1, 2) from J also (p. 602 sq.). Finally, *Lev.* xxvi. 3–45 is the work of J, and constitutes his hortatory conclusion to the laws which he had adopted from S, but it has been interpolated throughout, and especially in *v.* 32–45, by a later prophetic writer (p. 619 sqq.). *Lev.* xxvii. is P²'s, but he follows S in it, and borrows some of his regulations from that source (p. 628, 636 sq.). We must wait for the publication of Dillmann's commentary on *Num.-Josh.* to know which sections of *Numbers* and *Deuteronomy* he supposes to have been directly or indirectly drawn from S.

Following the objections—conclusive for the most part—urged by Horst (p. 36–47) and Kayser (*Jahrb. f. prot. Theologie*, 1881, p. 648–665), I would make the following remarks on this hypothesis. No one will say that it has simplicity or internal probability to commend it. On the contrary, it is as involved as it well can be. The redactor has two recensions of one and the same law-book before him, and he uses each in turn, so that he sometimes falls into repetitions and contradicts himself. On the other hand he treats his documents with great freedom, and sometimes drops out considerable portions altogether (*Ex. u. Lev.*, p. 550). Such a representation of the origin of *Lev.* xvii. sqq. can hardly be accepted unless imperatively demanded by the facts. And this it certainly is not. Dillmann starts from *Lev.* xviii.-xx. (p. 540 sq.), and then builds upon the result he has there obtained. But here, at the outset, he fails to demonstrate the use of the two recensions (SP² and SJ). It is clear enough, doubtless, that *Lev.* xviii.-xx. was put together and worked up by a collector, and also that certain foreign elements were afterwards inserted into it (see above), but it does not appear that the streams from which the collector drew had flowed from a single source, nor that P² was commenting upon another code—which is constantly in conflict with his own precepts, observe—whenever his hand or that of one of his followers can be traced in *Lev.* xviii.-xx.; and least of all does it appear that by the side of this supposed P²S we have also a JS, i. e. a recension of S in the prophetic spirit, whether by J or by some other such author. It is just this branch of the hypothesis—the most improbable intrinsically—that is most destitute of proof.— The significance of the hypothesis, however, lies not in these two recensions of the one document, but in the high antiquity assigned to the document itself. Dillmann would willingly sacrifice P²S and JS if he could establish S as 'of hoary antiquity.' But conversely, even if we accepted the two recensions, it would not follow that their original had come down from the earliest times. Dillmann had still to prove the high antiquity of S—and he has not proved it. The Israelitish literature does not support, and therefore opposes it. On the relation of D to S in *Lev.* xviii.-xx. see § 14, n. 6, on his relation to S in *Lev.* xxiii., see below, n. 8; and further, [273] n. 9 and 10. The facts to which attention is there called disprove the high antiquity claimed for S by Dillmann, and with it his whole hypothesis.

⁷ The name was suggested by Klostermann (*Zeitschr. f. luth. Theol.* 1877, p. 416), and has been adopted, with good reason, by others. Its appropriateness is apparent, for instance, from *Lev.* xix. 2; xx. 7, 8, 26 xxi. 6-8, 15, 23; xxii. 9, 16, 32 (xi. 44, 45; *Num.* xv. 40). But even where sanctity is not spoken of, it is still before the lawgiver's mind: e. g.

in *Lev.* xviii., xx., where marriage with relatives is condemned as unclean, and in xxii., where the use of the kodashîm is regulated. Cf. Horst, p. 47-51.

[8] The two positions here laid down as to the relation between P[1] and *Deuteronomy.*—viz. (1) that P[1] is later than D, and (2) that he is nearer to him than P[2] is—must be severally illustrated.

With regard to (1), I may refer at once to § 14, n. 6, where the position that D was not acquainted with *Lev.* xvii., xviii.–xx. is defended by citations that, in some cases, clearly demonstrate his priority, whereas there is no proof whatever of the opposite relationship. The comparison of D with *Lev.* xxi. sqq. leads in general to the same result. In *Lev.* xxi. severer demands of purity are laid on the priest than on the layman, and the ordinary priests are distinguished from him 'who is greater than his brethren;' whereas no trace of either of these conceptions can be discovered in D. In D the use of nebéla is forbidden to all alike (*Deut.* xiv. 21[a]); whereas in *Lev.* xxii. 8 nebéla and terépha are forbidden specifically to the priest (on *Lev.* xvii. 15, 16—due in its present form to P[2]—cf. § 14, n. 5). The regulations concerning the pentecost and feast of tabernacles in *Lev.* xxiii. 9-22, 39-43 are more detailed than the corresponding precepts in *Deut.* xvi. 9-12, 13-15, and therefore in all probability later, for in the nature of the case religious usages gradually become more and more accurately determined, and such was in point of fact the course which the Israelitish festal legislation took. The sabbatical year of *Lev.* xxv. 1-7, 18-22 seems to have been unknown to D. At any rate he makes not the smallest allusion to it in his regulations concerning the year of release, xv. 1-11. And is it not highly probable, in itself, that this extension of the sabbath rest to the very soil is a later application of that sabbatical idea which lay so close to the heart of the priests? Cf. *Lev.* xix. 3, 30; *Ex.* xxxi. 12-17; xxxv. 1-3; *Num.* xv. 32-36; and on the relation of *Lev.* xxv. 1-7 to *Ex.* xxiii. 10 sq., see § 11, n. 23.

(2) The mutual relations of P[1] and P[2] in *Lev.* xxiii. have already been explained in § 6, n. 28. I would now further point out that in *Ex.* xiii. 3-10; *Deut.* xvi. 1-8 the feast of maççôth is fixed in the month Abîb, and in *Deut.* xvi. 9-12 Pentecost is fixed seven weeks after the beginning of the harvest, without any definite indication of the days on which the two feasts are to be celebrated. This is completely in harmony with their original character; for, as agricultural feasts, they were necessarily dependent on the harvest and could not possibly be held on a previously determined day. It was not till after the centralisation of worship at Jerusalem that any inconvenience could arise in the matter, and D makes no attempt as yet to obviate it—apparently supposing that the maççôth week and pentecost would be officially announced from Jerusalem year by year in accordance with the condition of the barley [274] and wheat fields. For the same reason 'the feast of ingathering' has no fixed date in *Deut.* xvi. 13-15, and was doubtless intended by the lawgiver to be proclaimed in like manner. Accordingly when P[1], in *Lev.* xxiii., assigns no fixed day either for pentecost or tabernacles, he is following the earlier lawgivers, whereas P[2] deserts their footprints and sacrifices, or at least compromises the true character of the festivals for the sake of regularity and

uniformity. So again the feast of tabernacles lasts seven days according to P¹ (*Lev.* xxiii. 39–41) as it does in *Deut.* xvi. 15, whereas P² (*Lev.* xxiii. 35, 36, from which *v.* 39 has been interpolated) departs from them and specifies eight days. In this connection we may note that in 1 *Kings* viii. 65 sq. 'the feast,' i. e. the feast of tabernacles, lasts seven days, and on the eighth day Israel returns homewards, whereas in 2 *Chron.* vii. 8–10 the eighth day is absorbed into the festival and Israel is dismissed not on the 22nd but on the 23rd of the seventh month. The regulations which the earlier narrator presupposes (those of D and P¹, to which *Ezek.* xlv. 25 still adheres), are unquestionably older than those with which the later Chronicler makes the account of his predecessor square (those of P²). Dillmann (p. 575 sqq.) does not admit the distinction between P¹ and P², and therefore thinks it possible that *Lev.* xxiii. 9–22, 39–43, as well as the rest of the chapter, belongs to P². Yet he sees the difference between these verses and the others, and therefore supposes that P² borrowed them from S. But if this were so then *v.* 39–43 certainly would not come after P²'s ordinances as to the feast of tabernacles, in *v.* 33–36, and the colophon of his whole festal legislation, in *v.* 37, 38. It is true that no law of Pentecost from P² precedes *v.* 9–22, but this is no proof of Dillmann's hypothesis. No more is the absence of maççôth and phésach in the fragments of P¹. The redactor of *Lev.* xxiii. might reproduce both P² and P¹ in a single instance (*v.* 33–36 and 39–43) without its following that he must do so always. And what could be more natural than that, as a rule, he should only adopt one of them? The harmonising shifts to which Dillmann is reduced are conclusive evidence against his theory. 'The day after the sabbath,' in *v.* 11, 15, which, as we learn from *v.* 10 and *Deut.* xvi. 9, can be no other than the first day of the harvest week, Dillmann explains by *v.* 5–8,—with which, however, the writer himself would have brought it into connection, had such been his meaning. The 'seven days' of *v.* 39–41, and the indefinite formulæ 'when you gather in the produce of the land' and 'in the seventh month,' *v.* 39, 41, are sacrificed to *v.* 33–36 and to *v.* 39, which has been interpolated from them. Such explanations can content no one who has once seen the true bearings of *v.* 9 sqq., 39 sqq. The relation of P¹ to D on the one side and to P² on the other, which comes out so clearly in *Lev.* xxiii., is further illustrated by the following facts : *a.* P¹, though priestly in origin and character, has a number of precepts in common with D, whereas the parallel passages between P² and D are very few ; *b.* the exaltation of one of the priests above his brethren, which distinguishes P¹ from D (see under (1)), is carried much further yet in P² ; *c.* P²'s year of jubilee, in *Lev.* xxv. 8–17, 23–55, is further removed than P¹'s sabbatical year in *Lev.* xxv. 1–7 from *Deut.* xv. 1–11, 12–18.

[275]   ⁹ In the nature of the case the several laws in *Lev.* xvii. sqq. give no unequivocal evidence as to the age of the lawgiver. They are conceived in general terms and are written in the person of Moses. Neither have the exhortations *Lev.* xviii. 1–5, 24–30; xix. 2, 37 ; xx. 22–26 any date stamped upon them. It is clear that the settlement in Canaan is merely represented as still in the future, but it does not appear how far back in the past it really

lies. It is otherwise with the concluding discourse in *Lev.* xxvi. 3-45. Here too Moses is the speaker, the conquest of the land is in the future, Israel's attitude towards Yahwè's ordinances and judgments is uncertain, and so forth. But involuntarily the author, like the writer of *Deut.* xxix. sq., iv. 25 sqq., etc., allows his own historical position to shine through. He knows that Israel has sacrificed on bamôth and in sanctuaries, has reared chammanim and served idols (*v.* 30 sq.). He not only anticipates the dispersion of Israel and the devastation of his land (*v.* 33), but can regard this depopulation and lying fallow of the land as the penalty for the neglect of the sabbath law, as the payment in full of what the soil owes to Yahwè (*v.* 34, 35, 43). This last trait is decisive. The trespass could not be assumed as a fact when the law had only just been given, nor even while it was still open to observe it though it had already been neglected for a time. We cannot fail to recognise, under the form of a prophecy, the writer's account of the fact which he actually witnessed—the land lying fallow. The same conclusion is supported by *v.* 36 sqq. (parallel with *Deut.* xxix. sq.; iv. 25 sqq.; cf. § 7, n. 22 (4)), where the punishment is past and only the penitence and restoration are future: Israel, then, is in exile. Horst (p. 65 sq.), on the strength of these very verses, places *Lev.* xxvi. 3-45 shortly before the captivity, perhaps under Zedekiah, but in this he fails to do justice to their contents or to distinguish between what was necessarily involved in the form selected by the writer and what we may infer as to his own date from the underlying assumptions on which he goes. Wurster (op. cit., p. 122 sq.) declares for the early years after the return and appeals in support of this date to the practical character of P¹'s precepts concerning the priests, the sacrifices, the feasts, etc.; and also to his demand, in *Lev.* xvii. 3 sqq., that there should be no slaughtering save at the sanctuary—a demand which might have been made just after 536 B.C., but at no other time. On this last point see § 6, n. 28 and § 14, n. 6. Wurster's theory, which really differs but little from my own, is very seductive, and might be accepted were it not opposed to *Lev.* xxvi. 3-45, which shows us that Israel's time of punishment is not yet over.—Though I do not think a comparison of *Lev.* xxvi. with the denunciations in *Deuteronomy* decides the question of priority either way (but see Wellh., *Prolegomena*, 405 [381 sq.]), yet the language quite confirms the date we have assigned, as I shall presently show with respect to P¹ as a whole. This is granted by Dillmann too (p. 618 sqq.) as far as *Lev.* xxvi. goes. But he thinks that the later words only occur sporadically in *v.* 3-31, and that it is not till we come to *v.* 32 sqq. that they become more frequent. He therefore supposes that this discourse was composed in the eighth century, and was interpolated, expanded and supplemented during the captivity. But this hypothesis is without foundation. The passage is a single whole. See נגע, *v.* 43, 44, as in *v.* 11, 15, 30; קרי, *v.* 40, 41, as in *v.* 21, 23, 24, 27, 28; *v.* 36, 37 in connection with *v.* 17; *v.* 43, 44 in connection with *v.* 15. But the progress of the whole discourse pleads more powerfully than any detached expressions for its unity. *V.* 31 is not a conclusion. The covenant struck in [276] *v.* 9, broken in *v.* 15, and avenged by the sword in *v.* 25, cannot be severed from its restoration in *v.* 42, 44, 45 ; and if these latter verses are part of the original, then all that precedes and prepares for them from *v.* 32 onward must be so too. Dillmann's view of *Lev.* xvii. sqq. encounters an obstacle in *Lev.* xxvi. 3–45 which cannot be put aside, and which should have sufficed to make him reconsider his whole hypothesis.

The general character of P¹'s l a n g u a g e is indicated by the fact that it is mainly on the strength of linguistic evidence that he has been identified with Ezekiel (n. 10). It is an unquestionable fact that his laws and ex-hortations contain a number of words that appear for the first time in the writers of the Chaldæan period (D, Jeremiah, and yet later authors). The value to be attached to this evidence will be discussed in n. 11. I shall con-fine myself here to enumerating a few examples. The following words are taken from Giesebrecht's table (cf. n. 11): מדינת נפש, אכלה, בקרה, הבדיל, הבריל, קרבן, חקים, ברית מוך, מכך, מקק, פעלה, פרך, תושב, מושבת, התורה, נָכָר, רגם, רדה, רכל, משורה, משכית, שקץ, Piel and שֶׁקֶץ, with which the parallel passages and Giesebrecht's explanations should be compared. We may further note גלולים (*Lev.* xxvi. 30; *Deut.* xxix. 16 [17]; *Jer.* l. 2 ; *Ezek.* passim; *Kings* six times) ; געל (*Lev.* xxvi. 11, 15, 30, 44; *Jer.* xiv. 19 ; *Ezek.* xvi. 45 ; *Job* xxi. 10; and in another sense 2 *Sam.* i. 21) ; אזרח (*Lev.* xvii. 15; xix. 34 ; xxiii. 42 ; *Ezek.* xlvii. 22 ; *Psalm* xxxvii. 35 [?] ; P² *passim*) ; חסר (Aramæan ; *Lev.* xx. 17 ; *Prov.* xiv. 34 ?) ; נָדָּה (*Lev.* xviii. 19; xx. 21 ; *Zech.* xiii. 1; *Lam.* i. 17 ; *Ezek.* and P² *passim*; *Ezr.* ix. 11 ; 2 *Chron.* xxix. 5) ; יען וביען (*Lev.* xxvi. 43 ; *Ezek.* xiii. 10 ; xxxvi. 3) ; פגול (*Lev.* xix. 7 ; vii. 18 ; *Ezek.* iv. 14 ; *Isaiah* lxv. 4) ; קוא (*Lev.* xviii. 25, 28 ; xx. 22 ; *Prov.* xxiii. 8 ; xxv. 16 ; *Job* xx. 15 ; *Jonah* ii. 11 [10] ; רצה (Kal, and Hiphil in another sense, *Lev.* xxvi. 34, 41, 43 ; cf. Dillm. ; Niphal, *Lev.* xix. 7 ; xxii. 23, 27 ; i. 4 ; vii. 18 ; *Isaiah* xl. 2) ; תועבה (*Lev.* xviii. 22, 26, 27, 29, 30 ; xx. 13 ; appears as early as *Isaiah* i. 13 ; also in *Gen.* xliii. 32 ; xlvi. 34 ; *Ex.* viii. 22 [26] ; but only becomes frequent, through the influence of D, in *Jeremiah, Ezekiel,* etc.). See further n. 10.

¹⁰ The identity of P¹ and Ezekiel has been maintained, after Graf (*Ge-schichtliche Bücher,* p. 81–83) by Bertheau, in his review of Graf's work (*Jahrb. f. d. Theol.* 1866, p. 150 sqq.), Colenso (*Pentateuch,* vi. (1871) p. 3 sqq.; App. p. 1–8), Kayser (*Vorexil. Buch.,* p. 176–184; *Jahrb. f. p. Theol.* 1881, p. 548–553) and, most recently of all, by Horst (p. 69–96), though the last-named scholar differs from his predecessors in regarding Ezekiel as the collector of the laws in *Lev.* xvii. sqq., and the writer only of the discourse in *Lev.* xxvi. 3–45. On the other hand, Graf's hypothesis is combated or rejected by Nöldeke (*Untersuchungen zur Kritik d. A. T.* p. 67–71) ; by myself (*Godsdienst,* ii. 94–96 [*Rel. Isr.* ii. 189–192]); G. C. Steynis (*De ver-houding van de wetgeving bij Ezech. tot die in den Pent.,* p. 124 sqq.); Well-hausen (xxii. 440 sq. ; *Prolegomena,* 399 sqq., [376 sqq.]); Klostermann (*Hat Ezechiel die in Lev.* 18–26 *am deutlichsten erkennbare Gesetzessamm-lung verfasst ?* in *Zeitschr. f. luth. Theol.* 1877, p. 406–445); Reuss (*L'hist. sainte et la loi,* Introd. p. 252 sq.); Smend (*Der. Proph. Ezekiel,* p. xxv. sqq., 314 sq.); Delitzsch (*Stud.,* p. 617 sqq.), but whereas Nöldeke,

Klostermann, and Delitzsch assign the priority to *Lev.* xvii. sqq. the [277] others give it to Ezekiel.—The positions laid down in the text rest upon the following considerations :—

(1) The similarity in style, vocabulary, and phraseology is very remarkable. See, more especially, C o l e n s o, vi. 3 sqq.; and H o r s t, p. 72 sqq. Ezekiel and *Lev.* xxvi. have twenty-two expressions in common that occur nowhere else in the Old Testament, and thirteen more that occur nowhere else in the Pentateuch. In the nature of the case coincidences between the prophet and *Lev.* xvii. sqq. are less frequent, but amongst them are the following : הלך בחקות (*Lev.* xviii. 3 ; xx. 23 ; xxvi. 3 ; *Ezek.* v. 6, 7 and in ten other places) : אשר יעשה אתם האדם וחי בהם (*Lev.* xviii. 5 ; *Ezek.* xx. 11, 13, 21 (25) ; compare *Ezek.* iii. 17 sqq. ; xviii. 9, 13, 19 sqq., 31 sq. ; xxxiii. 8 sqq., 12 sqq.) ; גלה ערות פ" (*Lev.* xviii., xx., *passim* ; *Ezek.* xvi. 36, 37 ; xxii. 10 ; xxiii. 10, 18, 29) ; the use of המקרש, of הלל with יהוה שם or with מקרש יהוה, etc., etc. Specially noteworthy too are *Lev.* xxvi. 39 = *Ezek.* iv. 17 ; xxiv. 23 ; xxxiii. 10 ; *Lev.* xxvi. 11 = *Ezek.* xxxvii. 26, 27 (xxv. 4) ; *Lev.* xxvi. 4, 20 = *Ezek.* xxxiv. 27. Mutual independence is out of the question in such a case.

(2) This resemblance is accompanied by linguistic differences. Some of the idioms of *Lev.* xxvi. do not appear in Ezekiel ; such are ישן נושן (*v.* 10 ; cf. *Lev.* xxv. 22) ; ואין רדף (*v.* 17, 36, 37) ; הלך קרי (*v.* 21, 23, 24, 27, 28, 40, 41), etc. Ezekiel never uses אני יהוה alone, though the phrase ' and ye (they) shall know that I am Yahwè' occurs times without number. Nor does he use עמית. More might be urged of a like nature. But I would not venture to assert that these divergencies exclude the identity of P[1] and Ezekiel, especially if we refer the ' legislation of sanctity,' and the prophecies to different periods of Ezekiel's life. I attach more importance to the difference in artistic power, which in my opinion raises *Lev.* xxvi. 3–45 above Ezekiel's denunciations. But neither is this conclusive against identity of authorship ; for Ezekiel may have risen above himself on occasion. It is only on condition of our finding other proofs that P[1] and Ezekiel are not the same that we can bring in these formal divergencies as confirmatory evidence.

(3) These other proofs are not wanting. At the outset we must note the ascription of ' the legislation of sanctity' to Moses. We are not in a position to say that Ezekiel would have felt a scruple against this, but we can say that as far as we know he never made use of this form of utterance, and that a priori we have no right whatever to expect it from him. In xl.–xlviii. he makes Yahwè himself announce the regulations of the restored theocracy. What could have induced him, a few years earlier or later, to relegate similar precepts to the Mosaic age? If these latter are earlier than xl.–xlviii., then Ezekiel, as the organ of Yahwè, is himself made to annul a portion of them ; if on the other hand they are later, then he must have cancelled his first draft. But in that case, why did he not withdraw it? Though it is conceivable enough in itself that a prophet should introduce Moses as a speaker, yet such a *bis in idem* as G r a f and the rest assume is in a high degree improbable.

(4) Add to this that with all their affinities Ezekiel and P[1] differ in [278]

their precepts. It is not without reason that Smend (op. cit.) speaks of
' a whole series of important differences in matter.' If these differences
were all of a similar kind they might be chronologically explained on the
supposition that, either in xl.–xlviii. or in *Lev.* xvii. sqq., Ezekiel had modified his former ordinances in one definite direction. But this is not the
case. It is only now and then that the divergent ordinances seem to stand
in any such relation to each other, and even then the priority seems to
belong now to *Lev.* xvii. sqq., and now to *Ezek.* xl. sqq. P¹ never mentions subordinate priests (Levites),—not even in *Lev.* xxii. 1–13, whereas
Ezekiel introduces and justifies the distinction between priests and under-
priests (xliv. 9 sqq., cf. n. 15). In P¹ maççôth and tabernacles have no
fixed date (cf. n. 8); in Ezekiel they have (xlv. 21, 25); in P¹ we find
the sheaf of the first-fruits and the feast of pentecost (*Lev.* xxiii. 9 sqq.),
which Ezekiel does not mention, probably for the same reason which made
him loosen the connection between the two other high festivals and the
cultivation of the land.—On the other hand, P¹ is in advance of Ezekiel in
the law of the sabbatical year (*Lev.* xxv. 1–7 ; cf. xxvi. 34 sq., 43), to which
the prophet never refers, unless he alludes to it in xlvi. 17 (§ 11, n. 24),
where in any case he says nothing of the land lying fallow. But above all
there is the distinction drawn between the priests and the High Priest, in
Lev. xxi. 1–9, 10–15, of which Ezekiel knows nothing whatever. That this
is no accident appears from *Lev.* xxi. 5, 10 compared with *Ezek.* xliv. 20
(פרע forbidden in the latter passage to all the priests, in the former to
the High Priest alone), and from *Lev.* xxi. 7, 13, 14 compared with *Ezek.*
xliv. 22 (the prohibition of marriage with a layman's widow is cancelled
in *Leviticus* as far as the ordinary priest is concerned, and intensified in
the case of the High Priest into the prohibition of marriage with any
widow). In the same way a comparison of *Ezek.* xlvi. 14 with *Lev.* xxiii.
13 points to a difference of authorship. In *Ezekiel* the mincha that accompanies the lamb of the daily morning sacrifice consists of a sixth of an
ephah of meal and a third of a hîn of oil, whereas in other cases the
mincha is expressly left of undefined amount, *v.* 5, 7, 11 ; but in *Lev.*
xxiii. the lamb of the firstlings is accompanied by a mincha of two-tenths of
an ephah of meal, with oil poured over it, and a quarter of a hîn of wine
(a precept which, in its turn, deviates from that of P², *Ex.* xxix. 40 ;
Num. xxviii. 5, 9, 13 sqq.; xxix. 4 sqq., where the mincha to go with a
lamb is fixed at one-tenth of an ephah of meal, a quarter of a hîn of oil,
and a quarter of a hîn of wine). The difference in the quantities of meal
prescribed is just what might be expected between two writers : in defining the amount of oil Ezekiel goes further than P¹; his silence about
the wine as an element in the sacrifice is not accidental, for elsewhere too
he omits it. Even in xlv. 17 הנסך seems to mean the oil (cf. Smend),
and xx. 28 certainly implies no approval of the customary libation. Further,
compare xliv. 21 with *v.* 29.—Horst (p. 91 sqq.) allows most of these
points of difference, but he thinks they put no difficulty in the way of the
hypothesis he defends, viz. that Ezekiel was the collector and not the author

of the 'legislation of sanctity.' But in that case what could make him subsequently deviate from the laws he had himself collected? Why fix the amount of the mincha differently and pass the High Priest by in silence? Why not follow *Lev.* xxiii. 9 sqq. in including Pentecost amongst the high festivals to be celebrated by communal offerings?

(5) If the supposition that P[1] and Ezekiel are identical thus falls to the [279] ground, the question remains to which of the two we must give the priority. Ezekiel's assumption of the legislator's office in xl. sqq. is best explained on the supposition that the priestly toroth had not been codified before his time. He thus appears to be the elder. We have also seen that some of P[1]'s precepts represent a more advanced stage of development than Ezekiel's (see under (4)). So far all the indications agree; but we likewise noted some points on which Ezekiel is in advance of P[1] on the road that leads to P[2]. This does not force us to reverse our decision, however, for it is quite conceivable that in these special points P[2] attached himself to Ezekiel, whereas P[1] adhered to the older tradition. And, again, the date inferred from *Lev.* xxvi. 3-45 (n. 9) confirms the priority of Ezekiel; for the author of this discourse has a longer exile behind him than Ezekiel has. Hence it follows that in *Lev.* xxvi., where P[1] coincides with Ezekiel, he is imitating him—sometimes word for word. And as a matter of fact (cf. Wellhausen, *Prolegomena*, 404 sq., 407 sq. [381, 383 sq.]) it is clear, for instance, that *Ezek.* xxxiii. 10 is the original which the prophet himself in xxiv. 23 and P[1] in *Lev.* xxvi. 39 make use of. Not a single valid objection can be urged against this view of the relations of P[1] and Ezekiel. It is perfectly true that *Ezek.* xviii. 6, 7 and xxii. 7-12 respectively imply that the commandments now contained in *Lev.* xviii. 19, 20; xix. 13, 15, 35; xxv. 14, 17, 36; and *Lev.* xviii. 7, 9, 15, 19, 20; xix. 16, 30, 33; xx. 9, 10, etc., were by no means evolved after Ezekiel's time, but could be assumed by him as well known to his contemporaries pretty much in the form in which we have them in P[1] (cf. Horst, p. 81-83). But no one maintains that P[1] invented these and other such precepts. They may even have been in writing long before his time, like the tora which D incorporated in xiv. 3-21 (§ 14, n. 5); but the date of P[1] himself must not be confounded with that of his sources. In the same way we must grant to Klostermann (op. cit., p. 436 sqq.) that the formula אני יהוה appears in an earlier form in *Lev.* xviii. sqq. than in Ezekiel; but it is not the creation of P[1], who borrowed it from the older lawgivers (cf. *Ex.* xx. 2). Again, it is true that Ezekiel, both in this and many other cases, is dependent either on older toroth or on his prophetic predecessors, and Klostermann seems to regard the fact—on which he dwells with great emphasis, p. 413 sqq.—as conclusive. But how does this prove that Ezekiel was not followed, in his turn, by a later lawgiver? Delitzsch (p. 619) thinks that this 'inversion of the true relationship' makes the drastic changes in Ezekiel's festal and sacrificial legislation initiated by P[1] entirely inexplicable, but I answer that we are no more bound to regard P[1] as a slavish copyist of Ezekiel than Delitzsch himself is bound to make Ezekiel uniformly follow P[1]. Moreover we know—and this is conclusive—that P[2] likewise departed from Ezekiel in very important particulars.

In the priestly elements of the Hexateuch which remain
after the withdrawal of P[1], we have already (§ 6) seen reason
to recognise the several portions of a single whole, a historico-
legislative work (P[2]) that begins with the creation of heaven
and earth, passes on, after a rapid survey of the history of the
[280] primitive world and the patriarchs, to the narrative of Israel's
release from Egypt and the legislation of Moses, and ends
with the settlement of Israel in Canaan. But in our previous
investigation we never proved that these legislative and
narrative passages (1) really belong to each other, and (2)
once constituted a single and independent whole. All this
we tacitly assumed or merely sought to render probable *primâ
facie*. We have now reached a point of our inquiry at which
we can give the full proof.

But first we must ask whether we are justified in assuming
as our point of departure the date which we fixed for the
legislation in § 12, chiefly on the strength of the narratives
concerning Ezra and Nehemiah. We have no hesitation in
answering in the affirmative. We shall take the post-
exilian origin of P[2]'s laws, and *a fortiori* of those of
his followers, as our point of departure, looking forward
to a closer chronological definition in due course. For no
single objection that can throw any doubt upon this date
has been urged. The language of the priestly legislator
cannot, in the nature of the case, lead to any absolute certainty, but it raises no difficulty whatever against the supposition that he lived in the sixth or fifth century B.C.[11]
The same hypothesis is in some cases supported and in others
demanded by the relation of P[2]'s ordinances to those of P[1]
and of the prophet Ezekiel, and more generally by the consideration of their contents taken in connection with the established
facts of the history of Israel and of the Israelitish religion.
Not till the period we have named could any system of
legislation treat the people as a religious community (or

congregation) rather than as an independent body politic[12]; assign the foremost place to the High Priest[13]; make the centralisation of worship, as an accomplished fact, its point of departure[14]; explain the difference between priests and Levites genealogically and enforce it with the utmost rigour[15]; make such provisions as we find in P² for the support of priests and Levites alike[16]; and, finally, regulate the whole worship after the pattern observed in these laws[17]. In all these essentials, as well as in minor matters[18], P²'s legislation stands in such relations to the ordinances of *Deuteronomy*, of Ezekiel and of P¹, as its later origin, within the sixth, or the first half of the fifth century, would demand and would [281] alone explain.

[11] Cf. C. V. Ryssel, *De Elohistæ Pentateuchici sermone* (Lips. 1878); F. Giesebrecht, *Zur Hexateuchkritik. Der Sprachgebrauch des hexateuchischen Elohisten* (*Zeitschr. f. alttest. Wissensch.* i. 177–276); S. R. Driver, *On some alleged linguistic affinities of the Elohist* (Journal of Philology, vol. xi. 201–236). In the present note we shall only deal with that portion of the subject of the above-named essays which refers to the laws of P², and the narrative sections inextricably intertwined with them. The language of his narratives, especially from *Gen.* i. to *Ex.* vi., will be expressly examined hereafter (n. 21), inasmuch as it has been alleged in proof of the high antiquity of these passages. Only a part of the laws on which we are engaged were committed to writing by P² himself. Some were incorporated into his work, or incorporated into the Hexateuch along with his work, at a subsequent period, while others are of yet later origin, and must be regarded as amplifications or modifications of his precepts. But here, in discussing the question whether the language of these laws presents any obstacle to the recognition of their post-exilian origin, these differences may be ignored.

Well-founded objections are urged by Giesebrecht (p. 177 sqq.) against the method followed by Ryssel in his plea for the high antiquity of P². Ryssel (p. 19 sqq.) distinguishes three 'ætates' in the history of the Hebrew language, 1. from the earliest times to the year 700 B.C.; 2. from 700 B.C. to the end of the sixth century, so that Haggai and Zechariah (i.–viii.) are still within the limits of this 'ætas'; 3. from 450 B.C. to the close of the Old Testament literature (*a.* the memoirs of Ezra and Nehemiah; *b.* Chronicles and Ecclesiastes; *c.* Daniel and Esther). He then proceeds to ask whether P² belongs to the 3rd period, and answers in the negative. But (1) seeing that no one supposes P² to be a contemporary of the Chronicler, Ryssel has only the fragments of Ezra and Nehemiah left for comparison, and they are

U

far too limited in extent to furnish a standard, and (2) the question is not whether P² and Ezra are one and the same person, or even whether they are absolutely contemporary, but whether there is anything in P²'s language to prevent our supposing that he is later than *Deuteronomy,* Jeremiah, Ezekiel, and Deutero-Isaiah. It is to this point that the inquiry should have been directed.—Now when we consider the obvious tendency of Ryssel's essay, it is highly remarkable that his results should be so unfavourable as they actually are to the high antiquity of the laws in P². He discovers a whole series of formations and grammatical peculiarities in them which are special to his second 'ætas' (p. 35 sqq.), a list of Aramæisms that is not to be despised (p. 70-72), and even some phenomena that belong exclusively to his third 'ætas' (אֲשֶׁר יֵשׁ, *Num.* ix. 20 sq.; הוּא הַלַּיְלָה הַזֶּה, *Ex.* xii. 42; p. 61, 63; cf. also p. 68, on מִקְרָא, מֹסַע, מַשָּׂא, שָׁרֶת, and p. 77, n. 1 : 'Attamen concedendum est in quibusdam particulis ad librum Numerorum pertinentibus pauca inesse posterioris ætatis vestigia, quæ in recentissimis demum libris reperiantur. Quibus solis si quis, aliis disquisitionis partibus prorsus neglectis (!), nitatur, eum eo posse adduci, ut has partes statuat post exilium [i. e. after the year 450 B.C.] esse conscriptas haud negaverim'). But Ryssel thinks that these idioms occur exclusively in a single group of laws, concerning the tabernacle, [282] the priests and the Levites, which he therefore refers to the second 'ætas,' while deriving the rest, together with the narratives in *Gen.* i.–*Ex.* vi., from the first 'ætas.' To the question which laws belong to this later group, we receive, strangely enough, somewhat divergent answers. The final list (p. 80) embraces the laws in *Ex.* xii. (in part); xxv.–xxxi.; xxxv.–xl. ; *Lev.* viii.–x.; xxvii.; *Num.* i.–x. 28; xv.–xix.; xxvi. sqq. (i. e. xxvi.–xxxvi.). But in note 2 (*ibid.*) *Num.* xv. 1–16 ; xxviii. sq. and xxxii. sq. are included amongst the earlier passages; and on p. 78 we read not that *Lev.* viii.–x., xxvii., but that '*Lev.* v. sqq. exceptis capite undecimo aliisque legum partibus' belong to the later group; while on p. 45 the 'particulæ' (*sic*) in which the forms תְּלוּנָה, תְּנוּאָה and the like occur, are thus summed up : 'Ex. 25–30, 35 sequ.; Lev. 5, 7, 10, 22, 23; Num. 5, 6, 14–28 sequ.' This vacillation, however, is not altogether inexplicable. The truth is that it is hazardous in the extreme thus to divide P²'s laws between two 'ætates.' The criteria relied on are wholly inadequate, as Ryssel himself appears to feel when (p. 81) he seeks support for his divisions from Wellhausen whose results, however, differ totally from his own. But the strangest is yet to come. The grammatical and linguistic peculiarities which are accepted as conclusive, would lead to a different conclusion from the one which Ryssel arrives at. In *Lev.* i.–vii., which is finally relegated to 'ætas 1,' the following traces of the later usage, recognised as such by Ryssel himself, occur: פָּגוּל (p. 41), מַרְחֶשֶׁת (p. 43), תְּנוּפָה, תְּרוּמָה (p. 44 sq.), תְּשׁוּמתִּיר (p. 44 sq.), מִלּוּאִים (p. 51), אַשְׁמָה, טֻמְאָה (p. 49), מִשְׁחָה (p. 49), פִּדְיֹן (p. 47), הִגִּיעַ intrans. (p. 54), מַחֲצִית (p. 41), אֶזְכָּרָה (p. 46), לְעֻמַּת (p. 79 n.), מִן abundans (*Lev.* iv. 2 ; v. 13, p. 62 n. cf. 67) and the Aramæisms חָזֶה and הַתּוֹרָה. Even if the evidential value of some of these forms should be invalidated, more than enough would still remain to expose the utter uncertainty of Ryssel's conclusions. What he grants concerning a single group of laws, he ought, from his own point of view, to extend to all P²'s legislation.

While Ryssel concerns himself chiefly with the forms and grammar of P², and only devotes a few pages—chiefly of a polemical character—to his vocabulary (p. 69-76), Giesebrecht, on the other hand, makes it his special task to acquaint us with the latter. With this view he takes all the commonest words in P² (and some in P¹)—omitting technical terms, however, which admit of no comparison with other books of the Old Testament—arranges them alphabetically, and then states, in separate columns, whether, and if so where, each of them occurs in writings (1) earlier than 700, (2) between 700 and 600 B.C., (3) of the exilian and post-exilian period. Finally, there is a column in which we are told whether the words, or significations, in point are known in Aramæan. The result of this comparison is thus summed up (p. 206): 'In the early period the points of contact between the prophetico-poetic literature and the chohistic lexicon amount to almost nothing; in the eighth century they are still of very moderate frequency; in Deuteronomy they rise to a number which almost doubles that of the earlier literature; and thenceforth they rise steadily from Job, Proverbs and Jeremiah to Deutero-Isaiah and Ezekiel.' The same gradual ascent is traced through the historical books (p. 206 sqq.). These facts are incontestible. Giesebrecht's table is carefully drawn up, and the result summarised above remains true, even if we think that here and there he may have gone too [283] far in excluding parallel passages from the earlier prophetic and historical literature which he regards as corrupt or interpolated. The question remains, however, what evidential value can we ascribe to these facts. To my mind their importance is chiefly negative. They seem to prove, not that P² belongs to the exilian or post-exilian period, but that it is vain to attempt to vindicate a high antiquity for his work, and place it, for instance, in the eighth century B.C., on the strength of linguistic evidence. We may see from Driver's essay (op. cit.) that the conclusion which Giesebrecht draws from his parallels, is open to dispute in a large number of the cases when taken separately. It is not proved, and strictly speaking it is not susceptible of proof, that the numerous words which P² has in common with the writers of the sixth century were not really in use in earlier times; for their absence from the older literature may be simply accidental; neither is it proved that the eighteen Aramæisms noted by Ryssel and the ten others added by Giesebrecht (p. 220-228), all of them really are Aramæisms and not good old Hebrew words which the earlier writers knew but did not use because they did not require them for their purpose, which differed much from that of P². Linguistic comparisons, therefore, do not furnish a positive or conclusive argument. But they do furnish a very strong presumption against the theory that the priestly laws were written in the golden age of Israelitish literature. As long as P² is regarded as a contemporary of Isaiah, the ever increasing number of parallels must remain an enigma. A constantly recurring phenomenon is not satisfactorily explained by accident or by very special causes. It must rest on some general basis. If it should appear on other grounds

(n. 12 sqq.) that the legislation of P² is post-exilian, it will also follow that
Giesebrecht is right in bringing the characteristics of the author's vocabulary into connection with the period in which he lived, and that any other
explanation of it, though possible in the abstract, is incorrect in point of fact.

¹² הָעֵדָה (on which cf. Giesebrecht, p. 243–245) or עֲדַת בְּנֵי יִשְׂרָאֵל is P²'s
usual designation for the community of Israel. It occurs about a hundred times.
Primarily the word signifies the Mosaic Israel, encamped in the desert, but
the condition, attitude and needs of his own contemporaries are always before
the legislator's mind as he speaks of the עֵדָה. What these are is indicated
negatively by the absence of such regulations as those of *Deut.* xvi. 18–20;
xvii.; xviii. 9–22 (on judges, kings and prophets) and positively by the
ordinances themselves, which—as Reuss expresses it in Ersch u. Gruber,
Encycl. Sect. II, Band xxvii. 337—were obviously intended 'not for a great,
far-spreading nation, but for a people drawn close together, within easy
survey, and to some extent evidently dwelling together at a single place, a
people amongst whom private property in land and the rights of inheritance
based upon it were established, yet to whom, as to a nascent community,
agrarian laws that testify to certain theoretical principles, but are in conflict
with all experience, destined to secure equality of possessions and to avert
pauperism, might approve themselves in the abstract, though impossible to
carry out. Such conditions had never been realised either at Sinai or since
David's time. The laws were written for political conditions in which
communal autonomy existed but not national independence.'—The עֵדָה, and
with it the age of the legislator, is further characterised by the regulations
[284] concerning the gêrîm, who are subject to the same laws as the native members
of the community, or in other words are incorporated into it (*Ex.* xii. 49;
Lev. xxiv. 22; *Num.* ix. 14; xv. 29, etc.).

¹³ 'Princes' or 'heads,' נְשִׂיאֵי הָעֵדָה (on the word itself see Giesebrecht,
p. 237 sq.), appear as the representatives and leaders of the עֵדָה in P², even
before they have been appointed by Moses in *Num.* ii. (*Ex.* xvi. 22; xxxiv.
31; xxxv. 27; *Num.* i. 16, 44) and frequently afterwards (*Num.* iv. 34, 46
and *passim*; *Josh.* ix. 15, 18, 19, 21; xvii. 4; xxii. 30, 32). In the legislation
their continued existence is at least once assumed, *Lev.* iv. 22, but their duties
are nowhere defined. So much however is clear: that the High Priest is
placed above them, and takes the first rank in the community. In *Lev.* iv. he
precedes 'the whole community of Israel' and the nasi' (*v.* 3, 13, 22). Aaron
is always mentioned, during his life, together with Moses, and so is his son
and successor Eleazar after him (*Num.* xxvi. 1, 63; xxvii. 2, 19, etc.), and when
Moses dies Eleazar takes the first place (*Num.* xxxiv. 17; *Josh.* xiv. 1; xix.
51; xxi. 1). In harmony with all this the law of the cities of refuge, *Num.*
xxxv. 9–34, mentions the death of the High Priest as the *terminus ad quem* of
the homicide's abode in asylum (*v.* 25, 28, 32; *Josh.* xx. 6). The law, as a
whole, is certainly an amplification of *Deut.* xix. 1–13 (*Ex.* xxi. 13, 14) and
the regulation just referred to shows that it was written when the High
Priest was the chief magistrate, i. e. after the Babylonian captivity. But in
determining the date of P² we have to consider the High Priest's relation-

ship to his colleagues, as well as his political significance. The evidence concerning the pre-exilian organization of the hierarchy has been collected and illustrated in § 11, n. 15. The conclusion there arrived at that in the kingdom of Judah the High Priest was no more than the head for the time being of the priesthood (of Jerusalem), *primus inter pares*, is in perfect harmony with the fact that he is never mentioned either in Deuteronomy or by Ezekiel. The silence of the latter, more especially, is wholly inexplicable if P²'s regulations date from before the captivity. P¹ is the first who distinguishes 'the priest who is greater than his brethren' from the rest, attributing a higher degree of sanctity to him and making severer demands upon him (*Lev.* xxi. 1 sqq., 10 sqq.). P² goes still further. He gives the High Priest a special official robe, which carries with it the exclusive privilege of consulting Yahwè by the urim and thummîm (*Ex.* xxviii. 1–39, xxxix. 1–26, 30, 31 ; on urim and thummîm in the præ-exilian period see my *Godsdienst*, i. 99 sqq. [*Rel. Isr.* i. 96 sqq.]) ; and to this robe he evidently attaches great importance (*Num.* xxvii. 21 ; *Lev.* xxi. 10, interpolated from P²) ; moreover he has the High Priest alone consecrated to his office with the holy oil (*Ex.* xxix. 7 ; *Lev.* iv. 3, 5, 16 ; vi. 13, 15, [20, 22] ; viii. 12 ; xvi. 32 ; xxi. 10, 12 [probably interpolated from P²] ; *Num.* xxxv. 25 ; cf. § 6, n. 13). This exaltation of the High Priest corresponds to the rank given him in the state, and for that very reason is only intelligible in a post-exilian system of legislation.

[14] The single priestly ordinance that expressly confines the offering of sacrifices to the one sanctuary is due to P¹, *Lev.* xvii. 8, 9. P² begins his legislation with precepts about the ôhel mo'êd (*Ex.* xxv. sqq.) and takes for granted that it is to be the only place of sacrifice. מקרא קדש, 'holy or religious assembly' (*Ex.* xii. 16 ; *Lev.* xxiii. 2–4, 7, 8, 24, 27, 35–37 ; [285] *Num.* xxviii. 18, 25, 26 ; xxix. 1, 7, 12), means an assembly of the people at the one sanctuary. This is so completely a matter of course that it is not even explained. The idea that P² makes the pascal meal a domestic celebration (*Ex.* xii. 1 sqq.) and is in this respect less centralising than *Deuteronomy* (xvi. 1–8) is incorrect. Even in *Ex.* xii., where the special passover of the exodus occupies the field, a מקרא קדש is enjoined on the first and seventh days of Maççôth (*v.* 16) ; as soon as a sanctuary existed, the slaughter of the pascal lamb (v. 6) had to be performed there ; this satisfied the demands of unity, and the meal itself might then be enjoyed in the private houses of the holy city ; and indeed, it was only so that it could be celebrated by every one at once. Dillmann's supposition (*Ex. u. Lev.* p. 108 sq.), that P²'s pascal meal was only transplanted to the city of the temple by the centralisation of a later period, is in conflict with *Num.* ix. 7, 13, where the lamb is called קרבן יהוה ; for Dillmann will not seriously maintain that such a korbán could be made ' in any place.'

[15] Cf. § 11, n. 14, and above n. 4. The progress of the legislation about priests and Levites is really perfectly simple, and would have been taken in the same sense by every scholar long ago, had not the traditional date assigned to P² opposed it. We take it as proved that Aaron does not appear as the ancestor of the lawful priests in any one præ-exilian work, and

that according to *Deuteronomy* the sons of Levi, without distinction, though not all of them priests, are all of them qualified for the priesthood. Cf. § 3, n. 16. The suppression of the bamôth, and the limitation of the cultus to the temple of Jerusalem, which Josiah carried through in obedience to Hilkiah's book of law, drove many priests, some of whom were Levites, from their posts, and deprived them of their subsistence. If they had been dealt with in the spirit of the deuteronomic precept, xviii. 6–8, they would have been admitted to the service of the temple and placed on an equality with the priests of Jerusalem. But this was not what really happened—at least not altogether ; for though Josiah brought the bamôth-priests to Jerusalem, yet they did not go up to the altar of Yahwè, albeit they ate their portion (of the priestly revenues to wit) in the midst of their brethren (2 *Kings* xxiii. 8, 9; for מצות read מניות after Geiger, *Jüd. Zeitschr.*, ii. 287–289). This is not unnatural. The priests of the temple would have acted on lofty principles indeed, had they shared all their own privileges with these brethren from without, who had hitherto been their rivals. We have no express information as to the position assigned to the former priests of the bamôth during the years 620–586 B.C. ; but we may take for granted that they, and still more their sons, did not spend their lives in idleness, and live upon charity, but began to do service in subordinate capacities. Then in 572 B.C. (*Ezek.* xl. 1), when Ezekiel drafted the scheme of the restored theocracy, he laid it down in perpetuity that they were to rank beneath 'the sons of Zadok,' i. e. the priests of the temple of Solomon, and were only to perform the lower offices about the temple ; and he appealed to their trespasses while the bamôth were yet standing to justify their degradation from the higher functions (xliv. 10–16, and the parallel passages). Now although this ordinance of Ezekiel's accords with the practice from 620 B.C. onwards, yet [286] as a regulation it is, and purports to be, something new. Ezekiel knows absolutely nothing of a primeval law underlying the distinction between priests and under-priests. In other words, the laws of P^2 are unknown to him. Should it be urged that the prophet excludes a portion of the Aaronites from the priesthood, inasmuch as he only admits the Zadokites as priests in the new temple, I answer that he never speaks of Aaron at all, but expressly opposes the sons of Zadok to the rest of the Levites. He does not say that the degraded priests are henceforth to take rank with Levites who are not descended from Aaron, as he would have done had he known of the distinction. Indeed Ezekiel's testimony can only be disposed of by the sorriest shifts. See, for example, Ives Curtiss, *The Levitical priests*, p. 68–79; Bredenkamp, *Gesetz und Propheten*, p. 188 sqq.; Delitzsch, *Studien*, p. 279 sqq. and *à propos* of the last named essay, my remarks on the whole subject in *Th. Tijdschr.* 1883, p. 212–217.—But now observe that in the lists of the exiles who returned from Babylon, the Levites appear separately, after the priests (*Ezr.* ii. 36–39, 40; *Neh.* vii. 39–42, 43 ; cf. *Ezr.* viii. 15 sqq.). Does not this show that these two classes had been recognised as distinct before the captivity? And according to 2 *Kings* xxiii. 8 sq. there had in fact been, from 620 B.C. onwards, Levites in the temple who did not go up to the altar of Yahwè, i. e, who were not priests. Why should not this be the class referred to in *Ezr.* ii. and *Neh.* vii.? If 'the Levites,' without further qualification, strikes us as an inadequate designation, we must remember that the list has not come down to us in its original form (cf. my *Godsdienst,* ii. 84–89 [*Rel. Isr.* ii. 174–182]) and we may well suppose that its language in this particular has been brought into agreement with that of P², whose ordinances are of course assumed by Ezra himself (viii. 15 sqq.). This hypothesis, however, is not necessary. Even without it the rubric 'Levites' is clear enough, and their very small number when compared with the priests (74 against 4289) is incompatible with P²'s regulations, but is in perfect harmony with our representation of the course of things.—The genesis of P²'s conception hardly requires any further explanation. The difference of rank and qualification, existing *de facto,* which Ezekiel had attempted to justify historically, rests in P² on a genealogical basis, and is thus for the first time rendered thoroughly legitimate and unassailable. Aaron, who really had served as priest, according to the tradition (*Deut.* x. 6, cf. *Ex.* xxxii. 1 sqq.), becomes in P² the first High Priest and the ancestor of all the legal priesthood (*Ex.* xxviii., xxix.; *Lev.* viii. sq., etc.); while the Levites, in their turn, are chosen out by Yahwè himself, but only for the lower offices of the sanctuary (*Num.* iii. sqq., etc.); the limit of their qualifications is carefully drawn, and the severest punishment threatened should they transgress it (*Num.* xviii., cf. P³ in *Num.* xvi. 6 sqq.). As the result of the whole antecedent development, this conception is perfectly clear and intelligible; it is only if we accept it as reflecting the reality that we get into difficulties. Its harmony with the demands of the time was the measure of the readiness with which it was accepted. After a time, still further advances were made in the direction indicated by P². The singers and porters, who are distinguished from the Levites in *Ezr.* ii. 40–42; *Neh.* vii. 43–45, and elsewhere, have become Levites in the time of the Chronicler (1 *Chron.* xxv.; xxvi. [287] 1–19, and elsewhere), that is to say, they have been incorporated into the tribe of Levi by means of fictitious genealogies (cf. my *Godsdienst,* ii. 105 sq. [*Rel. Isr.* ii. 203 sq.])—a fact which confirms the historical character of our assumption that the priestly lawgiver sought his end by the employment of similar means.

In all that precedes we have assumed that Ezekiel and P², though formally differing, substantially agree, or in other words that P²'s Aaronites are identical with Ezekiel's Zadokites. But it is also conceivable that the Aaronites might include priests from other sanctuaries besides that of Jerusalem, and especially from Northern Israel, and that these latter together with the Zadokites were called 'sons of Aaron' in view of the fact that the priesthood of Northern Israel recognised Aaron as their ancestor. That they actually did make such a claim is rendered highly probable by *Ex.* xxxii. 1 sqq. (cf. above, p. 245 sq.), and if the same idea survived the fall of Samaria and retained its vitality at the sanctuary of Bethel, for instance, down to the time of Josiah (cf. 2 *Kings* xxiii. 15, 19, 20), it would be far from unnatural that it should be so modified and expanded as to include the Zadokites and some of the Judæan bamôth-priests, and should then force its way into the tora. This hypothesis is worked out in detail by O o r t in his essay on 'the Aaronites' (*Th. Tijdschr.* xviii. 289–335), but it has not yet been so tested and examined from every side as to justify us in substituting it for the ordinary conception.

[16] The Levites received the tithes of corn, wine and oil, *Num* xviii. 20–24, and according to *Lev.* xxvii. 30–33 of cattle also; while the priests had a tithe of these tithes (*Num.* xviii. 25–32), as well as the firstlings of clean beasts, the ransom of the first-born of men and of unclean beasts, *Num.* xviii. 15–18; *Lev.* xxvii. 26, 27, the first-fruits, *Num.* xviii. 12, 13; the heave-offerings, *Num.* xviii. 11, 19; things laid under the ban, *Num.* xviii. 14; the hide of the burnt-offering, *Lev.* vii. 8; all the flesh of trespass and guilt-offerings, *Lev.* vi. 24–26, 29; vii. 6, 7; *Num.* xviii. 9, 10; a part of the food-offering, *Lev.* vi. 16–18; vii. 9, 10, 14; the breast and right shoulder of the thank-offerings, *Lev.* vii. 28–34; *Num.* xviii. 18. Cf. also *Num.* xv. 20, 21. How far all this departs from the præ-exilian regulations appears from *Deut.* xviii. 3, 4, where the priests have the shoulder, the jaw and the belly of the thank-offering, the reshîth of corn, wine and oil, and the reshîth of wool; and also from § 3, n. 17, 18, where the laws of tithes and firstlings are compared. Thus, without reckoning the priestly and Levitical cities, of which more anon, the revenues of priests and Levites have been notably increased in P². This is enough in itself to render the later origin of the legislation probable (cf. n. 4), and a comparison with Ezekiel shows that it did not arise till after the captivity. The prophet assigns to the priests the food-offering, the trespass and guilt-offering, things under the ban, and the best of the first-fruits, of the heave-offerings, and of the dough (xliv. 29, 30; cf. S m e n d, p. 367 sq.). That is to say, he does not venture to divert the tithes and the firstlings from their original destination, still maintained in *Deuteronomy*, known to him from his own experience as an element in the life of the people, and very naturally regarded by [288] him as incapable of being diverted. It was only when a fresh start was made, after the return from the captivity, that the idea could be entertained of making the people relinquish the ancient but now no longer unbroken usage, and surrender to the priesthood—relatively increased in numbers and power— what had before been consumed at the sacrificial feasts.

On the forty-eight priestly and Levitical cities, see § 3, n. 19. When we consider the absolute silence of all the præ-exilian witnesses, and the indirect but clear contradiction of *Deuteronomy*, we can but regard the legal precept in *Num.* xxxv. 1–8, and the account of its execution, *Josh.* xxi. 1–40, as representing a priestly demand that could have no immediate practical result, but which might perhaps at some future time, under different circumstances, be put into practice. In so far these regulations stand in line with those of Ezekiel, xlv. 1–8; xlviii. 8–22, from which in other respects they diverge altogether, for Ezekiel assigns the priests and the Levites a territory of their own, where they all live together. W e l l h a u s e n shows, in a striking passage (*Prolegomena*, 165–170 [159–164]), that Ezekiel's simple and lucid ordinance is the original, which P² artificially modifies. P² could not have an ordinary tribal district assigned to Levi in the Mosaic age. This would have been too glaring a contradiction of the history to which he himself does homage by adopting the deuteronomic formula in *Num.* xviii. 20, 23. And yet Levi must not be allowed to rank below the other tribes, and so he receives a heritage of his own in the territory of·each of them, in those very cities in which he had sojourned as a stranger before the Captivity (*Deut.* xviii. 6, and the parallel passages). In selecting these cities P² was sometimes guided by a tradition which pointed them out as the sites of ancient sanctuaries, and therefore as asyla, but in other cases he chose them at his own discretion.

[17] On this point cf. § 11, n. 19-22, 25, 26, and above all, W e l l h a u s e n, *Prolegomena*, 54 sqq. [52 sqq.] (Sacrifice), 85 sqq. [83 sqq.] (The Sacred Feasts), whose brilliant demonstration must be read in its entirety and cannot be repeated here; also R o b e r t s o n S m i t h, *The Old Testament in the Jewish Church*, p. 208 sqq., 379 sqq. The difference of principle with regard to sacrifices and festivals between the præ-exilian practice and *Deuteronomy* on the one side, and the legislation of P² on the other, can only be explained on the supposition that this latter is something more than the codification of perhaps primeval priestly rules and usages, that it expresses and introduces a different fundamental conception from that which had been current before the captivity, and that this difference is due to a temporary suspension of Israel's national existence and its restoration on a new basis. In other words, the phenomenon presupposes the deportation to Babylon and the return to the fatherland. Thus, and thus only, can we explain the institution of a new cultus—and this expression is no exaggeration—in which the ritual, and as a consequence the priest who has charge of it and who conducts it, comes to the front, and the initiative of the private Israelite retires into the background; and in which the modified conception of Yahwè's being and Israel's relation to him expresses itself in a changed estimate of the various kinds of sacrifice and a new arrangement of the festivals. This complete revolution is already in progress in Ezekiel, the prophet-priest of the captivity; and in P² it is an accomplished fact. On the sacrifices, cf. *Ezek.* xlvi. 1-15 and *Lev.* i. sqq., especially *Ezek.* xlvi. 13-15 (daily morning burnt-offering with the food-offering [289] that belonged to it), and *Ex.* xxix. 38-42; *Num.* xxviii. 3-8 (daily morning and evening burnt-offering with food-offering). In this latter precept, and, generally, in his regulation of the ritual, P² goes further than Ezekiel. On the festivals cf. *Ezek.* xlv. 18-25, and *Lev.* xvi., xxiii.; *Num.* xxviii., xxix. (S m e n d, *Ezech.*, p. 377 sqq.). The purification of the sanctuary on the first day of the first and the seventh months (*Ezek.* xlv. 18-20) is the germ from which the great day of atonement, *Lev.* xvi., was developed. In fixing the day of the month on which Maççôth and Tabernacles are to begin the prophet leads the way (xlv. 21, 25), but P² adds an eighth day to Tabernacles (*Lev.* xxiii. 36 [39]), and regulates the sacrifices to be offered on behalf of the community less simply and naturally than Ezekiel does. See further, n. 8.

[18] After the investigations of n. 12-17, there only remain a few of P²'s laws, which can be compared with older ordinances, or the date of which can be

otherwise determined. *a.* On *Num.* xxxv. 9–34 compared with *Deut.* xix. 1–13,
see n. 13.   Apart from the place taken by the High Priest in the latter law,
it betrays itself as a later recension of *Deut.* xix. 1–13 alike by the minuteness
of its regulations and distinctions and by the dominant idea of cleanness.
—*b.* On the year of jubilee, *Lev.* xxv. 8–55, see n. *4 g.*   The view I have there
expressed is opposed to the opinion most recently defended by J. Fenton
(*Early Hebrew Life*, 1880, p. 70–74), that both the year of jubilee and the
ordinance of the sabbath year (op. cit., p. 64–70) rest upon the primitive
communal possession of the land and its periodical partition, which the great
land-owners had suppressed, but which the lawgivers attempted to revive in
modified forms (cf. *Isaiah* v. 8 ; *Jer.* v. 25–28).   From this it would follow
that the law in question, though not Mosaic, yet dated from the reign of the
first kings.   But if so, how comes it that the prophets never appeal to any
such law in their denunciations of the grasping conduct of the great men ?
And even apart from this Fenton's hypothesis is wholly inadmissible.   In
Lev. xxv. 8–55 there is not a trace of an attempt to restore the past, of communal possession, and so forth.   All this is arbitrarily called to the rescue
and forced upon the legislator into whose mind it never entered.   The law
goes on the supposition that the individual is the owner of his land, and can
dispose of it freely.   This power of free disposal it proceeds to take away from
him, on the ground that the land is Yahwè's, and that the Israelites only have
the use of it (*Lev.* xxv. 23), and because the interests of stability and of the equal
distribution of wealth amongst the people of Yahwè require it.   Like so many
other regulations in P[2] this scheme could never have arisen while the national
existence flowed on without a break ; but when it had been violently interrupted, and a new beginning was to be made, the introduction of a new social
order might be conceived.   The character of the law, then, really leads us to
the same date that, from our point of view, is necessarily involved in the
mention of the day of atonement (*v.* 9) and of the Levitical cities (*v.* 32–34).
—*c. Num.* xxxi. (the war with Midian and the precepts on military matters
and the division of booty that rise out of it) cannot well be compared with
[290] *Deut.* xx.   The two laws have hardly a single point of contact.   But the post-
exilian origin of the priestly law is obvious from its contents, especially from
the proportion of the Levites' share in the booty to that of the priests (*v.*
28–47), viz. $\frac{1}{50} : \frac{1}{500}$, which agrees with the assignment of the tithes to the
Levites and the tithes of the tithes to the priests, *Num.* xviii. 20–24, 25–32.
—*d. Num.* xxvii. 1–11 ; xxxvi. must be looked upon as riders to the law of
the year of jubilee, to which an allusion is made in *Num.* xxxvi. 4, and accordingly they must be at least as late as that law itself, on which see *b.*

We have already seen that this priestly legislation is set in
a historical framework so closely connected with it that
the two must have a single author (§ 6, n. 11, etc.).   And
accordingly this inseparable connection is all but universally

recognised[19]; and, now that our detailed establishment of the date of the priestly laws has given it a new significance, it must emphatically be maintained against the few who dispute it. For it is incorrect to assert that the date we have arrived at for the laws is inapplicable to the priestly narrative. Not only the historical sections of P² in *Exodus, Numbers* and *Joshua*, as to which indeed there is no dispute[20], but the sections in *Gen.* i.–*Ex.* vi. which belong to P² are post-exilian. The evidence of language is, to say the least, in no way adverse to so late an origin of the passages in question[21], and it is unequivocally supported by their contents whether taken by themselves or compared with the parallel narratives in J E. The priestly author builds upon J E throughout. He selects the main facts of his narratives, strips them of anything that seems unsuitable or offensive from his own point of view, and works up what remains in accordance with a scheme which could not possibly have been conceived in the period before the Babylonian captivity whilst ideas of the past were still dominated by the living tradition[22].

In all this we have assumed, what is indeed almost univer-sally allowed, that P² existed as an independent historico-legislative work before it was taken up into the Hexateuch. The opposite opinion, that regards the narratives and laws of P² as mere additions to the deuteronomico-prophetic Hexa-teuch[23], is not chronologically impossible; for this older Hexateuch was unquestionably in existence when P² wrote down his laws and narratives; but it absolutely misconceives the relation in which P² stands to his predecessors, and [291] entirely fails to do justice to the mutual connection of the several parts of his work and the systematic disposition of the whole. Though not unsuited, as the event showed, for com-bination with the Hexateuch as it had previously existed, the priestly work was certainly not designed by its author for any such purpose[24].

[19] In the first instance it was denied by Graf. In his *Geschichtliche Bücher* he only placed the priestly laws in the post-exilian period, and with respect to the priestly narratives simply held by the then (1865) prevalent opinion which regarded them as part of the 'Grundschrift' of the Hexateuch. Subsequently he withdrew from this position, influenced partly by Nöldeke's '*Untersuchungen*' and Riehm's review of the *Geschichtliche Bücher*, and recognised the unity of the legislative and historical elements of P². Cf. my *Godsdienst*, ii. 96 sqq.; 201 sqq.[*Rel. Isr.* ii. 192 sqq.; 291 sqq.] and *Th. Tijdschr.*, iv. 407 sqq. The opinion he had relinquished was, however, long maintained by Dr. Colenso, at least as far as *Gen.* i.–*Ex.* vi. is concerned (cf. § 6, n. 2–4); and in a certain sense it is defended by Ryssel also, for we have seen in n. 11 that he refers a portion of P², particularly its historical sections, and very specially those that appear in *Gen.* i. to *Ex.* vi., to the first 'ætas' of the Israelitish literature, thus separating them from the priestly laws which belong to the second 'ætas.' Against the distribution of the laws between two 'ætates,' see n. 11 ; and on the alleged gap between the laws and narratives, which Ryssel assumes chiefly on grammatical grounds, see n. 20–22.

[20] Colenso, more especially, may be noted as agreeing with us in regard to these historical sections; but not so Ryssel, who appears to refer them, together with the priestly narratives in *Gen.* i.–*Ex.* vi., to the first ' ætas ' (cf. n. 11, 19). But he does not produce a tittle of evidence for their higher antiquity, nor does he meet the difficulty which the intimate connection of legislation and history in *Exodus, Numbers,* and *Joshua* presents to any attempt to sunder them. If *Ex.* xxv.–xxxi., etc. belong to the second ' ætas,' so must *Num.* xx. 22–29 (which presupposes the delivery and execution of the directions as to the high-priestly garments); *Num.* xxvi.; xxvii. 15–23 (which rest on the passage cited above and on *Num.* i. sqq.) ; *Num.* xxxi. (which I suppose no one will maintain to be older than the laws of the second 'ætas'), etc., etc. The connection between the legislative and historical passages is in any case close enough to justify us in assuming their unity as long as no single objection to it has been produced.

[21] In drawing up the table already referred to (n. 11) Giesebrecht assumes the unity of P²; and had the assumption been incorrect, then the comparison of P²'s vocabulary with the other books of the Old Testament would have yielded different results with respect to the historical passages and the laws. But this is not at all the case. Of the hundred words, or thereabouts, included in Giesebrecht's list, some forty are either peculiar to *Gen.* i.–*Ex.* vi., or occur both there and elsewhere in P². They are here given in alphabetical order : מאור, אחז Niph., אחזה, אכלה, אנח, בדל Hiph., מושבות, תולדות Hiph., ילד Hiph. and subst., דשא מגורים, גוע, ברא, בהו, פרך, פרן, (Gen. xxiii. 8), פגע, נשיא, נקבה, נאקה, מין, כבש, מירה, זכר, תושב [292] קוה Niph., and מקוה חקים ברית מקנה and קנין, רדה, רחף, רכש verb and subst., רקיע, שיבה, שכך, שרץ verb and subst., תחו. To these might be added מאד מאד(ב), *Gen.* vii. 19; xvii. 2, 6, 20 ; *Ex.* i. 7 ; *Num.* xiv. 7, cf. *Ezek.* ix. 9; xvi. 13 ; מכסה, in *Gen.* viii. 13, as well as *Ex.* xxvi. 14 ; xxxv. 11, etc.; the formula ונכרתה הנפש ההוא, in *Gen.* xvii. 14, as well as *Ex.* xii.

15, 19 and elsewhere in the laws of P²; נכר בן, in *Gen.* xvii. 12, 27, as well as *Ex.* xii. 43 ; *Lev.* xxii. 25 ; נפש, 'person,' *Gen.* xii. 5 ; xvii. 14 ; xxxvi. 6 ; xlvi. 15, 18, 22, 25–27 ; *Ex.* i. 5 and *passim* in the laws of P²; עצם היום הזה ; *Gen.* vii. 13 ; xvii. 23, 26 in the laws of P² and *Ezek.* ii. 3 ; xxiv. 2 ; xl. 1 ; למשפחותם, *Gen.* viii. 19 ; x. 5, 20, 31 ; xxxvi. 40, as also in *Ex.* vi. 17, 25 ; xii. 21 and *passim* in *Numbers* and *Joshua*. It is possible that some of these words are only absent from the earlier literature accidentally ; others may be averred to be ancient, and their use in the later writings may be attributed to imitation of the Pentateuch. But taken together they prove conclusively that the language of P² in *Gen.* i.–*Ex.* vi., as a whole, is most closely related to that of the laws in P², and stands perfectly in line with it with reference to the successive periods of Israelitish literature.

²² With respect to the narratives from P² in *Gen.* i.–*Ex.* vi. two opinions stand opposed. According to the one their comparative simplicity and sobriety show them to be more ancient than the corresponding accounts in JE. The former contain the historical kernel and the latter the subsequent amplification and embellishment. The other opinion is the one briefly expounded in the text of this section and more fully developed in my *Godsdienst*, ii.·65–83, 96–102 [*Rel. Isr.* ii. 157–173, 192–201]. My position, as far as it refers to *Gen.* i.–*Ex.* vi., was controverted by Colenso, *Pentateuch*, vi. App., p. 116 144, who was answered in his turn by Kosters in *Th. Tijdschr.* vii. (1873) 28–59. Colenso translated this article in his *Contributions to the Criticism of the Pentateuch* (p. i.–xix.) and added a rejoinder (p. 1–22). Cf. also *Pentateuch*, vii. App., p. 129–139. Finally, Wellhausen has dealt with the mutual relations of P² and JE in his *Prolegomena*, 312–384 [297–362]. That P² and JE run parallel, even in details, is undeniable ; and hence it follows that they did not spring up independently of each other. P² is either the basis of JE or an excerpt from it. The first hypothesis might be accepted if P² were really more historical, or at any rate closer to the living popular saga than JE. But the opposite is the fact. P²'s genealogies are as unhistorical and artificial as those of the Chronicler. His chronology is obviously a product of the later systematising spirit. His representation of historical persons and events is bereft of all life and spontaneity and completely dominated by his theory of the graduated progress alike of the history of mankind and of the divine revelation. A narrative in which God appears successively as Elohim, El Shaddai, and Yahwè ; which accurately registers the ages of the primal race before the flood, and of the forefathers of Terah and the patriarchs, together with the months and days of the flood ; which makes sacrifices to the deity begin in the Mosaic age ; and from which every trace of hostility between Abram and Lot, Isaac and Ishmael, Jacob and Esau, Joseph and his brothers, has been carefully removed :—such a narrative is not only remote from its [293] ultimate source but could not be so much as conceived as long as the original meaning of the sagas still lived. But see, further, the works referred to above.

²³ This hypothesis was defended by Graf, *Die s. g. Grundschrift des Pentateuchs* (in A. Merx, *Archiv*, etc., i. 466–477) ; combated by me in *Th.*

Tijdschr., iv. (1870) 511–519; and brought forward again by Maybaum, *Die Entwickelung des altisr. Priesterthums* (1880), p. 107–120. The last-named scholar asserts that 'the priestly codex' contained ritual laws alone, and no 'history of origins.' These laws were united with JE + D by a redactor, who at the same time supplemented and expanded the older narratives or added historical statements of his own; and since he was himself a priest these latter show affinities with the 'priestly codex' and sometimes coincide with it in linguistic usage (e.g. *Gen.* xvii.). A portion of what we have assigned to P² seems to Maybaum properly to belong to E. This origin of the supposed 'Grundschrift,' he thinks, explains its fragmentary character and its inconsistency with JE.

²⁴ Maybaum, as may be gathered from n. 23, has not worked out his idea. Had he attempted to do so it would have become obvious at once that the sections and verses usually assigned to P² cannot in any way be regarded as additions from the hand of R. However far we suppose R's activity to have extended we can never make it probable or even conceivable that he enriched the narrative of JE in *Gen.* i.–*Ex.* vi. with statements and details unconnected with or even contradicting it, simply out of his own head and without his documents supplying the smallest occasion for it. How can the first narrative of the creation be regarded as an addition to the second? Or *Gen.* v. as an addition to *Gen.* iv.? Or P²'s portion of *Gen.* vi.–ix. as a series of supplementary amplifications of JE's narrative of the flood? They do not present the smallest appearance of any such intention. How Maybaum can affirm that his view removes the running contradiction between JE and P² is simply inexplicable. It leaves it in all its crudeness and makes it doubly perplexing by supposing that it was wantonly introduced by one whom we should rather have expected to remove or veil the want of harmony already existing. To this we must add Maybaum's failure to comprehend the mutual relations of these passages, which he regards as additions with no independent cohesion or purpose. Their true character need not be further illustrated after what has been said in § 6. Are we really asked to believe that the systematic and connected whole that is formed by the component parts of P² in *Gen.* i. sqq. (cf. Colenso, *Pentateuch*, v. p. 197–211; Wellhausen, *Prolegomena*, ibid.) is nothing but a string of fragments, flowing from one pen indeed, but neither written *uno tenore* nor conceived in mutual connection with each other? It is nothing short of absurd. See, further, the very just remarks of Budde, *Urgeschichte*, p. 276 sqq.

We may take it as demonstrated, then, that the historico-legislative work that we have called P² really constitutes a single whole and at first existed in an independent form. But this was not the end. After its composition P² underwent a rather complicated literary process of which we know nothing with certainty except the final outcome that lies [294] before us in the present Hexateuch. Starting from this, however, we may distinguish more than one stage in the history of P², such as its combination with D + J E; its absorption of P¹ and other priestly torôth which are now worked into the context of P² but formed no part of it originally; and finally, the recensions and amplifications of P² and all that had been added to it by later legislators and narrators. Nothing is more natural than that the mutual relations of the subdivisions of this process and consequently the progress of the history of P² should be only approximately ascertainable. In any attempt to trace this history we must return to the reformation of Ezra and Nehemiah, in 444 B.C. or one of the years immediately following. The law-book then introduced is closely connected with P² (§ 12, n. 10), but what is the nature of this connection? Setting aside for the moment the later recension and expansion, to which we shall return presently (p. 307), we may divide this question into two others: (1) Was P² combined with J E + D in Ezra's book of law? and (2) was P², as contained in that book, already amalgamated with P¹ and other laws of priestly character but of diverse origin? The former question may be answered with high probability in the negative, the latter in the affirmative. For (1) the identification of Ezra or one of his immediate predecessors with the redactor of the Hexateuch finds no support in what we read concerning him[25], and (2) the priestly laws which are not from the pen of P², and, more specifically, the ordinances of P¹, were practically indispensable parts of the book of law which he read, and are directly required by *Neh.* viii. 14–18, compared with *Lev.* xxiii. 39–43[26]. Taken in connection with Ezra's fortunes this would lead us to conjecture that some considerable number of years before he journeyed to Judæa, say between 500 and 475 B.C., P² was compiled in Babylonia, and was afterwards

amalgamated there, either by Ezra himself or some other, with
P¹ and other priestly torôth, and in this form was brought by
Ezra to Judæa in 458 B.C. But it is also possible that the amalgamation with P¹ and the other priestly laws was not effected
[295] till between the years 458 and 444 B.C., and took place in
Judæa. This hypothesis, in either form, is commended by its
intrinsic probability, and there is not a single fact known to
us that militates against it[27].

[25] Ezra is a reformer. He departs for Judæa in order to regulate all its
affairs in accordance with the Tora, and to secure its practical observance
(*Ezr.* vii. 10, 25, 26); his first task is the dissolution of the marriages with
foreign women (*Ezr.* ix., x.); and subsequently he renews his activity on the
same lines in conjunction with Nehemiah (*Neh.* viii.-x.). Now it is true that
this does not positively exclude such a task as the redaction of our Hexateuch,
but it is hardly probable, to say the least, that Ezra should have had the capacity
and inclination to accomplish it. The deeper we pierce into the character of
this redaction (cf. § 16), the less can we believe that it emanated from a man
of action. Cf. Reuss, *L'hist. sainte et la loi,* i. 256 sqq.; *Gesch. der heil.
Schr. Alt. Test.,* p. 460 sqq.

[26] We have seen already (§ 6) that in *Exodus–Numbers,* side by side with
the laws and narratives that unquestionably belong to P², there are a number
of sections, likewise of priestly origin, which for one reason or another cannot
be regarded as original constituents of that work. Some of them must be
looked upon as later completions or corrections of P², such as *Ex.* xii. 14–20,
43–50 (§ 6, n. 7); xxx., xxxi. (n. 13); xxxv.-xl. (n. 15), etc. Others again are
less directly dependent upon P². They treat their subject matter independently. They are in conflict with P² on some perhaps minute points, or
they only half fit or do not fit at all into its plan and miss such characteristics
as the historical introductions with which its author is in the habit of pro-
viding his ordinances. Cf. Wurster in *Zeitschr. f. alttest. Wissenschaft,* 1884,
p. 112-118. In this category are *Lev.* i.–vii. (§ 6, n. 17-19); xi.–xv. (n. 22);
Num. v., vi. (n. 31, 32); some few other laws in *Num.* (cf. n. 38, 40); finally
and principally P¹ (see above, n. 5-10; § 6, n. 24-28). The question when
these passages were amalgamated with P², which could not be answered in
§ 6, must now be approached.

We have at least one witness in this matter outside the Hexateuch itself.
Neh. viii. 14-18 alludes to a law in which on the one hand the celebration of
the feast of the seventh month during eight days, viz. from the fifteenth to the
twenty-second, is prescribed (cf. ix. 1), and in which on the other hand the
dwelling in tabernacles during the celebration of the festival is enjoined. The
reference therefore includes both *Lev.* xxiii. 33–36 (P²) and *v.* 39–43 (P¹, worked
over in the sense of P², cf. n. 8). Now *Neh.* viii. is not an exact official report

of what took place at Jerusalem; nor are v. 14, 15 a literal citation of *Lev.* xxiii. 40, which they reproduce freely, though the difference between the two texts has been much exaggerated by J. Halévy in the *Rev. de l'hist. des rel.*, iv. 38 sqq, and still more by Delitzsch, *Studien*, p. 177 sq.   In the main, however, *Neh.* viii. is perfectly trustworthy (§ 12, n. 12 sq.), and we may therefore assume on the strength of v. 14–18 that P¹ was united with P² in Ezra's law-book, unless proof should be forthcoming from some other quarter that this cannot be the case.   No such proof, however, can be produced.   On the contrary the probability seems to be in favour of this combination.   We can [296] quite understand that P² might conceive and execute the project of explaining the religious institutions of his people historically, and at the same time unfolding his ideal of the community consecrated to Yahwè.   But when it came to the practical introduction of his scheme it was impossible not to see how far from complete it was.   It contained, as far as we know, no detailed precepts as to sacrifices, no definitions as to the clean and the unclean, as to matrimony, as to the privileges and duties of the high-priest and other priests, the sabbatical year, and so forth.   It is of course possible that these subjects as well as others were originally dealt with in P² and that its precepts were forced to make way for those which we now possess in *Lev.* i. sqq., xi. sqq., xvii. sqq. ; but it is not probable.   For if that had been so the chapters in question would have sometimes preserved P² and sometimes P¹ or some other priestly lawgiver, just as the redactor does in *Lev.* xxiii., for instance.   And since this is not the case we conclude that these tôrôth supply genuine gaps in P², and thence again that their incorporation preceded the practical introduction of the priestly tora.   Cf. Wurster, op. cit., p. 128.—Of course this does not necessarily imply that the amalgamation was effected just in the form in which we find it in our Pentateuch.   The redaction was a long and continuous process (§ 16) and the later amplifications and supplementings of P, on which more anon, extended to those portions of it in which P² was combined with passages drawn from elsewhere (e. g. *Lev.* xxii. 29, 30; xxiv. 1–4, 5–8).   All I mean to assert is that in the year of the reformation the amalgamation, in one form or another, had already taken place.

²⁷ The conjecture that P² was written in Babylonia, rests upon the close connection between this document and Ezra which the accounts establish.   At the invitation of the people he produces the book of law (out of the temple ?) and reads aloud from it (*Neh.* viii. 1, 2).   And though it is only in the spurious edict of Artaxerxes, *Ezr.* vii. 14, 25, that we are told in so many words that he had brought it with him from Babylonia, yet we may infer as much from *Ezr.* vii. 6, 10, 11, and from the title הספר which is given him in *Neh.* viii. 2, 5; xii. 36 (in the latter passage by Nehemiah himself).   When Halévy (op. cit., p. 35 sqq.) denies our right to infer from these texts that Ezra and the law-book stood in any specially close relation to each other, he loses sight of the mutual connection of the texts.   If *Ezr.* vii. 6, 10 sq., etc. had not been followed by *Neh.* viii.–x., or conversely if these latter chapters had not been preceded by this description of Ezra's office and purposes, then it

might perhaps have been possible to regard him simply as one of many who devoted themselves to the study of the Tora, and strove to enforce its observance. But as the case really stands, such an interpretation is simply a misconception of the historical evidence.—If, then, the law-book, which was unknown in Judæa, cf. *Neh.* viii. 14–18, was brought out of Babylonia, then it must have been written there. It would be a mistake to reject the idea as improbable. Ezekiel, too, sketched his ideal of the new theocracy, xl.-xlviii., in Babylonia; and it was there that the legislation of sanctity rose (cf. n. 9). What is more natural than that such a work as P² should also have been written in the land of the captivity? The school of Ezekiel did not die out; [297] nor was it transported bodily to Judæa in 536 B.C.; for other 'teachers' (מבינים) came with Ezra to Jerusalem (*Ezr.* viii. 16). Possible lawgivers, therefore, were not wanting, and the motives which had caused priestly torôth to be committed to writing before 536 B.C. were still in force. Cf. my *Godsdienst*, ii. 22 sq., 61–64 [*Rel. Isr.* ii. 117 sq., 153-156].—As to the moment at which P² was reduced to writing we must, of course, be content with conjectures. In taking the years 500-475 B.C., I am guided by the consideration on the one hand that P² is later than P¹ (cf. n. 12 sqq.), and on the other hand, that time must be left for the amalgamation of the two. Possibly we should even ascend a little higher. The present redaction of *Gen.* i. 1-ii. 4ᵃ was preceded by an older one, in which the (eight) creative acts were not distributed over six days (cf. Dillmann and Wellh., xxii. 455-458). But, again, our present redaction is itself comparatively old, for it is presupposed in *Ex.* xx. 11; xxxi. 17. We must therefore distinguish various stages in what I have called the reduction of P² to writing. And this becomes easier if we place the first composition sufficiently early, always within the prescribed limits.—The years from 475 B.C. onwards remain for the amalgamation of P¹ and P², and I have left the alternative between 475-458 and 458-444 B.C. open. The latter period covers the years that elapsed between the events recorded in *Ezr.* ix. sq. and those in *Neh.* viii.-x., during which, as far as we know, Ezra did not take any active steps. This inaction is connected with the political confusion that reigned in Judæa, and its disastrous consequences alluded to in *Neh.* i. The conjecture that Ezra availed himself of this period of enforced leisure to prepare the way for the introduction of his Tora, and that its reduction to a suitable form was one of the measures he took to this end, was formerly hazarded both by Graf (Merx, *Archiv*, i. 476) and by myself (*Godsdienst*, ii. 137 sq. [*Rel. Isr.* ii. 232 sq.]), and it is still capable of defence in the sense that the supplementing of P² by P¹ may fall in this interval. But inasmuch as both collections alike grew up in Babylonia, they may also have been welded together there, and their union may have been the work of the circle from which Ezra came. The introduction of the priestly laws was not the outcome of a momentary impulse, but was planned and deliberated on beforehand. It may be regarded as the final cause of the second return of exiles under the guidance of Ezra, and if so, we may well suppose that the preparations for it were well advanced before the departure from Babylon.

It yet remains for us to trace the subsequent history of
Ezra's law-book. Even in § 6 we saw that there are sundry
priestly passages, both legislative and narrative, which cannot
be regarded as originally belonging to P² and must be later, not
earlier, than it. We afterwards discovered that here and there
in the books of *Ezra* and *Nehemiah* deviations from our present
Hexateuch may be observed, which can only be explained on
the supposition that in the time of Ezra and Nehemiah and
the oldest chroniclers of their doings some of the ordinances of
the Hexateuch were not yet in existence or at any rate were [298]
not yet accepted as binding (§ 11, n. 3). These two sets of
facts converge upon the conclusion that the priestly law-book
underwent very considerable modification and extension even
after the year of the reformation. There is nothing to
surprise us in this. On the contrary it lay in the nature of
the case that as soon as the priestly law was put into force
gaps would be revealed in it and the need of corrections and
additions would make itself imperatively felt. The oral
priestly tora, from which Ezra's law-book was largely drawn,
was still open as a source of these additions, and if it could
not give what was wanted, then for a time at least the
same necessity that defies law might in this instance create
it²⁸. There can be no doubt that it was the scribes of
Jerusalem, most of them of priestly descent, who undertook
this extension of the law-book²⁹. The question what passages they appended, or in other words what sections were
added to the priestly law-book after the year of the reformation, can only be answered with perfect certainty in those
cases in which the critical analysis of the priestly components
of the Hexateuch (§ 6) and the evidence of the books of *Ezra*
and *Nehemiah* coincide. This is the case with respect to the
institution of a daily morning and evening burnt-offering (*Ex.*
xxix. 38–42 ; *Lev.* vi. 1–6 [8–13] ; *Num.* xxviii. 1–9), the poll-
tax of half a shekkel (*Ex.* xxx. 11–16) and the tithes of cattle

(*Lev.* xxvii. 32, 33)[30]. But even where the earlier post-exilian literature yields no evidence, critical analysis alone here and there raises the later insertion of a section above all reasonable doubt[31]. On the other hand the analysis does not lend itself to the conclusion that might be drawn from *Neh.* viii. 14–18 (though not necessarily involved in it), that the whole body of precepts concerning the day of atonement (*Lev.* xvi. and the parallel passages) was absent from Ezra's law-book[32].

Special difficulties surround the determination of the *terminus ad quem* of this supplementing process. It must be distinguished from the continued diaskeue, which will be dealt with in § 16, inasmuch as it was exercised exclusively on the priestly laws, and aimed at filling in the gaps that experience had revealed in them ; but yet we must not [299] suppose that it came to an end as soon as our present Hexateuch was brought into existence by the interweaving of the priestly law-book with J E + D. On the contrary it was still possible, and, as a fact, it still continued, afterwards. We must suppose, however, that the material and most important additions had already been made before that date (presumably about 400 B.C.), and that subsequently the additions became gradually less important and more purely formal in character[33]. This continued at any rate into the third century B.C.[34] ; but the recension of the priestly laws, together with the diaskeue as a whole, steadily declined in significance till at last it debouched into those comparatively innocent and insignificant alterations which are usually considered as falling under the history of the text[35].

[28] The character of the later additions to the priestly law-book will be best explained by a few examples. In addition to those dealt with in n. 29, we may here notice the following (cf. *Th. Tijdschr.*, iv. 1870, p. 487–511):—

Num. viii. 23–26, the service of the Levites extending from their twenty-fifth to their fiftieth year, a later modification of the precept in *Num.* iv. 3, 23, 30, 35, 39, 43, 47, which made their thirtieth year the beginning of their time of service. The small number of Levites (cf. *Ezr.* ii. 40 ; *Neh.* vii. 43 ;

Ezr. viii. 15 sqq.) made this alteration necessary, and in still later times occasioned their entrance upon duty as early as in their twentieth year. Since it was then no longer possible to introduce a new regulation into the law, this last modification was attributed to David in 1 *Chron.* xxiii. 24–27 ;

Num. xxviii., xxix., the catalogue of the festival offerings of the community, must certainly be regarded as a later supplement to the tora on the feasts, in *Lev.* xxiii. If it had had the same origin as the latter, it would have followed it immediately. The contradiction between *Num.* xxviii. 27–30, and *Lev.* xxiii. 18, 19, would raise the matter above all doubt, were it not due to the fact of the verses in *Leviticus* having been interpolated from *Numbers,* in which process a very natural mistake crept in (§ 6, n. 40) ;

Ex. xxxv. 1–3, and *Num.* xv. 32–36 (the prohibitions of kindling fire and gathering wood on the sabbath) are *novellæ* on *Ex.* xxxi. 12–17, where all work, מלאכה, is forbidden in general. They must have been intended to remove an uncertainty as to the meaning of ' work ' ;

Num. xv. 22–31, expanding and explaining *Lev.* iv. 13–21, 27–31. The trespass-offering is extended on the one hand to *peccata omissionis,* and on the other hand expressly limited to involuntary trespasses ;

Num. v. 5–10 provides for the case in which the offender, in the absence of the Israelite whom he has injured, and of his goël, would not be able to pay them the fine ; and it decrees that in this case he must pay it to the priest. It is therefore a supplement to *Lev.* v. 14–26 [v. 14–vi. 7].

See, further, § 6, n. 13 sqq., whence a whole string of examples may be [300] taken. They are no more homogeneous than those we have cited, but all alike may be explained by the practical requirements revealed or developed soon after 444 B.C., and provided for either by the incorporation of a tora which had previously only been delivered orally, or by the framing of a new precept to meet the demands of the time.

[29] According to the Jewish tradition I should have named the men of the Great Synagogue as Ezra's helpers and successors. But I have shown elsewhere (*Verslagen en Mededeelingen der K. Acad. van Wetenschappen,* Afdeeling Letterk., 2ᵈᵉ reeks, vi. 207–248) that this designation was originally applied to those who were present at the assembly described in *Neh.* viii.–x., at which the Tora was read and accepted, and that the later ascription to them of an active part in the guidance of the people and the continuation of Ezra's work is quite unjustified. The only real organs of the movement were the priests and the scribes, and though in later times these two orders diverged from and were often openly opposed to each other, yet originally they frequently pulled together and in many cases, as in that of Ezra himself, the two functions were combined in the same person. Nevertheless it was not as priests but as scribes that they employed themselves on the Tora, that they prepared copies of it and supplemented what was wanting in it. But they worked in the priestly spirit,—not only in the sense of understanding religion in the priestly as opposed to the prophetic way, but also in

the sense of upholding the interests and privileges of the priests against all others, including the Levites. See *Num.* xvi.–xviii., and compare § 6, n. 37.

[30] Cf. my *Godsdienst,* ii. 219 sq., 267–272 [*Rel. Isr.* iii. 6 sq., 49-62]. I must content myself now with touching upon the proofs that are there given at greater length.

a. A doubt whether the morning and evening burnt-offerings (with the food-offering pertaining to them) were prescribed from the first in the priestly law-book, is roused by *Ezek.* xlvi. 13–15, where a morning burnt-offering only is ordained. From 2 *Kings* xvi. 15 it appears that in the time of King Ahaz, and presumably in that of the historian also, a burnt-offering was made in the morning and a food-offering in the evening ; and apparently Ezekiel wished to maintain this usage; at any rate his precept in no way interferes with it. On the other hand it might be gathered from 1 *Kings* xviii. 29, 36 ; 2 *Kings* iii. 20, that long before that time a food-offering had already been instituted in honour of Yahwè in the morning as well as the evening (כעלות המנחה, in the former passage of the late afternoon, in the latter of the early morning). But in these passages 'mincha' is not contrasted with the burnt-offering, and therefore signifies no more than ' offering' in general. Moreover, I agree with Robertson Smith (*Encycl. Brit.,* xiv. 85, n. 3), that the purity of the text, at any rate in 2 *Kings* iii. 20, is very doubtful : כעלות השחר would be far more suitable. Be this as it may the evening sacrifice was still known as מנחת הערב after the captivity (*Ezr.* ix. 4, 5), even on into the second century B.C. when the evening burnt-offering was unquestionably established (*Dan.* ix. 21). The survival of this name is best explained on the supposition, suggested by 2 *Kings* xvi. 15, that the mincha originally was, and throughout successive centuries continued to be, the proper evening sacrifice. It seems that it remained so after the introduction of the priestly law; for in *Neh.* x. 34 [33] the people pledge [301] themselves to contribute 'to the perpetual (daily) food-offering and the perpetual burnt-offering.' The two offerings are therefore distinguished from each other, and that too, since the food-offering is mentioned first, as evening and morning sacrifice. Add to this that various considerations prevent our regarding the three passages in which the two-fold burnt-offering is prescribed as original components of the priestly code. *Lev.* vi. 1–6 [8–13] is a ritual direction to the priest, that serves, like other torôth in *Lev.* vi., vii., to supplement *Lev.* i.-v., and this is enough in itself to suggest its later origin ; *Num.* xxviii. 3–8 is included under the general verdict passed on *Num.* xxviii. sq. (cf. n. 28) ; *Ex.* xxix. 38–42, finally, is very strangely placed, is textually later than *Num.* xxviii. 3–8 (cf. Popper, op. cit., p. 190 sq.), and was apparently inserted in *Ex.* xxv. sqq., from the passage in *Numbers,* because the two-fold tamîd is said in *Num.* xxviii. 6 to have been 'ordained on Mount Sinai.'

b. On *Ex.* xxx. 11–16, cf. Graf, *Geschichtliche Bücher,* p. 63 ; Popper, op. cit., p. 194 sqq. The section is misunderstood by the author of *Ex.* xxxviii. 21–31 (§ 6, n. 15), as Dillmann, too, confesses (*Ex. u. Lev.,* p. 364 sq.). But the last-named commentator maintains (p. 317 sqq.) that the precept is only intended for the special census to be held by Moses, and is out of place amongst the ordinances concerning the tabernacle. This is a mistake. We ought rather to take the position of the precept as an indication that the author was not considering an isolated case, but the cultus in general, to which, of course, *Ex.* xxv. sqq. refers; and accordingly what he is giving us is a general ordinance in the form of a direction given to Moses. He therefore means to impose a yearly tax in support of the cultus (על־עבדת אהל מועד, *v.* 16) upon every male Israelite, and so he was understood by the Chronicler (2 *Chron.* xxiv. 6, 9) and the Jewish tradition. But in *Neh.* x. 33 [32] the people freely undertake to contribute a third of a shekkel per head for the purpose, whence it follows that *Ex.* xxx. 11–16 was not yet incorporated in the law-book, but was subsequently inserted in it when the necessity of raising the temple tax had become evident.

c. In *Deuteronomy* tithes of corn, wine, and oil, i.e. of the fruits of field and tree, are the only tithes demanded (xiv. 22–29; xxvi. 12–15; cf. xv. 19, 23). If P^2 had intended to claim the tithes of cattle likewise for the Levites, he must have said so expressly in *Num.* xviii. 20 24, 25–32. As his ordinance stands it cannot be understood in any other sense than that of *Deuteronomy*, except for the difference as to the destination of the tithes. And we see from *Neh.* x. 38–40 [37–39]; xii. 44–47; xiii. 5, 12 that it was so understood at the time of the introduction of the book of law and immediately afterwards. But in that case *Lev.* xxvii. 32, 33 can only be regarded as a *novella*, increasing the revenues of the Levites by the tithes of oxen and sheep. The Chronicler was acquainted with it, and therefore very naturally supposed that it was observed under the pious King Hezekiah (2 *Chron.* xxxi. 5, 6). The choice between this view and Dillmann's (*Ex. u. Lev.*, p. 637 sqq.) may safely be left to the reader.

[31] No rule can be laid down here, for everything depends upon the impression received from the analysis in question. Where such various criteria of later origin as the unnatural position of a law, its more or less marked linguistic divergency from the context, its conflict or imperfect harmony with the unquestioned portions of the book, all coincide, then there can be no doubt in [302] the matter. But even a single criterion may be conclusive, e.g. the departure from *Num.* iv. in *Num.* viii. 23–26 (n. 28), etc.

[32] The inference in question is indicated by Zunz in *Zeitschr. der deutsch. Morgenl. Geselsch.*, xxvii. 682, and positively formulated by Reuss, *L'hist. sainte et la loi*, i. 260 sq.; *Gesch. der heil. Schr. Alt. Test.*, p. 475. In the latter passage he sums up his proofs as follows: 'A careful study of the account of the promulgation of the law in *Neh.* viii. sq., which evidently flowed from the pen of an eye-witness (x. 1, 33), shows that the great fast of the day of atonement, without any further ceremonies, is expressly fixed on the twenty-fourth day of the seventh month, *after* the feast of tabernacles, and immediately following the reading of the book of law. No room is left therefore for the feast of the tenth day (*Lev.* xvi.); after which indeed the feast of the twenty-fourth-day would have been wholly superfluous . . . Add to this that

Ex. xxx. 10 speaks quite differently of the yearly day of atonement, and that
the very minute sacrificial code of *Num.* xxviii., xxix (see especially xxix. 7 sq.)
shows no trace as yet of the highly significant ceremony of *Lev.* xvi. . . . The
fact that 2 *Chron.* vii. 9 likewise excludes the festival of atonement is
a proof of its dependence upon some older document.'—The conflict here
spoken of between *Lev.* xvi. and the other priestly laws does not appear to
me really to exist. *Ex.* xxx. 10 alludes to the already existing tora upon the
day of atonement and supplements it by the direction that the High Priest
must also cleanse the altar of incense, which is not mentioned in *Lev.* xvi.
(§ 6, n. 23). *Num.* xxviii. sq. is the catalogue of the communal sacrifices
on holy days, and the rites of *Lev.* xvi. could not, therefore, be reimposed
in it, but the author's acquaintance with them appears from xxix. 7, 11, where
he speaks alike of the fasting and of 'the sin-offering of atonement,' in
conformity with *Lev.* xvi. *Lev.* xxiii. 27–32 ; xxv. 9, likewise presuppose
xvi. The question therefore is whether that chapter, together with all
the other passages that allude to it, was absent from Ezra's book of
law. Its position and its connection with the preceding laws would not throw
any suspicion on it (cf. § 6, n. 23), so that if we reject it it must be entirely
on the strength of *Neh.* viii. 13 sqq. But now consider the character of
the assembly there described and the intention of those who presided over it.
The day of atonement was a new institution, unknown alike to Ezekiel and
P¹, regulated for the first time in *Lev.* xvi. The book of law in which
this tora was embodied had still to be introduced. Could the reading of
the book of law be interrupted by the celebration of this very exceptional
ceremony ? Must not the ceremony itself, rather, be deferred until the
new order of things had been accepted by the people and thus come into
practice ? With the feast of tabernacles it was another thing. It was a
joyous, popular festival that had long been celebrated by all Israel, though
never before in accordance with *Lev.* xxiii. 40, and moreover it was in
perfect harmony with the character which the great assembly was to take,
according to *Neh.* viii. 9–12. But, says Reuss, there was a day of humiliation held on the twenty-fourth of the month (*Neh.* ix. 1–3), and how is
that to be explained if the book of law had fixed the tenth for it ? I answer
that this day of humiliation was the special and immediate preparation for
entering into the covenant ; that it had little or nothing in common with the
day of atonement, and that its celebration has therefore no bearing either
[303] way on the question whether *Lev.* xvi. was contained in Ezra's book of law or
not. The *argumenta e silentio* on which I have myself relied from time to
time—most recently in n. 30—are really quite different in character from any
that can be drawn from *Neh.* viii. 14 sqq.

³³ The distinction here made is not absolutely essential. We may, if we
like, include all the alterations made at or after the amalgamation of Ezra's
law-book with JE + D under the name of the 'redaction' or 'diaskeue,' especially since, as we shall see in § 16, the redaction in the narrower sense
(harmonising the heterogeneous elements of the Hexateuch) was likewise
conducted in the priestly spirit. But inasmuch as the priestly law-book

existed for a time, according to the view we have taken, as an independent work, and during that period was supplemented and extended, but was not subjected to redaction in the narrower sense explained above, it seems natural to distinguish between this completion or continuation, even in its second period, and the redaction which was then going on contemporaneously with it. And indeed there is an essential difference between additions to P[1] and P[2] such as *Lev.* xxiv. 1–4, 5–9 on the one hand, and such a narrative as that of *Josh.* xxii. 9–33 on the other, although sometimes of course the line is difficult to draw.—I abstain from all attempts to arrange the additions to the priestly law-book chronologically. We can generally determine with sufficient certainty what is and what is not primary, but it would be rash to attempt to distinguish between the secondary, the tertiary, and the still later elements. The supposition commends itself that the alterations of matter are earlier, as they are certainly more important, than the alterations of form. The freedom which the scribes allowed themselves in expanding the book of law must have been gradually restrained, and as the number of copies increased it would limit itself spontaneously. Merely formal completions, on the other hand, would be regarded with less jealousy and might therefore be continued longer. Such considerations would lead us, for instance, to regard *Ex.* xxxv. sqq. as later than *Ex.* xxx., xxxi. (cf. § 6, n. 13, 15), etc.

[34] The *terminus ad quem* is the work of the Chronicler, which presupposes the Hexateuch in its present form (§ 11, n. 4). Now the date of the Chronicler cannot be determined with certainty. But a comparison of the LXX. with the Masoretic text, especially in *Ex.* xxxv.–xl., shows that the work of supplementing continued down into the third century B.C. Cf. § 6, n. 15, and, further, § 16, n. 1 sqq.

[35] See the further development of this view, which is equally applicable to the diaskeue of the Hexateuch and the supplementing of Ezra's law-book, in § 16, n. 1 sqq.

§ 16. *The redaction of the Hexateuch.*

The results of the inquiry now completed (§ 13 sq. and 15) show that in the year of the reformation of Ezra and Nehemiah (about 444 B.C.) the deuteronomico-prophetic sacred history and the historico-legislative priestly work both existed independently. The union of these two gave rise to the present Hexateuch. The question when and how this took [304] place must be answered in the present paragraph.

More than one consideration must have rendered an early amalgamation of DJE with P urgent. Probably the authors of P never intended to cancel or suppress the older laws and narratives. But yet their work departed notably from that of their predecessors. As long as the two retained their independence they challenged mutual comparison, and the great difference between them could not but be observed. If this difference were regarded as amounting to contradiction, then the prestige of the two works alike must suffer under it and the authority of the more recently introduced legislation specially must be shaken. There was but one means of averting this danger ; viz. to weld together these independent but related works into a single whole which might then claim, without fear of challenge, the place which Judaism assigned to the documents of Yahwè's revelation to the fathers. It is therefore highly probable that the Sopherîm lost no time, and that before the end of the fifth century they had produced the Hexateuch.

Almost everything that we can establish with regard to this work of redaction must be deduced from the Hexateuch itself ; but this makes it all the more incumbent on us not to neglect the few hints that are presented us from outside. The combined evidence of the books of Chronicles, the Samaritan Pentateuch, and the Alexandrine translation of the Hexateuch, prove that in the third century B.C. the Hexateuch as we know it was in existence. They fix a *terminus ad quem* which we must in no case overstep [1]. But at the same time the Samaritan Pentateuch and the Alexandrine translation, when compared with each other and with our *textus receptus*, show that the Hebrew texts of the third century did not agree with each other. They displayed, of course, the usual type of variants, due to the carelessness or caprice of the copyists ; but beyond these they manifested [305] divergencies of far greater extent and significance which can only be understood as the results of deliberate recension of the text conducted with a relatively high degree of freedom and in accordance with certain fixed principles [2]. Now in former times it was usual, if not universal, to hold the Samaritans or the Greek translators, or the copyists of the manuscripts they followed, responsible for these divergencies, while our own *textus receptus*—allowance being made for subsequent corruptions—was regarded as substantially identical with the recognised text of the Scribes in the third century B.C. and still earlier. But we have no *a priori* right whatever to assume any such contrast, and *a posteriori* it is contradicted by the prevalence of so-called Samaritan or Alexandrine readings in Judæa itself[3]. The true conclusion is rather that the text of the Hexateuch, not only here and there but throughout, was handled with a certain freedom in the third century, and yet more so previously, being still subject to what its guardians considered amendments.— Now this is perfectly natural if, but only if, we think of the redaction of the Hexateuch not as an affair that was accomplished once for all, but as a labour that was only provisionally closed at first and was long subsequently continued and rounded off[4]. Even apart from the evidence borne by the divergent recensions of the text, this view, as we shall presently see, is supported by phenomena which appear in all three recensions alike. The redaction of the Hexateuch, then, assumes the form of a continuous diaskeue or diorthosis, and the redactor becomes a collective body headed by the scribe who united the two works spoken of above into a single whole, but also including the whole series of his more or less independent followers. It is only in exceptional cases, however, that the original redactor can be distinguished with certainty from those who continued his work. For the most part we shall have to club them together and may indicate them by the single letter R[5].

---

[1] On the Chronicler see § 11, n. 4. The Alexandrine translation of the Pentateuch was made in the first half of the third century B.C., that of the Book of *Joshua* later, but perhaps still within the third century. At what [306]

period the Samaritans adopted the Pentateuch from the Jews, and to what
date the text of their Pentateuch ascends—which is not exactly the same question—cannot be determined with certainty. The *terminus a quo* may be taken
as fixed by the secession of the priest Manasse, and by the building of the
temple on Gerizim (Flavius Josephus, *Arch. Jud.*, xi. **7**, 2 ; **8**, 2–4). But it
cannot be proved that the acceptation of the Tora was contemporaneous with
that event, nor, if it was, that the text thenceforth developed itself independently of Jewish influence. The internal differences amongst their own manuscripts show that the Samaritans themselves did not leave the text unaltered.
Thus, in ranking the Samaritan Pentateuch with the *Chronicles* and the
LXX. as a witness dating from the third century, we can only plead
probability, not certainty. But the conclusion derived from the examination
of these three witnesses will hardly be combated. It is that g e n e r a l l y
s p e a k i n g and with the reservation of those divergencies to be further
examined in n. 2–4, it is one and the same Tora, divided into five books,
which is implied in the citations of the Chronicler and which lies before us now
in the Alexandrine, Samaritan, and Masoretic recensions ; and further that
the book of *Joshua* employed by the Chronicler is likewise identical with the
Alexandrine and Masoretic book. The Samaritans, as is well known, adopted
the Tora only, so that the absence of the book of *Joshua* from their literature
has no critical significance whatever. Their own book of Joshua (ed.
J u y n b o l l, Lug. Bat. 1848) dates from a much later period.

² On the Alexandrine version of the Pentateuch cf. T. C. Töpler, *De Pent.
interpr. Alex. indole crit. et herm.* (Halle, 1830) ; H. G. J. Thiersch, *De
Pent. vers. Alex. libri iii.* (Erl. 1841) ; Z. Frankel, *Ueber den Einfluss der
paläst. Exegese auf die alex. Hermeneutik* (Leipz. 1851) ; J. Popper, *Der
bibl. Bericht über die Stiftshütte* (Leipz. 1862), p. 124 sqq. ; J. C. Schagen
van Soelen, *De oorsprong der Grieksche vert. van den Pentateuch volgens
de LXX.* (Leiden, 1864 ; containing, on p. 14 sqq., a refutation of the
opinion defended by Graetz, *Gesch. der Juden*, iii. 615 sqq., as to the date of
the translation). On the book of Joshua in the Alexandrine version, cf.
J. Hollenberg, *Der Character der alex. Uebers. d. B. Josua* (Moers, 1876) ;
on the Samaritan Pentateuch, Gesenius, *De Pent. Samar. origine, indole
et auctoritate* (Halle, 1815) ; Popper, op. cit., p. 60–84 ; S. Kohn, *De Pent.
Samar. eiusque cum verss. ant. nexu* (Breslau, 1865) ; H. Petermann,
Versuch. einer hebr. Formenlehre nach der Aussprache der heut. Samar.
(Leipz. 1868), p. 219–326.

³ The true conception and interpretation of the mutual relations of the
three texts is set forth by Geiger, *Urschrift und Uebers. der Bibel*,
p. 97–100, and *passim* ; cf. *Zeitschr. d. deutsch. Morgenl. Geselsch.*, xix. 611–
615 ; and Popper, op. cit. However natural it may have been to begin by
testing the Alexandrine and the Samaritan by the Masoretic text, and
regarding the divergencies of the two former from the later as the result, in
every case, of intentional or unintentional corruption of the *textus receptus*,
which was accepted as genuine, yet it is obvious, on a moment's reflection,
that we have no right to apportion light and darkness thus. The Alexandrian

translators were believing Jews, just as much as their contemporaries the Palestinian Scribes; and the Samaritan Pentateuch, which was derived from Judæa, was at least as much revered in its new fatherland as amongst the Jews themselves. *A priori* we should expect that the text would be subject to essentially the same method of treatment in Egypt and in Samaria as in Judæa; or, if there were any difference, that it would only be one of degree, [307] corresponding to the r e l a t i v e l y g r e a t e r p u r i t y which actually does distinguish the Masoretic alike from the Greek and from the Samaritan text. Add to this that any specific difference of treatment in Judæa on the one hand, and in Alexandria and Samaria on the other, would not have escaped the notice of the Scribes, and would have given rise to protests on their part. But nothing of the kind appears, for the divergencies of the Alexandrine text mentioned in the Talmud (Geiger, *Urschrift*, p. 439 sqq.) are very insignificant, and the Samaritans are only reproached with having substituted Gerizim for Ebal in *Deut.* xxvii. 4, and the corresponding passages. The significance of this silence is heightened by the fact that Flavius Josephus usually follows the Greek text, in the Pentateuch as elsewhere, though he was not unacquainted with the Masoretic recension (cf. my essay *De stamboom van den Masor. tekst des O. T.* in the Verslagen en Mededeelingen der K. Akad. van Wetenschappen, Afd. Letterk., 2de reeks, iii. 321 sqq.), and that the chronology of the (Palestinian) book of Jubilees rests on the Samaritan text of *Gen.* v. and xi. (*ibid.*, p. 325 sqq. and Dillmann, *Beitr. aus dem B. d. J. zur Kritik des Pentateuch-Textes*, Sitzungsber. d. k. preuss. Akad. d. Wiss., 1883, p. 323–340). Every attempt to erect a wall of partition between the Jewish and the other recensions turns out to be futile.

⁴ Had the redaction of the Hexateuch been effected *simul et semel*, the guild of copyists would surely have confined itself strictly to its proper task, and would not have taken the liberties to which the divergent recensions bear witness. On the other hand, the method actually pursued is the natural continuation of a diaskeue which long maintained its vitality, though in the nature of the case it must have been gradually ebbing. Compare, for instance, *Gen.* xlvii. 7–11; *Josh.* v. 2–9; xx., in the Masoretic and in the Alexandrine texts. The latter represents, throughout these passages, an earlier stage of the harmonising diaskeue; and on the other hand the Masoretic recension of *Gen.* i. 1–ii. 4ᵃ is earlier than the Greek.

⁵ We have to assume a redactor or harmonist for the union of J and E, and again of JE and D. But the redactor of whom we are now speaking differs from both of them, for he had DJE and P before him, and he effected their union in the spirit and in the interest of P. We may therefore call him Rp in distinction from Rd (the deuteronomic redactor of D + JE) and Rj (the redactor of J + E, whom we have also indicated by JE). Cf. Jülicher, *Die Quellen von Ex.*, i.–vii. 7, p. 3 n. We have already remarked (§ 15, n. 33) that Rp's task may be theoretically distinguished from that of P's continuators, but that in point of fact it often coalesces with it. As a rule, however, the manipulation of the text which in one way or another subserves the amalgamation of DJE and P, or at any rate might have been dispensed with had

that amalgamation never taken place, may readily be distinguished from the completion or expansion of the priestly ordinances themselves. See the remarks in n. 12, on *Num.* xxxii. 5–15 ; xxxiii. 1–49 ; *Josh.* xxii. 9–34.

R's task has already been described, in general terms, as the welding together of the two works that lay before him. His purpose, then, was at once to preserve his material virtually intact and to combine it in such a way as to produce a veritable whole.

[308]

This account of R's objects at once explains certain details noticeable in his work. After *Gen.* xvii. 5, 15 the names 'Abraham' and 'Sarah,' which are there substituted for 'Abram' and 'Sarai,' are employed throughout, even in passages which are not taken, as *Gen.* xvii. is, from P. In the same way 'Israel' might have superseded 'Jacob' after *Gen.* xxxii. 25–33 [24–32]. And the name of the successor of Moses might have been given as 'Hoshea' before *Num.* xiii. 16 and as 'Joshua' afterwards. But this is not found to be the case. The motives which induced R for the most part to leave these names as he found them cannot be determined with certainty, but may be assigned conjecturally[6]. In like manner the use of הוּא and נַעַר for both genders, which is the rule in the Pentateuch (not in *Joshua*), though there are exceptions to it, as well as the use of הָאֵל instead of the customary הָאֵלֶּה, would have to be ascribed to R did it ascend as far back as the period of his activity. But this cannot be proved, nor indeed is it probable ; for in R's time the masculine and feminine pronunciation of the third personal pronoun and of the three consonants נַעַר, and the two-fold pronunciation of הָאֵל, were not as yet distinguished in writing at all. It was not till the later time in which Hebrew gradually ceased to be the language of the people that הָא was replaced by הוּא or הִיא as the case might be, and the distinction made between נַעַר and נַעֲרָה and between הָאֵל and הָאֵלֶּה. It is impossible to say for certain why הִיא and נַעֲרָה were then avoided, at any rate generally, in the Pentateuch, and הָאֵל occasionally written for הָאֵלֶּה. It is possible that הוּא, נַעַר, and הָאֵל were regarded as older forms and were therefore used by preference in the Tora, to which extreme antiquity was assigned. But if so we must pronounce the idea mistaken, for the forms in question are not archaisms. Nor can we regard them as due to the redaction of the Pentateuch at all, unless we take the word in its very widest signification and make it cover the whole præ-Masoretic history of the text[7].

In any case these matters are but of trifling and wholly [309] subordinate interest. If we are to understand the work of R as a whole we must not be content with the general description given above, but must arrive at a more sharply defined conception of the real nature of his task. When he set his hand to the work, the deuteronomico-prophetic sacred history (DJE) had long been recognised and highly revered, whereas the priestly historico-legislative work had only quite recently been promulgated and put into practice. The problem was how to make P share in the reverence that DJE already commanded. In other words P must be incorporated with DJE. This was required in the interest of P, and there can be no doubt that it was carried out by some one imbued with the spirit of this document. R, then, belonged to the school of Ezra, to the priest-scribes of Jerusalem. And indeed they were the only men to whom it could even occur to execute such a work, for no one else would either feel called to it or be competent to undertake it[8].

The Hexateuch itself must teach us whether this more definite conception of R's activity, which seems to spring from the nature of the case, is really the correct one. We have to inquire, therefore, whether R actually follows the rules which flow spontaneously from this view of his task, i.e. (1) whether DJE is kept as far as possible intact, and (2) whether, when unity of design imperatively demands some sacrifice, the changes are made in the spirit and in the interests of P.

A survey of the Hexateuch, as a whole, is enough to justify an affirmative answer to these two questions. It embraces a great number of narratives and laws which the authors of P cannot possibly have accepted with complete satisfaction, and which they would not have combined with their own legislation and historiography of their own free choice[9]. It is true that we need not suppose these writers to have been fully aware of the inconsistency of their own conceptions with those of D and his 'prophetic' precursors. But that the latter always attracted them is hardly conceivable; and if, [310] in spite of this, these older laws and narratives have found a place in the Hexateuch, the fundamental explanation of the phenomenon must be found in the fact that they were already in possession of the field and only needed to maintain the place they occupied. But it also shows that R, however much he sympathised with P, did not absolutely identify himself with the priestly view of things, but was content to secure for it the place which it must take, but which it could not transcend, when made a part of the whole. His conservatism with respect to DJE, to which we owe the apparently almost complete preservation of that work[10], hardly admits of any other explanation. But it is equally clear, even from a general survey, that we were right in describing him as belonging to the spiritual kindred of P; for he scrupulously inserts even the minor fragments of P in the places that seem best to fit them when the more detailed notices of the older documents might have seemed to a less zealous disciple to have rendered them superfluous and warranted their omission[11].

This general survey, however, really furnishes nothing more than a presumption as to the method followed by the redaction. To arrive at certainty we must examine the work of the redactors in detail, and must make the phenomena which appear in connection with the amalgamation of DJE and P the subject of a close inspection in view of the maxims we have laid down. In the nature of the case there must be many of these phenomena which bear no unequivocal testimony and which might, at need, admit of some other interpretation; but whereas our view of the method pursued by the redactors is directly confirmed and even demanded by a great mass of the evidence, it does not appear to be contradicted by any single fact[12].

⁶ We must bear in mind that the name of 'Jacob' did not become obsolete, like 'Abram' and 'Sarai,' so that even the writers who mention the change of name, i.e. J (*Gen.* xxxii. 25–33 [24–32]) and P² (*Gen.* xxxv. 10), may still have used the name 'Jacob' as well as 'Israel.' Whether they actually did so or not is a question which could only be decided if we possessed their works in the original form. In the sections compounded of J and E the way in which 'Jacob' and 'Israel' alternate raises a suspicion that the one name was [311] occasionally substituted for the other when the two documents were combined (e.g. *Gen.* xlv. 27, 28; xlvi. 2, 5; xlviii. 2). It seems clear, on the other hand, that P still uses the name 'Jacob,' even after *Gen.* xxxv. 10 (*Gen.* xxxv. 22–29; xxxvi. 6; xxxvii. 1, 2, etc.; *Ex.* i. 1, 5; ii. 24; vi. 3). In any case, therefore, R had precedent to follow in preserving the two names.—*Num.* xiii. 16 would, properly speaking, require that 'Joshua' should be replaced by 'Hoshea' throughout *Ex.* xvii., xxiv., xxxii., *Num.* xi., and conversely that 'Joshua,' not 'Hoshea,' should stand in *Deut.* xxxii. 44. It is probable, however, that 'Joshua' was so firmly established as the name of the successor of Moses that R did not venture on the strength of P in *Num.* xiii. 16 to substitute 'Hoshea' for it. *Deut.* xxxii. 44 stands quite alone, and 'Hoshea' may perhaps be simply a clerical error (LXX., Ἰησοῦς; Samaritan, יהושע).

⁷ There are eleven exceptions to the rule that הוא is used for the feminine as well as the masculine (*Gen.* xiv. 2; xx. 5; xxxviii. 25; *Lev.* xi. 39; xiii. 10, 21; xvi. 31; xx. 17; xxi. 9; *Num.* v. 13, 14). נער, for 'girl,' occurs twenty-one times, viz. *Gen.* xxiv. 14, 16, 28, 55, 57; xxxiv. 3 (bis), 12; *Deut.* xxii. 15–29 (thirteen times); נערה only in *Deut.* xxii. 19. The form האל is found in *Gen.* xix. 8, 25; xxvi. 3, 4; *Lev.* xviii. 27; *Deut.* iv. 42; vii. 22; xix. 11, and never outside the Pentateuch; אל, without the article, is read in 1 *Chron.* xx. 8 only.—As to the antiquity of these readings we may note that at any rate הוא for היא and נער for נערה are mentioned in the Talmud (cf. Delitzsch, *Stud.*, p. 395) and therefore belong to the *textus receptus*. But the definitive settlement of this text did not take place till as late as the second century A.D., and it cannot be shown that the manuscripts upon which it rested were much older. In the Samaritan Pentateuch היא and נערה and האלה are written

throughout. This may be due to the correction of an apparently irregular text, but should anyone maintain, on the other hand, that the departure from the usual orthography is subsequent to the period at which the two recensions parted, it would be impossible to show that he was mistaken.—As long as the forms in question were regarded as genuine archaisms there seemed no room to doubt that the *textus receptus* was the original ; but with respect to הוא as a feminine this opinion is now generally abandoned (cf. D e l i t z s c h, p. 393 sqq.) ; and although נער, as an epicoen, is still regarded as a survival from the ancient language (p. 398 sq.) the preliminary proof that such a usage ever really existed at all, or in other words that ' girl,' though w r i t t e n נער, was ever p r o n o u n c e d otherwise than (ה)נַעֲרָ, is not forthcoming ; there is no reason whatever to ascribe a high antiquity to האל, and here again the question rises whether it really differs from הָאֵלֶּה at all. D e l i t z s c h allows (p. 396) that in the ancient MSS. הא was in all probability written, and that it was left to the reader to supply the vowel û or î as the case might be ; and in my opinion it is just the same with נער. Cf. C h w o l s o n, *Die Quiescentes* הוי *in der atthebr. Orthographie*, p. 10 sq. The simple fact, then, is that whoever for distinctness' sake inserted the *quiescentes* at some later date, departed from the general rule in the Pentateuch. It is possible that the motive of this breach of uniformity rested on an idea that in former times הוא and נער were often used as feminines and that the vowel after האל was often omitted (D e l i t z s c h, *ibid.*). But what importance are we to attach to such an idea ? and what are we to think of the few passages in which היא occurs and of the [312] unique נערה ? Does anyone seriously suppose that a tradition existed, with respect to those divergent texts, prescribing the resolution of הא into היא and the writing of נערה in those special passages ? At the present stage of our inquiry the only significance we can attach to these alleged archaisms is derived from the evidence they bear to the separation of the Tora from the other books of the Old Testament, especially the book of *Joshua*, with which in other respects it is so closely connected. Cf. n. 13, 14.

⁸ Cf. § 15, n. 29 on the sopherim and the direction in which they worked·
—The position of affairs hardly seems to need further explanation. Even the warmest upholders of P could hardly demand more than equality with DJE. It is true that Haggai and Zechariah (i.–viii.) contain no references to ' the book of the Tora,' i. e. *Deuteronomy*, and the last-named appeals to ' the former prophets ' instead (i. 4-6 ; vii. 7, 12), but the fact remains that DJE had long been recognised and was, as it were, in possession of the field. P c o u l d n o t have been made to eject it from this position, even if anyone had wished it ; and it is not probable that anyone did. Cf. n. 9–11.

⁹ The contrast—sometimes sharp—between DJE and P hardly needs to be pointed out again. We have only to recall the conflicting stories of the creation, the difference between the patriarchs of P and those of JE, the length of the sojourn at Sinai and the contents of the Sinaitic legislation in the two works, the regulation of the cultus in the Book of the Covenant and in P, the numerous ordinances of D which could not be reconciled in practice with those of P but must be superseded by them, the two conceptions of the partition of

the land in *Joshua*, etc. Indeed it is no exaggeration to say that P attempts a running and unbroken rectification of DJE.

[10] It is very improbable that any important part of DJE dropped out when it was combined with P. D presupposes JE and alludes to most of the details it contains, either expressly or incidentally; so that if any narrative has been dropped out of JE, as offensive, the allusion in D must likewise have been excised, which is conceivable, no doubt, but does not approve itself as probable. And moreover there is a running parallelism between DJE and P (cf. Wellhausen, *Prolegomena*, 312 sqq. [297 sqq.]), which implies that P reproduced his own version of everything he found in DJE and thus had rendered its expurgation superfluous. P has his manna (*Ex.* xvi., cf. *Num.* xi.), his ôhel mo'éd (*Ex.* xxv. sq., cf. xxxiii. 7–11), his ark of the witness (*Ex.* xxv. 10–22, cf. *Num.* x. 33–36; *Deut.* x. 1–5), his Balaam (*Num.* xxxi. 8, 16, cf. xxii.–xxiv.) and so on. Of course all this must be taken with due qualification. It was impossible for R to include everything. A number of details which the two documents had in common could not be given more than once, and the contradiction was sometimes so palpable that one of the two notices must be modified or shortened. But when we see what contradictions R allowed to stand, and therefore must have acquiesced in, we cease to fear that he was often driven to violent methods of mutilation in order to give unity to his compilation. A quicker critical perception on his part would have cost us the irreparable loss of important narratives and laws from DJE.—Abundant specimens of R's conservatism will be furnished by n. 12. Is it not remarkable, for instance, that in *Gen.* xxxiv. J's representation (massacre of the men [313] of Shechem by Simeon and Levi) is supplemented and amended instead of being replaced by R's own representation (the vengeance exacted by all the sons of Jacob)? Cf. *Th. Tijdschr.*, xiv. 280 sq.

[11] We may take, as specimens, *Gen.* xii. 4[b], 5; xiii. 6, 11[b], 12[a]; xvi. 1, 3, 15, 16 (indispensable now, but only because the corresponding accounts in JE have been omitted); xix. 29; xxxi. 18, etc.; *Ex.* xvii. 1; xix. 1, 2[a]; *Num.* xxii. 1; *Josh.* iv. 19, etc.

[12] The method we must follow in this note is decided for us. We must run through the whole Hexateuch and inquire where and how R has intervened. Thus the principles he followed will reveal themselves spontaneously, and we shall also see from time to time why we cannot suppose his work to have been completed all at once, but are forced to think of it as a continuous diaskeue. Where R has confined himself to intertwining the documents that lay before him I shall abstain from any more detailed description of his work. I certainly need not justify myself for now and then leaving the choice open between several possible conceptions of the method followed by the redactors.

Genesis. If ii. 4[a] was originally the superscription of i. 1–ii. 3 (אלה תולדות is elsewhere a superscription, and וְאֵלֶּה ת" cannot be anything else), we must suppose that R transplanted it, and so made it into a colophon destined to separate the second story of the creation from the first. This is more probable than that it stood as a colophon in P[2] itself. The contents of the two narratives required that i. 1–ii. 3 should come before ii. 4[b] sqq. R left the second story as he found it, except that he altered ' Yahwè ' into ' Yahwè Elohîm ' (ii. 4ᵇ, 5, 7-9, 15, 16, 18, 19, 21, 22; iii. 1, 8, 9, 13, 14, 21-23), thereby giving it to be understood that the Creator of man, Yahwè, in this second story, was no other than the Elohîm of i. 1-ii. 3 (' Yahwè, who is Elohîm ').—The recasting which iv. has undergone preceded R in point of time (§ 13, n. 26); the latter took this chapter as he found it, but omitted the continuation and conclusion of the genealogy of Seth, except the explanation of Noah's name, which he inserted (v. 29) in the list he had taken from P (v.). —In vi.-ix. 17 R united the two stories of the flood as well as might be into a single whole. This working up of the two stories now and then produced a mixed text, i. e. resulted in the introduction of the language and characteristic ideas of one narrative into a verse taken from the other. Thus we find ברא and P²'s characteristic enumeration of the different kinds of animals in JE, vi. 7 (cf. Dillmann on the passage); so too זכר ונקבה in vii. 3; and conversely JE's distinction between the clean and unclean beasts is introduced into P², in vii. 8; and again in vii. 23 the two documents may both be recognised. Cf. Budde, *Bibl. Urgesch.*, p. 248 sqq. —Then, after taking ix. 18-26 from JE and v. 28, 29 from P² (where these verses immediately followed v. 1-17) he gives us x. which is again compounded from the two documents; then JE's account of the tower of Babel, in xi. 1-9 is followed by the genealogy of Shem, down to Abram, taken from P², in xi. 10-26. V. 27-32, as already shown (§ 6, n. 1), is taken partly from JE and partly from P². With respect to xii., xiii. we have only to remark that R incorporated the continuation of P²'s narrative as successfully as was possible under the circumstances. He was obliged to pass over for the time the notice of Lot's deliverance from the destruction of the cities of the plain, that [314] immediately followed xiii. 11ᵇ, 12ᵃ in P²; but he introduced it later on (xix. 29).—At this point R departed from his ordinary method; and in xiv. he has given us a fragment of a post-exilian version of Abram's life, a midrash, such as the Chronicler likewise had amongst his authorities (2 *Chron.* xxiv. 27). Ch. xiv. does not belong to JE, from which it differs in point of form, besides being excluded by xviii. sq. But neither can it be taken from P², for it falls outside the scope of the work and is written in a wholly different style. Moreover, it is of very recent date, however archaic it may be in form. The names ברע and ברשע (v. 2) are symbolical. Mamre and Eshkôl, and presumably Aner also (v. 13, 24), are transformed from places into men. The previous inhabitants of the Transjordanic district (v. 5, 6) appear to have been adopted from *Deut.* ii. 10-12, 20. V. 18-20 is intended to glorify the priesthood of Jerusalem and to justify their claiming tithes. Affinities with P² are betrayed in the use of רכוש (v. 12, 16, 21), נפש (v. 21), ילירי ביתו (v. 14). This last phenomenon might, indeed, be explained on the supposition of R's having worked up some more ancient fragment; but this could only be allowed if the antiquity of the passage were really established, which is far from being the case. Cf. Nöldeke, *Untersuchungen*, p. 156-172; *Zeitschr. f. wissensh. Theol.*, 1870, p. 213 sqq.; *Th. Tijdschr.*, v. 262 sq., and on the historical value of the story,

E. Meyer, *Gesch. des Alterthums*, i. 165 sqq.—In xv. R has again gone to work more drastically than usual, though in another way. He has taken the chapter in the main from JE, but has allowed himself to introduce certain modifications, as we see by the formulæ אֲשֶׁר יָצָא מִמֵּעֶיךָ (*v.* 4; cf. xxxv. 11; xlvi. 26; *Ex.* i. 5); רְכוּשׁ גָּדוֹל (*v.* 14, in P² *passim*); שֵׂיבָה טוֹבָה (*v.* 15, cf. xxv. 8); nor can the very peculiar enumeration of the inhabitants of Canaan (v. 19–21) be from JE, who usually mentions six nations (§ 13, n. 29); it is probably very late. It is even a question whether the chapter has not undergone more than one recension; for the four hundred years' slavery (*v.* 13, cf. *Ex.* xii. 40) harmonises ill with the return in the fourth generation (*v.* 16), which latter, however, holds its ground in other sections of late origin likewise (*Ex.* vi. 13 sqq.; see below), presumably because it is the earlier conception of the two (*Ex.* i. 8 sqq.; ii. 1 'the daughter of Levi,' Moses' mother).—At this point R drops into his former method again. In xvi. he took up P²'s account of Ishmael's birth (cf. n. 11); xvii. he took, without alteration, from the same work (יהוה, *v.* 1, is simply a clerical error of later date for אלהים); xviii., xix., he adopted unaltered from JE, except that he found room, in xix. 29, for P²'s notice of Lot's deliverance; xx.–xxii. he also took from JE, except that he inserted xxi. 1–5, in the main from P², but not without certain small modifications (§ 6, n. 1). The adoption of xxiii. from P² necessitated the omission of JE's notice of Sarah's death. In xxiv. (JE), *v.* 67 might be taken as referring to this latter—which in that case must have come just before it—were it not that the form of this verse shows it to have been modified by another hand. In JE הָאֹהֱלָה stood alone, and the second half of the verse (וַיִּנָּחֵם—אַמֵּר) was wanting, unless with Wellhausen, xxi. 418, we suppose that in JE Abraham died before Rebecca's arrival and that the second half of *v.* 67 ran, וַיִּנָּחֵם—אָבִיו. This latter hypothesis is supported by the fact that according to *v.* 36ᵇ Abraham had already 'given all that he had' to Isaac, before the departure of the servant. On this supposition R omitted the mention of Abraham's death from JE and [315] altered *v.* 67—clumsily enough—to suit the change, while leaving 36ᵇ unaltered because he took it simply as a promise. His reason for all this was that according to P²'s chronology Abraham did not die until a considerable time after Sarah's death and Isaac's marriage, so that his death could not be mentioned till after xxiv. And there accordingly it stands recorded, in the words of P², xxv. 7–11ᵃ. But before he comes to this R inserts yet another notice of Abraham's descendants in *v.* 1–6, without concerning himself about the chronological difficulties created by this arrangement of the stories. In *v.* 5 he uses the formula adopted by JE in xxiv. 36ᵇ; but *v.* 6, in which concubines in the plural are mentioned, must be taken direct from the document that R is here following.—V. 7–11ᵃ is followed in *v.* 11ᵇ by a note which presupposes xvi. 14 and must either have been drawn from JE or supplied by R with JE in view. In *v.* 12–17 we have P² again; *v.* 18 which joins on badly to *v.* 17 is brought from elsewhere by R and connected with xvi. 12, the literal fulfilment of which it displays. The heading of Isaac's history (*v.* 19, 20) is from P², but the sequel (*v.* 21–34), all except *v.* 26ᵇ, was taken from JE, because it contained details which were wanting in P². Wellhausen (xxi. 418, n. 1) is of opinion that R here allowed himself to transpose the narratives of JE, in which xxvi. 1–33 must originally have preceded the birth of Esau and Jacob. This is highly probable. In that case R keeps to the order of events given in P², where the birth of the twins follows at once on the account of the marriage; and in taking over xxv. 27–34 as well as *v.* 21–26ᵃ from JE he failed to notice that the Rebecca of xxvi. has no grown up sons. For the rest, he left xxvi. 1–33 unaltered, and tacked on P²'s account of Esau's marriages to it, *v.* 34, 35, thus preparing the way for Jacob's departure for Padan-aram (cf. xxviii. 1 sqq.). Then he allows the reason for that departure given by JE to follow in xxvii. 1–45. This elaborate narrative having threatened to obliterate the recollection of xxvi. 34 sq. R reproduces the substance of the latter in xxvii. 46, and makes it the direct preparation for the despatch of Jacob as told by P², xxviii. 1–9. As to Jacob's journey to Laban, his abode with him and his return to Canaan, R gives the preference in xxviii. 10–xxxiii. 20 to the detailed narrative of JE rather than to the very brief notice of P², from which latter he merely borrows xxxi. 18, though using terms of P²'s and possibly following him in xxxiii. 18 also. *V.* 19, 20 is from JE again—including 'father of Shechem' in *v.* 19 if the saga of Dinah and Shechem followed at this point in JE, otherwise the words must have been added by R (Dillmann, *Genesis,* 351).—On xxxiv. see *Th. Tijdschr.*, xiv. 257–281 and the writers there cited, together with Dillmann's criticism, op. cit., p. 348–55. But Dillmann, too, believes that R has been hard at work on this chapter, with two accounts before him, viz. P²'s, from which he borrowed *v.* 1ᵃ, 4, 6, 8–10, 15 (14)–17, 20–24, but the conclusion of which he omitted (?), so that we cannot tell how it ran, and J's, from which he took *v.* 2ᵇ, 3, 5, 7, 11–13 (14), 19, 25, 26, 30, 31, adding *v.* 27–29 of his own and making the consequential formal alterations in *v.* 5 and 13. But I cannot see any pos-

[316] sibility of separating these verses, 27–29, and the corresponding expressions in *v.* 5, 13 from the first mentioned account, and I must therefore assign *v.* 1 and 2 in part, 4, 5, 6, 8–10, 13 in part, 14 in part, 15–17, 20–24, 25 in part, 27–29 to R, i. e. to one of the later diaskeuastæ of the Hexateuch. We may leave it an open question whether the original account that underlies all this had itself represented the circumcision of Shechem (not of all the citizens, as Dillmann has it), as a condition laid down in good faith by the sons of Jacob. In any case we must regard these later elements' as intended to rectify the older account from JE, which agreed with xlix. 5–7 in its representation of the affair. R now brings in xxxv. 1–4, which completely ignores the events at Shechem, whence it is clear that they were not mentioned in the document (E) from which the passage was originally derived, but *v.* 5 contains a reference to xxxiv. in its present form and must therefore be regarded as an addition by R, who then allows JE to resume the thread in *v.* 6–8. Here he inserted P²'s account of Elohîm's appearance to Jacob, and the change of the latter's name to Israel, *v.* 9–15, but not altogether without alteration. In *v.* 9 he added עוד with

reference to xxviii. 10 sqq.; *v.* 14, though perhaps suggested by JE, cf. § 10, n. 17, is due in its present form to the hand of R; the rearing of a maçcéba and the libation of oil agrees with xxviii. 18, while ויסך עליה נסך serves at any rate partially to connect this action with the legally established cultus, cf. *Num.* xxviii. 7 and the frequent use of נסך in P². Since *v.* 13ᵇ is a mere repetition we may suppose that in P², *v.* 15 followed *v.* 13ᵃ immediately.—In *v.* 16–21 the narrative of Jacob's journey is continued from JE; and *v.* 22ᵃ, designed to explain xlix. 3, 4, is also borrowed thence. On the other hand *v.* 22ᵇ–29 is taken by R from P², in spite of its being superfluous on some points after the chapters xxix. sqq., and inconsistent with them in others. It is certainly rather surprising that directly after giving such proof of his close attachment to P², R should assert his independence of that document in xxxvi., by not only supplementing its notices of the Edomites, but in some cases superseding them by others (§ 6, n. 1). He must have had his reasons for this, but we can only guess what they were. Meanwhile, the amplification of Esau's genealogical tree testifies to his love of 'documentary' material, which will soon be still further illustrated.—The heading of the next section of Genesis, xxxvii. 1, 2ᵃ, was supplied to R by P², but JE furnished him with the greater part of the substance of the section itself. Ch. xxxviii., inserted between xxxvii. and xxxix. in obedience to chronological propriety, is taken entirely from JE. In the remaining chapters (xxxvii., xxxix.-l.), of which Joseph is the hero, P²'s narrative is again welded into the more elaborate accounts of JE. The method here followed by R is simple. He inserted the verses which have been indicated in § 6, n. 1, as belonging to P², wherever they seemed best to fit, and this was no hard task since P² presented little more than an abstract of JE, constructed on quite the same model. But R did not confine himself to this. We have already seen, § 13, n. 7, that in *Gen.* xxxvii. 14 he probably substituted Hebron for some other place as the abode of Jacob; and perhaps *Gen.* xlvi. 1–5 was also modified in some degree by him for similar reasons (cf. *ibid.*). In accordance with the tradition (cf. *Deut.* x. [317] 22), P² had given the numerical strength of Jacob and his clan, at the time of the migration to Egypt, at seventy souls (*Ex.* i. 5); and R thought fit to draw out the list of these seventy and insert it in the most suitable place (xlvi. 8–27). In xlviii. 7, again, we have an addition from his hand, for this verse, though borrowed from xxxv. 16, 19, betrays acquaintance with P² also, by the use of the word מפדן; that is to say it has passed through the hands of R. It could only be ascribed to P² himself, to whom the immediately preceding verses (3–6) are due, if it really belonged to them; but so far is this from being the case that we are rather tempted to ask how R could have inserted it in so inapposite a place. See the answer to this question in Budde's essay, '*Gen.* xlviii. 7 *und die benach-barten Abschnitte,*' (*Zeitschr. f. alttest. Wissenschaft,* iii. 56–86) in which it is shown to be highly probable that *Gen.* xlix. (1ᵃ, 28ᵇ) 29–33 followed straight after xlviii. 3–6 in P²; that *v.* 31ᵇ then ran ושמה קברתי את־לאה ואת־רחל; that R struck out 'and Rachel' because of *Gen.* xxxv. 16 sqq., and replaced it by xlviii. 7; that originally R placed the passage from P², thus

modified (xlix. 28–32 ; xlviii. 7), together with xlviii. 3–6 after xlviii.
1, 2 ; and finally that when *Gen.* xlix. 29–32 was subsequently placed
after the blessing of Jacob (*v.* 1ᵇ–28ᵃ), xlviii. 7 was left where it
was and thus came to occupy its present very singular position. There
is not the smallest objection to this supposition of a second redactor
modifying (and indeed essentially improving) the order of the verses first
determined on. On the contrary, it is highly probable that such rearrange-
ments were far from unusual. It is only in exceptional cases, however,
that the originally selected and subsequently deserted order has left a trace,
as in this case, which enables us, at least conjecturally, to restore it. See
also § 6, n. 1 on *Gen.* xlvii. 7–11 in the LXX. and Masoretic text.—No
other additions by R can be detected with certainty in xxxvii., xxxix.–l.
Giesebrecht (*Zeitschrift f. alttest. Wissensch.*, i. 237, 266, n. 2) believes that
R's hand was at least as busy in these chapters as in xiv., xv., xxxiv. *A priori*
it is far from improbable that the fascinating story of Joseph was much
read and was not left intact in the process. It seemed to court amplification and embellishment. And as a fact xxxix., for example, and xl.–xlii.
are more diffuse than the documents from which they are drawn, as otherwise known to us ; and this may well be explained as due to R's revision,
unless we are to suppose that he had been forestalled by the Judæan
editors of E and J (cf. above, p. 146–147). Moreover, we now and
then strike upon expressions which do not occur elsewhere in the præ-
exilian writings, and on traces of later constructions ; see xxxvii. 2 (first,
' with his brothers,' then ' with the sons of Bilhah and the sons of Zilpah ;'
and at the end דבתם רעה, in which דבה [*Jer.* xx. 10 and later writers] excites
less suspicion than the absence of the article before רעה ; and indeed Joseph's
tale-telling is likely enough to be a touch subsequently added the better to
explain his brothers' hatred) ; xxxvii. 18 (נכל is a late word ; and התנכל
followed by את is strange) ; xl. 13 ; xli. 13 (כֵּן in the sense of ' post ' or
' place,' only in *Dan.* xi. 7, 20, 21, 38 besides) ; xl. 20 (הֻלֶּדֶת, which
Giesebrecht, p. 236, connects with the really late הוליד, but since it is
a Hophal form, I cannot regard it as conclusive, though it is certainly
[318] strange) ; xli. 8 (the Niphal of פעם, *Dan.* ii. 1, 3 ; *Psalm* lxxvii. 5 [4] ;
but Piel in *Judges* xiii. 25, so that I cannot allow any evidential value
to this word either) ; xli. 46, 47 (here the datum as to Joseph's age—
borrowed from P²?—coincides with the use alike of P²'s formula, ' Pharaoh, King of Egypt,' and of לקמצים ; cf. *Lev.* ii. 2 ; v. 12 ; vi. 8 [15] ;
Num. v. 26) ; xlii. 5, 6 (needless repetition ; שליט, cf. *Eccles.* vii. 19 ; viii.
8 ; x. 5 ; and also *Ezek.* xvi. 30 ; and *Dan.* passim) ; xlii. 19 ; xliii. 14
(אחר or אחר with אחיכם, a late construction ; in the last-named passage
אל שדי, which only occurs in P² elsewhere, and which we must therefore presumably refer to R) ; xlv. 19–21ᵃ ; xlvi. 5 (derived by Dillmann in
Genesis, 3rd edit., p. 447, from P², but in 4th edit., p. 413, rightly assigned to
JE. The pual of צוה, *v.* 19, would indicate P² or R [cf. *Ex.* xxxiv. 34 ; *Lev.*
viii. 35 ; x. 13 ; *Num.* iii. 16 ; xxxvi. 2], but the text is corrupt and should
probably be amended from the LXX. and the Samaritan ; so that it is only

in כן ויעשׂו and in עלי־פי at most that the influence of R, who was acquainted with P[2] and imitated him, can be traced) ; xlv. 23 (מזון, elsewhere
only in 2 *Chron.* xi. 23 and in the Aramæan *Dan.* iv. 9, 18 [12, 21]) ; xlv.
26 (פוג, ranked with the later words by Giesebrecht, p. 237 ; see, however, *Hab.* i. 4). But these passages are, after all, very few in number,
relatively to the extent of the stories of Joseph, and we must therefore regard
Giesebrecht's representation of R's influence as much exaggerated.

Exodus. R begins by inserting the shorter parallel notices of P[2] into the
narrative of JE. The first section he takes up, i. 1–7, proves that we were
right in denying the list in *Gen.* xlvi. 8–27 to P[2] and assigning it to R. The
writer of i. 1–7 cannot be fresh from the enumeration of the seventy souls that
made up the house of Jacob. Ch. i. 13, 14 ; ii. 23[b]–25, which followed i. 1–7 in
P[2], easily found their place in JE's narrative. But at this point R was compelled to sacrifice a portion of P[2] to JE, from which he took iii. 1–vi. 1. Ch. vi.
2 sqq. is not the direct continuation of ii. 23[b]–25, for Moses appears as already
known to the reader. And the form of ii. 25 also indicates some omission, for
something more must have followed after וידע אלהים. Jülicher (A. p. 29–
34), starting from the very just observation that vi. 13 25 was not originally
a part of the context in which it now stands (see below), goes on to surmise
that in P[2] these genealogical data preceded vi. 2 sqq., to which they served as an
introduction ; R could find no room for them anywhere in iii. 1–vi. 1 and therefore placed them after vi. 2 sqq., which latter section, he thought, best fitted
on to the preceding narrative of JE. Against this we must urge that alike in
vi. 13 and in v. 20 sqq., 26, 27 Moses and Aaron appear as Yahwè's emissaries,
whereas in vi. 2 Yahwè reveals himself to Moses alone, and the call
of Aaron is not hinted at before vi. 12 and is not announced until vii. 1 sqq.
P[2], therefore, cannot have assumed, before vi. 2 sqq., that the two brothers
were to be the joint deliverers of Israel, nor is the necessary preparation for
vi. 2 sqq. to be found anywhere in vi. 13–25. All this, however, is negative
and we have not yet discovered the true view to take of the last-named section.
Dillmann (*Ex. u. Lev.*, p. 53 sqq.) is the most recent advocate of its ascription to P[2] ; but he would make it follow vii. 1–5, when Moses and Aaron have
both been brought upon the stage. This hypothesis overcomes the objection
urged just now against Jülicher ; but it leaves the extraordinary position of [319]
the passage unexplained. Dillmann makes R responsible for it, and says
that he had already supplemented P[2]'s text from J, in vi. 6 sqq. and was now un-
willing to let vii. 1–5 follow ' because by doing so he would have completely
mixed up two distinct accounts, and moreover v. 13, regarded as the immediate
answer to v. 12[b] (in the spirit of C [= J]), would have been severed from it by
too great an interval.' 'He contented himself therefore with simply adding
ואני ערל שׂפתים from v. 30, and then appending the objection of Moses and
God's answer to it from A [= P[2]] (vi. 30[b]–vii. 5) together with his own introduction, v. 28–30[a] ; but at the same time he indicated by the words ביום דבר,
v. 28, how he thought the two accounts might be combined without subjecting
Moses to the reproach of renewed faint-heartedness ; all which is extremely
characteristic of R's remarkable conscientiousness.' On this I would remark

(1) that certain expressions do no doubt occur in *v.* 6 sqq. which are not else-where used by P² (viz. נשׂא יד, הביא אל, הציל, סבלות). But it does not appear that they are borrowed from J, nor have we any reason to suppose that this latter narrator, who makes Midian the scene of the call of Moses, records any confirmation of that call in Egypt. The more natural supposition is that in *v.* 6 sqq. R supplements P² from some other priestly account of the summons of Moses, related to Ezekiel (cf. § 15, n. 5). But (2), however this may be, we can in no case allow with Dillmann that the amalgamation of two texts in *v.* 6 sqq. accounts for the transposition of *v.* 13–27. A dislike of mixing up two accounts is a most extraordinary motive to allege, since that is exactly what R was *ex hypothesi* engaged in doing in *v.* 6 sqq. Moreover this intermingling is not averted by the interposition of *v.* 13–27, inasmuch as after all the chief substance of *v.* 12 is repeated in *v.* 28–30, and it is there-fore no more appropriate for vii. 1–5 to follow the latter than the former. Finally (3), vi. 13–27, whether placed before or after vii. 1–5, remains an extraordinary passage which fits but ill into the framework of P². If it belongs there at all we must suppose that the clans, at any rate, of the other tribes as well as of Reuben and Simeon were enumerated, and that R, after including Levi, omitted the rest. But there is nothing to support any such idea. Judging by the evidence before us we can come to no other conclusion than that the section was written for the sake of being inserted here, and therefore by R, though probably not by the first redactor, but by one of the later diaskeuastæ who was less scrupulous in preserving the connection of the narrative, and therefore thought he had done enough when he had repeated the main purport of *v.* 10–12 in *v.* 28–30. The details he communicates in *v.* 14–25 are for the most part derived from the Pentateuch itself, and in the remaining cases (the name of Aaron's wife, *v.* 23, and of Eleazar's father-in-law, *v.* 25), they are taken from Levitical genealogies, a number of which were in circulation after the captivity (cf. 1 *Chron.* v. 27–vi. 38 [vi. 1–52], etc.). The (unhistorical) figures in *v.* 16, 18, 20 are anything but inconsistent with this account of the origin of the passage.—The way in which the two texts are amalgamated in vii.–xi. may easily be gathered from § 6, n. 6. Nothing is more natural than that here, too,—as in *Gen.* vi.–viii. for example—the characteristic terms of one document should here and there be imported by R into a text borrowed from the other. Thus we have שׁרץ (P²) in vii. 28 [viii. 3] (JE); מושׁבות (P²) in x. 23 (JE);

[320] cf. Giesebrecht, op. cit., p. 190, 197, 226 sq.; also מגפה in ix. 14, a word never used by JE, but occurring in P², *Num.* xiv. 37; xvii. 13–15 [xvi. 48–50]; xxv. 8 sq., 18, 19 [xxvi. 1]; xxxi. 16; elsewhere only in *Ezek.* xxiv. 16; *Zech.* xiv. 15. Equally natural, from R's standpoint, is the repeated introduction of Aaron (dictated by P², who always makes him accompany Moses), in those sections of JE in which this alteration had not already been made; for we must remember that JE, in contradistinction to his documents, had already initiated this process (§ 8, n. 11), so that R had only to follow in his foot-steps in cases where the amalgamation of JE with P² made the mention of Aaron seem desirable (viii. 4, 8 [8, 12]; ix. 12, where אליהם, made necessary

by *v.* 8–11, is due to R).—In xii. the verses 21–27 must have been introduced
by R; for we have already seen (§ 9, n. 4) that they are later than *Deuteronomy* and are related to P², but form no part of the latter, with which they do
not completely agree. R may have considered them the complement of *v.* 1–
13 and inserted them here on that account. This implies that he found *v.* 14–
20—and in that case we must add *v.* 43–50 also—included in P²; and even
those who think that these verses originally stood elsewhere (§ 6, n. 7) must
admit the likelihood that their present position had already been assigned them,
on account of their affinity with *v.* 1–13, before the priestly tora was proclaimed. R could therefore confine himself to interweaving his texts, and only
seems to have dealt more drastically with *v.* 40, 41. The representation of the
abode of Israel in Egypt as lasting four hundred and thirty years (cf. *Gen.* xv.
13, four hundred years), does not agree with the exodus in the fourth generation which P² assumes everywhere and which is expressly mentioned in *Gen.*
xv. 16; *Ex.* vi. 13 sqq. This estimate, therefore, is apparently due not to P²
but to the diaskeuastæ, though probably not to the first of them, but to some
later redactor. The LXX., Samaritan, and other witnesses prove that the text
of xii. 40, 41 was still undergoing so-called correction long after the captivity.
Cf. Dillmann, *Ex. u. Lev.*, p. 120 sqq., and in the *Sitzungsb. der K. Press.
Akad. d. Wissens.* 1883, p. 339 sq.—In xiii.–xv. R followed his usual method
(cf. § 6, n. 8); הזכרים in xiii. 12, 15, and all xv. 19 (parallel to xiv. 16, 21,
22, 29) may be from his hand.—In xvi. he allowed himself more freedom. It
is certain that the basis of this chapter is taken entirely from P², not even
partially from JE (though Dillmann, p. 164 sqq., still defends this latter
hypothesis); but the version in P² was shorter than the present form. Cf.
Th. Tijdschr., xiv. 281–302; Jülicher, B, p. 279–294. No agreement has
yet been reached as to the extent of the additions, and it therefore remains
doubtful whether the original narrative preceded the Sinaitic legislation in P²,
as xvi. now does, or came after it. For *v.* 22–30 presupposes the sabbatical
commandment, and *v.* 32–34 the construction of the tabernacle, so that if these
verses come from P² the first fall of manna was there represented as subsequent to the legislation. But if that be so then the fact to which the elaborate
chronological statement of *v.* 1 refers must have disappeared, whereas *v.* 35
makes it highly probable that it is rightly attached to the fall of the manna.
This is an additional reason for regarding the whole of *v.* 22–30, together with
v. 4, 5 and *v.* 32–34, as due to the recension of P²; to which source we must also
refer *v.* 31 and 36, on account of the singular position they occupy; we must
likewise admit that only one of the two dates in *v.* 35 can be original; and
finally the almost hopeless confusion of *v.* 6–12, in as far as it is not due to
corruption of the text, indicates repeated recasting and supplementing. All
these additions cannot be from the same hand; *v.* 4, 5, 22–27, 28–30 belong [321]
to each other and are evidently intended to enforce the rigid observance of the
sabbath; *v.* 32–34 stands alone and is meant to stimulate admiration of the
manna or of Yahwè's faithful care for his people; neither of these supplements
appears to be due to the first redactor; the free treatment of xvi., therefore,
must be attributed to the later diaskeuastæ who are included under the letter

R.—In xvii.–xxiv., as we have already seen (§ 6, n. 10), only a few traits from P² have been incorporated in JE's narrative. The method pursued by R, in this section, needs no explanation, with the single exception of xx. 11, our judgment on which must partly depend on our conception of R's work in *Ex.* xxv. sqq. In general terms, it is obvious that R has inserted P's whole Sinaitic legislation (*Ex.* xxv.–xxxi.; xxxv.–*Num.* x. 28) into the previously existing narrative of the events at Sinai, without, however, bringing the latter into agreement with the widely divergent representations of the former. And this is why the repeated command to march for Canaan (*Ex.* xxxii. 34; xxxiii. 1, cf. *Deut.* x. 11) is not acted upon, in our present Pentateuch, until far later, *Num.* x. 29. It is equally clear that R availed himself of Moses' stay of forty days on Mount Sinai, *Ex.* xxiv. 12 sqq.; xxxii. 1 sqq. to make Yahwè convey the precepts concerning the tabernacle and the priests to him, and that in order to do so he has detached xxv.–xxxi. from the account of the carrying out of the injunctions (in xxxv. sqq.) and has inserted it between xxiv. and xxxii. Now nothing could be more natural than to suppose that in thus combining P and JE, the redactor so modified one or the other of his documents, if not both, as to remove their most flagrant contradictions. With respect to these modifications, we may note (1) that the mention of 'the testimony,' i. e. the Decalogue, in *Ex.* xxv. 16, 21; xl. 20 is not one of them. This designation occurs some forty times in P² and certainly raises no difficulty in itself. Nor can we say that the thought of Moses receiving 'the testimony' on Mount Sinai and afterwards depositing it in the ark is foreign to P². When this document was drawn up JE and D had long given currency to the idea in question, and there was no reason whatever to reject it. It is even a question whether P² did not include 'the testimony' in his own law-book, and whether it was not dropped out by R when he united JE and P. In that case R must have been indebted to this priestly recension of the Decalogue for the reference to *Gen.* ii. 1–4ᵃ with which he enriched the text of JE (*Ex.* xx. 11) which had already been interpolated from D when he adopted it. If on the other hand *Ex.* xxv. 16, 21; xl. 20 are to be regarded as allusions to the 'testimony' which the reader was supposed to know simply by tradition, then *Ex.* xx. 11 must be regarded as an addition by R himself. (2) From what has just been said about עֵדֻת it follows almost of necessity that the designation לֻחוֹת הָעֵדֻת in *Ex.* xxxi. 18; xxxii. 15; xxxiv. 29 is not due to JE but to R. If the handing over of 'the testimony' was mentioned in P² (see under (1)), then this notice (now lost) may have had a direct influence on the form of xxxi. 18; xxxii. 15; but if not, then R must [322] have followed the linguistic usage of P² in xxxi. 18, as he intertwined his two documents, and must then have brought the mention of 'the tables' in JE, xxxii. 15, 16, into conformity with the other passage.—(3) The last of the texts mentioned under (2), xxxiv. 29, belongs to a section (*v.* 29–35) which was pronounced in § 6, n. 14, for very sufficient reasons, not to belong to P², but which we cannot assign to JE either. The combination of the characteristics of both documents (see above, § 6, n. 14) makes it very probable that the passage was written by some one familiar with them both, i.e. by one of the younger diaskeuastæ. Its contents quite agree with this origin. The reflection of Yahwè's glory from the face of Moses is a corollary from the tradition about Yahwè's intercourse with his servant that has left no trace in the other Pentateuchal narratives (such as *Num.* xiii. sq., xvi.), and the later we place its origin the easier it is to e plain it.—(4) *Ex.* xxxiii. 7–11 is borrowed from E, but not without o missions. 'The ark of Yahwè' goes along with the ôhel mo'éd and was doubtless mentioned by E, but it has dropped out of the narrative that lies before us. Cf. *Th. Tijdschr.*, xv. 204–212 and the writers cited there. If the ark still held its place in JE when P[2] was united with it then R must have struck it out in consideration of *Ex.* xxv. 10–22 ; xxxvii. 1–9. But it is far from improbable that before the combination of D with JE, or on occasion of that combination itself, the ark had had to give way (cf. *Th. Tijdschr.*, ibid.), and in that case R had no need to modify *Ex.* xxxiii.—Nor had he any occasion to modify *Ex.* xix–xxiv. and xxxii.–xxxiv. elsewhere. His hand has indeed been traced in xix. (13[b]) 20–25 ; xxiv. 1, 2, 9–11, where Aaron is accompanied by 'the priests' and his sons Nadab and Abihu, who are supposed to be taken from P[2]. But P[2] knows of no priests before *Lev.* viii., and there is no reason to assert that Nadab and Abihu were only mentioned in P[2]. We may therefore refer the verses in question to JE. Nor was any modification made in P, so far as we can discover, when it was taken up into DJE. No doubt *Ex.* xxv. sqq. and xxxv. sqq. have been amplified by later elements and worked over more than once (§ 6, n. 12–15 ; 15, n. 33) ; no doubt, too, this process was at any rate in part later than the insertion of P into DJE ; but it stands in no causal or consequential relation to this insertion and we need not re-discuss it here. For the same reason we pass in silence over

  Leviticus and Num. i. 1–x. 28,

and may go on at once to

  Numbers x. 29 sqq. The connection between x. 29–32, 33–36; xi. 1–3, 4–35 leaves something to be desired (cf. Wellhausen, xxi. 567 sqq.) ; but all these pericopes come from JE and were taken thence, perhaps with abbreviations, by R. He does not seem to have ventured upon any great alterations. Giesebrecht (p. 232–235) refers *v.* 33 in its present form to the later diaskeue. The word הוּר in the sense of ' to spy ' is no doubt a characteristic term of P[2]'s (*Num.* xiii., xiv. twelve times, xv. 39) and does not appear elsewhere except in later writers (*Job* xxxix. 8 ; *Eccles.* i. 13 ; ii. 3, 6 ; vii. 25 ; in *Judges* i. 23 ; I *Kings* x. 15 [2 *Chron.* ix. 14] the reading is uncertain). But an earlier writer might use the verb in the sense of ' track out,' ' search' which is demanded here ; and that JE actually did so use it is rendered highly probable by the parallel passage [323] in *Deut.* i. 33 ; the 'three days' journey' between the ark and the camp is astonishing enough, but it must be explained as a false reading, derived from *v.* 33[a], where the words are in their place.—In xi. 10, למשפחתיו (cf. *Gen.* viii. 19 and P[2] *passim*) is perhaps an addition of R's, but in other respects both that chapter and xii. were incorporated without alteration, unless we are to ascribe xii. 1, which is singular enough in itself, and does not agree with *v.* 2 sqq., to R or one of his successors. The despatch of the spies was recorded in JE as well as in P[2], so that R had to weld the two accounts together in

Num. xiii., xiv. (cf. § 6, n. 37). The denunciation in xiv. 26–35 and the statement in *v.* 36–38, both which are derived from P², were expanded either by R himself or some later diaskeuast: עד־מתי (*v.* 27); the oath in *v.* 28 ; נשׂא יד, *v.* 30 ; זנות, *v.* 33, and other such turns of expression are not in P²'s sober vein ; but at the same time they are so completely amalgamated with his conception of the event that they can only be regarded as later embellishments of it.—Between xiii. sq. and xvi. R placed certain priestly ordinances (xv.) which are disconnected alike with what precedes and with what follows them, but which could be inserted here just as well as anywhere else. In xvi.–xviii., on the other hand, we have another composite passage before us (§ 6, n. 37). The account of the revolt of Dathan and Abiram in JE furnished an opportunity for inserting P²'s somewhat similar narrative of the contest of Korah and his followers with the tribe of Levi, together with the laws that belonged to it. It is not absolutely demonstrable, but it is highly probable, that the character of P²'s narrative was left unaltered on this occasion, and that, accordingly, Korah and his band were still represented by R, not as Levites, but as Israelites sprung from different tribes. In that case it was a later diaskeuast who made Korah and his followers Levites and transformed their contest with Levi for a share in the ritual into a contest with Aaron and his descendants for the priestly dignity. He gave the narrative this new turn by describing Korah in *v.* 1 as ' the son of Yiçhar, the son of Kohath, the son of Levi,' by adding *v.* 8–11 and by working over *v.* 16–18. The section xvii. 1–5 [xvi. 36–40] was also added by him, or at least in his spirit. For details cf. *Th. Tijdschr.*, xii. 139–162.—In contrast to xviii., which is closely connected with P²'s portion of xvi. sq., and is moreover united to it by xvii. 27, 28 [12, 13] (from R's hand ?), xix. stands entirely alone, and we must therefore regard its insertion in the same light as that of xv.—It appears from § 6, n. 42 that R must have taken great liberties with JE and P² when combining them in xx. 1–13, but it is hardly possible accurately to separate his share in the narrative that lies before us from the contributions of his two sources. On the other hand he took over xx. 14–21 from JE and *v.* 22–29 from P² unaltered, and hence the version of the events at Kadesh alluded to in *v.* 24 differs from the one communicated in *v.* 1–13. Ch. xxi., likewise, is largely borrowed from JE, and its composite character is to be explained by the divergencies of J and E and the additions made by their redactor. But to R himself we must attribute the [324] insertion of *v.* 10, 11 (a portion of P²'s narrative, cf. xx. 22–29 ; xxii. 1), and also of *v.* 4ª, which is a reference to xx. 22–29. This latter section was inserted by R in the midst of JE's narratives, and was thus brought at any rate into some kind of connection with them. The case is much the same with xxii.–xxiv.; only xxii. 1 is taken from P² and inserted here, in its most fitting place, and a few touches are added in *v.* 2 sqq. to make it square with P². In JE's narrative Balaam was summoned by Balak alone and in the exclusive interests of Moab (cf. *Deut.* xxiii. 5, 6 [4, 5]; *Josh.* xxiv. 9, 10). Balak's deliberation with ' the elders of Midian ' (*v.* 4) and the despatch of Midianite by the side of Moabite elders (*v.* 7) conflict with this, and are ignored in the sequel, from xxii. 8 to xxiv. We can therefore only regard them as a timid attempt to connect the representation of JE with *Num.* xxxi. 8, 16; *Josh.* xiii. 21, 22. The question whether this attempt was made by the first redactor or one of his successors cannot be answered with certainty. The latter supposition is supported by the feebleness with which the design is carried out, and perhaps also by the fact that the texts followed are amongst the latest portions of P. Or is it possible that Balaam really appeared as the seducer of Israel as early as in P^2 itself? We should know the answer to this question if the two accounts from which xxv. is compiled had come down to us in their original form. But the end of one (taken from JE, *v.* 1–5) and the beginning of the other, taken from P^2, *v.* 6 sqq., have been omitted. The result is a singular patchwork which leaves the answer to the above question doubtful. We may, however, regard it as probable that R would not have sacrificed P^2's Balaam altogether, and that, accordingly, he cannot have been mentioned in the verses that preceded xxv. 6; whence it would follow that R had no occasion to modify JE's representation by the additions in xxii. 4, 7. In this case xxv. 16–18 must also be denied to R^1 and assigned to a later diaskeuast; for these verses are the announcement of xxxi. and are inseparable from it, so that if they had been taken from P^2 and incorporated by R^1 it would follow that P^2 contained an account of Balaam, to which xxxi. 8, 16 would then refer.—On xxvi. cf. § 6, n. 41, where it is noted that *v.* 9–11 is not P^2's, but is due to the redaction which joined the two component parts of *Num.* xvi. together. But on closer examination we see that these three verses are not from a single hand. The author of *v.* 9, 10 includes Dathan and Abiram amongst Korah's band, and therefore cannot have held this latter and his followers to have been Levites. His position is that of the first redactor of *Num.* xvi. On the other hand the writer of *v.* 11 ('and the sons of Korah perished not') goes on the assumption that at any rate Korah himself was a Levite, and he wishes to explain how it could be that after the captivity there was still a Levitical clan of the B'ne Korah. Hence it follows either that he is the author of *Num.* xvi. 1ᵃ, 8–11, etc., or that he is dependent on him. In other respects R made no change in xxvi., and he likewise took up xxvii. 1–11, 12–23, and the laws of xxviii. sq.; xxx. just as he found them in P; whence it happens that in xxvii. 14 reference is made to a version of what occurred at Kadesh, differing from the one we now possess in xx. 1–13, and showing Moses and Aaron in a less favourable light. Of xxxi. (and xxv. 16–18) we have already spoken; there can be no doubt at all as to the secondary or tertiary character of the chapter, but the possibility still remains that it [325] may have been incorporated with P^2 before R accomplished his task, though the single reference to the war against Midian in *Josh.* xiii. 21, 22 does not favour the hypothesis.—To what has been said in § 6, n. 42 on *Num.* xxxii. I have nothing essential to add. The distinction there drawn between the first redactor of the story (R), who here combined JE and P^2 more intimately than was his wont, and the younger diaskeuast who added *v.* 6–15 under the influence of *Num.* xiii. sq. in its present form (and attached his interpolation to what went before by recasting *v.* 5) is now seen to be in complete analogy

with the phenomena observed elsewhere in the Hexateuch. *Num.* xxxiii.
1–49 has likewise been dealt with already, § 6, n. 43. The number of the
stations reaches forty-two, or if the starting-point, Ramses, be not reckoned,
forty-one. This figure comes so near to forty that the question forces itself
upon us whether the author of the list did not intend to give just that number
of names (cf. the number forty in *Num.* xiii. 25 ; xiv. 33, 34). In that case
there must be a mistake in one name, perhaps in Yam Suph, that appears so
oddly in *v.* 10, 11 (cf. *Ex.* xv. 22 and Kayser, op. cit., p. 98). This use of
the number forty would then be a fresh proof of the unhistorical character
and the later origin of the list. Its ascription to Moses (*v.* 2) is easily explained if R did not draw it up independently, but based it upon a record he
found ready to his hand and filled it up from the accounts he had himself
adopted.—On xxxiii. 50–xxxvi. consult § 6, n. 39, where it will be seen that
R may have taken all this from P² without alteration. Should it be thought
unlikely that P² imitated P¹'s linguistic usage (xxxiii. 52, 55, 56), we may
suppose that R himself expanded the introduction to the law regulating the
partition of the land (as he certainly did *Ex.* vi. 6–8 and other sections
already mentioned).

Deuteronomy. Nothing was more natural than that when R approached
the deuteronomic portion of DJE he should wish to bring it into chronological connection with his preceding narrative. This is effected by the date
in *Deut.* i. 3, 4, which attaches itself to *Num.* xxxiii. 38 (cf. xx. 22–29) and
agrees in point of form with P² (§ 7, n. 15). Whether R's hand has also been
busy with *v.* 1, 2, it is impossible, in the present corrupt condition of these
verses, to determine. From *v.* 6 onwards, R simply takes D as he finds him.
It would not be surprising in itself if here and there he had interposed,
whether in the historical preface (i.–iv.), or in the hortatory introduction
(v.–xi.), or in the law-book itself (xii.–xxvi., xxviii.), or, finally, in the appended pieces (xxvii., xxix. sqq.) ; for there was certainly no lack of inconsistencies with what had gone before for him to remove. But it appears, as a
fact, that he systematically abstained from any such attempts. The different
sections of *Deuteronomy* have come down to us, speaking generally, in their
original form, and have not lost their characteristics in the process of union
with P. It is only a passage here and there that raises a doubt whether the
diaskeuastæ have left things just as they found them :—

a. Ch. iv. 1–40. The points of contact with P² are more numerous here
than in any other portion of *Deuteronomy.* *V.* 3 might be understood as an
allusion to the chastisement described in *Num.* xxv. 6 sqq. ; but the writer
[326] may have had in view the continuation of *Num.* xxv. 1–5, which we no longer
possess. In *v.* 16, besides סמל which only occurs elsewhere in *Ezek.* viii. 3,
5 ; 2 *Chron.* xxxiii. 7, 15, we have זכר ונקבה, a formula of P² ; in *v.* 17, 18
תבנית (*Ex.* xxv. 9, 40 ; *Ezek.* three times ; *Isaiah* xliv. 13 ; 2 *Kings* xvi. 10 ;
Josh. xxii. 28 ; *Chronicles* ; *Psalms*) ; in *v.* 17, צפור כנף (with double בל
Gen. vii. 14 ; *Ezek.* xvii. 23 ; "צ כל־כנף, *Ezek.* xxxix. 4 ; xxxix. 17 ; "כ "צ
only *Psalm* cxlviii. 10) ; in *v.* 18 רמש (passim in P² ; the substantive רֶמֶשׂ
also in *Hos.* ii. 20 [18] ; *Hab.* i. 14 ; 1 *Kings* v. 13 [iv. 33]) ; in *v.* 25, הוליד

(passim in P²) and נוֹשֵׁן (elsewhere only in *Lev.* xiii. 11 ; xxvi. 10) ; in *v.* 32, ברא אלהים (as in *Gen.* i. 1, etc.).   Now as far as I can see the supposition that these verses have been interpolated, finds no support in their relation to the rest of iv. 1–40.   The phenomena we have noticed must therefore be explained in some other way.   *Deut.* i. 6–iv. 40 is exilian (§ 7, n. 22 under (4) and § 14, n. 12), and there is nothing to prevent our supposing that it issued from Ezekiel's circle.   In this case its approximation to the language of P² may rest upon the same grounds as the similar phenomenon in Ezekiel himself, and need not involve any direct dependence upon the priestly codex.   *Deut.* xiv. 3–21 (§ 14, n. 5) is another proof that the priestly style is older than the priestly law-book.

b. Ch. iv. 41–43 could only be assigned to R on proof of acquaintance with *Num.* xxxv. 9-34.   And no such proof is forthcoming (§ 7, n. 17, under *d*).   Nor is the use of הבדיל a proof of R's workmanship, for this verb, though exceedingly common in P², is also found in *Deut.* x. 8 ; xix. 2, 7 ; xxix. 20.

c. Nor can x. 6–9 be assigned, even in part, to R.   With regard to *v.* 8, 9, which is deuteronomic alike in form and substance, this needs no further proof ; and *v.* 6, 7 is inseparable from the rest.   Its contents, moreover, conflict with P² (cf. *Num.* xx. 22–29 ; and also xxxiii. 38) whom R is in the habit of following.   Eleazar ben Aaron figured in the older tradition concerning the Mosaic age (*Josh.* xxiv. 33), and we need not be surprised that it should present him, like Aaron himself, in the character of a priest.   Cf. § 7, n. 6.

d. On the other hand xxvii. 11–13, and *v.* 14–26, most certainly spring from the later diaskeue (cf. § 7, n. 22, under (2), (3), and § 14, n. 11), either of DJE or of the whole Hexateuch.   The latter alternative is supported, in the case of xxvii. 14–26, by the affinity of this interpolation with *Lev.* xviii.–xx., and also by the fact that it was still unknown to the author of *Josh.* viii. 32–35.   See p. 338.

It is only towards the end of *Deuteronomy* that R resumes his usual method.   He inserts the command to ascend Mount Nebo (xxxii. 48–52) immediately before the account of the death of Moses (xxxiv.)—for xxxiii. seems to have been inserted after the final redaction.   We cannot determine whether this command was repeated once more in P² itself, after *Num.* xxvii. 12–14, or whether R composed *Deut.* xxxii. 48–52, in imitation of the other passage ; but the former alternative is the more probable, as the passage in *Deuteronomy* is too independent for a mere copy, and moreover in *v.* 51 it presupposes *Num.* xx. 1–13, not in its present, but in its original form.   It still remains possible that R may have added a little himself, and specifically the words 'the mountain of Nebo, which is in the land of Moab over against Jericho,' *v.* 49.—In the account of the death of Moses, likewise, a few traits [327] from P² have been added by R (xxxiv. 1ᵃ, 7ᵃ, 8, 9, cf. § 6, n. 44).

Joshua.   In tracing R's labours through this book, we must distinguish between the first half, i.–xii., and the second, xiii.–xxiv.

In i.–xii. R might well be content, in general, with simply adopting the detailed narrative of DJE and weaving in a few details from P², viz. iv. (13?) 19 ; v. 10–12 ; ix. 15ᵇ, 17–21, 27ᵃ,—the insertion of which last verses necessitated some small harmonising changes. Cf. § 6, n. 48. Beyond this, he now and then permitted himself deliberately to modify the language of the accounts he took up, or involuntarily substituted more familiar terms for those he found in them. Some such touches are probably due not to the first redactor, but to his successors. This furnishes the true explanation of iv. 16, ארון העדות (for יי "א; see above, on *Ex.* xxxi. 18, etc.); v. 4-7 (cf. § 7, n. 26), where the verses are not unjustly characterised as deutero-nomic ; but this does not necessarily imply that they were already embodied in DJE,—and that too in their present form (cf. LXX.)—when the latter was united to P; for the interpolation may be of later origin, and probably is. In that case it dates from a period when the influence of P² (*Gen.* xvii.) had established the idea that circumcision was instituted by Yahwè as the sign of the covenant, and was faithfully observed as such in Egypt. Note that in *v.* 4, הזכרים agrees with P²'s usage) ; vii. 1, 18 (מטה, follows the usage of P²); vii. 25 (רגם אבן, as in *Lev.* xxiv. 23 ; רגם is extremely common in P², but only occurs once in *Deuteronomy* (xxi. 21) ; *v.* 25ᵃ is pleonastic, too, which is another reason for regarding it as a later addition) ; viii. 33 (cf. § 7, n. 30; one of the revisers of the passage betrays his dependence upon P² by the expression כגר כאזרח); x. 27 (עד עצם היום הזה for עד היום הזה is a reminiscence of P²); x. 28, 30, 32, 35, 37; xi. 11 (and x. 39, where the reading should be the same ; הנפש after P²'s usage); xi. 21-23ᵃ, cf. § 7, n. 26.

R's task in compiling xiii.-xxiv. was harder. What has been said in § 6, n. 51-53 ; § 7, n. 27, may be supplemented by the following remarks. R had before him an account by P², in which the partition of the land was repre-sented as a single act, which took place at Shiloh. It was impossible to follow this account without completely abandoning that of DJE, and to this he could not make up his mind. He therefore accepted the version of DJE so far as to divide the act of taking possession of Canaan into two stages, the first referring to Judah and Joseph, and the other to the seven remaining tribes. Accordingly he went to work as follows. He left the introduction (xiii. 1-7) in the form into which D had brought it; following it up by a description of the Transjordanic district compiled from DJE and P², xiii. 9-33. *V.* 21ᵇ, 22,—the connection of which with what precedes is unsatis-factory, both grammatically and logically—is a later addition, after *Num.* xxxi. 8. The 'kings' of Midian R changes to 'princes,' so that they may rank amongst the נסיכי סיחן and be included in their defeat. He omits the heading of P²'s introduction to the partition of the land (=xviii. 1), or rather postpones it, in order that the first act of the settlement of the tribes may be played through in Gilgal, in accordance with the conception of DJE.

[328] The rest of P²'s introduction he then takes up, xiv. 1-5, and follows on with a section from DJE on the heritage assigned to Caleb, xiv. 6-15, in which either R or some later reader has inserted, 'and concerning you,' *v.* 6, under the influence of P², *Num.* xiii. sq. The account of Judah's and Joseph's heritage that now follows, xv.-xvii., is a combination of the two documents ; but, as already shown, it is not always possible to identify them severally. P² is indicated by מטה in xv. 1, 20, 21 ; xvi. 8; xvii. 1 ; while xv. 13-19

(containing an allusion to xiv. 6–15), 63 ; xvi. 9, 10 ; xvii. 11–13, 14–18 are
certainly not taken from P². R has been less successful here than elsewhere
in welding the two accounts together—at least, if we may judge by the text
as we now have it. Ch. xvi. 4 (P²), in which Manasseh precedes Ephraim,
should have been followed at once by the description of Manasseh's heritage,
which, according to xvii. 1ᵃ, did actually occupy the first place in P². But in
xvi. 5–8, it is Ephraim's territory that is dealt with. Can this really be the
original order ? In xvii. 1 sqq. there is likewise so much confusion that one
cannot but ask whether the text is sound. If *v.* 1ᵇ is regarded as a
parenthesis, then ' for the tribe of Manasseh ' (*v.* 1ᵃ) is limited by ' for the
rest of the sons of Manasseh' (*v.* 2ᵃ), who are then enumerated in *v.* 2ᵇ, to the
number of six. In form *v.* 2 strikes us as belonging to P², like 1ᵃ, but on
the other hand it conflicts with *v.* 3, 4, which is unquestionably from P²
(cf. *Num.* xxvii. 1–11). *V.* 5, 6, is also difficult. The number of ten
'portions' agrees with *v.* 3, 4, if the five daughters of Çelophechad received one
portion each and were thus placed on an equality with the brothers of their
grandfather Hepher, who were also five in number (*v.* 2) and would thus
make up the ten. But no motive is assigned for any such equal sharing, nor
is there any mention elsewhere in P²'s partition of the land of ' portions '
being assigned to the several mishphachôth. *V.* 6, in which ' the rest of the
sons of Manasseh' balances Machir, who stands alone in *v.* 1ᵇ, is also peculiar
and is perhaps best explained as a gloss on *v.* 5. These difficulties prevent
our pronouncing a definitive judgment upon R's work in xvi., xvii. It may
be that Wellhausen (xxi. 599) is right in detecting the hand of ' a redactor
hostile to the Samaritans,' who is not to be identified with R¹.—We have
already seen that at this point R took up xviii. 1 (P²) and why he did so.
For the rest the introduction, xviii. 2–10, is taken from DJE (p. 255) ; and the
description of the territory of the seven tribes, xviii. 11–xix. 51, is compiled
from the two documents (§ 6, n. 50). Ch. xx. and xxi. 1–40 [42] come from
P² ; *v.* 41–43 [43–45] on the other hand is a deuteronomic colophon that
followed xix. in DJE. The continuation of these three verses is found in
xxii. 1–6. In taking over this passage, R here and there modified the
language (*v.* 1 משה, *v.* 4 אהוה, as in *v.* 9, 19). The whole of *v.* 7, 8, must
be assigned to him, or rather to a later diaskeuast. *V.* 7ᵃ is a very superfluous
reminder, which was probably added still later than *v.* 7ᵇ, 8 itself, for the
suffixes in the latter refer not to half or all Manasseh, but to the Transjordanic tribes mentioned in *v.* 1–6, and the passage is intended to remove the
appearance of Joshua's having blessed these tribes, but sent them away
empty handed. Note that the word נכסים seems to be very late (only [329]
occurring in 2 *Chron.* i. 11, 12 ; *Eccles.* v. 18 [19] ; vi. 2). The narrative that
follows next, *v.* 9–34, is wrongly regarded as composite by Knobel (*Num.*,
Deut., *Josh.*, p. 475 sqq.) and Kayser (op. cit., p. 106 sqq.), and may be
best compared with the recasting of *Gen.* xxxiv. (see above, p. 326) and
of *Ex.* xvi. (p. 331), and with *Num.* xxxi. and xxxii. 6–15. The writer
is dependent on P², whose language he imitates, but not servilely. Cf. אחז
Niphal, v. 9, 19 ; מרד verb and substantive, *v.* 19 (read ואתחנו אל-התמרדו),

22, 29; תבנית *v.* 28, etc., and see § 6, n. 53. His point of departure is
v. 1–6, which belongs to DJE, and therefore, though one of P²'s epigoni, he
must be reckoned amongst the later diaskeuastæ of the Hexateuch.—The close
of Joshua's history, xxiii., xxiv., is taken by R unaltered from DJE. There
must have been an account of Joshua's death in P² likewise, but the more
elaborate statements of the older documents made it unnecessary to insert it,
—unless indeed xxiv. 29ᵇ is derived from it.   On xxiv. 33, cf. § 6, n. 51.
The treatment of xxiv. 28–31, as a parallel to *Judges* ii. 6–9, and of the other
parallel passages in *Joshua* and *Judges* (*Josh.* xv. 13–19,=*Jud.* i. 10–15;
Josh. xv. 63=*Jud.* i. 21; *Josh.* xvi. 10=*Jud.* i. 29; *Josh.* xvii. 12 sq.=*Jud.*
i. 27 sq.; *Josh.* xix. 47=*Jud.* xvii. sq.) belongs rather to the criticism of
Judges than of *Joshua.*

The redaction of the Hexateuch further includes the division
of the Tora into five books and its separation from the book
of *Joshua.*

As to the latter point, it was no part of the original
intention either of the prophetic narrators, or of the Deuteronomist, or of the priestly law-giver, to make the settlement
of Israel in Canaan the subject of an independent work. On
the contrary, they looked upon Joshua's activity as inseparable
from that of Moses, and regarded an account of it as the
indispensable complement of the narratives of the patriarchs,
the deliverance from Egypt and the legislation. But yet the
character of Judaism involved the ultimate separation of the
Tora if not from the history of the preceding and accompanying events with which it was quite inseparably bound
up[13], at any rate from that of the succeeding ages, beginning
even with the conquest and partition of the land. The redaction therefore severed what had previously been regarded
as a single whole, and what we too have been perfectly
justified in handling as such. Whether the redactor of *Joshua*
is the same as the redactor of the Pentateuch may be left
undecided. If they were two then they were kindred spirits
and worked on one and the same method. And on the other
hand, even if the Redactor of the Tora included the book of
[330] *Joshua* in his labours, he nevertheless distinguished between

these two works and it was part of his plan to separate them[14].

The dimensions given to the Tora by the combination of DJE and P must suggest the desirability of breaking it up. The Redactor took this view, and was easily led to five as the proper number of books. Two of these, the first and the last, fixed themselves. The central portion might equally well have been split into two (*Ex.* i. 1–*Num.* x. 10 and *Num.* x. 11–xxxvi.), but in that case the two parts would have been of very unequal length, and both alike would have differed notably in this respect from *Genesis* and *Deuteronomy*. Probably this was one of the considerations which induced the Redactor to prefer a three-fold division of the central portion of his work, and he proceeded to execute it in a perfectly satisfactory manner. He marked the end of *Leviticus* by a colophon and that of *Numbers* by another, but had no need to accentuate the close of the other books[15].

[13] Attention has been called to this close connection in § 1 and subsequently *passim.* It is not kept sufficiently in view by those who regard the present existence of the separate Tora as a proof that it was never united with *Joshua* at all, and who therefore object to the two being included under the single name of 'the Hexateuch.' It is true that the work never existed as a single whole split up into six parts, and to that extent the name in question is not strictly accurate. But it is equally true that the legislation in all its stages— and in the highest degree in the first and third—was combined with history and in a way subordinated to it. Purely legislative writings did not exist, and all the documents of the Pentateuch, though in different degrees, were historico-legislative. The continuation of the history till after the settlement in Canaan is in perfect keeping with this character; and an attempt to change that character and draw up a purely legislative work would have involved the mutilation of the documents. But when the Tora came to be regarded as the divine revelation, in the proper sense, it was possible to break off at the death of the law-giver, where legislation and history ceased to be absolutely inseparable, and to make an independent work of the rest of the history.

[14] We are speaking here, of course, of the first redactor. It lies in the nature of the case that the later diaskeuastæ did not cover the whole ground and in some cases only dealt with a single passage.—Now, that this first redactor separated the Tora from *Joshua* may be inferred at the outset, at any rate with high probability, from his date; for Judaism was established

[331] and had already assigned its special place and its peculiar authority to the Tora, when he undertook his task. Confirmatory evidence is borne by the differences between the Tora and the book of *Joshua* in details which must be referred to the redaction. On the so-called archaisms of the Penta-teuch, cf. n. 7, where we have seen that R is presumably not responsible for these peculiar forms. The same may be said of other orthographical distinctions: ירחו is *defective* (ירחֹ) in the Pentateuch, and *full* (יריחו) in *Joshua*; for שֶׁמַע (*Gen.* xxix. 13, etc.) and קְנָא (*Ex.* xx. 5; xxxiv. 14) we read in *Joshua* שֹׁמַע (vi. 27; ix. 9) and קנוא (xxiv. 19); and the first distinc-tion, at any rate, is not accidental but must be attributed to the wish on the part of the punctuators to separate the Tora from the other sacred books. But it is more significant that 'Yahwè, the god of Israel,' only occurs twice in the Pentateuch (*Ex.* v. 1; xxxii. 27), and fourteen times in *Joshua* (vii. 13, 19, 20; viii. 30; ix. 18, 19; x. 40, 42; xiii. 14, 33; xiv. 14; xxii. 24; xxiv. 2, 23); for two of these passages in *Joshua* (ix. 18, 19) are taken from P[2], whence it follows that it was R, and not JE or D, who introduced this formula, or at any rate applied it so freely,—and yet it is only in *Joshua*, not in the Tora, that he did so. Finally, the redaction of *Joshua* seems to allow itself greater freedom than that of the Tora. Such pheno-mena as we have discovered in *Josh.* xiii., xvi. sq., xviii., xxii. 7 sq., 9 sqq., do not occur in the Pentateuch, or at any rate not quite in the same way. It is therefore very possible that R is in some degree at least responsible for the confusion which reigns in certain narratives in the first portion of *Joshua*, viz. iii. sq., vi., viii. 30-35, xi. 21-23. This cannot be actually proved, for, as we have seen, the traces of R's linguistic peculiarities are few, and perhaps the copyists may be responsible for the relative corruption of the language. The facts I have pointed out, however, tend to support on every side the theory of a distinction between the redaction of the Tora and that of *Joshua*, though only in the very limited sense explained above.

[15] Cf. § 1, from which the explanation of the statements in the text can easily be drawn. The happy choice of resting-places strikes us at once. *Ex.* i. opens a veritably new division, viz. the history of the people of Israel. The com-pletion of the sanctuary, *Ex.* xl., naturally closes the second book. The laws of *Lev.* i. sqq. divide themselves clearly from what precedes. *Num.* i. 1 is the first chronological statement after *Ex.* xl. 17 and at the same time the heading of a new book. Finally, the line between *Num.* xxxvi. and *Deut.* i. is obvious at a glance. Of the two colophons, the second, *Num.* xxxvi. 13, com-pletely answers to our expectation: בערבות מואב על ירדן ירחו, as in xxii. 1; xxvi. 3, 63; xxxiii. 50; xxxv. 1, all in P whence 'the commandments and ordinances' referred to were taken. On the other hand the last words of *Lev.* xxvii. 34, 'on Mount Sinai' surprise us, for we want 'in the desert of Sinai,' or more specifically ' in the ôhel mo'éd (pitched in the desert) ' (cf. *Lev.* i. 1). Obviously the writer of *Lev.* xxvii. 34 is following *Lev.* xxvi. 46 (cf. xxv. 1), where 'Mount Sinai' is mentioned by P[1] as the place where Yahwè made his will known to Moses; and he applies this statement to *Lev.* xxvii. also, though this latter chapter was not taken from P[1].

INDEX

Of Principal Passages in the Hexateuch dealt with in this Volume.